Cisco Internet Applications and Solutions Self-Study Guide: Cisco Internet Solutions Specialist

Michael Wilkes

Cisco Press

Cisco Press
201 West 103rd Street
Indianapolis, IN 46290 USA

Cisco Internet Applications and Solutions Self-Study Guide:
Cisco Internet Solutions Specialist

Michael Wilkes

Copyright © 2003 Cisco Systems, Inc.

Published by:
Cisco Press
201 West 103rd Street
Indianapolis, IN 46290 USA

Printed in the United States of America 1 2 3 4 5 6 7 8 9 0

Library of Congress Cataloging-in-Publication Number: 2001092524

ISBN: 1-58705-066-8

First Printing September 2002

Warning and Disclaimer

This book is designed to provide information about the Cisco CISS Applications Essentials and CISS Solutions exams. Every effort has been made to make this book as complete and as accurate as possible, but no warranty or fitness is implied.

The information is provided on an "as is" basis. The author, Cisco Press, and Cisco Systems, Inc. shall have neither liability nor responsibility to any person or entity with respect to any loss or damages arising from the information contained in this book or from the use of the discs or programs that may accompany it.

The opinions expressed in this book belong to the author and are not necessarily those of Cisco Systems, Inc.

Feedback Information

At Cisco Press, our goal is to create in-depth technical books of the highest quality and value. Each book is crafted with care and precision, undergoing rigorous development that involves the unique expertise of members from the professional technical community.

Readers' feedback is a natural continuation of this process. If you have any comments regarding how we could improve the quality of this book, or otherwise alter it to better suit your needs, you can contact us through e-mail at feedback@ciscopress.com. Please make sure to include the book title and ISBN in your message.

We greatly appreciate your assistance.

Trademark Acknowledgments

All terms mentioned in this book that are known to be trademarks or service marks have been appropriately capitalized. Cisco Press or Cisco Systems, Inc. cannot attest to the accuracy of this information. Use of a term in this book should not be regarded as affecting the validity of any trademark or service mark.

Publisher	John Wait
Editor-in-Chief	John Kane
Executive Editor	Brett Bartow
Cisco Systems Management	Michael Hakkert, Tom Geitner
Production Manager	Patrick Kanouse
Acquisitions Editor	Michelle Grandin
Development Editor	Jill Batistick
Project Editor	San Dee Phillips
Copy Editor	Marcia Ellett
Technical Editors	Matt Bandy, Bryce Lynn, Canon Menon, Umar Ruhi
Team Coordinator	Tammi Ross
Cover Designer	Louisa Klucznik
Production Team	Octal Publishing, Inc.
Indexer	Heather McNeill

CISCO SYSTEMS

Corporate Headquarters
Cisco Systems, Inc.
170 West Tasman Drive
San Jose, CA 95134-1706
USA
http://www.cisco.com
Tel: 408 526-4000
      800 553-NETS (6387)
Fax: 408 526-4100

European Headquarters
Cisco Systems Europe
11 Rue Camille Desmoulins
92782 Issy-les-Moulineaux
Cedex 9
France
http://www-europe.cisco.com
Tel: 33 1 58 04 60 00
Fax: 33 1 58 04 61 00

Americas Headquarters
Cisco Systems, Inc.
170 West Tasman Drive
San Jose, CA 95134-1706
USA
http://www.cisco.com
Tel: 408 526-7660
Fax: 408 527-0883

Asia Pacific Headquarters
Cisco Systems Australia,
Pty., Ltd
Level 17, 99 Walker Street
North Sydney
NSW 2059 Australia
http://www.cisco.com
Tel: +61 2 8448 7100
Fax: +61 2 9957 4350

Cisco Systems has more than 200 offices in the following countries. Addresses, phone numbers, and fax numbers are listed on the Cisco Web site at www.cisco.com/go/offices

Argentina • Australia • Austria • Belgium • Brazil • Bulgaria • Canada • Chile • China • Colombia • Costa Rica • Croatia • Czech Republic • Denmark • Dubai, UAE • Finland • France • Germany • Greece • Hong Kong Hungary • India • Indonesia • Ireland • Israel • Italy • Japan • Korea • Luxembourg • Malaysia • Mexico The Netherlands • New Zealand • Norway • Peru • Philippines • Poland • Portugal • Puerto Rico • Romania Russia • Saudi Arabia • Scotland • Singapore • Slovakia • Slovenia • South Africa • Spain • Sweden Switzerland • Taiwan • Thailand • Turkey • Ukraine • United Kingdom • United States • Venezuela • Vietnam Zimbabwe

About the Editor

Michael Wilkes has spent the last twenty years wandering the Internet and watching it mature. He is an architect of systems integration and a self-proclaimed log file evangelist in the engineering department for Organic, Inc. Michael has built relatively few web pages himself, but has measured and analyzed billions of web pages for hundreds of sites. Most of those web pages were analyzed while working as the senior data manager for Internet Profiles Corporation auditing traffic for AOL, CNN, Microsoft, Yahoo!, and many others. Working for Organic, Inc. since 1998, he has organized and managed several teams of engineers responsible for hosting and maintaining web sites for Sprint, McDonalds, Harley Davidson, Kinko's, Colgate, Starbucks, Washington Mutual Mortgage, Sony Playstation, British Telecom, Blockbuster, and nVidia Corporation. Michael started his telecommunications career working for a think tank in the U.S. Department of Education and is an executive officer of CLIQ Services Cooperative, a worker-owned company he started with several friends in 1997. He holds a B.A. degree in Philosophy from the University of Wisconsin-Madison and an M.A. degree from Stanford University.

About the Technical Reviewers

Matt Bandy is a systems integrator for weddingchannel.com, specializing in database administration and small-scale custom applications development.

Bryce Lynn, after leaving the Computer Science Department at the University of California at Davis somewhat short of enough credits to graduate, spent several years learning the networking trade while working in network implementation, and later operations, for Wells Fargo Bank. At the height of the dot-com boom, Bryce left the bank and took a position as a hosting engineer for Organic, Inc., where he designed, implemented, and sometimes maintained server environments for large e-commerce web sites. Bryce is currently lead network engineer for Organic's corporate information services department. Bryce is also an avid softball player, and will rarely turn down an offer to buy him a beer.

Canon Menon lives in Toronto, Canada with his lovely wife Beatrice and three children. He has been involved in software design for nearly two decades and has worked on most known technology platforms during a rewarding career that included working with technology leaders, such as IBM and FedEx. He has an M.B.A. degree in information technology and is also a PMP (Project Management Professional). He teaches Software Design, Project Management, and E-Commerce in his spare time, and loves to share interesting stories from his eventful career with his students.

Umar Ruhi is a software engineer by profession and has been working as an internet services consultant for the past five years. He specializes in the deployment of open-source backend technologies for e-commerce and runs his own business in Toronto (www.netbizstudios.com). He has completed projects with several companies in North America. He has been a Visiting Research Scholar at Johns Hopkins University and he teaches e-business technology courses at various universities and community colleges in the greater Toronto area. Umar is an IBM Certified e-business Solution Technologist, a Novell Certified eBusiness Strategist, Cisco Certified Network Associate, Sun Certified Solaris System Administrator, and CIW Certified Instructor. His qualifications include a B.S. degree in computer science and an M.B.A. degree in e-business, and he continues his post-graduate research work in knowledge management.

Dedication

I would like to dedicate this work to Ingrid, for the inspiration you provide to enjoy the spice of life. Your patience and support while I worked on this book were as nourishing to me as any food or water. I would also like to acknowledge the ever-present support of my parents and family. Thanks especially to my mom and dad for letting me use the phone line for all those nights when I was online and nobody had invented DSL internet access yet.

Acknowledgments

This book would not have been possible without a host of circumstances that involve many people. With their help and support, I have been able to reach the finished product and know that, because it was not my effort alone, it is a good product. As others have before, I too accept the blame for any errors that remain.

I would especially like to thank my editors at Cisco Press. Thank you to Jill Batistick, my development editor, for your constant eye toward making my transitions smoother and the structure more logical. And thank you to Michelle Grandin, my acquisitions editor, not only for your support and direction in launching and tracking this effort, but also for having wandered across my resume and giving me the chance to be an author. Although I had long-considered writing a book involving such topics, it was never a reality until I spoke with you.

Equally important to managing the "signal-to-noise" ratio in these pages is the work of my reviewers. Thank you for your diligent minds, your attention to detail, and your excellent suggestions. I was lucky to secure your efforts and am pleased to count myself among your peers.

As I write this, I have yet to learn the names of those who will bear the burden of translating this work into an actual printed thing of many pages of text and some nifty figures and tables, but I thank you for your efforts now and always.

Lastly, I'd like to thank someone with whom I've only spoken briefly, but whose influence upon my life is unsurpassed. Thank you to Steve Noonan, wherever you are now, for introducing me to the Internet that fateful day in 1981 when I bought my first (300 baud) modem at the tender age of 13. It was not until about 12 years later that this hobby of mine would become my career, but it was that day that computers and computer networks the world over were revealed to me in great awe and potential.

Michael Wilkes
March 2002
Oakland, CA

Contents at a Glance

Table of Contents

Introduction

Just about every project I've worked on over the past few years could have benefited in some way from this book to give to the client, the project managers, or the development team. While there are no great secrets revealed within these pages, the simple gathering together of this information into one volume, focused on the applications essentials of building Internet business solutions, can have a very beneficial impact. It is often the case that a talented group of people will work on a project together, and even with the right ideas, resources, and execution, they are unable to create a successful solution. *Cisco Internet Applications and Solutions Self-Study Guide: Cisco Internet Solutions Specialist* attempts to prepare you for the CISS certification, but also serves to bind a team and their project with a successful solution.

Audience

This book's primary audience is the networking professional who is tasked with a project where participation includes more than just network administration responsibilities. Increasingly, businesses need a hybrid network engineer with a good understanding of application development fundamentals. A secondary audience can be found among system architects, application developers, and project managers who want to be more familiar with the concepts, techniques, and tools used by network engineers involved in their project. Both of these audiences find themselves challenged by the complexity of building Internet-based applications and realize that knowing more about areas beyond their core competence is a key ingredient to their continued success and growth.

Organization

This book is organized into six major parts. Each of these parts explains an aspect of developing Internet-based applications. Each part is divided into chapters, as described here.

Part I: Introduction

These chapters establish the context for building Internet-based applications and provide history and background on business applications architecture. Cisco certifications are introduced, and the CISS certification program, in particular, is explained. The bulk of the information presented in this part addresses the distributed computing model in building three-tier Internet business solutions and web applications.

Chapter 1, "Overview of CISS and Cisco Certifications"

Chapter 2, "Models for Business Applications Architecture"

Part II: Applications Engineering

This part of the book carries the heaviest load of information about applications essentials. The software development lifecycle is introduced in Chapter 3, and is discussed as it relates directly to the roles and responsibilities of a CISS working on a software project. No other part of this book will introduce more terminology, concepts, or technologies than is contained in these four chapters on applications engineering. Mastering the content presented here is essential to understanding the objectives of the CISS certification.

Chapter 3, "Application Design and Development"

Chapter 4, "Application Requirements"

Chapter 5, "Build or Buy?"

Chapter 6, "Internet Business Solutions"

Part III: Application Management and Support

Application and system management addresses the post-launch aspects of Internet-based software applications. An overview of the issues involved in managing and supporting an application or service helps ensure that a CISS is prepared to fulfill the application maintenance requirements. Specific topics covered in this part include system monitoring, software distribution, and application configuration management.

Chapter 7, "Application and System Management"

Part IV: CISS Case Studies

The CISS certification deals with both the theory and practice of application development. The practice of application development is addressed in this part of the book in five case studies. These case studies illustrate many of the central concepts and themes presented in the CISS course materials, as well as offer a much-needed practical context for thinking about application design and development.

Chapter 8, "CISS Case Studies"

Part V: CISS Exams

As an essential aid in preparing you for taking the CISS certification exams, this part of the book contains two sets of sample exam questions, one based on the course materials for CISS Applications Essentials, and the other based on the course materials for CISS Solutions. CISS Applications and Essentials covers all the topics found in this book, whereas CISS Solutions is concerned solely with the role of a CISS during the testing phase of the software development lifecycle.

Chapter 9, "CISS Applications Essentials Sample Exam Questions"

Chapter 10, "CISS Solutions Sample Exam Questions"

Part VI: Appendixes

The editors and contributors of this book have compiled a list of books recommended for further reading on many of the topics covered. More detailed treatments can be found in these books, and you are encouraged to supplement your knowledge with these works. The appendixes also include all answers to sample exams and chapter review questions. Also included is a short piece in Appendix E on Public-Key Infrastructure (PKI) because this topic is an essential component in the increasingly complex world of application security, not only for e-commerce, but also for all forms of secure applications and transactional systems.

Appendix A, "Recommended Further Reading"

Appendix B, "Solutions to CISS Applications Essentials Sample Exam"

Appendix C, "Solutions to CISS Solutions Sample Exam"

Appendix D, "Answers to Chapter Review Questions"

Appendix E, "Public-Key Infrastructure"

The Glossary includes terms referred to in the text.

Cisco Internet Solutions Specialist

Successful completion of the three CISS certification examinations results in the designation of CISS. As a CISS-certified network engineer, you can feel confident that you have become familiar with the major elements of software applications design and development for use with Internet business solutions. Internet-based applications and web services are built upon the careful practice of software application development and will yield incredible results for businesses seeking to participate in the widespread adoption of Internet protocols and the power of web-based applications. The CISS certification was designed to provide a means of qualifying the skills and experience required to build successful Internet business solutions.

CISS Applications Essentials Course

CISS Applications Essentials covers the A to Z of the CISS certification. This course presents the majority of the information needed to become a certified CISS. Although CISS Architecture Essentials and CISS Solutions go into their respective topics in greater detail, this course raises the same topics that the other two courses cover and should be considered the base CISS course.

CISS Solutions Course

CISS Solutions focuses on the role of a CISS during the testing and validation of Internet-based applications. During the basic software development lifecycle, the test phase is the fourth phase of six total phases—and the one in which a CISS can be expected to play the greatest part. This course contains two modules: testing and validation, and responsibilities and tools. This course provides great insight into the practical skills and techniques required of a CISS.

Conventions Used in This Book

This book is organized into six major parts. If you are unfamiliar with application architecture, application development, or network administration, you will probably gain the most benefit by reading each part in order, beginning with Part I. If you are already familiar with application architecture, however, you can focus on the specific sections of interest, starting with Part II. Those already familiar with network administration might want to skim Part III, paying greater attention to sections on application management and less on system management. The layout of the parts enables you to quickly locate the needed information.

The text is sprinkled with notes and sidebars that highlight information that might be of particular importance to you. Sometimes, these notes and sidebars point out potential problems. Others clarify terms used within the text. These sidebars and notes are generally not covered in the review questions or sample exams.

Each chapter also contains a set of review questions. These questions are designed to highlight the major concepts in each chapter. These review questions assist you in reviewing for mastery of the subjects covered in the chapter. The answers to the chapter review questions are in Appendix D.

Introduction

CHAPTER 1

Overview of CISS and Cisco Certifications

> If the 1980s were about quality and the 1990s were about re-engineering, then the 2000s will be about velocity. About how quickly business itself will be transacted. About how information access will alter the life-style of consumers and their expectations of business. Quality improvements and business-process improvements will occur far faster. When the increase in velocity is great enough, the very nature of business changes.
>
> —Gates, Bill with Collins Hemingway. *Business @ The Speed of Thought: Using a Digital Nervous System.* Time Warner Company; March 1999.

Since the opening of the first 24-hour stores, business owners have accepted that competition drives businesses to provide more services to more customers in more ways than was conceivable when money was first created. The "velocity" described in the quote at the beginning of this chapter is certainly true of the software industry, but it also accurately describes one of the fundamental forces affecting all businesses. The velocity of change, competition, innovation, and demand are apparent as business in general continues to evolve, and as business in particular continues to adapt to these forces.

Despite the spectacular hype that led to the rise and fall of Internet companies after the turn of the millennium, the Internet's impact on business and the velocity of business transactions has been significant. Not all Internet businesses are here to stay, but Internet-based business solutions have arrived, and nobody can deny that they have changed the nature of business.

Cisco Systems Inc. has developed the Cisco Internet Solutions Specialist (CISS) certification to address the need for networking professionals who participate in the design, deployment, and support of Internet-based applications and services. Cisco created the CISS certification after developing one of the most respected network professional certification and training programs. Thousands of professionals have studied for and passed the various levels of Cisco network certifications to provide validation of their skills and experience. Because of the high quality and high standards demanded by a Cisco certification, industry leaders trust Cisco credentials and require them for placement in top positions within their companies.

Feedback and information gained from network professionals about real-world business needs led to the creation of the Cisco certifications, which are designed to provide system and network administrators with the training and tools to handle the challenges of their ever-evolving jobs. (The CISS certification is but one of those certifications.) Cisco engineers have experience with both core business applications and innovative business practices.

Internet-based applications and services are rapidly evolving into enterprise-wide Internet business solutions. Internet business solutions either create or migrate business services into highly available, interactive, and efficient business processes and transactions. The CISS certified professional might act in one or more of the many roles of solution implementation: driver, consultant, implementer, program manager, trainer, and tester. Along the way, the CISS certified professional helps businesses find competitive advantages and maintain growth through Internet business solutions.

This chapter discusses the following:

- Cisco training and certification
- Details about the CISS program
- How to use this book

About Cisco Training and Certifications

Several tracks and programs comprise the full range of Cisco training and certifications. The main certification tracks address the needs of all levels of network professionals and are categorized as expert, professional, and associate, as shown in Figure 1-1. With the addition of specialist certificates, Cisco has expanded the offering by making in-demand subject specializations available that provide the benefit of the same quality and high standards found in other Cisco training and certification:

- **Expert**—This is the highest level of achievement for network professionals, certifying an individual as an expert or master. The Cisco Certified Internetwork Expert (CCIE) represents both in-class training and testing, but also involves a laboratory component in which successful participants must troubleshoot and solve actual network problems introduced into the laboratory network setup.

- **Professional**—The level below expert for Cisco certification contains the professional certifications. These include the advanced or journeyman-level certifications, such as the Cisco Certified Internetwork Professional (CCIP), Cisco Certified Design Professional (CCDP), and the Cisco Certified Network Professional (CCNP).

- **Associate**—The first step in Cisco networking begins with the Associate level. Think of this as the apprentice or foundation level of networking certification. Further certifications are the Cisco Certified Network Associate (CCNA) and the Cisco Certified Design Associate (CCDA).

- **Qualified Specialist Certificates** — A variety of Cisco Qualified Specialist designations show knowledge in specific technologies, solutions, and job roles. These specialist certificates include the Cisco Cable Communications Specialist (CCCS), Cisco Internet Solutions Specialist (CISS), Cisco Security Specialist (CSS), Cisco SNA/IP Design Specialist (CSDS), and Cisco SNA/IP Support Specialist (CSSS).

Figure 1-1   *Cisco Training and Certifications Levels*

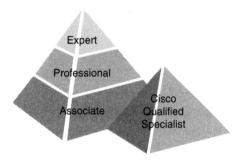

CISS Program Features

The Cisco Internet Solutions Specialist certification validates skills and knowledge in developing Internet business solutions and focuses on four key areas of systems planning: applications, tools, operating systems, and networks. This specialist has the technical expertise to integrate applications with the underlying network architecture, providing a foundation of knowledge to accelerate deployment of e-business projects. CISS designations are valid for two years. To recertify, you must pass the current version of the CISS exams. The CISS certification complements the Cisco Internet Quotient program (Cisco iQ) by providing several case studies as a part of the CISS three-course training program.

This section of the chapter covers the following about the CISS program:

- Goals
- Course format
- Applications essentials
- Solutions
- Exams
- Features and benefits of certification

CISS Program Goal

A CISS certification enables you to assist businesses with optimizing their Internet business solutions, such as implementing a workforce optimization application or introducing Internet-based customer care services. The intent of the CISS certification is not to solve all application problems but to change network architecture as appropriate to support Internet business solutions. As a CISS professional, you will have the fundamental knowledge to become conversant in both network and system architecture and the applications side of an Internet business solution. You will be capable of identifying the key personnel who can assist in building a sound Internet business solution.

CISS Course Format

The CISS Architecture Essentials course and CISS Solutions course are entirely web-based and include a combined 80 hours of online learning. They do not include instructor facilitation or hands-on lab exercises but do provide user interactivity through mouseovers and interactive practice questions. The CISS program consists of three distinct courses:

- Course 1—CISS Architecture Essentials
- Course 2—CISS Applications Essentials
- Course 3—CISS Solutions

Courses 1 and 2, "CISS Architecture Essentials" and "CISS Applications Essentials," can be taken interchangeably; they are not sequential. If you have an experienced background in architecture or applications, you can choose to take the exam for Course 1 or 2 to qualify to take Course 3, "CISS Solutions." Course 3 is required. After completing the Solutions course, the next step toward receiving your CISS certification is to pass a proctored certification exam.

This book combines the content for Courses 2 and 3 but follows the general structure of Course 2 to illustrate the importance of the materials covered in Course 2. Course 2 addresses all of the topics for the CISS certification in some manner and can be thought of as the heart of the certification. The materials in Course 3 represent a detailed look into the testing phase of the software development life cycle model from the point of view of the CISS specialist. The remainder of the Course 3 is composed of five case studies, which are included in this study guide in Chapter 8, "CISS Case Studies."

CISS Applications Essentials

Unless testing out of Course 1 or 2, taking the CISS Applications Essentials course is generally the second step for individuals who want to receive the CISS certification. The course teaches the fundamental concepts and applied design guidelines necessary to certify an individual's Internet application knowledge in the following areas:

- General Application Concepts
- Application Architecture
- Application Design and Enablers
- Development Life Cycle Model
- Sourcing Models
- Internet Business Initiatives
- System and Application Management

You should be conversational across all referenced areas after completing the course.

The knowledge gained in this course prepares you to take the CISS Application Essentials exam and CISS Solutions course, and to apply strong Internet application skills to real-life situations. In particular, after completing this course, you should be able to do the following:

- Speak conversationally about application concepts and architectures, the development life cycle, and major Internet business initiatives.
- Articulate system and application management guidelines and application design considerations that must be considered when recommending an appropriate Internet business strategy based on client specifications.

CISS Solutions

The CISS Solutions course is the only required step for individuals preparing for the CISS certification examination. The online portion of the course teaches CISS responsibilities in the different phases of the Life Cycle Model, as well as the tools that a CISS can use to fulfill those responsibilities. The facilitated session portion of the course allows students to apply the skills learned in Courses 1, 2, and 3 of the certification program in a case study format.

Course 3 gives you the opportunity to work with other students and produce solutions to realistic and meaningful case study scenarios. You will interact with and receive feedback from subject matter specialists. After taking this course, you should not only be prepared to take the CISS Solutions exam but also to apply strong Internet business strategy skills to real-life situations.

The CISS Solutions course is a blended solution course that includes instructor facilitation and web-based content. The web-based content includes user interaction through user mouseovers and practice questions, including drag-and-drop questions. After completing this course, you should be able to do the following:

- Describe the responsibilities of a CISS in the different phases of the Life Cycle Model.
- Identify techniques and tools used when performing the tasks of a CISS.
- Apply the knowledge and skills learned in Courses 1, 2, and 3 to case study scenarios and deliverables to produce Internet business strategy solutions.

CISS Exams

The CISS certification involves the following three course examinations:

- CISS Architecture Essentials
- CISS Applications Essentials
- CISS Solutions

CISS Features and Benefits of Certification

CISS certification provides important benefits common to all Cisco certifications. The industry's respect and awareness of the value of a Cisco certification is a prime benefit that qualifies you for successful employment. Although you might already have the experience and skills to perform the tasks of a particular job, the addition of the Cisco certification gains the attention of the hiring manager sorting through resumes of candidates applying for a position. With Cisco certification, network professionals can do the following:

- Gain and qualify new skills
- Provide project leadership
- Deploy best-of-breed Internet business solutions

Because Cisco training and certification is the result of Cisco's collective experience and history in developing knowledge and expertise found in real-world applications using Cisco network devices and operating systems, the CISS program represents a complete set of topics and lessons. The course developers have brought not only their own knowledge of the principles and techniques to design and develop Internet-based applications and services, but they have also employed the work of teams of technical reviewers and editors to ensure that the final product is technically accurate and easy to understand.

How to Use This Book

This book provides a study guide to prepare you for the CISS Course 2 and Course 3 examinations. All of the chapters and sections presented here are based on the official Cisco course materials. Additional materials and topics are presented at the end of select chapters so that you are clearly aware of which material is intended for examination preparation and which material is incidental information about Internet business solutions from the author's personal experience. These sections are titled "Applied Solutions."

Almost all the figures and diagrams in this book are from the online course materials, so you have the benefit of a portable, offline study resource and repository for future reference. The book contains an index, glossary, and appendices to help locate specific terms or find various sections that address CISS exam topics. Review questions are placed at the end of chapters to allow you to self-test your mastery of the topics introduced in the chapters.

Chapter 9, "CISS Applications Essentials Sample Exam Questions," and Chapter 10, "CISS Solutions Sample Exam Questions," present sample CISS examination questions. Sample exam answers are located in the appendixes. These solutions ensure that you'll know about the nature of the questions that make up the examinations.

NOTE   CISS Applications Essentials and Solutions readers are highly recommended, though not required, to have a general working knowledge of application architecture and basic networking in client-server environments. You should also have a basic understanding of commonly used Internet protocols and computer network administration. The Cisco Press title, *Internetworking Technologies Handbook*, Third Edition, or the Cisco Training Class, "Understanding Networking Fundamentals," is recommended reading and preparation for this book. CCNA certification is a sufficient, but not necessary, prerequisite. However, the CISS certification is generally expected to be pursued after you pass the CCNA exam.

CISS and This Study Guide

This book is divided into five parts with ten chapters and six appendices. The parts of the book and the chapter topics are as follows:

- Part I—Introduction
  - Chapter 1—Overview of CISS and Cisco Certifications
  - Chapter 2—Models for Business Applications Architecture

- Part II—Applications Engineering
    - Chapter 3—Application Design and Development
    - Chapter 4—Application Requirements
    - Chapter 5—Build or Buy?
    - Chapter 6—Internet Business Solutions
- Part III—Application Management and Support
    - Chapter 7—Application and System Management
- Part IV—CISS Case Studies
    - Chapter 8—CISS Case Studies
- Part V—CISS Exams
    - Chapter 9—CISS Applications Essentials Sample Exam Questions
    - Chapter 10—CISS Solutions Sample Exam Questions
- Part VI—Appendixes
    - Appendix A—Recommended Further Reading
    - Appendix B—Solutions to CISS Applications Essentials Sample Exam
    - Appendix C—Solutions to CISS Solutions Sample Exam
    - Appendix D—Answers to Chapter Review Questions
    - Appendix E—Public-Key Infrastructure (PKI)
    - Appendix F—Glossary

Cisco iQ Program Overview

The prevailing model of competition in the Internet economy is more like a web of inter-relationships than the hierarchical command-and-control model of the industrial economy. Unlike the traditional value chain, which rewarded exclusivity, the Internet economy is inclusive and has low barriers to entry. Like an ecosystem in nature, activity in the Internet economy is self-organizing. The process of natural selection takes place around profit and value. Profit for companies, however, centers on value for customers in the ecosystem of the Internet.

The Cisco iQ program is a product of two metrics: operations ecosystem and market eco-system. *Operations ecosystem* is a term that expresses how a company uses the Internet to optimize its internal operations. *Market ecosystem* is a company's ability to expand and create value for the entire ecosystem. The potential for success in the modern business economy is measured by the quality of a company's ecosystem. The *Internet ecosystem* is the business model of the Internet economy. It is an ecosystem because it has complex relationships between companies' systems that have independent, dependent, and synergistic aspects.

As the Internet ecosystem evolves both technologically and in population, it will be even easier and likelier for countries, companies, and individuals to participate in the Internet economy. One trillion dollars in technical infrastructure is already in place, ready and available for anyone to use at any time—free of charge. That's why new ideas and ways of doing things can come from anywhere at anytime in the Internet economy. The old rules don't apply anymore. How quickly a company can target, acquire, service, and grow customers will be measured by its Internet quotient.

Cisco iQ Web Site

The Cisco iQ web site demonstrates how Internet technology can solve critical business problems. It provides the guidance, insight, and knowledge you need to implement successful Internet business strategies for your organization. Business strategies on the Cisco iQ web site are grouped by Internet Basics, Business Solutions, Trends, Case Studies, From the Experts, and Tools and Resources. The web site also features iQ Magazine and is designed as a portal site around the Cisco iQ initiative and program partners. The Cisco iQ web site URL is www.cisco.com/warp/public/750/iq.

Summary

The CISS program provides an industry-recognized certification to train professionals to participate in the design, creation, and maintenance of Internet business solutions. The Cisco Internet Solutions Specialist program details, as well as the context for the CISS certification within the larger scope of all Cisco training and certifications, should be familiar to you at this point. The CISS training track consists of three courses: "CISS Architecture Essentials," "CISS Applications Essentials," and "CISS Solutions." This study guide covers the materials used in Courses 2 and 3. A significant portion of this study guide covers the role of the CISS engineer during the testing and validation phases of a project. Because the certification concerns a variety of Internet-based applications and services, five case studies are presented to help ground the discussions in real-world examples.

CHAPTER 2

Models for Business Applications Architecture

A business application is any software application or service that provides a business task, logic, or function. Business applications can be executed in a number of ways, depending on the application requirements, plans for changes to features and functionality, and development constraints, such as budget or timeline.

This chapter defines the various software architecture options available for business application development and explores the components of business transactions in the following sections:

- Centralized Computing Model
- Distributed Computing Model
- Components of business transactions

Centralized Computing Model

In centralized computing, applications and data storage are executed on a central server instead of on local workstations and terminals. Prior to the advent of the personal computer revolution in the 1980s, computers were something that few organizations, let alone individuals, could afford. Mainframe computer resources were extremely centralized, expensive, and hard to operate and maintain. The Centralized Computing Model is based on resource scarcity and is characterized by "dumb" terminals and punch card data entry devices. User experience was mostly limited to an ASCII text and keyboard interface, with no GUI or pointing device.

One of the major benefits of a centralized computing model is ease of support because only a few actual computers need to be managed. Upgrades to a word processing application used by a server and 100 workstations, for example, need only be performed on the server. Thin client computers are similar to mainframe workstations in this respect, because companies realize that the Total Cost of Ownership (TCO) for full-featured desktop PCs is greater over time than for thin client workstations. The difference with early mainframe workstations is that the thin client user can run GUI applications and modern operating systems, but the application-processing and data storage functions still reside on a central server.

Another advantage to centralized computing is related to security. Managing a secure environment on a centralized computer system is easier than on a distributed computer system because a centralized system generally has fewer components.

A disadvantage to the Centralized Computing Model is that if an application error occurs, it occurs for all users simultaneously. For this reason, the shared aspects of a centralized computer system resulted in reduced fault tolerance compared to that achieved with distributed systems. Early mainframe computer users also suffered from the effects of other user load. If one person executed a command that required a great deal of the computer's available resources, all users experienced degraded performance. Data loading and storage represented another limitation in early, centralized computing environments. Disk drives were nowhere near today's sizes in terms of capacity and physical size. Tape operators were required to work in rooms with large farms of reel-to-reel computer tape drives, and data storage and retrieval needed to be scheduled in advance of application processing. You did not have the luxury of browsing a directory with gigabytes of documents and simply double-clicking on a file.

Thanks to the steady advances in integrated circuitry etching and design, computer chips have become smaller and faster. Moore's Law of a doubling in density of computer chips every year or so has held true for almost 40 years. Centralized computing has become less practical over time because the cost of computing power is no longer a prohibitive factor to owning your own computer, or a company owning thousands of computers.

Distributed Computing Model

The Distributed Computing Model is based on multiple components and servers that each provide part of the entire processing required by an application or service. It is an outgrowth of basic assumptions upon which the Internet was designed. Noncentralized computing lends itself to highly available, noncentralized calculations, and transaction processing. The popular architecture of three layers, or three tiers (presentation, logic, and data), is based on the Distributed Computing Model.

Specifically, this chapter discusses the following:

- Peer-to-peer applications
- Distributed applications
- Client/server architecture
- Web-based applications

Peer-to-Peer Applications

Peer-to-peer applications are characterized by having no centralized structure because each node in a network is capable of communicating directly with any other node. They take advantage of the widespread acceptance of Internet protocols and the increasing availability of inexpensive high-speed connections to the Internet. Internet protocols were designed to allow each node within the network to operate without need for any centralized coordination or control. This makes the Internet the ideal topology for peer-to-peer networks and peer-to-peer applications.

Peer-to-peer applications function with each participating server or device as an equal participant. In a peer-to-peer networked application, each server is both client and server depending upon whether it is requesting information (client) or serving information (server). The most infamous example of a peer-to-peer application is the music-sharing program, Napster. Napster software spread quickly as music lovers the world over began sharing MP3-encoded songs of their favorite bands and performers through peer-to-peer connections. Although Napster no longer continues to enjoy its center-stage status because of legal injunctions imposed to comply with recording industry pressures, many new music-sharing, peer-to-peer applications have appeared to take its place.

Peer-to-Peer Applications

Some of the more clever programs avoid maintaining centralized database listings of files shared on their peer-to-peer networks, making legal injunctions to interrupt the sharing of music, images, documents, and movies more difficult.

For the network administrator, for peer-to-peer applications such as Napster and the programs that have followed, the major repercussion concerns bandwidth usage. A company with a high-speed connection to the Internet must be careful to manage the bandwidth used by these programs. Traffic-shaping routers and bandwidth management practices centered around quality of service (QoS) come into play here, as more than just firewall rules become necessary to avoid sacrificing bandwidth to these programs and enthusiastic employees. Some of these programs also render your computer and network vulnerable to hacking by opening unauthorized ports.

From a security standpoint, peer-to-peer applications, such as instant messaging, present a significant security and privacy risk. Although instant messaging can provide a useful medium for communications and collaboration within an organization, the immediate adoption and use of the technology without adequate attention to its impact on security policies and the unrestricted sharing of private information can be devastating. More than one company has discovered the truth behind the phrase "Information wants to be free" as they attempt to recover from incidents involving instant messaging and chat rooms where information has been unwittingly shared with competitors and customers.

Distributed Applications

A *distributed application* distributes its processing across multiple networked computers. Distributed applications can concurrently serve multiple users and, depending on their design, make optimal use of processing resources.

Distributing an application enables you to select which parts of an application will be grouped together logically and where these groups will run. You distribute an application by creating groups and dividing application resources or tasks among the groups. Creating groups of servers enables you to partition a very large application into its component business applications. You can, in turn, partition each of these applications into logical components of manageable size and optimal location.

The Distributed Computing Model has been applied to scientific research efforts such as the search for signs of extraterrestrial intelligence, prime number discovery, finding a cure for anthrax, and many other scientific pursuits requiring massive amounts of computational power. These scientific research efforts harness the power of PCs the world over, making use of idle CPU power that might otherwise be used to perform the mundane task of a simple screensaver. The model has also led to talk of computational grids akin to electrical grids, where various sources provide or extract units of energy and, in the case of computational grids, computing power.

Each of the following shows how the concept of distributed applications can be interpreted and implemented differently:

- You can manually schedule time on a remote scientific instrument and collect the data locally. You can then transfer that file to a data repository using File Transfer Protocol (FTP). When the file is in place, you can use it as input to a simulation or post-processing program on a high-performance computer, again storing the output manually to an archive. You can then retrieve your data from the archive to do basic visualization. However, with a properly designed distributed application system, all these resources could be scheduled and accessed in a coordinated way, requiring less effort from you on the intermediate steps to your finished product.

- You might want to interact with your colleagues using audio, video, and shared applications. With remote collaboration applications, you can. Commercial and nonprofit groups develop such distributed applications for use on the emerging landscape of high-speed networks.

- A scientific research institute must sometimes run a large simulation program frequently to analyze research data. The simulation program will not be able to run in a reasonable time given the computing resources at only one high-performance computing center. By implementing a distributed application system that links resources at multiple centers through high-speed connections, the institute is able to use a larger aggregate computing resource to do one large simulation.

The next sections discuss distributed applications and distributed applications architecture in terms of the following topics:

- Application tiers
- Reasons for distributed applications
- Benefits of distributed applications
- Role of middleware in distributed application architecture

Application Tiers

Typically, a distributed application is divided into three tiers or levels: presentation tier, business logic tier, and data tier.

Figure 2-1 shows a three-tier distributed application architecture.

Figure 2-1   *Three-Tier Application Architecture*

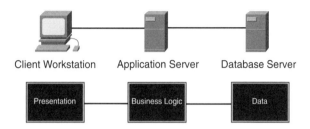

- **Presentation tier**—The presentation, or client, tier (sometimes referred to as the *front end*) is a logical layer of a distributed system that typically presents data to and processes input from the user. Usually, the presentation tier requests data from a server based on input and formats and displays the result. E-mail programs and web browsers are examples of the presentation tier of distributed applications.

- **Business logic tier**—The business logic, or middle, tier is a logical layer between a user interface or web client and the database in a distributed system. This tier is typically where business objects are instantiated. The business logic tier is a collection of business rules and functions that generate information and operate upon receiving information. Business rules can change frequently and are encapsulated into components that are separate from the application logic itself. The business logic tier is also known as the *application server tier.*

  An application client, an application server, or an application support server can implement this tier. For example, a database application can use a database client to convert user selections into Structured Query Language (SQL) statements. A database access server can support communication between the client and a database server, and the database server can use reporting software to process the information requested by a client.

- **Data tier**—The data tier is a logical layer of a distributed system that represents a computer running a Database Management System (DBMS), such as an SQL server database.

Why Distributed Applications?

Business needs are driving the trend toward enterprise-wide distributed applications. These factors represent common business drivers:

- Most modern enterprises are already distributed and need distributed information systems to support them.

- Competition creates an increased focus on the importance of customers and, consequently, on the information resources and services that are required to support interactions with customers.

- Companies hope to exploit the newest computing technologies to improve their business processes so they can stay competitive or become more efficient and profitable.

A common example of an enterprise-wide distributed application is a business process that offers customers a single point of contact within an enterprise, even though a customer business might actually require services to be provided by many different parts of the organization. To support such a business goal requires enterprise-wide information processing. Systems must be created to organize, maintain, locate, relocate, relate, summarize, and display the right data wherever it is needed. Systems must meet the needs of larger business processes while ever growing transaction volumes and databases can span terabytes. Distributed application architecture is required to fulfill these needs.

Benefits of Distributed Applications

Listed are five benefits of distributed applications:

- **Scalability**—You can distribute the processing of a particular interface across multiple server groups and, if desired, across multiple machines. This feature allows you to distribute the processing load, which can prevent the processing problems that result when concurrent, resource-intensive applications compete for the available CPU, memory, disk input/output (IO), and network resources.

- **Ease of development and maintenance**—Separating the business application logic into services or components that communicate through well-defined messages or interfaces allows you to similarly separate and simplify development. When you choose an architecture that isolates your business rules in one layer, long-term maintenance can be much easier. Code requiring change as rules change is more obvious, and you can feel more confident that you will not be affecting other areas of the application.

- **Reliability**—When multiple machines are used and one fails, the remaining machines can continue operation. Similarly, when multiple server processes are within a group and one fails, the others are available to perform work. Finally, if a machine should fail, but there are multiple machines within the application, these other machines can be used to handle the load.

- **Reusable components**—Developers who choose distributed application development create components that can be reused in other applications. This is an important goal for creating modular, reusable code.

- **Coordination of autonomous actions**—If you have separate applications, you can coordinate autonomous actions, as a single, logical unit of work, among applications. *Autonomous actions*, also called *autonomous agents*, involve multiple server groups and multiple resource manager interfaces. Such software takes action without user intervention and operates concurrently with the user, either while the user is idle or taking other actions. Workflow is a good example.

Role of Middleware in Distributed Application Architecture

Middleware is connectivity software consisting of a set of enabling services that allow multiple processes running on one or more machines to interact across a network. As shown in Figure 2-2, middleware runs on the business logic tier of a three-tiered architecture. Middleware addresses the needs of the networked enterprise to create, integrate, and manage large-scale, distributed applications in heterogeneous environments. Middleware connects disparate applications, such as web-based applications and mainframe-based legacy applications. It is also used to develop and manage new applications that are robust, scalable, and highly available.

Figure 2-2   *Business Logic Tier*

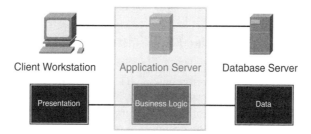

    Client Workstation   Application Server   Database Server

Presentation   Business Logic   Data

There are three types of middleware:

- Application
- Database
- Presentation

Application middleware differs from database and presentation middleware in a significant way. Database and presentation middleware let user-written components communicate with supplied database engines or web browsers. The developer has little design flexibility because the software vendor (or an industry standard like HTML or SQL) has already defined most of the rules (the formats and protocols) for the communication.

Application middleware is more like a general-purpose programming language. It lets two user-written components communicate in any way that suits the application designer and developer. Choosing a communication style is a key application design decision, particularly in deciding whether to implement synchronous or asynchronous connections.

Application middleware can be further divided into the following subcategories.

- **Data access**—Structured Query Language (SQL) performs only database access.

  Data Access middleware uses data-oriented application programming interfaces (APIs) that can be proprietary and/or standardized. It accesses data stored in a Relational Database Management System (RDBMS) using SQL. Java Database Connectivity (JDBC) is another API that connects middleware with database applications.

  Each of the major distributed RDBMS vendors has a proprietary SQL API, such as Microsoft SQL Server, Oracle Server, Sybase SQL server, and so on. Most of the vendors can also use Microsoft's "standard" Open DataBase Connectivity (ODBC) API, in addition to RDBMS-independent SQL APIs provided by third-party vendors.

  Data access products are used when the only component needing distribution is the data. The advent of stored procedures has enabled some ability to execute program logic over the network but is limited to SQL data manipulation and vendor-specific implementations.

- **Remote-procedure call (RPC)**—Enables the logic of an application to be distributed across the network. Program logic on remote systems can be executed as simply as calling a local routine.

- **Messaging-Oriented Middleware (MOM)**—Provides program-to-program data exchange, enabling the creation of distributed applications.

  MOM falls within the communication services middleware and typically includes message passing and message queuing. MOM generally uses a basic send-and-receive set of communication commands to send data to programs. MOM supports queued messages and is primarily designed to support deferred communication. Messages under a MOM system are placed into a queue and retrieved whenever the server requests them. Whether the server is available at the time the message is sent is irrelevant.

  Figure 2-3 shows that MOM typically resides in both portions of a client/server architecture and supports asynchronous calls between the client and server applications.

  Queued messaging is good for the mostly disconnected user who uses low-speed and wireless links. In addition, MOMs are especially adaptable to event-oriented development models.

Figure 2-3   *Messaging-Oriented Middleware*

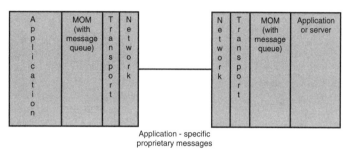

Application - specific
proprietary messages

Some of the major MOM vendors and their products include Digital DECmessageQ, IBM MQSeries, Oracle Mobile Agents, and Sybase Enterprise Messaging Services (EMS). MOMs are typically platform independent in that queues can exist between multiple platforms (for example, mainframe to UNIX, mainframe to NT, and so on).

- **Transaction Processing monitor (TPM)**—Provides tools and an environment for developing and deploying distributed applications.

    TP monitor-based middleware products are transaction-oriented. The TP monitor adds the surrounding semantics of "begin transaction" and "end transaction" to basic commands such as send and receive. These semantics allow several command chains to be grouped together as one transactional unit, and the application itself does not have to include transaction integrity logic. TP monitor generally uses MOMs or RPCs as underlying infrastructure but adds management and control functionality.

    Put simply, a TPM is an environment that inserts itself between the clients and the server resources to manage transactions and resources, provide load balancing and fault tolerance, and so on. The typical TP monitor model does not know how to handle objects; it knows how to handle only requests in the most efficient means possible.

    Figure 2-4 shows a TP monitor approach to handling transactions in a distributed environment.

    In a simple client/server system, many clients issue requests, and one server responds. However, when you scale from 50 to 500 clients or more, this model breaks most operating systems. TP monitors solve this scale-up problem by modifying the simple request-response flow using techniques that have evolved over the last few years. They also introduce tools for designing, configuring, managing, and operating client/server systems.

Figure 2-4   *TP Monitor-Based Middleware*

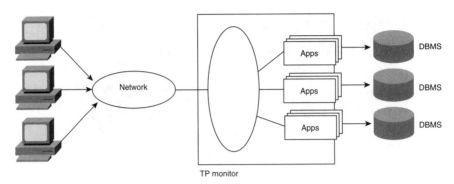

Some of the TP monitor vendors and their products are IBM CICS, Bea Systems'
Tuxedo, and Transarc ENCINA.

- **Object Request Broker (ORB)**—Enables the objects that comprise an application to
  be distributed and shared across heterogeneous networks.

  ORB is object-oriented. The ORB architecture enables pieces of programs, called
  objects, to communicate with one another regardless of what programming language
  they were written in or on what operating system they are running. The approach is
  similar to the way the RPC-based products distribute function calls to various platforms,
  except objects are distributed instead.

  An ORB acts similarly to a telephone exchange. It provides a directory of services and
  helps establish connections between clients and these services. Figure 2-5 illustrates
  some of the key ideas.

Figure 2-5   *ORB Middleware*

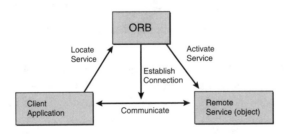

Several competing ORB architectural standards exist, including Microsoft Common
Object Model (COM) and the Object Management Group (OMG) Common Object
Request Broker Architecture (CORBA). Microsoft COM provides a natural interface

to desktop-based visual application development tools, but COM has almost no presence on UNIX systems.

OMG CORBA is a platform-independent middleware solution, but it does not provide as simple an integration with Windows applications and tools as COM.

The scope of the problem to be solved determines which type of middleware will be used.

Client/Server Architecture

Client/server is a network computational architecture in which each computer or process on the network is either a client or a server.

Servers are powerful computers or processes dedicated to managing disk drives (file servers), printers (print servers), or network traffic (network servers). Servers provide services to clients on a network. *Clients* are devices or entities on a network that request services from a server. Clients include PCs/workstations, PDAs, and so on. Clients rely on servers for resources, such as files, devices, and even processing power for server-based application processes.

Clients and servers can be located on the same processor, different multiprocessor nodes, or on separate processors at remote locations. The client typically initiates communications with the server; the server rarely initiates a request with a client. A server can support many clients and act as a client to another server. A client can also request resources from multiple servers.

Servers can be multipurpose (one server offering multiple services such as file and print) or single-purpose. Servers can also be dedicated and nondedicated. Dedicated servers service only the network. Nondedicated servers service the network and also act as a workstation.

Detailed discussions of client/server architecture and applications are presented with the following topics:

- Examples of client/server applications
- Components of client/server applications
- Benefits of client/server applications
- Two-tier client/server architecture
- Three-tier client/server architecture
- Multiple-tier client/server architecture
- The benefits and uses of thin and thick clients

Examples of Client/Server Applications

The client/server design is central to most applications and programs that use networks. Some examples of client/server applications follow:

- Netscape or Internet Explorer browser can retrieve a web page from a World Wide Web server.
- Ping program can verify a remote computers operation.
- Nslookup program can perform name and address resolution.

Client/server is simply the distribution of resources (files, programs, bitmaps, and so on) around a computer-based network and the management of those resources to the benefit of the enterprise.

Client/Server Architecture Components

A basic client/server architecture is a two-tier architecture. A client, or front-end portion, interacts with the user, and a server, or back-end portion, interacts with the shared resource.

A client is a process (program) that sends a message to a server process (program), requesting that the server perform a task (service). Client programs usually manage the user-interface portion of the application, validate data entered by the user, and dispatch requests to server programs. The user sees and interacts with the client-based, front-end process of the application. The client process contains solution-specific logic and provides the interface between the user and the rest of the application system. The client also manages the local resources that the user interacts with, such as the monitor, keyboard, workstation CPU, and peripherals. A key element of a client workstation is the Graphical User Interface (GUI).

A server process (program) fulfills the client's request by performing the task requested. Server programs generally receive requests from client programs, execute database retrieval and updates, manage data integrity, and dispatch responses to client requests. Sometimes, server programs execute common or complex business logic.

Server-based processes can run on another machine on the network. This server could be the host operating system or network file server; the server is then provided both file system services and application services. In some cases, another desktop machine provides the application services. The server process acts as a software engine that manages shared resources, such as databases, printers, communication links, or high powered-processors. The server process performs the back-end tasks that are common to similar applications.

Benefits of Client/Server Applications

Client/server computing arose because of a change in business needs. Businesses today need integrated, flexible, responsive, and comprehensive applications to support the complete range of business processes.

Because client/server computing tries to address problems experienced by developers working on nonclient/server applications, here is a list of some of the problems found with pre-client/server applications and systems:

- Applications were developed to model vertical applications and business processes.
- Applications were built in isolation.
- Applications were implemented as monolithic systems.
- Applications were complex.
- Supporting technology was based on a centralized control model.

In addition, traditional monolithic enterprise applications are expensive to maintain and difficult to further develop without understanding the entire application. These problems are addressed in the client/server architecture by separating the GUI, business logic, and data repository from each other. This architecture allows a change to the GUI without requiring any changes to the other layers.

In general, the development and implementation of client/server computing is more complex, more difficult, and more expensive than traditional, single-process applications. The only reason to build client/server applications is because the business demands the increased benefits of applications that can handle complexity.

The benefits of client/server application architecture follow:

- Client/server architecture is aligned with both the user view and the business process view.
- Client/server architecture allows organizations to modify business rules without changing the entire system.

Client/server techniques, when implemented correctly, can change the way companies do business, so they can enhance their competitive position and do business more profitably. Successful applications impact company business both internally and externally. The client/server application model can potentially improve business processes, add efficiencies, increase productivity, and improve the bottom line.

Two-Tier Client/Server Architecture

Three types of client/server application architectures exist: two-tier architectures, three-tier architectures, and multiple-tier architectures.

In a two-tier architecture referring to a client/server architecture, the user interface runs on the client and the database is stored on the server. The actual application logic can run on either the client or the server. Figure 2-6 shows a two-tier client/server architecture.

Figure 2-6   *Two-Tier Architecture*

User Interface   Data
Business Rules

With two-tier client/server architectures, the user-system interface is usually located in the user desktop environment, and the database management services are in a more powerful server machine that services many clients. Processing management is divided between the user system interface environment and the database management server environment. The database management server provides stored procedures and triggers.

The two-tier client/server architecture is a good solution for distributed computing when workgroups are 12 to 100 people interacting on a LAN simultaneously. It does, however, have several limitations:

- When the number of users exceeds 100, performance begins to deteriorate. This limitation is a result of the server maintaining a connection through *keepalive* messages with each client, even when no work is being done.

- Implementing processing management services using vendor proprietary database procedures restricts flexibility and choice of Database Management System (DBMS) for applications.

- Current implementations of the two-tier architecture provide limited flexibility in moving (repartitioning) program functionality from one server to another without manually regenerating procedural code.

Three-Tier Client/Server Architecture

Today, to meet the needs of the business, application architecture must reflect the complete range of business requirements. A three-tier architecture is a newer client/server architecture and consists of three well-defined and separate processes, each running on a different platform. The three-tier architecture does not, however, mandate a three-tier physical design. Two tiers, for example presentation and business logic tiers, can exist on the same physical server.

The three-tier design has many advantages over traditional two-tier or single-tier designs:

- The added modularity makes it easier to modify or replace one tier without affecting the other tiers.

- Separating the application functions from the database functions makes it easier to implement load balancing.

- The three-tier client/server architecture improves performance for groups with a large number of users (in the thousands), and improves flexibility when compared to the two-tier approach.

A limitation of three-tier architectures is that the development environment is reportedly more difficult to use than the visually oriented development of two-tier applications.

The three layers in a client/server application architecture (as shown earlier in the chapter) are reproduced in Figure 2-7. This application architecture does not demand multiple hardware platforms, although such technology can be utilized if the environment is robust and reliable and the business is prepared to pay the additional costs associated with workstation and LAN technology.

Figure 2-7   *Three-Tier Architecture*

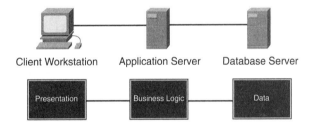

Client Workstation   Application Server   Database Server

Some additional facts are as follows:

- **Presentation**—The presentation layer, or user interface layer, provides the human/machine interaction. The presentation layer handles input from the keyboard, mouse, or other device and output in the form of screen displays.

  This first layer is the GUI of the application; it can also be called the data capture layer. This means that the data is captured and converted from a human representation to a computer representation.

- **Business logic**—The application layer gives the application program its character. For example, application logic makes the difference between an order entry system and an inventory control system. This layer is often called the business logic layer because it contains the business rules that drive a given enterprise.

  This layer applies the business rules to the data captured in the first layer. It is responsible for converting the data to a business context and adding information about the business rules. The user does not interact with the software in this layer at all. However, this layer is critical because it validates the data to make sure that the data is in the correct form and that validation is applied to the data both coming from, or going to the server. The business rules must be only rules; they must not process the data.

- **Data**—The data layer is the bottom layer that provides the generalized services needed by the other layers, including file services, print services, communications services, and, perhaps most important, database services.

  This layer processes the data, which is now in a technology context. The process is not dependent on the actions of the user interface. The processing does not need to be logical in human terms. This layer is all about storing the data and calculating results.

NOTE   When most people hear the term client/server, they only think of database services as the bottom data layer. That is a narrow view. The client/server architecture applies to all kinds of services, including file services and print services.

As previously discussed, in the three-tier architecture, a middle tier was added between the user system interface client environment and the database management server environment. You can implement this middle tier in a variety of ways, such as using transaction processing monitors, message servers, or application servers. Therefore, different variations of three-tier client/server architectures also exist:

- **Three-tier with Transaction Processing monitor technology**—The most basic type of three-tier architecture has a middle layer consisting of Transaction Processing monitor (TP monitor) technology. The TP monitor technology is a type of message queuing, transaction scheduling, and prioritization service where the client connects to the TP monitor (middle tier) instead of the database server. The monitor accepts the transaction, queues it, and takes responsibility for managing it to completion, freeing up the client. TP monitor technology also makes other provisions:

  — Updates multiple DBMSs in a single transaction

  — Connects to a variety of data sources including flat files, nonrelational DBMSs, and the mainframe computers

  — Attaches priorities to transactions

  — Facilitates robust security

  Using a three-tier client/server architecture with TP monitor technology results in a considerably more scalable environment than a two-tier architecture with direct client-to-server connection. For systems with thousands of users, TP monitor technology is reportedly one of the most effective solutions.

- **Three-tier with message server**—Messaging is another way to implement three-tier architectures. Messages are prioritized and processed asynchronously. Messages consist of headers that contain priority information and the address and identification number. The message server connects to the Relational DBMS (RDBMS) and other data sources. The difference between TP monitor technology and the message server is that the message server architecture focuses on intelligent messages, whereas the TP monitor environment has the intelligence in the monitor and treats transactions as incompetent data packets. Messaging systems are good solutions for wireless infra-structures because a dedicated, always-on link is not required.

- **Three-tier with an application server**—The three-tier application server architecture allocates the main body of an application to run on a shared host rather than in the user system interface client environment. The application server does not drive the GUIs; it shares business logic, computations, and a data retrieval engine. Advantages include less security to worry about because of less software on the client, more scalable applications, and cheaper support and installation costs on a single server than maintaining each on a desktop client. Use the application server design when security, scalability, and cost are major considerations.

- **Three-tier with an Object Request Broker architecture**—Currently, the industry is developing standards to improve interoperability and determine what the common Object Request Broker (ORB) will be. Developing client/server systems using technologies that support distributed objects holds great promise because these technologies support interoperability across languages and platforms, in addition to enhancing system maintainability and adaptability. Two prominent distributed object technologies currently exist:

  — Common Object Request Broker Architecture (CORBA)

  — Component Object Model/Distributed Component Object Model (COM/DCOM)

The industry is working on standards to improve interoperability between CORBA and Microsoft's COM/DCOM. The Object Management Group (OMG) has developed a mapping between CORBA and COM/DCOM that is supported by several products.

Multiple-Tier Client/Server Architecture

The growth and acceptance of the Internet in both businesses and homes is changing the face of many industries. With a browser on virtually every desktop, companies can deploy a multi-tier architecture in which web servers act as a middle tier, managing interactions with web-based clients.

Figure 2-8 shows a multiple-tier client/server architecture.

Figure 2-8   *Multiple-Tier Architecture*

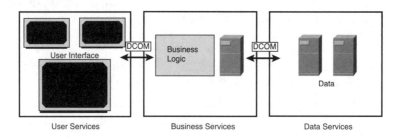

A web-based client architecture can have three or more layers. This multi-tier architecture provides many benefits over a traditional (two-tiered) client/server architecture:

- Installing and deploying the user interface is virtually instantaneous—only the web interface in the middle tier needs to be updated.

- Because the application itself is server-based, users always access the most up-to-date version.

- Without a *thick* client interface (also referred to as *fat* clients), deploying, maintaining, and modifying applications is easier, no matter where the client is located.

These benefits explain the growing popularity of the multi-tier architecture and why almost every client/server application provider has retooled, or is retooling, to support web-based clients.

Thin Clients and Thick Clients

In client/server applications, a client designed to be especially small so that the bulk of the data processing occurs on the server is called a *thin* client. In its purest form, a thin client refers to a desktop device that is only equipped to handle input and output for your monitor, keyboard, and mouse. Although the term usually refers to software, it is increasingly used for computers, such as Network Computers (NCs) and Net PCs, which are designed to serve as the clients for client/server architectures.

The traditional PC system is usually referred to as a *thick* or *fat* client. Specifically, in a client/server environment, a client machine that contains the program logic and performs most or all of the application processing while the server performs little or none is called a thick client. Again, the term usually refers to software but can also apply to a network computer with relatively strong processing capabilities.

Thin clients are PC-like devices that embody the idea of the network "appliance." Although like the PC in appearance and user functionality, the thin client is a clear demarcation from the PC at the technical level. Unlike PCs, thin clients cannot function without being connected to a server. Thin clients do not house hard drives or localized operating systems. Applications either run directly on the server and are used through a terminal program, or they are downloaded from the server and executed locally within the thin client's RAM.

The thin client, however, is far removed from its cousin, the mainframe terminal. Thin clients utilize Windows and UNIX-based graphical applications as a normal PC or workstation from the server side and not the client. Thin clients represent traditional host-based computing with a significant difference: full functionality with not only host-based applications, but also the full array of client/server and PC-based programs—all residing on the server and administered and configured there.

Why Choose Thin Client Computing?

Few would disagree that costs of client/server computing have begun to outpace the capacities of most organizations to keep up. PCs are generally underused in proportion to their processing and storage power, and they are very expensive to maintain.

In client/server computing, most applications are developed along the thick client model. Servers primarily function as repositories for data and shared code, while the clients (PCs and workstations) handle much of the processing. As programs have moved from text-based to GUIs, the PC has become thicker, and the costs of configuring and maintaining the PC to run a multitude of memory-intensive, locally loaded programs have risen exorbitantly. Adding to this cost is an upgrade cycle for both hardware and software that requires an almost constant allocation of resources and time.

As PC technology improves and software becomes "thicker," upgrade cycles become more relentless, asset volatility reaches unjustifiably high levels, and the total cost-of-ownership figures are genuinely frightening. This result has compelled many organizations to explore alternatives to the thick client general-use machine.

Thin-client technologies offer an approach that moves beyond client/server toward a network-centric model, reducing ownership costs and centralizing network resources. In a thin-client environment, you would have a thick server. The thick side of the environment handles all the application processing. All application overhead, file processing, report production, and so on, takes place on the server. All user interface mechanisms take place on the client workstation. In this type of environment, the network is not bombarded with traffic from file read/write requests or print requests. That processing is done on the server side. In most network environments, thin clients can lead to dramatic performance improvements.

Two types of thin clients exist:

- **Network computers**—A network computer (NC) is a client device designed to take advantage of its being part of a distributed-computing client/server network. A true network computer system complies with the NCRef1 standard. These machines are usually designed to run Java software and not Windows applications, and can look completely different than PCs.

  IBM, Sun, and Acorn Computers manufacture NCs. Sun thin clients, commonly known as JavaStations, are the biggest market leaders in this field.

  NCs contain RAM, a processor, and input devices. NCs are connected to the network through an Ethernet port and boot directly from the server. After the boot process begins, the server downloads the NCs operating system into the thin-client RAM. Requested applications are also downloaded in this manner.

  Because the NC is not dependent on a single processor architecture or operating system, different devices, based on many different systems, have been designed. An NC advantage is that it can use RISC (reduced instruction set computer) processors that often offer equivalent performance to an Intel CPU without the cost.

- **Net PC**—The Net PC is a platform that was codeveloped by Microsoft and Intel in response to the NC. The concept involves sealing up a traditional PC and making it easier to manage. Unlike the NC, Net PCs run on the Windows operating system, reducing training costs of users familiar with Windows PCs.

  Net PCs are completely reliant on the server for everything they do. When booted, a Net PC notifies the server that it is present on the network. No operating system download occurs. The Net PC emulates the Windows NT environment that is running on the server. The Windows environment and its associated variables are contingent on the user login profile and the published applications available, similar to the "roaming profiles" model used on NT and Windows LANs.

  Processing on the Net PC is limited to keystrokes, screen paints, and mouse clicks. The server does the rest. A typical Net PC comes preconfigured with four to eight MB RAM, a processor, and input devices. The Net PC also houses a ROM chip that can contain data, such as a static IP address and configuration information for local peripherals such as storage devices and printers.

The key difference between a PC and a Net PC is that the Net PC is centrally administered. Users cannot install their own software; it must be downloaded from a server first. In addition to the inability to install software, the hardware is also sealed.

Benefits and Uses of Thin and Thick Clients

To cut costs and make better use of both technical support personnel and existing computers, organizations are beginning to adopt thin client computing. Organizations can simplify their networks and computing systems by eliminating substandard machines and outdated software from the network without sacrificing access.

With thin client computing, organizations can escape endless, pricey workstation upgrades. To upgrade hardware, they only need to upgrade servers, not individual computers or clients. The client does not need to do more than process keystrokes, mouse clicks, screen refreshes, and sound. The benefits of building thin client systems are highly dependent on what data is processed and the nature of the processing.

Some applications are much better implemented with a thick client approach. Because the network provides more bandwidth capability, the client machine can perform additional tasks that previously were unattainable. For example, as video on demand becomes more prevalent for training and web broadcasting, the capability of the client machine to decode MPG video and audio streams is a must. A true thin client would not have this capability.

Because more plug-ins are available for Netscape and Internet Explorer browser-based software, a thin client is not capable of performing these tasks. For example, when viewing a Portable Document Format (PDF) file in a browser window on a personal computer, the browser actually launches a local copy of Adobe Acrobat Reader to provide the code to view the document. On a true thin client, the serving side would need to perform this function. Thick client technology is also used for CAD (Computer-Aided Design), engineering applications, and scientific research applications.

Web-Based Applications

The web application is a fairly new concept and has no widely accepted, standard definition. Some people view a web site as an example of a web application, while others make a clear distinction between web sites and web applications.

In relation to the Applications Essentials course, a web application runs on the World Wide Web. A web application is a kind of client/server application that runs inside a browser or, more accurately, that displays inside a browser because most of the processing occurs on the server. It usually involves extracting information from a database, performing an action against that information, and displaying the results. Online stores are web applications. Collaboration systems that allow employees of a company to find and share data through the Internet or intranet are also web applications. Figure 2-9 shows the overall architecture of a web application.

Web applications typically reduce the amount of work necessary to maintain a site, and present more targeted and accessible information to site visitors. Web applications often allow visitors to customize a site to satisfy their particular tastes or needs. In many instances, web applications allow collaboration or interactivity on a scale that has never before been possible.

Figure 2-9   *Web Application*

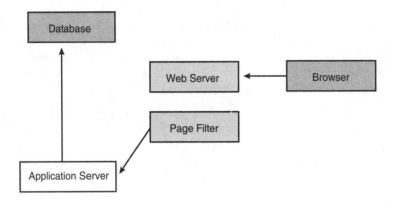

Generally, there are five different types of web applications:

- **Public applications**—Public applications are sites that provide services for thousands of clients around the world. The FedEx web site, www.fedex.com, is an excellent web application. It directly ties with the internal Federal Express tracking system, allowing businesses and individuals to inquire about the location of their packages without the help of a FedEx employee.

- **Enterprise applications**—Enterprise applications are intranet sites, operating inside an organization at the enterprise level. An intranet is any private network that supports web applications. Similar in many ways to public applications, web applications that run on intranet sites can include human resources systems, procurement systems, and other company-wide functions.

- **Group applications**—Group applications serve a workgroup or office. These include a number of common functions, such as scheduling or document management systems and functions specific to a particular group. Usually accessed over a local network by a small number of users, these applications are generally maintained by the members of the group they serve, with little or no IT support.

- **Personal applications**—Personal applications are run by a single user. A single user deploys personal applications such as calendaring and other personal productivity functions. The applications usually run on a desktop PC, but the web interface makes them easily accessible from anywhere on the local network, and potentially from anywhere in the world. (The distinctions between group and personal applications are not clear—personal applications generally have a single data owner.) These applications can include MyYahoo!, AvantGo, or StarOffice.

- **Embedded applications**—Embedded applications run on appliance-like devices that are not general-purpose computers; examples include printers, scanners, facsimile machines, and networked storage devices. Increasingly, these devices are being built with network access and a web-based user interface.

NOTE   The distinction between web sites and web applications is subtle and relies on the ability of a user to affect the state of the business logic on the server. For those systems where the web server (or an application server that uses a web server for user input) allows business logic to be affected through web browsers, the system is considered a web application. For all web applications, the user must impart more than just navigational request information. Web application users typically enter a varied range of input data. This data might be simple text, check box selections, or even binary and file information. In essence, a web application uses a web site as the front end to a more typical application.

The following sections outline issues related to web-based application basics:

- Web application advantages
- Web application architecture
- Web application enabling technologies
- Web application programming languages

Web Application Advantages

Web applications have numerous advantages:

- They extend the life and usefulness of legacy systems by extending them to the web and to the world.
- They entail high return on investment. According to International Data Corporation (IDC), businesses are seeing a 240 percent return on investment from intranet applications (web applications), compared to 90 percent for client/server applications.
- They leverage the benefits of the web in applications. The web has these benefits: (1) ubiquity, (2) standards-based, and (3) universal client (web browser). Because of these benefits, web applications are usually platform-independent and support multiple operating systems. The applications also allow wider management, data accessibility, and improved end-user and customer support.
- They cut costs on hardware resources. Web applications do not require high-end PCs on every desk. They run on any device that can host a browser—a low-end PC, a laptop, a network computer, or even a handheld device.
- They entail flexibility, scalability, security, and stability. Web applications are based on open standards.

Web Application Architecture

Web application architecture will become significantly more elaborate with new technologies. This section reviews a fairly complete and complex architecture that contains most of the concepts and components that are expected to be the cornerstones of web applications.

Figure 2-10 shows the web application architecture.

Figure 2-10 *Web Application Architecture*

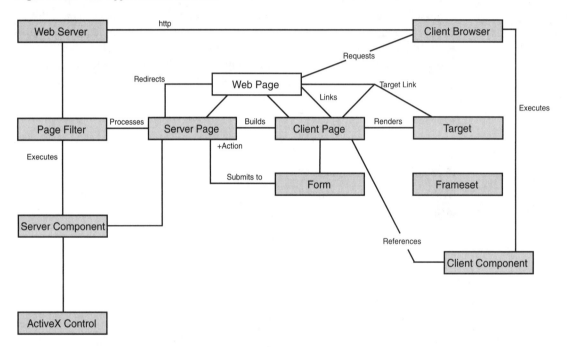

A web application architecture includes these major pieces:

- Pages
- Forms
- Components
- Frames

The first piece of a web application architecture is the *page*, by far the most fundamental component of a web application. Browsers request pages from servers. Web servers distribute pages of information to browsers. The makeup and organization of web pages make up the user interface for the application. In web applications, the browser acts as a generalized user interface container with specific user interfaces being defined by each page's content.

In addition to static HTML pages, web applications utilize dynamic scripted pages extensively. The scripted pages contain code that is executed by the web server (or likely delegated to a scripting engine or page filter) that accesses server resources (database servers) to ultimately build an HTML formatted page. The newly formatted page is sent back to the browser that requested it. The two types of dynamic scripted pages are *server scripting* and *client scripting*.

For server scripting, all activity on the server, as affected by the user, occurs during the page request. Business logic on the server is activated only by the execution of scripts inside the pages requested by the browser. This server processing updates the business state of the server and prepares an HTML formatted page (user interface) for the requesting browser.

The server is not the only component in a web application that executes scripts. The browser can execute scripted code in a page. When the browser executes a script, however, it does not have direct access to server resources. Typically, scripts running on the client augment the user interface as opposed to defining and implementing core business logic.

Scripts on the client are appropriate for immediate data validation or for assisting navigation. Client scripts often simply embellish the user interface but provide little, if any, business logic behavior. This is changing, however, as client-side scripting becomes more powerful and client-side resources become a bigger part of the overall application.

The second piece of a web application architecture is the form. Any serious web application accepts more than navigation input from its users. Web applications often elicit textual, selectable, and Boolean information. HTML forms are the most common mechanism for collecting this type of user input.

An HTML *form* is a collection of input fields that is rendered in a web page. Basic input elements include a text box, text area, check box, radio button group, and selection list. Each form is associated with an action page. This action page represents the name (and location) of the page that receives and processes the information contained in the completed form. The action page is almost always a dynamic page, containing server-side scripts (or compiled code).

Figure 2-11 shows a form with a text box, a selection list, and four check boxes, as well as the submit and reset buttons.

Figure 2-11 *HTML Form*

The user submits a completed form back to the server with a page request for the action page. The web server finds the page and interprets (or executes) the page's code. The code in the page can access any information in the form that was submitted with the request. This is the major mechanism for obtaining user input in a web application. Data collected through the form can be passed to the server insecurely through a Common Gateway Interface (CGI), or securely through a Secure Socket Layer (SSL) or similar technologies.

The third piece of a web application architecture is the component. A *component* is an encapsulated piece of code that performs some function for an application. This function could be processing a business rule, such as the computation of a sales tax, or it could be retrieving information from a database for an application. A component's key characteristic is that when it is created for use, the code for the component and the information associated with the component are packaged together. If there are multiple versions of the same component in use at one time, each one keeps its information separate from the others. There is no danger of information in one polluting the information of another.

All business logic does not have to be interpreted from scripts in web pages. Larger and more enterprise-savvy web applications use a third, middle tier of components. This middle tier exists between the user interface and the database system and is typically a set of compiled components that run on an application server.

The following describes the two types of components that are available to you in web-based applications:

- Server components can be reused in multiple applications or in multiple modules of the same application. If server-side scripting were used exclusively, a code maintenance danger would quickly occur, as snippets of script are cut and pasted between ASP or PHP pages. HTML-formatted web pages can also specify components for execution on the client machine. The most common of these components are Java Applets and ActiveX controls. Both are self-contained, compiled components that run at the browser's request. Depending upon browser and component configuration, these components can have access to browser or client machine resources.

- Client components are useful in providing user interface functionality not readily achievable with standard form or HTML elements. A client component can be a display control that visualizes a three-dimensional model. It can also represent a user interface control to specify dates with a control window that pops up a miniature calendar from which dates can be clicked. Some client components have no visual display and are used to retrieve client machine configuration information. The insecurity of some client-component technologies, such as ActiveX, has been demonstrably exploited, and the benefits of using such components should be weighed against the risks they bring.

- Server components extend your scripting capabilities by providing a reusable means of gaining access to information. For example, the database access component enables scripts to query databases. Whenever you want to query a database from a script, you can use the database access component; you do not need to write complex scripts to perform this task. You can call components from any script or programming language that supports automation.

- Server-side scripts handle interpretation and processing on the server before transmission to the browser. The script can add or change the contents of a page before the browser receives it. In fact, the browser is completely unaware that any server-side processing was performed. To the browser, the processed result is indistinguishable from a static web page.

- Client scripts are JavaScript (or VBScript) code embedded in the HTML-formatted page. The code is executed in response to browser-generated events (document loaded, button pressed, and so on). With the acceptance of the new Dynamic HTML specification, client scripts can access and control nearly every aspect of the page content. Additionally, DHTML further opens up access to the browser object model itself, enabling client-side scripts to interact with other browser resources.

The fourth piece of a web application architecture is the *frame*. Using frames enhances the user interface capabilities on the client. Frames and the ability to target browsers enable the user interface designer to have multiple web pages active and open at the same time. The browser divides its rectangular client window (where web pages are rendered) into distinct frames (or subrectangles). Any web page can specify a frameset, and a frameset can be embedded inside other framesets (a process called *nesting*).

Scripts and components in any of these pages can interact with scripts and content in others. In HTML, this is all managed by associating a target with each frame in a browser window.

NOTE   A proper discussion of the use of frames in user interface design is beyond the scope of these discussions. However, know that the use of frames constitutes a major design decision in a web application, because it indicates that multiple pages are simultaneously available to the user. Frames also affect the ability to perform site traffic analysis and extract meaningful path analysis information about how users browse a site. Therefore, frames might not be the best design choice at all times.

Web Application Enabling Technologies

Web applications are built on these key infrastructure elements and synergies:

- **Web browser**—A software application used to locate and display web pages. The two most popular browsers are Netscape Navigator and Microsoft Internet Explorer.

  A web browser is the interface by which a user interacts with a web application. A web browser has two major functions: communicate user requests to a web server and render formatted information returned by the web server.

Again, in web applications, the browser acts as a generalized user interface container with specific user interfaces being defined by each page's content.

- **Web server**—A computer that delivers (serves up) web pages. Any computer can be turned into a web server by installing server software and connecting the machine to a network (private or public). Many web server software applications are available, including public domain software from NCSA and Apache, and commercial packages from Microsoft, Netscape, and others.

  A web server accommodates requests from users, retrieves requested files or applications, and issues error messages.

  When a web server receives a request for a web page from a browser such as http://www.yahoo.com/index.html, it maps the Uniform Resource Identifier (URI) to a local file on the host server. In this case, the file, index.html, is somewhere on the host file system. The server loads this file and serves it out across the network to the user's web browser. The browser and web server, talking to each other using Hypertext Transfer Protocol (HTTP), mediate the entire exchange. This workflow is shown in Figure 2-12.

Figure 2-12 *Static Content*

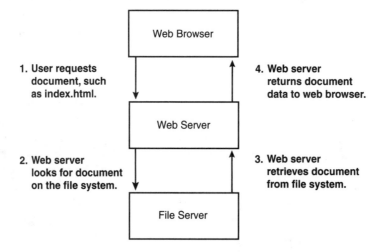

- **Web servers serving dynamic content**—For dynamic content, the process is basically the same as with nondynamic web server content. Instead of finding the file on the file system, the web server identifies other programs, such as CGI programs, to execute the requests. Those programs then transmit their output through the web server to the user's web browser that is requesting the dynamic content. Figure 2-13 shows what happens when a browser requests a page dynamically generated from a CGI program.

Figure 2-13 *Dynamic Content*

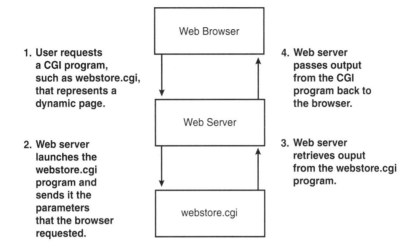

1. **User requests a CGI program, such as webstore.cgi, that represents a dynamic page.**

2. **Web server launches the webstore.cgi program and sends it the parameters that the browser requested.**

4. **Web server passes output from the CGI program back to the browser.**

3. **Web server retrieves ouput from the webstore.cgi program.**

- **Servlet engines**—A Java servlet engine is a program that runs Java servlets. A Java servlet is a java applet that runs within a web server environment (analogous to a Java applet that runs within a web browser environment).

  A Java servlet engine is usually installed on the web server. Its sole function is to run Java servlet and JavaServer Pages. The servlet engine creates the servlet configuration object and uses it to pass the servlet initialization parameters to the init method. The initialization parameters persist and are applied to all invocations of that servlet until the servlet is destroyed. If the initialization is successful, the servlet is available for service. If the initialization fails, the servlet engine unloads the servlet.

- **Application server**—An application server is a middle-tier application program run on a mid-sized machine that handles all application operations between browser-based computers and a company's back-end business applications or databases. Because many databases cannot interpret commands written in HTML, the application server works as a translator, allowing, for example, a customer with a browser to search an online retailer's database for pricing information.

  An application server's main function is to communicate with one or more relational databases to generate the dynamic content needed from the existing data sources and information systems running in your environment, and to communicate with a web server to provide services to the client.

  An application server's design helps developers to isolate the business logic in their projects (usually through components) and develop three-tier applications. Many application servers also offer additional features, such as transaction management, clustering and failover, and load balancing.

- **Combining web servers and application servers**—Web servers and application servers can be combined into one, although usually, they are separate servers. A web server typically serves up HTML (including certain dynamic HTML such as CGI scripts) and images for viewing on a browser. An application server typically contains raw business/application programming and mainly processes data using objects or code that represent application logic. Note the following advantages of separating the application server from the web server:

  — It aids in performance. For example, web servers are usually highly tuned to server data from disks, such as HTML pages and images. Such a server is tuned to speed up input/output (I/O) operations. In contrast, application objects usually operate on pure logic—they take data in from a stream, process it, and send new data back out. This is a CPU rather than an I/O-intensive activity. The application server is best served when it is tuned for CPU usage.

  — It adds to the stability of an application. Application servers are tested by their respective vendors to work in the context of executing application logic, and are thoroughly debugged in that context. Likewise, web servers are heavily tested within the context of serving documents either dynamically or statically. Joining the two in one server can cause unexpected bugs that neither vendor has tested for.

  — It adds to the security of the application and data. When the web and application servers are separated by a firewall, a compromise of the web server by an intruder does not necessarily lead to the compromise of the application server, which can contain sensitive business logic, and allows direct access to the database server(s).

- **Database server**—A computer in a LAN dedicated to database storage and retrieval is called a database server. The database server is a key component in a client/server environment. It holds the Database Management System (DBMS) and the databases. Upon requests from the client machines, the server searches the database for selected records and passes them back over the network. The database server is the data layer of an "n-layer" client/server application architecture.

Web Application Programming Languages

The common languages used in programming web applications include, but are not limited to the following:

- **HTML** (HyperText Markup Language)—An authoring language used to create documents on the World Wide Web.

HTML defines the structure and layout of a Web document by using a variety of tags and attributes. The correct structure for an HTML document starts with <HTML><HEAD>(enter here what the document is about)</HEAD><BODY> and ends with </BODY></HTML>. All the information you want to include in your web page fits in between the <BODY> and </BODY> tags.

Hundreds of other tags are used to format and lay out the information in a web page. For example, <P> is used to make paragraphs, and <I>some text</I> is used to italicize fonts.

HTML creates only static web pages. However, a new form of HTML, Dynamic HTML, has evolved. Dynamic HTML refers to new HTML extensions that enable a web page to react to user input without sending requests to the web server. Microsoft and Netscape have submitted competing Dynamic HTML proposals to the World Wide Web Consortium (W3C), which is producing the final specification. However, HTML specifications are taken as a rather loose guideline. Significant extensions to official HTML specifications have been in widespread use since HTML 1.0. These common terms remain in use:

— **Content**—Makes up the actual core of a document and includes all the words, images, and links that a user can read and interact with.

— **Hyperlink**—A link from one document to another, to any resource, or within a document. Hyperlink text is usually highlighted in some fashion. The default is usually blue, underlined text, but your display can vary.

— **Block-level elements**—These elements provide structure to an HTML document. Block-level elements can contain other block-level or inline elements nested under them. Examples include a division element <div>, a span element <span>, and a paragraph element <p>.

— **In-line**—Inline elements, as opposed to block-level elements, cannot contain any other HTML elements. Almost always used in the context "in-line image," this refers to a resource that is placed directly into a document.

— **URI**—A standard way of easily expressing the location and data type of a resource. URIs, in general, take the form "protocol://address" where protocol could be HTTP, FTP, or Real Time Streaming Protocol (RTSP), and the address is the server and path name (if any) of a given resource or page.

● **CGI and PERL**—CGI (the abbreviation of Common Gateway Interface) is a specification for transferring information between a web server and a CGI program. A CGI program is any program designed to accept and return data that conforms to the CGI specification. CGI programs are the most common way for web servers to interact dynamically with users. For example, many HTML pages that contain forms use a CGI program to process the form's data after it is submitted.

Many people associate CGI with Perl (Practical Extraction Report Language) because Perl is used to create a majority of the CGI scripts found on the web. However, CGI is not language specific—it is merely a protocol for allowing the web server to communicate with a program. CGI scripts can be written in any language. Common choices, in addition to Perl, include C, Java, Python, and Visual Basic.

One problem with CGI is that each time a CGI script is executed, a new process starts. Starting new processes on a web server adds extra overhead. For busy web sites, this can noticeably slow down the server. A more efficient solution, but one that it is also more difficult to implement, is to use the server application programming interface (API), such as Internet Server API (ISAPI) or Netscape Server API (NSAPI). Using Java servlets is another increasingly popular solution.

Perl is probably the most popular language for writing a CGI program. Perl is a programming language, written by a man named Larry Wall, especially designed for processing text. Perl, like HTML, is an interpretive language that facilitates building and testing simple programs.

- **Java/JavaScript**—Java is a high-level programming language developed by Sun Microsystems. Java is an object-oriented language similar to C++ but simplified to eliminate language features that cause common programming errors. Java is a compiled language and has several features that make the language well suited for use on the World Wide Web. Small Java applications called Java applets can be downloaded from a web server and run on your computer by a Java-compatible web browser, such as Netscape Navigator or Microsoft Internet Explorer. Java is designed to be distributed, portable, and secure.

JavaScript is a scripting language developed by Netscape to enable web authors to design interactive sites. Although it shares many of the features and structures of the full Java language, it was developed independently. JavaScript can interact with HTML source code, enabling web authors to embellish their sites with dynamic content. JavaScript is endorsed by several software companies and is an open language that anyone can use without purchasing a license.

JavaScript can add simple programs and functions to HTML pages. It is not compiled, so the execution of javascript is fairly slow. JavaScript must be embedded with the HTML page; the code has to be inside the same file or at least read at the same time as the HTML page. Like most scripting languages, JavaScript solves problems by joining existing resources, rather than by creating resources to solve the problem. As an example, JavaScript can be used to control the browser or to dynamically modify the documents that the browser displays. Java, in contrast, can be used to build a browser.

Java and JavaScript have very little in common besides the name. Java is a full-featured, object-oriented, programming language capable of living inside or outside a web browser. JavaScript, in contrast, is a limited, object-based, scripting language.

- **ActiveX**—A loosely defined set of technologies developed by Microsoft. It is not a programming language but a set of rules for how applications should share information. ActiveX enables interactive content for the World Wide Web. ActiveX enriches web sites using multimedia effects, interactive objects, and sophisticated applications that create a user experience comparable to that of high-quality CD-ROM titles. ActiveX ties together a wide assortment of technology building blocks to enable these "active" web sites.

  ActiveX includes both client and server technologies and consists of the interactive objects in a web page that provide interactive and user-controllable functions to enliven the experience of a web site.

  ActiveX Documents enable users to view non-HTML documents, such as Microsoft Excel or Word files, through a web browser. Active Scripting controls the integrated behavior of several ActiveX controls and Java applets from the browser or server.

  Java Virtual Machine (JVM) is the code that enables any java-compatible browser, such as Internet Explorer with ActiveX controls enabled, to run Java applets and integrate Java applets with ActiveX controls.

  ActiveX Server Framework provides several web server-based functions, such as security and database access.

  VBScript, a scripting language related to ActiveX, enables web authors to embed interactive elements in HTML documents. Just as JavaScript is similar to Java, VBScript is similar to Visual Basic. Currently, Microsoft Internet Explorer supports Java, JavaScript, and ActiveX. Netscape Navigator supports only Java and JavaScript, although plug-ins can enable support of VBScript and ActiveX. The difference between Java applets and ActiveX controls is that Java applets can be written to run on all platforms, whereas ActiveX controls are currently limited to Windows environments.

  ActiveX controls represent a specific way of implementing ActiveX technologies. An ActiveX control can be automatically downloaded and executed by a web browser. Programmers can develop ActiveX controls in a variety of languages, including C, C++, Visual Basic, and Java. An ActiveX control is similar to a Java applet. Unlike Java applets, however, ActiveX controls have full access to the Windows operating system. This access gives them much more power than Java applets, but with this power comes a certain risk that the applet might damage software or data on your machine.

In an effort to control this risk, Microsoft developed a registration system so that browsers can identify and authenticate an ActiveX control before downloading it. Unfortunately, two false certificates were generated and distributed, allowing controls to appear as originating from Microsoft. ActiveX and Visual Basic have been exploited in numerous virus programs, and represent a significant security risk to Windows users and their computer networks. The "I love you" virus, for example, was written in Visual Basic Script and takes advantage of ActiveX controls and vulnerabilities in the Windows security architecture to gain access to other programs such as Microsoft Outlook in order to propagate itself. Many derivatives of this kind of virus have been found, and security administrators are constantly working to restrict the damages, both to actual data and to network bandwidth degradation. The scale of these problems is no trivial matter, and Microsoft is working to find ways to maintain interactive and dynamic functionality without sacrificing security.

Components of Business Transactions

Whether centralized or distributed, business application transactions are at the heart of doing business, and have various common elements and concepts. These elements determine the network design.

As an example of the implications of business transaction elements on network design, if a customer database is queried upon user login, that transaction is greatly impacted by whether the database is close (network-wise on the same 100 Mbit segment) to the application servers. If customer order history is also a required application feature, the size of each order transaction between the application servers and database servers dictate aspects of geographic redundancy and the costs of data replication versus the costs of high-speed private links between systems.

The network architectures required to execute transaction-based systems vary depending on these key elements. Whether the transaction is entirely new, or is a web-based, redesigned core business process, attention must be paid to these essential application and network concepts.

Specific subsections discussing the components of business transactions include the following:

- Database systems
- Transactions
- Object-oriented design
- Object-oriented programming
- Data modeling
- System enablers

Database Systems

A database is a collection of information organized to allow a computer program to quickly select desired pieces of data. You can think of a database as an electronic filing system.

Fields, records, and files organize traditional databases:

- **Field**—A single piece of information
- **Record**—One complete set of related fields
- **File**—A collection of related records

For example, a telephone book is analogous to a file. It contains a list of records, each of which consists of three fields: name, address, and telephone number. Other examples of database applications follow:

- Computerized library systems
- Automated teller machines
- Flight reservation systems
- Computerized parts inventory systems

To access information from a database, you need a Database Management System (DBMS). This system is a collection of programs that enables you to enter, organize, and select data in a database. That functionality is why some people define a database as a set of related files created and managed by a DBMS.

To best present the information about database systems, this section is divided into the following:

- What is a DBMS?
- Features of a DBMS
- Components of a DBMS
- Types of databases
- The role of SQL
- Deployment considerations

What Is a DBMS?

DBMS programs enable you to store, modify, and extract information from a database; that is, DBMS software controls the organization, storage, retrieval, security, and integrity of data in a database. DBMSs range from small systems that run on personal computers to huge systems that run on mainframes or high-end servers.

From a technical standpoint, DBMS types can differ widely. The terms relational, network, flat, and hierarchical all refer to the way a DBMS organizes information internally. The internal organization affects how quickly and flexibly you can extract information.

You request information from a database using a stylized question (a query). Here is an example of a query:

```
SELECT * WHERE NAME = "SMITH" AND AGE > 35
```

This query requests all records in which the Name field is SMITH and the Age field is greater than 35. The set of rules for constructing queries is known as a query language. Different DBMS types support different query languages. A semistandardized query language called Structured Query Language (SQL) is supported by many DBMS types.

The information from a database can be presented in a variety of formats. Most DBMSs include a report writer program that allows you to output data in report form. Many DBMSs also include a graphics component that allows you to output information in graphs and charts.

Features of a DBMS

The major features of a DBMS follow:

- **Data security**—The DBMS can prevent unauthorized users from viewing or updating the database. Using passwords, users can access the entire database or database subsets called subschemas; for example, in an employee database, some users might be able to view salaries, whereas others can view only work history and medical data.

- **Data integrity**—The DBMS can ensure that no more than one user can update the same record at the same time. It can keep duplicate records out of the database.

- **Interactive query**—Most DBMSs provide query languages and report writers that let you interactively interrogate the database and analyze its data. This important feature gives you access to all management information, as needed.

- **Interactive data entry and updating**—Many DBMSs provide a way to interactively enter and edit data, allowing you to manage your own files and databases. However, interactive operation does not leave an audit trail and does not provide the controls necessary in a large organization. These controls must be programmed into the application's data entry and update programs.

- **Data independence**—The data-structure details are not stated in each application program. The program asks the DBMS for data by field name; for example, a coded equivalent of "give me customer name and balance due" would be sent to the DBMS. Without a DBMS, the programmer must reserve space for the full structure of the record in the program. Any change in data structure requires changing all application programs.

Components of a DBMS

The database engine is that part of a DBMS that actually stores and retrieves data. Most DBMSs include an API, which enables programmers to directly control the engine without going through the user interface. A DBMS typically includes five main components:

- **Data Description Language (DDL)**—Describes the structure of the database.

- **Data Manipulation Language (DML)**—Provides the necessary commands for all database operations, such as storing, sorting, retrieving, updating, and deleting database records.

- **Query Language**—Structured Query Language (SQL) and Query By Example (QBE) are examples of query languages.

- **Data dictionary**—Data dictionary is a central repository for information, schemas, and relationships.

- **Utility programs**—Utility programs include support for interactive processing, database security, backup and recovery, audit trails, data integrity, and shared updates, which means more than one user can use the database simultaneously.

Network Data Manipulation Language

A network data manipulation language consists of a set of operators for processing data represented in the form of records and links. Examples of such operators include the following:

- Locate a specific record given a value of some of its fields.

- Move from a parent to its first child in a link.

- Move from one child to the next in a link.

- Move from child to parent within a link.

- Create/delete/update a record.

- Connect an existing child record into a link.

- Disconnect a child record from a link.

- Disconnect an existing child record from one occurrence of a given link type, and reconnect it to another.

These operators are typically all record-level (as suggested by the examples themselves), as in the hierarchical model.

Types of Databases

DBMSs can differ widely in how they organize information internally. There are four basic types of databases.

The earliest database, the *hierarchical database*, can be structurally represented as an upside-down tree with each row of objects linked to objects directly beneath it. It is sometimes referred to as a tree model and is very similar to the concept of the "family tree," like Explorer in Windows. As you go down the tree, the details of the file become more specific. This allows you to progress through a series of questions, or parameters, that specify an exact file to reach the desired data.

Figure 2-14 shows the layout of a typical hierarchical database.

Figure 2-14 *Hierarchical Database Layout*

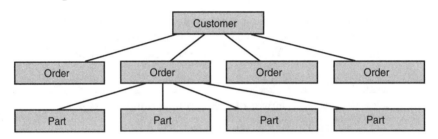

Here are some facts about a hierarchical database:

- A record to which several lower-level records are linked is called a *parent*.
- All records linked below the parent record are called *children*.
- The highest-level parent in the hierarchical model is known as the *root*. The root is the beginning of the model and the record you would start with if you began using the model.
- The lowest-level records are called *leaves*. The leaves have no children records and, like a tree, are only linked to their parent branch.
- Children records are linked to their parent by adding what are known as *pointer fields* to the records. The links are maintained between parent and child records by these pointer fields.

Hierarchical databases are generally used on mainframes. Such databases have considerable advantages.

- A hierarchical database substantially decreases programming effort and program maintenance because of its environment maintaining data independence.

- A hierarchical database promotes database integrity because there is always a link present between parent and children records. The hierarchical model proves efficient when a database contains a large volume of data in one-to-many relationships.

However, although the hierarchical model relieves the designer and programmer from data-dependence problems, it still requires knowledge of the physical level of data storage. The hierarchical model has these additional disadvantages:

- Does not support many-to-many relationships

- Allows each child to have only one parent and, therefore, cannot deal with some real-world problems that are based on children with more than one parent

- Is complex to manage and maintain, and can lack flexibility

- Requires extensive, time-consuming, and complicated programming activities if you want to change or modify the database

- Maintains high data redundancy

The second database type is the *network database*. A network database stores information by linking all related records with a list of pointers. These records can be in one or more files, located on one or more servers. A network database can make use of the World Wide Web to locate the files to which they are pointed.

Figure 2-15 below illustrates a network database structure.

Figure 2-15 *Network Database Structure*

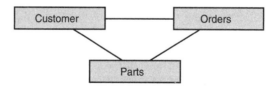

You can regard a network database structure as an extended form of the hierarchical data structure. In many ways, the network database model was designed to solve some of the serious problems with the hierarchical database model. Specifically, the network model solves the data redundancy problem by representing relationships in terms of sets, rather than hierarchies. In addition, instead of using a single-parent tree hierarchy, the network model uses set theory to provide a tree-like hierarchy, with the exception that children records (called *member records*) can have more than one parent record (called *owner records*). This relationship allows the network database to support many-to-many relationships.

The network database model also incorporates certain integrity rules. Similar to the hierarchical model, the network model includes built-in support for specific referential integrity, by virtue of its primary data structure, the link. For example, you can enforce the rule that a child cannot be inserted unless its parent already exists.

The network database model is generally used on mainframes and has several advantages over the hierarchical database model:

- Supports many-to-many relationships, while the hierarchical database model does not
- Contains a superior data access type and flexibility to that found in the hierarchical model
- Enforces database integrity because the user must first define the owner record and then the member
- Achieves sufficient data independence to partially isolate the programs from storage details

The network database model still has shortcomings:

- Difficult to design and use properly
- Difficult to make changes in a database (some changes are impossible)
- Complex structure for the programmer

The third database type is the *relational database*. The relational database stores data in the form of related tables. Data is organized in two-dimensional tables or relations. Each row is called a *tuple*, and each column is called an *attribute*. Think of a relation (relational table) as a file, tuples as records, and attributes as fields. Relational databases are powerful because they require few assumptions about how data is related or how it will be extracted from the database. As a result, the same database can be viewed in many different ways. A single database in a relational system can be spread across several tables. This differs from flat-file databases, in which each database is self-contained in a single table.

Figure 2-16 shows a relational database structure:

Figure 2-16 *Relational Database Structure*

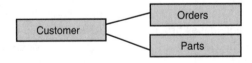

Figure 2-17 below shows a snapshot of the tables of a relational database.

Figure 2-17 *Relational Database Tables*

Order Customer Table

Order#	Customer#
93-1123	AA2340987
93-1123	AA2340987
93-1154	AA2340987
93-2321	T12389790
93-2342	T12389790
93-4596	T12389790

Customer Table

Customer#	CustomerName
AA2340987	Intex, Inc.
GV1203948	Alpha, Inc.
MT1238979	Sonet

Order Table

Order#	Part#	Qty.	Customer#
93-1123	037617	81	AA2340987
93-1123	053135	36	AA2340987
93-1154	063364	32	AA2340987
93-2321	087905	39	T12389790
93-2342	006776	72	T12389790
93-4596	055622	81	T12389790
93-1154	067587	29	T12389790
93-2321	005449	33	T12389790
93-2342	036893	52	AA2340987
93-4596	06525	29	AA2340987
93-4596	090643	33	AA2340987

The relational database model, implemented through a relational Database Management System (RDBMS), performs the same basic functions as the hierarchical and network models' DBMS, in addition to other functions that facilitate the implementation and use of the relational database. The relational database model is the most popular model in the software market.

The following list summarizes the relational table's characteristics:

- A table is a two-dimensional structure composed of rows and columns. Each table row (called tuple) represents a single entity within the entity set.
- Each column represents an attribute, and each column has a distinct name.
- Each row/column intersection represents a single data value.
- Each table must have a primary key that uniquely identifies each row.
- All values in a column must conform to the same data format.
- Each column has a specific range of values, known as the attribute domain.
- Each row carries information describing one entity occurrence.
- The order of the rows and columns is immaterial to the DBMS.

A *key*, or a field that identifies a record, must be used to retrieve records from a relational database. A primary key is best for retrieving the desired data because it uniquely identifies every record in the table. Two records can't have the same value in the primary key column. DBMSs require that each table possess a primary key.

In some cases, more than one value is required to uniquely identify the contents of a table. These are called *composite keys*; for example, the last name, first name, and department in a table of professors' records.

To link records from one table to records of another table, both tables must have a field (or column) containing the same types of data. That field must also be the primary key in one of the tables. In the other table, the field is called the *foreign key.*

Relational databases can run on many platforms, including PCs, and they are well suited to client/server computing models. The relational model's power and flexibility make it the predominant design approach in the modern business world.

The relational model has many advantages:

- **Simple and easy to maintain**—You can modify or add new entities, attributes, or tables at any time without restructuring the entire database.

- **Reduced redundancy**—Because the data between tables can be easily connected, the relational model provides a minimum level of controlled redundancy to eliminate most redundancies commonly found in file systems.

- **Structural independence**—Unlike the hierarchical and network database models, the relational database structure is of no interest to users. Therefore, the relational model achieves the structural independence not found in the other database models.

- **Easy to design**—Because the relational model achieves both data and structural independence, designing and managing the contents of the database is much easier.

Although it is powerful and flexible, the relational model has disadvantages:

- It requires substantial hardware and operating system overhead because the RDBMS hides most of the system's complexity. A more powerful computer is required to perform all the RDBMS-assigned tasks. Consequently, the relational database system tends to be slower than other database systems.

- The easy-to-use asset of the relational model presents a problem in that relatively untrained people can generate badly designed reports and databases. As the database grows, lack of proper design slows the system down and produces the data anomalies.

The fourth type of database is the *object-oriented* variety. Certain information systems have complex data structures not easily modeled by traditional data structures. The newer object-oriented database can be employed when hierarchical, network, and relational structures are too restrictive. In addition, the increased emphasis on process integration is a compelling reason to adopt object-oriented database systems.

There are many examples of object-oriented database adoption:

- Computer-Integrated Manufacturing (CIM) focuses on using object-oriented database technology as a process-integration framework.

- Advanced office automation systems use object-oriented database systems to handle hypermedia data.

- Hospital patient-care tracking systems use object-oriented database technologies because they are easy to use.

All these applications are characterized by having to manage complex, highly interrelated information, which is a strength of object-oriented database systems. Object-oriented database systems provide feasible solutions to complex problems for users.

Object-oriented databases incorporate several key elements associated with, and stemming from, object-oriented programming (OOP), such as complex objects, abstract data types (ADT), encapsulation, and inheritance. These networked databases can link a variety of data objects, such as text, graphics, photos, video, and sound, and associate them with an object. An object-oriented database is managed by an object-oriented Database Management System (OODBMS).

Figure 2-18 shows an object-oriented database structure.

Figure 2-18 *Object-Oriented Database Structure*

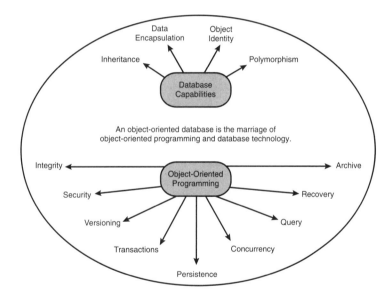

An object-oriented data model's design is the first step in applying an object-oriented database to a particular problem area. Developing a data model includes these major steps:

- Object identification
- Object state definition
- Object relationships identification
- Object behavior identification
- Object classification

An object-oriented data model has three main components:

- Static properties, such as objects, attributes, and relationships
- Integrity rules over objects and operations
- Dynamic properties, such as operations or rules, defining new database states (based on applied state changes)

Object-oriented databases have the ability to model all three of these components directly within the database, supporting a complete problem/solution modeling capability. Prior to object-oriented databases, databases were capable of directly supporting static properties and integrity rules, and relied on applications to define the dynamic properties of the model. The disadvantage of delegating the dynamic properties to applications is that these dynamic properties can't be applied uniformly in all database scenarios because they are defined outside the database in autonomous applications. Object-oriented databases provide a unifying paradigm that allows you to integrate all three aspects of data modeling and apply them uniformly to all the database users.

An OODBMS's objective is to provide consistent, data-independent, secure, controlled, and extensible data management services to support the object-oriented modeling paradigm.

An OODBMS must fulfill two basic criteria:

- It must be a DBMS containing these facilities: persistence, secondary storage management, concurrency, recovery, and ad-hoc query facilities.
- It must be object-oriented equipped with these facilities: complex objects, object identity, encapsulation, types or classes, inheritance, overriding combined with late binding, extensibility, and computational completeness.

Object-oriented databases are modular and cost-effective. They have the following advantages:

- Object-oriented databases can easily handle one-to-many relationships combined with many-to-one relationships.
- Object-oriented databases are often better equipped for multimedia than other database structures. The world of information is also made up of data, text, pictures, and voice. Many traditional DBMSs manage text in addition to data, but few manage both with equal proficiency. For example, although a relational DBMS can provide a Large Object (LOB) field that holds multimedia data, it is not equipped to store multimedia data because extensive use of the LOB field strains the processing. An object database can handle data, text, graphics, voice, and video with the same ease that modern systems handle data.
- Object-oriented databases can directly represent complex behaviors by incorporating behaviors into the database, which substantially reduces the complexity of applications that use the database. In an ideal scenario, most of the application code deals

with data entry and display. All the functionality associated with data integrity and data management is defined within the basic object model. This approach has several advantages: all operations are defined once and reused by all applications, and changes to an operation affect all applications and simplify database maintenance. (Although, most databases require the applications to be recompiled.)

- Object-oriented database applications development entails high productivity because of frequent code reuse and the ability to cope with greater complexity resulting from incremental refinement of problems.

- Object-oriented databases' polymorphism and dynamic binding allow increased design flexibility.

- Object-oriented databases benefit both developers and users because of their natural structures and simplicity of representing data as objects.

Although an object-oriented database has many advantages, it does have some drawbacks:

- OOP skills required. (In general, most skills today are with relational database.)

- Huge investment because not much data is presently in object form.

- Poor query and reporting tools.

- Limited concurrency control and transaction management; consider how to lock all or part of an object.

- Performance unproved.

- Steep learning curve (not like Microsoft Access).

The Role of SQL

SQL means Structured Query Language, and is pronounced either 'see-kwell' or as separate letters. It is a nonprocedural, standardized query language for manipulating and retrieving data from a relational database.

Figure 2-19 shows a sample Employee table in a relational database.

Figure 2-19 *Relational Database Employee Table*

Name	Age	Occupation
Will Williamson	25	Electrical Engineer
Dave Davidson	34	Museum Curator
Jan Janis	42	Chef
Bill Jackson	19	Student
Don DeMarco	32	Game Programmer
Becky Boudreaux	25	Model

The six rows are the records in the Employee table. To retrieve information from this table, you must use SQL to write queries and execute the queries against the database. Two examples of sample SQL statements follow:

- To retrieve a specific record from this table, for example, Dave Davidson, instruct the DBMS to retrieve the records where the Name field is equal to Dave Davidson. The following SQL statement makes this query:

  ```
  SELECT * FROM EMPLOYEE WHERE NAME = "DAVE DAVIDSON"
  ```

- If the DBMS is instructed to retrieve all the fields in the record, the employee's name, age, and occupation are returned to the user. The following SQL statement makes this query:

  ```
  SELECT * FROM EMPLOYEE
  ```

Historically, SQL has been the favorite query language for DBMSs running on mini-computers and mainframes. Increasingly, however, SQL is being supported by PC database systems because it supports distributed databases (databases that are spread over several computer systems). This enables several users on a LAN to access the same database simultaneously.

The SQL language is widely used to access and manipulate relational databases. Several levels of SQL are defined, and these levels are generally upwardly compatible.

The first basic version of SQL is ANSI X3.135-1989, "Database Language — SQL with Integrity Enhancement." It is usually referred to as SQL'89. The functionality of SQL'89 includes schema definition, data manipulation, and transaction management.

The second version of SQL is ANSI X3.135-1992, which describes an enhanced SQL and is known as SQL'92. The enhancements include schema manipulation, dynamic creation and execution of SQL statements, and network environment features for connection and session management.

A third version of SQL is currently under development by ANSI and the International Organization for Standardization (ISO). This version is referred to as SQL3. The enhancements of SQL3 include the ability to define, create, and manipulate user-defined data types in addition to tables.

The SQL language continues to evolve, pulled in two directions by vendors who add new features to give competitive advantage to their offerings, and by the ANSI committee seeking to keep the language standardized (and growing) in a common way.

SQL defines standard components and facilities for RDBMSs. SQL database components include schemas, tables, and views. A schema describes the structure of related tables and views. Tables hold the actual data in the database. (They consist of rows and columns. Each row is a set of columns, and each column is a single data element.) Views are derived tables and can be composed of a subset of a table, or the result of table operation (for example, a join of different tables).

The SQL standard describes facilities to perform five specific functions:

- A **schema definition** defines the structure of the database, integrity constraints, and access privileges.
- **Data retrieval** retrieves data from a database with a standard query interface.
- **Data manipulation** populates and modifies the contents of a database by adding, modifying, or deleting rows and columns.
- **Schema manipulation** modifies the structure, integrity constraints, and privileges associated with the tables and views in the database.
- **Transaction management** defines and manages SQL transactions.

The most commonly used statement in SQL is the SELECT statement, which retrieves data from the database and returns the data to the user. In addition to the SELECT statement, SQL provides statements for creating new databases, tables, fields, and indexes, and statements for inserting and deleting records. ANSI SQL also recommends a core group of data manipulation functions. Many database systems have tools for ensuring data integrity and enforcing security that enable programmers to stop the execution of a group of commands if a specific condition occurs.

Database Deployment Considerations

When deploying a database, consider the following issues that affect the ease and speed of database operation:

- Tuning
- Network overhead
- Data warehousing
- Parallel processing
- Backups
- Physical storage
- Security

Monitoring the performance of production databases is crucial. Database tuning is an essential follow-through to performance monitoring. Tuning is the only way to ensure maximum database performance and efficient use of the system resources. In reality, most database tuning is reactive rather than proactive because tuning is a complex, time-consuming process.

Tuning requires time, specialized skills, and adherence to a structured methodology for monitoring performance, collecting data, and implementing changes. Database performance tuning can be divided into three major categories:

- Database-access optimization, such as index tuning and SQL reusability

- Database instance tuning for shared pool, I/O and sort operations, parallel query, and operating systems
- Database structure tuning for storage sizing and database objects placement

Generally, two areas can be "tuned" to improve database performance.

- **Database server**—Database server tuning entails adjusting the database software installation and the configuration of the database server to better interface with the operating system. The goal is to ensure optimal use of the machine and the operating system's resources.
- **Database**—Database tuning entails adjusting the implementation of the objects in the database to improve the applications' access to these objects.

The amount of data required to effectively tune a database is enormous. Data from multiple sources must be pulled quickly and efficiently, with no impact to the production environment. The volume of data required and collection process complexities are often enough to discourage regular database tuning. Note that the following data must be collected:

- **Database schema and instance data**—The database schema and instance data are extracted from the data dictionary, V$ dynamic performance tables, and other sources. Instance data includes the current instance-parameter settings and V$table statistics, which are used to analyze the optimal settings for important instance parameters.
- **Database workload**—Database workload is a key factor in many tuning decisions, such as assessing the relative importance of a particular table, which is then used to determine the table placement and the type and number of indexes required. Workload data includes the volume of application transactions that use the database.
- **System environment data**—System environment information includes system configuration data (the number and capacity of disks, memory, and CPU power). A thorough picture of the power and various capacities of the system environment is essential to database tuning decisions, such as allocating memory to the various instance memory structures.

Many facilities for database server and performance tuning are provided by the popular DBMSs, such as CA-OpenIngres 2.0, Informix OnLine 5.0, Borland InterBase 6.5, Microsoft SQL Server 2000, Oracle9i, Centura SQLBase 7.0, and Sybase SQL Server 11.

Oracle Expert is such a tool. Oracle Expert is an Oracle Enterprise Systems Management application for automated performance tuning. Oracle Expert can analyze and solve performance problems detected by Oracle Performance Manager, Oracle TopSessions, and Oracle TRACE. Oracle Expert automates the process of collecting and analyzing data, and contains a rules-based, inference engine that provides "expert" database tuning recommendations, implementation scripts, and reports.

The second issue that affects the ease and speed of database operation is network overhead. Network packets are bursts of electrical voltage organized into discrete packages governed by countless network protocols. Packets can be broken into user data and network overhead. *User-data packets* carry the files and print jobs that travel across the wire. The other packets are dedicated to *network overhead*. For example, NetWare servers use Service Advertising Protocol (SAP) packets to broadcast their file and print services, and routers use routing information protocols, such as IGRP, EIGRP, RIP, OSPF, RTMP, and NLSP, to communicate with other routers.

Put another way, network overhead is the proportion of the network bandwidth used for management and is unavailable for the transport of user data. Particularly in the case of bulk transfers, which already deal with large amounts of data, you want to keep network overhead low.

Take steps to reduce the network overhead as much as possible. Two elements are associated with optimizing communications within the network. At the hardware level, you need a fast network. At the software level, you need a way to send numerous short messages without incurring processor overhead.

Overhead's major culprit is the operating system itself, which has about three times the overhead of the TCP protocol. You can substantially reduce processing overhead by implementing header prediction. In addition, you can reduce overhead if careful thought is put into the implementation of the buffer layer.

The odds that an incoming packet is destined for the same TCP connection as the previous packet are approximately 90 percent. Using this information, you can cache a pointer to the Transmission Control Block (TCB) used by an incoming packet and compare that information with the next incoming packet. If the compare fails, you perform a search to find the appropriate TCB. This saves you tremendous overhead.

Operating system timers, if not carefully designed, can actually use as many CPU cycles as TCP. Since a timer is used for every TCP packet, this can be a major source of overhead.

Memory accesses, in relation to TCP computing times, are a huge source of overhead. Combining tasks, such as copying and computing the checksum, even if it only saves one memory read, can reduce the total overhead by several factors of the total time it takes for the actual TCP computation.

Although seemingly a good idea, moving protocols such as TCP onto silicon to create hardware protocol processors can have detrimental effects on overhead and provide unnecessary complexity. TCP software implementations work just fine if they are implemented correctly.

The third issue affecting the ease and speed of database operation is data warehousing. A *data warehouse* is a collection of data designed to support management decision-making. It combines many databases across an entire enterprise.

A more technical definition of data warehouse is a subject-oriented, integrated, time-variant, nonvolatile collection of data in support of management's decision-making process:

- **Subject-oriented**—Focuses on a subject defined by users and contains all data needed for the users to understand the subject.

- **Integrated**—Data is combined across systems and transactions.

- **Time-variant**—A history of the subject over time, not a single moment in time.

- **Nonvolatile**—Does not change while a query is running.

- **Supports management's decision-making process**—Focuses on planning for the future, not day-to-day operation.

The potential advantage of data warehouses, or data marts, is obvious, but their implementation is not easy. Several issues must be considered in data warehousing implementation.

One of the biggest mistakes of many large data-warehousing projects is a false assumption that requirements are fixed; when, in fact, the needs are continually evolving. Data warehousing is an ongoing, organizational process, not a one-time solution to a problem.

Facilitating access to data for authorized purposes also facilitates access for unauthorized uses. The corporate database is a valuable asset. Enabling access amounts to weakening security and puts the asset at greater risk. Corporate data security is always an issue, but a data warehouse multiplies the potential loss from a security breach. However, too much emphasis on maintaining security means denying access and reducing the value of the data warehouse to those for whom it was created.

Another potential problem is the "nice-to-know" syndrome, where a program is developed and data is collected only for developers to discover that the information gathered has no impact on the decision problem that prompted the study.

Data warehouse initiatives have discovered that some of the most valuable data is not transactional, nor even internal to the organization. Instead, key information might include Internet postings, clippings from trade journals, and even images. These diverse data types substantially magnify demands on the data warehouse. One significant and difficult technical issue is how to index poorly structured data, such as images and text, so that it can be searched and analyzed.

The growth of data warehouses strains the ability of single-processor and single-computer systems to handle the load. Data warehouses often grow to enormous sizes and are accessed by larger and larger numbers of users. Data warehouses holding several hundred gigabytes of data are now common. Complex queries are run on these data warehouses to gather business intelligence and to aid in decision-making. Such queries require considerable processing time to execute (otherwise called overhead). More and more organizations are turning to parallel-processing technologies to give them the performance, scalability, and reliability they need.

Parallel processing, the fourth issue that affects the ease and speed of database operation, is becoming increasingly important in the world of database computing. Parallel processing takes a large task, divides it into several smaller tasks, and works on each of those smaller tasks simultaneously. This divide-and-conquer approach's goal is to complete the larger task in less time than it would have taken in one large chunk. By executing these queries in parallel, you reduce the elapsed time, while still providing the required processor time.

Parallel execution overhead can be divided into the following three areas:

- **Startup cost** refers to the time it takes to start the parallel execution of a query or DML statement. Time and resources are needed to divide one large task into smaller subtasks that can be run in parallel. Time is also required to create the processes needed to execute those subtasks and to assign each subtask to one of these processes. For a large query, the startup time might not be significant in terms of the overall time required to execute the query. For a small query, however, the startup time can result in a significant portion of the total time.

- **Interference** refers to the slowdown that one process imposes on other processes when accessing shared resources. Although the slowdown resulting from one process is small, a large number of processors can cause a substantial impact.

- **Skew** refers to the variance in execution time of parallel subtasks. As the number of parallel subtasks increases (perhaps as a result of using more processors), the amount of work performed by each subtask decreases. The result is a reduction in processing time required for each of those subtasks, as well as for the overall task. However, variations in the size of these subtasks always occur. In some situations, these variations can lead to large differences in execution time between the various subtasks. The net effect of this occurrence is that the processing time of the overall task becomes equivalent to that of the longest subtask.

Additional Terms

A *data mart* is a data repository that serves a particular community of knowledge workers. It is a database, or collection of databases, designed to help managers make strategic decisions about their business. While a data warehouse combines databases across an entire enterprise, data marts are usually smaller and focus on a particular subject or department. Some data marts, called dependent data marts, are subsets of larger data warehouses.

Data scrubbing is the practice of monitoring a data warehouse and removing data that is not trustworthy or current.

Two-tiered data warehousing consists of a data warehouse, where multiple sources of data have been extracted, transformed and cleansed, and one or more data marts, where subject-specific data is deployed to business users.

A *data mall* incorporates multiple, smaller data marts providing information for specific user needs, while using the data warehouse to store large amounts of commonly accessed data. A data mall's objective is to build a hybrid data warehouse/data mart solution that is integrated, scaleable, manageable, quick to deliver, and able to support the demands of end users and corporations. The process of implementing a data mall is different than implementing a first-generation data warehouse, and must be planned for accordingly. The data mall is not a complicated theory, but a modernized approach to balancing and supporting the unique needs of business users and IT professionals.

The fifth issue that affects the ease and speed of database operation is *data backup*. In every database system, the possibility of a system or hardware failure always exists. If a failure occurs and affects the database, the database must be recovered and restored. Backups protect your database from media failures or other media errors. A media failure can physically damage one or more of your database files or render them unusable. In this case, you can use the most recent backup to replace the damaged files and reconstruct your database.

The two main types of database backups are full backups and incremental backups. In addition, your database can be online or offline when you want to perform a backup. These types are defined as follows:

- **Full backups**—A full backup creates a copy of all data and journal files (that is, data files, online redo log files, control files, and so on), providing a copy of the entire database at one point in time. It is probably the easiest and most reliable way of backing up a database. Full backups archive the entire database, so they require a large amount of storage space. In addition, this backup technique is not usually feasible because of database availability requirements or the volume of data to be backed up. However, you can restore a database relatively quickly using a full backup because you can simply copy the backup files over the damaged originals. You can restore a database to the point in time you performed the full backup and copied database files.

- **Incremental backups**—An incremental backup creates a copy of only the journal files that have changed since the last backup. These files provide a copy of the changes made to the database since the last backup. Because an incremental backup only contains changes made to the database you must perform a full backup prior to the incremental backup to restore your database at a later time.

   Incremental backups require only a small amount of storage space to archive journal files. However, restoring from archive journal files can take more time than a full backup to restore a database because the DBMS must take the time to roll over all transactions in the back-up journal files. You can use an incremental backup with a full backup to restore a database to any point between the time of the previous full backup to the time the incremental backup was completed.

- **Offline backups**—An offline backup must be performed after a database has been shut down. The database administrator must schedule a time to shut down the database and notify all users so they can disconnect from the database. Offline backups can be inconvenient for users because they must remember to complete all active transactions and disconnect from the database before it is shut down. Offline backup is also known as *cold backup*.

- **Online backups**—An online backup can be performed while a database is running. The database administrator does not have to shut down the database, and users do not need to disconnect. Online backups are more convenient for users because no action is required on their part. A DBMS must explicitly provide the capability to back up a database online because it is still running and still has users connected. This is also referred to as a *warm backup*. The online backup is performed from a snapshot of the database.

A database backup policy needs to be prepared for backing up a database system. The following factors influence database backup policies:

- **Database availability requirements**—If a database needs to remain available at all times during weekdays, for example, full backups can be performed only on weekends when the database can be shut down.

- **Data volumes**—The total volume of data requiring backup must be compared with the available storage capacity of the backup media. You must determine whether the backup storage capacity (for example, one DAT tape per backup session) is sufficient for the volume of data held in the database. If the backup storage capacity is insufficient, a concept for partial database backup must be prepared. This might involve backing up the data of individual applications or individual sectors of the database in rotation, or backing up only modified data. The possibilities of partial backup depend on the database software in use.

- **Maximum permissible data loss**—Here, you must specify whether a loss of data accumulated in the course of one day is permissible in the event of damage to a database, or whether the database should be restorable right up to the last transaction. The latter option is generally chosen in cases where high demands are placed on data availability and integrity.

- **Restart time**—The maximum permissible time taken to restore a database after a crash must be specified to meet the applicable availability requirements.

- **Possibilities of backing up provided by the database software**—Standard database software does not generally support all conceivable possibilities of data backup, such as partial database backup. Individual cases require a check as to whether the prepared database backup policy can be implemented with the available mechanisms.

This information can be used as a basis for defining a database backup policy, which should include a specification of the following items:

- Persons responsible for carrying out data backups
- The intervals at which database backups are to be performed
- The database backup techniques

- The times at which database backups are to be performed
- The data volume to be backed up in each session
- Documentation on performed data backups
- Storage locations for the database backup media

Here is an example of a backup policy:

- Backup from Monday to Saturday: Starting time: 3:00 a.m.

  Perform a backup of all relevant data using the online database backup feature of the DBMS. The database is not shut down.

- Backup on Sunday: Starting time: 3:00 a.m.

  Shut down the database and perform a full, offline backup.

Physical storage is the sixth issue affecting ease and speed of database operation. With businesses staking their futures on information-intensive applications, such as data warehousing, Internet-based commerce, document processing, and teleconferencing, the demands on storage are exploding. Storage already often accounts for 40 to 60 percent of computer system costs. For applications moving to incorporate imaging, video, multimedia, or virtual simulation, storage requirements are poised to grow—not twofold or threefold—but one-hundred, one-thousand, and even ten-thousand fold!

Physical storage for databases and backups can be on hard drives or tape systems. Companies in both the mainframe and open system enterprise environments have improved performance and cost-effectiveness of storage through *Redundant Array of Independent Disks (RAID)* technologies. RAID enables multiple small disks to operate together as one large disk. RAID technology also improves a storage system's resilience to disk failure by using multiple disks and data distribution and correction techniques.

However, as the demands on storage grow, the limitations of RAID become self-evident. Inherent architectural trade-offs begin to surface, such as performance versus data protection; read versus write performance; and large versus small data transfers. All these situations limit the performance, efficiency, and cost-effectiveness of traditional RAID storage. For many, the write penalties of RAID, wasted capacity of 1:1 mirroring, and expense/performance limitations of disk caching and buffering are becoming increasingly unacceptable.

The storage server is a new technology that is expected to deal with these problems. With its own central or distributed intelligence and storage management software, a storage server manages a network of intelligent devices throughout the array to enable real-time storage operation optimization. This capability, combined with the ability to logically distribute data streams across any number or combination of physical disks, enables optimal performance through the following means:

- Highly efficient parity calculation
- Elimination of unnecessary read/write operations
- Highly parallel, asynchronous operations

- Concurrent support for multiple RAID levels (0, 1, 3, 5, 7) at the data-set level
- Concurrent support for multiple levels of data mirroring (intramirroring, local, remote, cross-host [cluster], reflective mirroring, and replicated mirroring) at the data-set level

Mirroring is creating a replica of each data block so that all operations are stored on two different disks. If one of the two disks fails, lost data is retrieved from the other. When the failed disk is replaced, a replica of all the data blocks on the good disk is made on the new disk. (In theory, any number of replicas of the same block can be made on the same number of disks.)

Although mirroring statistically offers high reliability, it comes at the expense of losing half the raw capacity of the array. The amount of storage lost in mirroring is substantially higher than the storage lost when the array operates in parity calculation mode.

Transactions

A *transaction* is a logical unit of work, as defined by C.J. Data, a founder of relational systems. Transactions are necessary for all sorts of business activities. For example, an online bookstore needs transactions to perform many activities, including the following:

- Ordering books from suppliers
- Transferring inventory from suppliers
- Accurately updating available book inventory
- Charging customers appropriately for purchases
- Fulfilling customer orders and communicating order status

Once a merely theoretical topic for discussion at the onset of the computer age, the platform-independent application has become a modern reality. Layers of programming abstraction have succeeded in segregating the presentation layer from the application and transaction layers. Individuals can now write code once, and if they adequately adhere to industry programming standards, they can expect that same code to run on multiple platforms, regardless of hardware architecture or vendor. This represents a revolution in programming, resulting in code being liberated from hardware-based specifications and constraints. Your company's core business logic processes can be represented in code that can readily take advantage of changes and advances in software and hardware technology, without prohibitively expensive rewriting and migration costs.

To guide you through learning about transactions, information is discussed in the following categories:

- ACID Properties
- Transaction Models
- Chained Transactions

- Transaction Integrity
- Types of Application Transactions
- Distributed Transactions

ACID Properties

To ensure that a transaction never has an unexpected or inconsistent outcome, you need transactions that have ACID (atomicity, consistency, isolation, and durability) properties:

- **Atomicity**—A transaction is a unit of work with a series of operations. Operations within a transaction usually share a common intent and are interdependent. By performing only a subset of these operations, the system can compromise the overall intent of the transaction. Atomicity eliminates the chance of processing a subset of operations. A transaction must be done or undone completely and unambiguously. If any operation fails, the effects of all operations that make up the transaction must be undone, and data must be rolled back to its previous state.

- **Consistency**—A transaction must preserve all the invariant properties (such as integrity constraints) defined on the data. On completion of a successful transaction, the data must be in a consistent state. In simplest terms, a transaction must transform the system from one consistent state to another consistent state; for example, a money-transfer application must not arbitrarily move decimal points during the transfer.

- **Isolation**—A transaction must appear to execute independently of other transactions that might be executing concurrently in the same environment. Transactions attain the highest level of isolation when they can be serialized. At this level, the results obtained from a set of concurrent transactions are identical to the results obtained by running each transaction serially. This requires that (1) during the course of a transaction, the intermediate (possibly inconsistent) state of the data must not be exposed to all other transactions, and (2) two concurrent transactions must not be able to operate on the same data. Because a high degree of isolation can limit the number of concurrent transactions, some applications reduce the isolation level in exchange for better throughput.

- **Durability**—The effects of a completed transaction must always be persistent; that is, a transaction is also a unit of recovery. If a transaction commits, the system guarantees that its updates will persist, even if the computer crashes immediately after the commit. Specialized logging allows the system restart procedure to complete unfinished operations, making the transaction durable.

These ACID properties guarantee that a transaction is never incomplete, the data is never inconsistent, concurrent transactions are independent, and the effects of a transaction are persistent. Furthermore, such properties ensure predictable behavior, reinforcing the role of transactions as all-or-none propositions designed to reduce the management load in the face of many variables.

If a transaction violates any of these properties, undefined (usually bad) behavior can result.

Using a Database Management System (DBMS) as an example is useful to see how the ACID properties apply to a specific database transaction that involves transferring money from one bank account to another. The transfer is two separate actions, a debit from one account and a credit to another, which comprise a single transaction.

Figure 2-20 shows the two-step money transfer transaction.

Figure 2-20 *Two-Step Money Transfer Transaction*

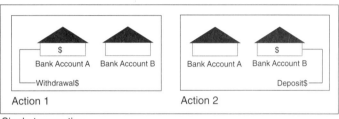

In this scenario, both actions must be completed for the desired result to be achieved. If Action 1 is completed, but Action 2 is not, the customer loses money. If Action 1 is not completed, but Action 2 is, the bank loses money.

Transaction Models

Three common transaction models have different answers to two questions: When should a transaction be committed or aborted? When should changes made by one transaction become visible for other transactions?

Each model is discussed as follows:

- **Flat transactions**—A flat transaction denotes the atomic unit of work performed by many entities and is controlled from one point. It contains any arbitrary number of actions that are taken as a whole and considered to be one action.

  In a flat transaction, all work done within a transaction's boundaries occurs at the same level—which is why it's considered flat. The transaction starts with a **begin_transaction** command and ends with either a **commit_transaction** or an **abort_transaction** command. You cannot commit or abort parts of a flat transaction. If any part of the transaction fails before the transaction completes and commits, whatever was done by the transaction before the failure is effectively erased. The work can be performed by many different servers and distributed across many different platforms. Figure 2-21 shows two flat transactions. One is committed and the other one is aborted.

Figure 2-21 *Two Flat Transactions*

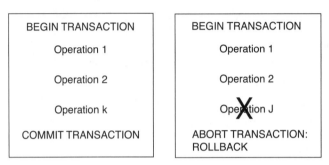

Most alternatives to the flat transaction extend the flow of control beyond the simple unit of work, either by chaining units of work in linear sequences of minitransactions (chained transactions) or by using nested subtransactions (nested transactions).

- **Nested transactions**—Within nested transactions, the main transaction is composed of several subtransactions. Each subtransaction can recursively call other subtransactions. If the main transaction aborts, all subtransactions abort. The effects of a subtransaction on a given database are permanent only when the subtransaction and all its ancestors have committed. The failure of an individual subtransaction does not necessitate the failure of the main transaction. The main transaction can try to find another way to make the subtransaction succeed. This feature of nested transactions gives them an advantage over flat transactions. Figure 2-22 illustrates the structure of a nested transaction.

Figure 2-22 *Nested Transaction*

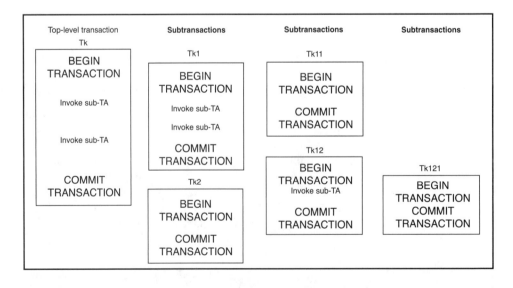

• **Chained transactions**—Chained transactions are similar to hard-save points. The work is broken into pieces with each piece being under control of a flat transaction. After a piece of work is complete, it is committed, or rolled back, without regard to the state of the other pieces. If the chained transaction succeeds and is committed, and if the transaction under which the original requester is working is rolled back, the committed work remains durable. That is, the transactions are isolated, and one has no affect on the other.

Figure 2-23 shows a chained transaction. The first transaction in the chain has been started. Start of the second one will be triggered by the commit of the first.

Figure 2-23 *Chained Transaction*

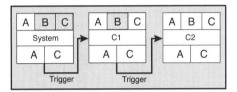

Chained transactions have merit in satisfying certain functional requirements. Chained transactions are often used when there is a requirement to log information into a database that must remain durable, regardless of the result of other work performed.

Figure 2-24 shows a client that initiates a transaction and makes a request of Service A. Service A performs a task and requests that Service B write some information that must remain durable if Transaction 1 fails. The structural dependencies of both transactions are not strong. Each behaves like a flat transaction. Transaction 2 can occur in parallel with Transaction 1 or at a later time.

Figure 2-24 *Chained Transaction Illustrated*

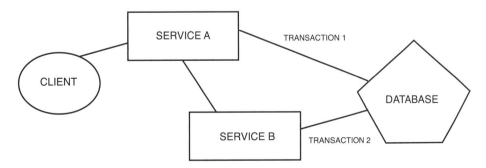

Transaction Integrity

Transaction integrity refers to the extent to which a transaction flowing through a network reaches its intended destination without impairing its function, content, or meaning.

Enterprise applications often require concurrent access to distributed data shared among multiple components to perform operations. These applications must maintain the integrity of the data, as defined by the business rules of the application. A transaction is legal only if it obeys the business rules of the application integrity constraints. Illegal transactions are not allowed and, if an integrity constraint cannot be satisfied, the transaction is rolled back.

Transaction integrity is becoming a requirement in Business-to-Business (B2B) enterprise applications. Data integrity must be kept between various distributed components of an application across the network.

There are three common methods that ensure transaction integrity:

- **Journaling**—A journal for a computer includes a record of changes made in files, messages sent, and so on. It can recover previous versions of a file before updates were made or reconstruct the updates if an updated file gets damaged.

  Transaction journaling provides the capability to log database updates to either files or disk partitions. It tracks the facilities that ensure transaction durability. The transaction journal's intention is to provide an updates log that can be made available for database recovery, in the event that the system uncontrollably fails. Using transaction journaling provides the means to recover in seconds rather than hours after an unexpected restart (a power failure, and so on). Transaction journaling also provides increased file-system integrity with solid audit controls. Mission-critical applications require transaction journaling and the ability to enforce data integrity constraints. Without those features, you do not have secure, robust databases. Following are the three common types of journaling:

  - **After-image journaling** allows users to reapply modifications that have been made to a file. This type of journaling allows users to recover files that are inadvertently deleted, lost, or corrupted.

  - **Before-image journaling** allows users to reverse modifications that have been made to a file. This type of journaling allows users to return a file to a previously known state. This capability is useful if a file is updated with incorrect data. Application modifications are not necessary to use before-image journaling.

  - **Recovery unit journaling** allows users to maintain transaction integrity. A transaction can be a series of file updates to one or more files. If any failure occurs during the transaction, recovery unit journaling rolls back the partially completed transaction to its starting point. This rollback allows complex transactions to be completed as an atomic event. Therefore, partially completed transactions can be avoided. Recovery unit journaling requires application modification.

- **Rollback**—If a transaction fails to complete, the entire transaction and its history are deleted, and the committed resources are released. Any committed subtransaction will not be affected, although uncommitted subtransactions will also be rolled back.

  In a database scenario, rollback is a feature in a DBMS that undoes the entire last transaction and returns the database to the way it was before the transaction. It is performed automatically when a transaction is interrupted by machine error. Alternatively, you can roll back the trailing portion of an uncommitted transaction to a marker, called a save point, to maintain the integrity of the data.

  Transactions can be rolled back explicitly at the request of the application or user, or automatically by the database manager when an error occurs and the application is no longer able to communicate with the database. Following are specific scenarios in which rollback can occur:

  — Statement-level rollback because of statement or deadlock execution error

  — Rollback to a save point

  — Rollback of a transaction because of a user request

  — Rollback of a transaction because of an abnormal process termination

  — Rollback of all outstanding transactions when an instance terminates abnormally

  — Rollback of incomplete transactions during recovery

  All types of rollbacks use approximately the same procedures. This is what occurs when rolling back an entire transaction, without referencing any save points:

  — The database undoes all changes made by the SQL statements in the transaction by using the corresponding rollback segments.

  — The database releases the transaction's locks of data.

  — The transaction ends.

  This is what occurs when rolling back a transaction to a save point:

  — The database rolls back only the statements executed after the save point.

  — The specified save point is preserved, but all save points established after the save point specified are lost.

  — The database releases all table and row locks acquired since that save point but retains all data locks acquired before the save point.

  — The transaction remains active and can continue.

- **Triggers**—Triggers are commands that can be contained within another command. They are similar to stored procedures. A trigger stored in the database can include SQL and Procedural Language/SQL (PL/SQL), or Java statements to execute as a unit, and can invoke stored procedures. However, procedures and triggers differ in the way that they are invoked. A user, an application, or a trigger explicitly executes a procedure. Triggers (one or more) are implicitly fired (executed) when a triggering event occurs, no matter which user is connected or which application is being used. The trigger is transparent to the client.

In an object-oriented context, a trigger is an operation linked to an object type that is automatically invoked on instances of that type when certain events occur. A trigger definition specifies the name of the trigger and the event that will trigger its execution. Four kinds of events can be specified: create, update, delete, and commit. Create events trigger the execution after creation. Update and delete events trigger execution before any changes are made to the actual stored object. Commit events trigger execution before the commit is performed. All triggers and events refer only to that part of the object associated with the type in question, and have these specific uses:

— Generate derived column values automatically

— Prevent invalid transactions

— Enforce complex security authorizations

— Enforce referential integrity across nodes in a distributed database

— Enforce complex business rules

— Provide transparent event logging

— Provide sophisticated auditing

— Maintain synchronous table replicates

— Gather statistics on table access

— Modify table data when Data Manipulation Language (DML) statements are issued against views

— Publish information about database events, user events, and SQL statements to subscribing applications

— Check the attempted operation and undo it (roll back the transaction) if there is referential data inconsistency or bad data

— Keep duplicated or precalculated data automatically up to date

Types of Application Transactions

The three common types of application transactions follow:

- **Lookup**—Lookup, or query, transactions are the messages and trigger events used between querying applications and filler applications.

These transactions can be used as a user or agent tool for requesting information, generally as a formal request to a database. These transactions can also be basic interactive and batch facilities that allow users to query files and databases, and create terminal and printed-report output.

- **Update**—An update can be performed in two ways. Under certain conditions, changes can be made directly to the rows of database tables. In the second way, when a direct table row update can be made, the operation is done quickly, with little overhead to perform the operation. An update directly to the rows of a table is referred to as an update in place.

You can also change the rows of a table through an indirect, or deferred, update. This update makes a change by deleting the row to be modified and inserting a new row with the new values in place. A deferred update is slower because two operations are required to make a change to a table's row.

The conditions under which a direct update can be performed are primarily determined by restrictions set on the database table. The restrictions occur because the database table is distributed in some form such as in a clustered or replicated database. These conditions must be met for a direct update to be performed on a table:

— The updated column cannot be part of a clustered index.

— The update trigger cannot be defined on the table.

— The table cannot be set up for replication.

Several conditions must be met for an update in place that changes a single row. Again, these restrictions are created by the database and table type requirements being at odds with the way an update in place occurs.

— For a table column that is defined using a data type of variable length, the updated row must fit in the same database page.

— If a nonclustered index that allows duplicates is defined for the column, the updated column must be a fixed-size data type or be composed of multiple fixed data types.

— If a unique, nonclustered index is defined on the column and the WHERE clause of the UPDATE statement uses an exact match for a unique index, the updated column must be a fixed-size data type or composed of multiple fixed data types. The column in the WHERE clause can be the same column as the updated column.

— Byte size of the updated row value cannot be more than 50 percent different from the original row, and the total number of new bytes must be equal to or less than 24.

These set conditions must be met for updates that change multiple rows to be performed in place:

— The updated column must be a fixed-length data type.

— The updated column cannot be part of a unique, nonclustered index.

— If a nonunique, nonclustered index is defined on the column, and the UPDATE statement's WHERE clause is not the same column as the updated column, an updated column must be a fixed-size data type or composed of multiple fixed data types.

- **Add**—Add is a type of transaction for inserting data. You can add data using an INSERT statement. Instead of executing the query, iterating over the record set, and extracting the values, you tell the DBMS that you are inserting data, set the values, and execute the statement for each new record.

Distributed Transactions

Distributed transactions are an extension of traditional transactions. A distributed transaction is composed of several subtransactions, each running on a different site; that is, a distributed transaction involves multiple transaction resources running on two or more distinct nodes, such as an application server and a relational database. Distributed transactions are particularly important in maintaining consistency across multiple resource managers.

By allowing transactions to span servers, you can make sure that updates are executed on all database objects. As with standard transactions, distributed transactions must follow the ACID rules. As you might imagine, distributed transactions add an entire new layer of variables to the development and deployment process.

Figure 2-25 shows a distributed transaction that spans two machines and two databases.

Figure 2-25 *Distributed Transaction*

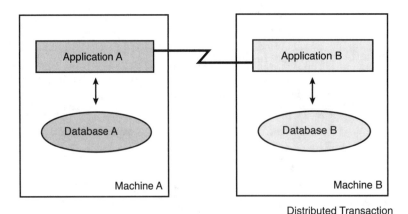

Distributed Transaction

In the figure, Application A runs on Machine A using Database A locally. As part of its processing, Application A must update Database B on Machine B. Application A uses a second application, B. By running under a transaction manager, such as Microsoft Transaction Server or IBM CICS, the processing in both applications can take place inside a single transaction. When Application A commits the transaction, the transaction manager coordinates the updates in both databases. Other applications see the updates in both databases as they appear simultaneously. In addition to protecting the integrity of the data in each database, the distributed transaction ensures that the external view of the data is always consistent.

Distributed transactions are vital for maintaining consistency across multiple resource managers. However, their functionality factors must be considered. Distributed transactions are completely synchronous. In the figure, Application A cannot continue until all the application processing on Machine B is complete and all the processing associated with the commit has finished. The time taken to log and commit changes to disk can be appreciable, and the applications must wait until the process is complete.

Distributed transactions require transaction managers who can communicate and cooperate in processing the transactions. Operations support for distributed transaction managers carries its own costs, both in software and in complexity of managing the logs and archives necessary for data recovery. In addition, all the components involved in the transaction must be available simultaneously. Both the applications, both the databases, and the transaction manager must run at the same time. If any component is unavailable, the transaction cannot be processed. Although not a problem if the components are all geographically local, this can be a major issue for international applications that span countries and time zones.

The cost and complexity of distributed transactions is justified for many applications, particularly when high-value operations are involved. Transfer of funds between organizations is a good example. When large monetary amounts are involved, you want to know exactly where the funds are at all times.

You should understand the following distributed-transaction processing concepts:

- **Transaction demarcation**—A transaction can be specified by what is known as transaction demarcation. Transaction demarcation enables work done by distributed components to be bound by a global transaction. Demarcation is a way of marking groups of operations to constitute a transaction. The most common approach to demarcation, called programmatic demarcation, is to mark the thread executing the operations for transaction processing. The established transaction can be suspended by unmarking the thread and resumed later by explicitly propagating the transaction context from the point of suspension to the point of resumption. The transaction demarcation ends after a commit or a rollback request to the transaction manager. The commit request directs all the participating resource managers to permanently record the effects of the transaction's operations. The rollback request makes the resource managers undo the effects of all operations on the transaction.

- **Transaction context and propagation**—Because multiple application components and resources participate in a transaction, the transaction manager must establish and maintain the state of the transaction as it occurs. This is usually done in the form of transaction context. Transaction context is an association between the transactional operations on the resources and the components invoking the operations. During the course of a transaction, all the participating threads share the transaction context. The transaction context logically envelops all the operations performed on transactional resources during a transaction. The underlying transaction manager usually maintains the transaction context transparently.

- **Resource enlistment**—Resource enlistment is the process by which resource managers inform the transaction manager of their participation in a transaction. This process enables the transaction manager to keep track of all the resources participating in a transaction. The transaction manager uses this information to coordinate transactional work performed by the resource managers, and to drive two-phase commit and recovery protocol. At the end of a transaction (after a commit or rollback), the transaction manager delists the resources and breaks the association between the transaction and the resources.

- **Two-phase commit**—Committing a distributed transaction has two distinct phases, as shown in Figure 2-26.

Figure 2-26 *Two-Phase Distributed Transaction*

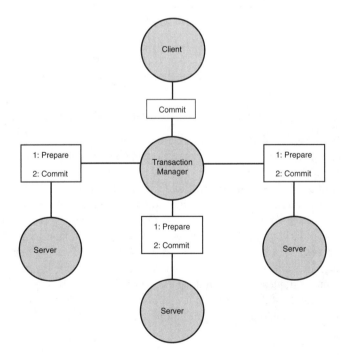

— Prepare phase—The transaction manager (global coordinator, initiating node) asks participants to prepare (to promise to commit or rollback the transaction, even if there is a failure). The coordinator asks all nodes to commit the transaction if all participants respond to the coordinator that they are prepared. If any participants cannot prepare, the coordinator asks all nodes to roll back the transaction. The figure illustrates a transaction that succeeds. In the first round of interaction, the transaction manager queries the server.

— Commit phase—The transaction manager commits the transaction. In this two-phase commit protocol, when the application requests the transaction commit, the transaction manager issues a prepare request to all the resource managers involved. Each of these resources can in turn send a reply indicating whether it is ready to commit. The transaction manager issues a commit request only when all the resource managers are ready for a commit. Otherwise, the transaction manager issues a rollback request, and the transaction is rolled back.

NOTE   In a typical flat or nested transaction, no action is taken until an explicit **begin_transaction** command is received. Chained transactions can begin without any explicit **begin_ transaction** command.

Object-Oriented Design

Object-orientation is a popular technical term that can mean different things depending on how it is being used. However, the term generally describes a system that deals primarily with objects, and where the actions you can take depend on what type of object you are manipulating. For example, an object-oriented draw program might enable you to draw many types of objects, such as circles, rectangles, triangles, and so on. Applying the same action to each of these objects, however, would produce different results. If the action were **Make three-dimensional**, for example, the result would be a sphere, box, and pyramid, respectively.

A more technical definition of object-orientation is an approach to writing software based on objects and classes, or the use of objects and classes in analysis, design, and programming. Object-orientation presently represents the best methodological framework for software engineering. By providing first-class support for an application domain's objects and classes, the object-oriented paradigm entails better modeling and system implementation. Objects provide a strict focus throughout analysis, design, and implementation by emphasizing the state, behavior, and interaction of objects, and providing seamlessness between activities.

NOTE	The use of objects distinguishes object-orientation from other techniques, such as traditional structured methods (process-based or procedural programming where data and function are separate, such as C programming language); or other techniques, such as knowledge-based systems (logic programming that is rule-based, such as Prolog); or mathematical methods (functional programming, such as fp, ML, Haskell).

The discussion in this section is divided into the following subsections:

- What Is Object-Oriented Design?
- Key Concepts in Object-Oriented Design
- Benefits of Object-Oriented Design
- Object-Oriented Design Methods and Tools

What Is Object-Oriented Design?

Object-oriented design (OOD) is constructing software systems as structured collections of abstract data type implementations, or *classes*. The following points must be noted in this definition:

- Emphasis is on structuring a system around the types of objects it manipulates (not the functions the system performs on them) and on reusing entire data structures together with the associated operations (not isolated routines).

- Objects are described as instances of abstract data types; that is, data structures known from an official interface rather than through their representation.

- A basic modular unit, called the *class*, describes one implementation of an abstract data type (or, in the case of *deferred* classes, a set of possible implementations of the same abstract data type).

- Word collection reflects how classes should be designed, as units that are interesting and useful on their own, independent of the systems to which they belong, and reusable by many different systems. Software construction is viewed as the assembly of existing classes, not as a top-down process starting from the beginning of a class construction.

- Word structured reflects the existence of two important relations between classes: the client and inheritance relations.

Object-oriented design is a methodology that focuses design on the data (objects) and on the data interfaces. To make an analogy with carpentry, an "object-oriented" carpenter would be mostly concerned with the chair that the carpenter was building, and, secondarily, with the tools used to make it; a "nonobject-oriented" carpenter would think primarily of the tools used. Object-oriented design is also the mechanism for defining how modules "plug and play."

Corporations face several problems in software development:

- Software is difficult to develop, modify, and maintain.
- Most software is delivered late and over budget.
- Programmers have to create entirely new software each time because code can't be reused.

These issues are born of the traditional structured programming approach that corporate America has been using for years. Structured programming is a top-down, modularized approach that breaks a program down into components until the components cannot be decomposed anymore. The top-down approach made a vast improvement to the quality of software but caused potential problems in large systems. Structured programming can seldom design a complete system without actually implementing the system. If a design is found to be incorrect after programming has started, the design must be entirely restructured, costing corporations time and money.

With these issues looming, corporations are willing to try another approach to developing more cost-effective, efficient software that will be delivered on time. Corporations need to have a competitive advantage over their competitors by delivering products faster and must adapt quickly to new changes.

The need to develop easy-to-extend-and-change software systems has driven interest in new approaches to software development and design. The object-oriented technology has emerged as one of the most promising paradigms for design and implementation of large-scale systems. With the object-oriented approach, the design of the entire system can be modeled at a higher level. Any potential problems with the design can be fixed at this level without having to start any programming. In addition, because people naturally think in terms of objects, they can more easily understand an object-based system than a procedure-based one. For example, people see a car as a system with an engine, gas tank, wheels, and so on. Most people would not see a car as a series of procedures that make it run.

Key Concepts in Object-Oriented Design

Object-oriented concepts are important in learning and understanding object-oriented technology. These are the key concepts:

- Object
- Method
- Class and instances
- Message
- Encapsulation

- Inheritance
- Polymorphism

Object—Generally, any item that can be individually selected and manipulated is an object. It directly relates to the real-world entities. Objects are the physical and conceptual things found in the universe around us. They can be a person, thing, or concept. For purposes of modeling a company, a CEO could view employees, buildings, divisions, documents, and benefits packages as objects.

In object-oriented design, an object is a self-contained entity that consists of both data and procedures to manipulate the data.

Figure 2-27 illustrates an abstract object.

Figure 2-27 *The Object-Oriented Object*

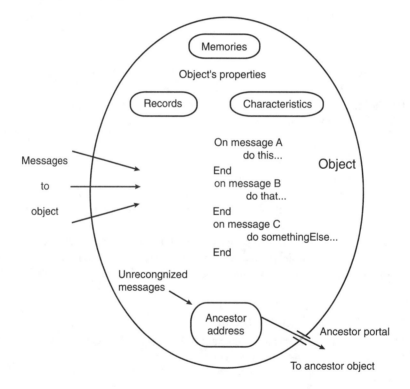

The state of an object is one of the possible conditions in which an object may exist; for example, if a light bulb is the object, one of the possible conditions (states) for it would be "on." The state is represented by the values of the properties (attributes) of an object. State changes are reflected by the behavior of an object.

The behavior of an object defines how an object acts and reacts. The behavior is determined by the set of operations the object can perform on itself. The object's behavior is also known as its interface, functions, and methods; for example, if a printer is an object, its behavior (function) is to print whatever it receives.

Method—A method is defined as part of a class and is a programmed procedure with access only to the data known to the object in which it is included. Having access to only the data known to the object ensures data integrity among the set of objects in an application. Methods can be re-used in multiple objects.

Class—A class is a set of similar objects. A class consists of both a pattern and a mechanism for creating items based on that pattern. Instances, individual items within a class, are created by the class's creation mechanism. An instance's corresponding class determines its structure and capabilities.

Objects are instances of a class; for example, the attribute for the ANIMAL class is having four legs and a tail. The class's behaviors are sleeping and eating. Possible instances or objects of the ANIMAL class include a cat, an elephant, and a horse. Similarly, subclasses of ANIMAL would be cat, elephant, and horse.

The class definition specifies both the memory structure and the set of attributes and allowed operations for objects of the class. The operations and data in a class can be private, so only objects belonging to the same class can access them, or public, so objects of any class can use them.

Figure 2-28 shows the contents of a typical Java class in Java.

Figure 2-28 *Class in Java*

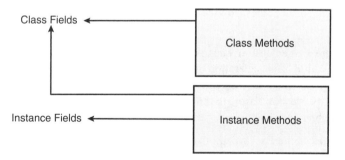

The analogy between classes and objects, and types and variables is obvious: classes and types are declarations that are instanced by objects and variables, respectively.

Class—An instance of a class can also be a class. A metaclass is a class whose instances themselves are classes. When you use the instance creation mechanism in a metaclass, the instance created will itself be a class. The instance creation mechanism of this class can, in turn, create instances—although these instances might or might not themselves be classes.

A concept similar to the metaclass is the parameterized class. A parameterized class is a template for a class, wherein specific items have been identified as necessary to create nonparameterized classes based on the template. You can view a parameterized class as a "fill in the blanks" version of a class. You can't directly use the instance creation mechanism of a parameterized class. You must first supply the required parameters, resulting in the creation of a nonparameterized class. After you have a nonparameterized class, you can use its creation mechanisms to create instances.

Messages—Objects communicate through message passing. This occurs when an object receives a message. A message is an action asking objects to behave in some way. Specifically, a message is a request for the receiver object to carry out the indicated method or behavior and return the result of that action to the sender object. For example, a person object sends a light bulb object a message to turn on. The light bulb object has a behavior that will change its state from off to on. Then the light bulb object turns itself on and indicates to the person object that its new state is on.

Constructors and deconstructors are special messages invoked automatically when an object is created (by declaration or by explicit allocation using the new operator) or destroyed (by exiting the scope of the object or by explicit de-allocation using the delete operator) to ensure that the object is initialized or de-allocated correctly. The explicit inclusion of these essential operations gives the class definition a consistent and complete structure.

An object-oriented program execution involves receiving, interpreting, and responding to messages from other objects.

Encapsulation—Clear distinction between an operation's specification and implementation is necessary. Encapsulation refers to building a capsule or a conceptual barrier around a collection of things. Encapsulation allows suppliers to present clearly specified interfaces around the services they provide. The procedures of an object are fully visible to a consumer, but its data is not.

In object-oriented design, encapsulation hides the implementation details of an object. Encapsulation is the separation of the external aspects of an object, which are accessible to users, from the internal implementation of the object, which is hidden from users. Only an object's interface is visible to other objects. The only access to manipulate the object data is through its interface.

Encapsulation forms a type of data-independence: if the interface does not change, the applications are not required to change; if any of the applications change, the object specifications don't have to change, as long as the application works on the same interface; and if any of the implementation details of an object change, neither the interface nor the applications must change.

Encapsulation protects the internal state of an object from being corrupted by other programs. Other programs are also protected from changes in the object implementation, thereby reducing the ripple effect. Program maintenance is easier and less expensive because changes in the object data or implementation are modified only in one place.

Programs using these object functions care only that the object does what it is supposed to do because encapsulation allows objects to be viewed as black boxes. Object-oriented programs failing to deliver any particular advantage over procedural language programs is an example of poor object encapsulation.

Inheritance—To achieve the goals of reusability and extensibility, and to avoid rewriting the same code, wasting time introducing inconsistencies, and risking errors, use techniques to capture the striking commonalities that exist with groups' similar classes. Inheritance is one of the object-oriented features that allow you to do just that.

Inheritance is a code reuse mechanism that builds new objects out of old ones. Inheritance defines a relationship among classes, where one class shares the structure or behavior of one or more other classes. For example, the "feline" class inherits all the behavior and attributes of the ANIMAL class. The feline class also exhibits a meow behavior that was not in the ANIMAL class. So, all instances of the feline class feline have four legs, a tail, sleep, eat, and meow, while instances of the ANIMAL class have only four legs, a tail, sleep, and eat. Inheritance also provides a more flexible and adaptable system, and enables polymorphism. A common pitfall of OOP is that a particular class will conflict with the attributes of a desired subclass. In the case of the previous example, "bird" is a proper subclass of ANIMAL, but a bird has only two legs, not four. The attribute, "has four legs," should not be assigned to the ANIMAL class because all instances should share any attribute assigned to the class.

A class can inherit properties and operations from an ancestor class and can have its operations inherited by other classes. Inheritance from a single direct ancestor is called *single inheritance*. Inheritance from more than one direct ancestor is called *multiple inheritance*. Class inheritance is essentially a static form of inheritance. New classes inherit properties when they are defined rather than at run time.

Figure 2-29 illustrates the object-oriented idea of inheritance. Occurrences of items to a dealership are VEHICLES, and beneath the VEHICLE class are subclasses for CAR and BOAT. The CAR subclass can be further partitioned into subclasses for VAN and SEDAN.

The VEHICLE class contains the data items unique to vehicles, including the vehicle ID and the year of manufacture. The CAR class, because it is a VEHICLE, inherits the VEHICLE data items. The CAR class can also contain data items, such as the number of axles and the gross weight of the vehicle. Each time a subclass is created, it inherits all the data items and behaviors from the appropriate higher classes. Because the VAN class is a CAR, which in turn is a VEHICLE, objects of the VAN class inherit all the data structures and behaviors relating to the CAR subclass and VEHICLE class.

Several variations of inheritance occur in object-oriented languages, including dynamic, selective or partial inheritance, and monotonic inheritance.

Figure 2-29 *Inheritance in Object-Oriented Design*

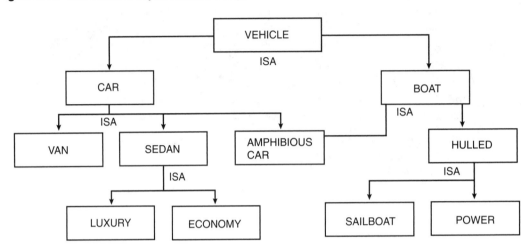

Dynamic inheritance is the mechanism that allows objects to alter their behavior in the course of normal interaction with other objects. The two forms of dynamic inheritance are *part inheritance and scope inheritance*. Part inheritance occurs when an object changes its behavior by accepting new parts from other objects. Part inheritance is nothing more than an exchange of values between objects. An object can dynamically inherit new instance variables and methods from other objects. In scope inheritance, the object's behavior is determined, in part, by the environment or its acquaintances. When changes in the environment occur, the object's behavior changes. For example, a paragraph in a document can inherit its font and style from an enclosing environment. If the paragraph is moved to a footnote, new properties are inherited.

Partial inheritance is a variation of class inheritance. With partial inheritance, often referred to as refinement by cancellation, properties inherited by the subclass can be dropped so that they are no longer properties of the child class. For example, a QUEUE is defined to inherit from a LIST and inherits properties and the length operation. However, the insert and delete operations are suppressed. Partial inheritance is convenient for code sharing and is supported by C++.

Monotonic inheritance is a variation of class inheritance whereby a child class inherits every property from its ancestor class.

Polymorphism—Polymorphism means the ability to take many forms. In OOP, this refers to an entity's ability to refer to instances of various classes at run time. Polymorphism enables a single message to invoke many different behaviors. For example, you have a SHAPE class with a draw behavior. The draw behavior will draw any instances of SHAPE. If TRIANGLE, RECTANGLE, and CIRCLE classes are inheritances of the shape object, all will have the behavior of the shape. Within the inherited classes of TRIANGLE, RECTANGLE, and

CIRCLE, the draw behavior is rewritten to draw a triangle, rectangle, and circle, respectively. If a triangle object calls the draw behavior, a triangle is drawn for the rectangle, a rectangle is drawn, and so on. The individual implementation of each shape is hidden behind the single interface or behavior, draw. Other programs can generically invoke an object's operation without knowing the object's type.

Two forms of polymorphism occur in object-oriented languages: inclusion polymorphism and operation polymorphism:

- Inclusion polymorphism is implemented using inheritance. This kind of polymorphism allows an object to be treated as belonging to several types at one time. An object that is an instance of one class can be used as if it is an instance of another class, provided that the first object has a subclass relationship with the second object.

- Operation polymorphism implies that operations can be applied to distinct types that correspond to disjoint sets. Operations with the same name can be applied to different objects that have no relation in terms of inclusion. The two forms of operation polymorphism are overloading and parametric polymorphism.

Additional Concepts

Additional concepts that will not be discussed in detail in this section include the following:

- **Subject**—Subjects are a mechanism that partitions large, complex models. Subjects also help organize work packages on larger projects.
- **Service**—A service is a specific behavior that an object is responsible for exhibiting.
- **State**—The state of an object is the value of its attributes.
- **Transition**—Transition is the change of a state.

Benefits of Object-Oriented Design

Characteristics of object-oriented design include reuse, quality, and an emphasis on modeling the real world (or a "stronger equivalence" with the real world than other methodologies). Additional characteristics include a consistent and seamless object-oriented analysis (OOA) /OOD/OOP package, naturalness (the "object concept"), resistance to change, encapsulation, and abstraction (higher cohesion/lower coupling).

The object-oriented design has these benefits:

- **Faster development**—The development time is shortened because software is built from standard objects, existing, reusable models of corporate processes, and rapid model prototyping from the methodologies.
- **Increased quality**—Higher quality is achieved because programs are created out of existing, tested components.

- **Easier maintenance**—Easier maintenance is achieved because code must be changed in only one place. Changes to existing systems can be made without rebuilding the system.

- **Enhanced scalability**—Larger systems are easier to build and maintain because their subsystems can be developed and tested independently.

- **Greater appeal to human cognition, naturalness**—Programmers can design programs that naturally reflect the inherent objects and relationships found in real-world systems. OO models mirror the business systems.

Object-oriented design is not, however, inherently error free or without disadvantages. Poorly designed object-oriented programs do exist. One trade-off found with OOP is that application performance is generally sacrificed for the sake of an environment rich with objects and classes.

Object-Oriented Design Methods and Tools

This section reviews object-oriented design methods and examines object-oriented design tools. Upon completing this section, you will be able to describe the UML and the CASE tool used in object-oriented design.

Unified Modeling Language—Although there are many object-oriented methodologies, such as Booch, Buhr, Wasserman, and the HOOD method, the Unified Modeling Language (UML) has become the industry standard design and analysis notation. UML joins the concepts of Booch, Object Modeling Technique (OMT), and Object-Oriented Software Engineering (OOSE), resulting in a single, common, and widely usable modeling language for users of these and other methods.

The UML language specifies, visualizes, constructs, and documents the artifacts of software systems, nonsoftware systems, and business modeling. It represents a collection of best engineering practices that have proven successful in modeling large and complex systems. UML provides the application modeling language for the following types of modeling:

- Business process modeling
- Class and object modeling
- Component modeling
- Distribution and deployment modeling

The UML includes the following elements:

- **Model elements**—Fundamental modeling concepts and semantics
- **Notation**—Visual rendering of model elements
- **Guidelines**—Usage idioms within the trade

The UML notation provides several diagrams for different purposes, such as dynamic or static system views. Figure 2-30 provides an overview of the UML notation that contains the essential classes and their associations. The association types are elements of class diagrams that show the model's static structure. Classes are represented as boxes, divided in up to three fields, where the upper field contains the class name, the middle field contains the attribute names, and the lower field contains the method names. The attribute and method fields can be omitted.

Figure 2-30 *UML Notation*

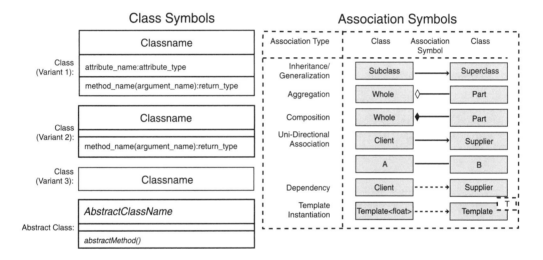

Computer Aided Software Engineering Tool (CASE)—In layperson terms, CASE is a tool that aids a software engineer in maintaining and developing software, much like mechanic use their tools to maintain and develop vehicles, aiding their respective techniques. CASE tools, once considered a luxury, are increasingly necessary in today's software engineering environment.

CASE tools offer many benefits for developers building large-scale systems. As spiraling user requirements continue to drive system complexity to new levels, the CASE tools enable you to abstract from the entanglement of source code to a level where architecture and design become more apparent and easier to understand and modify. The larger a project, the more important using CASE technology becomes.

CASE tools are important for object-oriented design, as well. As developers interact with portions of a system designed by their colleagues, they must quickly seek a subset of classes and methods and gain an understanding of how to interface with them. In a similar sense, management must be able, in a timely fashion and from a high level, to look at a representation of a design and understand what is occurring. For these reasons, CASE tools, coupled with methodologies, enable you to represent systems too complex to comprehend in their underlying source code or schema-based form.

A major obstacle to the creation of standards-based object-oriented design CASE tools is the wide variety of approaches and methodologies. Some OOD methodologists, or their organizations, have released their own CASE tools (for example, Rational ROSE and Object International OOA Tool). Some CASE vendors have chosen to automate the approaches from several different methodologists, such as Mark V Systems, Ltd. ObjectMaker and Protosoft Inc. Paradigm Plus.

Object modeling CASE tools will probably continue to support multiple methodologies into the foreseeable future. Even when the UML achieves its expected market penetration, other methodologies will probably continue to have strong followers.

In terms of language, object modeling CASE tools must improve their support for mixed-language development, which involves Java, C++, Visual Basic, and so forth.

Some useful techniques can be employed in the object-oriented design process. A partial list follows:

- **CRC cards**—Creators found Class Responsibility Collaboration cards to be the essential dimensions of object-oriented modeling. CRC cards are index cards that represent class responsibilities and the interaction between the classes. These cards are an informal approach to object-oriented modeling. The cards are created through scenarios, based on the system requirements that model the system's behavior.

- **Interaction diagram**—An interaction diagram consists of blocks, stimuli (signals between blocks), and input and output from the environment. The rules govern an interaction diagram:

  — Every bar is either a block or the system border.

  — Every block can have a description.

  — No more than one system border can exist.

  — A stimulus is either a named signal or message, and can have additional parameters.

  — A stimulus is either input for, or output from, an operation.

  — Blocks that are not part of any operation are not allowed.

  — Two blocks can be connected by a message; a block can be connected to the system border by a signal. (However, in rare situations, a signal can connect two blocks, or a message can connect the system border and a block.)

  — An interaction diagram always has one time axis. (Sometimes, the time axis is implicit; that is, no exact times are given.)

  — One or more gridlines can exist.

- **Class diagram**—The class diagram, a central modeling technique, runs through nearly all object-oriented methods. This diagram describes the objects in the system and the various static relationships that exist between them. Three principal relationships are important:

  — Associations (A customer might rent a number of videos.)

  — Subtypes (A lawyer is a type of person.)

  — Aggregation (A tire is part of a car.)

- **Patterns**—A pattern-based modeling, or a parallel computing pattern, is a reusable, application-independent component that provides a commonly used parallel structure. It is implemented as a reusable code-skeleton for quickly and reliably developing parallel applications. The benefit is twofold:

  — Each pattern is well documented through examples, usages, and so on. This provides a user with in-depth knowledge about the pattern. Successive usage of the same pattern in different applications reduces learning time.

  — The reusable, application-independent components hide most of the low-level, parallel-related details from the user. These low-level detail implementations are often tedious and error-prone from the very start. Using reusable components reduces development time.

- **Evolutionary development**—Evolutionary development is done as a series of increments. Each increment builds a subset of the full software system. An increment is a full lifecycle of analysis, design, coding, testing, and integration. Developers can work independently on implementing and testing classes during a cycle, and incorporate them for system testing at the end of the cycle.

Object-Oriented Programming

This section introduces object-oriented programming, discusses the difference between structured programming and object-oriented programming, and reviews the common object-oriented programming languages.

In object-oriented programming (OOP), programmers define the data type of a data structure and the types of operations (methods) that can be applied to the data structure. The data structure becomes an object that includes both data and functions. In addition, programmers can create relationships between objects. For example, objects can inherit characteristics from other objects.

A principal advantage of OOP techniques over procedural programming techniques is that OOP enables programmers to create modules that do not need to be changed when a new type of object is added. A programmer can simply create a new object that inherits many of its features from existing objects. This makes object-oriented programs easier to modify.

Figure 2-31 illustrates the object-oriented programming concept. OOP makes up a "web" of interacting objects, each housekeeping its own state. Program objects interact by sending messages to each other.

Figure 2-31   *Object-Oriented Programming*

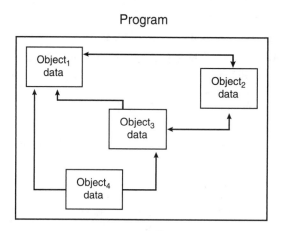

History of object-oriented technology—Object-oriented technology is a popular topic today, but its inception began in the late 1960s with the simulation programming language, Simula, which was the first object-oriented language providing objects, classes, inheritance, and dynamic typing. It was intended to convey object-oriented design. In the early 1970s, another programming language, SmallTalk, furthered the idea of using software objects simulating real-world objects. In the mid-1980s, other OOP languages, such as C++ and Eiffel, emerged. Recent additions are Java and Python.

OOP versus structured programming—OOP is described as being "in the 1980s what structured programming was in the 1970s." A coding discipline, structured programming limits transfers of control to a small set, such as sequence, conditional, or iteration. Applying this discipline yields low-level code structures that are easier to understand (and, therefore, easier to debug and maintain). Reasoned arguments for adopting structured programming involve measures of code complexity, the applicability of formal and informal verification methodologies, the expressive power of various sets of control constructs, and anecdotal evidence concerning the understandability of code. Structured programming became a serious undertaking with the proof that any program can be written using only a small set of control structures: the set (sequence, iteration, and conditional) yields programming languages, such as Pascal, C, and Algol; the control set (function composition, recursion, and conditional) yields LISP and its derivatives.

OOP, a code-packaging discipline, allows a designer to impose a reasonable structure on large software systems, based on the notions of encapsulation and inheritance. OOP provides several useful software development innovations:

- It provides a useful operational definition of module (a class is a module).

- It establishes an organizing principle for task decomposition (minimizing communication and dependencies among modules).

- It enforces a useful, formal separation between architecture, implementation, and realization (implemented in the separation between public and private members of a class, and in the separation of class declaration from class realization).

Object-oriented design (OOD) simplifies the structure of large software systems, just as a decade ago, structured programming simplified the structure of code segments. In addition, OOD separates and clarifies system design responsibilities, making managing software teams more straightforward, and provides some new tools for thinking about software design.

NOTE   The difference between structured programming and OOP is in how the data and functions are kept. Structured programming keeps data and functions separate. The data is usually placed before any of the functions are written. Sometimes, it is not intuitively known which data works with which function. OOP places related object data and functions together within one unit.

OOP Languages—To perform OOP, you need an object-oriented programming language (OOPL). Object-oriented theorists identify three fundamental aspects of an object-oriented language:

- User-defined data types (classes)

- Inheritance

- Polymorphism

Java and C++ are two of the more popular object-oriented languages:

- **C++**—Added classes to C as early as 1985, and by the 1990s had emerged as the market leader in object-oriented languages (if not all of programming) with powerful features, including multiple inheritance, exceptions, templates, operator overloading, and namespaces. Its popularity was due in part to its compatibility with the large existing base of C programmers and the widespread use of UNIX, which ran on many machines.

Although C++ is not an entirely new language, it represents a significant extension of C abilities. Consider C to be a subset of C++, which supports essentially every wanted action, and most of the unwanted actions, of its predecessor but provides wide-ranging language improvements and added OOP capability. However, using C++ does not imply that you use its OOP features. You can create structured code that uses only non-OOP C++ features.

- **Java**—Created as a simplification of C++ that could run on any machine, providing a write once-run anywhere capability. This development was originally instituted to support multitudes of devices (still true today), and with the rise of the World Wide Web, it enabled Java to become the standard web programming language with applets that could run in a browser, on any platform. Java provides first-class support for object-orientation rather than C++'s hybrid approach, which added object-orientation to C but retained the underlying C structured, programming base language. Java also has several advanced capabilities, including reflection and support for graphics, distributed programming (Remote Method Invocation), components and distributed middleware (Enterprise JavaBeans), threading, and the World Wide Web (applets). Java is now used in most application programming areas but does not have the low-level facilities, such as pointers, required for systems programming. It was originally an interpreted programming language, although some vendors now provide native-compiled executables, and Sun provides hot spot run-time optimized run-time environments (Java Runtime Environment). Java is now competing with C++ as the most popular OOPL.

Data Modeling

A *model* is a symbolic or abstract representation of something real or imagined. A person often builds a model to visualize a design before constructing the real thing. For example, for a city architect planning designing building, a computer-simulated helicopter ride 200 feet above planned streets can reveal potential areas of traffic congestion and unusable parks.

Similarly, a data model helps you visualize data structures to gauge how completely and accurately the models reflect your information system problem space. A *data model* is an abstraction of an aspect of the real world (system) and specifies the data structure needed to support a business area.

The data model is, essentially, a set of plans or specifications for a database that will meet the needs of the business. Today, most databases are relational, but the real world is not. (A relational database stores data in the form of related tables. Each table is called a *relation*. Each row is called a *tuple*, and each column is called an *attribute*.) Data models are built to map business concepts into relational objects.

A data model is not just a smaller copy of something but a formal representation with the following functions:

- Hides uninteresting detail
- Substitutes symbols for bulkier components
- Highlights important facts
- Promotes understanding of the whole

To help you understand the intricacies of data modeling, the discussion is broken into the following sections:

- What Is Data Modeling?
- Components of a Data Model
- Benefits of Data Modeling
- Types of Data Modeling
- Entity Relationship Method
- Transforming an ERD into Relations
- Other Data Modeling Methodologies
- Object Role Modeling

What Is Data Modeling?

Data modeling is a technique applied to capture the information concepts and rules of a business area, leading to a description of data structures used to define a database.

Data modeling is also the process of identifying and formalizing data requirements with a conceptual modeling tool. Data modeling is an intrinsic part of the database design process, and the first step in OOP.

Data modeling's purpose is to obtain a comprehensive view of the data that exists in an organization's working environment. This all-encompassing view enables suitable computer systems to be developed to support the organization's activities.

For an information system to be useful, reliable, adaptable, and economical, it must be based on sound data modeling. Just as constructing a home requires a detailed architectural plan, a complex data infrastructure requires a detailed data model. A well-developed data model is the architectural blueprint that enables a stable and flexible database and application development.

The modeling phase of information system design is crucial to ensure an accurate representation of the user's business perspective. Some reasons for data modeling follow:

- Thoroughly comprehending the user's perspective of the data
- Studying data apart from physical considerations

- Understanding who uses the data and when
- Preventing data duplication in the database
- Providing complete, accurate, and essential data input for physical design

Components of a Data Model

Figure 2-32 shows the data model.

Figure 2-32 *Data Model*

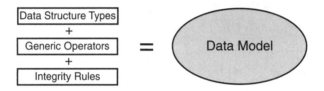

As stated by E.F. Codd, "a data model is a combination of at least three components":

- A set of data structure types.
- A collection of operators that can be applied to any instance of the data types to retrieve, derive, or modify data from any part of those structures, in any combination desired.
- A set of integrity rules that define the consistent database state. (These rules are general in that they apply to any database using the model.)

Essential attributes of a good data model include abstraction, transparency, and effectiveness:

- **Abstraction**—Expresses a concept in its minimum, most universal set of properties. A well-abstracted data model is economical and flexible to maintain and enhance because it has few symbols to represent a large body of design. You save repetitive labor, minimize opportunities for human error, and enable broad-scale, uniform change of behavior by making central changes to the abstract definition.

- **Transparency**—Being intuitively clear and understandable from any point of view. A good data model enables its designer to perceive design truthfulness by presenting an understandable picture of inherently complex ideas. A data model that exists merely as a single, global diagram with all content smashed into little boxes is insufficient. To provide transparency, a data model must enable examination in several dimensions and views:

  — Diagrams by functional area and related data structures
  — Lists of data structures by type and groupings

— Context-bound details within abstract symbols

— Data-based queries in the data describing the model

- **Effectiveness**—An effective data model does the job for which it was commissioned accurately, reliably, and economically. It is tuned to enable acceptable performance at an affordable operating cost. An effective data model is durable and ensures that a system built on its foundation will meet unanticipated processing requirements for years to come. A durable data model does not need constant reconstruction to accommodate new business requirements and processes. Furthermore, as additional data structures are defined over time, an effective data model is easily maintained and adapted because it reflects permanent truths about the underlying subjects, rather than temporary techniques for dealing with those subjects.

Benefits of Data Modeling

The following are benefits of using data models:

- Facilitates communication among knowledge workers in different business areas by sharing commonly defined data. A data model uses a language (notation) designed to record and present concepts and constraints.

- Increases business opportunities by relating data across functional areas and supporting cross-functional queries.

- Eliminates unnecessary redundant data and sources of error and confusion to improve data quality.

- Enables business process reengineering by eliminating nonvalue-adding processes (redundant data entry and unnecessary interfaces).

- Allows effective data resource management by creating a model that represents the enterprise data, rather than requiring that decentralized business areas be responsible to know and manage their disintegrated portions.

- Elicits and documents requirements by capturing a precise statement of requirements for those who must satisfy them.

- Reduces the cost of change. Changing a data model is cheaper and easier than changing an implemented system. Variations on a model can be developed and "tried on" before expending the effort and money to building the final product.

- Leads to an information system design that is understandable, flexible, and stable.

Types of Data Modeling

The three steps in the data modeling process result in a series of progressively formalized data models, as shown in Figure 2-33. These data models are obviously closely related to the three levels of the data modeling process: conceptual data models, logical data models, and physical data models.

Figure 2-33 *Data Modeling*

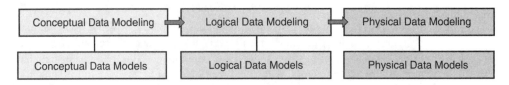

The terms conceptual, logical, and physical are frequently used in data modeling to differentiate between levels of abstraction and detail in the model. No general agreement or accepted authority defines these terms. Nevertheless, data modelers generally understand the approximate scope of each. The conceptual model is concerned with the real-world view and understanding of data; the logical model is a generalized, formal structure in the rules of information science; and the physical model specifies how this structure will be executed in a particular DBMS instance.

Each data model abstraction level is discussed in detail in the following paragraphs.

Conceptual data modeling—Conceptual data modeling defines, in broad and generic terms, the scope and requirements of a database (or information system).

A conceptual data model shows how the business world sees information. It suppresses noncritical details to emphasize business rules and user objects. The model typically includes only significant entities that have business meaning, along with their relationships. Many-to-many relationships work to represent entity associations.

A conceptual model can include a few significant attributes to augment an entity's definition and visualization. You do not need to inventory the full attribute population of such a model. A conceptual model can have identifying concepts or candidate keys noted, but it explicitly excludes a complete identity scheme, because identifiers are logical choices made from a deeper context.

Entity relationship (ER) modeling is probably the most popular conceptual data modeling method. It involves four work aspects:

- Identifying entities (An entity is a person, a place, an event, a thing, and so on.)
- Identifying attributes.
- Determining relationships.
- Drawing an entity relationship diagram (ER diagram).

Figure 2-34 shows a portion of an ER diagram.

Figure 2-34 *ER Diagram*

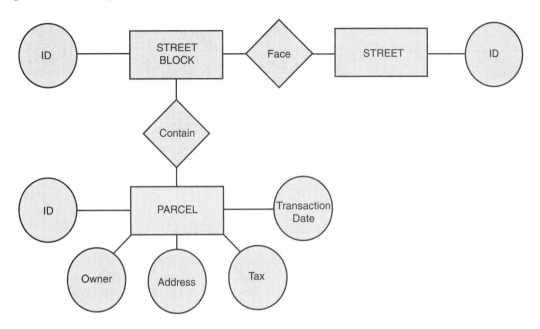

Logical data modeling—Logical data modeling specifies the user's view of the database (or information system) with a clear definition of attributes and relationships. A logical data model is developed by mapping the conceptual data model (such as the ER diagram) to a software-dependent design document. Figure 2-35 illustrates the logical data model of entity, PARCEL, defined in the conceptual model.

A logical model is provable in data science mathematics. Given relational databases' current predominance, logical models generally conform to relational theory. A logical model contains only fully normalized entities. Some of these entities can represent logical domains, rather than potential physical tables.

For a logical data model to be normalized, it must include the full population of attributes to be implemented, and those attributes must be defined in terms of their domains or logical data types (for example, character, number, date, picture, and so on).

A logical data model requires a complete scheme of identifiers or candidate keys to uniquely identify each occurrence in every entity. Because many entities have choices of identifiers, the logical model indicates the current selection of identity. Propagation of identifiers as foreign keys can be explicit or implied.

Figure 2-35 *Logical Data Model*

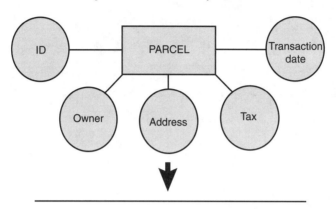

Logical Data Model of Entity PARCEL

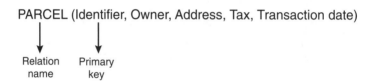

PARCEL (Identifier, Owner, Address, Tax, Transaction date)

Relation
name

Primary
key

Because relational storage cannot support many-to-many concepts, a logical data model resolves all many-to-many relationships into associative entities that can acquire independent identifiers and other attributes.

A logical data model is a generic, relational schema (in at least a first normal form) that processes the following functions:

- Replaces many-to-many relationships with associative entities
- Defines a full population of entity attributes
- Can use nonphysical entities for domains and subtypes
- Establishes entity identifiers
- Does not specify any Relational Database Management System (RDBMS) or configuration

Physical data modeling—Physical data modeling specifies the database's internal storage structure and file organization. Logical data modeling is a comprehensive process that consolidates and refines the conceptual data model.

Physical data modeling is the database design process that defines the tables used to store the data in the following terms:

- **Data format**—The data format, specific to a DBMS
- **Storage requirements**—The volume of the database
- **Physical location of data**—System performance optimization by minimizing the need to transmit data between different storage devices or data servers

A physical data model is also known as a data dictionary, item definition table, data specific table, or physical database definition. A physical data model is both software and hardware specific. This means the physical models for various systems look different from one another. Figure 2-36 shows an example of a physical schema.

Figure 2-36 *Physical Model*

Example of a Physical Model

Item Definition Table:

COLUMN	ITEM NAME	WIDTH	OUTPUT	TYPE	N.DEC	ALT NAME
1	PARCEL-ID	10	15	B	-	-
11	AREA	10	15	F	2	-
21	LU-CLASS	3	5	C	-	-
24	OWNER-LN	15	20	C	-	-
29	OWNER-FN	15	20	C	-	-
44	ADDRESS-1	30	35	C	-	-
74	ADDRESS-2	30	35	C	-	-
104	TRNS-DATE	8	10	B	-	-
112	ASS-VALUE	10	15	I	-	-
122	TAX-RATE	5	10	F	3	-
127	TAX	8	10	F	2	-

Explanatory Notes:

PARAMETER	DESCRIPTION
Item name	Any name to 16 characters
Width	No. of space used to store item values
Output	No. of spaces used
Type	Data item type:
C	Character
I	Integer
B	Binary
N	Number
D	Date MM/DD/YYYY
F	Floating point
N.DEC	No. of decimal points

In database context, a physical data model is a database design for a DBMS product or site configuration. A physical data model is a single, logical model instantiated in a specific database management product (for example, Sybase, Oracle, Informix, and so on) in a specific installation.

The physical data model specifies implementation details, which might be features of a particular product or version, and configuration choices for that database instance. These choices include index construction, alternate key declarations, modes of referential integrity (declarative or procedural), constraints, views, and physical storage objects, such as table spaces.

Entity Relationship Method

Many forms of symbolic notation have been developed to enable data models to represent various levels of abstraction. The entity relationship (ER) method is one of the most popular and earliest data modeling approaches to database design. Peter Chen first published the ER approach in 1976. It is a high-level data modeling language that can be used to understand and simplify data relationships and complex systems.

The ER model views the world as consisting of entities and relationships between them. Entities are "things" that can be distinctly identified (a chamber, a wire, a point, a track, a vertex, and so on). Relationships are associations between entities. "Point belongs to track" is an association between a point and a track. The graphical representation of an ER model is called an entity relationship diagram (ERD). Figure 2-37 shows a sample ERD.

Figure 2-37 *Sample ERD*

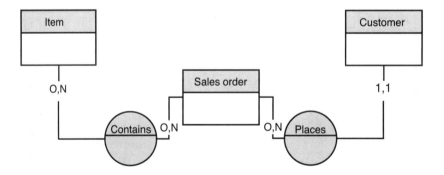

Here is an example of a real-world situation: Mr. Joe Jones resides in the Park Avenue Apartments, located on land parcel #01-857-34 and owned by the Apex Company.

In this example, "Joe Jones," "Park Avenue Apartments," "land parcel," and "Apex Company" are entities, whereas "occupant," "building," "parcel," "owner," "resides," "located on," and "owned by" define relationships.

Figure 2-38 shows an ERD of the real estate example.

Figure 2-38 *Simple ERD*

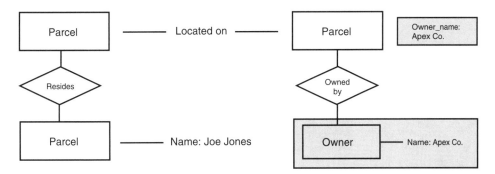

The basic ER modeling approach describes data in terms of the following three components:

* **Entities**—Entities are conceptual data units or data objects.

* **Relationships between entities**—Relationships depict the structural association that exists between entities.

* **Attributes of entities or relationships**—Attributes describe the characteristics or properties of entities or relationships.

Each component has a graphic symbol and a set of rules for building an ER model, such as an ERD. Entities are represented as rectangles, relationships as diamonds, and attributes as ellipses. Each is discussed in turn in the following paragraphs.

Entities—Entities are conceptual data units or data objects, such as Person, Place, Object, Event, or Concept, about which the organization wants to maintain data. They consist of a number of attributes.

In general, the term entity refers to an entity type. An entity type is a collection of entities that share common properties or characteristics. An entity instance, on the other hand, is a single occurrence of an entity type.

An entity type corresponds to a table or relation within a relational database. An entity instance corresponds to a row or record within that table. An entity within an ERD is depicted as a rectangle, as shown in Figure 2-39.

Figure 2-39 *An ERD Entity*

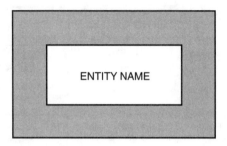

Attributes—Characteristics that describe an entity type. In a relational database, attributes
correspond to the field names (column titles) within the data table. Attributes within an
ERD are depicted as ovals attached to the entity shape or in a separate list, as shown in
Figure 2-40.

Figure 2-40 *An ERD Attribute*

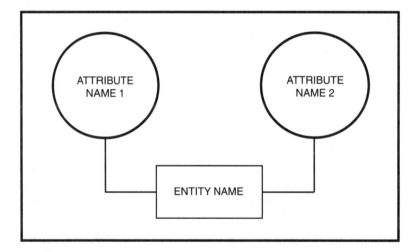

Selecting/identifying the primary key helps determine the appropriate attributes for each
entity. The primary key is the attribute that uniquely identifies each entity instance.

Each attribute that is a possible primary key is called a candidate key. Sometimes, more than
one attribute must be combined to create a primary key. Primary key attribute names are
generally underlined.

Relationships—Entities and attributes by themselves simply provide data; they have little meaning without the addition of the relationship. All entities are related to other entities, and these relationships provide additional information to the data.

A relationship associates the instances of one or more entities. A relationship is depicted in the ERD as a diamond shape, as shown in Figure 2-41.

Figure 2-41 *ERD Relationship*

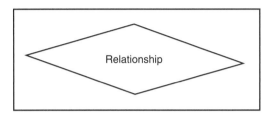

The key concepts to understanding relationships between or among entities are the degree of the relationship and the cardinality of a relationship.

The degree of relationship refers to the number of entity types involved in the relationship. The common ones follow:

- **Unary (degree one)**—The entity has a relationship with itself.
- **Binary (degree two)**—Two entities have a relationship.
- **Ternary (degree three)**—Three entities have a simultaneous relationship.

Most entity relationships are binary. In addition, relationship cardinality is the number of instances of entity B that can, or must, be associated with each instance of entity A. Each relationship has a minimum and a maximum cardinality. The minimum cardinality can be zero, one, or many. The maximum cardinality can also be zero, one, or many.

Transforming an ERD into Relations

A relational database consists of one or more relations, or data tables. A *relation* is a named two-dimensional table that consists of named columns and an arbitrary number of un-named rows. Remember that a relation exists even if no data is entered in it.

The following properties must be associated with relations:

- Entries (cells) are single-valued, or atomic.
- Entries in columns are from the same domain.
- Each row is unique (no duplicates).
- Column sequence is not significant.
- Row sequence is not significant.

Well-structured relations have a minimum amount of redundancy and allow users to modify, insert, and delete rows without error or inconsistency.

Normalization ensures well-structured relations (tables). It assigns attributes to entities. These attributes transform into column names, and the entities transform into relations. Normalization reduces data redundancies and helps eliminate data anomalies. The levels of normalization are first normal form (1NF), second normal form (2NF), and third normal form (3NF). Although, higher normal forms exist, the three listed are most commonly applied to business applications.

Consider the following:

- 1NF Definition
  - All the key attributes are defined.
  - No groups repeat in the entity. Each row/column intersection can contain one and only one value, not a set of values.
  - All attributes depend on the primary key.
- 2NF Definition
  - Relations are in 1NF.
  - Second normal form normalizations include no partial dependencies. No attribute is dependent on only a portion of the primary key.
  - Relations whose primary key is a single attribute will be in 2NF if it is in 1NF.
- 3NF Definition
  - Relations are in 2NF.
  - No transitive dependencies exist.
  - Transitive dependency occurs when a nonkey attribute is dependent on another nonkey attribute. For example, consider that the attribute Wage is dependent on the attribute Job Grade. Job Grade determines Wage, yet neither Job Grade nor Wage are primary keys or part of a primary key. This is a transitive dependency.

Normalization eliminates the potential for data redundancy and the errors that can result. Normalization also eliminates unwanted many-to-many relationships and attribute redundancy.

Each entity type is transformed into a relation with the designated primary key. Nonkey attributes become additional column headings.

Basic Terminology Review

Definitions of basic ER modeling language follow:

- **Entity type**—A type of person, place, thing, event, or concept about which an enterprise wishes to keep information.

- **Entity instance**—A particular occurrence of an entity type. All entity instances share a common meaning, have the same attributes, and follow the same rules. Instances are (conceptual) records in the system.

- **Relationship type**—An association between two (not necessarily distinct) entity types. It describes the reason for, and rules behind, associating things.

- **Relationship instance**—The connection between entity instances. All instances of a relationship share a common definition and rules.

- **Domain**—A value set from which an attribute can draw its values over time. It records not only the possible values of a piece of data, but also those values that are sensible to the business. In summary: A domain specifies the set of valid values for an attribute.

- **Attribute type**—A descriptive property or characteristic about an entity. It is the lowest level of detail that the enterprise records as data.

- **Attribute instance**—A specific attribute value. All attribute instances are drawn from a specified set of valid values (domain) for the attribute type.

- **Cardinality**—A relationship qualifier that expresses the maximum degree to which two entity types can be related. In the most general sense, "many" instances of one entity type can be related to "many" instances of the other entity type. More specific cardinality is used to constrain this general case. Cardinality says "at most, how many" of this thing can be related to "at most, how many" of that thing.

Other Data Modeling Methodologies

Many forms of symbolic notation have been developed to enable data models to represent various levels of abstraction. The entity relationship (ER) method is only one of them. Following are other common data modeling methods:

- Information engineering
- IDEF1X modeling
- Object role modeling

Each is discussed in the following paragraphs.

Information Engineering—Information engineering (IE), developed by James Martin, streamlines the ER theme by discarding the arbitrary notion of the complex *relationship*. Martin models them as simply associated entities. Every relationship in IE is binary, involving two entities (or possibly only one, if reflexive). Martin also simplified the graphic notation in his diagram style.

Figure 2-42 shows a sample IE diagram.

Figure 2-42 *Information Engineering Diagram*

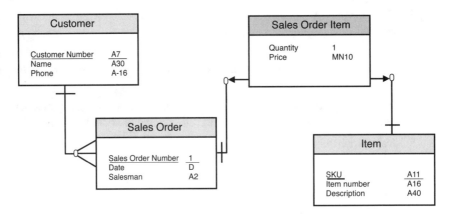

Widely practiced, IE is reasonably concise, consistent, and has a minimum of clutter. However, it lacks important notations for attributes and unique identifiers. IE also refers to a system development methodology. In this context, it develops an integrated information system based on the sharing of common data. It differs from more traditional methodologies in that it emphasizes the need to integrate information and its relationships with functional processes. Martin further states that IE is "...an interlocking set of format techniques in which enterprise models, data models, and process models are built up in a comprehensive knowledge base and are used to create and maintain data processing systems."

IE begins with the development of the enterprise model, which describes the mission and goals of the organization. The model establishes why actions are performed and how the mission is being accomplished. IE continues with the data and process models as the primary mechanisms to communicate information system requirements and design concepts between users and developers.

A data model typically consists of entities, relationships, and attributes. Entities are things about which an organization stores or processes information. Relationships identify how various entities are associated with each other. Attributes describe the characteristics of data items. During the lifecycle of a system, a series of three data models, also known as schemas, are developed to convey and document system design information. These are the conceptual, logical, and physical models.

Process models depicting the functionality of the system and the flow of its data are created and integrated with the data model to ensure creation of a stable information system. IE establishes target architecture for the new system, and subsequent data and process model iterations are created and analyzed to ensure graceful migration from the current environment to the new system.

IDEF1X, another common modeling technique, was developed in the late 1970s and early 1980s by Bob Brown. IDEF1X was later extended by various parties into a set of tools and standards that were adopted by the U.S. Air Force as the required methodology for government projects.

IDEF1X is a method for designing relational databases with a syntax that supports the semantic constructs necessary in developing a conceptual schema. IDEF1X is most useful for logical database design after the information requirements are known and the decision to implement a relational database has been made. The IDEF1X system perspective focuses on the actual data elements in a relational database. If the target system is not a relational system (for example, an object-oriented system), IDEF1X is not the best method.

An entity in IDEF1X refers to a collection or set of similar data instances that can be individually distinguished from one another. Instances are individual members of the set. A box in IDEF1X represents a set of data items in the real-world realm. An attribute is a slot value associated with each individual member of the set. The relationship that exists between individual members of these sets is given a name.

Figure 2-43 shows a sample IDEF1X diagram.

Figure 2-43 *IDEF1X Diagram*

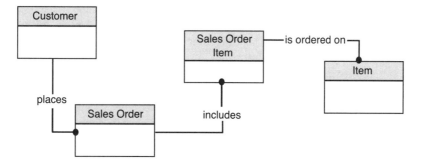

IDEF1X's support for modeling logical data types by using a classification structure or generalization or specialization construct is a powerful feature. This construct is an attempt to overlay models of the natural kinds of things that the data represents, whereas the boxes, or entities, attempt to model types of data. These categorization relationships represent mutually exclusive subsets of a generic entity or set. Subsets of the superset cannot have common instances; for example, the generic entity PERSON has two subsets representing complete categories: MALE and FEMALE. No instance of the MALE subset can be an instance of the FEMALE subset, and vice versa. The unique identifier attribute for each subset is the same attribute as that for a generic entity instance. The characteristic components of IDEF1X data modeling has the following characteristic components:

- **Entities**—In IDEF1X, entities are either identifier-independent or identifier-dependent. Instances of identifier-independent entities can exist without any other entity instance, while instances of identifier-dependent entities are meaningless (by definition) without another associated entity instance. Dependence and independence are specific to a model.

- **Connection relationships**—Solid or dashed lines with filled circles at one or both ends denote how entities (sets of data instances) relate to one another. Connection relationships are always between two entities. The connection relationship beginning at the independent parent entity and ending at the dependent child entity is labeled with a verb phrase describing the relationship. Each connection relationship has an associated cardinality. The cardinality specifies the number of instances of the dependent entity that are related to an instance of the independent entity.

- **Categorization relationships**—Allow the modeler to define the entity's category. An entity can belong to only one category; for example, the entity CAR is the generic entity in a category showing different types of cars. Each category entity must have the same primary key as CAR. The category entities are distinguished by a discriminator attribute, which must have a different value for each category entity.

- **Attributes**—Properties used to describe an entity. Attribute names are unique throughout an IDEF1X model, and the meaning of the names must be consistent. For example, the attribute "color" has several possible uses for hair color, skin color, or a color in a rainbow. Each use has a range of meaningful values, and the entity must be distinctly named. Each attribute is owned by exactly one entity. The attribute "social security number," for example, could be used in many places in a model but would be owned by only one entity (for example, PERSON). Other occurrences of the social security number attributes would be inherited across relations. Every attribute must have a value (No-Null Rule), and no attribute can have multiple values (No-Repeat Rule). Rules enforce creating proper models. In a situation where it seems that a rule cannot hold, the model is likely wrong.

- **Keys**—A group of attributes that uniquely identify an entity instance. There are primary and alternate keys. Every entity has one primary key displayed above the horizontal line in the entity box. Entities can have alternate keys that also uniquely identify the entity, but they are not used to describe relationships with other entities.

In a connection relationship, the parent's primary key migrates to the child. If the relationship is categorical, the child's primary key is the same as the generic key. If the relationship is an identifying relationship, the child's primary key must contain attributes inherited from the parent.

In addition to the fact that a key must uniquely identify an entity, all attributes in the key must contribute to the unique identification (Smallest-Key Rule). When deciding whether an inherited attribute should be part of a key, consider whether that attribute is necessary for unique identification. It is not sufficient that the attribute contributes to the unique identification of the parent. Note the following two dependency rules:

— The Full-Functional-Dependency Rule states that if the primary key is composed of multiple attributes, all nonkey attributes must be functionally dependent on the entire primary key.

— The No-Transitive-Dependency Rule states that every nonkey attribute must be functionally dependent only on key attributes.

- **Foreign keys**—Foreign keys are not really keys at all, but attributes inherited from the primary keys of other entities. Foreign keys are labeled (FK) to show that they are not owned by the entity. Foreign keys are significant because they show the relationships between entities. Because entities are described by their attributes, if an entity is composed of attributes inherited from other entities, that entity is similar to those entities.

Object Role Modeling—Conceptual modeling approach, object role modeling (ORM), pictures the application world as a set of objects that play roles (parts in relationships, which can be unary, binary, or higher order). ORM is a well-proven technique for conceptual modeling from rudimentary data elements and business rules. In ORM, an object is anything that can be stored as data. The modeler does not need to differentiate entities from attributes because they are all objects to ORM.

ORM provides both graphical and textual languages that enable models to be expressed naturally. For data modeling purposes, its graphical language is more expressive than ER.

Figure 2-44 shows a sample ORM diagram.

ORM has a greater capacity than other models to describe business rules and constraints. It also captures a much larger range of structural features and constraints than ER-based methods.

However, ORM has its drawbacks. With ORM, describing entities independently of relationships is difficult. The language describes *facts*, where a fact is a combination of entities, attributes, domains, and relationships.

Figure 2-44 *Object Role Modeling*

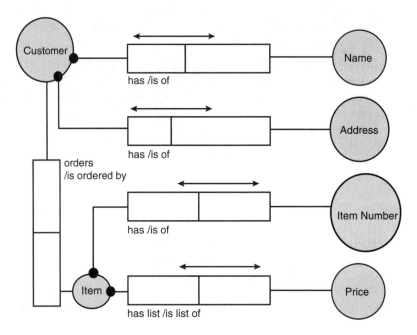

System Enablers

This section reviews process threads that link applications to the operating system and hardware drivers that link applications to the hardware platform. This information is important to your study of distributed computing because system enablers are essential to building robust and efficient distributed applications. Without such knowledge, you can't take full advantage of the processing capabilities of modern hardware.

The discussion is organized into the following categories:

- Threads
- Single-Threaded Design
- Multithreaded Design
- Why Use Multiple Threads?
- Use of Single-Threaded and Multithreaded Design
- Threads Sharing
- What You Need to Know to Use Multithreaded Programs

Threads

A *thread* is a single, sequential, independent flow of control within a process, composed of a context and a sequence of instructions to execute. Within each thread is a single point of execution.

A thread is similar to a real process in that a thread and a running program both exhibit a single, sequential flow of control. However, a thread is considered "lightweight" because it runs within the context of a fully developed program and takes advantage of the resources allocated for that program and the program environment.

As a sequential flow of control, a thread must secure some of its own resources within a running program; for example, it must have its own execution stack and program counter. The code running within the thread works only within that context. Some texts use execution context as a synonym for thread.

A thread is an encapsulation of the flow of control in a program. Threads isolate tasks. The exact meaning of the term thread is not generally agreed upon but is sometimes called an execution context or a lightweight process.

A Human Analogy

A bank with one person working in it (traditional process with single thread) has lots of "bank stuff," such as desks and chairs, a vault, and teller stations (process tables and variables). A bank provides many services, including checking accounts, loans, savings accounts, and so on (the functions). The one person doing all the work has to know how to do everything, and doing so, might take extra time to switch among the various tasks. Two or more employees (multiple threads) would share the same "bank stuff," but they could specialize in their different functions. If all the employees came in and worked on the same day, lots of customers would get serviced quickly.

Single-Threaded Design

A single thread is a single stream of program execution, one statement after the next after the next. Single-threaded programs execute one path through their code at a time. A single thread has a beginning, a middle sequence, and an end, and at any given time during the runtime of the thread, there is a single point of execution. A thread itself is not a program; it does not run on its own, but within a program. Figure 2-45 shows a single-threaded process.

The traditional flow of control within a program is a process with a single context of registers following a single path through the code. This is referred to as the process-based or single-threaded model.

Figure 2-45 *Single-Threaded Process*

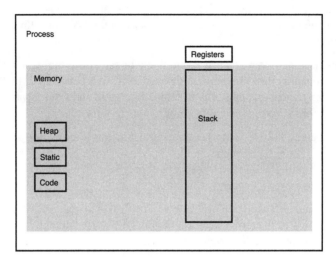

For an application in a single-threaded model to handle multiple tasks, it would have to break up those tasks into multiple processes, coordinate with signal handlers to provide concurrency, or handle those tasks serially (one after the other).

Multithreaded Design

A multithreaded model process allows multiple, concurrent execution paths, or threads, through the same process, allowing a single process to handle multiple tasks without having to program it to serially move from one to the other. Figure 2-46 shows a multithreaded process.

A multithreaded program design might have several threads running through different code paths simultaneously. In a typical process in which multiple threads exist, zero or more threads might actually be running at any one time. This depends on the number of CPUs, the computer on which the process is running, and also on how the thread system is implemented. A machine with n CPUs can, intuitively enough, run no more than n threads in parallel. However, it can give the appearance of running many more than n simultaneously by sharing the CPUs among threads.

When you write a multithreaded program, 99 percent of the programming is identical to what it was before being rewritten. The other 1 percent is spent in creating threads, arranging for different threads to coordinate their activities, and handling thread-specific data and signal masks.

Figure 2-46 *Multithreaded Process*

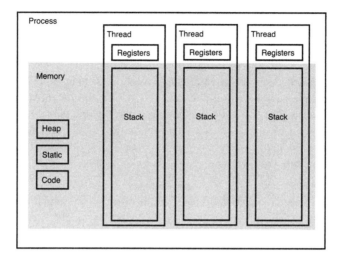

Why Use Multiple Threads?

Most designs must account for multiple streams of program execution. There are several reasons for using multiple threads in a program:

- Multiple threads give the appearance of doing more than one task at a time; for example, your application can serve multiple clients at the same time.

- Threads also give you a clean, simple way to design your application's main function, along with other functions that you would like the application to be aware of or check on from time-to-time (like a background calculation or another mundane chore).

- Threads improve the timeliness and response time when a higher-priority part of an application needs to run.

Green Threads Versus Native Threads

Depending on the application environment, a project needs to decide whether to use green threads or native threads. Green threads are implemented by the Java runtime system itself. Native threads are supported by the underlying operating system, making them more efficient than green threads (if the underlying operating system has a good threading implementation). Green threads are generally considered safer, as fewer things are likely to go wrong (especially with a distributed application in a heterogeneous environment). With green threads, however, I/O can become suspended unless calls are trapped. Another consideration is whether multiple CPUs are available to the application. Native threads make use of multiple CPUs if they exist. Green threads, on the other hand, scale well on single-CPU machines because they consume fewer system resources.

Use of Single-Threaded and Multithreaded Design

Most traditional programs execute as a process with a single thread. Single-threaded applications, such as database management systems by Oracle and the popular Apache Web server, are built using many single-threaded processes. These applications use many CPUs to create multiple processes that execute in parallel.

Single-threaded design is a cost-effective solution for many applications and is generally easier to implement than multithreaded design. One significant benefit to developers of single-threaded design is in the area of debugging. Without thread-aware debuggers, debugging a multithreaded program can be a frustrating experience. Even with a reasonable debugger, application developers who are not experienced with threading can find themselves in a foreign environment, even when developing the simplest application.

Single-threaded design also has disadvantages. The main drawback is that when a single-threaded program requests a service from the operating system, it must wait for that service to complete, often leaving the CPU idle. For example, single-threaded applications that do something lengthy when a button is pressed typically display a Please Wait cursor and freeze while the operation is in progress.

Multithreaded applications, such as databases by Informix and Sybase, use few processes with many threads, allowing many CPUs to execute in each process, speeding execution for parallel code. The Java programming language facilitates multithreaded programming, too. The Sun implementation of the Java virtual machine allows Java applications to use as many processors as necessary to speed execution.

Any program in which many activities are not dependent upon each other can be redesigned so that each activity is executed as a thread.

For example, you can easily create a multithreaded Distributed Component Object Model (DCOM) server capable of providing services to potentially unlimited clients (limiting factors being memory and processing power). Two types of threads can be used in this situation:

- When a client connects to a multithreaded DCOM server, the server creates a thread, which is often called a client thread. The client thread is responsible for servicing that client.

- A request thread is also created when the server initializes and creates before any clients connect to the server. These limited request threads are the threads shared by the potentially unlimited clients.

Thread Sharing

Servers usually rely on services provided by other servers, such as a relational database server. Connections to these underlying servers are expensive in terms of resource use and must be used sparingly. For example, 100 clients connected to a server require 100 corresponding connections to the underlying database server.

This connection is clearly impractical; in most cases, it is impossible and represents a tremendous waste of resources because those database connections are unlikely to be used all the time by all the clients. A better solution is for clients to share these precious resources.

A pool of connections that all clients can share is needed. This sharing must be transparent to the clients, who need not be aware of such implementation complexities. When a client connects to the DCOM server, the client does not create a new connection to the database server. Instead, the connection pool manager asks one of the threads created earlier to do the processing and return the results, which are, in turn, passed back to the client.

A multithreaded application has several advantages over a single-threaded application:

- **More natural programming style**—Imagine an application that has several disjointed tasks, such as doing computations, reading input from a socket, refreshing the Graphical User Interface (GUI), and so on. In a single-threaded model, the application must take on the responsibility of switching between these various tasks, but a multithreaded application tasks can be set up to operate mostly independent of one another.

- **The ability to gain concurrency**—A single-threaded application must do one task, wait for completion, and then do the next task. For example, in an application that must read data, modify it, and write it back out, a single-threaded application might spend much of its time blocked on Input/Output (I/O). A multithreaded version of the same application gains concurrency by scheduling the next read while the previous write is completing.

- **The ability to parallelize an application**—In a computation-intensive application, dividing a task among the various processors on a multiple-processor system is advantageous. The single-threaded model cannot do this within the process because the process is scheduled as a single unit on only one processor. A multithreaded application can run different threads of the same process in parallel across multiple processors.

One of the main disadvantages to a multithreaded design is the complexity of multithreaded programming and its difficulty for users to learn. Threads can be difficult to use. Developing multithreaded applications without understanding all of the aspects of multitasking is almost impossible. In addition, threads tend to make programs harder to debug.

What You Need to Know to Use Multithreaded Programs

If you are an application architect, be familiar with the following issues:

- Concurrent program design schemes
- How threads are scheduled
- What scope a thread runs under
- What data threads have access to (which is mainly an implementation issue)

If you are a programmer, be familiar with the following issues:

- Synchronization mechanisms
- Correctness analysis theory
- Debugging strategies
- Implementation details

Despite the disadvantages, threads can be invaluable. They can improve your program's perceived performance and can sometimes simplify a program's code or architecture.

NOTE   You can gain the benefits of concurrency on either a uniprocessor or a multiprocessor system, but parallelism can only be achieved on multiprocessor systems. In both concurrent and parallel applications, however, performance (or throughput) improvements are often achieved by multithreading.

Hardware Drivers

A hardware driver, or device driver, is a program that controls a device. Every device, whether it is a printer, disk drive, or keyboard, must have a driver program. Many drivers, such as the keyboard driver, come with the operating system. For other devices, you might need to load a new driver when you connect the device to your computer. In DOS systems, most drivers are files with .SYS extensions. In Windows environments, drivers often have a .DRV extension.

A driver acts as a translator between the device and programs that use the device. Each device has its own set of specialized commands that only its driver knows. In contrast, most programs access devices by using generic commands. The driver accepts generic commands from a program and translates them into specialized commands for the device. Figure 2-47 illustrates the relationship among the hardware, device drivers, and interfaces.

Figure 2-47 *Device Drivers Relationship*

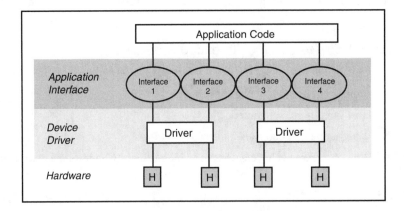

Hardware drivers are software programs that interface with the computer hardware devices. Without the proper drivers, devices such as a keyboard, a mouse, video cards, and sound cards will not work.

The device drivers issue commands to the device controllers and see if they are carried out properly. The device driver knows the specific hardware details for managing the device.

When an I/O request is made (hard drive, CD-ROM, keyboard stroke, a mouse movement or click, or print), the device driver determines what commands to issue and writes the commands to the device controller's registers. The driver then blocks the device until the interrupt comes back to unblock it. In some cases, the operation is immediate, so the driver does not need to block the device. If the driver blocks, it is awakened by the interrupt of the device controller.

Deployment Issues of Hardware Drivers

Device-independence is a key concept in the design of hardware device (I/O) software. You can write programs that read files from different hardware devices (I/O) without having to modify the programs for each different device type. The operating system, not the application, is responsible for these different devices and their device drivers.

All device-dependent code goes in the device drivers. Each device driver handles one device type or one class of closely related devices. The device driver accepts the input from the device-independent software in the layer above it and sees that its request is executed. If everything works successfully, the driver will have data to pass to the device-independent software.

Basic hardware driver functions include the following:

- Perform I/O functions that are common to all devices and provide a uniform interface to the user-level software.
- Perform device naming, which is the mapping of symbolic device names to the proper driver.
- Supply protection by keeping users from accessing devices they are not supposed to access.
- Hide the fact that different block devices have different sector sizes and provide a uniform block size to higher layers. Hide differences in character device stream rates from the higher layers.
- Provide read and write buffers so that data written to these devices is sent in blocks, and provide buffers for character devices, so that data input and output will not cause delays.

- Provide storage allocations, because when a file is created and filled with data, new disk blocks must be allocated to the file. To perform this allocation, the operating system needs a list of free blocks per disk. The algorithm for locating the free block is device independent and can be run above the device driver.

- Provide allocating and releasing of dedicated devices. Only a single process can use some devices at any given moment. The operating system decides if the device is being used and rejects or accepts requests by processes for the device.

- Perform error handling. The device driver does most error handling. If the device driver fails to complete the I/O request because of an error, it informs the operating system.

User-Level I/O

Some of the I/O software can be found in libraries that are linked to user programs. A user program that invokes a function such as printf, scanf, or write is invoking the I/O functions that are contained within a library.

The spooling system is another type of user-level I/O. The spooler or print daemon prints files that are placed into a spooling directory. The spooler is the only process with access to the printer and controls the output of all files that are written by other user-processes to the printer.

Summary

Application architecture models range from centralized to distributed computing solutions, with many tradeoffs regarding the benefits of each architecture. Although centralized computing was considered a computing model from the early days of computer mainframes and dumb terminals, the idea of a network PC has rejuvenated discussions of the benefits of centralized computing. This rejuvenation is due in part to the realization that the total cost of ownership of a regular PC workstation is significantly higher than that of a network PC or network computer because of administrative time and resources spent maintaining systems.

Peer-to-peer and client/server applications architectures represent some of the latest innovations and developments, taking advantage of the topology of the Internet and increasing availability of high-speed connections. A major portion of Internet business solutions are being built as client/server applications in a distributed computing model with a three-tier architecture. The basic three-tier architecture consists of the presentation tier, the business logic tier, and the data tier.

Another development in client/server architecture is a move away from thick client applications toward thin client applications and web-based applications. You can update and maintain these applications with less effort (for reasons related to software distribution costs and remote configuration management) and consume fewer resources on client workstations.

Web-based applications and services being developed have the advantage of providing a way for companies to continue using legacy systems by simply writing a new "front end" to their systems. Middleware software provides the connectivity between web servers and the legacy systems. These kinds of Internet business solutions also leverage the widespread adoption of web browser software and open standards, such as SSL, for encrypted connections and dynamic HTML technologies. Programming languages geared toward web-based applications and services are also continually being refined and introduced to solve problems and provide richer experiences than were afforded by static HTML web pages and simple Perl/CGI forms. Java and javascript represent two of the major technologies being used to build web-based applications.

This chapter also presents detailed information about database systems because database systems are required for almost all forms of business applications, whether they are web-enabled or not. The four types of database models are hierarchical, networked, relational, and object-oriented. Each of these types has its own unique advantages and limitations, but relational databases are most popular because their power and flexibility is well matched with the needs of modern business. The introduction to database systems is meant to acquaint the CISS with the technologies and tools that actual database administrators will use on projects. Of more direct importance to the CISS engineer is the section on database deployment considerations. Evaluating all the areas that affect the ease of deployment and maintenance of a database will certainly reward the effort.

At the heart of a business application model is the modeling of the actual transactions that will be processed. The transaction models discussed familiarize you with the concepts and terminology used by the application architects and developers. Network design is affected by the choices made at the transaction level, and the frequency and size of the transactions dictate many important requirements for the application.

Directly related to the discussion of application transactions are the sections on object-oriented design and object-oriented programming. The object-oriented design fundamentals are relevant to almost all Internet business solutions because some aspect or component of the solution involves object-oriented programming. Although more than a brief introduction to object-oriented design and programming is beyond the scope of this book, this section does define the key concepts of object, method, class, message, encapsulation, inheritance, and polymorphism. It also covers some of the reasons for choosing to write applications in object-oriented programming languages, taking care to point out trade-offs and possible pitfalls.

No discussion of distributed applications design is complete without addressing data modeling. This section introduces data modeling and the components of various approaches to data modeling. Data modeling and object-oriented programming are closely related. Building the data model is generally the first step toward creating a distributed application. Several common data models are presented so that you can speak knowledgeably about conceptual, logical, and physical data models, and the methods employed by each model.

The final two sections address two low-level application concepts: threads and hardware drivers. These are considered low-level concepts because they operate close to the raw machine-code operations and processes of a system. If object-oriented design is a high-level abstraction of objects and properties, threads and hardware drivers are where these abstractions and properties become actual configurations and platform-specific settings for operating system settings and software components.

Review Questions

1   Which definition best describes a distributed application?

   a. PC user accessing application from the server

   b. Cooperative processing

   c. Retail channel sales of software applications

   d. Web browser

2   Which is not a key benefit of moving to distributed applications?

   a. Reliability

   b. Cost-saving

   c. Scalability

   d. Reusability

3   Which is not a purpose of middleware in relation to addressing the needs of networked enterprises?

   a. Migrating distributed applications

   b. Developing distributed applications

   c. Integrating distributed applications

   d. Managing distributed applications

4   Which is not one of the five categories of middleware classifications?

   a. RPC

   b. MOM

   c. TPM

   d. OMG

   e. ORB

5 Which statement is false?

a. A client usually waits for a server to initiate requests.

b. A client relies on servers for resources, such as files, devices, and processing power.

c. A client manages the user-interface portion of the client/server application.

d. A client workstation usually has a graphical user interface.

6 Which is not a client/server application?

a. Ping

b. Internet Explorer browser

c. Nslookup

d. MS Access

7 Client/server computing is the logical extension of modular programming. With this architecture, what requests a service?

a. The user

b. The server

c. The client

d. The system administrator

8 Which layer allows you to tell the difference between an order entry application and an inventory control application?

a. Presentation

b. Business logic

c. Data

d. Enhanced data streams

9 Which is not an advantage of a three-tier architecture over a two-tier architecture?

a. Improved performance for groups with a large number of users

b. Greater flexibility to update business rules

c. Easier code programming

d. Enhanced capability to implement load balancing

10 Which example typifies a thin client?

    a. A UNIX-based workstation

    b. JavaStations

    c. A VMS terminal

    d. A traditional PC

11 Which company develops network computers?

    a. Oracle

    b. Microsoft

    c. Cisco

    d. Sun Microsystems

12 Which statement about web applications is false?

    a. Every web site is a web application.

    b. An online store is an example of web applications.

    c. Web applications have the capacity to provide extensive collaboration or interactivity.

    d. A web application uses a web site as the front end to a more typical application.

13 Web applications are developed to display on what?

    a. Client/servers

    b. Browsers

    c. Mainframes

    d. High-end PCs

14 Which is not a key component of the web application architecture?

    a. Server components

    b. Web pages

    c. Web forms

    d. Graphical user interface (GUI)

15 Which component of the web application architecture is mainly used to collect user input?

    a. Frame

    b. Form

    c. Client Component

    d. Server Component

16 A Java servlet engine is a _____ .

    a. Search engine

    b. Program

    c. Web server

    d. Web application

17 Which web application language is not a programming language?

    a. Perl

    b. ActiveX

    c. JAVA

    d. HTML

18 CGI can be written in many languages, but the most popular one is _____ .

    a. Visual Basic

    b. Perl

    c. C

    d. Java

19 In which scenario is a transaction considered illegal?

    a. Goods or services are incorrectly shipped or performed.

    b. Integrity constraint cannot be met.

    c. One of the B2B partners rejects the transaction.

    d. Data is passed between distributed components.

20 When an update to a row can be performed quickly and with little overhead, this is called _____ .

    a. Indirect update

    b. Deferred update

    c. Update in place

    d. None of the above

21 Query transactions are not used to create _____ .

    a. Terminal outputs

    b. Records

    c. Printed reports

    d. Transaction summaries

22 Which statement about distributed transactions is false?

    a. A distributed transaction is more complex than a traditional transaction in terms of management.

    b. A distributed transaction is a transaction that involves multiple transaction resources running on two or more distinct nodes.

    c. Distributed transactions are important in maintaining consistency across multiple resource managers.

    d. A distributed transaction is different from a traditional transaction in that it does not have to conform to the ACID rule.

23 What transaction model does not need an explicit **begin_transaction** command to start a new transaction?

    a. Chained transactions

    b. Nested transaction

    c. Flat transaction

    d. Team transaction

24 Which statement is false?

    a. Database management systems allow multiple users to simultaneously retrieve a record.

    b. Database engines are the parts of database management systems that actually perform the storing and data retrieving functions.

    c. Databases are collections of information organized to make data easily retrievable.

    d. Database management systems allow multiple users to simultaneously update a record.

25 Which element is not a component of a typical DBMS?

    a. Data Description Language

    b. Data Manipulation Language

    c. Data dictionary

    d. Query Language

    e. Data

26 Which one is not an advantage of a relational database?

    a. It reduces redundancy. Because the data between tables can be easily connected, the relational model provides a minimum level of controlled redundancy to eliminate most of the redundancies commonly found in file systems.

    b. It is faster than the other database systems because it requires minimum hardware and operating system overhead.

    c. It is simple and easy to maintain. You can modify or add new entities, attributes, or tables at any time without restructuring the entire database.

    d. It is easy to design the database because the relational model achieves both data and structural independence.

27 What statement about backup is false?

    a. An incremental backup alone is necessary to restore a database in case of failures.

    b. A full backup must be performed offline.

    c. An incremental backup creates a copy of only the journal files that have changed since the last backup.

    d. A full backup archives the entire database providing a copy of all data and journal files.

28 What situation does not limit the performance, efficiency, and cost-effectiveness of traditional RAID storage?

    a. Performance versus data protection

    b. Large versus small data transfers

    c. Read versus write performance

    d. Centralized versus distributed data management

29 What statement about object-oriented design is false?

    a. In object-oriented design, data and function are not separated.

    b. Objects are the central focus throughout object-oriented design.

    c. Object-oriented design indicates a top-down design process from the beginning of the class construction.

    d. Object-oriented design is based on a uniform underlying representation (classes and objects).

30 What language is the first object-oriented language?

a. Eiffel

b. Simula

c. SmallTalk

d. C++

31 What statement is not a benefit of object-oriented design?

a. Fundamental infrastructure

b. Reduced development time because of data structure reuse

c. Superior quality because programs are created out of existing and tested elements

d. Uncomplicated preservation of the scheme because changes to existing systems can be made by restoring the system

32 What statement about object and class is false?

a. The class definition specifies the set of attributes and allowed operations for objects of the class.

b. Polymorphism has the ability to take many forms as a single message to execute a specific function.

c. An object is a self-contained entity that consists of both data and procedures to manipulate the data.

d. A class is an abstraction of a real-world entity that can be either concrete or abstract.

e. Instances are the individual items that are created using the class's creation mechanism.

33 What statement about the CASE tool is false?

a. CASE technology is an important tool for large schemes.

b. CASE tools were once considered an easy approach, but are now a necessity.

c. CASE tools are hindered by their narrow mixture of techniques.

d. CASE tools methodologies provide a way to present sophisticated processes.

34 What definition best describes a parallel computing pattern?

a. A central modeling technique that runs through nearly all object-oriented methods

b. A full lifecycle of analysis, design, coding, testing, and integration

c. A reusable code-skeleton for quick and reliable development of correlative applications

d. Indications between blocks and input and output from the environment

35 What definition best describes the difference between structured programming and OO programming?

   a. Structured programming discipline allows reasonable structure on large software systems based on the idea of encapsulation and inheritance, while object-oriented programming discipline limits control transfers to a small set.

   b. In object-oriented programming, all the data is usually placed before any of the functions are written.

   c. In object-oriented programming, the information and tasks are kept apart, while in structured programming they are combined into one unit.

   d. In structured programming, information and tasks are maintained independently, while in object-oriented programming they are kept together.

36 What language is not an object-oriented programming language?

   a. Java

   b. C++

   c. Perl

   d. SmallTalk

37 What statement about data models is false?

   a. A data model is a specification of the data structures needed to support a business area.

   b. A data model is to a database designer what blueprints are to a builder.

   c. A data model is built to map business concepts into relational objects.

   d. A data model is a miniature of the actual data itself.

38 What element is not a key component of a data model?

   a. Integrity rules

   b. Cost

   c. Data structure types

   d. Operators

39 What attribute is not essential to a good data model?

   a. Effectiveness

   b. Reusability

   c. Abstraction

   d. Transparency

40 What statement is not a benefit of data modeling?

a. Data modeling allows each department to be accountable for its portion of the data.

b. It leads to better system design that is understandable, flexible, and stable.

c. It facilitates requirements clarification and documentation.

d. It facilitates communication among knowledge workers.

e. It reduces the cost of change.

41 What model is both software and hardware dependent?

a. Conceptual model

b. Logical model

c. Physical model

d. Transaction model

42 What model allows many-to-many relationships?

a. Conceptual model

b. Physical model

c. Logical model

d. Transaction model

43 What element is not one of the three components of an ER model?

a. Relationship

b. Cardinality

c. Entity

d. Attribute

44 The important ingredients of data modeling consist of which set?

a. Entity type, instance, and attributes

b. Domain, relationship, and cardinality

c. Relationship, entities, and attributes

d. Unary, binary, and ternary

45 What method is used as a system development methodology in which enterprise models, data models, and process models are built up in a comprehensive knowledge base and are used to create and maintain data processing systems?

   a. Information engineering

   b. IDEF1X

   c. ORM

   d. Entity relationship method

46 In what modeling method is it difficult to describe entities independently from relationships?

   a. Entity relationship method

   b. Information engineering

   c. IDEF1X

   d. ORM

47 What item does not fit in with IDEF1X?

   a. Relational systems

   b. Object-oriented systems

   c. No-Repeat Rule

   d. No-Null Rule

48 Why is a thread sometimes called lightweight?

   a. It runs within the context of fully developed programs.

   b. It is an inexpensive code.

   c. It is easy to use.

   d. The design is not important.

49 What statement about threads is false?

   a. Multithreaded models allow a single process to handle multiple tasks.

   b. Multithreaded programs can have several threads running through different code paths simultaneously.

   c. Multithreaded designs divide tasks into multiple processes and coordinates with signal handlers to provide concurrency.

   d. Multithreaded programs can avoid blocked input/output (I/O) by scheduling the next read while the previous write is finishing.

50 What disadvantage is there to a multithreaded design?

   a. Complex learning curve.

   b. CPU is inactive until the task is completed.

   c. Set up to operate independently.

   d. Expensive.

51 What statement is true?

   a. A program with many conditional functions can be modified as a thread.

   b. An advantage to using a single-threaded design is that the essential part of the OS that is responsible for the resource allocation is affected.

   c. Single-threaded program requests must wait for one job to complete before another can begin.

   d. Native threads are implemented by a Java runtime system instead of the operating system.

52 What device does not make I/O requests to hardware drivers?

   a. Monitor

   b. Printer

   c. Telephone

   d. Keyboard

   e. Disk drive

53 What function is not fundamental to hardware device software?

   a. Deny access to some devices

   b. Capture misbehaved requests

   c. Sponsor dissimilar interface to the user-level software

   d. Allocate and release dedicated devices

Applications Engineering

CHAPTER 3

Application Design and Development

Software is the result of a process. Good software development is the result of a structured process. Software development can be described as a lifecycle, germinating from the original idea for an integrated application, a game, or a service.

Software development lifecycles take the form of various models, each with their own unique characteristics and patterns. Choosing the right lifecycle model for your business application is a decision that must reflect careful questioning about the nature of the business application being considered. Just as you would not expect palm trees to grow in the arctic tundra, you should not expect all lifecycle models to be equally valid options for your project.

The factors that influence your choice are sometimes hard to identify, or perhaps change over time as the project progresses. Remembering the forces that guide your development lifecycle helps guard against frustration and failure.

Knowing the impact that development decisions have upon network and infrastructure planning is one of the jobs of a CISS professional. Every member of a software development team, from project management to code developers, has both the responsibility and the right to pay attention to the software lifecycle phases and issues of overall project management.

The role of the CISS throughout the various phases of the development lifecycle is explained in detail in this chapter, using the following Basic Lifecycle Model:

- Business Modeling and Requirements Phase
- Analysis and Design Phase
- Development Phase
- Test Phase
- Implementation Phase
- Maintenance Phase

| NOTE | After reviewing these phases, you'll also take a closer look at other lifecycle model facts at the end of the chapter. |

Although development and testing are two distinct phases in the model, they are generally performed iteratively in practice. Unit testing and integration testing are usually performed throughout the development phase. System testing and UAT (User Acceptance Testing) are performed in the test phase. At the end of formal testing, if the requirements are not met, the next step is to return to the development phase to modify the code, network components, and system components.

The model serves as a framework with guidelines to follow when designing Internet business solutions. The model serves to ensure that all essential issues necessary to planning, designing, and implementing an optimal Internet business solution are considered. This model is chosen not because it is the most popular model for software applications development, but because its parts are found among a variety of models. Other models simply make different decisions as to the length and depth of the basic development phases.

Before the text jumps into the modeling and requirements phase, a side trip into the activities performed by a CISS is in order.

Activities Performed by a CISS

This section briefly reviews the many different roles of a CISS and typical activities that a CISS might perform in an Internet business solution project. After completing this section, you should be able to list typical activities performed by a CISS in a project. Not all projects entail having a CISS adopt each of these roles, but knowing what they are and how they differ helps make sure that the project has not ignored them.

The discussion is further divided into the following sections:

- CISS Roles in an Internet Business Solution Project
- Typical Activities a CISS Performs
- Focus on Testing

CISS Roles in an Internet Business Solution Project

Effective Internet business solutions are the result of sound planning, thoughtful design, rapid development, reliable implementation, and ongoing maintenance and support. A CISS is expected to provide input in each phase of the complete software development lifecycle. A CISS must be conversant in both network technologies and application technologies and have sound business knowledge to interact with customers effectively.

Furthermore, a major responsibility of a CISS is to help customers to plan and implement Internet business solutions. This entails work on a spectrum of problems that range from well-structured problems to ill-structured or unstructured problems. An example of a well-structured problem is a client requesting that an existing application or service be integrated with a newly acquired or developed service. This kind of problem has fixed rules and boundaries, which are similar to developing a technical specification. An example of an ill-structured or unstructured problem is a client requesting that an order process be made easier. With this kind of problem, you can expect to be surprised and challenged by the lack of boundaries and fixed rules.

A CISS can take different roles in different Internet business solution projects. In most cases, a CISS is an active player who provides input on various aspects of each phase of a software development lifecycle. In many cases, a CISS can act as a facilitator who assembles experts from relevant disciplines to successfully complete the project. In some cases, a CISS can take the lead role or take the project manager role, and push the design and development of the solution through to the final customer approval.

NOTE   Project management is an area replete with methods, techniques, and tools of its own. Finding many training programs available on project management is easy. Information on project management discipline and certification can be obtained from the Project Management Institute's (PMI) web site at www.pmi.org. This book does not cover any project management-related knowledge or skills, even though they are important in an Internet business project.

Typical Activities a CISS Performs

Following are typical activities that a CISS might perform during each phase of an Internet business solution project:

- Business Modeling and Requirements Phase
  - Advise on nonfunctional requirements — Provide input on identifying non-functional requirements, such as performance, availability, security, and scalability.
  - Review current state — Assess the current state of the organization, competencies of the information technology (IT) staff, current systems, processes, tools, and standards.
  - Advise on system concept — Provide input on the system concept and resulting impact of the solution to the organization. Review the system concept for completeness and validity.
  - Advise on project plan — Provide input on project management plan. Verify completeness and accuracy.

- Analysis and Design Phase

  — Advise on platform selection—Provide input on which types of hardware, software, servers, software applications, and operating systems are appropriate for the project.

  — Advise on security design—Provide input on the security aspect of a specific design or implementation. Identify obvious types of security vulnerability in the system architecture and in applications.

  — Perform current network assessment—Participate in the current network assessment activity. Determine whether the current network and system architecture support the application solutions.

  — Deliver application architecture design—Lead the application architecture design discussion and eventual design.

  — Deliver network design—Lead the network design discussion and eventual design. Make sure the design is valid, and reasonable—and complies with the current network technology.

- Development Phase

  — Steer application architecture design—Provide advice and assistance on platform selection, network architecture, and security design as the system and network infrastructure is modified, upgraded, or built.

- Test Phase

  — Perform transaction profiling—Provide input on transaction profiling. Identify types of transactions and understand how various transactions affect the systems, network, and applications.

  — Validate user or test scenarios—Verify that the test scenarios are representative of the way the application is used in the real world. Each testing scenario must be a description of the predicted usage of the network by an application. Be aware of the trade-offs of the number of test scenarios and cost.

  — Perform testing and validation—Create a complete testing and validation plan from the business and system perspective. Team with others to complete the testing and validation. A critical task in this phase is load testing on the entire system.

  — Validate transaction performance—Ensure that the transaction performance criteria (that is, response time) are met during application performance testing.

  — Validate nonfunctional requirements—Ensure that the system requirements (that is, response time, availability goals, security) are met during system testing (that is, user load testing, availability testing, security testing).

- Implementation Phase

  — Implementation planning—Specify and coordinate the activities for delivering and installing the solution, including hardware, software, and documentation.

  — Deliver network and system management plan—Create a complete network and system management plan, and make sure it is implemented.

- Maintenance Phase

  — Issue resolution—Resolve any noncritical issues or bugs that remain after the client has accepted the application.

  — Troubleshooting—Troubleshoot enterprise-level problems. Identify what the problems are and know who must be responsible for solving the problems.

  — Upgrade and patch—Perform regular software, network, and operating system upgrades and patches.

NOTE   This is not a complete list nor does it imply that a CISS has to perform all these activities. The project and the customer mainly determine a CISS role and activities. As projects vary, a CISS can assume different roles and perform different sets of activities.

Focus on Testing

Of the six phases presented in this Basic Lifecycle Model, the testing phase is given the largest treatment. This is because practically one half of the CISS Solutions book is devoted to software testing and validation. Testing and validation is broken down into the following categories:

- **Application Performance Testing**—Testing the upper limit of projected user traffic and scenarios

- **Security Testing**—Testing to see if access levels are appropriate and unnecessary services closed down

- **User Load (Stress) Testing**—Testing greater than the upper limit of projected user traffic and scenarios

- **Availability (Failure) Testing**—Testing simulated and real failure scenarios

Somewhere, in between the requirements phase and the maintenance phase, a software project is launched and declared live. Reaching go live with full functionality, no bugs, on time, and on budget is almost impossible. Changes always end up affecting one of these criteria, and a compromise must be reached. Either the demo won't be ready in time for the board of directors meeting, or the holiday shopping season starts and your site still provides only 80 percent of the planned functionality, or some other event causes a slip in the schedule, or a creep in scope without the requisite resource allocation. But with all this said, you must still stick to your plans and make sure that they reflect reality. Update the plans according to what the resources can reasonably deliver. This is the only way to keep client expectations from getting out of control, and the only way to avoid catastrophic failure and the collapse of your project.

Business Modeling and Requirements Phase

The business modeling and requirements phase is the level of the Basic Lifecycle Model that provides a representation and needs assessment of an application. That representation allows the decision makers and application specialists in the business to capture, organize, and visualize the web-based application as if it were functioning within their business.

Business modeling identifies and organizes the knowledge of the people conducting the business into a concrete form. It converts business practices into a comprehensive knowledge database by constituting an agreement within the business about its organization, processes, information requirements, current business environment, and potential gains or losses. The purpose of a business model thus becomes to highlight, as a tangible structure, an entire business.

A typical business model involves knowing how to

- Automate business processes to help people capture, organize, and visualize information about the business.

- Empower business people so that they can understand, communicate, and control their business activities sufficiently to enable support and service to their customers.

- Understand the business, the organization, and the information technology.

- Develop an equipment and software system to affect the business purpose and supporting graphics.

An auto parts business might construct a business model that represents a data communications link among all its warehouses. Besides detailing the communications systems required, it might also provide the following details:

- Demonstrate how the application solved the company's parts inventory coordination problem.

- Evaluate the potential decrease in overhead and increase in revenues.

- Inform a discussion on the impact that the system might have on company personnel.

- Inform a discussion on the impact that the system might have on company personnel requirements.

- Recommend operational procedures for using the system.

Preliminary business models can have a loose structure, which allows for valuable approximations and estimates. As the application project evolves, better insights can be incorporated into the model.

After the company acquiring an application accepts the business model, the business model provides the additional, important function of documenting an application. This documenting is done in a business-oriented format that can later provide the basis for future application development.

To help illustrate this phase, it is broken into the following sections:

- Inputs to the Business Modeling and Requirements Phase
- Outputs from the Business Modeling and Requirements Phase
- Issues of the Business Modeling and Requirements Phase
- Responsibilities During the Modeling and Requirements Phase
- Techniques and Tools for the Modeling and Requirements Phase
- Introduction to Tools

Inputs to the Business Modeling and Requirements Phase

The inputs to the business modeling and requirements phase consist of the business need, business organization, business capabilities and resources, and the business environment in which the business application is implemented.

To begin developing the business model, which contains the preliminary requirements to support the business application specifications development, the model developers need the following inputs:

- Business-need stated as functionality and new products needed
- Current business organization and purpose
- Current business capabilities and resources
- Stated requirements and desires of all internal constituencies that might impact or be impacted by the application
- Definition and distinction of the context business and core business

Consider the content of the last bullet in the preceding list. A computer motherboard is an example of a core business product for a computer manufacturer. However, the boxing and mailing of the computer motherboards to the wholesale distributors represents a context business for that computer manufacturer.

Context business consists of those activities in which the company has no desire to compete, but are necessary to the function of the organization or production of its products or services.

A *core business* consists of those products or services with which the business has an objective to be the best, and therefore maintain a substantial competitive edge over all competition.

Personnel involved in the business modeling process must ensure that they do not limit inputs or manufacture inputs to favor any specific application provider. This prohibition extends to the organization of the modeler. Adding capabilities or partnering with another provider is ultimately superior than providing a customer with a deficient business model upon which to base decisions about acquiring business applications.

Outputs from the Business Modeling and Requirements Phase

The outputs from the business modeling and requirements phase consist of an organized presentation of any information concerning the proposed business application. The outputs allow the key decision makers to determine the value of the application. Additionally, the product and services development, marketing, and production personnel receive the information required to develop strategic advice for key decision makers. The outputs from this phase include information about the following:

- **Product or services**—The business modeling and requirements phase has, as its first and most essential component, the definition of the product or service that an application provides to satisfy the business need or business opportunity.

- **Gain or loss potential**—The business part of the business modeling and requirements phase presents the potential for gain or loss from the investment required to develop and implement an application. The terms of the gain or loss estimate can take one of several forms, from straight return-on-investment to the degree of protection of the share of a core business interest from competitors. The estimate of potential for loss has equal value to the business decision makers. The rest of the application business model defines the processes and issues involved in attempting to achieve the projected gain and avoid the possible loss.

- **Feasibility**—As the potential for gain can determine the desirability and excitement of developing and implementing an application, the feasibility instills realism into the decision-making process. The decision about the desirability of implementing an application becomes a weighted product of both potential for gain and the feasibility. As an example, though the potential gain from providing motorists with bug-free windshields might be huge, the feasibility of producing that product might be so low that the business decision might reject the proposal. Conversely, an application with high feasibility, for example, producing another decibel gain from existing amplifiers, might have so little potential for gain that the business decision might reject the amplifier.

- **Critical success factors**—Critical success factors are those items that an application absolutely requires for completing the application implementation; that is, any condition that can prevent the end product or service from being provided. The model must provide the following data:

  — Identity of the critical success factors

  — Means of tracing critical success factors throughout the rest of the lifecycle

  — Process for testing the satisfaction of the requirement associated with the critical success factors

- **Risk analysis and control**—The business model requires a preliminary assessment of risks and a plan to mitigate the potential effects of risks. This business model's business plan can list risks to application success, such as obsolescence of equipment or software prior to lifecycle completion; the means of continued assessment of the risk; and the points in the lifecycle to assess the potential damage of each risk.

- **Relevant baselines**—The business model must list, for the business decision makers and application developers, the baseline criteria against which to compare the performance of an application and its components. The baselines can be derived either from current performance of the company that is acquiring an application or from similar business organizations in the industry.

Issues of the Business Modeling and Requirements Phase

The business model remains dynamic throughout the basic application lifecycle. Although the results of the business modeling and resource requirements phase provided the information which defined and sold the application development and implementation project, subsequent insights gained in the analysis, design, and development phases can improve the application and require changing the model.

Business model presentation emphasis can vary depending on whether the audience is the administrative, product/service/marketing, or production personnel. If presenting to representatives of more than one of these company groups, the presenter must have supporting information and data of interest to the business agenda of each group.

Responsibilities During the Business Modeling and Requirements Phase

In the business modeling and requirements phase, the CISS can play a part in gathering, modeling, and analyzing business area information to help identify and prioritize requirements. Techniques, such as interviews and facilitated sessions, can gather information about strategy, operations, processes, data, system performance, functionality, and costs.

It is possible that the CISS can be involved in all aspects of the business modeling and requirements phase of an Internet business solution project. During this phase, the CISS has the following three major responsibilities:

- Keep the requirements gathering focused on business, functional, and information models.
- Provide leadership on gathering system requirements.
- Validate completion of the business modeling and requirements phase.

In the previous bulleted list, a requirement is "a condition or capability to which a system must conform." Many different kinds of requirements exist; however, system requirements typically fall under two categories:

- **Functional requirements**—Functional requirements specify actions that a system must be able to perform, without taking physical constraints into consideration. These requirements describe what the system does, who is using it, and what needs the system satisfies. Important performance goals, such as time or space efficiency, security, and reliability, can be included. Decision makers and stakeholders usually determine functional requirements. Questions and guidance from the CISS help ensure feasibility and completeness.

- **Nonfunctional requirements**—Nonfunctional requirements apply to the systems component of the solutions. These requirements are constraints on various attributes of the outlined functions or tasks, such as constraints on the speed or efficiency of a given task. Nonfunctional requirements are commonly called the qualitative aspects of a system—availability, security, recoverability, testability, and scalability, to name a few. Moreover, such requirements frequently include quantitative aspects. Nonfunctional requirements include the following:

  — *Performance*—What is the speed, availability, response time, and recovery time of various software functions, and so on?

  — *Attributes*—What are the portability, correctness, maintainability, and security considerations?

  — *Interfaces*—How will the solution interact with people, the system hardware, other hardware, the network, and other software?

  — *Design constraints imposed on an implementation*—Are there any required standards in effect, implementation language, policies for database integrity, resource limits, operating environments, and so on?

Business models, functional models, and information models are representations of actual business elements within each of the respective areas. These are broad terms that encompass various techniques and are described in the following list:

- **Business model**—Basically, the business model shows how the enterprise generates revenue. Text, diagrams, a business plan, and financial analysis can all be part of the business model.

- **Functional model**—The functional model provides detailed information about the processes and functions performed by the system or proposed solution. This model can be expressed using process flow and data flow diagrams, use cases, text, or various techniques.

- **Information model**—Generally, an information model can be any diagram or text that describes objects, attributes, relationships, or information flow.

This collection of data allows decision makers and technical experts to capture, organize, and visualize business processes, functional divisions, geographic impact, financial impact, and information flow throughout the organization. Data gathered around the current state becomes the input for configuring the eventual solution and determining the scope and costs.

Very often, a business has its own methodology for working through the software development lifecycle. Many possible methodologies exist. Following are some popular examples:

- **Rational Unified Process (RUP)**—A software engineering process that provides a disciplined approach to assigning tasks and responsibilities within a development organization. Its goal is to ensure the production of high-quality software that meets the needs of its end users, within a predictable schedule and budget.

- **Rapid Application Development (RAD)**—A software development process that allows usable systems to be built in as little as 60 to 90 days, often with some compromises. To ensure high responsiveness, projects are designed with fixed timescales, sacrificing functionality if necessary. This arrangement allows the development team to focus on the functionalities that have the highest business value and to deliver those functionalities rapidly. RAD limits the amount of change, and the scope and requirements creep, by shortening the development cycle. A key to RAD is the potential supply of reusable components because RAD tools quickly generate usable programs to meet requirements.

- **Protocycling**—An iterative process by which prototypes develop into production systems. This is an approach where you develop a prototype of the application by using a limited subset of data and model structure to demonstrate the power of the software and application. Migrating the prototype to production is part of the protocycling approach. The developers continue to build upon the prototype, adding more data, calculations, and structure until it reaches the point where it can be rolled out as an application to the users.

In whatever case, the CISS must learn the customer approved methodology and communicate it as needed and at the appropriate time. If no approved methodology is available, the CISS must rely upon a fundamental understanding of the software development lifecycle, with its tasks and expected outcomes of each phase.

Communicating expectations of the business modeling and requirements gathering process is vital to gaining cooperation and moving forward in gathering requirements. The CISS must communicate those expectations to each segment of the team.

The CISS must review the proposed solution relevant to the enterprise and its current processes and systems to provide adequate input at any level or phase. The CISS must understand the following considerations:

- **Type of enterprise involved**—Manufacturing, logistics, wholesaler, retailer, professional services, and so on—and how it competes in the marketplace
- **Functional processes**—Who and how they are performed
- **Current architecture, system, and applications**—What comprises the existing environment

If there are areas in which the CISS has little experience or knowledge, it is important to recognize the deficiency, identify internal expertise, recommend additional resources, or develop the needed skills internally.

The CISS must help keep processes in scope and identify requests that can divert the project from the scope of the original objective.

The CISS must ensure that the proposed goal is technically feasible at the early stage. Reality checks are conducted when expectations or requirements begin to approach thresholds that might be obstacles to successfully completing the project. The CISS must quantify impact in terms of cost, system efficiencies, end users, competencies, and critical success factors. The following are some questions that are frequently reviewed to determine impact:

- Is the actual resource expenditure versus planned expenditure acceptable?
- Is the vision of the product stable?
- Do the stakeholders agree on the project objectives?
- Is the architecture stable and sufficient to support the proposed solution?
- Is the selected architecture scaleable to accommodate growth?
- Are major risk elements being addressed and credibly resolved?
- Is the system concept, scope definition, priorities, and estimated schedule acceptable?
- What is the projected impact on the employees—re-engineering of jobs, layoffs, hiring?
- How does this solution mesh with the current infrastructure including the corporate culture, IT capability, and management systems?

The CISS can take on a leadership role in gathering systems requirements. The following tasks are included in leading the system requirements gathering:

- Assess the current system, processes, people, and tools.
- Analyze functional requirements data as it relates to systems.
- Define expectations of the system.
- Define nonfunctional requirements.

To help plan a solution, the CISS must understand the context of the project. This understanding includes the current state of the software-development organization, including its people, its processes, and its supporting tools.

It is also important to understand the problem areas and potential areas for improvement and to have information about external issues, such as competitors and trends in the market. The assessment of the current state becomes input for planning.

When this task is complete, the CISS must be familiar with each element presented in Figure 3-1.

Figure 3-1   *Elements to Assess*

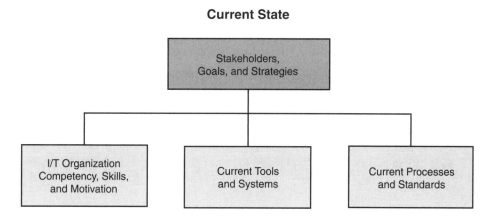

The functional requirements are the basis for the entire solution project. Meeting those requirements is paramount to successfully completing the project. To analyze these requirements, the CISS must follow these steps:

Step 1   Review use cases, documentation, functional and business requirements, and business strategy.

Step 2   Understand the specific functions, tasks, or behaviors that the system must support.

Step 3   Identify the problem areas and potential areas for improvement.

Step 4   Examine each requirement, including its potential impact on people, technology, and processes.

Step 5   Identify how these requirements affect the system and whether a transition or change in people, process, or technology is needed.

Step 6   Assess related cost.

The CISS' technical expertise is helpful in defining expectations of the system. The stakeholders can provide broad performance goals that must be refined and detailed before defining nonfunctional requirements. To define system expectations, the CISS needs to do the following:

- Create brief descriptions of the functionality that is required by outlining the most important features of the system.

- Detail special needs such as security, interaction with existing databases, use of existing design elements, time or space efficiency, reliability, availability, or implementation languages.

The functional requirements are specific to the customer and the tasks required of the system. The nonfunctional requirements vary depending on the functionality and complexity of the system. Examples of nonfunctional requirements include availability, security, recoverability, scalability, predictability, efficiency, throughput, response time, recovery time, resource usage, extensibility, and maintainability.

The CISS must define interfaces: how the solution interacts with people, the system hardware, other hardware, the network, and other software. Also included are any design constraints imposed on implementation, such as required standards and policies, implementation language, resource limits, and operating environments.

Before progressing to the analysis and design phase of the software development lifecycle, the CISS must determine that all necessary results of the current phase have been accumulated. The following tasks must be accomplished to validate completion of the business modeling and requirements phase:

- Participate in a walkthrough of the business model, the functional requirements, and the nonfunctional requirements. Ensure that adequate information has been provided to generate system requirements.

- Ensure that Service Level Agreement (SLA) components are positioned, if one is to be used.

- Identify potential areas of reusability.

- Generate the system concept.

Before leaving the business modeling and requirements phase, the business models and functional and nonfunctional requirements for the current integration must be complete and ready for a formal walkthrough.

Walkthrough

A *structured walkthrough* is a technique for providing project participants an opportunity to examine a work product for errors. It is a quality review technique that is used in team reviews and formal reviews to look at the product from the perspective of requirements, standards, content, maintenance, and usability.

A process walkthrough is the step-by-step observation of the physical activities of a process. The objective is to provide all parties in the improvement effort with an overall, high-level understanding of the process, its terminology, resources, inputs, interim products, outputs, and general flow.

The goal of this review is to improve the quality of the deliverables and to document any issues discovered during this process. It is also at this stage that the deliverables are evaluated against the planned solution to ensure that the project is still on schedule. The CISS must ensure that the following questions have been addressed:

- Are there any required standards in effect, implementation language, policies for database integrity, resource limits, operating environments, and so on?

- Have all significant requirements related to functionality, performance design constraints, attributes, or external interfaces been identified?

- Have all realizable classes of input data in all realizable classes of situations been addressed?

- Have responses been included to both valid and invalid input values?

- Do all figures, tables, and diagrams include full labels, references, and definitions of all terms and units of measure?

- Have all outstanding issues or questions been resolved or addressed?

An SLA is a contract for performing minimal expected levels of service between a customer and a service provider. That service provider can be external or internal to the customer company. The SLA can determine how or if the service provider receives compensation.

If an SLA is being incorporated, the CISS must ensure that all components of the SLA are present. The CISS must verify that the following SLA components exist:

- Complete documented systems requirements that can be ranked, verified, and traced to their owner.

- Cost-effective process with which a person or machine can verify that the software products or services meet the requirements.

- Consistent agreement on project objectives and goals among the stakeholders and project team.
- System requirements that can be modified in structure and style and that have been reviewed to identify and minimize redundancy.

With the business modeling and requirements gathering complete, the components of the project solution must be reviewed for reusability.

Consider many levels when looking at potential areas or components for reuse. Reuse of system hardware, networks, data, objects, and source code are all areas of potential reuse. Modular-based system development is a common application delivery mechanism in the modern environment. Existing modules that can be reused can be identified at this point in the lifecycle.

Techniques and Tools for the Business Modeling and Requirements Phase

Throughout the business modeling and requirements phase, the CISS is working with the project team and decision makers to determine the business goals and project objectives, and the functional and nonfunctional requirements of the solution. Several techniques are employed to gather information from many different people. The following are some of those techniques:

- Interviews
- Surveys
- Shadowing
- Facilitated sessions
- Brainstorming

Interviews

The two types of interviews are *single* interviews, which involve one or two interviewees, and *group* interviews, in which three or more participants are interviewed simultaneously. Both interview types require the same steps:

Step 1   Prepare context-free questions (high-level).

Step 2   Conduct the interview.

Step 3   Summarize the findings.

Step 4   Confirm the interview results.

Information gathered during an interview can include, but is not limited to, topics such as goals and objectives; business functions; problems and concerns; critical success factors, information needs, organization structure, events, processes, entities, attributes, and relationships.

NOTE   Interviewing requires minimal commitment from the organization's personnel because the CISS is gathering the information. However, that also means the organization has little or no opportunity for group involvement and discussion.

Surveys

Surveys are an inexpensive method of obtaining limited information from a large number of users. Surveys can be performed through questionnaires or interviews. The questions should be prepared with advice from the organization. A survey should include an introduction (designed to cover all preliminary information needed by the respondent) and a set of questions for the specific population. There is some risk of poor-quality resulting information because of the lack of discussion.

Shadowing

Shadowing is an effective technique for observing and recording the activities of workers doing their jobs. Shadowing an end user is certainly an appropriate technique when attempting to gather all information about the actual tasks that an end user performs on a system. Observing the actions of someone performing a specific job is an effective means of gathering detailed information about processes and procedures. It certainly provides first-hand knowledge of system or process efficiencies and inefficiencies.

Facilitated Sessions

Facilitated sessions are effective techniques for gathering information about a process. This technique is a structured workshop led by a trained facilitator and involves people at all levels who are most knowledgeable about the process. With the right participation, facilitated sessions are efficient ways to gather accurate information about the process in a short period of time (usually two to five days).

The facilitated session process focuses on an intensive workshop but actually consists of three major activities: preparation, workshop, and follow-up. A successful three-day workshop can take several weeks of preparation and a week or longer to generate and review the resulting deliverable. Scheduled facilitated sessions must be held as early in the project as possible.

Facilitated sessions are an excellent technique for building consensus on these and other various needs:

- Strategy
- Operations
- Processes
- Data
- System performance
- Functionality

Because much of the work is left to the organization's personnel, a high-level of commitment of the organization's staff is necessary for facilitated sessions to be successful. It is also important to have an experienced facilitator leading the sessions.

Brainstorming

The premise for using brainstorming is that ideas generated by an uninhibited group are likely to be much more numerous and creative than those generated by an individual. It is an excellent technique to use for identifying problems, the causes of problems, and their solutions. Here is a partial list of what brainstorming can do:

- Create alternative interpretations
- Identify key issues
- Select problems to work on
- Identify criteria for decision-making
- Suggest possible solutions to a problem
- Create alternative action plans

Brainstorming involves spending a short amount of time, about 15 minutes, where everyone in the room is allowed to say whatever they feel is important to the project with no criticism or debate. After that, a facilitator leads the group in organizing and prioritizing the results. It is important to start out by clearly stating the objective.

The two styles of brainstorming are *freewheeling* and *written*. Freewheeling brainstorming involves verbal calling out of ideas by group members. For written brainstorming, group members individually write down their ideas and submit them.

Introduction to Tools

During the business modeling and requirements phase of an Internet business solution project, the CISS is working with the project team and decision makers to provide representation of an Internet business solution functioning within their business. Gathering data about the organization structure, processes, information requirements, current environment, business strategy, and potential gain or loss are all part of the information gathering process. The CISS can use these tools during the business modeling and requirements phase:

- Enterprise models
- Entity relationship diagrams
- Flowcharts
- Case models

Enterprise Models

Enterprise models create a visual, process-based model of the enterprise. These gain a high-level of understanding of the organization's processes and process performance.

There are several types of enterprise models, such as the enterprise model itself, enterprise profile, enterprise organization model, and enterprise process model. Following are some enterprise models:

- **Enterprise Model**—Describes the enterprise, outlining its profile, organization structure, and processes; also used to scope and plan the project.
- **Enterprise Profile**—Describes the enterprise in relation to company and industry information, major competitors, external customers, suppliers, and stakeholders to serve as a basis for discussion in enterprise strategy data-gathering sessions.
- **Enterprise Organization Model**—Provides a summary of the enterprise organizational structure and geographical distribution.
- **Enterprise Process Model**—Describes the enterprise high-level processes and business segments to assist in determining the scope of the project.

Figure 3-2 depicts an example of a manufacturing enterprise process model.

Use enterprise models for the following practical applications:

- To identify main processes and define the boundaries of processes
- To define process domains to show how processes can differ across markets and marketing channels, products and services, and geographic regions
- To determine key characteristics, such as inputs, outputs, resource consumption, full-time equivalents (FTEs), capital, and other cost elements, for each process
- To validate and document the characteristics of each process on the process model to better show the relationships between processes
- To identify the process owners and create a current state business process model

Figure 3-2   *Enterprise Process Model*

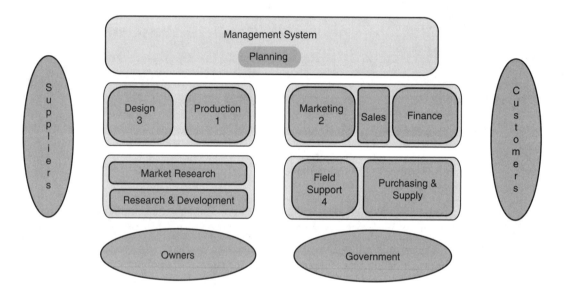

The Manufacturing Enterprise
Process Model

Entity Relationship Diagram (ERD)

The *entity relationship diagram (ERD)* of database design is a high-level, conceptual data model that provides information that is close to the way many users perceive the data. An ERD describes the exact logical structure of the database. Such diagrams can show the relationships between database objects (master, slave, one-to-many, many-to-one, and so on). Figure 3-3 is an example of an entity relationship diagram.

An ERD has three key concepts: entities, attributes, and relationships:

- An *entity* represents a real-world object or concept, such as a customer or a purchase order, which is described in the database.

- An *attribute* represents some property of interest that further describes an entity, such as the customer name or address.

- A *relationship* among two or more entities represents an interaction among the entities; for example, a relationship between a customer and a purchase order.

Figure 3-3   *Entity Relationship Diagram*

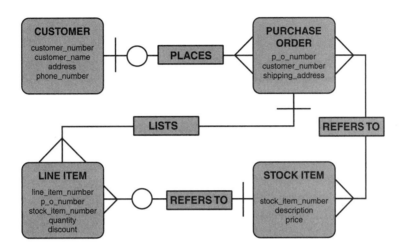

Flowcharts

The purpose of a flowchart is not to portray every aspect of the process, but to highlight major characteristics so that opportunities for business process redesign can be identified and defined. The flowchart should use standard flowcharting symbols to depict elements such as start/finish, movement, decision points, documents, storage, direction of flow, and data transmission. Figure 3-4 contains an order system flowchart.

This flowchart presents data as it flows through one specific process. A functional flowchart identifies how vertically oriented functional departments affect a process flowing horizontally across the enterprise. A typical functional flowchart shows the organizational units and functional site types involved as columns, with the process flowchart superimposed so that activities are placed in the column of the responsible business unit.

Use Case Models

The business Use Case Model is a model of the business intended functions. The business Use Case Model is an essential input to identify roles and deliverables in the organization. It describes the business in terms of its processes.

At least three categories of work related to business use cases follow:

- Commercially relevant business processes
- Support activities such as systems administration
- Management work that reflects how other business use cases are managed and started

Figure 3-4 *Flowchart*

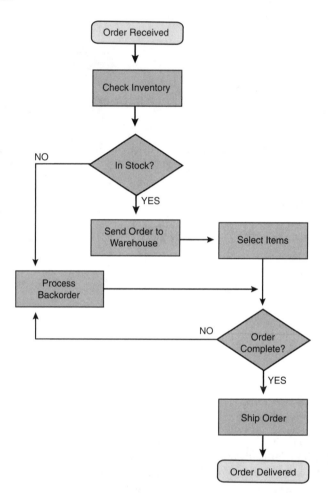

Use cases must conform to the business they describe and every activity within the business should be included. All use cases are identified so that taken together, use cases perform all activities within the business, many of which normally execute in parallel. There should be a balance between the number of use cases and the complexity of the use cases. Each use case must also be unique so that the survey of the Use Case Model gives a good comprehensive picture of the organization.

Use Case Models

Every business has many business use cases, many of which normally perform in parallel. Also, there can be an almost unlimited number of paths a use case instance follows. In modeling business use cases, you can assume that use case instances can be active concurrently without conflicting. At this stage of business development, you must focus on what the business must do. Later, you can try to understand how things must work in the business and discuss resource conflicts.

Analysis and Design Phase

The analysis and design phase consists of the research and analysis that produces the application design. The design should include the following:

- Application architecture
- System specifications
- Security design
- Software and database specifications
- Networking specifications
- Equipment specifications
- Operating procedures

The *analysis and design phase* gathers additional and more-focused information concerning the system designated in the business model. It then produces an application system specification consisting of a more detailed technical description of the system that is affecting and supporting the application.

As required, the analysis and design team updates the requirements during this phase.

During the analysis and design phase of an application project for a small bank that decided to add automatic bill-paying to its services, the design team prepared a specification for modification of one of its standard software packages to meet the needs of the local bank. During the process, the vendor design team informed the bank that it might also have to acquire some additional memory storage, most economically supplied by external devices that are connected to the main computer through the server system. This additional memory device for the new databases also required a server upgrade to handle data communications between it and the computer.

To help you understand this phase, the discussion is divided into the following sections:

- Inputs to the Analysis and Design Phase
- Outputs from the Analysis and Design Phase

- Issues of the Analysis and Design Phase
- Responsibilities During the Analysis and Design Phase
- Techniques and Tools for the Analysis and Design Phase

Inputs to the Analysis and Design Phase

The inputs to the analysis and design phase of the application development lifecycle consist of any information required to create a design that specifies all the required elements in the system to provide the application. This design must meet the specification requirements of the system developers in the development phase.

Besides the direction received from the business modeling and requirements phase, the following inputs can assist the analysis and design team in developing the application system specification. Designers and developers seldom create a system from a point at which nothing has been done ahead of time, but rather try to use previously existing objects:

- **Existing applications**—Knowledge of existing applications allows the analysts to leverage the existing applications into a new application without creating it entirely.

- **Programming code and objects**—Maintenance of a library of completed routine computer code and objects in the case of OOP greatly reduces the time and effort required by the software subject matter experts on the analysis and design team.

- **Training requirements**—Contact with the customer to determine their current employee skill set allows comparison to the new skills required by the application operating procedures.

- **Compatibility tests**—Specification of compatibility tests between existing and new equipment and software helps ensure proper performance of the existing equipment of the customer within the application. These tests include compatibility with other applications that are running in the customer environment.

- **Validation tests**—Specification of customer quality validation tests and user criteria promotes successful design to pass guidance.

Outputs from the Analysis and Design Phase

The primary output of the analysis and design phase is a system design from which the developers can create the system to provide the application or service.

The lifecycle plan expects the developers to complete various technical details normally associated with the development process and also make as-discovered recommendations for changes to the design specification for efficiency purposes. Nevertheless, the design specified in the analysis and design phase must be sufficient for a team of application design engineers to develop the application system.

The outputs from the analysis and design phase include these technical system design details to complete system development:

- System architecture
- System platform
- Equipment
- Software
- Network
- System communication inputs and outputs
- New equipment and software documentation
- Communication protocols and interfaces
- Estimate of development time and resources
- Security features required

These outputs from the analysis and design phase include sufficient performance detail to support training development:

- Equipment operation
- System operations
- Equipment maintenance
- Network configuration and maintenance

NOTE   The fact that the development phase can improve design and complete technical details does not relieve the obligation of the analysis and design phase to exercise the utmost discipline in providing a sufficiently complete design.

Issues of the Analysis and Design Phase

The analysis and design phase of the application development lifecycle has important issues associated with its use. These issues relate to the primary purpose of providing the development phase with sufficient design information to efficiently develop a complete application.

The application system design specification should not concentrate so hard on an attempt to provide every technical design detail such that the specification limits the application developer. During the development process, the systems design engineers complete technical details necessary to fit the application information into the environment into which the application works. This level of specification results from development for the business environment rather than the design specifying the environment.

The analysis and design personnel must not completely disengage from the project when the design specification goes to the development phase. As the development process adds detail or recommends changes to the design specification, the analysis and design phase personnel must both ensure that the changes do not depart from the intent of the approved business model, and also update design documentation to reflect approved design changes.

Responsibilities During the Analysis and Design Phase

During the analysis and design phase, the CISS further analyzes the information and requirements gathered during the business modeling and requirements phase, and works with the project team to plan and design the Internet business solution. The goal is to design a system that fulfills user requirements and that is effective, usable, reliable, and maintainable.

The analysis and design phase of the software development lifecycle is crucial to successful development and implementation. Throughout this phase, the CISS has four major responsibilities:

- Analyze business requirements in relation to system architecture.
- Develop a project management plan.
- Design a robust and maintainable system.
- Design a system architecture and application solution that satisfies business requirements.

To analyze business requirements in relation to system architecture and to identify areas of reuse and risk, the CISS has three major tasks:

- Assess the current system architecture relative to requirements.
- Validate data flow diagrams, data dictionary, and data modeling against requirements.
- Verify process modeling and process descriptions against requirements.

The CISS must assess the existing system architecture or the architectural strategy that the enterprise wants to employ. Functional and nonfunctional requirements must be analyzed in relation to the current architecture, the existing processes, and the organizational structures for the following purposes:

- Identify possible areas of reuse of hardware and software.
- Identify areas of risk.
- Determine whether the current network and system architecture supports the proposed application solutions.

As the team is progressing through the requirements, the CISS must again verify the completeness, consistency, and stability of the requirements because they all are used throughout design.

A definite priority for the CISS and the design team is correctly interpreting the information requirements, forming data elements that satisfy those information requirements, and building a creative design that adheres to the system concept. The CISS must validate each step of the process beginning with the data flow diagrams (DFDs), data modeling, and data dictionary.

Figure 3-5 illustrates a DFD for an e-commerce web site with three inputs and a single output. Additional DFDs are required to adequately depict the entire set of processes or transactions in an e-commerce web site.

Figure 3-5 *DFD*

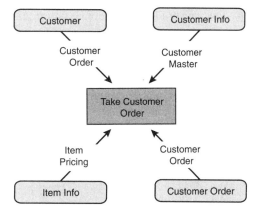

More information on this topic is presented in the following sections:

* DFDs
* Data Modeling
* Data Dictionary

DFDs

DFDs depict the input data necessary to generate the required output of the system and the functions that the system performs. A DFD specifies how data flows among components at one level of a decomposition of activities. After validating these diagrams, the CISS and the team must perform the following tasks:

* Produce a sample display screen that can be used by the users who input data into the system.
* Present a sample of the output that can be generated by the system, and explain why it is important and how it is used.
* Determine data requirements.

Data Modeling

Data modeling tools provide developers with a means to create an application foundation by graphically depicting organization business processes and data requirements and how they relate to each other. The data modeling tool acts as a blueprint (or detailed plan) for the database, just as a blueprint acts as a graphical representation of all the requirements for a house. This model becomes the detailed plan for the database.

The CISS must work with the *database administrator (DBA)* or data architect to establish data constraints, ensure that data values are within defined ranges and types, and verify the existence of referential integrity for the database. The CISS also must verify the following elements:

- Data elements that satisfy the information requirements and are sharable across organizational/process boundaries
- Complete and normalized data design
- A physical database design that meets the constraints of the business
- Optimal technology usage (database management system [DBMS], languages, operating system, environment)
- Efficient data access, distribution, and storage
- Performance requirements and constraints of processing transactions
- Security requirements
- Structures consistent throughout the design
- Sufficient consideration given to growth and expansion

Data Dictionary

A *data dictionary* describes data stores and the external entities that are included in the DFDs. This dictionary contains a list of all tables in the database, the approximate number of records in each table, and the names and physical attributes (length, type, default value, and so on) of each field. Though the data dictionary does not contain actual data from the database, it contains detailed information for managing and accessing the data. This view is generally referred to as *metadata*.

The CISS must work with the DBA or data architect to validate the translation of requirements into data attributes. The CISS, along with others from various areas of the organization, participate in structured walkthroughs.

NOTE   A *structured walkthrough* is a technique for providing project participants an opportunity to examine a product for errors and to ensure compliance to requirements. This technique is a quality review technique that you use in team reviews and formal reviews to examine the product from the perspective of requirements, standards, content, maintenance, and usability.

A process walkthrough is the step-by-step observation of the physical activities of a process. The objective is to provide all parties in the improvement effort with an overall, high-level understanding of the process, its terminology, resources, inputs, interim products, outputs, and general flow.

Following are the participants of a structured walkthrough:

- **Presenter**—Selects the deliverable, selects and invites the other participants, provides the materials to the participants, and responds to questions
- **Coordinator**—Controls the meeting
- **Documentor**—Records any potential problem areas
- **Attendees**—Identifies potential problems

Throughout the analysis and verification of processes, the CISS must keep attention focused on meeting the expectations of stakeholders and managing the scope of the project. After process descriptions and process models are verified, the CISS must perform the following tasks:

- Estimate what volumes of activity can be expected for the system.
- Determine areas of risk within the defined data flow.
- Identify areas of potential reuse of equipment and source code.
- Validate compliance to requirements.

The project plan is actually a part of the overall project management plan. This project plan describes the approach to the solution development and is the primary plan that managers generate and use to direct the project efforts. The project plan must meet these key objectives:

- Guide project execution.
- Document planning assumptions.
- Document planning decisions regarding chosen alternatives.
- Facilitate communication among stakeholders.
- Define key management reviews as to content, extent, and timing.
- Provide a baseline for progress measurement and project control.

The CISS works with the project manager to develop a project management plan. This responsibility includes the following tasks:

- Document assumptions regarding scope.
- Confirm the relative project priorities.
- Identify the project dependencies.
- Create the preliminary schedule of development projects.
- Confirm business goals, project objectives, and opportunities or problems.

The CISS must document all assumptions made during the definition of the project's scope. When establishing the deliverable scope of the project, the CISS must make many assumptions concerning the project. These assumptions have a key impact on the size and amount of work to be performed during the project. Documented assumptions become part of the project plan and help to track any changes in scope and other areas of the project.

Together, the project manager and the CISS re-evaluate the initial priority assigned to each project in the context of the overall solution. Next, they establish the relative priority of each project in relation to other projects underway.

Project dependencies help determine priority and are necessary to establishing a timeline and required resources. Following are the steps necessary to establish project dependencies:

Step 1 Define the infrastructure priorities.

Step 2 Determine the infrastructure projects, which must be completed before development projects can be executed.

Step 3 Define the development project dependencies.

Step 4 Determine the logical sequencing of development projects and resource dependencies.

Step 5 Define any functional or technical dependencies determined by this sequencing.

The CISS can provide input into the preliminary schedule, which is crucial to further project planning. Outlining execution sequence, timeframe, and resources help to determine scope. Creating a preliminary schedule encompasses each of the following subtasks:

- Create a Gantt chart that shows each development project as a series of bars that represent simultaneous, sequential, and dependent tasks.
- Use the preliminary estimates developed as part of the project definition process to estimate the duration of each project.
- Incorporate dependencies.
- Use a project management tool to define dependencies from project to project.

- Use finish-start dependencies where one project must end before another can begin, and start-to-start and finish-to-finish dependencies where projects must run in parallel.

- Rearrange the projects on the schedule to obtain a resource requirement graph that is in line with available resources.

Figure 3-6 shows an example of a basic Gantt chart.

Figure 3-6   *Gantt Chart*

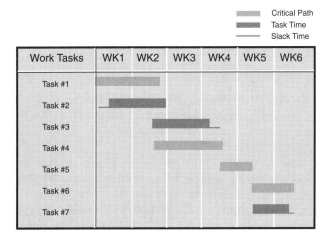

There can be an extended time between project planning and execution. Sometimes, stakeholders change, or perhaps, strategy, priorities, or objectives change. The CISS must confirm agreement on these elements before progressing. To do that, the CISS (or project manager) must perform the following functions:

- Verify goals, critical success factors, and other strategic information with the project sponsor.

- Verify the currency and validity of the business goals, critical success factors, opportunities, and problems that the project is expected to address.

- Confirm the project objectives with the project sponsor.

A robust system implies that the system is designed for high-volume, multi-user operation. It also refers to software that is without bugs and can handle abnormal conditions without locking up the system or causing damage to data. A robust system is thoroughly tested and has built-in safeguards against system failure.

A maintainable system is one that is flexible, accommodates change, is intuitively understandable, and promotes effective software reuse. A maintainable system is generally modular in design and includes detailed documentation.

Maintenance costs associated with an application can constitute a large percentage of the overall cost of ownership. Following are the objectives of designing a robust and maintainable system:

- Minimize future system maintenance costs.
- Ensure security, recoverability, and backup.
- Incorporate a design that is as modular and scalable as requirements allow.

Throughout the analysis and design phase, the CISS looks for all design factors that might present opportunities for decreasing maintenance costs and resources. Designing a robust and maintainable system definitely incorporates that principle. Following are the tasks involved in designing a robust and maintainable system:

- Ensure the design is modular and scalable to the degree requirements allow.
- Provide input on prototyping and testing strategies.
- Verify that security issues are addressed.
- Ensure that disaster recovery plans and a backup process is in place.

The design must incorporate plans for a resilient Internet business solution that is flexible, accommodates change, is intuitively understandable, and promotes effective software reuse. A modular design, assembled in a well-defined architecture component infrastructure, can help give a company a competitive edge. A scalable design results in a system that is capable of expanding to meet the higher demands and rapid growth of the future.

The CISS provides input into the design strategies that develop an application. Very often, prototyping is done to simulate systems or processes so that users can understand and critique the system or processes created. Prototypes provide an opportunity to test alternative solutions and generate more accurate requirements. The CISS takes an active role in this process to ensure that the best solutions to the problems are identified.

Typically, the CISS also provides input into the testing strategy. Certainly, this involves recommending a test database, hardware and software testing tools, and data extraction software tools. Special software modifications might be required to support testing, such as software for generating application transaction loads. Alternatively, pre-existing load generators, such as network simulators, can be used.

Prototyping

Prototypes can be divided into four general categories that are based on the objective of the prototype:

- **Validation prototype**—Created to confirm that what has been done is correct or will be with some minor changes. This type of prototype is typically discarded shortly after being used.

- **Requirements gathering prototype**—Places the emphasis on discovery. With the underlying assumption that we do not know what is right initially, this type of prototype is typically evolved during analysis and then discarded.

- **Proof of concept prototype**—Determines if something will work. This type of prototype is commonly developed to test unknown or suspect areas and is discarded after the answers are gained.

- **Production prototype**—Evolves into a fully functional application. This type of prototype is expected to produce useful service.

The CISS ensures that all security issues are addressed in the design and that no unnecessary or redundant security exists. Security requirements must be determined for handling confidential data, preparing source data documents, and storing data conversion listings. The security requirements must state data privacy needs with respect to entity types. The CISS must make the following verifications:

- Ensure that access to sensitive data and systems is restricted to appropriate personnel.

- Verify identification of the users and *information systems (IS)* managers responsible for reviewing and approving the data conversion process.

Providing input and ensuring that a *disaster recovery plan (DRP)* exists is important. A DRP is a plan for duplicating computer operations after a catastrophe occurs. The DRP must outline how to manage natural disasters, such as fire or an earthquake, blackouts, hardware failure, theft, viruses, or key personnel leaving the company. This plan includes routine offsite backup and a procedure for activating necessary information systems at another location. There is generally a direct correlation between the detail level of this plan and the importance of the application or system to the business.

The CISS must ensure that backup and recovery procedures are planned and documented for any data that cannot be reproduced outside the system. Backup and recovery can be executed at varying degrees and costs. The CISS must be aware of the costs and methods available for performing these services.

Small projects often succeed because they reduce confusion, complexity, and cost. The solution to the problem of building large systems is to employ those same techniques that help small projects succeed, minimize complexity, and emphasize clarity. That being the case, the following are objectives of the design of system architecture and the application solution:

- A system design that meets functional and nonfunctional requirements

- An architecture and system that is as simple, clear, and efficient as the specified requirements allow

Anticipating design requirements and creating a manageable architectural framework for your solution is crucial. The tasks involved in designing a system architecture and application solution that satisfies the business requirements are as follows:

- Provide leadership on the architecture and application design.
- Verify that the design fulfills business and system requirements.
- Participate in specification of any hardware or software upgrades or purchases.
- Generate a design document.

The CISS must provide leadership to the architecture and application design teams. With knowledge of the overall process of developing Internet business solutions, the CISS can provide guidance or direct team members to required information or expertise as needed. The CISS and the project manager typically work closely together, with the CISS leading the technical issues, and the project manager leading the administrative issues.

To be effective, the CISS must work toward earning the respect of the project team, project manager, stakeholders, user community, and management team. The obvious considerations for architecture and application design are the hardware, software, and network issues. However, it is also important to consider the culture of the organization, the capabilities and knowledge of the IT staff, and the management systems of the organization.

The design is actually the foundation of the solution. To ensure customer satisfaction, that design must fulfill both the business and system requirements. The results of all the work the CISS and the design team have done must be incorporated in the solution design. Depending on the size and complexity of the Internet business solution, there can be many factors that must be addressed within the design. The following are some typical factors that a CISS must verify:

- Security requirements of the organization and the application
- Functional requirements—core functions or events occur in the application and are provided the data attributes required to fulfill the events
- All nonfunctional requirements such as scalability, availability, and response time
- Any known future requirements such as availability
- Efficient network technology
- Error messages that are clear and consistent throughout the application
- Database organization
- Platform
- Geographic locations
- Required interfaces and software customization
- Reuse of existing hardware and software where applicable
- Requirements and skill level of the end users of the system

The CISS must participate in specifying the hardware and software requirements to support each component of the application. Hardware items to be considered are the requirements for data storage devices, PCs, printers, database or application servers, and so on. Software includes the operating system and applications or upgrades needed to meet the functional requirements and necessary processing.

Often, the CISS provides specifications to vendors to obtain quotes and technical expertise as needed. All hardware and software licensing and maintenance agreements must also be considered in designing the solution to minimize the impact associated with these elements.

Techniques and Tools for the Analysis and Design Phase

Throughout the analysis and design phase, the CISS can use the following techniques:

* Prototyping
* Abstraction
* System modeling tools
* Project management software

Prototyping

An *application prototype* is a representation of an application system that simulates the main user interfaces so that users can understand and critique the system. Software tools enable the application prototype to be built quickly and easily modified to adapt it to end-user needs. Sometimes, tools are used that enable the application prototype to be successively modified until it becomes the full working application system. Application prototypes are generally developed to elicit more accurate user requirements or to test several design alternatives.

Abstraction

Abstraction is the process of building black box models that are abstract entities that can be understood and analyzed independently of the rest of the system. Architects use this process to communicate the design to the developers. Through specification of black box descriptions of the modules, abstraction simplifies the design of a complex system by reducing the number of details that must be considered at the same time. This reduces confusion and aids clarity of understanding.

System Modeling Tools

Data and system modeling tools provide developers with a means of creating an application foundation by graphically depicting an organization's business processes and data requirements and how they relate to each other.

Network and system modeling applications typically have the following functions:

- Predict end-user response times before deployment
- Visualize and report on application behavior in a distributed, multitiered network
- Tune applications for efficient operations over WANs
- Troubleshoot performance problems throughout an application development cycle

Server sizing/modeling tools are typically vendor specific and depend on many different factors, such as choice of operating system, the application's design, and the type of processor. Because of this, it is important to involve the vendor in the modeling and sizing of a server.

Project Management Tools

Project management software is a software application that assists in monitoring and controlling a project. After being properly configured, this software allows a project manager to control and track project-related metrics, such as resource usage, project cost, and task duration. Project management software, when used effectively, can dramatically reduce the effort required to maintain a project plan.

Development Phase

The development phase of an application development lifecycle finalizes the application system specification for use during implementation. A defining characteristic of the development lifecycle phase is that it increases in size and value with the size of the application system. An extremely small application requires no development phase because the implementation phase implements the application system specification received from the analysis and design phase, with no further development required. A large application requires more development before beginning the implementation.

Different application development efforts respond to different sets of issues with a nonlinear increase of the development effort as the application size increases, but the principle remains.

The development of software required to support an application is an example of the effect of the size of the application on the size and importance of the development phase. An estimate makes the effort required to generate 10,000 lines of computer code 50 to 75 times as great as that for 1000 lines of code; 10,000 lines of code are only 10 times 1000 lines of code.

The amount of effort required in the development phase depends on situational factors other than size. Accuracy of the effort in the development phase can affect the rest of the lifecycle.

In 1983, Gerald Weinberg documented a case in which a single incorrect character in a line of computer program code cost a large company $1,600,000,000 before they detected and corrected the problem.

The purpose of the development phase is to translate the application system specification into an application installation package. This translation allows the application to work effectively in the customer environment.

To aid your understanding of the subject, this section is broken into the following sections:

- Inputs to the Development Phase
- Outputs from the Development Phase
- Issues of the Development Phase
- Responsibilities During the Development Phase
- Techniques and Tools for the Development Phase
- Application Development Tools

Inputs to the Development Phase

The system specification provides the primary input to the development phase of the application development lifecycle. The development team must bring to the development efforts the knowledge required to assign the additional operating parameters that make the application perform most effectively. This category of input can include technical data required to configure or adjust equipment for the most efficient operation within the customer environment.

The development team might also require, as an input, local industry and governmental regulations. Safety and quality issues often fall into this category. Essentially, the development team must find and bring to the development phase any necessary specification not included in the application system specification.

As an example, a development team responsible for adding a motion sensing and reporting alarm system to a chain of hardware stores makes a discovery. The team finds that on visits to the various hardware stores in different locations, that local regulations differ on whether the system must have separate breakers in existing power distribution boxes or whether the system requires separate breaker boxes. The store managers do not know this information. Therefore, the development team must obtain the information necessary to complete the system specification.

Of course, the analysis and design team could have researched this power distribution information for each location and included it in the system specification. Normally, the preliminary system specification lists this as a required development issue. The third possibility exists of the development team requiring the implementation team to determine the local regulation and carry sufficient equipment and supplies to comply with whichever of the variety of regulations they discover for input.

Outputs from the Development Phase

The primary output of the development phase is the implementation package, which includes the completed system specification for the application. The development phase output includes additional necessary information, such as the implementation schedule, and customer validation criteria passed down from the business modeling and requirements phase.

The output of the development phase must include either everything the implementation team needs to implement the application or at least direction on how the implementation team can obtain the additional specifications as a part of the implementation effort.

If the development team changes the intent of the specification received from the analysis and design phase, or makes any cost changing modification to the specification, the development team must supply the changed specification back to the analysis and design team.

As an example, the development phase for a project to install a telephone transmission line can possibly specify this data to the installation crew:

- Transmission receiving and sending systems
- Transmission media, for example, fiber-optic cable
- Transmission route
- Anticipated quantities of equipment and supplies
- Right-of-way considerations
- Special tools required
- Installation schedule

Issues of the Development Phase

Conflict between objectives of the preceding phase, analysis and design, and the following phase, implementation, represent the most critical issue faced in the development phase. The system specification received from the analysis and design phase results from the primary intent of translating the perceived customer desire into the application specifications. The implementation phase pressures the development team to provide a system specification that requires the most technically efficient and trouble-free system. Trying to meet both these goals can lead to conflicting design specifications.

As an example, an analysis and design team might have specified less reliable equipment to accommodate customer desire to keep the initial cost to a minimum. The implementation team can continue to object to the development team that the system specified requires three times the maintenance cost because of the equipment failure rate. Although both phases have valid professional positions, the development team must find the most feasible way to accomplish program objectives.

Responsibilities During the Development Phase

In the development phase, developers generate, integrate, debug, document, and complete unit testing on software programs that are specified because of the previous analysis and design phase. Server and network administrators size, configure, and implement server and network structures, as specified in the design document. The project team members focus on building and delivering a high-quality system, reducing delivery time, improving application design, and coordinating and controlling changes. For the development phase to be successful, the CISS might need to perform the following activities:

- Contribute to the physical integration of the architecture components defined in the design phase.

- Verify that all necessary resources exist to perform development in all areas.

- Confirm that change control processes exist.

- Ensure that documentation is created.

- Ensure that the design document is adhered to during the development phase.

- Confirm that each individual development group is performing adequate unit testing.

The development phase varies in size depending on the dimensions of the proposed application system. Thus, CISS responsibilities also vary depending on the dimensions and resources available for developing the new application system.

In the development phase, the CISS might need to contribute to the physical integration of the architecture components as they are defined in the design document. To accomplish this, the CISS might need to perform the following functions:

- Determine hardware sizing.

- Review design document implementation strategies with DBAs, network engineers, IS staff, and UNIX or Windows NT administrators.

To provide more details, the continued discussion is divided into the following sections:

- Hardware Sizing

- Change Control Processes

- Design Document Modification

Hardware Sizing

The CISS might need to determine hardware sizing including the number of servers, the number of CPUs, the amount of memory, and the appropriate bandwidth. Two different approaches can determine the sizing of the required hardware:

- The first method is to compare the new product with products (of known size) developed in previous projects. Compare the various characteristics of the products being compared, such as transaction frequency and number of resources used, number of users, database size or complexity, and expected numbers of online and batch programs. Use the known size of each old product to calculate the estimated size for the new one. Remember that it is important to compare products that are of similar complexity and that have been developed using similar approaches. (Variances in such things as the level of detail in use case descriptions can invalidate the comparisons.) It is also important to consider the future expansion of the system. It is rare that systems are oversized or have too much room for expansion. It is far more likely that more restrictive choices made at this step can cost more in later upgrades after the system is online.

- Use the analytical technique to estimate the product size. This approach requires that adequate information about the new product be available to use an analytical technique to estimate the product size. This technique uses a functional description of the software product and applies standard metrics to the product being evaluated.

Several activities might need to be performed during this phase:

- Determine the implementation approach (for example, phased, parallel, immediate cut-over) for each application, and describe the factors that can drive the implementation including technology, location, and organizational concerns.

- Determine the scope of the implementation effort. Determine the pace of the implementation for each application; for example, when is implementation likely to begin and which activities can be done concurrently? Document the plan and estimate assumptions.

- Work with project management to develop a schedule that shows the order of implementation for each component or business area application based on the development strategies.

Identifying all the necessary resources needed to perform development of the system is not always easy. The CISS can assist by performing the following tasks:

- Verify that processes are in place to manage development.

- Ensure that development teams receive the necessary training.

- Confirm that test procedures and test data for unit testing are in place.

Good project management works closely together with formal, disciplined processes that are performed consistently so that all interested parties know what deliverables are associated with each activity. In the modern fast-paced, competitive environment, a development methodology must be used that helps to handle critical issues and potential dangers that can adversely affect the outcome of the development phase. By using a development methodology, you can improve the quality, productivity, and economics of the software development lifecycle.

A CISS might need to collaborate with Internet business project managers to ensure their development in performing the following activities:

- Learn about effective light methodologies that balance rigor with speed.

- Use triage (sort, sift, select) so that resources are focused on the most critical functionality and features of the Internet business solution, and the nonessential features are de-emphasized or ignored.

- Learn how to negotiate under pressure with customers and end users to achieve a realistic balance of schedule and functionality.

- Learn how to accurately estimate resources and time requirements to meet expected goals.

A critical resource for performing development is *peopleware*, which is the human resource component. Project managers first need to select qualified people and then provide those people with the necessary training, resources, and work environment to perform their tasks. Developers need to be an integral part of each project team, and they need to be highly motivated so that high performance can be achieved.

Training for new employees and continuing education for all employees is an important aspect to ensure that the development team can cope with technical change. The CISS needs to ensure that all development team members receive the necessary training by implementing the following activities:

- Schedule required formal training as close as possible to the point in the project when it is needed. Treat training as tasks in the detailed project plan.

- Use a knowledge transfer approach to training. This provides informal training and information sharing. Some development methodologies encourage two developers to work together to develop a component for the project and thus share knowledge. Other approaches include identifying opportunities for cross training team members or sharing specific responsibilities across several team positions.

- Ensure information is being shared among project team members by scheduling frequent and regular briefing sessions.

With the dynamic environment used to develop Internet business solutions in today's world, training can be a critical success factor in determining the outcome of the project.

The CISS needs to confirm that test procedures and test data for unit testing are in place and that all development groups are performing the necessary unit tests. Unit testing is the most basic level of testing, and it is usually performed by the project team during the development phase. Its major objectives are to verify that the application software component's code works according to its specifications and to validate the program logic.

The advantage of unit testing is that it permits the testing and debugging of small units, thereby providing a better way to manage the integration of the units into larger components. It also enables the detection of discrepancies early in the development process, which helps to lower the overall cost of development.

Change Control Processes

Change control processes permit multiple copies of a document (for example, a design document, source code, configuration files, and various types of documentation) to exist.

Figure 3-7 shows a sample document undergo change control processes. This process must permit a document to be checked out for update purposes for unspecified periods of time, track the document, prohibit check out of the document by any other developer, assign a new version number when the document is checked in, and then save the document.

Figure 3-7   *Change Control Processes*

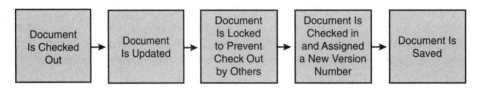

The CISS might need to confirm that such change control processes exist by performing the following tasks:

- Ensure that change control processes exist to handle modifications in the design document.
- Verify that change control processes exist to handle code and configuration updates.
- Confirm that change control processes exist to handle discrepancy reporting, tracking, and resolution.

Design Document Modification

Change control processes must exist to update the design document when changes occur in the project. Following are some of those changes:

- Scope changes, such as a requirements clarification or customer functionality changes
- Data relationships that are not available as expected
- Network segregation that has occurred

When the need arises to make modifications, follow the process to change the design document and update the version number.

When making code and configuration changes, it is important to manage those changes by making certain that each change is acceptable and is being tracked. This is essential in an environment in which change is inevitable. The CISS might need to verify that change control processes are in place and being followed.

The code change process describes how to control, track, and monitor changes to enable successful iterative development. This process establishes secure software modules for each developer by providing isolation from changes made by other developers.

A configuration change process allows developers to control updates to various kinds of configuration data such as network devices, servers, and routers. Developers also typically define several baselines during a project's lifetime. For example, a developer can have a production configuration and a testing configuration.

The CISS might need to confirm that there is a process in place for discrepancy reporting, tracking, and resolution with the ability to associate system changes with the discrepancy.

Various tools follow the progress of the project and aid in the identification of problem areas and possible design or requirements issues. These tools include how to report defects, how to manage defects through their lifecycle, and how to use defect data to track progress and trends.

Developers create various documentation of project requirements, designs, programs, and user information. Documentation is important for several reasons:

- Design, system, and program documentation aim to transfer knowledge from the original developer to the maintenance programmer.
- Help desk scripts enable the help desk staff to interact more effectively and efficiently with the end users.
- User documentation is important for reference materials and training purposes.

Figure 3-8 shows that project documentation is the domain of at least three discrete kinds of documentation.

Figure 3-8 *Kinds of Documentation*

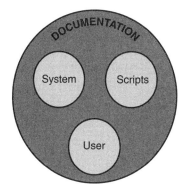

During the development phase, it is extremely important that the CISS ensure that developers perform the following functions:

- Keep the design document up-to-date. As development progresses, changes are made that require updates to the initial design. These updates must be incorporated into the original design document with appropriate tracking as to why the change was required.

- Create system and program documentation:
  - An ERD, which is created by the DBA
  - CRUD Matrix—Create, read, update, delete for database attributes
  - Configuration guides for software components
  - Failover, backup, and recovery procedures
  - Network diagrams
  - Application component or function descriptions

- Create appropriate user documentation that can include online tutorials, reference documentation, and information for training and transition requirements.

- Write help desk scripts that support the application by first line support or a help desk. These scripts must cover errors and problems that are expected to occur based on the nature of the application. Help desk scripts usually follow a decision flow that leads to corrective actions for the support personnel to start. Proper use of this process can greatly reduce the cost to support applications in the production environment. This process is also best used when integrated into the problem tracking and reporting process.

It is important to recognize the need to continuously review the prioritization as established in the design document and perform continuous triage (sort, sift, select) to ensure that the most critical requirements are actually implemented. Even when a system is developed in Internet time, there is a good chance that there can be changes in the marketplace, competition, government regulations, development project team, or the end user with decision-making authority. The solution is to perform triage on the user requirements at the beginning of the project and then repeat the process on a regular basis—at least monthly and perhaps as often as weekly, depending on the pace of the project. Thus, CISS tasks can include the following responsibilities:

- Monitor and verify project progress against the design document.
- Establish regular information exchange sessions.
- Confirm that a process exists to do walkthroughs of deliverables.

There needs to be a design document change process defined so that when an enhancement or issue arises, it can be addressed. The process must include submission, investigation, resolution, and approval steps.

When using prototyping, users and developers can easily become infatuated with the process and continuously add or change functionality. There is often a tendency to explore and add functionality beyond the original scope of the project as defined in the design document. The user must be conditioned early to expect that enhancements outside the scope can be processed through the design document change process; developers do not have the authority to agree to changes outside of that process. Project management has the following responsibilities:

- Must be constantly wary of scope creep issues that can cause the project to quickly become out of control

- Needs to ensure that the project includes all the work required, but only the work required, to complete the project successfully

- Must be primarily concerned with defining and controlling what is or is not included in the Design Document

Active participation by the CISS in the various aspects of the development process can help the CISS accurately access the progress of an application's development.

While ensuring that the Design Document is being adhered to, the CISS might need to confirm that a process is in place to do walkthroughs of deliverables. During this process, the project manager along with the project team examine the Design Document to verify that all the requirements are being fulfilled through the deliverables. Each deliverable is reviewed to ensure that it meets the stated criteria in the Design Document. If not, the team identifies the corrective actions that are required to achieve compliance. At the end of the meeting, important discussions and action items are recorded for future use.

During the development phase, the CISS might need to confirm that each individual development group is performing adequate unit testing by performing the following tasks:

- Ensure that unit test activities for all areas are included in the project plan.
- Review unit test scenarios and results.
- Conduct code reviews (at the module level).

The CISS can work with the project manager and the development team to ensure that unit test activities are included in the plan and that activities are tracked. The CISS might need to work with project teams in areas where the teams need additional support in determining adequate unit test requirements and corresponding appropriate metrics.

While confirming that each individual development group is performing adequate unit testing, the CISS can perform the following activities:

- Confirm that structured walkthroughs of the unit test scenarios are performed.
- Ensure that there is a process for tracking and reviewing the progress of the unit tests.

The CISS is an active participant in the structured walkthroughs of the scenarios that are used during unit testing. Unit testing scenarios cover system requirements and functional requirements. These walkthroughs help determine that the test scenarios cover all appropriate conditions.

Associated with each test scenario are the expected results. The actual results of the unit test are measured against expected results to validate that the requirements are being meet. These results are recorded and reviewed, and also help measure the application's progress.

Techniques and Tools for the Development Phase

The combination of best practices that have evolved in productivity approaches, quality improvement, and technology collectively form a set of techniques called *structured development methodologies*.

A structured development methodology is a set of rules, processes, and procedures that are followed by all members of a project team during the development phase. By using a development methodology, it is possible to improve quality, productivity, and economics.

A software development methodology has the following functions:

- Provides a framework for managing software-intensive projects
- Provides guidelines for planning, staffing, executing, and monitoring projects
- Provides a framework for managing risk
- Provides a basis for consistent software results
- Provides for scalability of projects

Several methodologies are listed; however, this list is certainly not all the methodologies:

- **Light Methodologies**—Represent a risk or reward approach to investing time, money, and resources in the various activities associated with the development phase. How much is too much—or too little? Light methodologies advocate just enough— just enough formality and rigor in architectural design, code walkthrough, testing, and other development activities, and just enough time reporting, progress reporting, status meetings, and other project management activities. These strategies must be re-examined every few years because the cost or benefit analysis changes as business conditions and technology change. The popular light methodologies are also reintro- ducing collaboration among developers by emphasizing teamwork among managers, customers, and developers. Any IT organization involved in Internet business develop- ment projects needs to investigate light methodologies. An example of a light meth- odology is eXtreme Programming.
- **RAD**—Also known as rapid prototyping, is a software development methodology that allows usable systems to be built quickly, often with some compromises. To ensure high responsiveness, projects are designed with fixed timescales, sacrificing

functionality if necessary. This allows the development team to focus on the functionalities that have the highest business value, and deliver those functionalities rapidly. RAD combats scope and requirements creep by limiting the amount of change by shortening the development cycle. One key to RAD is the potential supply of reusable components. RAD tools quickly generate usable programs to meet requirements.

- **Joint Application Development (JAD)**—A methodology that brings users and developers together for intensive, highly productive facilitated sessions to resolve the task at hand. Because JAD focuses on analyzing the task and providing a solution, it has benefits in developing improved application performance and increased motivation of the individuals taking part. A major advantage of the JAD approach is that it allows for the simultaneous gathering and consolidating of large amounts of information. And discrepancies are resolved immediately with the aid of a facilitator.

Most software development organizations spend a substantial amount of time developing documentation. Developers create the following types of documentation:

- Documentation of the source code and test data for future enhancements or changes to the system
- Help desk scripts to enhance user support
- User information for reference and training

Document version control programs have the same purpose as software version control programs. Document version control software applications typically have the following kinds of core functionalities:

- Document check-in or check-out tracks—Who has a document checked out and for how long? It also enables locking a document so that others cannot edit it.
- Security controls document access rights to other developers or groups in the organization.
- Document history provides a log of every activity performed on a document.
- Version tracking.

Videotaping is a new approach used in today's Internet time environment because there is so little time to create documentation. Some organizations videotape important design review meetings, JAD sessions, and other key meetings in which the system's technical aspects are discussed. Voice-recognition technology can transcribe the meeting's audio content. Those documents are then indexed so that future developers can quickly locate key information.

Web-enabled workflow-automation tools give customers an instant view of the current project status as long as the project team performs all its work within this environment. Customers can literally watch the progress by using their own web browsers. They do not have to wait for status updates from the project team. They can observe requirements being created, modified, and approved; they can observe design reviews, with metrics about the number of defects that were identified; and they can track defects to see whether any critical problems might threaten the project's success. The drawback to these tools is that explanations and analysis are not readily available to the customer. Subsequently, the customer must be familiar with the project details to get meaningful information from these tools.

Application Development Tools

To aid you in understanding the wide variety of application development tools, the material is divided into the following sections:

- Application Programming Development Tools
- Integrated Development Environment
- Computer Aided Software Engineering
- Version Control Software

Application Programming Development Tools

Programming tools encompass editors, compilers, and debuggers that are available to support most conventional programming languages. Object-oriented programming environments, fourth generation languages, graphical programming environments, application generators, and database query languages also reside within this category:

- Typically, a programmer uses some type of visual building tool for developing the graphical user interface (GUI) of an application. These tools allow a developer to drag and drop objects such as list boxes, buttons, and graphics to create a GUI.

- An *editor*, sometimes called a text editor, is a program that creates and edits text files. The term editor usually refers to source code editors that include many special features for writing and editing source code.

- A *compiler* is a program that translates source code into object code. The compiler looks at all the source code and collects and reorganizes the instructions. Thus, a compiler differs from an interpreter, which analyzes and executes each line of source code in succession, without looking at the entire program. The advantage of interpreters is that they can execute a program immediately. However, programs produced by compilers run faster. Every high-level programming language (except strictly interpretive languages) has a compiler. Because object code is unique for each type of computer and platform, many compilers are available for the same language. For example, there are C compilers from different vendors for PCs and others for Apple Macintosh computers from the same vendors.

- A *debugger* is a tool that helps developers find errors (bugs) in programs. Tools include compiler warning messages, file comparators (for comparing different versions of source code), and interactive debuggers (software and hardware).

Integrated Development Environment

An IDE is a collection of tools (such as editors, compilers and debuggers) that are integrated into one application, which speeds up development time. Figure 3-9 shows some components of an IDE.

Figure 3-9   *IDE*

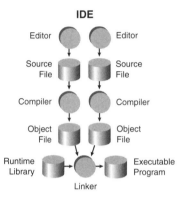

In Figure 3-9, the library is a collection of precompiled routines that a program can use. Libraries are particularly useful for storing frequently used routines because they do not need to be explicitly linked into every program that uses them. The linker automatically looks in libraries for routines that it does not find elsewhere. The executable program is a group of instructions that the computer understands and can execute.

Computer Aided Software Engineering

This can be as simple as a single tool that supports a specific software engineering activity, or as complex as a complete environment that encompasses tools, a database, people, hardware, a network, operating systems, standards, and myriad other components. CASE systems offer tools to automate, manage, and simplify the development process. Various companies offer CASE tools. While many CASE systems provide special support for object-oriented programming, the term CASE can apply to any type of software development environment.

Version Control Software

This is a critical facet of team software development. Using version control software prevents accidental file loss, allows backtracking to previous versions, branching and merging, and the managing of releases. Version control is highly desirable when developing software, web sites, or anywhere it is desirable to compare two versions of a file or return to a previous version.

Test Phase

The test phase of the business application development lifecycle integrates the components and operations of the application into a completed system, discovers and corrects any non-conformances, and prepares for the formal acceptance of the system. Testing and validation is the process of ensuring that the solution (applications and system) meets the business requirements (performance, security, availability, and so on) and that the solution fits into its environment (that is, it complies with established software and system requirements).

If you look at testing and validation separately, testing is the process of setting up and executing test scenarios in a controlled setting, and validation is the process of validating or confirming that the testing results meet certain business requirements.

The testing and validation phase has been consistently rated as the most important phase in a software development lifecycle. The advent of Internet commerce and the surge of Internet business applications have resulted in an enormous need for testing, validating, and managing the performance of web applications so that they are scalable, reliable, available, and perform flawlessly, even during peak usage times. Thus, testing and validation ensures solution integrity.

If an Internet application is not reliable, think about what can happen if customers have to wait for web pages to load and then cannot find their requested information or discover that their transactions did not go through. Or even worse, what if the web site is unavailable because of high traffic volumes? What if a hacker breaks into the system? With the competition only a mouse click away, customers expect pleasant user experiences and demand 24/7 access to your site. If you stumble, remember that they will leave your site as easily as they enter. Therefore, testing and validation is an indispensable phase required to ensure that your Internet business solutions meet business requirements and provide customer satisfaction.

Testing and validation is key to applications and systems performing as expected and not negatively impacting the productivity of business users or increasing their level of downtime because of system failures. Performing testing and validation gives you the ability to secure the following benefits:

- Ensure that the solution supports the peak usage level for which it is designed.
- Ensure that downtime meets the availability criteria.
- Ensure that security controls are in place as designed.
- Reduce unknown failures, and therefore minimize revenue and customer loss.
- Ensure that business requirements are met, and therefore increase overall client and customer satisfaction with the Internet business deployment.
- Lower support costs because fewer unplanned failures can occur.

The test phase for a business application, which is primarily a software addition to an existing system, can test the following components:

- Objectives
- Team responsibilities
- Procedures
- Schedules
- Products or services

The purpose of the test phase of the application development lifecycle includes the following objectives:

- Planning the test of the application
- Preparing the formal final acceptance testing procedures
- Testing the application components and the integrated system
- Verifying the content, structure, and interaction of operational mechanisms

Besides determining whether the application technically conformed to the application system specification, the test phase also ensures that the fully implemented application provides the quality of products and services agreed upon with the customer in the business modeling and requirements phase of the application lifecycle.

To aid you in understanding this topic, the material is divided into the following sections:

- Inputs to the Test Phase
- Outputs from the Test Phase
- Issues of the Test Phase
- Responsibilities during the Test Phase
- Techniques and Tools for the Test Phase
- Types of Testing

Inputs to the Test Phase

Besides the application system specification and any relevant information from the business modeling and requirements phase, the test phase must make another acquisition. This phase must acquire any information necessary to ensure that it can fully define the test objectives, test team responsibilities, test procedures, and test schedules.

The test phase planner must answer three questions before finishing gathering information about the application:

- What is the purpose of the test from the perspective of the application objectives and the customer objectives?

- How does each activity in the test plan tie to the requirements of the application from the business modeling and requirements phase?
- What criteria evaluates each test?

Although test phases vary for different application developments, a test plan can include the following inputs about the application:

- Name, purpose, and description (for example, range of values and accuracy) of each test input
- Source of the test input and the method for selecting the test input
- Determination of whether the test input is real or simulated
- Time or event sequence of test input

The input data is controlled to

- Test the items with a minimum/reasonable number of data types and values
- Exercise the items with a range of valid data types and values that test for overload, saturation, and other worst case effects
- Exercise the items with invalid data types and values to test for appropriate handling of irregular inputs
- Permit retesting, if necessary

Outputs from the Test Phase

The broad definition of the outputs from the test phase of the application development lifecycle is a checklist of requirements that must be satisfied before an application implementation is complete. The test phase personnel find these requirements in the application system specification, business model, and other requirements after the application passes from the business modeling and requirements phase of the lifecycle.

As an example, a model test plan used for a project to test a computerized assembly line control system required consideration of the following testing operational issues:

- Range or accuracy over which an output can acceptably vary
- Minimum number of combinations or alternatives of input and output conditions for an acceptable test
- Maximum or minimum allowable test duration, in terms of time or number of events
- Maximum number of interruptions, halts, or other system breaks allowed
- Allowable severity of processing errors as a function of criticality
- Conditions under which the result is inconclusive and retesting is required
- Conditions under which the outputs are to be interpreted as irregularities in input test data, in the test database or data files, or in test procedures

Issues of the Test Phase

The issues with which the test phase personnel must concern themselves relate to what they must detect. Different types of application quality tests catch different types of errors. Some tests, such as virus testing, are specific. Others are more general.

The test planner can easily get lost in the complexities of ensuring the specific functions of an application work. The real objective is to test how the application works within the end-to-end business process that it supports. Integrating formal software testing procedures and tools into a development process from the beginning can avoid a lot of extra cost and delays.

As an example, the steps that are used as part of a test plan to evaluate the operator interface with the customer database are to test operator actions and equipment operation required for each step, including commands, as applicable to the following:

Step 1   Start the test case and apply test inputs.

Step 2   Inspect test conditions.

Step 3   Perform interim evaluations of test results.

Step 4   Record data.

Step 5   Halt or interrupt the test case.

Step 6   Request data dumps or other aids, if needed.

Step 7   Modify the database/data files.

Step 8   Repeat the test case if unsuccessful.

Step 9   Apply alternate modes as required by the test case.

Step 10 Terminate the test case.

Responsibilities During the Test Phase

The test phase integrates the components and operations of the application into a completed system, discovers and corrects any nonconformities between the developed system and the business requirements as stated in the design document, and concludes with the formal acceptance of the system. Few stages in the software development lifecycle are more important than testing. Good testing equals a better return on investment, higher levels of customer satisfaction, and most important, better solutions. Ensuring quality is critical, especially for an Internet business solution where the consequences of defects can range from mere inconvenience and customer dissatisfaction to the loss of money and business.

The test phase varies in duration and difficulty depending on the dimensions and complexity of the proposed application system. However, the test phase usually has four major stages: plan the test, execute the test, analyze the test results, and perform acceptance testing.

During each of these test phase stages, the CISS might need to perform certain responsibilities to ensure the success of the project. Following are a few of those responsibilities:

- Confirm that the test plan is sufficient to test the system requirements as specified in the design document.
- Verify that testing is performed.
- Ensure that test results are analyzed.
- Collaborate with acceptance testing, as needed.

In Figure 3-10, the four basic stages of the test phase are shown as a pyramid of components that culminate in customer testing.

Figure 3-10 *Test Phase*

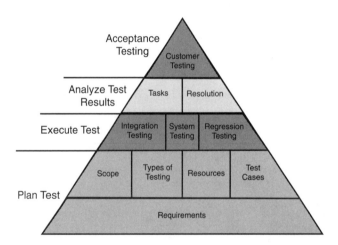

The test plan describes the objectives, scope, approach, resources, and schedule of the tests. This plan identifies the items and the features being tested and the tasks and the personnel responsible at each stage. It includes test cases and the expected results. It also specifies what criteria must be met for testing to begin, what constraints exist in the testing environment, and what can cause testing to cease prematurely. The test plan describes how the software is tested. Figure 3-11 shows the components of the first stage: planning the test.

Figure 3-11 *Planning the Test*

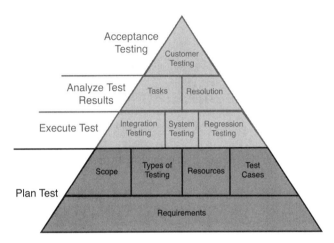

The test plan can be discussed in stages. Each stage is presented in the following sections.

Test Plan: Stage One

The first stage in the test phase is planning the test. During this stage, the CISS might need to support project management with the tasks of identifying system requirements, scope, approach, resources, test case scenarios, and a schedule of the testing effort by performing the following tasks:

- Ensure that all requirements as specified in the design document have been identified.

- Guarantee that the complete scope of the project is considered when developing the test plan.

- Discuss the various types of testing that can validate an application.

- Verify that sufficient resources are available for the test environment.

- Confirm the validity of test cases and test data.

The objective of this stage is to verify that the developed system successfully performs all the functionality that is documented in the design document. The test phase must also demonstrate that the SLA and operational criteria will be met.

The CISS needs to ensure that the design document is examined to review the system specifications and expectations for quality of product and services that were agreed upon with the customer during the analysis and design phase. The goal is to create the test objectives based on the functional and nonfunctional requirements specified in the design document. It must be possible to trace any test to a statement in the design document. This capability ensures that all specifications are tested, and that meaningless tests are not carried out. Periodically, these functional and nonfunctional requirements must be compared with the testing objectives as a reality check.

After the requirements are clear, the CISS needs to guarantee that the complete scope of the project is considered for the test phase; thus ensuring that each critical element is covered in the test plan. An Internet business application typically consists of multiple layers, such as database servers, web servers, application servers, and other components, to deliver the required functionality. Web software must be compatible with different browsers; for example, Internet Explorer and Netscape Navigator. Connectivity issues need to be considered, for example, broadband lines; so be sure that download sizes and times are assessed. The CISS must be aware that the scope of the test needs to include more than just testing the user interface.

The CISS might need to ensure that the following areas, depending on the scale of the developed system, are validated during the test phase:

- Desktop configuration
- Usability
- Documentation
- Error messages
- Destructive testing
- Performance testing
- Middleware testing
- Multisite testing
- Backup and recovery testing
- Volume testing
- Installation testing
- Security
- Data conversion

Depending on the scale and complexity of an Internet business solution, all or part of the preceding system considerations can be applicable. The CISS might need to provide guidance as to which areas are appropriate, given the circumstances of a specific solution and environment.

During the test phase, the CISS might need to verify that there are sufficient resources available for the test environment by performing the following tasks:

- Verify that adequate hardware, software, and people are available.
- Ensure that there is an awareness of any deficiencies of the test environment.

Figure 3-12 shows the resources incorporated in the test environment.

Figure 3-12 *Test Resources*

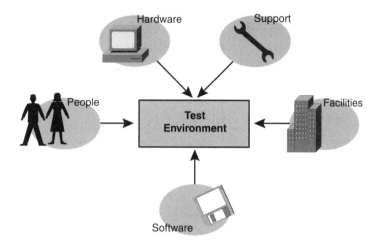

Following are some necessary resources:

- Client and server hardware including client workstations, application and database servers, web servers, gateways, LAN, WAN, and any other peripheral components that might be required to support the application

- Software including web servers, network operating systems, and any web browsers that users are likely to use

- People requirements that are defined with expectations, skills, and timeframes desired for each team member

- Facilities such as floor space, filtered power, air conditioning, and network connectivity

- Support services including management of the various versions and configurations that can be involved with a large scale application

- Any other special tools or equipment needed to support the test environment, such as test data generators

Often, it is not feasible to replicate the production environment for the test phase. Thus, deficiencies and shortcomings between the test and production environment must be well defined. Each exception must be documented and addressed in the test plan. On occasion, it might be necessary to identify tests that can be performed only in the production environment. These test items must be well defined and included in the acceptance test plan.

After the test objectives have been documented, the approaches have been established, and the necessary resources identified, the next step is to develop test cases—collections of tests that are catalogued by function or operation.

Test cases are formalized documents that record the test objectives, entry and exit criteria, constraints, inputs, expected results (based on the requirements, not the code), actual results, detailed descriptions of the test environment, analysis of results, and other desirable test attributes. Individual tests can be documented in more detail by use of test scripts. Because there can be many test scripts, it is important to use a good referencing system to keep track of them all.

Following are additional considerations:

- Ensure that a test case scrutinizes the code for things that are invalid and unexpected. The goal of testing is to find things that are wrong, not right. Thus, a validity test might search for fields that allow only numeric data—what happens when you enter characters in those fields?

- Because exhaustive testing is not feasible, tests must be carefully designed to capture the maximum number of errors in the most cost effective way.

- To verify the validity and completeness of test cases, use walkthroughs of test cases and inspections of test data.

- Save test cases for regression testing, both during the test phase and later, when enhancements are made to the production system.

The CISS might need to ensure that test data is a representative sample of production data. Good test data should not only include data to demonstrate positive results, but also cover invalid data and unexpected data conditions. Test data should include the following attributes:

- Traceable to requirements.

- Repeatable.

- Concise and complete: Cover as many test conditions as possible with the least amount of data.

- Verifiable.

Test Plan: Stage Two

The second stage in the test phase is performing the actual tests. The system is tested as a whole—the separate modules are brought together and tested as a complete system. The system needs to be tested to ensure that interfaces between modules work (integration testing), the system works on the intended platform and with the expected volume of data (system testing), and the system does what the user requires (regression testing).

During the test phase, the CISS might need to verify that methodical and comprehensive testing is being done by performing the following tasks:

- Ensure that integration, system, and regression testing are performed.
- Confirm that an incident or problem reporting process is in place and being used.
- Verify that documentation is validated.

Figure 3-13 shows the components of the second stage of a test phase: executing the tests.

Figure 3-13 *Executing the Tests*

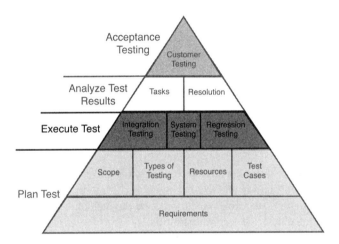

During the development phase, developers perform unit tests that verify the functionality of each individual module. When the code has passed the developer's scrutiny, it is time to move it into the hands of the testing organization. At this stage, sound entrance and exit criteria must be established. This information clearly states what condition the code must be in to enter this phase of testing (for example, all required functionality must be implemented, and compilation errors must not exceed a certain level of severity), and what condition it must be in to exit. (For example, there are no outstanding fixes for the code and the code must execute correctly.) Figure 3-14 shows the relationships between integration testing, system testing, and regression testing.

Figure 3-14 *Testing Relationships*

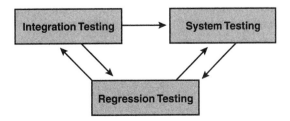

The CISS might need to ensure that the following types of testing occur:

- **Integration testing**—After all the individual programs have met the required criteria, integration testing is performed to see that the data flow from one program to another is correct. This is one of the most critical stages of the entire testing phase because it is the first stage in which all parts of the application are assembled and presented as a system. The testing group uses test scenarios to identify flaws in the system and verify the functionality of the system.

- **System testing**—After the integration test is over, the system as a whole is tested to ensure that the expected functionality is achieved. The nonfunctional characteristics of the system are tested and verified to ensure that they meet the requirements stated in the design document.

- **Regression testing**—Testing groups often perform regression testing throughout the test phase to verify that all known bugs are fixed—and stay fixed. A subset of the test cases ensures that any changes made to the code do not hurt previous functionality. Be sure to add to the regression test cases any new test scenarios that have been created to verify code fixes. If these enhanced test cases prove that the updates to the system have not changed an application's functionality, it is probably safe to assume that the code changes are valid.

The CISS must confirm that there is a process to log user issues, problems, suggestions, and requests for information, and to track them through to final resolution. This process must have the ability to categorize issues, describe the incident/problem, assign resources, anticipate due dates, and record resolutions.

The incident or problem reporting process is important not only because it tracks the progress, but also because it can help identify potential problem issues and trends. The number of incidents or problems reported must be closely monitored. Consistent problem areas, scope creep, requirements clarifications, and data issues are specific areas that can create issues during the testing phase. A process must be developed to manage incidents and problems, with escalation procedures defined. Ideally, the incident or problem reporting process is integrated into the overall change control process. This integration enables the tracking of corrective actions for specific releases or iterations of an application.

In general, testing of the documentation focuses on the accuracy, relevancy, user friendliness, and completeness of the documentation produced to support the system. Although all the other activities are taking place during the test phase, the supporting documentation should be inspected for inconsistencies, ambiguities, and errors. Update procedures should also be reviewed to help with the process of keeping documentation accurate. The CISS might need to perform the following tasks:

- Verify system documentation during the associated testing activity. Documentation of installation instructions and configuration parameters should be validated during the building of the test environment. Specific tests to validate backup and recovery should also verify support documentation.

- Confirm that help desk scripts are complete. Help desk scripts testing can often involve the creation of scripts that are used by a knowledge-based help desk tool. These scripts are similar to flowcharts that detail typical problems and solutions and identify when and how issues should be escalated.

- Ensure comprehensiveness of user documentation. User documentation such as field level help, user manuals, and other aids should be used in the appropriate scenario testing as a means of verifying their completeness.

Test Plan: Stage Three

During the test phase, the CISS might need to ensure that the results of the integration testing, system testing, and regression testing have been analyzed by performing the following tasks:

- Confirm that actual test results match the expected results.

- Verify that incidents or problems are resolved.

Figure 3-15 contains the components of the third stage of a test phase: analyzing the test results.

Figure 3-15 *Analyzing the Test Results*

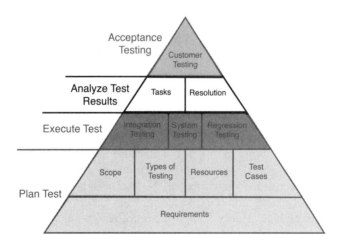

Each test case contains test scripts that include the corresponding expected test results. When a test script is executed, the actual results are analyzed and compared with the expected results to ensure that the actual results are valid and what the system is expected to produce. Document the results of the testing in the test case.

If a discrepancy is discovered when analyzing and comparing actual test results with the expected results, there must be a strategy to deal with the discrepancy. Any change, no matter how small, has its own lifecycle. First, design the change, which requires an understanding of the system and generating the solution to the problem. Second, modify the code or system. Each of these stages must be tested and carefully documented. Besides testing the changes, the entire system must undergo regression testing in case there are any unanticipated side effects caused by the solution for the incident or problem.

Test Plan: Stage Four

During the test phase, the CISS might need to support acceptance testing, as needed, by performing the following tasks:

- Verify that an acceptance test plan exists.
- Ensure that incidents or problems are resolved.

Acceptance testing is the final stage in the test phase before the system is returned to the customer. Following are several acceptance testing criteria:

- The actual customer team running the developed system in the customer environment must perform hands-on testing and acceptance.
- The actual software and hardware configuration must be tested.
- The actual procedures, manuals, operations, organization structure, and controls that exist, and that are required to meet the stated objectives of the system, must be used in the test.

The final stage of a test phase is acceptance testing, which is shown in Figure 3-16.

The acceptance test plan includes guidelines on how the acceptance tests are conducted and how the test results are recorded. The plan also specifies what the acceptance criteria will be. These criteria can include a link to the priorities given to various business criteria. There needs to be agreement on whether all the tests must be passed or whether some level of failure is acceptable; for example, a completion criterion can be that testing is complete only when all high priority tests have passed. The completion criteria are likely to depend on the business risks involved in implementing the new system.

The acceptance tests must focus on the user requirements relevant to both functional and nonfunctional requirements, as stated in the design document. When an incident or problem is discovered, the incident/problem report process must be followed. After successful completion of the acceptance testing, the customer accepts the delivered software system and gives final approval.

Figure 3-16 *Acceptance Testing*

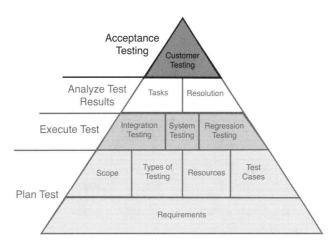

Types of Testing

Both the functional and nonfunctional requirements of a system must be tested to ensure that they match the customer requirements. Functional requirements are the actions that a system must be able to perform; that is, what a system does. Nonfunctional requirements handle the system components of the solution; for example, availability, security, and scalability. Testing of these nonfunctional requirements can require the use of a simulator (a system set up to mimic that of the user). The CISS must discuss various types of testing that need to be performed to validate a system. The following specific tests can be performed to ensure that the application and system meet these business requirements:

- **Application performance testing**—An application and network behavior are analyzed and diagnosed under a single-application, single-user environment.

- **Security testing**—The implemented security components, which comprise the security architecture, are validated as functioning according to design. Various assessment methodologies and tools are applied across the entire security architecture to ensure that all security mechanisms are installed and configured to protect the information resources as intended.

- **User load testing**—Excessive demands are made upon the application and system by increasing the number of users to predict systems behavior and performance and to identify and isolate problems. Sometimes, the term stress testing is used instead of user load testing.

- **Availability testing**—The components of an Internet business solution (applications, network, and servers) are deliberately failed in several ways (for example, failing network components so that the path of data has to change to an available one) to see if appropriate techniques for sustaining or restoring connections can function. The purpose of availability testing is to ensure that unplanned downtime does not exceed the designed availability goal for the entire system.

- **White box testing**—A structural testing that looks at the internal parts of the system—what is happening inside the program and the results of internal calculations. Knowing how the internal logic is structured allows the tester to generate test cases that are based on likely problem areas.

- **Black box testing**—Black box testing is nonfunctional testing that includes performance or availability, scalability, security, and disaster recovery. It is testing that does not include knowledge of how the system works internally, but rather the results as seen by the user.

- **Thread testing**—Often used during the integration of units, thread testing demonstrates key functional capabilities by testing a string of units that accomplishes a specific function in the application.

- **Incremental testing**—A disciplined method for testing the interfaces between unit-tested modules. This test involves adding unit-tested modules to a given module one by one and testing each resultant combination. There must be both white and black box versions of these tests.

- **Integration testing**—Can begin when the first developer tested software components are available. The test is not complete until all the components are finally integrated into a functioning system. There must be both white and black box versions of these tests. The following action items are the major objectives of integration testing:
  - Verify that the interfaces between application software components function properly.
  - Verify that the interfaces between the application and its external entities function properly.
  - Validate that the design specifications are being implemented.

- **System testing**—Usually follows integration testing. The system, as a whole, is tested to ensure that the expected functionality is achieved. The nonfunctional characteristics (for example, availability, security, and scalability) of the system are tested and verified to ensure that they meet the requirements stated in the design document. There must be both white and black box versions of these tests.

A CISS can use the following tools in the test phase:

* **Load testing tools**—Load testing software is designed to simulate several users or transactions on a system. It demonstrates system performance under a given set of conditions. By using a load testing tool, it is possible to simulate thousands of users or transactions on a system and perform detailed analysis of the results.

* **Automated functional testing tools**—Verify that an application functions as expected. Automated functional testing tools identify defects and verify business processes by automatically capturing, verifying, and replaying user interactions with an application. Automated functional testing is beneficial because numerous identical tests can be run on an application repeatedly.

* **Test data generators**—Populate a database with sample data. During the testing stage, it is important that test data is valid and useful and not just groups of random characters. Test data generators create meaningful test data and ensure that it meets the given criteria.

* **Test impact analyzers**—Gauge the impact of a code change before actually making the change. Using a test impact analyzer, it is possible to determine what potential effects a change will have on an application.

* **Incident tracking or reporting system tools**—Ensure that problems with the application detected during the testing phase, or later phases, are recorded, assigned to the appropriate developer, and resolved. These tools allow a project manager to track the resolution of problems and provide metrics on the progress of problem resolution.

To help you better understand the types of testing in detail, the remainder of the discussion is broken into the following sections:

* Application Performance Testing
* Documenting Application Performance Testing Results
* Security Testing
* Documenting Security Testing Results
* User Load Testing
* Documenting User Load Testing Results
* Availability Testing
* Documenting Availability Testing Results

Application Performance Testing

Application performance testing ensures that the application meets the nonfunctional requirements in terms of response time for a single-user environment.

Generally, a testing environment for a single application is set up, and five to ten typical transactions are identified. With each transaction, the behavior of the various components of response time for the transaction (network delay, server processing time, and client processing time) are observed and analyzed.

Application performance testing allows you to predict the effects of adding the application to the network (if it is a new enterprise application). Such testing also allows you to predict effects after making changes to an existing application, such as upgrading to a new version of the application, adding additional users, or changing the architecture of the application (that is, changing locations of servers or clients).

It also allows you to determine what level of service the application can be expected to deliver to its users based on the behavior of the application and architecture (network) over which it is running. It also allows you to isolate performance issues (such as an application server processing time) within the infrastructure (servers, clients, network) prior to solution deployment.

Certain items need to be measured in application performance testing:

- **Process time**—Process time of servers, clients, and the network are measured for each transaction processed.

- **Quantity of data (traffic size)**—Quantity of data flows in every key segment of the architecture (that is, between the client and the web server, between the web server and the application server, and between the application server and the database) is measured for each transaction.

- **Throughput**—Bits per second (bps) for every flow of the transaction are measured.

Application performance testing involves creating a characterization or workload for the behavior of an enterprise application (or for a set of representative application transactions). This characterization lets you predict the effect of the new application on the network behavior and also predict how the network behavior will affect the quality of service (QoS) delivered by the application.

The purpose of application performance testing is to validate whether the application meets the nonfunctional requirements in terms of response time for a single-user environment. Figure 3-17 shows the steps involved in an application performance testing process.

Figure 3-17 *Process of Application Performance Testing*

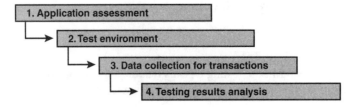

Application assessment is the process of identifying how a new application is used on the enterprise network. The purpose of application assessment is to determine how to test the application to successfully characterize the application behavior functioning within a given environment.

First, as a part of this assessment procedure, you determine how the application is deployed on the network in terms of the following data:

- Where users and servers are located
- How many users are at each location
- How frequently these users are expected to do various application tasks and transactions

Second, you also determine which transactions are representative of the way the application will be used by users (clients) on the network. These transactions (or a subset of them) form a benchmark that generates the traffic data that will become the basis for the application characterization. Understanding which transactions are likely to be used within the application, and the frequency with which these transactions will be done across the enterprise network, helps you to identify the specific application transactions that can be considered typical.

Finally, you need to define and understand the network environment in which your application will run when it is deployed, including the existing application traffic flows and how the introduction of your new application might affect that distribution.

The results of application assessment are a set of testing scenarios that you can use to help set up the testing environment for the application.

Each testing scenario is a description of the predicted usage of the network by an application in terms of the location of application users and application or database servers, the number of users at each location, and the frequency with which each user will run the application transactions under study. Also, the scenario must describe the network environment that the transaction traffic will cross (for example, 64-kBps circuits or T1 circuits). This information helps set up the test environment for the application.

As part of application performance testing, you must first identify a test environment where you can place your data collection device, run the application, process specific predefined test scenarios, and perform the data collection activities. If you cannot identify an appropriate test environment, you might need to create one.

An ideal test environment is one that is isolated from the overall production network, such as a development or pilot (trial) installation of the application, where you can capture application data without having to contend with competing traffic. You must be able to isolate the traffic created by the application transactions so that you can capture pure traffic samples that represent the data generated by the transactions, independent of the effects of other network traffic, network bottlenecks, propagation delays, and so on.

However, eventually the application will be deployed across an enterprise network where delays will be a factor. Network delays can affect the characteristics of your traffic, such as changing the application protocol behavior (windowing, retransmissions), so it is important to look at the traffic under these conditions. Therefore, although you want to isolate your test environment from the uncontrolled effects of other network usage, you do want to simulate the delays you anticipate encountering when the application is deployed. You can simulate these by using a WAN delay simulator (such as the Adtech Data Channel Simulator) in your controlled environment.

This test environment supports testing a three-tier application where the client communicates with the application server across a WAN environment. The setup has the following key components:

- **Client**—Generates application traffic by executing predefined transactions.
- **WAN Delay Simulator**—Adjusts bandwidth and inserts delays to simulate communication across your enterprise WAN.
- **Data Collection Device**—Captures the traffic data. It must be attached to the network at the appropriate point (most often between the client and the application server or database server) and must be capable of capturing all the information that is required to create a characterization of your application transactions.
- **Application Architecture Components**—Web server, application server, and database server are examples.

WAN Delay Simulator

The WAN delay simulator adjusts bandwidth and inserts delays to simulate communication across an enterprise network. In most real networks, circuits between different remote locations experience different degrees of delay, and the critical transactions of an application can meet service level goals on some circuits but not on others. Using a delay simulator lets you simulate the actual circuit speeds to your remote locations, and see how the application will perform over those circuit types (that is, a 128-kBps Frame Relay circuit with 120 ms of round-trip delay per packet).

Using a WAN delay simulator also lets you manipulate network delay to help you establish your service level goals. By testing network delays of various lengths, you can determine how much delay the user (or the application) can tolerate before the application becomes difficult or impossible to work with effectively.

Application data capture is the process of collecting traffic data that corresponds to the target transactions that comprise the application testing scenarios.

After you have installed, configured, and tested your data collection devices and established your QoS goals, you can begin capturing data. The actual data capture process involves the following steps for each transaction:

Step 1   Person monitoring the data collection device begins the data capture and tells the application user when the capture interval is beginning.

Step 2   Application user begins running a transaction; the person monitoring the data collection device records the start time of the data capture interval.

Step 3   Application user finishes the transaction or component activity and stops all use of the keyboard.

Step 4   Person monitoring the data collection device stops the data capture and saves the data to a file, or notes the end of the capture interval if saving the data is automatic.

Capturing the data for the transactions in the application benchmark requires a highly coordinated effort between a knowledgeable user who can process the tasks in the benchmark, and the person who is monitoring the data capture device and saving the captured data.

Figure 3-18 shows the data from an output file that was captured by using a Network Associates Sniffer Server.

Figure 3-18   *Sample Network Traffic Data*

1stFrm	LastFrm	Protocol	ApplID	ApplID2	Addr1	Addr2	Frms1	Frms2	Bytes1	Bytes2
13:15:05	13:16:23	TCP	Port 1219	Port 3700	[10.10.201.2]	[10.10.3.56]	76	78	19936	34093
13:15:33	13:17:08	NetBIOS-ssn	Port 1202	Port 139	[10.10.201.2]	[10.10.237.23]	229	208	17591	18508
13:15:51	13:15:53	TCP	Port 1222	Port 3700	[10.10.201.2]	[10.10.3.56]	12	11	1812	1335

The traffic analyzer must record the following critical pieces of data:

- Start and stop times for each conversation, to the second (shown in the columns 1stFrm and LastFrm, giving hour:minute:second)

- Network protocol being used

- Port numbers used by the application for the source and destination (shown under ApplID1 and ApplID2)

- Network layer addresses of the source and destination (Addr1 and Addr2)

- Number of frames and number of bytes in the forward and return directions (Frms1 and Bytes1 for the forward direction; Frms2 and Bytes2 for the return direction)

Essentially, you are collecting three types of data for each application transaction:

- Quantity of data flow on each key segment of the network
- Process time, which is the total of client process time, server process time, and network process time
- Throughput (kBps) for each key segment of the network

You should also collect the following data:

- Network errors such as network retransmission for each transaction.
- User perception information if a person is executing the transaction. Acceptable performance means that the user can use the application to accomplish a set of tasks without undue problems or unacceptable delays.

Data collection and analysis tools are important for collecting live data from networks. You need to use a data collection device such as a traffic analyzer or a sniffer attached to the network at the appropriate point (most often between the client and the application server or database server).

The data collection device must capture network layer conversation data between the source and the destination, and it must timestamp the conversation with the start and end times, to the second. It must also capture data bidirectionally (that is differentiating the data from client to server and from server to client).

After you have captured application-based data for target application transactions, you need to import the data into the performance analysis tool to extract useful metrics about the transactions. Cisco NETSYS Performance Service Manager is an example of such a tool that can be used in addition to the Optimal Application Expert tool.

Using your performance analysis tool, you can build a characterization for each target transaction. You can build a characterization for every transaction in your benchmark, or you can start with the transactions with the highest probability of occurring, or that are of the greatest interest in terms of testing on your network. These transaction characterizations represent the typical load that an individual application user can place on the network because of a specific application transaction.

Using the data from each application transaction, calculate or use a performance analysis tool to obtain the following metrics:

- Duration of the transaction in seconds for each testing scenario (for example, a Transaction Query Journal had a duration of 30 seconds in a LAN testing scenario, but had a duration of 300 seconds in a WAN scenario with a 64-kBps simulated circuit and 300 ms of delay)
- Type of media it was collected on (for example, Ethernet, Token Ring, Fiber Distributed Data Interface [FDDI])

- Networking protocol (typically interface processor for client/server applications, such as Service Advertising Protocol [SAP] R/3, PeopleSoft, or Extensity)

- Average packet size for each direction of transfer, forward and return (calculated from the number of frames for each direction)

- Total number of bytes transferred for each leg (from the client to the web server, from the web server to the application server, and from the application server to the database server) and each direction (forward and return) of the transfer

- Maximum bandwidth (throughput) for each leg and in either direction in kBps

- Process time of each component in the test environment (client, web server, application server, database server, network)

Essentially, you are looking at the results in terms of transaction size, the end-to-end response time, and the throughput for each transaction under each scenario. You can analyze the results in terms of whether the response time for target transactions meets your service level goals, and in terms of circuit use, especially for circuits where service level goals are not met.

Documenting Application Performance Testing Results

You need to create a testing report at the end of an application performance testing. Typically, it includes the following phases:

- Test objectives
- Test environment
- Test scenarios
- Test methodology
- Test results and conclusions

Test objectives—Test objectives need to be documented. Test objectives guide the test design, such as selecting test scenarios, determining test measurements, and so on. Therefore, it is important for you to list the test objectives in the final report. The objectives help people who read the document to better understand the purpose of the test and to be better prepared to assess the validity of the test design.

An example of application performance testing objectives is to determine the impact of different network conditions on the application to accurately define SLAs for customers.

Test environment—The test environment under which the test is conducted needs to be documented. The same test conducted in different environments can generate different test results. Therefore, it is important to document the test environment in a test report. Generally, a diagram of the test environment is included in the report. Descriptions for each critical component of the test environment and its configurations are also documented.

Test scenarios—Test scenarios need to be documented in detail. Different test scenarios generate different test results. The selection of test scenarios affects the test results and, in some cases, can even affect conclusions that have been reached. A sound, complete selection increases the validity of your conclusions, while a bad selection in test scenarios leads to false conclusions.

The test scenarios section must include these two key items:

- Complete the list of network environments under which you conducted your tests.
- Complete the list of transactions that are representative of the real usage of the application.

First, document the various network environments under which you have decided to conduct your test. For example, one network environment can be a WAN environment, 64 kBps with 125 ms delay, and another one can be a WAN environment, 100 kBps with no delay.

Next, document a list of transactions that need to be executed for each network environment. Typically, you present the description of the transaction, the steps to complete the transaction, and the type of the transaction in this section of the report.

Sample Test Scenarios in a Sample Report

Figure 3-19 shows a matrix of network environments and transactions that was followed during a real application performance testing. The application performance testing evaluates 13 transactions that are identified by the customer as representative of typical transactions. Each of the 13 transactions is conducted in 7 different network environments for a total of 91 combinations of tested transactions.

Figure 3-19 *Test Scenarios Report*

Network Environment	Transaction												
	1	2	3	4	5	6	7	8	9	10	11	12	13
Baseline (LAN)													
WAN Modem, 100 ms.delay													
WAN 64 K, 1 sec delay													
WAN 64 K, 500 ms delay													
WAN 64 K, 250 ms delay													
WAN 64 K, 125 ms delay													
WAN 256 K, 100 ms delay													

Test methodology—The descriptions of test methodology help people who read your testing reports evaluate the validity of your testing. Any results can be disputed if the methodology is not sound. Test methodology needs to be documented.

In this section of the testing report, you document the devices that collect the data and how the test is carried out (that is, through automated scripts on the client workstation or by knowledgeable users executing the transactions). You also document how many times each transaction is conducted, what kind of measurements are collected, and so on.

Test results and conclusions—Finally, test results need to be documented. This section of the report usually takes the largest amount of space in the test report. Testing results are usually documented in graphical format (that is, tables, charts, graphs) to facilitate the understanding and interpretation of the test results.

For a typical application performance testing, the following test results are usually presented:

- Transaction response time charts
- Total bytes per transaction charts
- Transaction response time comparison charts
- User perception data
- Overall conclusions

The transaction response time chart documents the response time for each transaction under a network environment. You must have one chart for each network environment that you tested.

Figure 3-20 shows a sample table. The table shows the response time for each of the 13 transactions in a WAN with a 64 kBps 1 second delay environment. The shaded transactions did not meet the SLA goals.

Figure 3-20 *Transaction Response Time Chart*

Transaction	Response Time (in seconds)
10	4029.45
8	3044.25
1	774.09
6	501.46
2	175.03
12	154.61
13	131.12
5	129.9
9	126.42
11	125.17
7	107.85
3	104.05
4	101.49

TABLE: Response times for [Fat Client]
NT transactions in WAN 64 kBps, 1 sec delay
scenario in order from longest to shortest

The total bytes per transaction chart shows the size of each transaction in bytes. The transaction size must stay the same regardless of which network environment is tested.

Figure 3-21 shows a sample chart. As you can see, Transaction 8 and 10 have the biggest size.

Figure 3-21 *Bytes per Transaction Chart*

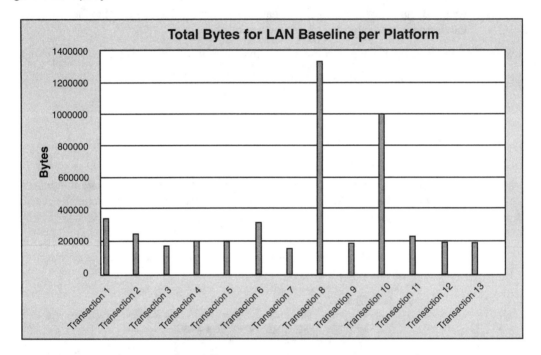

The transaction response time comparison chart compares one single transaction response time in different network environments.

Figure 3-22 shows such a chart for Transaction 10.

If you have collected user perception data on ease of use, special features, and so on, the data is presented in this section.

You must draw conclusions from the test results based on your analysis. The conclusions are focused on the objectives that were defined earlier in the report. For example, for various transactions in various network environments, the response time meets or does not meet the expected SLAs.

Figure 3-22 *Transaction Response Time Comparison Chart*

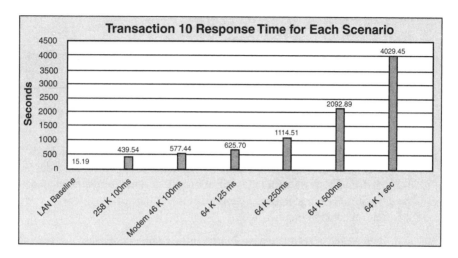

Security Testing

Security testing is the process of applying various assessment methodologies and tools across the entire security architecture to ensure that all security mechanisms are installed and configured to protect the information resources as designed and intended.

Security testing provides the assurance that the designed end-to-end security mechanisms are implemented and functioning as intended, to reduce the risk of any information resources being compromised. This testing ensures that an application can function securely from end-to-end when launched in a production environment.

Essentially, all security components across the Internet business security infrastructure need to be assessed. These components typically span the areas of systems, networks, applications, and operations. Such components can consist of security policies, standards, practices, configurations, tools, solutions, and services. In most cases, security vulnerabilities within each of these areas are identified and countermeasures are applied accordingly.

A comprehensive approach is recommended for security testing to ensure that the testing is adequately conducted on all components of an Internet business infrastructure. There are three guidelines in the approach. Figure 3-23 shows the security testing guidelines.

Figure 3-23 *Security Testing Guidelines*

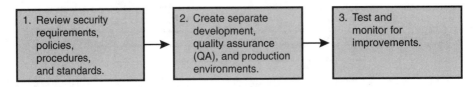

Consider the following steps:

Step 1   **Review security requirements, policies, procedures, and standards—**
Begin with reviewing the security requirements, policies, procedures,
and standards on both the application side and the infrastructure side
(that is, systems, networks, and operations) for how well they can be
enforced and complied with.

This is the first step in any security testing process because it is the basis
for which the entire security architecture and implementation are formed.
An approach that ignores this first step (which unfortunately happens too
often) usually results in significant retrofitting efforts after an application
is fully in production.

Step 2   **Create separate development, QA, and production environments—**
Security testing occurs in all three of these final target environments:

— **Development environment—**In the development environment,
the focus is on proof of concept, which includes the evaluation and
selection of security products or solutions.

— **QA environment—**In the QA environment, the focus shifts to
testing the configurations of the selected security components.

— **Production environment—**In the production environment,
besides validating configurations, the focus is also directed at
monitoring and taking corrective actions as required.

However, in many instances because of resource constraints, it is possible
for the development and QA environments to coexist or for the QA and
production environments to coexist. In worst case scenarios, all three
environments can coexist. Such a combined environment would breed
nothing but disaster!

Step 3   **Test and monitor for improvements**—This guideline is essentially the principle of Continuous Quality Improvement or Total Quality Management. There is always room for improvements in the area of performance to meet demands and also in adapting security to satisfy changes in applications or business requirements.

Here again, because of either resource constraints or plain shortsightedness, some choose to react to changes rather than practice a disciplined approach of consistent testing and monitoring for improvements.

Step 4   **The process of implementing security testing in a lab environment**— Implementing and testing a security architecture in a lab environment can be a staging process for promoting it to a development, QA, or production environment. The intent is to keep the lab environment isolated to create a controlled environment where iterative security tests can be performed without interference from unexpected variables.

Assuming that all required security components have been identified and procured, the following describes a simple four-step process of implementing and testing the designed security architecture in a lab environment. Figure 3-24 lists these security process steps:

(a) Coordinate the installation of security systems hardware and software for the application and the network infrastructure. Work closely with the application team to support the scheduled application project plan.

(b) Configure and enable the security components and services that support the application. Ensure that all systems are hardened for security; for example, apply software patches, configure baseline security settings, and disable unnecessary protocols and services.

(c) Perform iterative tests to validate and correct the configurations of security components. Ensure that security mechanisms are behaving as intended across all systems, applications, and the network (internal and external).

(d) Review any modifications made to security components and document any changes affecting the original design of the security architecture.

Figure 3-24 *Security Testing Process*

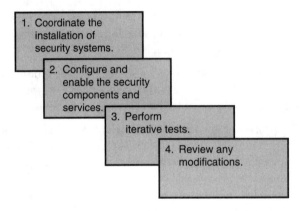

Step 5 **Validate and correct the functionality of security components**—The ultimate goal of security is to protect information assets. As such, it is vital that the implemented security controls are verified so as to success-fully achieve the protection of the intended information resources. This validation process essentially requires that the functionality of security components be validated and corrected across the entire Internet business infrastructure. Figure 3-25 shows the areas that require verification.

Figure 3-25 *Security Testing Venn Diagram*

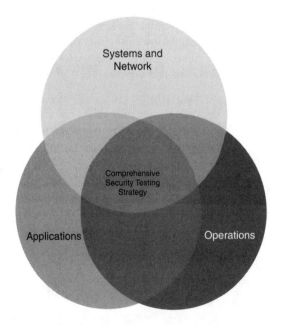

The following are the areas that require verification and the associated common security assessment methodologies for each area:

- **Systems and networks**—The common protection requirement in systems and networks is to mitigate the effects of threats and vulnerabilities. To ensure that implemented safeguards are effectively addressing known threats and vulnerabilities, the use of scanning and probing security tools is a method of performing security vulnerability assessments. Such security tools are designed to detect known vulnerabilities in systems and network services. These tools can provide a good status of how well the systems have been configured. Most tools categorize the vulnerabilities by risk level, such as high, moderate, or low. Additionally, some tools include recommended corrective actions to be taken to reduce or eliminate a specific vulnerability.

- **Applications**—To validate and correct the functional security in applications, you need to develop a comprehensive set of security test scripts that address and delineate the access control requirements in the application. Therefore, it is vital to review the business requirements for security during the development of the test scripts to ensure that adequate security scenarios are identified. Then, a functional security review can be performed that is based on these security scenarios.

- **Operations**—Validating and correcting functional security in the area of operations includes security policies and procedures, user account administration, physical access, change management, and disaster recovery planning. The common security assessment methodology for these areas is to perform some measurements that identify the level of compliance to each of these areas.

Although the validation and correction of all the areas that require verification can be performed in the development and QA environments, it is also prudent to perform them in production through a pilot phase. This action helps moderate the rollout into a production environment and offers opportunities to respond to unexpected problems in a manageable manner.

Documenting Security Testing Results

The documentation requirements for security testing results correlate directly to the areas in which the security assessments were performed. These areas are categorized as follows:

- Systems and networks
- Applications
- Operations

Systems and networks—The first and foremost documentation requirement in this area is the compilation of documented security standards and functional security requirements. These documents form the basis in describing what is being assessed. Hence, the documented results of the security assessments must map back directly to the requirements document. Besides what was assessed and by whom, other information that must be documented during the security assessments includes when and how the assessments were performed. Of course, any corrective actions taken, in addition to a rationale, must also be duly noted in the documentation.

Applications—Similar to systems and networks, the preliminary documentation requirement in the area of applications must comprise a compilation of documents describing the functional security requirements for the application. Then, the next set of documents must include the test scripts that were used, and the results of each script. The results must describe successes and failures, with cause of failures and corrective actions taken.

Operations—With operations, the required set of initial documentation includes the policy documents for security policies and procedures, user account administration, physical access, change management, and disaster recovery planning. The test results must document any areas of noncompliance, and the reason for noncompliance. Suggestions for improving compliance or modifying operational policies and procedures must also be noted.

User Load Testing

User load testing is a type of testing where excessive demands are made upon the Internet business application and system to ensure that it performs as expected when accessed by the maximum number of authorized users in the production environment.

The load conditions consist of hundreds to thousands of users using the system simultaneously to do both browsing and transactional activities. Load is usually created using virtual users—simulated clients that act like browsers to emulate the business processes performed by real users.

Applications that work well in a single-user environment might perform poorly when operating in a high stress environment with many users. User load testing allows you to observe the application and system behavior under load conditions and identify problems early in the process and before the solution deployment.

For most Internet business applications, the user experience is what matters most if the application deployment is to be successful. If the user experience is unfavorable because of applications and system stress problems, it is difficult to change their minds even after you have resolved the problems. Therefore, user load testing is essential to verify that application and system performance meets the required service levels under excessive usage.

The following items need to be measured in user load testing:

- **Control clients**—Response time of a control client executing while system is under load conditions.

- **Servers (database servers, application servers, web servers)**—Metrics to be measured for the servers are as follows:
  - CPU use
  - Memory use
  - Idle time
- **Network components (routers, switches, load balancing, caching, and firewall devices)**—Metrics to be measured for the network components are as follows:
  - Connections per second
  - Packets per second
  - CPU use
  - Memory use
- **Applications**—Application specific metrics, such as the number of concurrent database users.

User load testing is a type of testing where excessive demands are made upon the Internet business application and system. These demands are made to ensure that the application and system performs as expected in the production environment when accessed by the maximum number of authorized users.

User load testing must always be performed before deploying the application in a production environment. The basic purpose of user load testing an Internet business application is to accomplish the following objectives:

- Verify that the performance threshold in terms of response time for the user of the application meets SLA goals when the estimated maximum user load is placed on the system at one time.
- Ensure that the performance threshold remains at an acceptable level when the estimated maximum concurrent user load is placed on the system.

Figure 3-26 shows the four-step process of user load testing.

Figure 3-26 *User Load Testing Process*

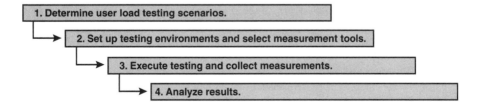

Apply these four steps when you conduct a user load testing:

Step 1 Determine user load testing scenarios.

Step 2 Set up testing environments and select measurement tools.

Step 3 Execute testing and collect measurement.

Step 4 Analyze the results.

The purpose of load testing is to observe overall system behavior under various user loads ranging from average to peak. Because the number of users and traffic levels can change in a matter of seconds in a live system, it is critical to test the worst-case scenarios to ensure that the system and application can handle it—and therefore provide a positive experience for end users.

To create load testing scenarios, you determine the maximum number of users that your system needs to support at peak time.

The two sources from which you can draw peak usage information are

- **Historical information**—If a system is currently up and running, you can use historical data to project future peak usage.

- **Current market analysis**—If you can get usage data about other businesses that are similar to your customers, you can use that information to project peak usage of the system.

If you do not have any credible information, you can do a best estimate. To do that, you first determine the population of the end users who might use your system. Concurrency rate is the number of users over time; for example, the predicted peak usage is 100,800 users/hour or 28 users/second. With this data, you can estimate the peak usage by using the formula (shown in Figure 3-27) Number of Simultaneous Users = Total Number of Users in Population * Concurrency.

Figure 3-27 *User Estimation Formula*

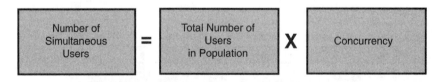

Besides determining the maximum usage, you also determine the typical transaction mix and the distribution of those transactions. You begin by defining how people use the system in real life. Identify the critical business processes and then break down the individual business processes into a series of transaction types. For each transaction type, identify a set of representative instances of that transaction type. The results must be a set of transactions that are representative of the way that the application will be used by users. For example, for a typical Internet commerce application, such as an online store, typical transactions are informational browsing and buying.

After you identify a set of typical or critical transactions, you determine the distribution patterns of those transactions, which means the percentage of each transaction at a given time. For example, for the same online store application, you determine, at a certain time, how many people are typically doing informational browsing transactions and how many are doing buying transactions (such as, 80 percent of users browsing the catalog and 20 percent of users buying items in the catalog).

Understanding what transactions are likely to be used within the application, and understanding the frequency with which these transactions are done across the enterprise network, helps you make reasonable assumptions for the application transactions mix. You use the application transactions mix later to generate load testing scenarios. Again, if possible, you base these assumptions on available, historical information.

NOTE   The list of transactions that you need to consider in user load testing is the same set that you identified in the application performance testing stage.

After you determine the maximum number of users and the transactions mix, it is time for you to construct load testing scenarios. Load testing scenarios are a set of tests that define the quantities of virtual users to be tested and the mix of transactions to be emulated by these users. After the transactions are scripted by using an automated load testing tool, these scripts emulate the unique behavior of real users that are using your application. For example, one test scenario might have 1000 users doing order entry, 250 users doing product configuration, and 2000 users checking order status.

Look at the online store application example again. Suppose you identified that the maximum number of users who will use the application simultaneously is 5000. There are two typical transactions, browsing and buying. Also, on average, 60 percent of the users will be performing browsing transactions, and 40 percent will be performing buying transactions at a given time. Therefore, the worst-case scenario for this example is 3000 users running browsing transactions and 2000 users running buying transactions at the same time.

Often, you cannot have just one worst-case scenario for load testing. You want to gradually increase the load until it hits the worst-case scenario load. If the system fails before peak usage is applied (that is, if the system and application fails at 3000 users as you are scaling to 5000 users), you need to know at what point in the testing the system failed. Therefore, for this online store case, you might need three basic test scenarios.

Besides the worst-case scenario, you might need two other scenarios, so that you can scale to peak usage:

- 3000 users total (1800 users doing browsing and 1200 users doing buying transactions)
- 1000 users total (600 users doing browsing and 400 users doing buying transactions)

TIP   It is best practice to slowly increase the load on the target system incrementally (for example, 100 users at a time). This provides you with better, more accurate data and enables the testing team to determine at which level of load performance problems exist. You should also maintain a load for sustained periods to determine how the performance varies over time.

You now consider the test environment and data collection tools needed in user load testing. After completing this section, you will be able to describe a required testing environment and data collection tools that can be used for user load testing.

User load testing is performed in a simulated production environment to determine how the production environment operates under different load conditions. Figure 3-28 shows a typical user load test environment.

Figure 3-28 *Load Test Environment*

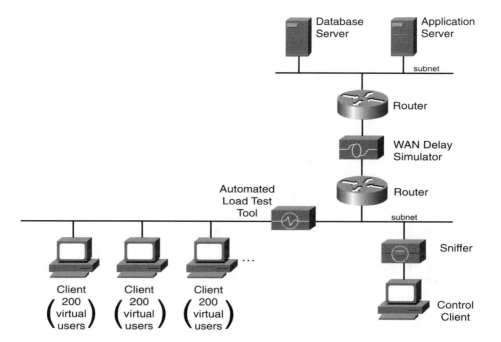

The testing environment is almost the same as the one used in the application performance testing. The differences are the following:

- Virtual users are needed to generate loads that act like browsers to emulate the transactions performed by real users. Each of these virtual users drives the application with real input for a transaction. Virtual users significantly minimize hardware and personnel resources required for load testing, as you can run hundreds or even thousands of them on just a few machines instead of using hundreds or thousands of desktop computers and operators.

- An automated load testing tool is needed to execute the testing and to gather measurement data about the virtual users.

- A control client is needed to perform transactions under each load condition. The data collected for a control client allows you to analyze the application performance at that point in the load testing. For example, during the application performance testing (no other users) a transaction takes 16 seconds, but when the control client executes the same transaction under load conditions (1000 additional users executing), the transaction time is now 220 seconds. The data collected can then be analyzed by using a method similar to the method described in the application performance testing, to determine which servers, clients, or network components are causing the performance to degrade.

There are three types of data collection tools in user load testing:

- Automated load test tools that collect measurement data on the virtual users
- Collection tools to collect the control client information (similar to application performance testing data)
- Collection tools to collect server usage data (for example, NT performance monitor)

Automated load testing tools emulate virtual users, measure response times for the transactions run by the virtual users, and keep track of how many transactions succeed.

If available with the tool you use, use the load testing tool integrated real-time monitors to gather performance data on the entire infrastructure, such as its web servers, application servers, database servers, and network devices. The performance testing tool can correlate this information with the performance data about the transactions that are run, which was gathered during the test. As a result, the tester can then pinpoint where the issues exist in the application architecture.

Data collection tools are important for collecting live data from networks. You need to use a data collection device, such as a traffic analyzer or a sniffer, that is attached to the network between the control client and the application or database servers to collect the necessary data.

Following is what the data collection device must be able to do:

- Capture network layer conversation data between the source and the destination
- Timestamp the conversation with the start and end times, to the second
- Capture data bidirectionally (that is, differentiating the data from client to server and from server to client)

Server usage data collection can be done with a performance monitor that is provided by the operating system of the server (UNIX, NT, and so on), by specialized agents that measure server metrics, such as CPU use and memory use, or by the automated load testing tool.

You next need to consider how to execute testing and collect measurement data. After completing this section, you will be able to explain how to execute load testing and identify the types of data that need to be collected.

After load testing scenarios are built and the testing environment is set up, you can run the testing scenarios and analyze the results. As issues are uncovered, they can be analyzed and the elements in the system that cause problems can be identified. After modifications are made, the tests must be run again to validate that the issues are resolved.

After you have carefully planned your testing strategy, actually running the tests is rather straightforward. The load on the target architecture must be gradually incremented by small groups. It is best testing practice to increase the load incrementally (for example, 100 users at a time). This gradual increase provides you with better, more accurate data and enables the test team to determine at which levels of load performance problems exist.

You must also maintain load for sustained periods to determine how the performance varies when under constant load. For example, hold at 1000 virtual users for approximately 15 minutes and continue to take all measurements.

Figure 3-29 shows the user load on the server during each second of a load test. Each load condition is held stable for 10 minutes before it is increased again.

Following is a partial list of the data that you need to collect on all elements of the architecture:

- Virtual users
- Control client data
- Servers
- Network components

Virtual users—Use automated load testing tools to collect data on virtual users. Collect data on the number of pass and fail for each transaction scenario and minimum response time, average response time, and maximum response time for each transaction scenario.

Figure 3-29 *Virtual Users Load Test*

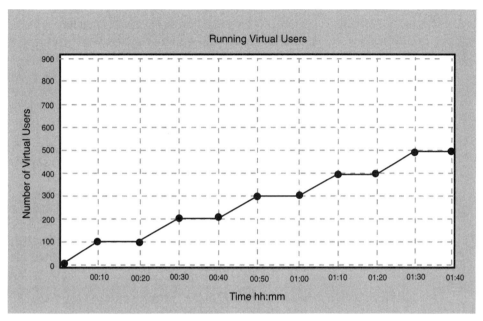

Control client data—Use data collection tools, such as a sniffer or traffic analyzer, to collect data on the control client. Besides the metrics listed, it is important to collect any network errors that occur during the different test scenarios. Collect data for the following:

- End-to-end response time (the total of client, web server, application server, and database server processing time)
- Throughput (kBps) for each key segment of the network

Servers—Following are the metrics that you need to measure:

- CPU use
- Memory use
- Idle time

Network components—Network components include routers, switches, load balancing, caching, and firewall devices. Following are the metrics that you need to measure:

- Connections per second
- Packets per second
- CPU use
- Memory use

You now analyze user load testing results. After completing this section, you will be able to describe how to analyze user load testing results.

The first task in analyzing testing results is to look at the values of all the measurements already discussed, virtual users, control client performance data, server performance data, and network performance data. The analysis starts with the response times of the transactions that the control client ran. If these values (that is, number of seconds) are all within the desired service level, the testing is considered successful, and the system can support the desired load. If not (for example, the transaction time exceeds the desired service level), additional analysis is needed to determine which component in the system is causing the performance to degrade.

This additional analysis includes looking at all collected data for the servers and network components, and possibly some application-specific metrics (for example, number of requests in queue for an application server). The goal is to find the component and the metric that is causing the performance to degrade. After that metric is identified (that is, database CPU use is above 95 percent during the testing run), a recommendation can be made for change, and the testing can be run again to see if the metric identified helps. This process continues until the control client transaction times are within the desired service level goal.

A typical load testing tool can generate the following types of reports:

- **Throughput Report**—Displays the amount of throughput (in bytes) on the web server during the load test. Throughput represents the amount of data that the virtual users received from the server at any given second. This graph helps you to evaluate the amount of load, in terms of server throughput, that virtual users generate.

- **Hits per Second Report**—Displays the number of hits made on the web server by virtual users during each second of the load test. This graph helps you to evaluate the amount of load, in terms of the number of hits, that virtual users generate.

- **Transaction Summary Report**—Displays the number of transactions that passed, failed, aborted, or ended with errors. The transaction summary quickly tells you if the architecture is scalable and working properly. Obviously, it is the goal of every transaction to pass. Transaction failures can be caused by the virtual user timing out (the virtual user never receiving a response from the target architecture), web server errors such as 404, 500, and so on, or network errors.

- **Transaction Performance Report**—Displays the minimum, average, and maximum response time for all the transactions in the load test. This is a graphical representation of the minimum, average, and maximum response times for each transaction. Ideally, the minimum, average, and maximum response times must be close together. The fact that they are not points to performance issues. Again, many of the performance problems are because of scalability issues or server tuning.

- **Transaction Response Time Average Report**—Displays the average time taken to perform transactions during each second of the load test. This graph helps you determine whether the performance of the server is within the acceptable minimum and maximum transaction performance time ranges defined for your system.

- **Transaction Response Time Under Load Report**—Displays the average transaction response times, relative to the number of virtual users, running at any given point during the load test. This graph helps you view the general impact of virtual user load on performance time and is most useful when analyzing a load test with a gradual load.

The throughput chart displays the amount of throughput (in bytes) on the web server during the load test. This graph helps you evaluate the amount of load, in terms of server throughput, that virtual users generate. Figure 3-30 is an example of a web server throughput chart.

Figure 3-30 *Web Server Throughput Chart*

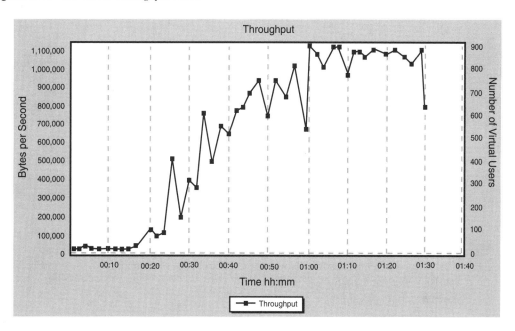

The hits per second chart shows the number of hits made on the web server by virtual users during each second of the load test. This graph helps you evaluate the amount of load, in terms of the number of hits, that virtual users generate. Figure 3-31 is an example of a hits per second chart.

Figure 3-31 *Hits per Second Chart*

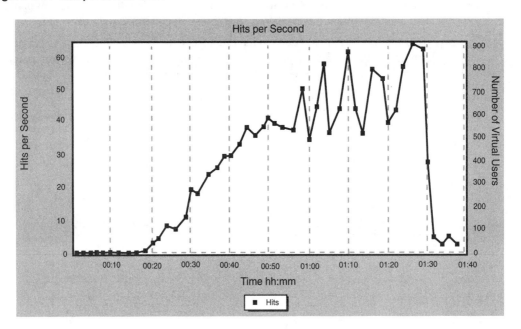

The transaction summary chart presents the number of transactions that passed or failed. Obviously, it is the goal of every transaction to pass. The transaction summary quickly tells you if the architecture is scalable and working properly. Figure 3-32 is an example of a transaction summary chart.

The transaction response time average chart displays the average time taken to perform transactions during each second of the load test. This graph helps you determine whether the performance of the server is within acceptable minimum and maximum transaction performance time ranges that are defined for your system. Figure 3-33 is an example of a transaction response time chart.

Figure 3-32 *Transaction Summary Chart*

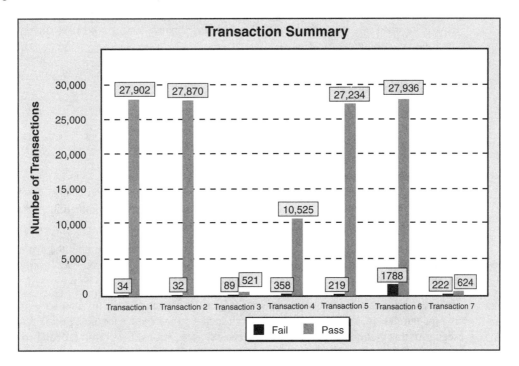

Figure 3-33 *Transaction Response Time Chart*

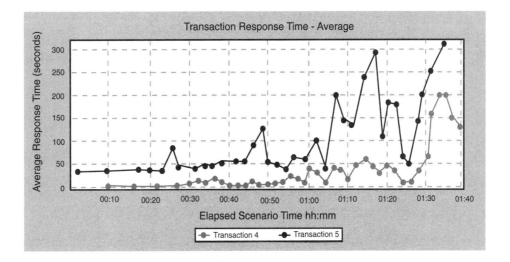

Documenting User Load Testing Results

A testing report is usually created at the end of user load testing. A user load testing report usually has the same structure as an application performance testing report, which includes the following components:

- Test objectives
- Test environment
- Test scenarios
- Test methodology
- Test results and conclusions

Test objectives—In the test objectives section, you document the objectives of the test. An example of a user load testing objective can be to verify that an Internet business web site has the ability to support the maximum user load while maintaining a defined SLA goal for all users.

Test environment—In the test environment section, you need to document the test environment. Typically, a diagram of the test environment must be presented. Descriptions of the components of the environment and their configurations must also be presented.

Test scenarios—In the test scenarios section, you need to specify the test scenarios, including the numbers of test scenarios (number of load testing) and a short description for each scenario (that is, number of virtual users, typical transactions that performed, and so on).

Figure 3-34 shows ten test scenarios in a real user load testing.

Figure 3-34 *Load Testing Scenarios*

Increment #	Control Clients	Virtual Clients
Baseline	1	0
Stress 1	1	500
Stress 2	1	1000
Stress 3	1	2250
Stress 4	1	4750
Stress 5	1	7250
Stress 6	1	8400
Stress 7	1	9505
Stress 8	1	10000
Stress 9	1	10100
Stress 10	1	10200

Scripts that emulate the virtual users also are presented. Figure 3-35 represents the steps performed by a typical load testing script.

Figure 3-35 *Typical Load Testing Script*

Client Task	Client Activity
1	Browse to test site: www.ciscopress.com.
2	Select "click here to register."
3	Select "Quick registration" using quick registration script.
4	Hit back button.
5	Select "News."
6	Hit back button.
7	Select "prizes" button at top of page.
8	Select "Books."
9	Select "earn tokens" button at top of page.
10	Select "help" button at top of page.
11	Leave site.

Test methodology—In the test methodology section, you document the method that scales the number of users and the devices that collect data. You also document the types of data that need to be collected (that is, performance data for the control client, performance metrics for the servers, and performance metrics for the virtual users).

Test results and conclusions—The test results section of a typical user load testing report includes the following:

- **Overall results and conclusions**—You begin by presenting the overall results and conclusions based on your analysis. For example, does the tested e-business site handle the proposed peak usage with acceptable performance level? The rest of this test results section presents the actual data that led to the above results and conclusions.

- **Web server results**—Provides a CPU utilization chart, number of connections per second chart, and memory utilization chart.

- **Application server results**—Provides several request charts.

- **Control client results**—Provides a control client performance metrics table (that is, duration, response time, total bytes transferred, time you did the capture). You have one table for each load test scenario.

  The test conclusions should also be based on log file data collected from the web, application, and database servers. Figure 3-39 shows important metrics for the control client behavior during Scenario 4 testing (4750 connections). The reference client was a Windows 95 workstation running one Quick Registration script at the times below in the Time Captured column. For each test run, the data was captured with a Network Associates sniffer.

- **Database results**—Provides a database CPU utilization chart and database interrupts per second chart.

Figure 3-36 through 3-41 contain charts of example test results.

Figure 3-36   *CPU Utilization Chart*

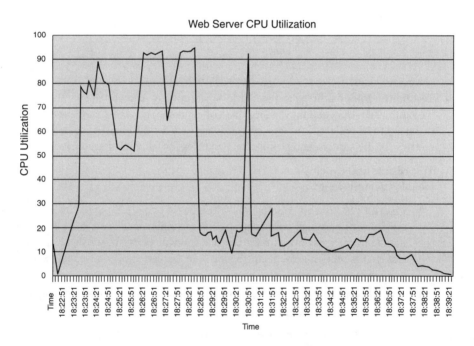

Figure 3-37 *Number of Connections per Second Chart*

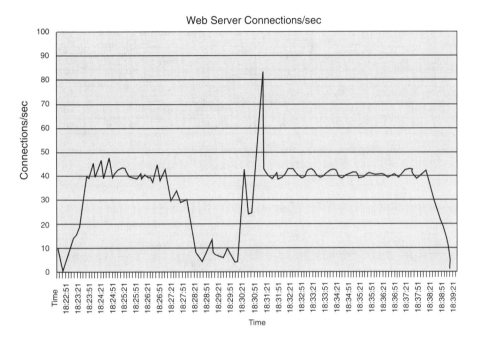

Figure 3-38 *Number of Requests Chart*

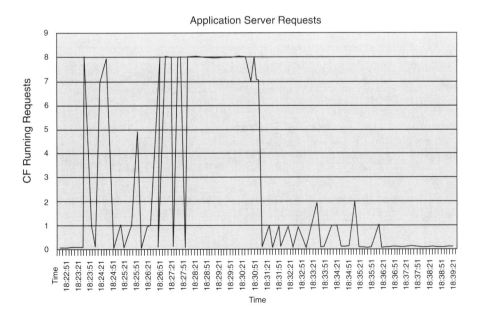

Figure 3-39 *Control Client Metrics Table*

Client Test Run	Duration (secs)	Frames	Bytes	Avg. Frame	App Turns	Time Captured
Stress 4_1	1.19	49	31668	646.29	7	18: 26: 18
Stress 4_2	24.98	53	31912	602.11	7	18: 27: 34
Stress 4_3_bad	0.01	5	1251	250.2	2	18: 30: 18
Stress 4_4	0.53	47	31,549	671.26	7	18: 31: 04
Stress 4_5	0.69	48	31,671	659.81	7	18: 32: 28
Stress 4_6	0.67	47	31,613	672.62	7	18: 33: 48

Figure 3-40 *Database CPU Utilization Chart*

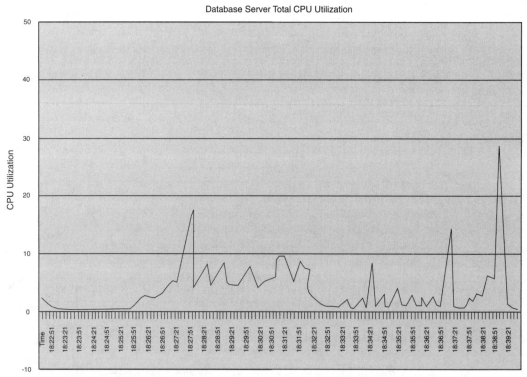

Figure 3-41 *Database Interrupts per Second Chart*

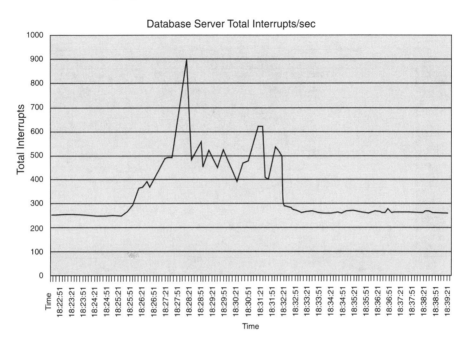

Following is a review of the charts shown from the Load Testing section:

- **Throughput Chart**—Displays the amount of throughput (in bytes) on the web server during the load test. This graph helps you evaluate the amount of load, in terms of server throughput, that virtual users generate.

- **Hits per Second Chart**—Shows the number of hits made on the web server by virtual users during each second of the load test. This graph helps you evaluate the amount of load, in terms of the number of hits, that virtual users generate.

- **Transaction Summary Chart**—Presents the number of transactions that passed or failed. Obviously, it is the goal of every transaction to pass. The transaction summary quickly tells you if the architecture is scalable and working properly.

- **Transaction Response Time Average Chart**—The transaction response time average chart displays the average time taken to perform transactions during each second of the load test. This graph helps you determine whether the performance of the server is within acceptable minimum and maximum transaction performance time ranges defined for your system.

Figure 3-42 through 3-45 contain additional charts of example test results.

Figure 3-42 *Throughput Chart*

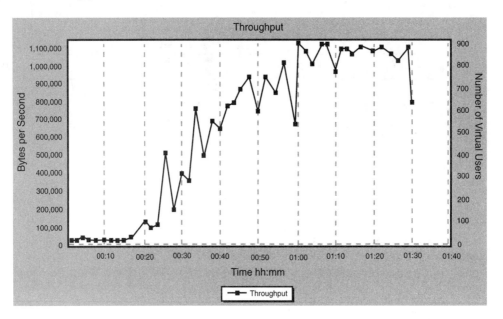

Figure 3-43 *Hits per Second Chart*

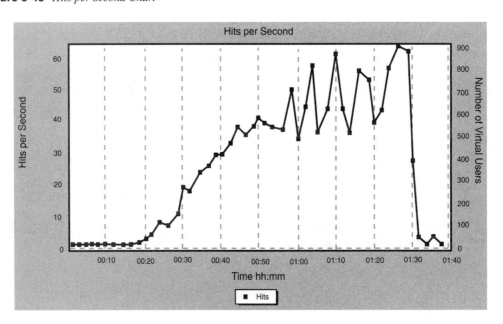

Figure 3-44 *Transaction Summary Chart*

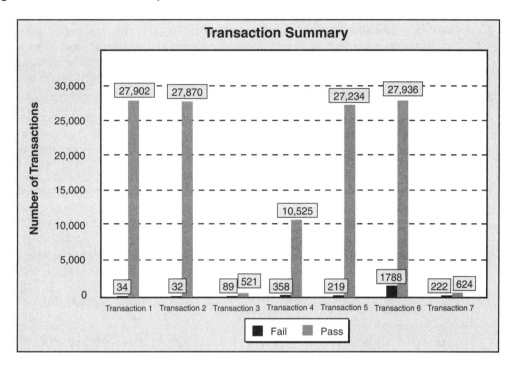

Figure 3-45 *Transaction Response Time Average Chart*

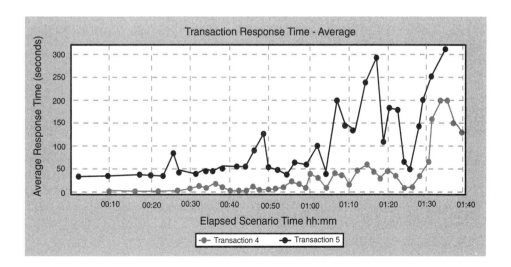

Availability Testing

Availability testing is a type of testing where the components of an Internet business solution (applications, networks, and servers) are deliberately failed in several ways to verify if appropriate techniques exist for the application and system to recover from failure and sustain existing connections. For example, network elements can be failed so that the path of data has to change to an available one. This action is taken to verify that the designed level of availability is achieved.

The purpose of availability testing is to ensure that unplanned downtime does not exceed the designed availability requirement for the entire system. For example, you can test to see if your standby database takes over in a timely manner (that is seconds or minutes based on the design) if you lose your primary database.

The explosive growth of Internet business, and the proliferation of new interface processor-based enterprise applications, is creating a heightened requirement for continuous availability of mission-critical data servers. Enterprises are implementing Internet business strategies to increase revenue, raise customer satisfaction levels, streamline their supply chain management, and optimize their workforce. Consequently, enterprises are experiencing ever-increasing demands from customers, suppliers, and employees for access to applications and data. This access requires scalable solutions with minimum system downtime. Therefore, availability testing is critical for any Internet business application implementation.

The availability testing allows you to verify that the solution meets the availability goal (An availability goal is commonly used as a percentage of uptime—99.5 percent.) Without availability testing, you do not know for sure if the designed solution meets the availability requirements.

Items that need to be measured in availability testing are the same as in user load testing. This sameness is because you are still applying a load and measuring the impact. The difference is that while the load is being applied, components of the system are being failed to look for designed redundancy that is not operating according to the availability goal.

From a practical point of view, availability testing involves breaking a stable system and observing what happens. For example, disturb the network by powering down a router, and monitor how the change is handled by the network and system: how traffic is rerouted, the speed of convergence, and whether any user connectivity is lost.

The purpose of availability testing is to ensure that unplanned downtime is within the limits of the availability goal (for example, 99.9 percent or less than 9 hours per year). Without this testing, it is unknown if all components will recover after failure in a way that will meet the availability goal (that is, the time it takes to switch to a new database server). Design and implementation are part of the situation, but without testing, you won't know if something might fail until a failure happens. The level of confidence in achieving an availability goal is much higher with good testing.

The process of conducting availability testing shown in Figure 3-46 includes the following four steps.

Figure 3-46 *Availability Testing Steps*

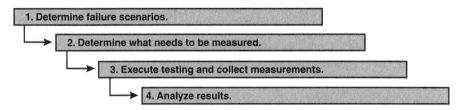

Steps two through four are exactly the same for user load testing as they are for availability testing. The difference between the two is that if redundancy has been designed into the system, you are forcing that redundant path or system to become active and then measuring again the same metrics as in user load testing (virtual user pass or fail and transaction times, control client performance, and server performance metrics). Also, for availability testing, it is important to keep track of the time that it takes for the system to become stable again after a disruption.

High availability is the continuous operation and access of computing systems and applications. For an application to be available, all components, including power, web servers, application servers, database servers, storage devices, and the end-to-end network, must provide continuous service.

Availability is a designed-in-product or solution attribute. Any attempt to add availability to a product after it is released or a solution after it is implemented can prove to be extremely difficult or impossible, especially for the type of high-availability levels that most businesses now need and expect. Therefore, to ensure high availability, the first step in any project is to clearly define an availability objective (for example, 99.9 percent or less than 9 hours unplanned downtime per year) based on service provider expectations and market needs.

After your client and you define and agree on the availability objectives, you need to design a high-availability solution. Designing a cost-effective network and system that supports high-availability objectives requires the right mix of technologies (including device-level fault tolerance and network and system-level redundancy) and complimentary operational procedures.

In many cases, successful implementation of a high-availability network and systems includes a balanced combination of the following:

- Definition and measurement of availability
- Fault management and diagnosis
- Device-level hardware reliability

- Operational best practices
- Network and system-level redundancy
- Network design and tuning
- Load balancing across redundant network devices
- Server fault tolerance

You need to test every aspect of the design during availability testing. Availability targets must include a clear definition for failure or outage. Because availability is typically observed from the end-user perspective, it deals mainly with service-affecting failures. Therefore, availability testing is essentially a series of simulations of various critical failures.

Following is a list of typical failure scenarios for an Internet business system:

- System component failure (web servers, application servers, database servers)
- Network component failure (routers, switches, load balancing devices, caching devices)
- Network connectivity failure (LAN cabling, dedicated WAN connections, Internet service provider (ISP) connections, Virtual Private Network (VPN) connections).

Examples of system components failure include the following:

- Web server host (power, hardware, or operating system failure)
- Web server software (software or data file access failure)
- Application server host (power, hardware, or operating system failure)
- Application server software (software or data file access failure)
- Primary database host (power, hardware, or operating system failure, cluster node interconnect hardware loss, and so on)
- Primary database software (database or data file access failure)

Examples of network components failure include the following:

- Network router (configuration, hardware, or power failure)
- Network switch (configuration, hardware, or power failure)
- Load balancing device (configuration, hardware, or power failure)
- Firewall device (configuration, hardware, or power failure)
- Caching device (configuration, hardware, or power failure)

Examples of network connectivity failure include the following:

- LAN cabling (connectivity failure [cut, short, open, and so on])
- Dedicated WAN connectivity (circuit down or high level of errors)
- ISP connectivity (ISP circuit down or high level of errors)
- VPN connectivity (VPN connection down or high level of errors)

Essentially, you are collecting data to find answers to the following three questions:

- Does the redundant device take over for the failed one, or is there a redundant path for data transfer?
- How long does it take for the new device or path to become operational?
- After the system is in a stable condition again after recovery from a failure, does the performance in terms of response time for user transactions still meet SLA goals?

Metrics that need to be measured are exactly the same as in user load testing.

The availability testing is built upon user load testing. You start your availability testing at a user load level that is the peak usage (for example, 5000 users). Such usage is determined during user load testing.

After you apply the peak usage load and have it at a stable condition, you fail a component (either network components, system components, or network connectivity) based on your test plan and see what happens while the peak number of virtual users are running. Essentially, you are changing the configuration of the entire system to see what happens after that.

NOTE   Internet business systems are complex, containing different browser types, web server components, application server components, database server components, and a complex network infrastructure. Failure in any one component can cause the application to fail. Therefore, you need to test every single point of failure that might take the system down and that redundancy has been designed for. Based on cost concerns, not all components in the system can be designed to be available under failure conditions. These components are single-points of failure and must be documented as high-risk components.

Data that needs to be measured in availability testing is the same as in user load testing. This sameness is because you are still applying a load and measuring the impact. The same tools that you use in user load testing are used in availability testing to collect data:

- Automated load testing tools emulate load and collect measurement (for example, fail and pass rate, response time, and so on) on virtual users.
- Sniffer or traffic analyzers collect performance data (for example, response time) for the control clients.
- Other tools collect server usage information (for example, CPU use, memory use, idle time, and so on).

When analyzing availability testing results, you are looking for answers to the following three questions:

- Does the redundant device take over for the failed one or is there a redundant path for data transfer?

- How long does it take for the new device or path to become operational?
- After the system is again in a stable condition after recovery from a failure, does the performance in terms of response time for user transactions still meet SLA goals?

Documenting Availability Testing Results

A testing report is usually created at the end of availability testing. It typically includes the following components:

- Test objectives
- Test environment
- Test scenarios
- Test methodology
- Test results and conclusions

NOTE   An availability testing report is similar to a user load testing report. You will see that the structure is exactly the same but the content within the test report is different.

Test objectives—An example of an availability testing objective might be to verify that an Internet business solution meets its availability goal (99.9 percent uptime, for example).

Test environment—Typically, a diagram of the test environment must be presented. Descriptions of the components of the environment and their configurations must also be presented.

Test scenarios—Includes the numbers of test scenarios (number of availability testing) and a short description for each test scenario (failure scenario) that you identified as critical. Besides descriptions, you might need to document all failure scenarios by using diagrams.

Test methodology—Documents the devices that collect data and the types of data that need to be collected (performance data for the control client, performance metrics for the servers, and performance metrics for the virtual users). You also document under what load condition you conducted the test.

Test results and conclusions—Includes the following:

- **Goal met**—Was the availability goal for this solution met? If the answer is yes, data is still presented and weak areas are pointed out for improvement. If the answer is no, the report documents why not and what needs to be fixed prior to retesting.

- **Overall conclusions**—Present the overall conclusions based on your analysis. You need to focus your conclusions on the test objectives, and present answers to the following key questions:
  - Does the redundant device take over for the failed one or is there a redundant path for data transfer?
  - How long does it take for the new device or path to become operational?
  - After it switches to the alternate device or path and is in stable condition, does the performance in terms of response time for user transactions meet the SLA goals?

An example conclusion of availability testing would be that the time it took for the system to recover in an automatic way did not meet the SLA goals under failure Scenario 3.

The rest of this test results section presents the actual data that led to these results and conclusions, including the following:

- Web Server Results
  - CPU utilization chart
  - Number of connections per second chart
  - Memory utilization chart
- Application Server Results
  - Number of requests chart
- Control Client Results
  - Control client performance metrics table (duration, response time, total bytes transferred, time you did the capture). You have one table for each load test scenario.
- Database Results
  - Database CPU utilization chart
  - Database interrupts per second chart

NOTE   As you might notice, the test results section includes the same set of charts as in user load testing because the kind of data you collect in availability testing is the same as in user load testing. The only difference is that you are focusing on different issues or objectives and forming different conclusions.

Implementation Phase

The implementation phase of the application development lifecycle consists of the following activities:

- Install the application.
- Receive application acceptance.
- Deliver equipment and systems documentation.
- Deliver operations and maintenance manuals.
- Provide operator and maintenance training.

The formal acceptance procedures used during the implementation phase can include four elements:

- Requirements-driven demonstration to show that the application meets requirements
- Documentation and manuals providing the application performance criteria
- Correction of performance not meeting criteria
- Formal written customer acceptance

The purpose of the implementation phase of the application development lifecycle is to specify, coordinate, and perform activities for delivering, installing, and getting acceptance of the application.

The implementation phase team considers the following early planning topics:

- **Support preparation**—Personnel, environmental preparation, equipment, and materials needed during installation of the application system
- **Delivery and installation planning**—Both the means of getting the physical requirements of the application system to the customer site and the method of assembling the application system at the customer site
- **Acceptance operator training**—Provision for application operator training both for the operators on the implementation team and for any participating customer personnel
- **Deliverable items list**—A checklist of the items required by the contract to give the customer when delivering the application
- **Implementation**—The implementation plan, which directs the implementation team activity and coordinates the various interrelated activities

Implementing complex applications, which are software additions to existing computer systems, require several distinct categories of manuals:

- **System manual**—Provides a specification of the system by programs, data files, equipment, clerical procedure, computer operation procedure, and so on.

- **Program manual**—Contains the detailed program specification of all programs used within the application system.

- **Data manual**—Documents all computer data captured, processed, or produced by the system.

- **Application operation manual**—Provides relevant information to the application operation staff.

- **Application user manual**—Provides relevant information to the system user; intended users are the staff of the user department.

- **Computer operating procedures manual**—Provides information and operating instructions related to the operating of the computer control system; intended users are the operating staff of the computer operation department.

To aid in the discussion of this important phase, the discussion is broken into the following sections:

- Inputs to the Implementation Phase
- Outputs from the Implementation Phase
- Issues of the Implementation Phase
- Responsibilities During the Implementation Phase
- Techniques and Tools for the Implementation Phase

Inputs to the Implementation Phase

The inputs to the implementation phase consist of those specifications and instructions that are required to install, test, and obtain customer acceptance of the application. These inputs, which include the combined development of the previous lifecycle phases, can be contained in the following manuals:

- Application system manual
- Software program manual
- Data manual
- Application operation manual
- Application user manual
- Test plan manual

The manuals portion of the input to the implementation phase of an application development lifecycle for a complex computer software application specifically includes the following:

- **System manual**—The major input for the preparation of the system manual is the system analysis and design report. This report is prepared during the system analysis and design phase, with necessary refinement and elaboration of details.

- **Program manual**—During the analysis and design phase, the program specification is prepared by the analyst and used by the programmer in program coding. The program specification also serves as a useful reference for future maintenance activities. The development team must tailor the program manual to fully describe any specific characteristics (for example, event handling and message passing) of the software development environment.

- **Data manual**—Describes the various forms of data, provides the source document involved in the system for data input purposes, and contains the data that is kept in the system for future processing. (These can be conventionally structured files or a database.)

- **Screen reports manual**—Contains all screens, reports, or documents output on printers, external media, or video display terminals.

- **Application operation manual**—Documents in detail the instructions of all the work performed by the computer operation staff in running the application system and also documents the work handled by the end user.

- **Application user manual**—Contains detailed instructions and an overall description of the procedures.

Outputs from the Implementation Phase

The outputs of the implementation phase provide the customer with items necessary to operate and maintain the application independently of the application provider after implementation. Although the customer retains the complete application and many of the items used during the implementation (for example, criteria manuals), this definition does not include items delivered from the development or test phase to the implementation phase for use during implementation.

With a complex software application, the following examples of outputs from the implementation phase to the customer show the volume and complexity of implementation phase output:

- System Manual
  - Equipment Configuration
  - Software Inventories
  - Security and Backup
  - Database Administration
  - System Constraints and Limitations
  - Function Point Analysis

- Program Manual
  - Program List
  - Program Specifications
- Data Manual
  - Source Document Description
  - Data File Description
  - Screen/Report Description
- Application Operation Manual
  - System Description
  - System Media Input and Output
  - System Output Reports
  - Operations Description
  - Run Job Specifications
  - Error Handling
- Application User Manual
  - System Summary
  - Equipment Configuration
  - Summary of Operation Procedures
  - Run Schedule
  - Computer Input Documents
  - Computer Output Documents
  - Terminal Operating Instructions
- Computer Operating Procedures Manual (or runbook)
  - Computer System Information
  - Computer System Operating – Normal
  - Computer System Operating – Abnormal
  - Computer System Operating – Restart
  - Data Backup Tape Handling
  - Operation Housekeeping Jobs
- Disaster Recovery Manual
  - Restart of System Programming
  - Recovery of In-Process Files
  - Restoration from Backup Files

Issues of the Implementation Phase

An extremely important issue for the implementation phase personnel is two-fold responsibility. The implementation team must conclude their company business by completing the application process. At the same time, they must satisfy the customer by ensuring that the application performs to specification.

To prevent misunderstanding of what the customer expects from the application and to ensure that the customer does not require more than originally contracted (sometimes referred to as *scope creep*), the following actions must be taken:

- High-level policies and standards must be identified in the development of the application throughout the project.
- Implementation plans must list standards that are applicable to the quality assurance and management of the application, including any engineering and technical standards.
- Implementation plans must also include a list of standards that are specifically related to the use of customer support environments with respect to the management, development, and quality assurance of the application.

The following additional topics that relate to the implementation process must be addressed:

- Sites and methods for installation
- Installation support
- Conversion of existing data to a new format, if applicable
- Acceptance process
- Final approving organization
- Provisions for training the implementation phase users and operators
- Change of management
- Any special requirements, such as safety and security

Responsibilities During the Implementation Phase

The implementation phase is the phase of the lifecycle model that covers the transition from the retirement of the old application and the activation of the new application or version. The CISS helps to manage this process and, thereby, allows for a smooth transition. The CISS's efforts enable the systems to be brought back to a known state in case of unforeseen problems.

The following are responsibilities that a CISS might have in the implementation phase:

- Ensure that comprehensive implementation planning is done prior to implementation.

- Verify that appropriate parties receive their required deliverables as specified in the design solution.

- Ensure that training environments are in place for users and support personnel.

The CISS is an active participant in the implementation planning process. This task includes working with the project manager to help create a plan that includes a list of tasks that are required to complete the implementation phase.

During the implementation phase, the CISS might need to ensure that comprehensive implementation planning is done prior to implementation by performing the following tasks:

- Verify that impact has been considered for operational environment considerations. Operational environment considerations are issues relating to the normal operating environment of the user domain. This includes normal application downtimes, user group characteristics, user traffic patterns, and time zone issues. The CISS can help identify these issues that can affect implementation schedules.

- Ensure that a notification plan is in place for downtimes, expected feature changes, and so on. Having a notification plan in place is important to make sure that all users are aware of scheduled maintenance and new releases. This plan is an existing plan that operations or support personnel use to make downtime notifications. Typically, this is an e-mail list of primary user groups. In the case of a true Internet application, this can be a web page that alerts the users that the system is temporarily unavailable.

  The CISS assists in the development and maintenance of channels of communication and can also ensure that processes are in place to help keep the required resources informed. All interested parties, including users and support members, are aware of the expected unavailability of the system and when new features will be activated. A large amount of coordination and communication is needed for an Internet business application to be successfully implemented.

- Confirm that operational and support resources are available. Additional resources need to be scheduled from operational and support areas. The success of an Internet business application implementation is usually dependent on having properly trained operational and support resources established. A CISS must help ensure that these resources are established at the right time. Additional staff might be needed in operations to handle the implementation tasks. Additional support staff might also be needed to handle the increase in queries about downtimes and new functionality.

- Ensure that well-defined migration procedures from the old to the new are in place. The CISS is responsible for making sure that migration procedures have been drafted so that moving to a new application or version of an application goes smoothly. It is tempting to think that a migration plan is not necessary, or that details of the migration might take more time to document than execute. But a well-defined migration procedure invariably results in a more controlled environment and higher quality results.

- Verify that the new solution is in place and functioning. Checking to see if the new application is in place is a simple quality check in the implementation process. It verifies that the correct version of the application has been installed and that it is in working order. The CISS can document how and what to perform during the check. This is important because it verifies that the installation is complete. If the test fails, the back-out plan must be followed. This task is performed as a final check only. It is not intended as a user acceptance test but as a check to verify complete installation.

- Ensure that a back-out or contingency plan is in place. The CISS must assist in determining contingency actions that might be needed during the implementation phase. This action includes planning how to handle problems that can occur during the implementation, providing input and recommendations on fallback positions, and planning how to recover from an unsuccessful implementation. Such actions ensure that the systems can return to their original (known) state in case of unforeseen problems with the new application. The back-out plan must be as detailed and comprehensive as the migration plan and must be tested and verified before any migration has begun.

Following are some examples of the deliverables that were specified in the design solution:

- **Installation procedures**—Detailed installation steps that the implementation team uses as a guide.

- **User documentation update**—Any functionality changes or additions to the application that are not described in previous user documentation.

- **Configuration data**—Information relating to the desired configuration of the new software. This gives the installation a set of required parameters to make all of the installations consistent.

- **Additional programs for migration**—Includes data conversion.

Verification that all the deliverables required to move into implementation are in place is critical to a successful implementation. Typically, there are several transitions occurring at this time within many groups. Complete and timely delivery of work products required by these groups aids in a smooth implementation.

In the implementation phase, the CISS might need to verify that appropriate parties receive their required deliverables, as specified in the design solution, by performing the following tasks:

- Ensure that the solution (code and configuration files) is packaged in a controlled (numeric) version environment. A historical trail of versions and the functionality therein will be tracked.

- Verify that there are distribution processes in place for deployment of the various types of coding and configuration files that you will want to deploy.

Having a packaged version and controlled releases provide for a uniform installation that is consistent and simplified. All associated files are released simultaneously and contained within the package. If necessary, producing releases in a packaged form allows for a smoother back-out of the new release.

The output of the development phase is a group of components that, when put together, constitute an application or system. Each component must be associated with other components to constitute a complete application or system. The following are various types of components:

- Installation scripts
- User documentation
- Configuration data
- Additional programs for migration: data conversion

The CISS ensures that a process is in place to control the packaging and tracking of components. This eases the installation (and back out, if necessary) processes by grouping the required application files together. Figure 3-47 depicts a sample version tree that starts with version 1.0 and includes versions developed through version 2.1.

Figure 3-47 *Sample Version Tree*

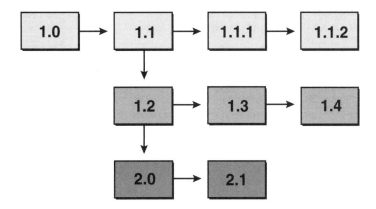

The CISS verifies that proper distribution methods are in place for the various components of the solution. These components can be of various types. The CISS assists in providing a process so that all components have a verifiable and repeatable distribution process. Some components might require their own installation procedures and might need to follow a specified order.

The training environment encompasses the training version of the production systems, the documentation regarding the production systems, and the system educational process.

Availability and accuracy of training environments can be critical in an Internet business application implementation. Training typically has to be scheduled in advance and requires an investment in time and resources. Having issues with the proper delivery of an application's training environment can cause a delay in implementation or an increase in costs. The CISS also verifies that training for support personnel has been accounted for.

During the implementation phase, the CISS might need to verify that training environments are in place and functional for the user environment and support personnel by performing the following tasks:

- Ensure that there is an approach in place to support the training environments.
- Ensure that support personnel (for example, help desk personnel) are adequately trained and prepared.
- Verify that the support desk has help scripts for the new solution.
- Verify that, prior to release, the users are trained on the new solution or the new functionality.

The CISS is involved in ensuring that the training environment reflects the released system. This also requires that the training environment have the same stability as the production environment. Without these two elements, training is inconsistent and possibly incomplete. Stability and valid data are two critical elements to having a successful training environment.

Training the support personnel on the new application (or version) is critical to the success of the implementation. This prevents misunderstanding by the user that the changed application is a broken application.

The CISS assists in helping to identify training requirements for systems resources for an Internet business application. After the needs have been identified, the CISS assists in the development of plans and strategies to address training requirements. Often, because of the pace of technology in today's environment, the area of training can be an opportunity to look for innovative methods to transfer knowledge.

User training is important to the ultimate success of the application. The training is not always completed before an application is released because of time constraints.

The CISS helps identify training requirements for users on the Internet business application. After the training requirements for users have been identified, the CISS helps develop the training strategies and plans.

Techniques and Tools for the Implementation Phase

Many implementation tools can ease the implementation process. No single tool replaces the process; however, these tools can aid in making implementations consistent and thorough.

A CISS might use a site survey checklist or automated software distribution tools during the implementation phase. Automated software distribution electronically distributes software to each workstation and server on the network. This distribution is done from a central location, which is more efficient because there is a lower likelihood of human error, and it eliminates the amount of time necessary to distribute the application.

There are many advantages of this method of software distribution:

- Delivers reliable downloads to remote users connecting with modems or communicating with slow connections
- Delivers and manages various types of applications across multiple operating system and hardware platforms
- Protects data during the transmission and verifies user identity and application authenticity
- Manages system resources to distribute applications in an efficient, coordinated manner

Maintenance Phase

The maintenance phase is the systematic provision of the effort to sustain the application and to support the operation of the application system that is installed in the customer environment during the implementation phase of the application development lifecycle. This effort involves the activities, procedures, products or services, and support environment requirements.

The maintenance phase begins to address activities just after acceptance of the application and before the sustained operation and support for the application. The maintenance phase can continue profitably for the provider and the customer as long as the customer's needs, the organization, or the environment requires change in the application.

The purpose of the maintenance phase of the application development lifecycle is to correct and modify the application to sustain its operational capabilities, and to upgrade its capacity to support the changing needs of the user.

The maintenance phase for a word processing software program starts immediately after distributors make their sale to businesses and private companies. The initial purpose might primarily include evaluation and correction of errors, bugs, and so on, in the software program that customers detect and report. As the market life of the software continues, the purpose of the maintenance phase can change to adding new features that customers demand or that competition offers. In the years that the software begins to decline into obsolescence, the maintenance phase can serve as the springboard to transition from supporting the older software to leveraging the software programming expertise into a new application development lifecycle.

To aid in the discussion of this phase, you'll find the subsequent discussion broken into the following sections:

- Inputs to the Maintenance Phase
- Outputs from the Maintenance Phase
- Issues of the Maintenance Phase
- Responsibilities During the Maintenance Phase
- Techniques and Tools for the Maintenance Phase

Inputs to the Maintenance Phase

The maintenance phase consists of two distinct input considerations:

- System maintenance organization
- System maintenance cycle

System maintenance organization—The maintenance organization is responsible for the overall management and quality control of the daily operation and maintenance activities of the application. Such a system maintenance organization monitors the operation and gathers, as inputs to the maintenance process, data required to analyze operational needs going beyond routine operation.

System maintenance cycle—Many of the inputs to the maintenance phase of the application development lifecycle must come from activity during the entire maintenance phase. The maintenance phase must follow a maintenance plan, which specifies the inputs it needs to perform maintenance. To get the required inputs, the maintenance team must closely monitor the following functions:

- System resources use, such as CPU, memory, data storage, and so on
- Network and transaction loading
- Printing and operator terminal requirements
- System security and control
- System response time

- System failure rate
- System downtime
- System tuning requirements

Outputs from the Maintenance Phase

The outputs of the maintenance phase do not include the completed performances within the maintenance phase, such as corrective maintenance and efficiency tuning. The maintenance phase does monitor operations to provide an output of codified data for record keeping and also for use in future similar applications. The maintenance does not redesign the system but does supply, as a major output, recommendations for change based on the continuing observation of application performance.

The following are some of the components of the change recommendation from the maintenance phase:

- **Change Request Form**—Formalization of the process and ensuring processing
- **Change Impact Analysis Report**—Evaluation of the effect of making or not making the change
- **Priority Rating of Change**—Gaining perspective of requirement and criticality of change
- **Periodic Control Report**—Monitoring the progress of the change disposition

Issues of the Maintenance Phase

The maintenance team needs to distinguish between the extremes of maintenance activity that can occur within the maintenance phase:

- Continuing attendance and monitoring until the formal maintenance phase ends and the maintenance team completely hands the application over to the customer
- Fire fighting that requires immediate corrective action of serious and unexpected problems

Continuous attendance and monitoring—After completing the attendance and monitoring portion of the maintenance phase, the maintenance team settles the application system into a regular operating pattern and then hands it over to the customer. The following are the major handover criteria:

- All documentation, programs, macros, security procedures, and so on conform to standards
- Documentation is complete and contents are consistent
- Production resources requirements are submitted to and agreed on by users
- System operates smoothly

Having satisfied the above criteria, the following documents must also be available for handover checking:

- Project evaluation report is endorsed
- Maintenance plan is approved
- System documentation is complete
- System test plan, data, and results are available
- Program sources, macros, data files, and so on exist
- List of maintenance items and outstanding requirements are agreed upon among user, development team, and maintenance team

Fire fighting—In case of fire fighting maintenance, the changes require immediate implementation because normal maintenance might not prove feasible prior to implementing the changes. The maintenance team must have the delegated authority to approve such urgent maintenance. All such urgent maintenance within the maintenance phase must have a plan for response within a reasonable amount of time, if not addressed in SLAs.

Responsibilities During the Maintenance Phase

The maintenance phase of the software development lifecycle is the phase that includes support, problem or metrics gathering, and the preliminary steps to form the next version of the software. Most software spends the majority of its useful life in maintenance.

The CISS can be responsible for performing a variety of activities in the maintenance phase.

Monitoring system performance tasks—System performance directly impacts customer satisfaction. It is a visible characteristic of the application. Along with security and transaction accuracy, performance is a key factor in the maintenance of a relationship with the customer.

During the maintenance phase, the CISS might need to monitor system performance in accordance with an SLA by performing the following tasks:

- Ensure that systems are available.
- Verify that the systems perform within acceptable criteria.
- Ensure that systems are in compliance.

Systems must be monitored to ensure that they are not only in working order, but also that they are available to the end user. In the Internet environment, a system might include the following components:

- Database servers
- Application servers
- Firewalls
- Network connectivity

SLAs are in place with hardware and software vendors to bring in proper support to keep highly available systems online. The following are some examples of high availability practices:

- Active server clustering
- Server failovers
- Database replication
- Server redundancy

These practices are not fault tolerant systems, but they do produce high percentages of uptime.

The SLA for the system specifies the acceptable performance envelope. The performance envelope is the range of performance, which is typically measured in user response times for typical activities, from the minimal acceptable levels to expected peak performance. The average performance is calculated from the performance envelope. The SLA dictates how much off of the average performance is allowed before steps must be taken to improve average performance.

These steps can include the following actions:

- Increased connectivity
- Increase in database servers
- Increase in application servers

As a general rule, average hardware use is allowed to reach 80 percent of the server's abilities, such as memory or CPU time, before being upgraded. This allows for unmeasured peaks, and it maximizes the use of current systems before purchasing new systems. Figure 3-48 shows a typical performance envelope with a U-shape.

Figure 3-48 *Typical U-Shaped Performance Chart*

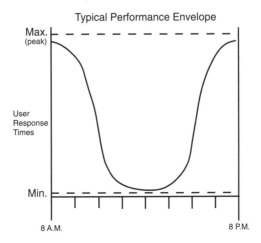

Production systems can be easily monitored for licensing compliance. Typically, there is a server license and some form of client license. These licenses vary for different vendors and implementation environments. Recent trends in major Internet software systems (databases, application servers, and so on) have been toward having a server license (based on the capacity of the server) with unlimited client licenses.

In any case, it is advantageous to know at any time the number of clients connected to the systems, the number of servers involved, and the relationship to purchased licenses.

Tracking hardware or software maintenance is less complex than determining client or server licenses, and there are usually annual or quarterly-based maintenance payments to the vendor. These payments are usually negotiated at the time of purchase of the software or hardware. Referring to the service contracts and payment history can highlight any discrepancies.

Ensure processes to support maintenance—Systems support is a major element of maintenance. Unsupported or under-supported applications are not standard. Customers expect supported systems to be available and stable. Applications that have poor backup and maintenance support do not last long in the ever-competitive market.

During the maintenance phase, the CISS might need to ensure that there are processes established to support the maintenance of systems in production by performing the following tasks:

- Validate backup and recovery procedures.
- Validate a disaster recovery plan (DRP) on a regular basis.
- Understand resource commitment to support systems in production.
- Proactively identify changes in current production environment and assess the impact that they will have on the systems in that environment.
- Perform preventative maintenance.

Resource commitment—To maintain proper working order, most high-availability systems require monitoring and operational and support resources. Automated monitoring packages are essential to supplement operational personnel.

Operational personnel work best performing varied and reactive tasks. Repetitive tasks, such as looking at a computer screen or checking for lights on a panel, can become tedious and increase the likelihood for mistakes to be made. Operational personnel are usually well suited for tasks such as managing backups and checking on monitoring programs.

Support personnel are required to communicate issues with the users, notify required parties, and to provide technical assistance for system problems when they occur. As the need arises, they can escalate a system problem (reported by operations) to key staff that are trained to resolve the situation, such as database administrators, application engineers, system administrators, and so on.

Change management—Change management is important to the maintenance phase because it stems the flow of ad hoc and frequent changes to the system. It does not prevent change; it helps to control change in such a way that it is reversible, planned, and historically documented. This provides an essential role in keeping the post-release system stable, yet adaptable, to problems encountered. There is a change management team that reviews each change to the production system (software, hardware, system environment) before it occurs. With a consensus, notifications are made and the released change occurs.

Any production system requires maintenance from time to time. Usually, it is to accommodate changes in the system but also to perform routine maintenance. The following are typical maintenance tasks:

- Updating indexes
- Defragmenting data
- Updating data stored on the application servers
- Updating service releases or patches
- Replacing malfunctioning hardware
- Purging or archiving old data

Preventative maintenance usually requires system downtime or, at the very least, must be performed while the system is in low use. Failover clusters can be used in situations where change must occur instantaneously.

Tracking and reporting process—Tracking problems is a crucial way to validate development and testing. A better tested and designed system has fewer problems in the field. Tracking these problems help a software group mature and correct any mistakes made in previous systems. Without problem tracking, customers can become frustrated with current problems, and they might go to the competition for future transactions.

During the maintenance phase, the CISS needs to ensure that there is a tracking and reporting process in place to communicate production issues by performing the following tasks:

- Ensure that problems are tracked and cataloged.
- Perform the review and analyze reports for trends.
- Implement corrective measures to address issues that are identified through trend analysis.

Reports that show the number and type of problems encountered with the system are created and reviewed on a regular basis. These reports are analyzed by support personnel to help prioritize the problems and to group them by similar solutions. This makes the problem resolution process more efficient.

The development teams also analyze these reports to get a good understanding of what sections of the software or application configuration need to be corrected. This also helps the development teams to dedicate proper resources to resolve these issues. An important step for the reporting process is to examine the trends of problems and to combine the problem data with system usage. You can identify significant correlations of problems and system usage by asking yourself the following questions:

- Is the number of problems increasing?
- Is the number of problems increasing with increased system use?
- Are there periods of time that more problems occur?
- Is there any statistical relationship between different sets of problems?
- On average, how many problems are experienced per transaction or user?
- Are average problems per transaction or user increasing?
- How quickly are problems resolved?
- Have any of the users experienced more than one problem?
- How many users are affected by each problem?

The ultimate goal of any support team is to resolve the problems. The development teams must be capable of making corrections to the software if all or most of the problems are to be fixed.

The most effective means of releasing fixed programs is to release multiple fixes at a single time. These group fixes or updates are commonplace in multi-user environments. Having periodic releases eases distribution problems and minimizes the number of releases to the users.

Problems that can be fixed that directly impact a larger number of users are given higher priority compared to low user count problems. Problems that have data integrity, security, or incorrect core functionality are given higher priority than problems that are cosmetic in nature.

Improvement of the existing application is important to the life of the application because it allows the application to have the ability to evolve and improve after its initial release.

Without this improvement, competitive products will continue to improve and eventually push the product out of favor with the users.

During the maintenance phase, the CISS might need to ensure that there is a continuous improvement process in place by performing the following tasks:

- Interact with end users.
- Identify potential targets of opportunity for enhancements.
- Examine how the application is used in the real world.

It is important to keep in touch with the end users during all phases of the development cycle, and maintenance is no exception. The CISS interacts with end users to get an overall perception of the system and ideas for improvement. The users can express their concerns about problems that persist with the system. There are several means by which the CISS can keep the lines of communication open.

Interacting with End Users

Support staff can use surveys with a small reward for participation (for example, a company logo item or a movie pass) to understand customer satisfaction and to spur feedback from the general population of users.

Another tool is to allow for direct customer feedback through e-mail or e-mail generation from a web page. Again, this is a direct feedback tool, but it is user-started and less standardized than a survey.

An additional form of discovery is to organize end-user groups. These groups can be virtual (company facilitated news groups on the web), in person (company facilitated meetings), or a combination of both. These groups are typically beneficial to the end users who have questions or who want information that they missed in training. If the company moderates the meetings, valuable feedback can be obtained by monitoring questions and responses. This is the most unstructured environment for feedback, but it can point to serious flaws or missing elements in the applications. These meetings also provide a forum to demonstrate new versions of applications and to gauge user reactions.

Despite the best efforts of the designers and engineers, user requirements change. These changes are either regulatory in nature or mandated by changing business needs. Because these requirements change, there is always an opportunity to target the differences between the requirements and the application. There must be a regular review of system and user requirements with application features to determine these changes. After a change in a requirement or a new requirement is discovered, the cost of the change is projected. If approved, the change is implemented. There has to be a continuous flow of new development for the application if the application is going to continue to be a valuable tool for the user. Programs that are static and not adaptive have a tendency to fall out of favor in a short period of time. Targeting the changes is a critical strategic role to keep the application in high demand.

Monitoring real-world use of the application is important to the long-term development of a product. This is because monitoring usage gives the development team an idea of how the application is being used, if there are areas that are not used, or if there are areas that are used far more than others. This gives the development team the opportunity to orient menus, screens, and tasks toward or away from that usage.

To effectively monitor the user, the CISS might need to perform one of the following:

- **In-depth observation**—In-depth observation is working beside the users as they use the system. This is labor-intensive, but it allows for interactive explanations of why certain tasks are performed.

- **Keystroke monitoring**—Keystroke monitoring is an automatic process by which a user's keystrokes are recorded and placed into a database. This database can perform an analysis of their actions, or it can re-create their actions. This option is difficult to manage, and it can be difficult to extract time-based information (how long it takes to perform tasks).

- **Video screen captures**—Video capturing is more efficient than in-depth observation, but it is hard to automate analysis (other than the capturing process) and it requires follow-up interviews.

Techniques and Tools for the Maintenance Phase

Many techniques and tools can help the development and support teams produce an effective maintenance program. Ultimately, use of a specific tool is not important, but they are all helpful in achieving the desired maintenance level.

System and network management tools include the following:

- Problem reporting and tracking tools
- Software license management tools
- Database management system (DBMS)
- Metrics database (faults database)
- Trend analysis

Systems management tools are used during the maintenance phase of the application to monitor the status and performance of hardware devices on the system. These devices can include routers, switches, servers, and any other device that is using Simple Network Management Protocol (SNMP) or Remote Monitoring (RMON). Larger monitoring systems typically have database and enterprise application extensions to allow for seamless monitoring of the network, servers, databases, and enterprise applications. Most commercial monitoring packages that are designed to monitor and analyze applications or databases have SNMP connectivity to the systems management tools.

NOTE	Cisco Network Management Products include the following:

- CiscoWorks2000

- Cisco Routed WAN Management Solution

- Cisco LAN Management Solution

- Cisco Service Management Solution

- Campus Bundle for AIX/HP-UX

- Cisco QoS Policy Manager

- Cisco User Registration Tool

- Cisco SwitchProbes

- CiscoWorks2000 Device Fault Manager

- CiscoWorks2000 Voice Manager

- CiscoWorks Blue

- CiscoWorks for Windows

- Cisco Netsys Service Level Management Suite

- Netsys Baseliner 4.0

- Netsys Connectivity

- Service Manager

- Netsys LAN Service Manager

- Netsys Performance Service Manager

During the maintenance phase, software defects can be identified by users and must be reported and tracked to ensure that they are resolved. Employing problem reporting and tracking tools is critical in the maintenance phase because they are typically one of the only means by which development teams get an accurate picture of how many and what type of bugs exist in the system after its release. This process also allows development teams to correct trends and larger problems that are not visible to the individual user or support personnel. At a minimum, these systems include and access the following types of information:

- Customer information, such as name and address

- Problem type, such as whether it was a question, an error that was encountered, or whether the system was unavailable

- What the symptoms were
- The resolution
- All support and development time spent on the problem

Software license management is the process of ensuring that software running on a particular PC or server is appropriately licensed for use on that machine. Tracking licenses of various applications manually can become a tedious and time-consuming task. Automated applications for software license management can reduce the time and resources spent on tracking licenses and automatically notify the appropriate personnel when there is a discrepancy. These tools are critical to keeping IT organizations within legal compliance of licensed software. Most license management tools can actively enforce compliance; as unlicensed users attempt to use a system, they can be blocked.

The function of the DBMS in the maintenance phase is to provide metrics such as database performance, available storage capacity, and memory use. Based on information gathered from the DBMS, a database administrator can determine when it is necessary to upgrade various components of the database and its associated hardware.

Software fault metrics need to be placed in an area that can be readily accessed. Having a relational database as a depository gives you several advantages. First, it allows for automatic information to be deposited. For example, the help tracking system can automatically place information about a version of software, severity, program area, and classification of a reported error. More information might be required to resolve the problem, but from a metrics point of view, keeping track of all problems such as this shows a lot of trending information.

Another advantage is the ability of the development teams to interpret the same data from a different perspective than the support team. Support software is oriented toward solving problems, and subsequently, the data behind the support system is not easy to extract to analyze metrics.

Support systems also have a tendency to be replaced or upgraded every few years, which leaves a need for a consistent historical storage for metrics information.

Trend analysis is defined as the process of looking at a business measure over a spectrum of time. Various types of metrics are often analyzed during the maintenance phase of an application:

- Processor use
- Memory use
- Disk swap file use
- Other performance related metrics

By examining trends in performance related metrics, it is possible to predict when it will be necessary to upgrade hardware devices on a system. Trend analysis can also help development teams design more efficient systems by showing real-world usage statistics of their products.

Basic Development Lifecycle Model

Every application development effort has a lifecycle, which is a process that includes all activities in the development cycle. This process is commonly called the Basic Lifecycle Model. As its main function, the Basic Lifecycle Model defines the order in which a project specifies, implements, tests, and performs its activities. The appropriate application lifecycle model can streamline a project and help ensure that each step moves the project closer to completion.

Successful business planners have always analyzed the need, examined the available solutions, and planned the implementation of an application to satisfy their business need. Previously, business demands changed slowly enough so that the business managers had sufficient time to try different approaches and almost evolve a plan as needs changed.

The lifecycle plan started as a tool to help decision makers respond in a business environment with greater competition. Such a plan provided a means for decision makers to acquire the right application to meet two goals: satisfy their business needs and avail themselves of opportunities before the competition. In time, formalized lifecycle models began to be used.

The first formalized lifecycle model was the Waterfall Model of software development. It was appropriately named for its cascading nature, with each step following the previous. This model came into existence because of repeated disorganized attempts at software development.

Following are some of the commonly used application lifecycle models:

- **Waterfall**—The Waterfall Model is a simplistic model, with each development step cascading from one step to the next.

- **Iterative**—The Iterative Model develops and implements the application by continually repeating the steps of the model with the goal of revising to produce the best outcome, which is based on insights gained during the process.

- **Spiral**—The Spiral Model is a form of the iterative model, which increases the scope of the project at each iteration after assessing the associated risk.

- **Prototype**—The Prototype Model initially develops a working but incomplete and inadequate version of the application. Subsequent steps, based on testing of the prototype, revise and enhance the application.

- **Cleanroom**—The Cleanroom Model is an adaptation of the other models in which the developers exercise extreme care to ensure that no errors or omissions occur in any step, thus producing a clean version.

- **RAD**—The RAD Model is a flexible model that attempts to expedite the application development and implementation process. It discourages any bureaucratic methodology or adherence to inflexible steps that might restrain the actions of the developer.

Further information on lifecycles is presented in the following sections:

- Continued Discussion of Lifecycle Models
- Input Differences Among the Lifecycle Models
- Key Outputs of the Lifecycle Models

Continued Discussion of Lifecycle Models

The following subsections provide more information on the stated topics:

- Waterfall Lifecycle Model
- Iterative Lifecycle Model
- Spiral Lifecycle Model
- Prototype Lifecycle Model
- Cleanroom Lifecycle Model
- RAD Lifecycle Model

Waterfall Lifecycle Model

The Waterfall Lifecycle Model (or Waterfall Model), also referred to as the classic lifecycle, performs essentially like the Basic Lifecycle Model. The Waterfall Model, however, requires sequential completion of the stages of the lifecycle model. That is, the next stage can begin only after completion of the previous stage. Because of this feature, the waterfall lifecycle model is described as the linear sequential model.

Application designers had no formal lifecycle models before the Waterfall Model. The Waterfall Model was derived from other engineering processes in 1970, and it contributed to the professional field of effort by providing a type of process that everyone can follow.

The Waterfall Model provides a simple process model that is widely used in conventional application development. Individuals use slight variations of the model, but it is essentially a one-way model without any feedback from the lower phases to earlier phases. This methodology assumes not only that the outcomes of a particular phase are correct and complete, but also that they will not be affected by insights gained later in the development process.

Regardless of what kind of system development lifecycle is used, the major goal of all organizations must be process improvement. The Waterfall Lifecycle Model improved the development process, thereby having a profound effect on productivity, creativity, profitability, and reliability. This improvement, in turn, had a positive effect on competitiveness.

The input requirements for the Waterfall Lifecycle Model are essentially the same as those of the Basic Lifecycle Model. The Waterfall Lifecycle Model is a simple system to process. Each phase must be completed before providing its outputs to subsequent phases because previous phases will not continue after the next phase begins.

The Waterfall Lifecycle Model generally requires an application development with the following characteristics:

- Simple in concept
- Easy to understand
- Effortless to apply
- Linear for definition of milestones
- Straightforward to manage

The discussion of the issues associated with the Waterfall Lifecycle Model points out its strengths and weaknesses, which stem from the lifecycle structure. The Waterfall Lifecycle Model has the following weaknesses:

- Does not work well with all individual projects
- Has problems with the lifecycle from an individual projects perspective
- Takes too long, needs many changes, requires high opportunity cost
- Has difficulty getting user participation
- Has difficulty determining user needs when nothing in the current environment resembles the new application
- Has empirical evidence suggesting high maintenance cost
- Is not robust
- Has no feedback loops
- Suffers the difficulty of needing the customer to state all the requirements in the initial requirements phase
- Cannot incorporate additional requirements realized at later stages of the project
- Requires delays in one stage of the project to result in delays in all the following stages

The Waterfall Lifecycle Model has the following strengths:

- **Visibility**—Because of the rigid structure and nature of the model to produce something deliverable during each phase of the lifecycle, the application has good visibility with respect to keeping track and managing the various tasks associated with the project.
- **Process order**—Provides a rigid structure that enforces a strict order of accomplishing phase objectives.

- **Focus**—Focuses on a single delivery point, accommodating the customer who wants the entire system delivered at once.

- **Structure**—Provides a more structured approach than a random attempt to develop an application.

Iterative Lifecycle Model

Business developed the Iterative Lifecycle Model as an alternative to the waterfall type of sequential lifecycle model. The Iterative Model accomplishes the following tasks:

- Accommodates changes in requirements and complexity with less disruption of the development process

- Produces evolving executable prototypes

- Adjusts plans continually in response to ongoing risk analysis

The Iterative Lifecycle Model incorporates the advantages of using executable prototypes from the more linear lifecycle models from which it evolved. With this model, the development process is planned, managed, and predicted. The model also involves the application user or customer throughout the entire development process.

Typical application development using the Iterative Lifecycle Model provides the following features:

- Continuously integrates inputs and lessons learned

- Produces frequent executable releases for formative assessment

- Assesses risks on each executable release

- Plans continued progress based on analysis results

- Effectively handles situations in which the user cannot know or cannot articulate the final product

It also measures progress in products, not documentation or engineering estimates.

The Iterative Lifecycle Model corrects the problems associated with the Waterfall Lifecycle Model. This model also facilitates the communication of requirements among users, designers, and developers.

Following are the typical benefits of the Iterative Lifecycle approach:

- Releases are a forcing function that drives the development team to closure at development iterations.

- Can incorporate solutions to problems, issues, and changes into future iterations rather than disrupting ongoing production.

- Project supporting elements, testers, writers, toolsmiths, contract managers, and quality assurance so that employees can better schedule their work.

The Iterative Lifecycle Model requires input for most of the same needs, products or services, organizational information, and environment information that all the other development projects require. The inputs described below assume an object-oriented approach, but iterative development applies equally to other approaches. Additionally, the Iterative Lifecycle Model requires a set of assumptions about the number of iterations that the development process can go through before releasing the application for use. Otherwise, the process can continue with a definitely declining rate of application improvement for each additional iteration.

During each iteration, the model requires continually updated inputs and additional input requirements that are discovered during the application design refinement process. In fact, the major feature of this method is that the steps are repeated several times until the project is completed. No work in any phase is completed until the process has ended; that is, no phase produces final documentation on its activity until the end result becomes satisfactory. At a higher level, the functional divisions where the iterative lifecycle might require continual inputs are listed here:

- Requirements Capture
  - Select or define the use cases to be implemented in this iteration.
  - Update the object model to reflect additional domain classes and associations discovered.
  - Develop a test plan for the iteration.
- Analyze and Design
  - Determine the classes to be developed or updated in this iteration.
  - Update the object model to reflect additional design classes and associations that are discovered.
  - Update the architecture document if needed.
  - Begin development of test procedures.
- Implementation
  - Automatically update system definitions from the design model.
  - Manually generate processes for operations.
  - Complete test procedures.
  - Conduct unit and integration tests.
- Test
  - Integrate and test the developed procedures with the rest of the system (previous releases).
  - Capture and review test results.

- — Evaluate test results relative to the evaluation criteria.
- — Conduct an iteration assessment.
- — Prepare the release description.
- Work allocation within an iteration
  - — Determine the work to be accomplished in an iteration by the requirements of (new) use cases to be implemented.
  - — Determine work to be accomplished in an iteration by the rework required.
  - — Prepare convenient work packages for developers.

Although a finished and refined application comprises the final output of the iterative application development lifecycle, each iteration of the lifecycle requires a distinct output prior to initiation of the next iteration. A plan that identifies the next iteration goal, processes, and evaluation criteria comprises that necessary output.

The following are factors that each iteration output plan must consider:

- Functionality in terms of prototype ability to accomplish the objective
- Performance in terms of the consistency of the prototype production
- Capacity as a measure of the amount of final product or service produced by the customer
- Quality measures in terms of how well the product or service conforms to the preset criteria
- External changes that have occurred during the current iteration
- Rework required for remaining iterations

Planning the increment of your lifecycle can be complex. Consequently, use the process architecture to help identify which groups need to be involved and to assess the impacts of the process on each lifecycle phase team.

The first iteration is usually the most difficult and requires that the entire development environment is in place. Planning for the first iteration includes the following considerations:

- Many tool integration issues, team-building issues, and staffing issues must be resolved.
- Teams new to an iterative approach are usually overly optimistic.
- Completion of the first iteration is delayed unless planners remain modest regarding the amount of development progress that can be achieved in the first iteration.

Spiral Lifecycle Model

The Spiral Lifecycle Model is an iterative lifecycle that repeats four steps: plan, design, review, and assess risk. Each iteration of the lifecycle builds on the progress of the previous iterations to expand the development until the last iteration completes all the project objectives. The Spiral Lifecycle Model adds to the iterative process the concept of expanding, in a controlled manner, the size of commitment to and potential investment in the developing application. The Spiral Lifecycle Model accommodates reuse, iteration, and independent evolution of existing systems. It also proves useful in a research project where all the requirements, options, and constraints are not known from the start. The model controls the commitment by doing a risk analysis at the end of each iteration of the lifecycle.

As a result of the risk analysis in each iteration, the model allows a decision as to what elements of the application to pursue and the extent to which to pursue them. Of course, the ultimate decision comes to finalize the development at the end of an iteration when the application meets requirements and further development does not justify further risk. In achieving its purposes, the Spiral Lifecycle Model acquires the negative side effect of not allowing rapid development of an application.

Figure 3-49 is an example of the Spiral Lifecycle Model.

Figure 3-49 *Spiral Lifecycle Model*

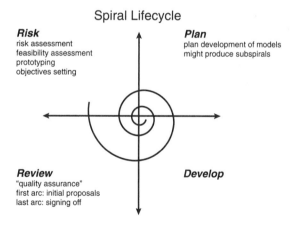

Prototype Lifecycle Model

The Prototype Lifecycle Model is an approach to development that quickly produces an easily modified and extensible model (representation, simulation, or demonstration) of the planned application. The development process then tests the prototype and modifies it to correct errors or to make it meet application requirements better. The prototype test and modification process continues until the application satisfies the project requirements. A project, however, must be large enough to justify the development costs of prototyping.

The Prototype Lifecycle Model makes understanding of the requirements easier, and clarifies many of the misunderstandings that developers have with each other and with the customer. The nature of the model also increases communication among developers and customers and allows the retention or discarding of the various versions of the prototype.

The Prototype Lifecycle Model provides additional development efficiency to the iterative method by limiting the iteration to only one phase of the lifecycle. By including consideration of all the major requirements of the application in the prototype, the development can move toward completion by testing and modifying the prototype iteratively until it meets requirements. The Prototype Lifecycle Model, by using a working model, allows the project decision makers to see an actual application at each step of the design and development. Therefore, when development concludes, the customer always has something useful.

Cleanroom Lifecycle Model

The Cleanroom Lifecycle Model is the process of completing and testing every activity in the lifecycle with such rigor and adherence to specification that no mistakes or inadequacies exist at the beginning of the next activity or phase of the lifecycle. Because the model tolerates no errors in design or procedures, the Cleanroom Lifecycle Model allows easy tracking because of the well-defined theory and process associated with the model. Although technically not a type of lifecycle in itself, where used, the Cleanroom process characterizes the lifecycle. The Cleanroom Lifecycle Model always produces a near perfect application that needs little maintenance. That is because of the thoroughness of activity in each phase. In achieving it's purposes, the Cleanroom Lifecycle Model acquires the negative side effect of requiring exhaustive documentation support and personnel from all related disciplines to ensure the desired degree of confidence in the activity results.

RAD Lifecycle Model

The RAD Lifecycle Model emphasizes rapid activity and accomplishment within each phase of the lifecycle to produce a minimally acceptable product within a short time. One of the main benefits of using the RAD model is the ability to seize a window of competitive opportunity with a quick product delivery. RAD is also a linear sequential model but differs from the Waterfall Model because this lifecycle intentionally compromises quality and completeness of the end product in favor of speed.

The RAD Lifecycle Model usually produces an application for less cost because of the enforced efficiency of the shortened period for design and development. Because of the lessened rigor during development, the application has higher maintenance costs and generally prohibits modularization of the application. This combination allows lower initial costs that are associated with acquiring an application and permits the owner of the application to pay the required extra maintenance with the revenue from a working application.

Input Differences Among the Lifecycle Models

The Waterfall Lifecycle Model does not repeat any phase. Input back to a previous step from a succeeding step of the Waterfall Lifecycle Model represents failure and requires an expensive restart.

In contrast, the structures of the iterative lifecycles, including the Iterative, Spiral, and Prototype, purposely use the output of the previous iteration as the major input to the next iteration.

In the Waterfall Lifecycle Model, the later in the lifecycle that a problem evolves and that a change becomes required, the more expensive the resolution becomes. With the iterative lifecycles, the structure tends to automatically take the change requirement as an input to the next iteration and handle it as business as usual.

The major differences of inputs to the iterative lifecycle and the inputs to other lifecycles exist with the Waterfall and RAD Lifecycle Models. Following are some of the differences:

- **System architecture**—The Waterfall and RAD Lifecycle Models define the system architecture during the activity of the lifecycle phases. However, the Iterative Lifecycle Model defines the system architecture as an early input. The Iterative Lifecycle Method then iteratively completes the details within that architecture.

- **Completion criteria**—The Iterative Lifecycle Model requires, as an input, completion criteria for each iteration cycle. The Waterfall and RAD Lifecycle Models only need functional completion criteria for each of the limited number of phases. In the case of the RAD, that inputted criteria can be compromised in favor of speed.

- **Budget**—With the Waterfall and RAD Lifecycle Models, the development budget comes as an input. The planners can even input the size of the budget for each phase. Because of the iterative method of approaching the application requirements, the amount of budget left can be reduced to determining whether additional iterations will take place.

The inputs required for the Prototype Lifecycle Model differ from the inputs to the other lifecycles:

- **All other lifecycles**—The Prototype Lifecycle Model requires a large fraction of the development budget up-front to develop the initial prototype. All other lifecycle models gradually use the budget either during successive iterations or during the later exclusively developmental activity. This input difference requires a higher degree of initial commitment to finish the project when using the Prototype Lifecycle Model.

- **Scope creep**—Particularly for the Waterfall, RAD, and Iterative Lifecycle Models, the customer inputs their requirements early, and the lifecycle process affects those specifications. With the Prototype Lifecycle Model, the customer frequently sees the iteratively improving prototype and enjoys the expanding satisfaction of their requirements. In this situation, the personnel developing the application must control the tendency of the customers to continue to input additional desires for the application with each iteration. (Of course, these additional desires can form the basis of additional application feature sales to newly educated customers.)

- **Requirements conflict**—The Prototype Lifecycle Model, by presenting an approximation of the final application, creates its own input requirements by revealing inadequate or conflicting requirements. The Waterfall and Spiral Lifecycle Models, in particular, might not discover these inadequacies or conflicts until late or at the end of the application development process.

In the rush to provide a working application, the RAD Lifecycle Model generates the following input considerations:

- **Criteria sacrifice**—Compromises some aspects of the development process, such as rigor in testing and documentation, to increase the speed of development and implementation of the application. This still represents a controlled compromise process in which the model has, as an input, the criteria that limits the sacrifice in quality and process.

- **Change request limit**—Must strictly limit change request inputs to achieve the application development time limit. Usually, the application developers must treat these change requests as inputs for postimplementation application modification efforts.

- **Multitalented developers**—Requires multitalented developers to apply all required development disciplines and expertise during the same short development time.

- **Current applications**—To save time by not starting anew, requires that its application developers make maximum use of current application component libraries.

Key Outputs of the Lifecycle Models

When the output of one phase becomes the input of a previous phase in the Waterfall Lifecycle Model, this represents the failure of the lifecycle to provide an efficient application development structure.

The uses of the outputs from the Prototype Lifecycle Model define the major differences of that lifecycle from the others:

- **Faulty or incomplete applications**—Right at the beginning, purposely and correctly outputs products that have faults or incomplete products that require later modification. This is in accordance with the final specification of the application.

- **Proof of concept**—Delivers an early proof of concept. This confirmation is lacking in other models until much closer to implementation.

- **Management assessment**—Helps management assess progress of the application development process through early and continuing visibility of the prototype.

- **Useful subproducts**—Through prototyping, produces useful deliverables even if the project runs out of money or time.

- **Funding**—Through the early prototypes, can provide enough visibility and proof of concept to attract funding for the developing application.

The outputs from the Cleanroom Lifecycle Model differ from the outputs from the other lifecycles in the following favorable ways:

- **Low error rate**—A low error rate that is tolerated when using the cleanroom concept within a lifecycle model tends to get reflected in the output of an error-free application.

- **Low maintenance**—Extreme dedication of the cleanroom process to producing an error-free application, which strictly conforms to the specification, results in the output of a low maintenance product.

In the rush to provide a working application, the RAD Lifecycle Model tolerates the following output characteristics, which the other application development lifecycle models were designed to avoid:

- **Faulty and incomplete application**—Delivered product can contain some faults because of compromises in quality of product development and adherence to specifications, which were made to get quick development.

- **Customer dissatisfaction**—Product meets the delivery schedule, which is the highest priority of the customer. Because of the rush to deliver a useful product, necessary compromises of quality and adherence to specifications require the delivery of an application that does not satisfy some of the less emphasized customer desires. The customer must know and agree to this at the beginning of the project.

- **Increased maintenance**—Controlled rush to deliver the application can force development effort reduction and cause an increased maintenance cost during application use.

- **Informal deliveries**—Formalities and ceremony that impress customers take time. The RAD Lifecycle Model implies that customers will accept informal deliveries.

- **Informal documentation**—One of the compromises with professionalism required by the accelerated development schedule of the RAD Lifecycle Model usually consists of accepting designer notes as initial documentation.

- **Reliability**—Application, which was rapidly developed using the RAD Lifecycle Model, might lack reliability. The goal, in such a competitive rush to market with the application, can be a sufficiently high success rate to provide initial market share and profitability.

Summary

The basic software development lifecycle model figures prominently in the design and development of Internet-based applications. Although lifecycle development models vary in particular ways, each with their own emphasis or assumptions, they all contain the basic phases introduced in the basic software development lifecycle. Familiarity with the basic model helps keep a project on track with the requirements for an application and provides direction when changes need to be incorporated along the way. This chapter presented the history and purpose of the six phases of the basic lifecycle model, and you should now be familiar with each of these phases. Once again, the phases are as follows:

- Business Modeling and Requirements Phase
- Analysis and Design Phase
- Development Phase
- Test Phase
- Implementation Phase
- Maintenance Phase

The role of the CISS professional, and the specific responsibilities, tools, and techniques used during each phase were covered in detail. Features of each phase, including the inputs, outputs, and issues to be considered when selecting the development methodology for a project have been outlined and the relevant differences explained. One of the major responsibilities of a CISS is helping customers plan and implement Internet business solutions. This responsibility sometimes entails acting as a technical lead on a project, but it can also entail a more facilitative role as a project manager.

The CISS professional, although having responsibilities during each phase, is clearly most concerned with managing the test phase of a project. Various types of testing, and the documentation required to guide decision making during the entire lifecycle of the project, are the principal contributions made by a CISS in building and delivering an optimal solution to a customer's needs.

Each project and customer, however, generally does not require a CISS to assume each and every activity and role presented in this chapter. Instead, as projects vary, so will the set of roles, skills, and techniques. In general, a CISS is responsible for troubleshooting, making recommendations based on research and requirements gathering, solving problems, and implementing project plans according to best practices and industry-accepted standards.

Some of the additional activities for a CISS on a project might include advising on hardware selection, security design, network design, and application architecture. And along with any advising on design issues such as these, the CISS is also required to validate various aspects of an application such as performance, security, and maintenance. The validation process involves the use of issue tracking software, and troubleshooting anything that might arise during the testing and validation of functional and nonfunctional requirements.

A short description of each of the basic software development lifecycle phases is useful to summarize the main points:

- **Business Modeling and Requirements Phase**—Business problems and opportunities for improvement and growth are defined. Information, both functional and nonfunctional, is gathered and modeled. System (nonfunctional) requirements, such as performance, availability, and security are identified and prioritized.

- **Analysis and Design Phase**—In this phase, information gathered in the business modeling and requirements phase is further analyzed. A rigorous model of data, process, and behavior that addresses the requirements of the business area is developed. The impacts of nonfunctional requirements on the information system infrastructure are examined. Then, conceptual solutions for problems and opportunities are defined. Alternative solutions are identified and compared to ensure that the best solution to the problem or opportunity that fits the enterprise vision is selected. For example, the project might go beyond just an Internet business solution (business to consumer) to include an enhanced intranet and an expansion of an extranet (business to business) solution. Finally, high-level physical architectures for applications, the network, and systems are then designed.

- **Development Phase**—In this phase, new applications are either built or selected, and packaged applications are customized. Systems and network infrastructures are modified, upgraded, or built. Documentation is written. Unit testing is performed to ensure that the individual software modules properly function. The development phase has three concentration points:
    - Functional—Solution needs to reliably perform its intended mission.
    - Creative—Solution must be the best within the constraints of the design document.
    - Technical—Solution needs appropriate technologies for its use.

- **Test Phase**—In this phase, the network components, system components, and new applications are integrated into a complete system. System testing (that is, user load testing, availability testing, security testing) is performed to discover and correct any nonconformities between the developed system and the business requirements. Documentation is validated during the appropriate testing. The final stage of this phase is the acceptance of the solution by the customer. During this phase, ensuring that the solution meets its nonfunctional requirements is the essential purpose. Although development and testing are two distinctive phases in the software development lifecycle model, they are generally performed iteratively in practice. Unit testing and integration testing are usually performed throughout the development phase. System testing and UAT (User Acceptance Testing) is performed in the test phase. At the end of the formal testing, if the requirements are not met, the next step is to return to the development phase to modify the code, network components, and system components.

- **Implementation Phase**—In this phase, the production environment is established, and the solution is installed and implemented. This activity includes the delivery of software, documentation, and manuals to be used during implementation and installation of the software applications. The purpose of this phase is to get your network and system up and running quickly and to get your application running successfully at an acceptable performance level. A migration process phase out is usually in place to ensure a smooth transition from old systems and applications to new systems and applications. Other supporting programs, such as training programs, are usually performed in parallel in this phase. Also, a plan that specifies the activities for delivering and installing the solution or software must be assembled and given to the organization. The plan usually includes the following:
  - Support preparation
  - Delivery and installation planning
  - User training

- **Maintenance Phase**—During this phase, the network, systems, and application are monitored to make sure that they are running efficiently and effectively. A continuous improvement plan is defined and implemented during this phase. This is a plan for supporting enhancements to the software and network, and it can be defined in terms of activities, methods, approach, controls, and support environment requirements. For example, corrections and modifications are made to the applications and systems to sustain their operational capabilities and to upgrade their capacity to support their users and customers. Solution changes range in scope from simple corrective action to major modifications to systems, networks, and applications. Most changes require a full lifecycle process.

Although the largest discussion in this chapter deals with the test phase, it should be noted that a definitive treatment of application testing is beyond the scope of this book. See Appendix A, "Recommended Further Reading," for works whose sole topic of discussion is software testing, practices, and procedures. The materials presented here, however, should go a long way toward preparing a CISS in the concepts, tools, and technologies of software testing.

Finally, after having taken the reader through the basic software development lifecycle, this chapter provides some additional material about the Waterfall and Iterative lifecycle models. This final section distinguishes these models on purpose, inputs, and outputs.

Review Questions

1 Which word best describes the quality that a lifecycle model adds to an application project?

   a. Cost

   b. Location

   c. Order

   d. Time

2 The application development lifecycle became a tool to help businesses respond to greater competition in which manner?

   a. More quickly

   b. More honestly

   c. More leisurely

   d. More publicly

3 Which grouping of application development lifecycle phases is in the order in which they normally occur?

   a. Analysis and design, development, test, implementation

   b. Implementation, maintenance, business modeling and requirements

   c. Business modeling and requirements, maintenance, development, implementation

   d. Development, implementation, maintenance, test

4 Which is the definition of the business modeling and requirements phase of the application development lifecycle?

   a. A demonstration of the application that allows the production specialists to determine the quality of the product or service resulting from use of the application

   b. A simulation of the application, without the expense of actual performance to the application, which allows the marketing personnel to determine the potential for revenue generation during the lifecycle of the application

   c. A requisition for contracting the application that allows the administration to determine the cost and schedule of implementation of that application

   d. A representation of the application that allows the decision makers and application specialists in the business to capture, organize, and visualize the web-based application as if it were functioning within their business

5 Which feature is not a purpose of the Application Development Lifecycle Model?

a. Providing the basis for future application development

b. Supplying the specifications to which the application will be built

c. Organizing the knowledge of the people conducting business

d. Discussing the impact the system would have on company personnel requirements

6 Which set of inputs is required for developing a business model to present to the potential user of an application?

a. Business need, business organization, company capabilities

b. Business need, business organization, equipment inventory

c. Business need, company capabilities, equipment inventory

d. Business organization, company capabilities, equipment inventory

7 Which set of desired outputs reflects the business modeling and requirements phase?

a. Customized procedures documentation, feasibility of the application, product or service

b. Customized procedures documentation, feasibility of the application, gain or loss potential

c. Customized procedures documentation, gain or loss potential, product or service

d. Feasibility of the application, gain or loss potential, product or service

8 Which phase of the application development lifecycle does the business modeling and requirements phase provide input?

a. Analysis and design

b. Development

c. Implementation

d. All phases

9 Which does the business modeling and requirements phase treat the model as?

a. Cost estimate

b. Dynamic specification

c. Equipment specification

d. Marketing tool

10 Which of the following is not a part of the typical application specification that results from the analysis and design phase?

   a. Quotation response request

   b. Software and database specifications

   c. Networking specifications

   d. Equipment specifications

11 Which accurately describes the analysis and design phase of the application development lifecycle?

   a. Produces a more detailed technical description of the system affecting and supporting the application

   b. Analyzes only the data received from the business modeling and requirements phase but restates it for technical clarity

   c. Attempts to reduce the requirements identified in the business modeling and requirements phase

   d. Modifies the intent of the business model from the business modeling and requirements phase

12 Which set of analysis and design phase inputs assist the analysis and design team in developing the application system design?

   a. Cost analyses, existing applications, and training requirements

   b. Cost analyses, existing applications, and validation test requirements

   c. Cost analyses, training requirements, and validation test requirements

   d. Existing applications, training requirements, and validation test requirements

13 Which phrase describes the output from the analysis and design phase of the application development lifecycle?

   a. Prototype of the application and all the technical specifications from which the developers can create the application

   b. Prototype of the application and basic technical information from which the developers can create the application

   c. System design and all the technical specifications from which the developers can create the application

   d. System design and basic technical information from which the developers can create the application

14 Which statement describes the level of design detail required during the analysis and design phase of the application development lifecycle?

a. The design specification should provide sufficient technical design detail that the developers will not need to develop any additional technical specification.

b. The design specification should provide sufficient technical design detail that the developer can develop the application but not so much that the developer cannot make necessary adjustments for the application environmental differences.

c. The design specification should provide general design information and wait until the development phase personnel request approval of their design.

d. The design specification should provide general design information and appropriately pass responsibility for finishing the design to the development engineers and the customer interface personnel.

15 What does the size and importance of the development phase do with an increase in size of the application?

a. Increases exponentially

b. Increases in proportion

c. Remains the same

d. Varies randomly

16 The purpose of the development phase is to translate the application system specification into an application implementation package that allows the application to work effectively _____ .

a. In the customer environment

b. In the development laboratory

c. On turnover to the implementation phase personnel

d. Under standard industry conditions

17 Which is the primary input to the development phase of the application development lifecycle?

a. Customer contact point

b. Equipment operating parameter

c. Local regulation

d. System specification

18 Besides the completed application design, the development phase output includes what set of additional pieces of data?

    a. Customer contracted cost, customer validation criteria

    b. Implementation schedule, customer contracted cost

    c. Implementation schedule, customer validation criteria

    d. Prototype operating parameters, customer validation criteria

19 What are the objectives of the analysis and design team and the implementation team, respectively?

    a. Designing the most technically efficient application; implementing to satisfy customer desire

    b. Designing to use company current equipment; implementing high reliability systems

    c. Designing to accommodate customer desire; providing the most technically efficient application

    d. Designing to use high profit margin systems; installing company current equipment

20 Which statement does not describe a benefit of testing and validation?

    a. Testing and validation ensures customer satisfaction.

    b. Testing and validation involves setting up the test scenarios and executing the test scenarios in a controlled manner.

    c. Testing and validation is a nice-to-have step that is dispensable for some Internet business solution projects.

    d. Testing and validation is the process of ensuring that the solution meets the business requirements.

21 Which does not represent a function of the test phase of the application development lifecycle?

    a. Corrects the application system specification

    b. Discovers any nonconformances to the application system specification

    c. Integrates the application components and operations

    d. Prepares for the formal acceptance of the application

22 Which is the purpose of the test phase of the application development lifecycle?

    a. Ensuring the adequacy of the test plan provided by the customer

    b. Preparing a formal final acceptance testing procedure

    c. Limiting the test size by including only the application system specification

    d. Proposing to the customer additional features for economical system performance enhancements

23 The test phase must acquire any inputs necessary to ensure that it can fully define _____ .

    a. Test objectives, test procedures, and test schedules

    b. Test appeal to customer, test objectives, and test schedules

    c. Test appeal to customer, test objectives, and test procedures

    d. Test appeal to customer, test procedures, and test schedules

24 What must be satisfied before an application implementation is complete in the test phase?

    a. Delivery milestones

    b. Cost restrictions

    c. Application requirements

    d. Service successes

25 Which group is in the correct order of function?

    a. Application system specification, work priority, initial customer intent

    b. Initial customer intent, work priority, application system specification

    c. Initial customer intent, application system specification, work priority

    d. Application system specification, initial customer intent, work priority

26 Which is the most important objective of testing an application prior to implementing it?

    a. Ensuring that each function performs to specification

    b. Obscuring weak portions of the application by emphasizing the robust portions

    c. Ensuring that test personnel use time-saving software to do evaluation

    d. Testing how the application works within the end-to-end business process that it supports

27 Which of the following is not a type of testing that is usually performed in the testing and validation phase?

   a. User load testing

   b. Availability testing

   c. Application performance testing

   d. Functional testing

   e. Security testing

28 The purpose of application performance testing is to ensure that the application meets the _____ .

   a. Functional requirements

   b. Functional requirements in a single-user environment

   c. Nonfunctional requirements

   d. Nonfunctional requirements in a single-user environment

29 Which item does not need to be measured in application performance testing?

   a. Process time

   b. Traffic size

   c. Throughput

   d. GUI friendliness

30 Security testing is the process of _____ .

   a. Applying assessment methodologies and tools that measure the cost of security components that are required to implement the designed security architecture across the entire Internet business infrastructure

   b. Validating that the implemented security components across the entire Internet business security infrastructure are manageable

   c. Applying assessment methodologies and tools across the entire security architecture to ensure that all security mechanisms are installed and configured to protect the information resources as designed and intended

   d. Validating that the assessment methodologies and tools used on the entire security architecture are reliable and capable of measuring the performance of each security component

31 Which statement does not define user load testing?

a. User load testing is a type of testing that ensures that the application and system perform as expected when accessed by the maximum number of authorized users in the production environment.

b. User load testing is essential to verify that the application and system do meet the service level agreement under excessive usage.

c. User load testing is a type of testing where you test the manageability of the application and system.

d. User load testing allows you to observe the application and system behavior under load conditions.

32 Which of the following is not a device on which you need to collect measurements during availability testing?

a. WAN simulator

b. Servers

c. Control clients

d. Network components

33 The output of an application assessment is a/an _____ .

a. Application architecture diagram of the application that will be deployed

b. Network architecture diagram of the network in which the application will be run

c. Set of typical transactions that are representative of the way that the application will be used by users

34 Which consideration is not needed when determining how an application will be deployed on a network during application assessment?

a. Locations of users and servers

b. Frequency with which users execute the application transactions

c. Number of users at each location

d. Number of servers at each location

35 Which component is not in a typical lab environment?

a. WAN simulator

b. Client

c. Production circuit

d. Server

e. Data collection device

36 Which type of data does not need to be collected in application performance testing?

   a. Throughput

   b. Network errors

   c. Menu options for the GUI

   d. Quantity of data

   e. Process time for each server and client

37 Which tool is not a data collection tool in application performance testing?

   a. Traffic analyzer

   b. Netsys

   c. Sniffer

   d. Test inputs

38 Which tool is an example of a performance analysis tool that analyzes metrics for collected data?

   a. RMON probe

   b. Optimal application expert

   c. Network modeling tool

   d. Prototype user

39 Which metric do you not need to obtain after the final results analysis in application performance testing?

   a. Transaction sizes for each tier of the transaction

   b. Processing time for each server and client component

   c. Average think time for a user

   d. Total transaction response time

40 Which step is the first in the recommended approach for security testing?

   a. Install and configure security components.

   b. Review security requirements.

   c. Set up testing lab environments.

   d. Generate test scenarios.

41   Which environment is not one of the three final target environments that are recommended in the best-practice security testing approach?

a. Production environment

b. Development environment

c. Lab environment

d. QA environment

42   Implementing and testing a security architecture in a lab environment can be a staging process for promoting it to a development, QA, or production environment. Which advantage best describes the staging process?

a. It provides an assurance that all three target environments have identical security components installed.

b. It provides an isolated and controlled lab environment where iterative security tests can be performed without interference from unexpected variables.

c. It provides ample time to ensure that testing occurs iteratively and accurately prior to promoting the security architecture.

d. It provides an identical replication of a real-world environment for the security testing to produce accurate and reliable results.

43   The verification process essentially requires that the functionality of security components be validated and corrected across the entire Internet business infrastructure. Which statement best describes why this verification process is essential?

a. It ensures that the security controls are successfully achieving the protection of the intended information resources.

b. It ensures that the operational framework is manageable and scalable.

c. It ensures that the systems, network, applications, and operations infrastructures are all assessed with a single security methodology.

d. It ensures that the application components are free of threats and vulnerabilities.

44   Which of the following is not a purpose of user load testing?

a. To verify that application functionality meets user requirements

b. To verify that performance in terms of response time for the user of the application meets SLA goals under load conditions

c. To determine whether current capability is sufficient for SLA goals

d. To measure the individual user experience as overall user load is increased on the system

45 There are four steps in a user load testing process:

Set up testing environments and select measurement tools.

Analyze results.

Determine user load testing scenarios.

Execute testing and collect measurement.

Which order of steps is correct?

a. A-B-C-D

b. A-D-B-C

c. C-A-D-B

d. A-C-D-B

46 Which of the following describes the two elements of a user load testing scenario?

a. Maximum number of users and transaction mix

b. Average number of users and transaction mix

c. Transaction mix and transaction distribution

d. Target population and concurrency rate

47 Which of the following describes a good practice to follow when testing?

a. Rapidly increase the load on the target system incrementally.

b. Have a fast ramp-up of users—1000+ at one time.

c. Always start with the peak number of users.

d. Ramp up slowly to the number of users to be tested.

48 Which of the following is not a component of the user load testing environment?

a. Control client

b. LoadRunner

c. Knowledgeable users

d. Virtual users

49 Which device collects data on virtual users?

a. Virtual users

b. LoadRunner

c. Control client

d. Traffic analyzer

50 In a load testing, you need to collect two types of data for virtual users. One is response time and the other one is _____ .

  a. CPU use

  b. Throughput

  c. Memory use

  d. Pass and fail of each transaction

51 When analyzing load testing results, you need to first look at the data collected to see if there is a problem. Which one of the following is not a type of data that you should examine at this point?

  a. User perception data

  b. Application performance data for control client (response time for client, server, network)

  c. Response time for each transaction executed by virtual users

  d. Pass and fail of each transaction

52 Which description is not appropriate for availability testing?

  a. Availability testing is to ensure that unplanned downtime is kept to a minimum.

  b. Availability testing is to ensure that security controls are operating correctly.

  c. Availability testing is to verify that application performance meets SLA goals under certain failure conditions.

  d. Availability testing involves breaking a stable system and observing what happens.

53 Which of the following is not a typical failure scenario?

  a. System components failure

  b. Network components failure

  c. User-error/process failure

  d. Network connectivity failure

54 Which of the following is not a network connectivity failure?

  a. Database server LAN connection failure

  b. Dedicated WAN circuit failure

  c. Database query failure

  d. ISP connection failure

55 Which of the following is not a measurement that you need to collect in availability testing?

   a. Application functionality

   b. Whether the redundant device is operating correctly

   c. The overall performance after the system is stable again

   d. The time for the switch-over to take place

56 Which of the following is not a task that you need to execute in availability testing?

   a. Fail components that have the most impact first.

   b. Test in a single-user environment.

   c. Apply the peak number of virtual users.

   d. None of the above.

57 A sniffer is generally used to collect data on _____ .

   a. Servers

   b. Routers

   c. The control client

   d. Virtual users

58 Which of the following is not a conclusion that you are trying to draw in an availability testing results analysis?

   a. Whether the response time meets the SLA goals under different load conditions

   b. Whether the speed of convergence is acceptable

   c. Whether any user connectivity is lost because of slow response

   d. Whether traffic is rerouted when a path fails

59 Which of the following is not a typical type of chart to be put in an application performance testing report?

   a. Transaction response time chart

   b. Total bytes per transaction chart

   c. Total number of users supported chart

   d. User perception report

60 Which of the following is not a conclusion that you are trying to draw in an application performance testing results analysis?

a. Whether any user connectivity is lost because of slow response

b. Whether the response time meets the SLA goals under different load conditions

c. Whether the speed of convergence is acceptable

d. Whether traffic is rerouted when a path fails

61 Which set of requirements is not a critical part of the documentation for security testing?

a. Security standard and functional security requirements for systems and network

b. Security policies and procedures, and user account administration

c. User perceptions toward security requirements

d. Functional security requirements for applications

62 Which chart is not a typical test results chart for user load testing?

a. The database server interrupts per second chart

b. User perception chart

c. The web server CPU utilization chart

d. The control client performance metrics table

63 Which of the following is not a typical test results chart for availability testing?

a. Database CPU utilization chart

b. Control client performance metrics table

c. Web server number of connections per second chart

d. Control client memory utilization chart

64 Which of the following is not a phase in the software development lifecycle?

a. Operation

b. Test

c. Analysis and design

d. Business modeling and requirements implementation

65 Which set of three components makes up the development phase?

a. Technical, functional, creative

b. Internet, extranet, intranet

c. Support preparation, market effectiveness, best practices

d. Master technology plan, operations strategy IT strategy, marketing strategy, business strategy enterprise's vision

66 Which of the following is not an activity that a CISS typically performs in an Internet business solution project?

a. Implementation plan

b. Security assessment

c. Application architecture design

d. Financial audit

67 Which of the following is not an activity that a CISS typically performs in an Internet business solution project?

a. Testing scenarios validation

b. Network and system management planning

c. Nonfunctional requirements identification

d. Router and switch configuration

e. Current network assessment

68 What statement is not a responsibility of a CISS in the business modeling and requirements phase?

a. Validate completion of the business modeling and requirements phase.

b. Lay out design and implementation details.

c. Keep the requirements gathering focused on business, functional, and information models.

d. Provide leadership on gathering system requirements.

69 Which of the following statements is not accurate?

a. A CISS does not participate in requirements gathering.

b. Functional requirements describe the core activities that the system must perform.

    c. Nonfunctional requirements describe constraints on the system such as availability or security.

    d. Business modeling and requirements is the first phase of the software development lifecycle.

70 Which statement does not describe the tasks involved in gathering systems requirements?

    a. Analyzing functional requirements data helps the CISS understand the specific functions, tasks, or behaviors that the system must support.

    b. Assessing current system, processes, people, and tools provides input to the planning process.

    c. Defining all nonfunctional requirements can be done without knowing the functional requirements.

    d. Defining system performance expectations can include elements such as security, availability, and space efficiency.

71 Which statement reflects the major tasks involved in validating completion of the business modeling and requirements phase?

    a. Walkthrough of SLA, identify reusable components, provide input on order of magnitude, define nonfunctional requirements

    b. Walkthrough of business models and requirements, identify potential areas of reusability, develop project plan, generate a system concept

    c. Walkthrough of business models and requirements, ensure SLA components are in place, identify reusable components, generate the system concept

    d. Ensure SLA components are in place, define system requirements, identify reusable components, develop project plan

72 Which of the following statements is not a major responsibility of the CISS during the analysis and design phase of the software development lifecycle?

    a. Analyze return on investment (ROI) data.

    b. Design a robust and maintainable system.

    c. Analyze business requirements in relation to system architecture.

    d. Design a system architecture and application solution that satisfies business requirements.

    e. Develop a project management plan.

73 Which task is not involved in analyzing business requirements in relation to system architecture?

a. Validate data flow diagrams, data dictionary, and data modeling against requirements.

b. Specify hardware and software requirements.

c. Assess the current system architecture relative to requirements.

d. Verify process modeling and process descriptions against requirements.

74 Which task is not one of the tasks involved in designing a robust and maintainable system?

a. Ensure that the disaster recovery and backup process is in place.

b. Provide input on prototyping and testing strategies.

c. Verify that security issues are addressed.

d. Ensure that the disaster recovery and backup process is in place.

e. Redefine nonfunctional requirements.

75 Which set of tasks comprises the responsibility of designing a system architecture and application solution that meets business requirements?

a. Verify that the design fulfills requirements, develop the application, specify the hardware and software needed, and generate the design document.

b. Lead architecture and application design, verify that the design fulfills requirements, specify the hardware and software needed, and generate the design document.

c. Verify that the design fulfills requirements, participate in prototyping, specify the hardware and software needed, and generate the design document.

d. Lead architecture and application design, specify the hardware and software, verify that the design meets requirements, and develop the application.

76 Which of the following is not a responsibility that a CISS can perform during the development phase?

a. Ensure that the design document is adhered to.

b. Confirm that change control processes exist.

c. Verify that all necessary resources exist to perform development.

d. Confirm that quality assurance testing has been performed.

e. Ensure that documentation is created.

77 Which task is not necessary for a CISS to perform when contributing to the physical integration of the architecture components defined in the design document?

a. Ensure that a change control process exists.

b. Determine hardware sizing.

c. Review design document strategies with the appropriate administrators and staff.

78 Which set of data does the CISS have to determine hardware sizing for?

a. Number of servers, amount of memory, number of users

b. Number of CPUs, number of servers, appropriate bandwidth

c. Number of users, appropriate bandwidth, number of servers

d. Amount of memory, number of users, number of CPUs

79 When reviewing the design document implementation strategies with the appropriate administrators and staff, the CISS might need to _____ .

a. Develop the preliminary maintenance schedule.

b. Determine the impact of the test phase.

c. Design a change control process.

d. Determine the implementation approach.

80 Which statement is not an activity included in Internet business project management during the development phase?

a. Learning to negotiate with customers and end users to achieve a balance between schedule and functionality

b. Using triage to focus on critical functionality and features

c. Learning about effective light methodologies

d. Contracting with outside vendors for support of application server pages

81 Which statement about a change control process is false?

a. The change control process tracks who has a document checked out.

b. After a document has been checked out, a change control process prohibits anyone else from checking out the same document until it has been returned.

c. The person who checks out a document updates the version number before returning the document.

d. The change control process saves the updated document after it has been returned.

82 Which data is the change control process not used to track changes in?

a. Updates to configuration files

b. Results of running test case scenarios

c. Modifications to the design document

d. Changes to code

83 Which statement is not valid about the tasks that a CISS performs while ensuring that the design document is being adhered to during the development phase?

a. Confirm that a process exists to do walkthroughs of deliverables.

b. Establish regular information exchange sessions.

c. Ensure that the code delivery is meeting scheduled deadlines.

d. Monitor and verify project progress against the design document.

84 Which task might a CISS not perform while confirming that each individual development group is performing adequate unit testing during the development phase?

a. Ensure that unit test activities are included in the project plan.

b. Confirm design specifications of test scenarios.

c. Review unit test scenarios and results.

d. None of the above.

85 A set of rules, processes, and procedures that are followed by all members of a project team during the development phase is a _____ .

a. Network change control process

b. Prototyping tool

c. Structured development methodology

d. None of the above

86 Which methodology is not a major structured development methodology?

a. Rapid application development

b. Change control process

c. Joint application development

d. Light methodologies

87 Which category of tools might a CISS not use during the development phase?

a. Application assessment tools

b. Documentation tools

c. Application development tools

d. None of the above

88 A new approach used by some organizations to create documentation is _____ .

a. Version tracking all the project team's documents

b. Audio taping conference calls

c. Video taping the project's technical meetings

d. None of the above

89 Which statement is not an application development tool?

a. Debugger

b. Scalability tool

c. Editor

d. Compiler

90 Which statement is not a responsibility that a CISS performs during the test phase?

a. Resolve testing issues by updating the design document.

b. Confirm that the test plan is sufficient to test the system requirements as specified in the design document.

c. Verify that testing is performed.

d. Ensure that test results are analyzed.

91 Which task is not necessary for a CISS to perform while confirming that the test plan is sufficient to test for the system requirements, as specified in the design document?

a. Verify that sufficient resources are available for the test environment.

b. Confirm that test cases are written and executed.

c. Discuss the various approaches/techniques that can validate an application.

d. Guarantee that the complete scope of the project is considered when developing the test plan.

e. Ensure that all requirements, as specified in the design document, have been identified.

92 When examining the scope of a project, be sure to consider _____ .

   a. Performance testing

   b. Staffing requirements

   c. Testing schedule

   d. Filtered power needs

93 Which resource is not necessary when verifying that sufficient resources are available for a test environment?

   a. Support services

   b. People requirements

   c. System and support software

   d. Help desk scripts

   e. Client and server hardware

94 When creating test cases, which consideration is not needed?

   a. Find those things that are wrong.

   b. Discard test cases after testing.

   c. Capture the maximum number of errors in the most cost effective way.

   d. Use walkthroughs of test cases and inspections of test data.

95 Which task is not necessary for a CISS to execute while verifying that testing is performed?

   a. Review the design document to identify functional and nonfunctional requirements.

   b. Verify that documentation is validated.

   c. Ensure that integration, system, and regression testing are performed.

   d. Confirm that an incident/problem reporting process is in place and being used.

96 The incident problem reporting process is important because it can _____ .

   a. Solve compilation errors

   b. Help identify problem issues and trends

   c. Create test scenarios to test discrepancies

   d. None of the above

97 Which statement does not apply to documentation?

a. User documentation should be verified while using the associated test scenarios.

b. Software program documentation is part of the configuration documentation.

c. Documentation of installation instructions should be validated during the building of the test environment.

d. Help desk scripts can include when and how issues should be escalated.

98 Which task is not necessary for a CISS to perform while ensuring that test results are analyzed?

a. Verify that incidents/problems are resolved.

b. Confirm that actual test results match expected results.

c. Identify documentation to include in the test.

d. None of the above.

99 Which task is not necessary for a CISS to perform while collaborating with acceptance testing?

a. Ensure that incidents/problems are resolved.

b. Guarantee that developers perform acceptance testing.

c. Verify that the acceptance test plan exists.

d. None of the above.

100 Which statement does not apply to acceptance testing criteria?

a. Developers establish the completion criteria.

b. The actual customer team that is running the developed system in the customer environment must perform hands-on testing and acceptance.

c. The actual software and hardware configuration must be tested.

d. The actual procedures and documentation that will exist and that will be required to meet the stated objectives of the system must be used in the test.

101 Which of the following might a customer receive during the implementation phase?

a. Marketing tools

b. Documentation

c. Design parameters

d. Business plan

102 What does the implementation team specify in the implementation phase?

   a. Implementation activities

   b. Application system specification

   c. Acceptance criteria

   d. Performance criteria

103 The inputs to the implementation phase consist of specifications and instructions that are required to perform what functions?

   a. Install, maintain, and test the application

   b. Install, obtain acceptance for, and maintain the application

   c. Install, obtain acceptance for, and test the application

   d. Maintain, obtain acceptance for, and test the application

104 The application provider gives the customer, as an output of the implementation phase of the applications development lifecycle, manuals and other items needed to operate and maintain the application _____ .

   a. Automatically

   b. Bimodally

   c. Experimentally

   d. Independently

105 The implementation phase links to the development phase to provide _____ .

   a. Implementation schedule changes

   b. Potential application additions

   c. Recommendations for change

   d. Reports of implementation progress

106 Which is an important responsibility of implementation phase personnel?

   a. Customizing the application to accommodate customer changes

   b. Completing the application implementation process with good business advantage

   c. Concluding their own company business as quickly as possible

   d. Satisfying all the expressed customer desires

107 Which task is not necessary for the CISS to ensure is in place during the implementation phase?

    a. Secure training environments for support personnel.

    b. Secure a comprehensive implementation plan.

    c. Secure a comprehensive requirements analysis.

    d. Secure training environments for users.

108 Which item does a CISS not need to verify is in place in a comprehensive implementation plan?

    a. Notification plan

    b. Development process

    c. Contingency plan

    d. Migration process

    e. Installation procedures

109 Which statement associated with verifying that the appropriate parties receive their required deliverables is true?

    a. All solution components have identical installation procedures.

    b. Solution components never need to follow a specified order for distribution.

    c. Verification that all the deliverables required to move into implementation is critical to a successful implementation.

    d. A tracking process for the solution versions can ease the installation process by distributing the required solution files to separate locations.

110 Which statement is false?

    a. A CISS must assist in developing plans and strategies to address training requirements.

    b. Production environments must have more stability than the training environment.

    c. Availability and accuracy of training environments can be critical in an Internet business application implementation.

    d. CISS must be involved in ensuring that the training environment reflects the released system.

111 A site survey checklist is used to do which of the following?

    a. Provide metrics including performance, storage capacity, and memory use.

    b. Provide all parties in the improvement endeavor a chance to examine the resources, implementation plan, and implementation process.

    c. Distribute software to all desktops and servers on the network from a central location.

    d. Identify gaps in required hardware, software, and support for a new solution.

112 Which is a benefit for the customer of the maintenance phase?

    a. Maintenance of the application environment after implementation

    b. Support for the application during implementation

    c. Support for the operation of the application during the test phase

    d. Sustaining the application from acceptance until no further changes occur

113 Which is not a purpose of the maintenance phase of the application development lifecycle?

    a. Redesigning the application to improve output

    b. Sustaining the application operational capabilities

    c. Making corrections to the application system

    d. Upgrading the application capacity to support the changing needs of the user

114 Which is the characteristic of the maintenance phase that is different from the input process in the other phases that are involved in the process of getting inputs?

    a. Monitoring

    b. Codifying

    c. Sanitizing

    d. Purchasing

115 Which represents an output of the maintenance phase of the application development lifecycle?

    a. Tuning the application for improved effectiveness

    b. Application servicing

    c. Repair activity

    d. Recommendation for change of application

116 Which of the following is not a major handover criterion?

a. Completed performances within the maintenance phase

b. All documentation conforms to standards

c. Smoothly operating system

d. Complete and consistent source documentation

117 Which of the following is not an item that the CISS might be responsible for ensuring is in place in the maintenance phase?

a. Tracking and reporting process

b. Requirements analysis document

c. Continuous improvement process

d. Processes in place to support maintenance of systems in production

118 The CISS ensures that systems

a. Are available

b. Perform within acceptable criteria

c. Are in compliance

d. All of the above

e. None of the above

119 Production systems should be backed up on a regular basis.

a. True

b. False

120 DRPs should be validated daily.

a. True

b. False

121 Change management prevents change from occurring.

a. True

b. False

122 Production systems require maintenance.

a. True

b. False

123 Which statement is a benefit of tracking and cataloging problems?

    a. Problems can be prioritized.

    b. Problems are documented so that they can be resolved.

    c. Appropriate personnel are notified when there is a problem.

    d. All of the above.

    e. None of the above.

124 Which term distinguishes the Waterfall Lifecycle Model from the Basic Lifecycle Model?

    a. Sequential

    b. Repeating

    c. Coincident

    d. Parallel

125 The Waterfall Lifecycle Model came into existence to deal with which problem in the software development process?

    a. Overly structured business processes

    b. Disorganized attempts at development

    c. Lack of focus the customer desires

    d. Tendency to develop documentation before code development

126 Which statement about the inputs to the Waterfall Lifecycle Model is true?

    a. The inputs to the phases of the Waterfall Lifecycle Model are the same as those for the same phases in the Basic Lifecycle Model.

    b. The inputs to all the phases of the Waterfall Lifecycle Model must be gathered before beginning the project because the process is sequential.

    c. The Waterfall Lifecycle Model has no inputs because of the random variable concept that enhance development options.

    d. The inputs to the Waterfall Lifecycle Model accrue as the various phases repeat during the development process.

127 Which sentence describes the outputs associated with the Waterfall Lifecycle Model?

    a. The outputs from each phase of the Waterfall Lifecycle Model become a unique section of the implementation plan.

    b. No outputs from any phase serve as feedback input to any earlier phase.

    c. Each phase outputs its own input data after modification for accuracy.

    d. The Waterfall Lifecycle Model has no outputs from any phase except the implementation phase because of the random development process employed.

128 Which is a weakness of the Waterfall Lifecycle Model?

    a. Produces something deliverable during each phase of the lifecycle

    b. Enforces a strict order of accomplishing phase objectives

    c. Provides no feedback loops

    d. Attempts to randomly develop the application

129 The Iterative Lifecycle Model forces which of the following development processes?

    a. Customer involvement avoidance

    b. Cost analysis based on continually upgraded engineering estimates

    c. Application requirements freezing after lifecycle starts

    d. Continual adjustment of plans based on risk analysis

130 Which three functions are purposes of the Iterative Lifecycle Model?

    a. Avoids continual assessment processes, corrects the problems associated with the Waterfall Lifecycle Model, and facilitates the communication of requirements among developers

    b. Allows recursion during the course of design and development, avoids continual assessment processes, and facilitates the communication of requirements among developers

    c. Allows recursion during the course of design and development, corrects the problems associated with the Waterfall Lifecycle Model, and facilitates the communication of requirements among developers

    d. Avoids continual assessment processes, corrects the problems associated with the Waterfall Lifecycle Model, and facilitates the communication of requirements among developers

131 Besides the usual inputs required by other business lifecycle models, the Iterative Lifecycle Model requires which input?

    a. A set of assumptions about the number of iterations allowed in the development process

    b. An expected rate of decline in application improvement for each additional iteration

    c. An estimate of the operational longevity of the initial prototype

    d. A firm definition of the end product of the iterative process

132 Which is a unique output of each iteration of the Iterative Lifecycle Model?

    a. Statement of remaining development budget

    b. Comparison of the current iteration goal with that of the previous iterations

    c. Plan that identifies the goal of the next iteration

    d. Assessment of differences in the final application and the current prototype

133 Which aspect of the Iterative Lifecycle Model can assist with assessing the contribution required of each lifecycle phase team for an application development?

    a. Process architecture

    b. Projected number of prototypes

    c. Client business organization

    d. Average of development team estimates

134 Which set of lifecycles has sequential phases?

    a. RAD and Waterfall

    b. Cleanroom and Spiral

    c. Iterative and Waterfall

    d. Iterative and Prototype

135 Which description characterizes the Cleanroom Lifecycle Model?

    a. Extensive modeling of the product

    b. Numerous development iterations

    c. Quick development

    d. Rigorous adherence to specifications

136 Which set of characteristics best match, in order, the Spiral, Prototype, Cleanroom, and RAD Lifecycle Models?

    a. Useful application during development, little maintenance, less initial cost, risk management

    b. Less initial cost, risk management, useful application during development, little maintenance

    c. Little maintenance, less initial cost, risk management, useful application during development

    d. Risk management, useful application during development, little maintenance, less initial cost

137 Which lifecycle model would you use if you did a research project but did not know all the requirements, options, and constraints at the start of the project?

a. Iterative

b. RAD

c. Spiral

d. Waterfall

138 Which lifecycle model tends to produce applications needing the least maintenance?

a. Spiral

b. Cleanroom

c. Iterative

d. Waterfall

139 Which set of three lifecycle models emphasizes repeating application development lifecycle activities until the application meets requirements?

a. Waterfall, Iterative, Spiral

b. Iterative, Spiral, Prototype

c. Prototype, Cleanroom, RAD

d. Spiral, Prototype, Cleanroom

140 Which application development lifecycle model requires a large fraction of the development budget at the beginning of the lifecycle?

a. Spiral

b. RAD

c. Prototype

d. Iterative

141 Which set of two application development lifecycle models requires multitalented developers with high levels of expertise?

a. Iterative and Waterfall

b. Iterative and Prototype

c. Spiral and Prototype

d. Cleanroom and RAD

142 Which lifecycle model would you not use if you desired to avoid the probability of the customer identifying additional application requirements during development?

a. Spiral

b. Waterfall

c. Prototype

d. Cleanroom

143 Which application development lifecycle model would an application provider use if they knew that they would need to attract funding before they could finish development of the application?

a. RAD

b. Spiral

c. Iterative

d. Prototype

144 Which application development lifecycle model can result in your meeting all the major project specifications and the customer still feeling somewhat dissatisfied with the application received?

a. Spiral

b. Iterative

c. Prototype

d. RAD

145 Which application development lifecycle model can produce several useful applications of lesser value while developing and implementing the final application?

a. Spiral

b. RAD

c. Iterative

d. Prototype

Applied Solutions

Application design and development in the early days of Internet-based applications is best characterized as cowboy programming. The ideas and technology were so new and so fresh that the excitement surrounding a project gave rise to unstructured development environments. The process of software development was not often adhered to, but also was often disdained by overly confident developers making sweeping eleventh-hour development decisions.

The incredible hype surrounding anything Internet-related combined with seemingly endless venture capital funding meant that the concept of process was sacrificed in the name of speed each and every time a decision was made. HTML specifications and standards that existed as the first Web sites started popping up on the Internet were pushed far beyond their intended uses. Indeed, in a time when not all web browsers were capable of displaying both .gif and .jpg images, one could argue that specifications and standards were irrelevant. What mattered then was getting a presence online as soon as possible: an imperative based on the velocity of deployment and change.

The practice of cowboy programming still occurs, but to a much lesser extent now that most companies have had to start from scratch on their web presence to deliver content and services in a real and sustainable fashion. The utility of adhering to process has returned to project management discussions and practice. Now, even the smallest projects expect to have real requirements gathering, controlled development processes, multiple rounds of testing, and documentation for each phase of the software development lifecycle. A more mature and sophisticated generation of Internet developers have had to begin dealing with the reality that accountants and lawyers are the key decision makers nowadays. Technology for technology's sake was fun and exhilarating for those that were fortunate enough to be working on early web projects, but that bubble has burst. This is not to say that innovation and excitement are things of the past, but that now an idea needs to withstand deeper questioning and testing.

Scenario 1: Prototype Model

Problem

A request for proposal (RFP) for a relatively small project for a client has been won based on a competitive search for a solutions partner. The RFP specifies use of software tools and technology that have only just been developed and released. The project was won largely because of the decision to rapidly produce a working prototype of the requested system. The project will hopefully turn out to provide multiple follow-up projects of larger scope and budget. Should the solutions partner switch development models now that the relationship has been established?

Solution

Because the RFP specified use of newly developed technology and software platforms just released by the software vendor (after acquisition of these tools and software from a start-up company that had itself not yet produced anything beyond version 1.0), the project team felt that the development model cannot be changed. Documentation for the software is light, and research indicates that only off-the-shelf implementations have been successfully deployed. Only with the prototype model can major problems with software customization and component integration be discovered and adequately managed.

Solution Details

Following are key facts to remember:

- Front-load development costs by using the Prototype Lifecycle Model to expose problems with product customization.

- Do not rely on client-provided test data and content but instead supply sample data and content internally so that end-to-end functionality can be reached as soon as possible.

- Develop a vendor relationship with the software provider and identify the most knowledgeable resources available with experience by using and implementing the version 1.0 software.

- Subscribe to any and all developer forums and discussion lists related to the products to investigate problems and issues that are not covered in the product documentation.

Scenario 2: Y2K and Y2038 Bugs

Problem

Software and operating system developers needed to be parsimonious with their usage of memory. Recall that at one point, it was considered common knowledge that a computer does not require more than 640 KB of memory for any given application that it might be required to run. Therefore, software representation of a year was limited to two digits. Although aware that the year 2000 was going to come along before long, it was commonly believed that nobody would still be using these original time and date libraries that were written in the 1970s.

Well, a funny thing happened on the way to the year 2000: lots of legacy systems and code survived. The problem with Y2K was that the two-digit year would roll over to 00, and certain assumptions about the natural order of things, such as billing statements and birthrates, would be violated by the fact that 00 comes before 99 instead of after. Stories about the potential disaster caused by the Y2K bug ranged from the humorously benign about how letters of acceptance to kindergarten students were being mailed out to the elderly, to the catastrophic end, to the orderly processing of data for commerce and identification.

The Y2K problem seems to have come and gone without much incident, but there is another such date rollover coming along which could have a far greater impact. In the year 2038, the UNIX time and date libraries that refer to time as represented by the number of seconds since epoch (00:00:00 January 1, 1970 is the start of the UNIX time epoch) will rollover. How will your Internet-business solutions project survive this event?

Solution

Just as with the Y2K rollover, system updates, patches, and upgrades will need to be applied to your systems and their software. In advance of the actual event, test systems should have their clocks advanced so that the rollover can be simulated and consequences (if any) determined. The Y2K rollover affected only non-UNIX time-based systems. However, it can be argued that although the Y2K rollover turned out to be nothing much, the impact of the UNIX time rollover in 2038 could be more substantial.

As with all maintenance issues, you need to keep abreast of the discussions and solutions being proposed to deal with this problem. Migration of systems to newer operating systems that use new time and date libraries is the preferred solution. Indeed, by the year 2038, it is quite conceivable that source code for software using old 32-bit integers for time routines might be lost forever, requiring reverse engineering efforts in some cases. Patching and upgrading UNIX kernel software is another solution.

Solution Details

Note the following key tips:

* Time libraries and routines will need to be represented by at least a 64-bit integer.
* Deep assumptions in software about the nature of time libraries will need to be examined and changed.
* Leap seconds are necessary but awkward, making it impossible to predict when a leap second will be required more than a few years in advance. This is because time is measured by atomic clocks but needs to be adjusted to keep in alignment with the earth's varying orbit.

Scenario 3: User Load Testing

Problem

The client has requested that their production environment be able to support 90,000 concurrent users without degraded performance or system failures. The project was to build an e-commerce web store that has one significant functional requirement that radically impacts all design and development: the database must support real-time inventory. Real-time inventory was defined as including the act of placing an item on the web store into a shopping cart, and thereby decrementing the web store database inventory for that item, and reporting the decrement to back-end order fulfillment databases.

As you can imagine, this was no simple extension of the concept of nightly updates and regular data feeds. This was a requirement to build something that had not been done before. The successful user load testing or stress testing of this production environment provided me with all sorts of applied solutions that could be related here. But space and NDAs prohibit me from going too deeply into the solution details. The question I can discuss here was how to structure and perform the user load testing so that a high confidence factor would be achieved for the systems to survive a site launch and subsequent estimated peak usage.

Solution

The problem is not just researching and specifying a set of servers and components that can handle 90,000 concurrent users, but also what to do with excess demand for site resources over and above 90,000 concurrent users. The solution details for the real-time database inventory are, as I've said, not privy to public consumption. Suffice it to say that the developers on my team were more than up to the challenge and produced a solution that was both elegant and robust.

The user load testing was a long and hard series of conference calls, lasting sometimes more than six hours as virtual users were ramped up slowly to the target concurrency and mixture of buy, browse, search, and register users. The first day of testing, however, shows the importance of being able to come up with custom monitoring tools to automate the analysis of transaction and error logs. The testing administrator was given the go ahead to start 100 virtual users into a mixture of transaction types. Within a few minutes, it was reported that all the users were failing to perform any of the transactions.

Using scripts which, from a centralized or bastion host in the production environment, went out to each of the web servers and retrieved the log file lines from the tail of each access and error log, it was quickly determined that the test scripts were failing to request valid product IDs. The log files indicated that the virtual users were requesting the variable name the test software uses, instead of the actual product IDs. Similar problems encountered during additional tests on other days were quickly resolved by having scripts that could automatically check hundreds of lines of log files on dozens of servers.

The next part of the solution was to build a throttling mechanism into the application server code so that a fully used set of application server instances would not return server error responses, but rather would direct additional user sessions to another web site with only static content and no database or application server demands. This was devised to handle the 90,001[st] and onward concurrent user sessions. After this mechanism was successfully triggered by the test software a few weeks later, the mechanism was intentionally set to not trigger at all, allowing the uppermost load testing concurrency tests to identify any bottlenecks in the processing of transactions in the database layer or the web server layer.

Finally, just before the end of user load testing, there arose what appeared to be a show-stopping problem with the web store code. Only trivial levels of virtual users could be supported by the latest code deployed to be tested on the production environment. A long night of theorizing and investigating possible reasons for the problem eventually produced a cause. Knowing that the changes introduced in the latest web store code base were minimal and could not cause this problem, a comparison of the database catalog contents was made to see if, despite strong admonitions and assurances about keeping out content changes during test cycles, a data feed had been run. Sure enough, the database admins were able to discover that a catalog database feed had been run and had propagated new records into the production database.

These records, it turned out, contained a special character which, when returned to the application server process, was interpreted as a java command that suspended all output threads. The database specification for allowed characters had been violated and, after the offending data records were backed out, the web store went on to successfully test at over 120,000 concurrent user sessions.

Solution Details

Note the usefulness of the following toward this solution:

- Netscape iPlanet Web Server Software
- ATG Dynamo Application Server Software
- Oracle Database Server Software
- Cisco Arrowpoint Load Balancer
- Sun Cluster for Oracle
- Mercury Interactive Load Runner Test Software
- Custom scripts to analyze web, application, and database log files and alerts
- Conference calls run from distributed test plans to participants (test admins, system admins, network admins, database admins)
- Strict control and tracking of test environment to ensure adherence to code and content freezes

CHAPTER 4

Application Requirements

Explicit business and operational requirements for any Internet business solution are key to its success. Surprisingly high numbers of software application projects start and sometimes launch without addressing the question of requirements.

You can learn your basic application requirements by conducting a needs assessment, which not only dictates the metrics upon which a project is judged a success, but also helps create a realistic project plan and schedule. The features and functionality requirements within a needs assessment must be detailed enough so that a basic understanding of feasibility can be evaluated before you begin the planning and testing phases.

The discussion in this chapter is divided into the following sections:

- Basic Application Requirements
- Integration Concepts

Basic Application Requirements

Most applications created to provide Internet business solutions share a set of basic features for specific, nonfunctional requirements. These minimum requirements exist, regardless of the application's specific purpose or functionality. The basic, nonfunctional application requirements are

- Security
- Reliability
- Availability
- Scalability
- Performance
- Manageability

Each of these requirements is an important criterion to consider when creating an application needs assessment, and in making sure that you identify the basic requirements. Each is discussed in the following sections.

Security

Security is measures and controls taken to protect economic or other important assets. The key to achieving a secure application is to ensure that you include security considerations during the application's design. Too often, the need to implement Internet business applications quickly to shorten time-to-market schedules leads developers to neglect application security. Unfortunately, this increases the likelihood of security flaws and vulnerabilities in the application, and of further costs.

As security problems emerge during production use, immediate patches and modifications are required to correct the problems. Such a reactive approach can cause reduced confidence in an application's reliability and integrity. Furthermore, the approach is a negative reflection on those who were responsible for the application's design and creation. Ultimately though, for those who rely on using the application, questions about security center around the lack of assurance that their personal information is adequately protected—many times even resulting in loss.

This section describes the fundamental security elements that require attention during an application's design. Carefully integrating these basic security functions with the application can offer secure and reliable use of the application. Practice research analysis to make the right decision based on a complete risk assessment.

NOTE   A thorough discussion of security is beyond the scope of this study guide. For references to several texts that address the subject of application security in great depth, see Appendix A, "Recommended Further Reading."

Security is also concerned with three broad topics: policy, procedures, and compliance. Policy details what you are protecting; procedure details how you plan to maintain your security policies; and compliance details how well you manage to execute your security policies. Your security procedures are the implementations of your security policies. The amount of effort required to secure your application and systems depends on the nature of the application. For example, applications that require no customer information require less rigorous configuration than applications that handle online banking or other financial transactions.

To help you understand the depth of this topic, the discussion is divided into the following sections:

- Security Policy
- Security Procedures
- Security Compliance
- Authentication and Trust

- Authorization Procedures
- Access Control Mechanisms
- Data Confidentiality
- Data Integrity
- Auditing
- Accountability
- Examples of Security Technologies

Security Policy

A *security policy* is a document used as a guide to ensure that you adequately formulate and consistently implement security practices. A security policy document is often called a "living document" because it is never finished; it changes and evolves as conditions and requirements change. A security policy is also a mechanism by which to generate consensus among a group of people, allowing various levels of management and operations to express their views and goals. A security policy document broadly defines relevant security responsibilities, terms, and standards and provides a basis for more specific security documents, such as remote access policies, acceptable use policies, nondisclosure policies, corporate and departmental security policies, web site security policies, and privacy policies.

Initially, web sites did not make overt efforts to develop and document security policies, but as web sites have matured and grown in sophistication, publishing web content or providing online services now involves a legal approval phase that comes after the technical QA and testing phase. The legal approval phase makes sure that content and services are compliant with stated and published policies. This is not necessarily a bad thing, but sign-off from the legal department or oversight committee has introduced another step in the release management process.

Within closed environments or internal business applications, explicit security policies were not considered absolutely necessary in all cases because the systems were considered private, and access to them seemed sufficiently restricted. However, with the introduction of VPNs, IRC, and remote access technologies, assuming that a private or internal application operates without risk of exposure to security compromise is no longer valid. If you are remotely connected to an internal application, you can bridge security zones without knowing that you are making the internal application vulnerable. Users greatly increased the spread of the "I love you virus" by accessing personal e-mail accounts while at work, infecting private and internal file systems with the virus.

Security Procedures

A *security procedure* is a defined list of steps to follow to maintain security or to respond to various situations where security has been breached. Security procedures are grouped as *administrative* or *technical*. CISS professionals should participate in documenting administrative procedures for creating and removing accounts, gaining physical access to computer systems, and handling problem escalation. Administrative security procedures govern such things as remote client access to application services. For example, create an access request form to keep an accurate list of who is authorized to access various features of an application in a controlled fashion. If you need to change remote client access, contact information is necessary so that communicating changes to passwords is graceful and without confusion.

Technical security procedures cover application operations, active and passive intrusion detection, and emergency response. Requesting remote access to a staging environment web instance is an example of a technical security procedure. Rather than have open access to staging, create firewall conduits and rules that limit access to only authorized remote IP addresses and address blocks. Firewall conduits must be created to uphold security policy, while still accommodating remote access needs. Within the Cisco PIX Firewall setup, you should not only apply IP names so that security logs and security audits are easier to read and check for anomalies, but also apply comments. An example of Cisco PIX firewall conduits and comments to allow a class C network for a San Francisco office and a client proxy server to access a staging web site is shown here:

```
conduit permit tcp host stage.web.site eq 80 sanfrancisco-office 255.255.255.0
conduit permit tcp host stage.web.site eq 443 sanfrancisco-office 255.255.255.0
:the above 2 conduits allow the SF office http and https access to staging site
conduit permit tcp host stage.web.site eq 80 host proxy.client.server
conduit permit tcp host stage.web.site eq 443 host proxy.client.server
:the above 2 conduits allow the client http and https access to staging site
```

Although creating firewall conduits instead of allowing world access to a staging site's services might mean more work for administrators, it is generally considered worth the effort. Only if the requestor comes from a dial-up environment with hundreds of possible IP address assignments would username and password authentication be preferable to firewall-restricted access procedures. Firewall conduits, however, are only one part of a good security solution. Simply creating firewall conduits is considered *passive* intrusion detection because an administrator must actually check the firewall logs to discover an intrusion. *Active* intrusion-detection tools should also be used because they are configured to automatically trigger alerts and notifications as they monitor server connections and firewall logs.

Security Compliance

Compliance is not a one-time security check but an ongoing effort to verify the maintenance of high security precautions. CISS professionals are expected to keep abreast of security exploits by reading the CERT Coordination Center advisories and browsing other security forums. Awareness of vulnerabilities is important to maintain security policy compliance.

CERT/CC and FIRST

CERT/CC (originally referred to the Computer Emergency Response Team) is a service provided by the University of Carnegie Mellon in Pittsburgh, Pennsylvania. CERT/CC (www.cert.org) was started in 1988 to facilitate rapid information flow about security activities and is primarily funded by the U.S. Department of Defense.

The Forum of Incident Response and Security Teams (FIRST, at www.first.org) was created to help grow and evolve the many incident response and security teams to reduce differences caused by their individual purpose, funding, reporting requirements, and audiences.

Do not delay applying patches or software upgrades after learning of relevant vulnerabilities. Security compliance means the difference between falling victim to a virus crafted by the latest attacker and being able to do business as usual.

Periodically audit the organization's compliance with the security policy, using both internal and third-party auditing services.

Authentication and Trust

Authentication verifies that the identity of an entity is truly whom it claims to be, and *trust* provides either direct knowledge about each communicating party, or the assertion of a trusted third party. Before an application can grant access to the resources it manages, the application must be made aware of who or what is requesting the access. In other words, requestors for access must identify themselves positively before they are trusted to access the application. Authentication takes two basic forms: who you are (fingerprint, retina scan, and so on), and what you have (username, password, smart card, and so on). The best security schemes require both forms of authentication.

Identification is a basic security requirement of any application. All requesting entities, whether a person, device, or process expected to access the application, must be assigned a unique identifier (UID). This unique identifier, such as a user ID or username, forms the basis for establishing what can be accessed and can also be used for auditing purposes. Additionally, with audit logging enabled, the unique identifier's owner can be held accountable for all accesses made by that identifier.

Consequently, the identifier's owner should be the only one able to use that identifier to access an application. This requirement is where authentication becomes involved. For example, to authenticate a remote host or person, a local host requests a username and password (from the other host or person) and verifies that the username and password are valid by comparing them to values stored on an authentication service or server. Authentication determines a user identity and then verifies that information. The username and password example relies on the fact that the password is only known by the owner of the username.

When considering authentication requirements for an application, remember that rather than build an entirely new authentication structure in the application, using external authentication services that are available to the application might be more desirable. For example, applications can call upon authentication services that are available at the operating system level, such as Windows NT domain login or UNIX user accounts. An advantage of choosing this option is that it offers a Single Sign-On (SSO) approach, meaning the requestor has one less username to remember, and one less logon procedure to encounter.

A trust relationship is required for two or more discrete security zones to share user information or device access. Explicit trust relationships must exist between multiple authentication domains or realms, and are central to sound security practice.

Hierarchical trust models are implicitly easier to manage than flat trust models. With the advent of Microsoft Active Directory Services, Windows trust domains have moved away from a flat trust model to a hierarchical trust model. Hierarchical chains of trust link digital certificates from a certificate authority (CA) or software application during secure, encrypted communications used in e-commerce transactions.

Authorization Procedures

An *authorization procedure* defines a formal request process to grant authentication privileges. Authorization procedures occur prior to using access controls. Ask the following questions when establishing authorization procedures:

- Who is allowed to request or approve access? Can end users request access for themselves? Depending on the privilege level of the access being requested, another entity will most likely have to approve the request. For example, access requests for end users should be submitted and approved by the responsible supervisor/manager or sponsor.

- How can an access request be validated? A customer requesting access to services should have a way to register and apply for the access. Sufficient information should be collected during the registration process to allow the requestor's identity to be authenticated, and for the requestor's entitled privileges to be verified (customer entitlement).

- How can the proper use of accessed resources be ensured? To ensure proper use of authorized access, authorized users must understand their responsibilities. Approval does not mean that authorized access can be exploited. End users must agree to usage conditions, as prescribed by surrounding business policies. Appropriate audit and system logs must be maintained and reviewed to ensure responsible usage. End users will be tempted to share their usernames and passwords when access problems occur. Warn against this, because it undermines the validity of security audit trails and tracking.

Access Control Mechanisms

Access control restricts access privileges to the resources available to an application. Access control mechanisms determine who can access what resources and perform what actions. This makes access control requirements a crucial part of ensuring that an application functions securely.

Access control mechanisms should do the following:

- **Define various privilege levels to different user security profiles**—For example, the select privilege to data in a table can be granted to Security Profile A; the select and update privileges can be granted to Security Profile B, and the delete privilege can be granted to Security Profile C. Typically, each security profile represents the access required by a group of end users with similar roles or functions. In the case of databases, create customized views of the original data tables being queried to support such roles or functions.

- **Assign a security profile to each end user**—Continuing with the previous example, users X, Y, and Z can be assigned Security Profile A; users K, L, and M can be assigned Security Profile B; and so on. Instead of granting access to individual user IDs, access is granted to each security profile, reducing the amount of effort required to maintain user accounts. Generally, where database security is concerned, a group ID or secondary authorized ID is granted the appropriate privilege to the database resource. For most other protected resources, an access control list (ACL) is maintained for each resource. In the ACL, each security profile is granted the appropriate privilege to that resource.

- **Manage user accounts and policies**—A facility must be available for managing user accounts. This facility must include the administrative functions of adding, modifying, deleting, and revoking or suspending user accounts. The following is a checklist of common security policies for password-based user accounts:

  - Account lockout must occur after five unsuccessful logon attempts.

  - Assigned passwords for new or reactivated accounts must be generated randomly.

  - New or reactivated accounts must require a new password to be entered at initial logon by the account's owner.

  - Passwords must have a minimum length of six alphanumeric characters.

  - Passwords must not be displayed when being entered but should be entered twice for verification. Passwords must be different from previously used passwords.

  - Passwords must expire after 60 days.

  - Passwords must be stored encrypted with a one-way encryption algorithm.

  - Password reset functions must be kept separate from full administrative rights, for help desk purposes.

- **Encrypt stored and transmitted data**—Where necessary, an application must have the capability to encrypt sensitive or confidential data. However, encrypting large amounts of data can cause severe overhead to occur during data retrieval. If encryption is required, a public-key encryption algorithm, such as RSA, or a symmetric-key encryption algorithm, such as Data Encryption Standard (DES), triple DES, RC4/5/6, or International Data Encryption Algorithm (IDEA), should be selected. Select an algorithm that performs well and is an industry standard (to ensure interoperability). As an alternative to software encryption, hardware-based solutions, such as encryption cards for web servers, can offload the processing demands of applications requiring strong encryption of large amounts of data.

Access control mechanisms should also apply to managing administrative or super-user accounts. Furthermore, such highly privileged accounts should be constrained to a limited number of personnel who are directly responsible for administering the user accounts, applications, or systems.

How these access control mechanisms are actually implemented and managed depends largely on the business policies that define an application's use and its access requirements. The more granular the access requirements are, the more complex the access control structure is, and the more resources are required to maintain the structure.

Data Confidentiality

Confidentiality is the characteristic of information being disclosed only to authorized persons, entities, and processes at authorized times and following authorized protocol. Whether an application manages customer data or internal company data, a business organization is responsible for protecting the privacy of such data.

Customers believe they possess the right to have their private information protected—this confidentiality might very well be a legal requirement. A business would do well to maintain a trustworthy relationship with its customers by respecting their right to privacy.

Company proprietary information that is sensitive in nature also deserves to have its confidentiality protected. Only authorized parties must be granted access to information that has been identified as confidential. Data encryption within the application also supports the data confidentiality goal.

Data Integrity

Integrity refers to the assurance that data is not modified in an unauthorized or unintended manner. In other words, integrity preserves the accuracy and completeness of the data. Even for data that may be classified as nonconfidential, applications must be designed to preserve the integrity of the stored data.

Integrity maintenance begins with the application. Applications must be designed to collect accurate and complete data. For example, data entry fields must contain logic to check for valid values. Edit checks include numeric only values, date checks/formats, a range of values, drop-down lists, and so on. Logical checks should ensure that interdependent data elements relate to each other sensibly. For example, it would not make sense for a person to indicate a 1970 birth year, and subsequently specify an age range of 19–25 (in the year 2002).

As with confidentiality, data integrity's goal is further achieved by properly implementing access control mechanisms. Applications must be designed to handle different privileged functions that affect data integrity, such as add, delete, or modify. Defining separate data entry panels or forms for each of these functions might be necessary.

Auditing

The purpose of auditing an application is to ensure that all functions available in the application operate and are being used as intended. Information assets must be controlled and monitored with an accompanying audit log to report any modification, addition, or deletion to the information assets. These logs must report the user or process that performed the actions. Affixing the date, time, and responsibility to an individual must be possible for all significant events. Audit logs must also be protected from alteration and destruction. To accomplish this protection, audit logs can be offloaded to an isolated log server where access is more restricted.

The outcome of auditing an application might include the following findings:

- Auditing an application might uncover inadequate separation of duties and responsibilities, as provided by the existing functional design in the application. Modifications in the application or security profiles might be necessary to correct this.

- An audit might reveal inappropriate assignment of privileges to end users because of a lack of well-defined authorization procedures.

- An audit might discover inadequacies or deficiencies in user account administration, such as the existence of accounts that must be deleted. Deficiencies can also include poor password management policies—minimum password length of two characters, passwords do not expire, passwords are stored in clear text, and so on.

- An application audit might further discover inappropriate access made by an authorized person.

Accountability

In CISS, accountability means the ability to uniquely trace an individual's or an institution's actions to that individual or institution. The ability to audit the actions of all parties and processes that interact with information leads to accountability. Roles and responsibilities should be clearly defined, identified, and authorized at a level commensurate with the information's sensitivity and criticality. The relationship between all parties, processes, and information must be clearly defined, documented, and acknowledged by all parties. All parties must have responsibilities for which they are held accountable.

With the advent of digital certificates and digital signatures, accountability can be enforced through nonrepudiation. Nonrepudiation essentially ensures that an event or transaction has taken place. With nonrepudiation abilities in place, the initiator or author of an event or transaction cannot deny he was responsible for that event or transaction.

To enforce accountability, you can require client-side certificates for secure access to important resources or transactions. In this situation, a server provides a digital certificate that the client identifies as trusted, and the client machine contains a digital certificate that the server acknowledges as coming from an appropriate trusted CA. This level of authentication, when combined with usernames, passwords, and firewall conduits, allows the utmost in trusted access control.

Examples of Security Technologies

This section examines examples of security technologies. See Appendix A for further security references, as this section only begins to discuss the complex issues involved in application security.

Security technologies are technical standards, tools, and services designed to provide security functions that enable secure applications. Security technologies serve as technical safeguards and countermeasures that protect information assets from compromise, loss, or destruction. Additionally, security technologies can manage complex security functions, such as security profile management.

Security technologies extend an application's functionality beyond its basic design. The final result is that the application is made more accessible and available through security. For example, a web-based application that conducts business involving sensitive information over the Internet would not be useable if its sessions were not encrypted with the Secure Socket Layer (SSL) protocol and technology. Using SSL enables the application to be more readily accepted and used.

A security service accepts and processes requests for security privileges. Security services include the following:

- **GSSAPI**—Applications use the Generalized System Security Application Programming Interface (GSSAPI) to take advantage of centralized security services. The GSSAPI enables an application to see its users' authenticated identity, check their privileges, and record their activities. Because the GSSAPI is product independent, the application does not need to know which product provides the services. The GSSAPI can use one security product in one context and a different one in another.

- Single Sign-On (SSO)—SSO's purpose is twofold. First, it centrally manages a multitude of user accounts that exist across multiple platforms, systems, and applications. Second, it allows the end users to sign on only once for authentication purposes. Their authorized rights to all systems and applications will then be accessible. SSO is ideal for an environment with multiple applications that possess their own user account security structures. The recommended approach to SSO is to ensure that you use stronger authentication methods with it (for example, digital certificates, smart cards, and biometrics). Kerberos and Lightweight Directory Access Protocol (LDAP) are common mechanisms deployed to achieve single sign-on.

A directory service provides access to users and applications by identifying resources on a network.

An example of directory services is the X.500 standard. The standardized infrastructure of the Open System Interconnection (OSI) application layer includes the Directory, a specialized database system used by other OSI applications, and by people, to obtain information about objects of interest in the OSI environment. Typical X.500 Directory objects correspond to systems, services, and people. Information found in the Directory includes telephone numbers, e-mail addresses, postal addresses, network node addresses, public-key identity certificates, and encrypted passwords.

You should know about the following technologies (each is discussed in turn in the following paragraphs):

- Public Key Infrastructure
- Intrusion-Detection Systems
- Virtual Private Networks

Public key infrastructure—Enabling public key infrastructure (PKI) in an application means that the application can employ digital certificates and digital signatures for encryption, identification, authentication, access control, authorization, accountability, and non-repudiation. This functionality positions the application to function securely and scale well into the future.

Specific terminology associated with public key infrastructure includes public key, private key, certificate authority, secure shell (ssh), Pretty Good Privacy (PGP), and keyserver. See the Glossary for a description of public key cryptography and encryption terminology, and Appendix A for several public key infrastructure references.

Intrusion-detection systems—A host-based intrusion-detection system (IDS) is an effective tool that monitors events in an application log for attacks, anomalous activities, abnormal resource utilization, and impaired availability. A network-based IDS can monitor for attacks against, and unusual behavior of, the application across network segments. An IDS furthers the application's availability by alerting for appropriate responses to potential threats before any major damage occurs. Specific terminology related to an IDS includes tripwire, honey pot, and packet sniffer. See the Glossary for a description of IDS and Appendix A for references to books about security.

Virtual Private Networks—Virtual Private Networks (VPNs) make applications securely accessible over the public Internet. For example, business partners and employees can access the company intranet using a VPN tunnel across the Internet. VPNs essentially extend the accessibility and availability of internal application resources securely over the Internet. Many VPN connections use IPSec, which encapsulates packets bound for remote VPN targets as an encrypted packet. Some firewalls, however, do not accept IPSec packets as legitimate, so other encryption algorithms must be used in these situations.

Prior to the development of VPN technologies, dialup connections provided secure remote access to company intranet applications. This involved multiple phone lines, both for the company and for the remote users. VPNs take advantage of pre-existing network connections, avoiding the expense of modems, phone lines, and long distance telephone connection charges.

Reliability

Reliability is the probability that a system or a system's capability functions without failure for a specified time. Reliability is also defined as the probability that an item will perform its intended function for a specified interval under stated conditions, and is measured by time-to-failure, in hours, cycles, miles, missions, and so on.

Consider reliability under the following criteria:

* Hardware Reliability
* Software Reliability

Hardware Reliability

Hardware is reaching reliability levels today that were unheard of a few years ago. Hardware reliability systematically reduces, eliminates, and controls system failures that adversely affect a device's performance. In cases where failures cannot be eliminated or controlled because of cost or design limitations, reliability engineering provides data for overall risk assessment.

When a complex hardware system begins its life, it often has a high failure rate in terms of defects per unit of time. As the defects are worked out, the failure rate drops to an acceptable level at which it can remain for many years. Because of its physical attributes and the forces of nature, components usually begin to wear out and the failure rate begins to climb. Although the failure rate's rise and fall varies from one hardware system to another, and the time frame associated with the system's useful life can vary by many years, the "bathtub-shaped" trend shown in Figure 4-1 is typical.

Figure 4-1   *Bathtub Curve*

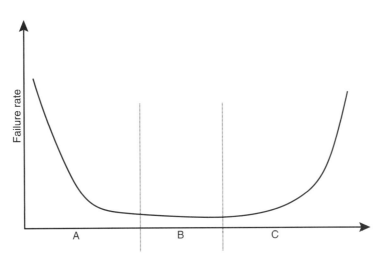

Software Reliability

Although hardware is becoming more reliable, software is, on average, becoming less reliable. Almost without exception, the main culprit is application software. Operating system facilities, which are exploited by many more users, are, consequently, better tested than most applications.

As applications offer more features, to accommodate the rapid growth in system resources, new code must be added. More code means more possibilities for bugs, leading to an increased risk of application software failure.

The decreasing reliability of application software does not mean that operating systems are totally without fault, rather that they contribute relatively few failures to the overall software failure number. Code analysis has determined that for each 1000 lines of code, one or two bugs exist. This would not be such a problem if software grew in increments of thousands of lines of code, but because of constant demands for greater functionality, short development windows, and emphasis on speed-to-market, software grows by millions of lines of code between major releases. Combating this trend is one of the software industry's greatest challenges.

Availability

Availability is the probability at any given time that a system or a system's capability functions satisfactorily in a specified environment. If you are given an average downtime per failure, availability implies a certain degree of reliability. Failure intensity, used particularly in the software reliability engineering field, is the number of failures per natural unit or per time unit. It is an alternate way of expressing reliability.

Enterprises implement high-availability networks for the following reasons:

- Prevent financial loss
- Prevent lost productivity
- Improve user satisfaction
- Improve customer satisfaction and loyalty
- Reduce IT support costs to increase IT productivity
- Minimize financial loss resulting from network unavailability
- Minimize lost productivity resulting from network unavailability

Availability is probably the most important property of your computer system. If a system is not available to run the intended workload or perform the tasks vital to your business, the system's speed or memory capacity won't matter. For example, consider the fiercely competitive arena of Internet business. If your web site is not available, or if you can't process an order because your backend server is down, you might lose a potential customer or damage the relationship you have with an existing one. All businesses, not just the Internet, need increased availability to stay competitive.

The following are factors within availability:

- User error
- Outages
- Ensuring availability through Service Level Agreements and failover methodologies

The text discusses each in turn.

User Error

Don't discount user error from discussions and plans regarding reliability. For systems with high availability requirements, mistyping one character can sometimes cause several hours of downtime, expending several year's worth of unplanned downtime. Rather than hope and pray that user error will not surface during the lifetime of your project, it must be taken as a given and dealt with like any other requirement or feature.

Expected user errors can be handled and managed as well-structured problems, with well-structured solutions. Computer-human interface research has identified many important design elements associated with user behavior and their likely errors. Identify and highlight end user error, as well as administrative user error, as significant areas for development and testing criteria.

Software developers feel that users should be responsible and aware of everything about an application's functions, but this bias comes from their own extensive familiarity with the application they are developing. Any developer who demands more intelligent users instead of writing more intelligent software will be sorely disappointed when asked to rewrite code to accommodate end user behaviors.

Outages

Outages are those periods of time when the system is not available to perform useful work. Whether your customers are external to your business or users of your own computer systems within your business, computer systems outage represents a major problem for an increasing number of computer users. Any period of computer system outage can directly translate into lost revenue for the business. Typical outages cost an average company 10,000 dollars per minute. This requirement for continuous access to computer systems spans both customers and computer systems. The need for computer availability has never been greater.

Major causes of outages include site failures, cut cables, power outages, fires, and floods, or large-scale disasters, such as earthquakes, hurricanes, and tornadoes. Although companies continue to increase their servers' availability, they find that site failures or disasters pose a very real threat to their competitive edge. Companies should take disaster survivability seriously when considering their availability strategy.

Ensuring Availability through Service Level Agreements and Failover Methodologies

Corporate availability strategies are usually covered by a disaster recovery plan that takes the offsite storage of critical data into account, but it can also include two alternative methods for application availability: Service Level Agreements, and failover methodologies.

Service Level Agreements—Integrating process improvement, best practices, technical expertise, and availability management tools provides the necessary ingredients for a healthy and highly available network. For customers committing to this rigorous process, most service providers provide health and availability assurances in the form of Service Level Agreements (SLAs).

The penalties for missed SLAs include additional high-availability technical resources to fix the availability issue, increased escalation, and financial penalties.

SLAs are the company's means to ensure the following:

- Clear performance goals
- Heightened awareness, attention, and accountability
- Strong linkage between network performance and availability goals and the customer's business requirements

Failover methodologies—A failover is completed by maintaining an up-to-date copy of a database, codebase, or network device on an alternate system for backup. The alternate system takes over if the primary system becomes unusable. This model utilizes duplicate network and server hardware configurations in which one device or server has the active role, and the other is a backup that monitors the active device or server's state. When the back-up device or server detects a hardware or software failure on the active server, it takes over the active server's role and identity. Components are configured to address the "virtual" device name or address, which is alternately hosted or served by the active or back-up server.

You can provide failover with a cluster. A *cluster* is a group of computers, usually referred to as *nodes* that are interconnected to provide a single computing resource. Clusters offer much higher availability than a single system, allowing avoidance of both planned and unplanned outages. High availability also refers to being able to service a component in the system without shutting down the entire operation. Given these requirements, a cluster is an ideal solution for customers.

To address the planned outage component, workloads can be moved to another cluster node while administrative changes occurs, allowing changes to be made while still maintaining a useful service. When the maintenance activities are completed, the workload can be moved back to its original location, if desired.

Redundant components handle unplanned outages. Redundancy in the cluster hardware (whether redundant servers, networks, storage, or adapters) allows work to continue transparently when one or more hardware or software components fail. A provided service continues by simply switching to other cluster components. If a node fails, service can be moved to another node. If a disk fails, service continues from another disk containing the same data, and so on. A cluster acts as a single, continuously available system in this respect. System resource availability is one of the greatest advantages of clustering.

Clusters provide easy management of your computing resources without restricting the systems' capabilities. You should be able to work with the individual components in addition to the cluster as a whole. Many people think that a cluster is beyond the scope of their requirements, or that it is only for large systems. This belief is unfounded. Any system that is important to a business qualifies for clustering.

Whether for a mission-critical enterprise server or a server for a small workgroup, clustering provides availability. The smallest workgroup servers can have enterprise-class availability characteristics through clustering. The ability to build clusters with small, cheap servers, or by reusing servers that are surplus to requirements elsewhere within the business, allows significant improvements in availability.

Cluster performance needs to be carefully planned and tested. Simulated failures must be tested regularly with clustering technologies because even minor configuration differences can affect whether failover is triggered as desired. A major problem with clustered environments is for a failover to be triggered, but for the alternative node or nodes to not pick up the active state. Expressing cluster configurations as strict statements of propositional logic is often necessary to build reliable cluster configurations. These configurations need to progress from the general to the specific. For example, cluster database triggers might first test for the existence of an active database application process ID before testing a particular tablespace's contents within that database. Appendix A contains the titles of several books that include extensive treatments of highly available systems design.

You can provide failover using a mirrored site. A *mirrored site* is a web site that is a replica of an existing site. The mirrored site is used to reduce network traffic, decrease hits on a server, or improve the original site's availability. Mirror sites are useful when the original site generates too much traffic for a single server to support. Such sites also increase the speed with which files or web sites can be accessed.

Users can download files quicker from a server that is geographically closer to them. For example, if a busy New York-based web site sets up a mirror site in England, users in Europe can access the mirror site faster than the original site in New York. Sites, such as Netscape, that offer copies or updates of popular software often set up mirror sites to handle the large demand that a single site might not be able to handle. Keep in mind, however, that geographic proximity does not necessarily mean faster network access speeds. A T3 connecting New York with Miami is faster than a T1 from New York to Washington, DC.

You can also provide failover using a backup. Backup types are based on the files selected for backup:

- **Full backup**—Backs up all selected files.

- **Differential backup**—Backs up selected files that have been changed. This backup is used when only the latest version of a file is required.

- **Incremental backup**—Backs up selected files that have been changed. If a file has been changed for a second or subsequent time since the last full backup, the file does not replace the already backed-up file; it is appended to the backup medium. This backup is used when each file revision must be maintained.

- **Delta backup**—Backs up only the actual data in the selected files that has changed, not the files themselves. This backup is similar to an incremental backup.

Recovery occurs with a backup when the need arises because of a planned business situation or unplanned event. Recovery times vary greatly depending on which schemes of which types of backups are performed. Daily full backups generally result in the shortest recovery time. Weekly full backups, with daily incrementals require application of the full backup, and then sequential applications of the incremental backups. If this involves the request and retrieval of offsite tapes and recovery media, an outage requiring a full recovery can take several days instead of several hours.

Rapid recovery options are expensive and must be carefully planned, and as data usage grows, they must be modified to accommodate growing data requirements and recovery demands. An important part of any disaster and recovery plan is to make periodic recovery procedure tests. These procedures must be tested for data integrity, as well as completeness. Finding out that the data can be recovered but that the configurations are unavailable can result in a situation where no viable recovered state can be attained.

Using fault tolerance can also provide failover. *Fault tolerance* is the ability to continue to perform a specified task even when hardware failure occurs. Fault tolerance improves reliability, availability, safety, performance, maintainability, and testability. A fault-tolerant system is designed by building two or more components, such as CPUs, disks, memories, and power supplies, into the same computer. In the event one component fails, another component takes over immediately. Many fault-tolerant computer systems mirror all operations. For example, each operation is performed on two or more duplicate systems so that if one fails the other takes over.

Many systems are designed to recover from a failure by detecting the failed component and switching to another computer system. These systems, although sometimes called fault-tolerant, are more widely known as *high-availability (HA)* systems. They require the software to resubmit a job when the second system is available.

A fault-tolerant system recovers from a fault in three steps:

1   The fault is detected.

2   The fault is isolated.

3   The fault is corrected.

True fault-tolerant systems are costly because redundant hardware is wasted if no failure occurs in the system. On the other hand, fault-tolerant systems provide the same processing capacity both before and after a failure, whereas high-availability systems often provide reduced capacity after a failure.

Hardware-based fault tolerance can react to component failures instantaneously, without the need for software-based recovery. Cluster-based solutions require anywhere from several seconds to many minutes to recover disk-based data and restart applications. Recovery time in a high-availability cluster varies based on application parameters, such as database size, transaction rate, and type of workload. A system's hardware-based fault tolerance is completely insensitive to these nonfunctional requirements and always provides uninterrupted service in the event of component failure.

Checkpoints can provide failover. *Checkpointing* is a simple technique for rollback error recovery. Rollback error recovery occurs when an executing program's state is periodically saved to a disk file from which it can be recovered after a failure. In the event of a failure, the last checkpoint serves as a recovery point. When the problem has been fixed, the restart program copies the last checkpoint into memory, resets all the hardware registers, and starts the computer from that point. Any transactions in memory made after the last checkpoint is taken are lost.

Programming abstraction provides a means to implement fault tolerance at various levels. At the application level, checkpointing can be done with C++ code using a preprocessor that inserts most of the checkpointing calls automatically. This saves the programmer time and work.

Another option to accomplish fault tolerance is to use a low-level checkpointing package to minimize the user's work. The problem with this option is that determining a consistent state is a major issue. Journaling file systems also provide this level of reliability at the disk level and reduce downtime greatly by not having to run lengthy disk integrity checks upon restart.

Another failover option is using hot swappable disks. A *hot swap* is the replacement of a CPU, hard drive, CD-ROM drive, power supply, or other device with a similar device, while the computer system using it remains in operation. Replacement can be necessitated by a device failure or, for storage devices, a need to substitute other data.

Hot swapping provides a rack or enclosure for the device that presents an appearance to the computer's bus or I/O controller that the device is intact while it is being replaced with another device. A hot swap arrangement where multiple devices are shared on a local area network is sometimes provided. Hot swap arrangements are sold for both Small Computer Systems Interface (SCSI) and Integrated Drive Electronics (IDE) drives. Hot swap versions of a redundant array of independent disks are also available.

Redundant Array of Independent Disks (RAID) provides failover by storing the same data in different places on multiple physical disks. By placing data on multiple disks, I/O operations can overlap in a balanced way, improving performance. Because having multiple disks increases the mean time between failure (MTBF), storing data redundantly also increases fault tolerance.

A RAID appears to the operating system as a single, logical volume. Some RAID configurations employ striping, which involves partitioning each drive's storage space into units ranging in size from one sector (512 bytes) to several megabytes. The stripes of all the disks are interleaved and addressed in order.

In a single-user system where large records, such as medical or other scientific images, are stored, the stripes are typically set up to be small (perhaps 512 bytes) so that a single record spans all disks and can be accessed quickly by reading all disks at the same time.

In a multi-user system, better performance requires establishing a stripe wide enough to hold standard-sized or large records. This allows overlapped disk I/O across drives.

The following are types of RAID:

- **RAID-0**—This technique has striping but no data redundancy. It offers the best performance but no fault-tolerance.

- **RAID-1**—This type is also known as disk mirroring and consists of at least two drives that duplicate data storage. There is no striping. Read performance is improved because both disks can be read at the same time. Write performance is the same as for single-disk storage. RAID-1 provides the best performance and the best fault tolerance in a multi-user system.

- **RAID-2**—This type uses striping across disks with some disks storing error checking and correcting (ECC) information. It has no advantage over RAID-3.

- **RAID-3**—This type uses striping and dedicates one drive to storing parity information. The embedded error checking (ECC) information detects errors. Data recovery is accomplished by calculating the exclusive OR (exclusive OR is known as XOR and is a boolean logic condition where either of two conditions are true, but not both) of the information recorded on the other drives. Because an I/O operation addresses all drives at the same time, RAID-3 cannot overlap I/O. For this reason, RAID-3 is best for single-user systems with long record applications.

- **RAID-4**—This type uses large stripes. You can read records from any single drive. This allows you to take advantage of overlapped I/O for read operations. Because all write operations have to update the parity drive, no I/O overlapping is possible. RAID-4 offers no advantage over RAID-5.

- **RAID-5**—This type includes a rotating parity array that addresses the write limitation in RAID-4. All read and write operations can be overlapped. RAID-5 stores parity information but not redundant data, but parity information can be used to reconstruct data. RAID-5 requires at least three, and usually five, disks for the array. It is most suitable for multi-user systems in which performance is not critical or few write operations are performed.

- **RAID-6**—This type is similar to RAID-5 but includes a second parity scheme that is distributed across different drives and offers extremely high fault- and drive-failure tolerance. Few, if any, RAID-6 commercial examples currently exist.

- **RAID-7**—This type includes a real-time, embedded operating system as a controller, caching through a high-speed bus, and other characteristics of a stand-alone computer.

- **RAID-10**—This type offers an array of stripes in which each stripe is a RAID-1 array of drives. This offers a higher performance than RAID-1 but at a much higher cost.

- **RAID-53**—This type offers an array of stripes in which each stripe is a RAID-3 array of disks. This offers a higher performance than RAID-3 but at a much higher cost.

Scalability

Scalability is the ability to change size or configuration to suit changing conditions. For example, a company that plans to set up a client/server network might want to have a system that not only works with the number of people who will immediately use the system, but also with the number who might be using it in ten years.

Scalability also refers to how well a hardware or software system can adapt to increased demands. A scalable network system can start with just a few nodes but can expand to thousands of nodes.

Scalability is an important feature because it means that you can invest in a system with confidence that you will not outgrow it. Scalability is the ease with which a system or component can be modified to fit a problem area. Achieving scalability is usually a combination of good database management (caching, connection pooling), shifting to multiple copies of the application server, using failover capacity, and utilizing load balancing.

This section discusses software scalability, network scalability, application architecture, and hardware scalability.

Software Scalability

Scalable application components can support more than a single instance of an application and retain context, which means retaining the conditions, parameters, and arguments used in a previous operation or query. Scalable application components include the software's capability to employ threads while the software is in operation. A *thread* is the work performed within individual processes.

Writing multithreaded applications enables more efficient use of resources and more scalable applications. Software components that can be distributed across multiple platforms are a characteristic of scalable software solutions. This allows hardware additions and resource expenditures to be strategically matched to the principal growth parameters that affect system performance and growth. Multiprocessing and multithreading are software mechanisms that can achieve the performance and scalability potential offered by Symmetric Multiprocessing (SMP) and Massively Parallel Processor (MPP) systems.

When a developer creates an application, much of the effort goes into defining the scalability of the application. Questions involving scalability include the following:

- How many records can the system hold?
- How many users can use the system at one time?
- How long will retrieving a piece of data from the system take?
- How well does the application grow?

In a traditional application, the developer provides answers to these questions when the system is being built. If the developer fails to address them properly, the application will not scale. As more users begin to access and place a greater load on the system, failures begin to occur. The system will buckle under the load of more users than it was designed to handle.

In a transaction-processing environment, the preceding questions are answered without the developer even having to think about them. The developer creates components that interact with the system as if they had exclusive access to the system and had the system's full resources available to it. The environment efficiently manages multiple objects' resources that could be active at any given time so that each one runs successfully. The environment can reuse objects, rather than create new ones, when they are needed, and destroy them after their work is completed. By managing the objects' lifetime, the environment ensures that as more objects are needed when more users access the system, the system will be able to support them.

Network Scalability

Mission-critical activity over the network is on the rise. A scalable network is more important than ever on both the Internet and on corporate intranets because new network applications, often with web browser interfaces, make networks easier to use. The result is that more people are on the network, generating more traffic per user, at an explosive rate. Many new products, protocols, and services have been created to help address this growing need for highly scalable network solutions.

Scalability Services

Cisco Systems, Inc. provides scalability services beyond the conventional hardware approach of increasing bandwidth and port density. Advanced Cisco IOS technologies help achieve performance capacity from network infrastructure with minimal upgrade requirements using Cisco IOS scalability services, protecting your investment for years to come. Such services include the following:

- **Tag Switching**—This highly scalable technology improves performance over large enterprise networks or over Internet service provider networks by speeding delivery.

- **NetFlow Switching**—This service streamlines the way packets are processed and features are applied. NetFlow switching provides high performance for switching and for higher-layer services, such as quality of service (QoS), security, and traffic management.

- **Express Forwarding**—This service is a new technique from Cisco for scaling Internet backbones through distributed packet forwarding. Express forwarding is one of the fundamental capabilities required for modern Internet routers and next-generation Internet routers to handle the increased load, dynamic traffic patterns, and new applications of the Internet.

- **Network Address Translation (NAT)**—This service allows enterprises and service providers to conserve valuable IP addresses by hiding internal IP addresses from public networks, such as the Internet. NAT reduces time and costs by easing IP address management.

- **Software-Based Compression**—This service increases performance by reducing the amount of traffic over expensive WAN lines.

- **DistributedDirector**—This service provides dynamic, transparent, and scalable Internet traffic load distribution of all IP traffic between multiple servers across topological distances.

Application Architecture

Application architecture plays an important part in an application's scalability. During the design phase, anticipated growth and other influences on an application's operational environment must be taken into account. Remember the following concepts while designing a solution to ensure a better level of scalability:

- Use servers and storage devices in your design that can be upgraded or added to without having a negative cost or time impact on your application. This design includes server clusters or servers that can easily add processors and memory.

- Consider using Operational Service Providers to provide some of your application architecture's operational components.

- Application Service Providers should also be considered during the design phase when appropriate.

Operational Service Providers and Application Service Providers are options that can give you a pay-as-you-go implementation, helping minimize cost and reduce risk. Using a three-tier client/server architecture with Transaction Processing monitor (TP monitor) technology results in an environment that is typically more scalable than a two-tier architecture with a direct client-to-server connection.

Hardware Scalability

From a hardware perspective, processor architecture can impact scalability. Symmetric Multiprocessing (SMP) and Massively Parallel Processing, or Massively Parallel Processor (MPP), architectures offer the potential for parallel execution.

Operating systems and databases can execute tasks on independent processes or threads. The system or database's performance and scalability increase. However, the work performed within individual processes (or threads) is constrained by the speed and resources of a single processor.

The number of processors your server supports also influences an Internet business application's scalability. Adding processors to your system might not always produce the results you expect. The reason for the poor performance is contention: lock, bus, or cache line contention. In contention, the processors fight over the ownership of shared resources instead of doing productive work. Having system monitoring tools in place and analyzing the data is essential for understanding scalability problems.

Storage Area Networks (SANs) are one hardware scalability solution. SANs are back-end network storage devices connected through a variety of standard peripheral channels and fiber channels. You can implement SANs in two ways: centralization and decentralization. A centralized SAN ties multiple hosts into a single storage system, which is a Redundant Array of Independent Disks (RAID) with large amounts of cache and redundant power supplies. The cabling distances allow local, campus-wide, and even metropolitan-wide hookups over peripheral channels rather than to overburdened networks. Storage networks enable a new approach to widespread sharing of large volumes of storage and, by implication, large amounts of data.

Performance

Application performance involves several components that can affect an Internet business solution's performance. User productivity and perception are key measures of the success of Internet business computer applications.

Unlike traditional system and network management, good performance management focuses on the area between an application being up and an application being down. Most organizations know when one of its applications is up or down but don't know what is happening in terms of application performance from an end-user perspective or know whether a significant new application will perform acceptably after it is deployed into the network.

The following performance issues are discussed:

- Baselining
- Architectural design strategies
- Key performance factors
- Custom-developed code
- Operating systems
- Hardware
- Application clients

Baselining

Baselining is a critical technique in determining application performance. Performance baselining involves taking measurements at regular intervals, over a long enough period of time to encompass the normal and busy times. For example, you might find high utilization at certain times every day, but month-end business activity increases utilization to a new, higher overall level. The baseline needs to identify these critical activity peaks.

The frequency at which you take samples and the ways in which you interpret the raw data directly influences the end result of a baseline measurement. For the baselining effort to yield meaningful results, you must do the following:

- Collect only the data that is pertinent.

- Collect data at an acceptable frequency. Network and application usage patterns tend to vary.

- Collect the data for an acceptably long period of time to ensure you have enough data to work with.

- Determine the level of service. Identify metrics and acceptable performance levels. These are typically used in a Service Level Agreement and can include file download times, network latency measures, and application or server response times.

Applications are continually being added and upgraded, and user community responsibilities and their locations are dynamic. Based on this, some form of baselining activity is needed full-time to design and properly maintain a viable infrastructure.

Architectural Design Strategies

Your enterprise's application performance is also affected by design strategies and implementation choices. These architectural options include the following:

- **Logical packaging**—Foundation of a high-performance application always includes good, logical packaging. Logical packaging groups related application services into common components.

- **Physical deployment**—Another important design strategy is to physically deploy the components on the network for optimum efficiency. Application components that have a lot of interaction should be deployed as close to one another as physically possible. For example, place your application servers on the same network segment as your database servers. If database servers cannot be located on the same network segment, data replication or multiple database servers can be employed to improve overall database performance.

- **Multiple instances and reuse**—Multiple instances of a program mean that the program has been loaded into memory several times. This provides increased throughput by allowing the application to work on multiple requests.

Custom-Developed Code

A system's components are often made up of custom-developed, or *coded* software. Poorly executed custom-developed application code falls into four major categories:

- Needless processing
- Redundant computation
- Excessive requests for system services, typically I/O
- Waiting for system service requests to complete

Implementing the following four concepts reduces the impact created by the problem areas described:

- Remove unnecessary or unexecuted code.
- Perform processing only when required.
- Perform required tasks online and move processing to batch process when appropriate.
- Perform required processing efficiently. "Tuned-up" reusable modules can improve quality and execution, and reduce development time.

Key Performance Factors

Upon exploring the idea of performance tuning and application optimization, you might think there are an endless array of possible configurations and parameters. Although this is essentially true, the following key performance factors account for the majority of performance gains that you can achieve:

- Compiler
- Workload growth
- Database
- Indexing
- Normalization
- Stored procedures and triggers

Each is discussed in the following paragraphs.

Compiler—Be aware of the compiler options available and how they are used. Turning off debug and removing all extraneous logging can greatly increase performance. Make sure that the correct version and appropriate libraries are included, especially operating system libraries and libraries for other supporting devices (such as video drivers). The execution modules' distribution and how the processing is dispersed can affect system performance.

Workload growth—Different kinds of workload growth affect application performance, including the following:

- **User population**—More users mean increased transactions, more component access, increased CPU consumption, more network traffic, and additional database access. For example, when the user population doubles, the network and database workloads probably double as well.

- **Database changes**—Databases grow in many ways, including data complexity, stored data volume, and database usage.

- **Transaction complexity**—Applications and their transactions tend to become more complicated. Newly added cross-application interfaces and their associated transaction coordination can create unnoticed resource consumption or blockage.

- **Component allocation**—With distributed components, on-demand component allocation consumes server computer resources. Without service queuing and object pooling, the server computer eventually loses efficiency and could fail.

- **Application population**—As applications become easier and less expensive to build, organizations use computers in new ways. These new applications increase the load on existing databases, server computers, and networks.

The workload your application experiences over time is generally predictable. After your application is up and running and establishes baseline performance statistics, you can identify workload growth trends and patterns using various performance analysis tools.

Database—Database access often imposes the largest performance penalty on your application. This is especially a concern with distributed applications where multiple clients simultaneously access common tables and rows. Although choosing the right data access technology solves an important part of your high-performance requirement, most of your application's database access speed comes from careful data-structure modeling, query optimization, and careful handling of multi-user concurrency situations.

Indexing—Indexing improves the time it takes to access data in the database. Indexes affect not only query performance but also the performance of update, insert, and delete statements. The proper or improper use of indexing on columns within a database can greatly affect the performance of a database. Typically, the primary key for each table is indexed. Foreign keys used with other tables are often indexed to improve performance.

Normalization—Database normalization organizes the contents of the tables for transactional databases and data warehouses. Normalization is used after the initial data objects have been identified in a database and usually duplicates data by creating additional tables. This data duplication should not be confused with redundant data, which is the *unnecessary* duplication of data. Normalization is part of a successful database design. Without normalization, database systems can be inaccurate, slow, and inefficient, and might not produce the results you expect.

A poorly normalized database and poorly normalized tables cause problems ranging from excessive disk Input/Output (I/O) and subsequent poor system performance to inaccurate data. An improperly normalized condition can result in extensive data redundancy, putting a burden on all programs that modify the data.

Businesses with bad normalization experience poor operating systems and inaccurate, incorrect, or missing data. Applying normalization techniques to Online Transaction Processing (OLTP) database design creates efficient systems that produce accurate data and reliable information.

Stored procedures and triggers—Stored procedures are pieces of application code that reside in the database. The stored procedures' advantage is that they cut down on the number of messages that are passed between the application process and the database server. Significant performance increases can be realized if the network is slow, or if several SQL statements are grouped together in a stored procedure.

You can also set triggers within the database to respond to certain events. Stored Procedures and Triggers together make up a powerful development tool.

Operating Systems

Configuring and tuning the operating system is critical to application performance. The operating system is the master control program that runs the computer. It is the first program loaded when the computer is turned on, and its main part, known as the *kernel*, resides in memory at all times. It can be developed by the computer's manufacturer or by a third party.

All programs must communicate with the operating system to function on the computer. The operating system usually offers some level of system resources configuration so you can set up the computer to serve specific functions efficiently.

Operating systems can be classified into the following categories:

- **Multiuser**—Allows two or more users to run programs at the same time. Some operating systems permit hundreds or thousands of concurrent users.

- **Multiprocessing**—Allows you to run a program on more than one CPU.

- **Multitasking**—Allows multiple programs to run concurrently.

- **Multithreading**—Allows different parts of a single program to run concurrently.

- **Real time**—Responds to input instantly. General-purpose operating systems, such as DOS and UNIX, are not real time.

The operating system is a foundation component of an Internet business application's performance. Resources configured and managed by the operating system are often involved with a performance issue. You can often tune or configure the operating system to support specific system requirements.

Most UNIX variants include some type of kernel-level tuning, along with basic tools to monitor CPU, disk, and memory usage. UNIX kernels tend to have many configurable parameters that you can fine-tune for specific applications.

A widespread misconception is that the Windows NT kernel is not configurable. The Windows NT kernel is largely self-tuning. The virtual memory, thread scheduling, and I/O subsystems all dynamically adjust their resource usage and priority to maximize throughput.

When benchmarking the UNIX and Windows NT operating systems, the differences between them are evident. The UNIX approach is to tweak kernel parameters for maximum advantage in the benchmark. The Windows NT approach is to let the kernel tune itself for whatever load is placed on it.

A variety of operating systems are available on the market. From a performance perspective, you should understand how the operating system is tuned, whether self-tuning or configurable, and realize that your Internet business application's performance can be greatly affected if it is not set up properly. Also consider Total Cost of Ownership (TCO). Service and support contracts often equal or surpass the cost of the operating system license.

The TCO for commercial operating systems is becoming increasingly expensive and, as a result, open-source Linux distributions are rapidly gaining market share. International Data Corporation estimates that Linux will have 32 percent of the server market by the end of 2002 and garner 9 percent of corporate IT budget spending. With over 60 percent of active servers running Apache according to Netcraft.com's long-running survey, a free web server running almost entirely on Linux operating systems is an attractive and popular combination. Linux service and support options have also arrived, making the decision to run Linux servers even easier for both small businesses and large corporations.

Hardware

A growing workload affects your application's performance by directly increasing hardware resource consumption. For example, if you have twice as many users as normal after a marketing campaign, you probably also have twice as many database accesses and double the amount of related network traffic.

Ultimately, your application's performance potential is largely constrained by the available hardware. It does little good to optimize your application if the hardware infrastructure is slow and inadequate. The following hardware factors affect performance:

- **CPU consumption**—High CPU use makes every task take longer.
- **Memory allocation**—Inadequate memory causes slow paging to disk.
- **Disk/Input/Output subsystem**—Too much disk input or output slows your application.
- **Network hardware**—Poor-quality network hardware limits throughput.

In a typical enterprise environment, the hardware available to your application is only upgraded occasionally. For most of your application's lifecycle, it will run in the same hardware environment. You should periodically monitor hardware resource consumption to ensure the current and future application performance you expect.

Facts about hardware and its affect on performance follow:

- **Hard disk**—Optimizing the hard disk can relieve server performance problems. Using RAID technology in combination with caching on the drive will improve hard drive performance. Increasing the amount of RAM can increase disk-bound application performance, allowing more data to be held in RAM. If you find that the percentage of time spent hitting the disks is high but the CPU and network utilization is low, look at your hard drives for issues.

- **Memory**—RAM configuration on the server can affect performance. If your server does not have enough memory, it will run slower as it swaps information to exchange files on its hard disk. This memory swapping to hard disk is called *virtual memory*. The performance impact occurs because your hard drive operates much slower than direct RAM access. Not only do the disk swaps interrupt the CPU from processing data, they also prevent the disk from accessing files and data needed by you and your users. If the amount of RAM in your system is so low that your computer spends most of its time reading and writing to its virtual memory, your system RAM is not going to be very useful. If you notice a high number of virtual memory page read faults when monitoring your system, this might indicate that more memory can help increase performance.

- **CPU**—CPU performance is the most important factor when you want to get the most work done in the shortest possible time. If performing a particular operation takes five seconds, is it worth spending an extra $10,000 to do the operation in three seconds? However, if the operation takes five hours and you could reduce the time to one or two hours, the additional expense might be worthwhile. Computational tasks are most affected by CPU performance. Be sure to consider investment protection. The CPU that seems adequate today might not meet your needs in the near future. Hardware development's rapid pace makes existing systems obsolete in a short period of time.

- **Network capacity**—Network capacity is reached when the network is saturated, and the performance will degrade regardless of the server's size. Remember the following capacity issues:
    - Be aware of the saturation of the network card. If you are running on a low-capacity card, you will saturate it quickly.
    - On applications that are accessed across a WAN link (virtually all Internet applications), the WAN link is the slowest network segment involved. Upgrading your server environment to Gigabit Ethernet won't do much good if your bottleneck is the T1 to the Internet. Your application design

should take the expected client connection speeds into account. For example, many people will access a public Internet application through 56 Kbps modems.

— Limiting connections is an excellent way to plan network capacity. Most browsers usually take up to four simultaneous connections to download text and graphics for a web page.

— Set connection timeout values in cases where connections do not break on their own. HTTP Keep-Alives happen when you open a browser session but keep the session running or connection established between the client and server.

— A new feature, called HTTP Compression, actually compresses data before it goes out on the wire. There's a trade-off, of course, because more CPU resources are required for the compression.

Cisco QoS

An integral part of the Cisco end-to-end quality of service (QoS) and intelligent network services, Cisco QoS Policy Manager (QPM) allows network administrators to protect business-critical application performance. By leveraging QoS mechanisms in LAN and WAN switching equipment along with application recognition technologies delivered through advanced Cisco IOS Software, QPM provides enterprise networks with centralized policy control and automated policy deployment.

A full-featured QoS policy system, QPM enables differentiated services for web-based applications, voice traffic, Internet appliances, and business-critical processes, ensuring QoS for network-intensive, critical applications. Relying on differentiated services to enforce QoS end-to-end, QPM delivers the key benefits of enabling advanced differentiated services across LAN and WAN policy domains, automating QoS configuration and deployment, and improving multiservice performance. Using QPM, network managers can quickly apply a mix of QoS policy objectives to protect business-critical application performance.

Now available as an add-in module to QPM is QPM-COPS. An integral part of the Cisco end-to-end QoS and content-aware network initiative, QPM-COPS provides intelligent traffic enforcement through application and user-aware, directory-enabled policy control.

Application Clients

An important Internet business applications consideration is the application client. (See Chapter 5, "Build or Buy," for a definition of application clients and the client-server model.) The client can vary in types of connectivity, hardware, operating systems, and a variety of other factors that can affect performance. Using the client's native system monitoring tools can be a great method to determine where performance issues exist on the client. Good application and code distribution methodologies can ensure that the proper software and software versions are available on the client.

Understanding the target client in the production environment is critical when upgrading or deploying an application. Memory, disk, CPUs, and applications that are expected to run concurrently must be taken into account. A variety of design techniques can be implemented to minimize the adverse performance impacts on the client in the overall performance equation.

The client is typically a shared component in any operating environment; decisions made by others often negatively affect your application in the environment. For this reason, a good monitoring methodology must be in place to support the client portion of any Internet business strategy.

Manageability

Software maintenance is the modification of a software product that improves performance or other attributes to adapt the product to a modified environment. An Internet business application's architecture can greatly affect maintainability and manageability. New technologies employed to meet increasing business demands often negatively affect an application's manageability. This consequence can occur when areas supporting a new architectural component force software or hardware upgrades.

Distribution and management of an Internet business application's elements need to be taken into account. The application distribution's level and volume need to be considered when the application's architecture is selected. Better methodologies are being developed every day to manage the changes required to support an Internet business application. Multiple reasons exist to support the software maintenance:

- Performing enhancements
- Adapting to change in the operational environment
- Correcting errors in the software
- Performing preventive maintenance in anticipation of problems

Performing software enhancements and making changes to accommodate other changes in the operational environment are inevitable, and usually desired. Error correction and preventive maintenance are areas that can always be improved upon. Commonly, 40 to 70 percent of a software application's budget is devoted to maintenance activity over the life of the software.

Many potential reasons exist for having maintenance performed on your software, including a lack of proper software testing and validation when changes are performed, or when new software is introduced into the production environment. The testing phase of software development is often compromised to meet project goals because it falls near the end of the delivery cycle.

Lack of realistic test scripts and data can create the need to maintain software. Nonproduction-like test environments can also create a need for software maintenance. Replicating the complete production environment in which software is expected to run is often impractical because of the large number of variables existing between the production environment and the test environment.

Improper, outdated, or missing documentation relating to the software can increase maintenance activity and cost. Documentation, such as requirements and design documents, is not always available when a maintenance opportunity arises. When documentation is available, it is often outdated and unreliable because it was not properly maintained when the software was modified.

Using standards and tools within an organization can help reduce the cost of software maintenance. Standards and tools provide known quantities and information about software entities that might be candidates for maintenance. A successful software project creates a coding style guide and enforces common coding practices across teams and developers to ensure high-quality work.

You should create software repositories, so that each developer is working with the exact same set of tools and utilities. Standard build environments are also important to keeping a project manageable, and for anticipating the need for a structured approach to environment variable naming and referencing. For example, templates for application start/stop scripts must be created so that software services and components can be killed and reset cleanly and consistently. Such scripts need to be created for web services, application services, and database services. All such scripts and environment configurations should be checked into version control software so that changes are tracked and matched with the corresponding code base.

Failing to manage or address software maintenance can cause an Internet business application to stagnate. Because of the large amount of maintenance activity required to keep the system up and running, there are no resources to pursue other development opportunities. Poor application maintenance practices increase the risk and lower the quality of an application by requiring more frequent changes in a less-controlled manner.

Manageability addresses not only software maintenance and management, but also the idea of designing applications and networked applications to be easily managed and maintained. This approach to application requirements for manageability expands to include several different areas. The manageability discussion in this section covers the following areas:

- Application Services Administration
- Application Integration Tools
- Network Manageability
- Licensing and Maintenance Agreements

- IT Operations Management
- Use of External Service Providers
- Environment Architecture Considerations
- Version Control

Application Services Administration

Application services administration covers a large area related to the configuration and maintenance of applications and services. With the introduction of new methodologies for implementing systems, many writing activities that require code in an application are now performed by modifying a package or service's configuration.

Database administration (DBA) associated with an application can create major issues if not planned and implemented properly. Database administration can consume a large amount of time and increase an application's cost because of changes to data attributes, data volume, backup, recovery, and data distribution.

Typical DBA responsibilities include the following:

- Installing, configuring, and upgrading database server software and related products
- Evaluating database features and database-related products
- Establishing and maintaining sound backup and recovery policies and procedures
- Taking care of the database design and implementation
- Implementing and maintaining database security (creating and maintaining users and roles, and assigning privileges)
- Tuning and monitoring database performance
- Tuning and monitoring application performance
- Setting up and maintaining documentation and standards
- Planning growth and changes (capacity planning)
- Working as part of a team and providing 24-hour support when required
- Performing general, technical troubleshooting interface with the database provider for technical support
- Facilitating sharing common data by overseeing proper key management and data dictionary maintenance

Application Integration Tools

Application integration tools can create manageability concerns for the Internet business application. Tools such as electronic data interchange (EDI), Common Object Request

Broker Architecture (CORBA), and Component Object Model (COM) require a considerable amount of configuration and management to work properly and to keep pace with the dynamics of a business operational environment. These files are often not maintained under proper configuration management practices and are poorly documented. To guard against some of the pitfalls associated with these tools, configuration management must maintain configuration and associated parameters. In addition, the parameters, values, and justification for the chosen values must be included.

Network Manageability

A system's network component is typically in a state of change as new applications become available and others are removed. Network management requires the creation of several different kinds of diagrams: physical, logical, system, security, and data flow. Physical network diagrams also include rack elevations, which detail the components that are placed within each rack in a server room. Network management involves using monitoring tools to access the network's performance. These tools, along with a solid network management and change control process, can minimize the impact of network administration.

The maintenance of elements, such as routing tables, firewalls, and connections, can create problems in the production environment if not diagramed, managed, and communicated properly. The following list details typical network management activities:

- Assessing network management functions (personnel, organizational, procedures, systems, and so on)
- Identifying, creating, and implementing automation and behavior models to improve environment management and reduce manual processes
- Updating network management application configurations documentation
- Capacity planning and optimization
- Controlling network management system configurations
- Troubleshooting applications
- Collecting system usage statistics and generating reports
- Maintaining and configuring backup network management systems
- Defining and generating network performance reports
- Analyzing system and network performance trends
- Identifying and resolving network faults for network uptime, stability, and customer satisfaction
- Optimizing complex network management applications
- Ensuring operational consistency

The following discussion provides examples of network diagrams for a basic e-commerce web site.

Figure 4-2 depicts an e-commerce network from the physical perspective. You should create and maintain a physical network diagram so that all administrative and support teams can readily identify the components and systems with which they work.

Figure 4-2   *e-commerce Physical Network Diagram*

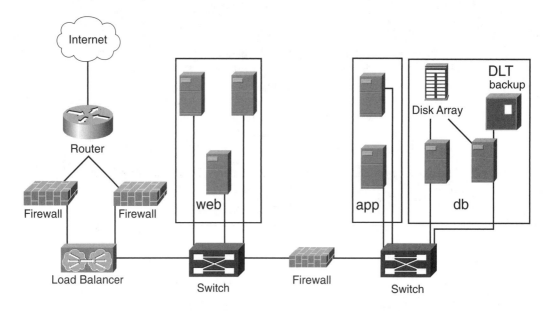

Figure 4-3 is a logical network diagram; it is necessary to understand the underlying structure of a set of servers used to create an Internet business solution, such as an e-commerce web site.

Figure 4-3   *e-commerce Logical Network Diagram*

Figure 4-4 shows information about the systems that comprise the example e-commerce web site. This systems inventory and basic system configuration information is necessary to know how each system is loaded, and whether there is additional capacity to add more CPUs, RAM, or disk space before needing to purchase additional systems.

Figure 4-4   *e-commerce Systems Information*

Name	Model	CPU	RAM	Disk	Service Contract
web-1	Sun Netra T1	1x400 MHz	512 MB	2x9 Gig internal	platinum
web-2	Sun Netra T1	1x400 MHz	512 MB	2x9 Gig internal	platinum
web-3	Sun Netra T1	1x400 MHz	512 MB	2x9 Gig internal	platinum
app-1	Sun E420R	1x400 MHz	2 GB	2x9 Gig internal	platinum
app-2	Sun E420R	1x400 MHz	2 GB	2x9 Gig internal	platinum
db-1	Sun E6500	1x400 MHz	2 GB	2x18 Gig internal	platinum
db-2	Sun E6500	1x400 MHz	2 GB	2x18 Gig internal	platinum
StorEdge Disk Array	A5000			45 Gig	platinum
fibre channel disk controller	PCI FC				
DLT 7000 Library	L280				
router	Cisco 2524				platinum
load balancer	Cisco CSS 11050		128 MB		platinum
switch-1	Cisco 2926				platinum
switch-2	Cisco 2926				platinum
firewall-1	PIX 520	266 MHz	512 MB		platinum
firewall-2	PIX 520	266 MHz	512 MB		platinum
firewall-3	PIX 520	266 MHz	512 MB		platinum

Figure 4-5 contains information about the data flow in the e-commerce production environment. A data flow diagram depicts the essential transaction directions between components.

Figure 4-5   *e-commerce Data Flow Network Diagram*

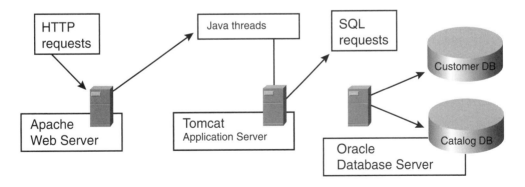

Figure 4-6 is a rack elevation diagram of the e-commerce web site. Rack elevation diagrams detail the use of available server room rack space and make sure that physical systems have sufficient space before installation occurs.

Figure 4-6   *e-commerce Rack Elevation Diagram*

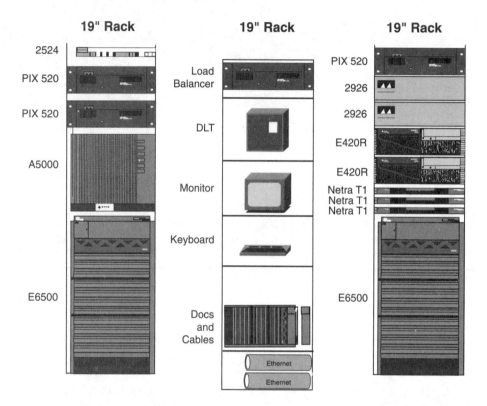

Licensing and Maintenance Agreements

A clear understanding of licensing associated with the tools provided by external vendors is important when considering changes and upgrades to an Internet business application.

Software licensing uses many different models, some of which are based on the number of physical machines involved, and others on the number and speed of CPUs. Being aware of the licensing model for key software and how upgrades and changes to accommodate growth affects your project costs is an important factor in choosing your software products. Database and middleware application licensing can cost as much as $100,000 per CPU.

You should also take the maintenance agreements associated with external software into account. A maintenance agreement is typically an annual agreement whereby the vendor agrees to provide specific support for its product, often including upgrades. A maintenance agreement's cost is typically between 5 to 25 percent of the total cost of the software package.

Maintenance agreements typically provide one of three levels of support, with "platinum" support being the highest. At this level, maintenance support is provided within one hour of a reported problem. Critical production systems generally require platinum-level support even if they are equipped with clustered or fault-tolerant components. Staging and development systems are usually maintained with "gold" or "silver" maintenance packages where service and support work is performed the next business day, or as available.

IT Operations Management

A specific team often manages the day-to-day operation of an enterprise Internet business application production environment. The operations management team typically provides the following services:

- 24-hour, 365-day coverage
- Console operations
- Tape handling, library, and storage
- Onsite maintenance staff
- Help desk services
- Technical support
- Backup and disaster recovery
- Application/component distribution

This group typically delivers the services related to the Service Level Agreement (SLA). Take the SLA into consideration from the initiation of any modification to the operating environment; otherwise, meeting the expectations detailed in the SLA might be difficult.

Use of External Service Providers

One method of handling an Internet business application's manageability is to use external service providers. The service providers have expertise in the areas in which they provide service. An Application Service Provider (ASP) can help a business handle the manageability issues associated with an application, allowing the business to focus on its customers. Remember, however, that risk is involved with allowing an external entity access to certain information about your business's core functionality.

Environment Architecture Considerations

During an Internet business application lifecycle, you must take an application that is currently in production, maintain that version, and create a subsequent "enhanced" version. You must consider the components management associated with maintaining a proper relationship among these environments.

Version Control

Version control is crucial to performing staged software code releases. A release schedule is the most often-used technique for supporting an application's manageability. Version control assists in the management of parallel environments. Enterprise-wide systems typically involve a number of components, and when upgrades are desired, they are sometimes difficult to develop and test in the upgraded environment while the environments needed to support the version in production are maintained.

A release schedule allows different areas of an enterprise to introduce enhancements and new versions, and test interfaces along with shared systems components that can be in the process of being upgraded at the same time. As technology advances, new methods for dealing with the multiple environment issue are becoming available. Creating environments in which to perform stress and volume testing presents a challenge because of the expense and resources involved in reproducing a production-like environment where proper conditions are present during testing and validation.

Integration Concepts

Application integration is when multiple, dissimilar applications work together as if they were one application. Application integration is mainly a function of traditional programming. Occasionally, one package will support the interfaces of one or two other packages. The current trend is to use message brokers and queues, applications servers, and other specialized integration products that provide a common connecting point. These prepackaged middleware solutions are widely used to enable an enterprise through the web.

The trend in the Internet business application arena is moving toward using *Enterprise Application Integration (EAI)*, which is interoperability and information synchronization across multiple applications—mainframe, packaged or purchased systems, and custom application systems. EAI enables information sharing within a business environment that includes a company, its suppliers, and its customers. EAI incorporates application integration within internal processes, as well as external entities that interface with the business.

To establish EAI, a tool or methodology must be in place to facilitate the process. EAI solutions enable the following services:

- **Message services**—These services provide the backbone of an EAI framework. This backbone transports messages between resources, reconciling network and protocol differences. Message services support features such as security, queuing, and guaranteed delivery.
- **Connectivity services**—These services provide the path and traffic management for message flow between integrated resources.
- **Security services**—These services provide user authentication, resource access control, and information encryption. This technology must also integrate with existing security implementations.

The following is a list of business benefits of using application integration:

- Extracting value from mergers and acquisitions
- Delivering new levels of customer care
- Benefiting from the investment in Enterprise Resource Planning (ERP) applications
- Exploiting the benefits of Customer Relationship Management (CRM)
- Delivering supply chain management benefits
- Integrating web-based information
- Delivering Internet business from old world business
- Achieving faster time-to-market of new products through an automated information flow
- Reducing cost and complexity compared with custom, point-to-point integration

From integration, managers usually hope to see the following:

- 25 to 50 percent reduction in time-to-market for new applications
- 25 to 60 percent lower development costs for integration infrastructure
- 10 to 20 percent reduction in infrastructure maintenance costs

An effective application integration strategy can position an enterprise to take advantage of new opportunities. Application integration projects emphasize the need for a common definition of information between applications. The greatest problems in enterprise application implementations come from difficulties in ownership and defining business rules and data, not from technology.

To illustrates integration's nuances, the discussion is divided into the following areas:

- Risk Factors
- Preplanning for Successful Application Integration
- Middleware
- Enterprise Resource Planning

Risk Factors

Consider the risk factors when looking at EAI. Risks should be factored in when approaching large-scale application integration:

- Is the patchwork of systems and databases developed without any architecture plan?
- Have attempts at small-scale integration occurred with less than optimal results?
- Are there conflicts between IT strategy and corporate strategy?
- Is there high acquisition and merger activity in the business area?
- Are there industry competitive pressures?

Preplanning for Successful Application Integration

Making the right decisions when it comes to application integration requires you to understand the various business requirements for applications. In addition, you need to know where they fit into the overall organizational context.

Achieving integration requires a comprehensive plan based on a proven methodology. The methodology should focus not just on the technology itself, but also on leveraging the technology to provide a solution that meets business requirements.

The following questions should be asked when considering application integration:

- How many applications need to be integrated?
- How much of the budget is available to build, integrate, and support the applications?
- What entry points are available into the applications being integrated?
- How current does the data need to be?
- Does the application's end user need an immediate confirmation that the transaction completed or failed?
- What level of integrity checks or native business logic needs to be applied on data passed between applications?
- Is the end user willing to accept separate user interfaces into separate applications on the desktop for executing the business process?
- Is application development and support structured along vertical business lines or horizontal layers of services?
- What resources—in terms of hardware, software, networks, number of staff, and staff skills—are available to address problems in application integration?
- Is unidirectional or bidirectional data flow needed?
- How important is having a single master copy or "single source of truth" for the data?

Middleware

Middleware is any program or application that connects or "glues" other programs or applications. Middleware is a methodology often incorporated into an enterprise application integration strategy because rewriting existing applications is generally prohibitively expensive.

Middleware can be classified into the following groups:

- **Message-oriented middleware**—Provides a common messaging interface and transport among applications. Typically supported features include store and forward, message queue management, and recovery. The messaging system can contain business logic that routes messages to the appropriate destinations and reformats the data. IBM's MQSeries is an example of message-oriented middleware.

- **Object-oriented middleware**—Enables processes to run anywhere in the network. These methods provide a way to execute programs (objects) written in different programming languages, running on different platforms, anywhere on the network. Examples of object-oriented middleware include Common Object Request Broker Architecture (CORBA), Distributed Component Object Model (DCOM), and Enterprise JavaBeans (EJB).

- **Transaction Processing (TP) middleware**—Provides integrity in a distributed environment by ensuring that transactions do not get lost or damaged. This type of middleware can perform many functions, including load balancing, high availability, and guaranteeing that all databases can be updated from a single transaction.

- **Database middleware**—Provides a common interface between a query and multiple databases. This method is typically implemented using either a hub and spoke architecture or a distributed architecture. This type of middleware enables data to be consolidated from a variety of disparate data sources into a single view. Database software that can provide database middleware services includes Oracle, DB2, SQLServer, MySQL, and PostgreSQL.

Enterprise Resource Planning

Enterprise Resource Planning (ERP) is an integrated information system that serves all departments within an enterprise. Evolving out of the manufacturing industry, ERP uses packaged software rather than proprietary software written by, or for, one customer. ERP modules can integrate with an organization's software with varying degrees of effort. ERP modules are also alterable with the vendor's proprietary tools, as well as proprietary or standard programming languages.

ERP systems include software packages in various combinations for manufacturing, order entry, accounts receivable and payable, general ledger, purchasing, warehousing, transportation, and human resources.

Summary

Successful Internet business solutions determine application requirements before starting the planning or development phases. Certain nonfunctional requirements, such as security, reliability, availability, scalability, performance, and manageability, are common among various types of applications and projects, and should be addressed in almost all cases. An application's needs assessment should identify the important characteristics relevant to the business tasks the application is meant to provide.

Many specific tools and technologies that exist to build networked applications are presented in each of the sections of this chapter, and you are directed to the books in Appendix A for more detailed treatments of these topics.

This chapter also presents items for consideration when working on a project with application integration requirements. Successful application integration relies on adequate planning to avoid risks and usually relies on introducing application middleware to mediate communications between existing programs and applications.

Although applications you will work on as a CISS have many diverse and unique functional requirements, a good foundation in basic application requirements (nonfunctional requirements) helps to identify and plan the development of application functions and features that make it useful and unique.

Review Questions

1 Which statement is a common approach when designing an application's authentication structure?

   a. Focus on creating and building the authentication structure within the application.

   b. Rely on the application's team to design and implement the authentication services.

   c. Focus on selecting the simplest and most cost-effective solution.

   d. Rely on external authentication services that are available to the application.

2 Access control mechanisms within an application should be able to support some basic objectives. Which of the following objectives is not an achievable objective?

   a. Detecting when end users share their access privileges

   b. Encrypting stored data

   c. Assigning a security profile to each end user

   d. Managing user accounts and policies

3 Data confidentiality and data integrity can be achieved through appropriately implementing authentication and access control mechanisms. Which of the following implementations does not support either of these two goals?

a. Performing periodic audit log reviews to prevent security breaches

b. Including edit checks, such as date checks and valid ranges, in data entry panels

c. Assigning access to sensitive data only to end users with a need to know

d. Enabling data encryption services within the application

4 To support auditing requirements, applications must provide certain logging conditions. Which of the following is not considered an essential condition?

a. Log the data, time, and location for all significant events.

b. Log all modifications, additions, or deletions made against the database.

c. Log all inquiries made against the database.

d. Log the identity of the user or process that performed an action.

5 What is the purpose of security technologies?

a. To make an application more accessible and available through security

b. To provide an application with a safer and more secure image

c. To enhance the look and feel of the application

d. To ensure that an application is completely protected from threats

6 An effective tool that monitors events in an application log for attacks, anomalous activities, resource utilization, and availability is an example of _____ .

a. Directory services

b. Virtual Private Networks

c. Public key infrastructure

d. Intrusion-detection systems

7 What is the correct definition of reliability?

a. Reliability is the probability that a system or a system's capability functions without failure for a specified time.

b. Reliability is the ability to service a component in the system without shutting down the entire operation.

c. Reliability is when the state of an executing program is periodically saved to a disk file from which it can be recovered.

d. Reliability is the ability to continue to perform a specified task even when a hardware failure occurs.

8 What is the correct definition of availability?

   a. Availability is the process of restoring a backup because of a planned business situation or an unplanned event.

   b. Availability is the probability that a system functions satisfactorily in a specified environment.

   c. Availability is a way to store the same data in different places on multiple hard disks.

   d. Availability provides a means for easier management of your computing resources, while not restricting the systems' potential capabilities.

9 Which of these choices is not a method used to achieve reliability and availability?

   a. SLAs

   b. Outage

   c. Backup and recovery

   d. Clustering

10 Which statement does not describe a scalability characteristic?

   a. Scalability is the ease with which a system or component is modified to fit a problem area.

   b. Scalability is a combination of things, including good database management.

   c. Scalability refers to how well a hardware or software system can adapt to increased demands.

   d. Scalability will not change in size or configuration to suit changing conditions.

11 Which question is not a factor to consider for scalability?

   a. How many records can the system hold?

   b. How well does the application grow?

   c. How many users can use the system at one time?

   d. How long can each user be on the system?

12 In relation to scalable software solutions, software components should be distributed across what type of platform?

   a. Multithreaded

   b. Single

   c. Threaded

   d. Multiple

13 Which method should not be considered to ensure a scalable network?

   a. Increasing the number of CPUs on your web servers

   b. Express forwarding

   c. DistributedDirector

   d. Tag switching

14 Which service allows enterprises and service providers to conserve valuable IP addresses by hiding internal IP address from public networks?

   a. DistributedDirector

   b. Tag switching

   c. Network Address Translation

   d. NetFlow switching

15 If you double the number of processors on your web server, performance should _____ .

   a. Decrease by half

   b. Increase, but less than double

   c. Increase exponentially by a factor of four

   d. Double

16 Which factor is not important for application performance?

   a. User productivity

   b. Application being up

   c. Perception

   d. Logic

17 What workload growth is related to increased transactions and more component access?

   a. User population

   b. Transaction complexity

   c. Component allocation

   d. Application population

18 What design factor determines how a database can affect performance?

   a. Workload growth

   b. Transaction complexity

   c. Indexing

   d. Application population

19 Which of these statements describes a multi-user operating system?

   a. It allows two or more users to run programs at the same time. Some operating systems permit hundreds or thousands of concurrent users.

   b. The operating system supports running a program on more than one CPU.

   c. It allows multiple programs to run concurrently.

   d. The operating system allows different parts of a single program to run concurrently.

20 Which of these actions is not a reason to support software maintenance?

   a. Performing enhancements to optimize

   b. Correcting errors in the software

   c. Adapting to change in the operational environment

   d. Adding an Internet interface to a legacy billing application

21 Application services administration can affect application manageability by which of these means?

   a. Taking care of the database design and implementation

   b. Not maintaining documentation and standards

   c. Working without a team

   d. Capacity planning

22 Which of these services is not typically provided by the operations management team?

   a. Changing the application code to add new functionality

   b. Providing console services

   c. Retaining an onsite maintenance staff

   d. Operating a help desk service

23 Which of these features is not required to support an application's manageability?

  a. Architecture

  b. Environments that perform stress and volume testing

  c. Global clientele

  d. Distribution and management

24 Which statement is not a description of application integration?

  a. Application integration is about interoperability and information synchronization across multiple applications.

  b. Application integration is about bringing together multiple disparate applications so that they work together, as if they were one application.

  c. Application integration provides the path and traffic management for message flow between integrated resources.

  d. Application integration must have a tool or methodology in place to facilitate this process.

25 What benefit is not linked to application integration?

  a. 10 to 15 percent reduction in IT budget

  b. 25 to 50 percent reduction in time-to-market for new applications

  c. Increased efficiency through consistent and accurate information available in real time

  d. Reduced cost and complexity compared to custom point-to-point integration

26 What question should not be asked when considering application integration?

  a. What resources are available to address the problem?

  b. How much space is on the hard drive?

  c. What entry points are available into the applications being integrated?

  d. How many applications need to be integrated?

Applied Solutions

Scenario: e-commerce Web Site Requirements

Problem

Your company has responded to a request for proposals to build an e-commerce web site for a company that currently has a modest web presence with no interactivity or e-commerce funtionality. Its business requirements indicate that it has allocated a sufficient budget to provide some degree of redundancy and fault tolerance, but not a complete cross-connected matrix of redundant hardware. Identify the basic application requirements and specify the hardware configurations needed to build a basic e-commerce platform for the client.

Solution

Figures 4-2 through 4-6 in this chapter represent a prototypical, e-commerce web site architecture with moderate levels of redundancy and fault tolerance in key locations. I have chosen to make the figures based on a Sun Solaris platform because it has time and again proven to be a reliable and scalable platform. This does not, however, mean that other operating systems can't be used in a similar arrangement of servers.

This basic architecture could easily be used as a baseline architecture for an Internet-based customer care application, a workforce optimization application (such as a time and expense reporting tool), a supply-chain management system, or an e-learning or e-publishing system. Only a few components would need to be added to accommodate these various purposes. Many of the single servers and components could be replaced with multiple servers or network hardware depending on the kinds of transactions being performed and the demands placed on each layer of the architecture.

Solution Details

The firewalls are configured in a failover setup, with one firewall serving as active and the other as standby. Redundant routers could be added to this front-end connection, if desired. Active and standby load balancers could likewise be added, depending on the application's needs and expected traffic levels. Three web servers currently make up the web farm, but another dozen could be added as the site scales for growth.

A firewall is placed between the web servers and the rest of the servers because the web servers are the only machines that need to have publicly routed IP addresses and represent the first point of attack or possible entry. The front-end firewalls would be configured to allow only port 80 (HTTP) and port 443 (HTTPS) traffic. Administrative access to the systems could be provided by means of a VPN tunnel, a dedicated back-end private network connection, or a dial-up ISDN connection. Even with a back-end private network connection, however, firewalls should be added on each side of the private link so that a compromise in the e-commerce site would not compromise internal development servers on the administrative team's network.

The application servers are configured with dual processors and 2 GB of RAM, as this layer is expected to perform the bulk of the work in processing user requests. Connection pooling on the application servers will reduce the impact of high-usage levels experienced by the database. Both the application servers and the web servers have two mirrored 9 GB internal disks.

The database is configured with dual, internal, mirrored 18 GB SCSI disks. The external fiber channel disk array is used for the data partitions, while the internal disks contain the operating system and database software. Depending on the application and transaction needs, the disk array can have more disks added. The disk should be configured as a shared node for high availability clustering. If a fault is detected by the clustering software (Veritas or Sun cluster, for example), the disk array is unmounted by the failed machine and handed over to the second database server.

Optional components that could be added to this architecture include the following:

- Dedicated intrusion detection servers (Host-based intrusion detection would be added to these machines after they have been "hardened" by shutting off unused services such as printer daemons, NFS daemons, email daemons, and so on.)

- An active/active database solution instead of active/standby. Oracle Parallel Server is an example of this kind of high performance, high availability solution.

- syslog log server for firewall syslogs, web logfiles, and application logfiles.

- Search server providing dedicated content index and search functionality.

- Image server providing dedicated image serving if the site is heavy on graphic images or images of catalog contents.

- Mail server for dedicated processing outbound and inbound e-mails.

- Additional database servers to host specific tablespaces instead of having all databases on one machine.

- logfile stats server to provide dedicated reporting and analysis of web site traffic.

- FTP server if application or service requires transfer of documents and data with clients or partners.

- Other specialized servers or segregated instances of web, application, or database services.

The core architecture does not really change, but you could develop a few more network connections alongside the web servers, or with the application and database servers. Additionally, a site does not need to necessarily use the Apache web server, Tomcat application server, or Oracle database.

Netscape web server, ATG Dynamo application server, Weblogic application server, DB2, or my SQL databases have all been used in projects I have worked on depending on budget, essential functionality, legacy compatibility, and so on. Restrictions on mixing and matching components have decreased over the last few years, so it is unlikely that you will choose two components and realize while installing one of them that no module or plug-in is available to connect it with another component.

CHAPTER 5

Build or Buy?

Deciding whether to insource or outsource all or part of an application requires the awareness of issues about expertise, maintainability, security, costs, time to market, and life expectancy. The question of whether to build or buy your applications, or components of your applications, requires understanding the application's many levels of detail and planning for the application within the context of your business strategy.

Over the last ten years, outsourcing has become more widely accepted among large companies for IT functions, as well as other business processes. Eastman Kodak was one of the first Fortune 500 companies to make the change by outsourcing its IT functions to IBM, DEC, and Businessland in 1988; however, effective use of outsourcing is not limited to large companies. Small businesses can benefit from outsourcing business processes, enabling them to focus on doing exactly what they are good at.

Insourced and outsourced applications can, when pursued without sufficient attention, introduce delays, limit functionality, and block overall business success. Knowing how to avoid problems for your project is the first thing you should learn. Knowing whether to build or buy is the second.

Internet business solutions comprise a mixture of contributors, making most projects co-sourced. This introduces potential risks because of control and scheduling problems and must be weighed against the costs of a more outsourced approach. An application service provider (ASP) can offer a significant portion of the required services and functionality, but sometimes development and security concerns make a shared environment unacceptable. Extension of application functionality can also be less rapid when working with an outsourced solution, as handing off information between development groups can hamper rapid execution.

Finding the right mix of developers and vendors can be difficult. One goal of this chapter is to present sufficient information about the factors involved so that you can make an informed decision for your project.

Deciding which pieces of an application development effort are built in-house and which are built through outsourced developers depends primarily on cost for most decisions. The accurate calculation of costs is not easy to estimate. This chapter's second goal is to help you identify any hidden costs or unexpected implications of your choice to build or buy.

This chapter is divided into the following sections:

- Insourcing
- Outsourcing
- Application Service Provider Outsourcing
- Network Implications of Sourcing Decisions

Insourcing

The insourcing model provides a framework with which a company controls, configures, and administers all parts of a business application. The insourcing model requires participation of the three main business facets: administration, products/services (including marketing), and production. To successfully complete its function within a business, an application needs the strong and equal support of all facets of a business.

The internal sponsor/developer considers the following before determining whether to insource:

- Core elements of a business
- Resource requirements
- Risk factors
- Security issues
- Delivery accountability
- Insourcing advantages
- Insourcing disadvantages
- Insourcing team-selection and training issues

Core Business Definition

A core business involves products or services with which the business has an objective to be best in the world and with which the business maintains a substantial competitive edge over all competition.

Businesses normally insource core business interests for four fundamental reasons:

- **Competency**—The company maintains its competitive edge by building and maintaining a knowledge and skill lead in core business areas.
- **Future business**—The company uses its skill and knowledge base in core business areas to develop additional business innovations.

- **Availability**—For some core business areas, the company will have trouble finding another company with sufficient ability in the core area to provide effective application support.

- **Protection**—The company might not want to enter into a business arrangement with an outsourcing company that will give outsourcing company employees expertise in any significant part of the core business and create a possible source of competitive expertise.

Insourcing Resource Requirements

The insourced business application requires that the company supply, from its own assets, expertise, production personnel, production equipment, computing capability, databases, support infrastructure, growth plans, and system updates.

Many companies do not know how much resource they provide for internal business applications. These applications often use resources that previously supported other business applications. Because the resources come from various parts of the business, not all get counted. Chief information officers often underestimate the resources they supply to any particular IS business application by as much as 50 percent.

The following two sections give an example of a successful insourced application and an unsuccessful insourced application.

Example of a Successful Insourced Application

Insourcing application costs are often simply absorbed as overhead. For example, an insourced application might require data communications over a telecommunications line. If a small company leases a 56 kBps line for $200 a month, the company IS department can multiplex the application data communications over that line. The fraction of the bandwidth consumed by the application can be added to the total communication through that pipe and not be noticed.

Example of an Unsuccessful Insourced Application Negative

Insourcing can prove to be a difficult or impossible task. Not all projects that begin as an internal effort should remain insourced. A bank CEO mandated that the IS department deliver across-the-board, comprehensive Internet service to all six bank departments. The internal IS technicians did all they could to maintain the internal LAN and associated equipment, but the current staff did not possess the required skills. Realizing that trying to hire additional IS staff would be difficult, expensive, and time consuming, the CIO included the existing IS staff in planning, but decided it was necessary to outsource the project.

Insourcing Risk Factors

You can generally classify risk factors as development failures, noncompetitive application failures, or need change failures. With a development failure, the company cannot successfully develop the application. Noncompetitive application failures occur when the implemented application cannot competitively provide the product or service. Need change failures arise when the need that induced implementation changes during the time needed to develop and implement the application.

Another primary risk factor is the inability to obtain personnel with the correct expertise. Competition for personnel with expertise in competitive business technologies makes recruiting personnel difficult and expensive. The same competitive forces make retaining expert technical personnel for the duration of the application development and implementation process difficult.

Taking the necessary time to develop a business application exposes the company to another risk—competing companies that implement the application first. By being first on the market with a new and needed application, first access to customers is ensured, as well as establishing name association with the application product or service.

Consider, also, the insourcing risk of obsolescence. The application solution can become obsolete before you realize the anticipated return on investment. This factor becomes particularly apparent in the computer and information services fields, where technology changes at an exponential rate. The combination of quick implementation and continual application maintenance serves as the best guard against this risk.

Insourcing Security Issues

Business applications can be a security risk through compromising system expertise or sensitive company information. The insourcing model allows the most secure environment of all the sourcing models. By definition, the insourcing model allows the company to control most application aspects by keeping everything associated with the application within the company. Nonetheless, you still need to be concerned about information selling and data encryption or disguise.

To further illustrate the security topic, the discussion is divided into the following sections:

- Security of Employee-Held Information
- Data Encryption

Security of Employee-Held Information

Company employees and contractors working for the company represent the knowledge and skills basic to the business application. Company employees operating the application can have access to the data generated by the application that contains sensitive company information. These employees take this information with them when they leave the company. They could also compromise the information while still employed.

Employee training concerning security issues and nondisclosure and intellectual property agreement requirements provides the best protection against exposure to this type of security issue. To handle critical company matters associated with the application, divide work and isolate employee involvement with the application to prevent any one employee from having access to all components. This prevents any employee from being able to violate company security.

Data Encryption or Disguise

For those situations in which the internally generated data associated with a business application is exposed to compromise, the company can either encrypt the data or keep it completely unformatted. Only those personnel with the decryption key can decipher the data. Completely unformatted data will, while providing no real security protection, provide ambiguous interpretations of application data for anyone intercepting it. This is only true where the data itself does not divulge its use or field type. For example, a series of yes and no values in a data record doesn't offer much meaning to the interceptor of such data.

Insourcing Delivery Accountability

Delivery accountability rests with the department responsible for using the application to generate revenue. Delivery accountability of all business applications within a core area typically belongs to the senior management person in that area. With the insourcing model, the senior manager in a core area assigns delivery accountability to a middle manager in charge of the business application. This delegation does not relieve the senior manager or chief executive officer of ultimate delivery responsibility.

Advantages of Insourcing

Using an insourcing model means you retain control of the project. A company can ensure that it maintains its status as primary provider (and maybe the only provider) in a core business area. Insourcing also allows a project to make changes to nonfunctional requirements as the project proceeds. Reporting requirements, for example, might have been initially gathered and specified in a project plan, but as the project nears completion, additional reports might be desired which, with an insourced project, are not hard to accommodate.

Disadvantages of Insourcing

Using an insourcing model means you must acquire and maintain the personnel expertise and equipment for the application. In the case of core business interests, you might already have or require the personnel expertise and equipment for normal operational purposes. For noncore business applications, this requirement becomes a serious capacity drain on other more important business resources. In general, the benefits of an insourced project come with added costs for those advantages.

Management of Team Selection and Training When Using Insourcing

An ongoing insourced project requires the right team selection and training. Team selection can take months to complete, depending on the skills and experience required for developing the application. If the technology chosen is not widely available, or the implementation requires advanced knowledge of relatively new development tools, team selection can cause delays.

You can move hiring forward by relaxing strict requirements. If, for example, the original request is for a Java programmer with x years of experience, a faster hire can be accomplished by seeking a good foundation in Java programming and the ability to learn quickly. In addition, using senior developers to mentor junior developers reduces hiring costs, and encourages common coding styles and practices on your team.

Budgeting for formal training is a good idea even with an experienced team of developers. As software development tools change, changes in the architecture and conceptual models employed by application development tools also change.

By providing the opportunity for ongoing skills training, you increase the value of your team members, create the chance for advancement to senior developer positions, and keep new hire costs lower (by creating vacancies on your team in junior-level positions).

Outsourcing

The outsourcing model provides a definable and controllable way for a company to use a combination of another company's expertise, equipment, software, and facilities to develop, implement, operate, or maintain a business application. Just as with the insourcing model, a company using the outsourcing model needs to involve and represent the requirements of all three facets of the business.

Companies with technical areas of core business interest typically outsource the following activities of their day-to-day operations:

- Traditional service activities performed in-house, such as accounting or employee benefits administration and payroll

- Complementary and departmentally common activities, such as copying, mailing, imaging, or record archiving

- Disciplines in which outsiders have greater expertise, such as equipment calibration, advertising, or legal opinions

When making a strategic decision about business function sourcing, consider the following before determining whether to outsource:

- Context business definition

- History of application outsourcing

- Resource requirements

- Risk factors

- Security issues

- Delivery accountability issues

- Outsourcing advantages

- Outsourcing disadvantages

- Managing team selection and training when using outsourcing

Context Business Definition

A context business involves activities in which the company has no desire to compete but are necessary to the organization's function or application product or service production.

The decision to outsource context business functions and processes is often based on the following four considerations:

- **Competency**—For the type of context business functions outsourced, companies can usually save money by relying on service providers whose competencies are greater than their own. For example, payroll services are a commonly outsourced context business function.

- **Currency**—Keeping current with changes in tax and labor laws is easier for service providers than for individual companies. Keeping current with the constantly changing terms and conditions is a common reason to outsource such functions.

- **Availability**—A benefits provider already has a significant infrastructure with which to administer a benefits plan and employee access to available benefits information. Providing similar availability within an organization is not cost effective for many companies.

- **Protection**—A contracted service provider can protect a company by the terms of a contract, which often explicitly indemnifies the company from the consequences of mistakes or the cost of remedies to problems with the service.

Evolution of Application Outsourcing

Business application outsourcing started with time-sharing the first mainframe computers. Companies that could not afford their own industrial-strength computer, but who needed the efficiencies of one, outsourced computer applications to a provider running a large and complex mainframe computer.

Now that computer and storage costs have decreased to affordable levels, the concept of outsourcing that which cannot be justified internally has become embedded in the industry. The concept has recently evolved so that companies not only outsource activities they cannot support but also those that can be performed more efficiently externally. The driving force for this policy is not just to save money, but also to free resources for core business activities.

Recently, a new class of companies started offering services on a different basis. Rather than continuing to contract capability or activity needs, service providers encourage companies to rent capability or activity on a periodic or even per-use basis. In this way, as the client company grows or increases its needs, the service provider automatically increases its business and revenue. This technique allows small, startup companies to initially afford the service. If that client grows, the service provider inherits the business.

An additional advantage to service providers is the automatic market for updates. Unlike companies that still use software they bought or leased years ago, the new business arrangement automatically upgrades the clients each time they use the service. The upgrade cost is included in the continuing service rental.

Renting applications over the Internet provides a quick way to acquire top enterprise applications with small up-front costs. Tom Gormley, of Forester Research, Inc., predicted that by 2001, 15 to 20 percent of packaged application software licenses would be rented. His research indicated that the application rental market would rise to $6.4 billion. Imagining that the evolution of outsourcing can come full circle is easy, as indicated by Microsoft's intention to move to subscription-based desktop applications in lieu of purchasing copies of software with future releases of common office suite applications, such as Word, Excel, and Outlook.

Vertical Networks, Inc.

Vertical Networks, Inc. develops integrated communications platforms for small- to medium-sized businesses. It anticipates becoming a billion-dollar business but plans to limit its operational infrastructure to that of a $50 million company. To do this, Vertical Networks plans to use outsourcing to build out from its core competencies of product development and marketing. Any noncore activities that it cannot outsource will provide the opportunity for Virtual Networks to partner with already established providers. This plan will result in a billion-dollar company with everything but $50 million related to the core competencies: an outsourced virtual company.

Outsourcing Resource Requirements

Defining the resource requirements for outsourcing involves comparing the requirements to deliver the same product or service using all internal resources. The short answer often equates to comparing the costs internally (of the hardware, software, operating system, development, implementation, operation, and maintenance) to the price charged by the application provider. That comparison does not figure in the inability to acquire and keep needed internal resources, and does not evaluate any potential loss should the application provider quit its provision.

To compensate for cost assessment inadequacies, add in the productive value of the resources freed by outsourcing and made available to core business activities. By so doing, the resource requirement will reflect the time savings realized in implementation. Evaluate how much the outsourcing will reduce the Total Cost of Ownership (TCO) to figure the actual gain in savings. In thoroughly considering the resource costs associated with outsourcing, you should address the following concepts:

- The cost of money
- Outsourcing Internet requirements
- Required internal personnel

The Cost of Money

As an advantage, outsourcing an entire business application avoids large up-front costs that often accompany such endeavors. These costs can include equipment and software purchase or lease, employee acquisition and support, and facility purchase or lease.

The savings gained by delaying up-front costs (by paying equal periodic payments to a provider) must be included in the equations used to make sourcing decisions. One possible way to account for the savings is to add the elimination of interest on the up-front costs to your calculations. Another approach is to figure in the amount of funds that would be unavailable for other operations if used in insourcing. However, most smaller ASPs cannot provide an entire business application complete with software licenses and equipment amortized into a periodic payment.

Outsourcing Internet Requirements

Businesses require real-time access to business applications. Older client/server applications might require a dedicated private and secure network, a factor which increases connection costs about ten times above Internet connection costs. Virtual Private Network (VPN) hardware and software, however, allows the Internet to function as a private network. Consequently, the need for (and cost of) private network lines has decreased dramatically. A VPN solution might not prove adequate for applications that involve large data transfers or thousands of concurrent application connections. In these cases, a dedicated circuit of sufficient capacity must be factored into the outsourcing resource requirements.

Required Internal Personnel

Outsourcing a business application allows existing personnel to work on core business interests rather than application support. Nevertheless, personnel responsible for the outsourced product or service must have adequate representation and oversee the application process.

Additionally, include the personnel that would have developed and implemented the application, if insourced, in the decision making. Their insights will be particularly valuable in defining the specifications and selecting the service provider. This helps create a better outsourced solution, prevent morale loss, and gain internal support for the application.

Outsourcing Risk Factors

Both the outsourced and insourced business application models share the risk that an application will not prove efficient or profitable. A company that internally manages its LAN illustrates the importance of maintaining application control. The network supports internal operations, communications, and data systems. When the company attempts to gain an advantage by granting access to internal applications (connecting all systems and employees to the Internet), it discovers a disadvantage it can't control: What had been nearly instantaneous internal LAN access slows other business communications. Consequently, the real risk of outsourcing must be carefully measured as only the additional or lessened risk that it provides after any side effects or unintended outcomes have had a chance to surface.

The risk factors that you must mitigate include the following:

* Provider compatibility
* Internal management resistance
* Component integration
* Provider stability

Provider Compatibility

For an outsourcing model to work, the provider must have both the right mix of capabilities and organizational compatibility with the client company. If the provider works, communicates, or responds to a changing environment in fundamentally different ways than the client company, misunderstandings and cross-purposing make the resulting solution much less effective.

The client company should carefully investigate and evaluate the provider prior to committing to the outsourcing arrangement. In addition, both client and provider should ensure compatibility with the managing department in advance. See the "Applied Solutions" section at the end of this chapter for an example of provider network compatibility.

Internal Management Resistance

A company must assess and manage the risk its own management might bring to outsourcing. Successful outsourcing must have strong and obvious top management support. Lower to intermediate managers tend to resist outsourcing. They fear loss of jobs, prestige, or power. The primary aid to fighting this resistance is education. Generally, outsourcing brings more opportunities for involvement in the core business, not fewer.

Application Component Integration

A newly acquired business application or component might not integrate smoothly with current business applications. For example, the data format and database design requirements can differ. This requires additional integration work for components to communicate effectively. Outsourcing requires constant attention to the issues of integration and the impact that changes to design can have on your project.

Stability of the Provider

New application providers face the risk that potential clients will withhold business until the provider displays a solid business success record. Similarly, providers offering new concepts (such as renting applications by usage) might find their current clients waiting for others to lead the way. The risk does exist that the new provider or newly offered application will fail to perform.

This point was well demonstrated with the spectacular failure in 2001 of several ASPs and MSPs. Despite a resounding chorus of predictions that hosting service providers could never satisfy anticipated customer demand for bandwidth or hosting facility server rack space, the bankruptcy of Global Crossing and Exodus Communications are an important warning for ASP clients, as well as for ASPs themselves. A stable and demonstrably successful business model has no substitute. A fevered environment of IPO greed and hyped business growth predictions will not suffice to overcome the laws of basic, good business practice.

Outsourcing Security Issues

The security risk associated with outsourcing is important to consider because exposure involves not only the applications and services, but also data exposure to an outside organization. Loss of control of the data can occur. Also, the risk of data exposure outside both the company and the provider is increased because data has become accessible by additional systems and users.

The software, data, and other operational information outsourced mostly reside on the equipment belonging to the application provider. In addition, it will generally be located at the application provider's facility. The company only licenses or rents the right to use the application and its components, and does not own the hardware or software assets.

In the basic outsourced application security arrangement, a few selected files and tokens of authenticity reside on the client company computers. Tokens of authenticity will necessarily reside in both the company and provider application environments. Because multiple application users have access to the selected files, only those tokens separate users from the company data and protect the integrity of the entire application process.

Further information on this topic is discussed in the following two sections:

- How to Supply a Secure Architecture
- How to Protect Sensitive Data

How to Supply a Secure Architecture

The typical information security architecture fills in any gap between the business application provider process and the company security policy. To the degree that the company policy mandates protection of customer information, the provider needs to modify its standard security measures to accommodate.

Consider the following areas for outsourced application security:

- **User identification and authorization**—Each user must supply a unique user name and matching password.

- **Access control list (ACL)**—Servers of both the user and provider contain a file with an agreed upon list of individuals allowed access to the servers or attached terminals.

- **Data encryption and digital signature**—Data encryption scrambles data algorithmically on the sender's end using a well-known algorithm and a shared, secret encryption key. The receiver's end uses the algorithm and key to unscramble the data to its original form. During a transmission interception, anyone without the encryption key will see only meaningless, scrambled data.

Modern cryptographic practice is to avoid the use of secret algorithms. Good practice is to use a well-known algorithm that has been reviewed by the cryptographic community and judged to be strong. An encryption algorithm is considered strong if it is impractical to decrypt data without knowledge of the shared secret key, and the key length is long enough to make an exhaustive search of the key-space ("brute force" attack) take longer than the useful life of the data.

The designers of CSS, the DVD encryption algorithm, did not follow this practice, however, and their encryption scheme was broken by a teenage boy who wanted to play his DVDs on a Linux machine, for which no players were available. Public-private key (or asymmetric) encryption, in contrast to the conventional (or symmetric) encryption previously described, uses pairs of keys for each sender and receiver, one of which is publicly available, while the other is known only to the owner. If the sender uses the receiver's public key to encrypt the data, only the receiver's private key can decrypt the data. Once again, the encryption/decryption algorithm is well known, and the security relies on keeping the private keys secret and on the difficulty of factoring large prime numbers.

Because of the greater complexity of public-private key encryption algorithms (and the resulting greater demand on processing resources), public-private key encryption is generally used to exchange the shared secret key for a conventional encryption algorithm, which the sender and receiver then use to encrypt and decrypt the actual data.

Public Key Infrastructure (PKI) can effectively integrate digital certificates, public-key cryptography, and trusted certificate authorities to create a secure environment. A detailed discussion of security is beyond the scope of this book, and certainly this chapter. Refer to Appendix A, "Recommended Further Reading," and Appendix E, "Public-Key Infrastructure," for references to application security design and hosting and application with an outsourced provider.

How to Protect Sensitive Data

Some business application providers host important information about the client company's customers. This information can include personnel information, financial records, credit histories, competitive business policy, and other equally sensitive information. The compromise of this information could ruin the company using the application. News that the provider had allowed compromise of the information could ruin the provider. The provider and the client company must know, agree to, and safeguard the security policies and procedures in advance of application operation. Compliance with the security control policies and procedures, and the restriction of physical access to computers and data, prevents most information compromise and outside attempts to break security measures.

Most companies do not allow transmission of untreated critical business application data over public transmission lines. Even dedicated network connections can get switched through communications facilities with other data. Physically discrete private transmission lines provide the highest level of protection. The following measures, however, usually provide adequate data protection during transmission over the Internet between the provider and the user:

- **Multiple firewalls**—The firewall is a hardware or software component that runs all the time, waiting for a client to connect. When the client requests a connection, the firewall performs basic authentication before the client can establish full connectivity. A single firewall offers some security, but security-minded companies set up multiple firewalls to provide added layers of protection. If an intruder gains access to one part of the network, data stored behind other firewalls remains secure. Using multiple firewall vendor hardware or software also thwarts security breaches because the tools and techniques used to break one firewall will not apply for subsequent firewalls.

NOTE	A firewall is not in itself a sufficient measure of security unless it is properly configured. In fact, it would actually provide a false sense of security unless its configuration represents the results of a well thought-out security policy and architecture.

- **Secure Sockets Layer encryption**—Secure Sockets Layer (SSL) is an open, non-proprietary protocol for providing data security between applications over protocols such as TCP/IP. This security protocol provides data encryption, server authentication, message integrity, and client authentication for a TCP/IP connection between a user interface and the user browser. SSL encryption should be used for both front-end application communication and back-end application communication.

- **Digital certificates**—Online companies get digital certificates from a certificate authority (CA), which verifies a company's identity and issues a unique certificate as proof of identity. This certificate is digitally signed by the certificate authority and represents a trust relationship. The browser uses the information in the certificate to encrypt a message back to the server that only the secured server can interpret. Using the information, the server and browser create a master key (code book) to encode and decode data transmissions. The key only works for the specific and continuous session.

Outsourcing Delivery Accountability

The delivery accountability for business applications, regardless of what sourcing model the company uses, ultimately belongs to the company, as represented by the chief executive officer. For the outsourced business application, the delivery accountability still rests with the company department responsible for using the application to generate revenue.

The oversight process for outsourced business applications tends to occur at a lower level of management than insourced business applications. The changed nature of the application operation allows this lower level of oversight. In the case of an outsourced business application, the manager in charge of day-to-day application operations needs to only ensure that the product or service meets the specification and occurs in a timely manner. The many other concerns, including equipment operation, software function, operator performance, and others, take place under the supervision of the provider.

Advantages of Outsourcing

Companies can outsource many of their information system functions that are not directly tied to their core business interests. By outsourcing, companies can improve their information services, obtain cost reductions, and acquire new technical capabilities. In addition, they can deploy information technology to focus efforts on improving critical aspects of their business performance. They can also market new technology-based products and services by leveraging provider assets without acquiring them.

As you evaluate outsourcing opportunities, consider the following advantages:

- Trial before purchasing
- Time to market
- Cost reductions
- Remote access

Trial Before Purchasing

Several clients who use the provider for an application share the application provider's up-front, equipment, software, management, and software costs. These costs get spread throughout the periodic costs charged to the clients by the provider. A client can try the business application without paying all the up-front costs by obtaining it from a provider, with the option of discontinuing.

Time to Market

By using a business application provider's technical expertise, companies can shorten the innovation cycle time by 60 to 90 percent. When a company perceives a business application product or service opportunity in the marketplace, rather than acquiring the necessary expertise, doing the research, and developing the application, the company uses a provider. With its already expert personnel and, perhaps, related existing applications, the provider begins an immediate and accelerated application implementation. The user company has done nothing but reach an agreement with the provider and perhaps provide an up-front fee.

Application Cost Reduction

By renting applications and services over the web, companies can quickly acquire advanced enterprise applications economically, with a modest up-front cost. Many small and medium-sized companies do not have the resources to create or purchase these advanced applications. The renting advantage, combined with the ability to have a virtual office, lets the small business appear to the outside world as a big company.

Remote Access

Organizations with highly dispersed work forces can take advantage of outsourcing their applications. For example, a service industry with little need for a physical presence could provide a nationwide sales force with a virtual office by outsourcing all their office support requirements from a provider over the Internet. The money saved by not renting an office can be used to pay the rent for the application.

Disadvantages of Outsourcing

Although outsourcing generally gets a project up and running quickly, most outsourcing agencies perform only minor software customization. If the purchasing company requires considerable customization work on the software, it will probably elect to purchase or license the software and have its own personnel tailor the software to its specific needs.

Disadvantages of outsourcing involve the following issues:

- Loss of control
- Bandwidth requirements

Loss of Control

By allowing a business application provider to provide its solution, perform associated activity, handle the data, and output the product or service, the user relinquishes considerable control of business operations in exchange for more efficient and profitable business relationships.

Bandwidth Requirement

Large bandwidth requirements represent a real disadvantage of outsourcing most applications. Presentation of value-enhanced information, such as full-motion, color video, requires large amounts of on-demand bandwidth. With sufficient bandwidth, the same display can take place thousands of miles away or in the home office. Bandwidth providers continue to build toward a high bandwidth, worldwide, fiber-optic network. Consequently, the present bandwidth requirement disadvantage will turn into an advantage with time. Of course, as more bandwidth becomes available, businesses will find more uses for it. Until then, teams with projects with large bandwidth requirements should investigate caching network services by ASPs, such as Akamai and others.

Management of Team Selection and Training When Using Outsourcing

An outsourced project also requires selection of internal personnel to participate in the outsourced business function. Forming the team can require some training and skills improvement if the team does not possess the experience necessary to work with the outsourced application provider tools and interfaces. Overall, an outsourced application project will not require an extensive period of training for the team to become familiar with the new business workflow incorporating the service provider. However, take care when making the team selection and in scheduling time to learn a new workflow.

Process and implementation mistakes are at their highest probability in the first weeks of a project because the process is new and unfamiliar. Make sure that the service provider assigns one or more staff members to be on-hand during the start of an outsourced application implementation. Questions about whether this field or that check box needs to be completed might otherwise go unasked, resulting in a poor implementation of the new process.

Application Service Provider Outsourcing

An ASP is a second party that markets a service to implement, host, and operate a business application using the ASP's equipment and facilities. The ASP offering includes the needed equipment, operations, and expertise to provide the application. The ASP user can contract to use all or part of the comprehensive service offering. Approached in the framework of this definition, the ASP concept represents the ultimate form of outsourcing.

ASPs align their operations to customer care by providing 24-hour-a-day operations and service, staffing customer care centers with application experts, and enhancing their applications and services on a continuous basis. ASP outsourcing is examined in detail in this section, by addressing the following characteristics and features:

- Technological reasons for ASP demand
- Business reasons for ASP demand
- Features of an ASP
- Applications typically provided by an ASP
- ASP resource requirements
- Employee cost reductions
- Minimum ASP resource requirements
- ASP risk factors
- Delivery accountability issues
- Advantages of an ASP
- Disadvantages of an ASP

Technological Reasons for ASP Demand

The following technology issues drive demand for outsourcing applications and application components through ASPs:

- Shortage of skilled and experienced IT expert workers in the industry despite layoffs and reductions in force
- Emerging technology best practices applications that involve high up-front costs for development and support
- Accelerating application deployment so that more resources can be focused on acquiring and servicing customers

- Increasing technology complexity that has made many small-scale deployments cost-prohibitive
- Access to leading edge technology applications and services

Business Reasons for ASP Demand

The following business issues drive demand for outsourcing applications and application components through ASPs:

- Minimizing development and ownership costs
- Stabilizing cash flow into fixed monthly costs
- Focusing on core business interests instead of technology
- Improving internal IT staff efficiency and focus
- Responding to increased global competition and global markets
- Increasing competitiveness and time to market
- Avoiding application development and ownership risk

Industry analysts expected small and middle-sized businesses to be the main market for ASP services, but large corporations and companies are beginning to emerge as the dominant ASP outsourcing subscribers.

Features of an ASP

ASPs develop best practices to deliver high value services. Figure 5-1 illustrates the features of an ASP.

Figure 5-1   *Features of an ASP*

SERVICE	SUPPORT
• Availability	• Technical
• Security	• Data Center
• Management	• Service Level
• Networked Storage	Agreement
• Shared Service	
• Dialup Software	
• Short-Term Use	
• Scalability	

The ASP services guarantee the following:

- **Availability**—Some ASPs can provide over 99 percent uptime through geographic redundancy and dynamic routing protocols. Partnerships with network peers allow ASPs to avoid single point of failure risks because of network bottlenecks and outages.

- **Security**—ASPs must ensure security to sell customers in the competitive applications market. ASPs add security provisions to existing platforms, such as Windows, Solaris, and Linux, by developing custom baseline configurations, applying security patches, and maintaining intrusion-detection systems.

- **Management**—ASPs provide a single, unifying management and administration function for entire corporations across multiple networks. Consolidated enterprise-wide management reporting tools and monitoring systems ease the burden of operating large corporate network services.

- **Networked storage**—Besides providing cheaper storage, which the user does not need to house or maintain, the ASP uses the storage to provide backup and disaster recovery for the customer. Large-scale storage solutions are often prohibitively expensive for many small- to medium-sized companies.

- **Shared service**—The ASP outsourcing applications feature the benefits of a shared service basis. The user can rent access to the application on a shared platform. This allows application access to the new user without up-front investments in licenses, equipment, software, servers, personnel, and personnel support.

- **Dial-up software**—*Dial-up* software refers to software that is available nearly immediately. Small businesses can rent major software systems rather than purchase licenses for them. This provides the ASP with continuous revenue for providing access to high-end software packages and lowers the software cost for the user.

- **Short-term use**—A company suddenly needing use of a particular application does not have to rush out to buy and implement an application for a short-term need. The ASP can provide the service immediately over the Internet for a fixed fee, day-by-day rental, or per-use charge.

- **Scalability**—The ASP's core application and service capabilities allow the user to increase or decrease use of the application or service continuously as needs change.

ASP application support for a company's business application features the following three services:

- **Technical support**—Because the application resides on the ASP servers, providers must supply the logistical technical support for the application performance. When upgrades occur, the provider will upgrade the application. Other than operating and performance changes, the user will never be involved in the technical upgrade. Adequate advanced notification must be given whenever upgrades will potentially impact the ASP's customers.

- **Data center support**—An ASP supplies a data support center 24 hours a day and 7 days a week. This service includes backups, redundant hardware, redundant data lines, and security measures and monitoring.

- **Service Level Agreement**—To assure users of quality service, the ASP must provide a Service Level Agreement (SLA) based on specified criteria for uptime, security, and availability. The SLAs are based on key performance indicators and specific triggers for immediate action, such as hardware failure.

Applications Typically Provided by ASPs

Typical ASPs provide the following applications:

- **Minimally customized application packages**—ASPs offer minimally customized application packages, such as Enterprise Resource Planning (ERP), time tracking applications, or Internet-based customer care solutions.

- **Vertical industry applications**—ASPs offer vertical industry applications, such as online documentation support and online documentation search applications.

- **Vertical industry portals**—ASPs offer vertical industry portals, such as business-to-business electronic commerce, financial services portals, and entertainment industry portals.

- **Horizontal industry portals**—ASPs offer horizontal portals providing special niche operations that many different businesses can use. Travel services represent an example of this type of ASP product.

Using an ASP application is much like using voicemail added to your telephone service. The voicemail technology does not reside in the phone on your desk. It might not reside in your building, but rather in the local telephone company office. You simply pay the phone company a monthly fee and the voicemail works as soon as you learn the operating procedures. Similarly, employees at companies that use the ASP-provided application simply learn how to use the system. Neither the user company nor the employees have to provide or maintain the application.

ASP Resource Requirements

Shifting application resource requirements from the user to the ASP represents a major reason for using an ASP. The ASP assumes responsibility for providing most of the resource requirements for the service and removes them from the user in exchange for payment. The user continues to bear resource requirements associated with proper operation and use of the provided application.

The following resource requirements shift from the user to the ASP:

- **Cost spreading**—By spreading the costs associated with providing the application across many users, the ASP manages to provide the application to each user at a greatly reduced cost (and makes a significant return in the process).

- **License fees**—The ASP can, but in most common practice does not, pay for and hold the licenses needed to support the application. In this case, the cost gets passed in some form of payment to all the users. For example, an ASP might pay for data backup services licenses, where the ASP pays for the backup server licenses, but the users pay for each backup client license depending on the number of machines needing data to be backed up.

- **Network**—The reduced requirement for in-house network bandwidth over the life of an ASP agreement constitutes a significant cost shift from the user to the ASP. It also allows both the ASP and the user to take advantage of high-end gigabit Ethernet network connectivity because of cost spreading.

- **Server costs**—The ASP provides all server hardware and software costs in the pure ASP arrangement. The ASP maintains the servers in its own facilities. Some network hosting ASPs also use virtual servers, allowing discrete hosting environments, but taking advantage of the savings from using shared physical hardware.

Employee Cost Reductions

Because, in the purely ASP outsourcing model, the provider maintains the application equipment, software, and service requirements, the ASP necessarily bears the requirement to acquire and retain the properly skilled employees needed to perform those functions. The cost of recruiting the skilled employees rests with the ASP. The user avoids the continuing costs of supporting the employees, hiring replacements, and providing benefits during the application provision agreement's life.

To place the employee savings in perspective, a user can purchase an Intel-based server cluster running the latest Windows software for approximately $20,000. Having made the investment, the user would have the usual difficulty of obtaining the skilled employees to run the cluster and must furnish at least three employees to provide the same 24-hour service provided by an ASP. The $20,000 initial investment increases by a minimum of $200,000 a year. The ASP provides the service for less and shoulders any difficulties.

Minimum ASP Resource Requirements

Prior to offering an application to users, the ASP must usually furnish the following resources in full operational status:

- Data centers for providing applications and related services
- Internet connectivity with sufficient speed (bandwidth) and redundant network connection providers to give acceptable application performance and availability
- A server that provides a platform for a secure application deployment engine

ASP Risk Factors

Using an ASP exchanges the risk of not doing well when implementing a business application for the risk of choosing an ASP that does not meet expectations. In effect, the risk becomes that of renting an application that does not work. Mitigate this risk by carefully selecting your ASP. Consider the following broad criteria when selecting an ASP:

- Commitment to quality
- Price
- References and reputation
- Contract terms
- Geographic location
- Cultural match
- Existing relationship

No absolute or correct answers exist in evaluating an ASP on the criteria in the preceding list, but the likelihood of a successful ASP relationship should become apparent after discovering the details. In addition, a successful project benefits from monitoring the risk potential of the following specific factors:

- SLA
- Loss of control possibilities
- Risk of ASP failure
- Partnering to reduce risk
- ASP security issues
- Software security aids

Service Level Agreement

A user company can reduce the risk of a misunderstanding, in which the ASP provides a business application that does not meet all the application needs. The user should thoroughly investigate the potential providers and their application results. The user should also request an SLA as part of the business agreement. The SLA guarantees performance specifications in business critical areas, such as application availability, system and communications uptime, and security of the data involved in the application process. Despite universal availability and promise of bandwidth by third-party data networks, bottlenecks and peak demand times can degrade real performance.

Loss of Control Possibilities

As with any other outsourcing arrangement, the user company willingly surrenders some control of the application. Transmission of sensitive customer information can leave user companies uneasy. User companies should request that the SLA be backed with an audit trail indicating successful data handling.

By using an ASP for a business application, the user company loses control of whether or when it updates the application. This occurs frequently in the case of a software application. The ASP makes its profit by supplying the application to several user companies. The degree to which it would have to make each user application different would decrease the profitability of providing the application. Consequently, all users will necessarily use the improved application when the ASP updates it. Some risk exists that the update will cause a disruption in user operations.

Risk of ASP Failure

A risk exists for the business application user that the ASP providing the application will fail and leave the user without the application to support its operation. In June of 2000, the Gartner Group predicted that more than 60 percent of the ASPs in the market would fail before the end of 2000. Despite this shakeout and provider consolidation, the ASP market is still expected to grow to approximately $25 billion by 2005.

The ASP business associated with "Internet business" will probably follow the success pattern of Internet business. The Gartner Group believes that part of Internet business success comes from hype and expects it to have peaked in the year 2000. Gartner analysts see a rapid decline through 2001 and 2002 because of a loss of confidence on the part of those previously persuaded by the initial successes and hype. They finally see the shakeout of noncompetitive providers in the Internet business followed by a gradual increase with sustained growth through 2010. The risk exists that some user companies will select their ASP from among those who fail during the forecasted decline. Some ASP failures have also contributed to legal battles surrounding patent infringements and other underlying technology comprising new ASP businesses and business models.

The Gartner Group E-Business Adoption Hype Cycle graph in Figure 5-2 shows the projected pattern of relative volume of Internet business through 2010. The graph annotations show some of the causal factors influencing the business during that period.

Companies should ensure that their relationship and contacts with an ASP remain flexible. Adopting an SLA with specific penalty clauses to address any service degradation that might occur is also a prudent step. Companies should maintain a list of backup ASP companies in the event of the failure of an ASP providing important business applications. A company could be left without its application or data in the event of an ASP failure. The company can complement the list of backup ASPs with an exit plan for each provider. These lists provide competitive comparison and leverage in the event of price increases by an ASP.

Users should periodically check the performance of the ASP in terms of the application specification to detect early signs of weakness. Although the ASP will provide the reports required by contract, users might choose to develop and use their own performance-monitoring tools.

Figure 5-2   *Gartner Group E-Business Adoption Hype Cycle*

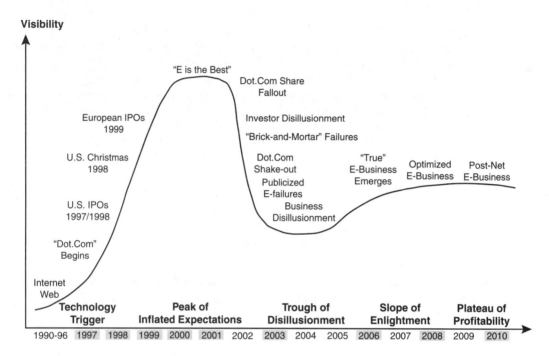

Partnering to Reduce Risk

Just as the ASP user company uses the ASP to get to the market more quickly with a business application for its customer, the ASP can turn to another ASP for help getting a business application to the market faster. In today's market, a company cannot afford to observe others in the same market and join them as another resource for the product or service. Six- to twelve-month development cycles, to prepare a changing technology application for use, will not produce a profitable return before product obsolescence. Consequently, successful ASPs aggressively partner with other ASPs to create online business applications that meet their customer needs in a timely manner. Selecting an ASP that has alliances with stable partners is a good sign of strength and long-term survivability.

ASP Security Issues

The security issues associated with using an ASP for a business application seem sufficiently large to keep companies from joining the growing trend of using ASPs. The Information Services (IS) departments of these hesitant companies do not readily trust sending highly valuable customer data over the Internet to the ASP. Compounding the transmission security issue, the industry trend for ASPs to merge or be taken over by a larger ASP means that the hesitant companies cannot ensure who will eventually have their valued customers' data.

The business application user and ASP need a coordinated organizational response to manage their risks to information security. Organizations enabling business applications that use data communications, especially over the Internet, need to extend their security architecture. Each needs to create and involve the efforts of an information security team under the leadership of a chief information security officer (CISO). This team, as a priority mission, should immediately deal with changed or deleted access to its systems, or to its partnering organization systems or employees.

Software Security Aids

ASPs need to incorporate software platforms that provide necessary security program administration. These software platforms must work as well remotely as when administered locally.

The ASP that effectively demonstrates complete protection of sensitive data sent to the ASP will inherit a large share of the available application business.

The ASP can use specific measures not only to effectively protect sensitive data, but also to assure the data owner about the following security issues:

- **Private leased lines**—Private leased lines almost ensure complete communicated data security. The user and ASP control both ends of the data line with no intermediary handling the data. The private leased line, however, costs the user about ten times as much as using the Internet. The ASP should offer that provision as a part of the application for a very careful user who is willing to pay the cost. However, because even private leased lines will eventually pass through shared hardware at the line-carrier level, it is good practice to employ data encryption over private leased lines as well.

- **Isolated data**—Data isolation on an exclusive server will protect it from exposure to anyone else accessing the server. The ASP will offer to provide this data isolation for any customer concerned about data compromise. This should also extend to data backup networks and data backup media, if required.

- **Firewalls**—For the user of an application over the Internet, the ASP provides provisions for multiple firewall protection and data encryption in the application package.

- **Digital certificates**—Digital certificates provide client authentication and data communication protection. The ASP can provide and arrange adequate user employee training on operating applications using digital certificates.

ASP Delivery Accountability

As with any outsourcing arrangement, the ASP agreement does not absolve the business application user of delivery accountability. Ultimately, the user company CEO is responsible for the entire performance of the company. Usually, delivery responsibility stays with the head of the user company department responsible for producing the package of products and services, including the ASP-provided application. The department head will hold a junior manager charged with monitoring the application responsible. The user company can have nonperformance penalties built into the ASP contract. Penalties, however, do not change the user's delivery responsibilities.

The ASP is responsible for all its activities—from understanding and capturing customer requirements to delivering application products or services. A single ASP normally concentrates on its core business and arranges the rest of the needs of its users with other providers as part of a complete package. For example, the ASP will usually arrange with a third party for the transmission system that carries the user data. While not providing data communications, the ASP remains responsible to its application user for delivery of the product or service, even if a data communications failure causes the default. The ASP guarantees the application product or service and accepts responsibility for delivery to the user.

Advantages of an ASP

The ASP represents a special case of the outsourcing model for business applications. The ASP can take over every aspect of the application for the user company. The ASP user contracts to use all or part of the comprehensive service offering. The advantages of using an ASP relate to the previously unusual concept of a business turning over control of its business activities to another business. Companies can transfer the burden and risk of buying everything needed to support a business application to an ASP. The up-front equipment, software, and employee ownership risk stays with the ASP. The ASP gives the user company the assurance of being able to try the application before buying it. In fact, the ASP allows the user to avoid the risk of ownership.

The relatively new field of ASP use resulted in a new business term, Risk on Opportunity (ROO). The ROO attempts to capture the value of an application in terms of the specification written for the application. ROO goes beyond measuring Return on Investment (ROI) measurements. When using an ASP, the investment stays low and inflates the ROI ratio. Although a high ROI remains a positive indication, it does not indicate the application's potential to capture the business opportunity it addresses. Of even greater importance, the ROO proves a more effective tool in comparing the value of the applications offered by various bidding ASPs.

The following is a list, categorized by benefit, of the basic advantages of using an ASP to obtain business applications. Other important advantages of a more specialized application, which deserve attention when considering whether to use an ASP, fall into one of these categories:

- **Focus on core competencies**—By allowing the ASP to provide a specific business application, the user company can focus more employee effort and resources on its core business interest.

- **Reduce cost**—By spreading equipment, software, and expertise expenses over many users, the ASP makes a profit and still reduces costs for each user.

- **Reduce risk**—By using established and effective security procedures and applying greater experience and expertise than the user company could, the ASP provides greater protection against important data compromise. The ASP has a greater probability than a user company of successfully implementing an application because of its already proven applications, greater focus, and technical expertise.

- **Provide universal accessibility**—ASPs use standard platforms, browsers, and data transmission protocols for all their applications. This allows near universal access from all local and remote sites.

- **Reduce implementation time**—Starting with standard applications and modifying them for the user, the ASP can implement a business application much more quickly than the user business.

- **Eliminate obsolescence**—The ASP automatically and transparently upgrades user company applications with advancing technology. To do this, the user forgoes customization, complies with the application's schema, and accepts the ASP best practice approach.

- **Provides scalability**—The great capacity of the ASP in their core area allows the user to increase or decrease application use continuously as the need increases.

Disadvantages of an ASP

The disadvantage of using an ASP to obtain a business application relates to surrendering control of the business activity to another company over which the user has only the promise of future business to influence decisions about the application. Control here also refers to a company's ability to customize the application. Responding to needs for software customization has proven to be one of the struggling points for most ASPs. Examples of ASP disadvantages follow:

- **Merger or partnering**—During the contract period with the ASP for the application, the ASP can decide to merge or enter into binding business arrangements with another company. Although the continuing ASP contract holder cannot change the terms of the contract, the user could find itself leasing a business application to handle its customer data from a direct competitor.

- **Complex system complications**—Obtaining a complex business application from an ASP could involve bringing in an application that proves incompatible with current user systems that interface with the new application. This forces current system duplication, or switching to additional systems that are compatible with the ASP-provided application. In short, bringing in the new ASP-provided application might cause the user company to need additional application acquisitions.

- **Automatic application updates**—The disadvantage of receiving automatic application updates from the ASP is the inability to schedule the updates. The user might want to delay an application update because of compatibility issues with current programs or customer interfaces. Usually, the user discovers the update incompatibilities after an automatic update that the user was unaware of.

- **No staffing control**—The customer does not have the ability to assess the competence and trustworthiness of the ASP employees that will actually administer the systems and software that they rent, and have access to sensitive data.

Network Implications of Sourcing Decisions

The network implications of the build or buy question are significant. As with the overall issue of application control in application sourcing, network control is near absolute with insourcing, but represents a major consideration and risk for outsourcing and ASP solutions.

To assess the network implications of a sourcing decision, consider the following questions:

- How important is total control of the application network architecture and network administration?

- How much network control can reasonably be relinquished?

- What SLA response times are acceptable for resolving network and application problems?

- Are network problems a significant factor to the smooth functioning of your business application?

- With an outsourced or ASP solution, how much more does a two-hour response time cost than a next-business-day response?

- How critical are the applications or application components to the overall business functions?

- Can critical application functions be supported by multiple outsourcing vendors to provide redundancy and fault tolerance?

- Are two ASP providers with basic SLA provisions cheaper than one ASP with high-level SLA coverage?

The risk associated with the answers to many of these questions can be mitigated in the design phase of an application. Application network architecture can accommodate any implications of the various sourcing options, but only if presented early enough in the design process. For example, a single-sourced customer care application can be hosted by one vendor in a clustered configuration of servers. Two or more vendors in nonclustered configurations can also host the same customer care application, with some design changes. The issue is not really which one is better, but which one is cheaper or easier to manage. The customer care application can be designed to operate in either network environment.

As you consider network implications of sourcing decisions, evaluate these issues, which are discussed in the following sections:

- Network development issues
- Network security issues

Network Development Issues

The specific business application being developed, or current business application being migrated, dictates the development network issues. Network implications can be a limited set of problems requiring solving, or pose questions about undertaking major network redesigns to accommodate changes. Creating network address assignment rules and building network architecture diagrams is essential to all sourcing models.

The first step for the CISS professional in analyzing the costs and benefits of insourcing versus outsourcing an application is to diagram the proposed networks. This highlights the hardware costs and indicates any network changes that might impact other business processes. If your company already outsources one or more business applications, the associated costs for adding another outsourced application are not that great. In this case, firewalls and development environments already exist, and can be utilized by adding additional network routes and firewall rules, or extending their capacity, if necessary. Providing adequate communication pathways and sufficient security measures represents the major cost of introducing a first-ever, outsourced application.

Network Security Issues

Corporate LAN security generally provides a hard exterior security layer and relatively soft interior security. Introducing an outsourced application, or even an insourced, Internet-based application, complicates that basic security assumption. For most projects to outsource an application, internal systems need to access remote systems, exposing internal systems to remote, potentially untrusted environments. WAN security is not all that much harder or more complicated than LAN security, but the benefit of being able to universally access and transfer data between servers and corporate systems is removed. Unsafe protocols and procedures, while possible within a protected corporate LAN, become entirely unacceptable.

Many applications, if first developed and deployed internally, don't make use of the full set of application security features and mechanisms. At the very least, host-level security is generally not a priority because the systems were built to reside within the corporate firewall. Now that internal systems will be talking with external systems, host-level security becomes very important. System security audits must be performed, and new procedures for hardening or tightening security on these systems must be developed and tested.

Security management also needs to be expanded, as it is good practice to make sure that systems participating in an outsourced application do not share the same administrative passwords as internal systems. This complicates security management by introducing a new set of security procedures and system accounts, if not a whole new set of hardware and software.

Summary

The discussion of sourcing factors and features introduces a number of important points. Knowing whether to build or buy raises issues relating to a trade-off between cost and control. To help summarize this chapter, Table 5-1 presents the advantages and disadvantages of insourcing and outsourcing. Rather than restate the various decision criteria to build or buy, contrasting statements are used to restate the observations and cautions presented in this chapter.

All the sourcing models require strong support from the three major functional divisions of a company: administration, products/services (including marketing), and production. Without equally strong support from all three divisions, resistance to the application will make it less effective.

Table 5-1   *Key Facts About Insourcing and Outsourcing*

	Insourcing	Outsourcing
Focus	Companies concentrate on offering and maintaining "best in the world" status in their core business interests. Consequently, they tend to use the insourcing model for all core business applications and complete all activities internally. Focus is on maintaining control and customizability.	Companies use the outsourcing model for assistance in producing context business requirements. Often, they will do the portions of the activities for which they already have capability and resources in place and outsource to complete the activities for which they lack capability. Companies also favor outsourcing activities if that means their employees can concentrate on core business interests. Focus is on reducing cost.

Table 5-1   *Key Facts About Insourcing and Outsourcing (Continued)*

	Insourcing	**Outsourcing**
Resource Requirements	The company that uses the insourcing model must provide all the resources required to develop, implement, operate, or maintain a business application. This includes employee resources and can prove expensive unless the application or related work keeps them fully occupied. The employee expense does, however, represent an investment in expertise that can later implement other business applications and provide the company with market opportunity.	The outsourcing model allows the user company to obtain parts or all the business application from an outside provider. The provider allocates resources that the user company does not have or does not to want to use for the business application. The company allocates a resource that it has, usually money, in exchange for the application parts. The ASP sourcing model allows the user wanting to acquire the business application to do so without supplying any specific resource. This model allows a money exchange for the delivery of the application product or service.
Risk Factors	Recruiting employees with the appropriate skill set is the largest risk a small to mid-sized company faces in implementing a business application in the competitive e-business environment. If the application requirements are outside the skills of the company's workforce, the implementation process cannot start until the company assembles the requisite expertise. Retaining employees is an additional risk factor for insourced projects, especially in technology expertise with a high demand.	The user company needs to avoid the risk that the outsourced business application will not integrate with existing user applications. Both the general outsourcing and ASP arrangements have the associated risk that the partner will fail or merge with another company. Companies reduce security risks associated with outsourcing by applying these compensating measures: User identification Access Control List Firewalls Data encryption
Delivery Accountability	Accountability is retained within the company by retaining control of the project. Final delivery accountability rests with the CEO.	Accountability is only partially transferred to the outsourced provider. Ultimate delivery accountability still rests with the company itself and the CEO.

continues

Table 5-1   *Key Facts About Insourcing and Outsourcing (Continued)*

	Insourcing	Outsourcing
Advantages	Insourcing allows greater control and customization. The insourcing model provides the best security environment for company data or customer data. The data resides in one location in only one computer system under the control of the company. Future business can leverage core skills and knowledge gained by insourced project teams.	Outsourcing offers reduced cost and rapid time to market. Employee resources are free to design and produce core business applications and services. Equipment and facilities for context business functions do not need to be maintained. Outsourcing leverages provider efficiencies, scalability, updates, and expertise.
Disadvantages	Insourcing can demand greater costs. A company is forced to expend resources on business functions that it needs for core business functions. Team selection and training can take months to complete. Hiring delays can, however, be avoided by planning to mentor junior developers instead of hiring senior-level talent.	Outsourcing forces a loss of control. Introducing a form of outsourcing reduces the security of the application data, both because another company has the data, and because the data must be communicated between the user and provider companies. The user company cannot completely control the data or the data processing with the outsourcing model.
Network Implications	Network design and control is maintained within the company, but still needs to be modified to accommodate new application requirements. Application bandwidth usage should be explicitly incorporated into resource requirements so that it doesn't affect other business applications and services.	Network design requires modifications and additional security measures to integrate outsourced applications and data sources. SLAs need to be established to avoid disruption to business functions. Third-party security audits should be performed to ensure compliance with policy.

Review Questions

1 For which business category would an organization use an insourcing model?

   a. Administration

   b. Context

   c. Core

   d. Personnel

2 Which reason explains why companies tend to underestimate the resources they use to support an internally sourced business application?

 a. Because the business application is new, accounting has no established accounts to debit for the application expenses.

 b. Only resources used by the developing application's final version get counted, and the development costs get assigned to overhead account categories.

 c. Some parts of the new business application support get charged to existing operating budgets.

 d. The department in charge of implementing the new business application wants to disguise the actual application costs.

3 Which of the following are associated with using an insourcing model for business application development and implementation?

 a. Application development failure, changed solution need, noncompetitive application

 b. Changed solution need, noncompetitive application, premature implementation

 c. Application development failure, noncompetitive application, premature implementation

 d. Application development failure, changed solution need, premature implementation

4 Which statement best explains why the insourcing model allows the business application the most secure environment of all the sourcing models?

 a. Customers sign standard nondisclosure statements before doing application business.

 b. The insourcing model retains application elements within the company.

 c. The internally sourced application model generates little product to compromise.

 d. With the insourcing model, only customers have access to company application information.

5 When companies use the insourcing model for business applications, to whom do they assign delivery accountability?

 a. Chief executive officer

 b. Customer representative assigned to the customer buying the application product or service

 c. Manager in charge of the applicable core business area

 d. Manager in charge of the business application

6 Which explanation best demonstrates why a company would want to use an insourcing model for a business application directly related to one of their core business interests?

a. Increasing accuracy of accounting resources expended on the application

b. Maintaining complete control of the business application

c. Reducing costs associated with the application

d. Retaining its personnel currently working in a core business area

7 Which areas of day-to-day operation do companies with technical, core business areas tend to outsource?

a. Basic technical research

b. Product customization

c. Product development

d. Record archiving

8 Which business application resource requirement consideration is favorable to outsourcing the application?

a. Allowing immediate write-off of up-front application costs

b. Boosting morale by not having to include existing personnel in the design process

c. Increasing application data security by using public facilities

d. Making resources otherwise required for the application available to support core business activity

9 Which risk is not linked to a company outsourcing a business application to a provider?

a. Failure of a new application provider

b. Intermediate manager resistance in the company

c. Provider incompatibility

d. Trial before obtaining the application

10 Which set of security measures is normally used to prevent customer information compromise in an outsourced business application?

a. Digital certificates, encryption, and multiple firewalls

b. Encryption, multiple firewalls, and private data lines

c. Digital certificates, multiple firewalls, and private data lines

d. Digital certificates, encryption, and private data lines

11 Which statement describes the difference between a business application's delivery responsibility using the insourcing model and a business application using the outsourcing model?

    a. With the outsourcing model, both the oversight of the application and the delivery responsibility occur at a much higher level of management.

    b. With the outsourcing model, both the oversight of the application and the delivery responsibility occur at a lower level of management.

    c. With the outsourcing model, the oversight of the application occurs at a lower level of management, and the delivery responsibility escalates to the chief executive officer.

    d. With the outsourcing model, the oversight of the application occurs at a lower level of management, and delivery responsibility stays with the same managers as with the insourcing model.

12 Which set of advantages does outsourcing deliver?

    a. Bandwidth requirements and innovation development time

    b. Remote access and innovation development time

    c. Remote access and download time

    d. Bandwidth requirements and remote access

13 Which set of three reasons drive companies to use ASPs?

    a. Best practices, emerging technology, and industry excess IT expertise

    b. Best practices, emerging technology, and increasing global competition

    c. Best practices, industry excess IT expertise, and increasing global competition

    d. Emerging technology, industry excess IT expertise, and increasing global competition

14 Which set of resource requirements would a company expect the ASP to supply?

    a. Internet connection, licenses, and networking

    b. Licenses, networking, and servers

    c. Internet connection, networking, and servers

    d. Internet connection, licenses, and servers

15 Which risk is involved when using an ASP to obtain a business application?

    a. ASP failure

    b. Leveraged ASP capabilities

    c. Performance monitoring tools

    d. Service Level Agreements

16 Which security issue provides the greatest objection of business application users to obtaining the application from an ASP?

    a. Unable to determine the ability of ASP employees

    b. Compromise of customer data

    c. Cost of leased data lines

    d. Need to keep user employees occupied with the application

17 Which statement best describes the way the ASP accepts responsibility from the user company for the delivery of the product or service the ASP provides?

    a. It guarantees the application performance.

    b. It returns the ASP fee to the user for the default period.

    c. It returns the ASP fee both to the user and to any customer for the default period.

    d. It takes no responsibility.

18 Which advantage does not result from obtaining a business application from an ASP?

    a. Eliminating obsolescence

    b. Providing universal accessibility

    c. Reducing risk

    d. Scheduling updates

19 Which sourcing model tends to require a company to maintain a larger staff of employees?

    a. ASP

    b. Contracting

    c. Insourcing

    d. Outsourcing

20 Which commodity does a company exchange for the risk associated with business application implementation in the process of using an outsourcing arrangement?

a. Payment

b. Profit

c. Time

d. Trust

21 Which causes the perceived loss of customer data security associated with forms of outsourcing models?

a. Data encryption

b. Employees leaving employment

c. Loss of data control

d. User tokens

22 Which statement best explains why companies assign business application delivery responsibility to lower levels of management if the company outsources the application?

a. The company CEO has no responsibility for outsourced applications.

b. The company has less direct management and supervisory activity.

c. Outsourcing's cost-saving philosophy dictates less management involvement.

d. The provider prefers a lower level point of contact with the user company.

23 Which major impact results from a company insourcing its context business?

a. Allows leveraging of provider company skills and expertise for core business

b. Prevents context business procedures from becoming obsolete

c. Requires employees to work on context business at the expense of core business

d. Requires employees to work on core business at the expense of context business

Applied Solutions

My experiences building Internet applications has certainly covered the entire spectrum of sourcing models. The first web sites that I worked on were 100 percent outsourced efforts because few companies in the mid-1990s had any experience in Internet technologies at all. These projects were perfect examples of the basic benefit of having another company design, build, deploy, and maintain a brochure-like web presence.

As the population of Internet-aware and Internet-savvy workers grew, more and more companies were interested in taking their web site operations inhouse and finding a small team to take over the project so that changes could be introduced more rapidly and with less cost. Some of these migrations from 100 percent outsourced to 100 percent insourced resulted in total failures.

The resource needs and technical experience required to operate even simple sites was found to be greater than anticipated. Sites lost functionality and failed to deliver rapid modifications because the site's new owners were not the ones who had built it in the first place. This led to the creation of many second-generation web site deployments for companies as total rewrites of the site code and contents. The point of the story here is that neither insourcing nor outsourcing are right or wrong. What matters most is knowing what a web site or application is expected to do now, and in the near future, to avoid total rewrites.

Now that both company web sites and company applications have evolved into sophisticated three-tiered architectures providing critical Internet business solutions, the question of sourcing remains mostly the same. The decision to build or to buy depends on knowing how much functionality and real-time transaction processing power you need, and how much you can afford to house internally versus finding a reliable outsourced vendor.

Scenario 1: Outsourced Database

Problem

A project wants to outsource the database layer of its business application because this layer does not represent any core business functionality for the company. The network connectivity between the company and the outsourced provider must be established using VPN gateways instead of private, leased communication lines. A network compatibility issue, however, has arisen. Both the company and the outsourced provider rely on an internal private IP network of 192.168.X.X address space. How can the outsourced provider connect to the company using VPN gateways to overcome this compatibility problem?

Solution

Employing Network Address Translation (NAT) rules on the VPN hardware can solve the potential routing and network addressing conflicts posed by this situation. However, network addresses must be assigned for systems on each of the two networks so that appropriate host routes can be added to establish connectivity and implement the outsourced database solution. NAT can translate traffic from either side of the VPN into the corresponding IP addresses reserved by the network administrators on the other side of the connection. So the IP address space being used does not matter for the company or its outsourcing application provider.

Solution Details

The following were useful in the solution:

* CISCO PIX Firewall 520 with 3 Network Interfaces
* CISCO IOS VPN module
* CISCO IOS NAT configurations and static IP configurations

Scenario 2: Internet Catalog

Problem

During the development of a large-scale, high-availability Internet catalog for a commercial web site, several vendors participate in the project, and each has specific network components for which they are responsible. One vendor is responsible for the production network hardware configuration and maintenance; another vendor for the production backup network configuration and maintenance; and a third is responsible for the production, staging, and development application environments. An integration problem is brewing here, as each vendor makes its own decisions about how to build its components without adequate communication with the other vendors. Adding to the problem are dependencies between the vendors because the application environment cannot be finalized until the production network configurations have been finalized. Any slippage in delivery dates for having the production environment ready for a code release will cause a slippage for the other vendors. How can these vendors coordinate their work and avoid falling behind schedule, and how do they avoid facing an integration problem after all the components are brought together?

Solution

The situation is quite common, and the solution is not technology-based. My participation in the successful launch of this Internet catalog was dependent on finding the client-side manager who was capable of taking 100 percent technical leadership of the project. However, finding this leader was not the only important step. Instituting weekly technology status meetings and, as the launch date approached, daily technology status calls was essential to keep all the vendors aware of each other's progress and find ways to solve problems as a group.

Solution Details

The following tactics were useful in the solution:

- Creating a technology team e-mail alias to facilitate communication between vendors
- Creating a detailed technology launch milestone checklist
- Holding weekly technology team meetings, taking minutes, and distributing meeting minutes promptly
- Holding daily technology team conference calls to discuss issues for each item on the milestone checklist

CHAPTER 6

Internet Business Solutions

Redesigning business services as Internet business solutions is a growing trend in a wide range of industries. With a focus on establishing a competitive edge, the latest business initiatives look to Internet-based solutions to achieve business goals. The CISS professional should be ready to assist an organization in developing its own applications and Internet-based services.

The benefits of migrating business services and applications to Internet-based business solutions include better customer information services, vendor and employee relationships, training environments, electronic publications, and commerce in general. You can incorporate business rules and logic with company databases to make customer personalization and relationship management comprehensive and easy to manage. All points of contact can be coordinated to provide a consistent message and level of service to each customer, vendor, employee, trainee, reader, or consumer.

This chapter covers the following Internet business solutions:

- Internet-based customer care
- Workforce optimization
- Supply chain management
- E-learning and e-publishing systems

Internet-Based Customer Care

Customer care is awareness that business should not spend all development and research resources on products and associated fees. Business focus on the customer is becoming a more competitive component in winning the business of modern customers.

Providing customer service for only eight hours each business day is no longer adequate now that business services have moved online. Good customer care now means near-instant messaging about their transactions. Transactions that once took several days to receive, process, and respond are now processed within minutes.

A full understanding of Internet-based customer care requires knowledge of the following:

- Need for Internet-based customer care
- Advantages of Internet-based customer care
- Internet-based customer care components
- Internet-based customer care lifecycle
- Elements of Internet-based customer care

Need for Internet-Based Customer Care

The need for Internet-based customer care has grown out of higher consumer expectations, and out of cost-cutting measures employed to keep the total cost of service and support low while still providing a full range of services.

Internet-based customer care encompasses people, processes, and technologies that support every type of interaction a customer has with an organization through every means of contact.

An Internet-based customer support solution offers many advantages:

- **Improved customer support response times**—Customers get nearly instant answers to questions or can request that their answers be picked up (or e-mailed later) at a later time, to avoid long customer wait times.

- **Responsive support team**—New customer support teams can be quickly activated to meet unexpected customer demands. Support teams can be anywhere in the world and do not have to be at centralized phone centers.

- **Outsourced customer support functions**—Customer support companies can be outsourced as a service more readily and can potentially reduce support costs.

- **Satisfy smaller company needs**—Customer support companies can pull the needs of smaller companies together to provide high-quality Internet-based customer support to start-up or emerging companies.

- **Customer relationship management**—Internet-based support systems easily fit into an Application Service Provider (ASP) model for customer relationship management (CRM). Many leaders in CRM solutions provide ASP-based CRMs at almost no incremental cost, providing further opportunities for emerging businesses.

In addition to these customer interaction advantages, the need for Internet-based customer care is based on three aspects of customer needs:

- Why customers demand more
- Why some businesses falter
- How to deliver more

Why Customers Demand More

Today's customers know and demand more than ever before. For example, customers expect around-the-clock support, faster product and services delivery, custom solutions to meet their unique needs, and efficient, hassle-free purchase and service transactions. The Internet dramatically reduces switching costs, allowing customers to compare competitive offerings and move to another supplier with relative ease.

Businesses face enormous pressure to respond appropriately and rapidly to increasingly complex and time-critical customer needs. To stay competitive in this open environment, companies must offer differentiated, 24-hour global service access.

New and global competition threatens to blur traditional boundaries and reduce barriers to emerging channels and business models that can be established rapidly. To compete in this environment, companies must offer competitive pricing for differentiated products and services.

Why Some Companies Falter

A traditional company faces a number of barriers to providing customers with an integrated and consistent experience across contact points. Most of these result from fragmentation of customer interactions into isolated groups based on separate functions (such as marketing, sales, service), separate contact points (such as web service, ATMs, call centers, dealers, agents and sales force), and separate communications media (such as phone, e-mail, web, fax, and video). As a result, companies face the following challenges:

- **Inconsistent sales and service levels**—Customers must frequently manage their own information requests within an enterprise to get them addressed (often repeating themselves several times before reaching the right people).

- **Fragmented customer messaging**—Conflicting or incomplete information originates and is disseminated by different parts of an organization.

- **Missed sales opportunities**—With no centralized information available about the customer, tailoring interactions to a customer's particular needs is difficult.

- **Inefficient business processes**—Companies often fail to effectively leverage information and coordinate resources across multiple business functions.

How to Deliver More

Internet-based customer care demands that businesses use all aspects of the Web to be successful. Three factors help companies to do this:

- **Availability of web-based applications to enhance business processes**—The Internet economy enables customer-facing applications through a web-based environment. All customer-facing business functions can be handled through web-based applications. A business using web-based applications is not required to deploy thousands of client software applications to address these functions. In recent years, web browser software has increasingly replaced dedicated client software used in client/server network services.

- **Increased access to customer information**—Sharing common customer information captured across all of these individual applications results in increased access. In addition, through web-based workflow and knowledge management systems, business users can transition seamlessly from one business function to another.

- **Increase of communication technologies**—New communications technologies integrated across all environments and media types enable the common capture of information and integration across all customer contact points. Key trends include the following:

  — Rapid infrastructure growth and customer adoption of the Internet and broadband service.

  — Convergence of data, voice, and video technologies.

  — Migration from traditional, centralized, circuit-switched customer call centers to open, standards-based IP contact centers. In addition to scaling poorly, proprietary PBX systems with custom software interfaces have historically been costly and slow to upgrade.

  — Emergence of unified messaging technologies that integrate e-mail, fax, paging, voice mail, and the web.

Advantages of Internet-Based Customer Care

Internet-based customer care benefits the business and customer, saving them time and effort. Internet-based customer care offers a comprehensive integration of marketing, sales, customer support, and service using networked applications over the Internet. Efficiency and revenue grow when implemented solutions address customers' service needs and make them more useful by making them more widely available. Today, not all customers want or use branch offices and telephone-based customer service. Millions of customers now want internet-based services in addition to the traditional customer service channels.

A defined and systemized business process for customer care creates company-wide processes and methodologies. Implementing Internet-based customer care enables companies to better manage these customer-care business processes.

Customer sales and support information systems have often been separate systems with their own data and application screens. Internet-based customer care allows all employees to use the same data sources as they investigate and process customer requests, but with different views of that data for each department. The system makes detailed and summary information available to all users, so updates and changes allow everyone to participate in a quick response to any customer issues.

A good customer care system is an important criterion upon which a company's valuation will be based. Hundreds of publicly traded companies and soon-to-be publicly traded companies can increase their market valuation with a strong commitment to customer service by providing helpful and easy-to-use customer care services.

You can build one application engine that supports multiple business units and customer groups. Sales teams, Value Added Resellers (VARs), and customers can all access the same front-end systems but see different aspects of the same data. This consolidation into one seamless front-end interface increases efficiency because multiple systems do not have to be created and maintained.

Internet-based customer care now handles customer service activities that sales and support teams used to handle. Repetitive tasks are reduced, leaving the sales and support teams to focus more of their time and energy on selling and personalized service.

Integration of company-wide databases in customer care applications creates cross-selling and up-selling opportunities. Simply put, Internet-based customer care increases revenue. As employees experience the benefits of Internet-based customer care, their job satisfaction and efficiency increases.

Internet-Based Customer Care Components

Customer relationship management integrates sales and marketing applications, as well as applications used in traditional customer support and service departments. The term *customer care component* applies to a set of application features and functionality, and each of the components described in the following sections can be thought of as part of an overall internet-based customer care system. The essential Internet-based customer care components are numerous, but the architecture and application software underlying them is common to almost all components.

The first essential Internet-based customer care module involves account names, addresses, phone numbers, e-mail addresses, and other notes—the basis of all customer care applications. Managing these accounts is easier when the information is centralized and accessible by anyone with appropriate account privileges. The *account* consists not only of the individual or company information, but also information about where a given product or service is being sold. Update privileges can be granted at the local workgroup levels or can require a centralized update process before becoming available to the entire company. Where necessary, separate offices can maintain separate accounts, but all accounts are still linked to the corporate headquarters. Regardless of time zone or geographic location, managers and sales teams can all benefit from Internet-based account management tools, services, and automated status messaging.

Contact management, the second essential Internet-based customer care module, strives to keep track of the contact person or persons for a customer account. A contact is generally a single person within a company, and a contact report details the events of meetings with the person pertaining to the goods or services being sold. Contact management is an important component in Internet-based customer care applications that allows sales and service teams to access up-to-date, detailed information to service customer requests.

Opportunity management is the third essential Internet-based customer care module, which details the process of knowing where in the selling process a given account and contact is at any given point in time. The details related to selling goods and services are found in opportunity management tools. Opportunity management's goal is to know how best to match up sales resources with sales opportunities. Internet-based customer care applications create enhanced sales monitoring opportunities. Managers and executives are given near-real time access to status of leads, lead assignment and sales territory delegations, as well as a contact's selling history.

The fourth essential Internet-based customer care module involves *marketing cycles*. These cycles are hard to manage and track, but become less unruly with Internet-based tools and applications. Targeted e-mails, newsletters, faxes, and other batch communications are best executed with accurate, up-to-date contact information. With the integration of customer sales and support tools, it is possible for sales staff, support staff, or even the customers themselves to enter updated information into the system. Effective marketing campaigns require a high degree of accuracy in customer contact data. Planning and executing marketing buys and campaigns should be informed by the success of previous efforts. The marketing management component of Internet-based customer care solutions controls the costs and results of marketing by using reports and analysis.

Sales force management, the fifth essential module of Internet-based customer care, keeps accurate and timely sales information. The knowledge gathered by a sales agent now lies within the organization and not with the agent alone, so you can build applications that immediately execute steps of the sales process automatically. Taking advantage of internet-based technologies accelerates customer services provisioning and tailoring product specifications. Networked sales communication channels provide managers with forecasting insights and help identify bottlenecks to processing orders and service requests.

Use sales force management for the following purposes:

- Generate and maintain the sales order processing cycle.
- Facilitate and automate processes and workflow in the sales cycle, including identification and tracking of opportunities and sales forecasting.
- Generate and manage cost estimates.
- Generate sales opportunities for sales professionals and all other customer-facing employees.
- Provide information details on customers, prospects, contacts, partners, and competitors.

- Provide relationship management roles and agents; activities and task delegation; messaging on status changes and communications history, meetings, calls, correspondence, visits, reports, and document management.

- Provide progress management, cost management, product planning, discount management, and more.

The sixth essential module of Internet-based customer care involves *developing a customer base*. Many enterprises compete in the market, and customer service maintains and attracts new clients. To do this, a company must maintain contact throughout the sales process. This end-to-end contact helps build closer relationships with customers and helps build and maintain new opportunities.

Customers make buying decisions based on their overall experience, which includes sales, service, recognition, and support. To compete in the fast-growing world of Internet-based customer care, companies need to maintain customer service and support for customers worldwide. Internet-based customer care systems built on templating technology, such as XML, can be used with content management tools to provide regionalized content in native languages, while still allowing for centralized content creation. This makes providing worldwide customer service a less daunting project.

Interactions with customers can employ the latest technologies:

- Person-to-person chat services offered, with web site phone call service and automated e-mail reply service

- Customer support web site available 24-hours a day with online call status monitoring available

- Help desk support for hardware and software

- Maintenance requests for field service parts, inventory, scheduling, and available on-site customer service

Internet-Based Customer Care Lifecycle

The Internet-based customer care process spans many stages. As a cycle, these stages are interdependent and continuous. As the transition from a given stage to the next occurs, insight is gained that enhances subsequent efforts. Through this understanding, the organization becomes increasingly sophisticated and profitable.

The customer's relationship with the company is maintained throughout the lifecycle. This involvement is possible because the organization stays up to date with the customer, understands ongoing needs, and provides the customer with the training and education based on their unique situation.

The key components of the lifecycle of an Internet-based customer care are shown in Figure 6-1. The text in the following sections discusses each in turn.

Figure 6-1   *Internet-Based Customer Care Lifecycle*

Target

eMarketing typically encompasses campaign management and general advertising. Its purpose is to help focus customer attention on the target company. Fulfilling that purpose can include the derivation of new services or product bundling offered to the potential customers to attract them to the target company. eMarketing's focus is to sell the products and services to broad customer groups.

eMarketing tools are available to find the appropriate target customers and sales management tools. Sales management tools can be used for reaching out directly across a sales force, across Internet commerce, Internet fulfillment, and Internet services, and across support tools to provide necessary transaction capabilities.

eSales typically encompasses sales tracking, contact management, and lead documentation or communication. eSales finalizes a commitment to a specific customer.

Acquire

The ability to acquire and provide services for clients through collaborative efforts between eMarketing and eSales management is an important factor. If an organization does not collaborate with others, the customer is not served with the best products and services. This failure defeats the purpose of integrating customer care with web-based functions and applications.

Develop

In a customer-focused marketplace, product and channel development must follow the customer's expectations to the fullest. Organizations develop products and services, and even new channels, based on the customer needs and service expectations.

Service

Access to information and appropriate training prepares organizations to steadily improve the way they deliver to customers. Delivering value is essential to the relationship with the client. Customers base value perceptions on a number of factors: quality of products and services, convenience, speed, ease of use, response time, and service excellence.

Retain

After the sale, the customer can check on orders and track shipping and fulfillment logistics. The same customer is equally supplied with the service and support capabilities and information that are required after a sale.

Grow

After the sale, the ability to stay with customers, to comprehend their ongoing needs, to provide them with training and education around the offerings the company provides, and to learn and grow with the customer as their business relates to future offerings will be required. E-learning and Internet community environments facilitate this growth.

Elements of Internet-Based Customer Care

This section introduces the elements of implementing Internet-based customer care applications. All these elements should be examined from the point of view of the network professional participating in the design, construction, and maintenance of Internet-based applications supporting customer care projects.

Here are the elements:

- Connectivity
- Capacity
- Availability
- Reliability
- Security
- Manageability

The Internet-based customer care system's connectivity requirements are dependent on the system requirements and overall design. If the Internet-based customer care is implemented on a thin client running on an intranet or the Internet, connectivity is a factor of the number of users times the amount of data transfer between the client and the server(s). Advanced features, such as screen-pops based on PBX information, increase the connectivity requirements. Network design is also affected by whether connectivity to a corporate, back-end customer information database is required. If only select information about a customer needs to be exchanged with back-end systems, software compatible with Lightweight Directory Access Protocol (LDAP) might provide sufficient connectivity.

The Internet-based customer care system must have enough storage and processing power (capacity) to handle the current user load and service for the next two years. This capability allows for normal growth of the system but does not dedicate resources prematurely.

The physical systems (network, database, and application servers) used must also be expandable. These systems are purchased or developed on a modular basis with capacities determined by the number of users and desired components. With network router and switch capacity, purchase of a router or switch that can have faster or denser "blades" dropped into place avoids the added expense of having to replace the entire router or switch when capacity needs to be increased.

The Internet-based customer care system must be available to users during the required business hours. If a global corporation uses this system, the opportunity for maintenance can shrink to nearly zero. These systems are considered high-availability systems because of the immediate customer impact. With some customers, using the Internet as their only channel of communication with the support teams only magnifies the importance of the continuous availability of these systems.

Failover systems with redundancy are appropriate for high-availability systems. Many companies employ multisite disaster recovery and support sites to route customers to the closest available site. Designing networks and systems for high availability allows companies to rotate components out of production use, upgrade or replace them, and rotate them back into service. Some high-end systems even provide hot-swapable components, such as CPUs and disks.

An Internet-based customer care system must be implemented on a reliable system that has failover redundancy. The systems need to be well designed and tested. In addition, the systems must be capable of delivering accurate and reliable results. A cheaper solution than fully redundant systems is to purchase and deploy standby network and system hardware. Having a "spare" switch or router on hand can reduce the impact of system failures to just a few minutes.

Any Internet-based customer care system that handles sensitive information (customer information, billing information, and so on) must ensure security. A high level of security must be present in the system to guarantee that information is not available to unauthorized users. Encrypted passwords (with history tracking and periodic expiration), menu security, and a database table access restriction by username are a minimal set of security features. Security must be configurable to the needs of the customer and the system's current purpose. Security should not become a management burden. Much of the security must be centralized and implemented according to user roles defined in the system (administrator, customer support user, employee user, and so on).

Security considerations can radically impact network design. Strong security requirements for tape backup and recovery systems, for example, call for a duplication of all networking interfaces in each system, and discrete routers and switches to ensure a private, secure backup solution. The CISS professional should present the relative risk and benefit of such expenditures in security and design discussions.

The Internet-based customer care system should include well-thought-out maintenance and flexibility provisions. Basic system monitoring and status reporting must be available at an administrative level. The Internet-based customer care system needs to be a maintainable system that requires little active cleanup of historical information. The applications must contain self-maintenance features to aid in system database maintenance. Furthermore, the system must be flexible, with an ability to grow from a functionality standpoint. Because most of these systems are modular, adding new areas of functionality is part of the design. For security, disaster recovery, and manageability concerns, backing up network and system configurations is an important consideration. Making this process manageable means automating it, hopefully without compromising system and network security.

Internet-Based Workforce Optimization

Cisco Systems, Inc. saves more than 75 million dollars annually, 2,500 dollars per employee every year, as a direct result of implementing workforce optimization applications. Forward-thinking businesses invest in web-enabled workforce optimization as a major competitive differentiator. State-of-the-art workforce optimization applications allow a company to succeed in this new environment.

Workforce optimization encompasses everything from facilitating routine administrative tasks, to managing complex business operations and decisions, to improving communications and learning—all enabled by an integrated, secure, global network. All workforce optimization initiatives share the goal to increase organizational effectiveness.

The workforce optimization solution denotes leveraging Internet technologies to maximize employee time so that they can focus on their jobs' core value. A truly optimized workforce has all the information needed to do a job, in addition to the tools required to complete a job most efficiently.

Workforce optimization applications streamline processes to reduce or eliminate time-consuming administration. Furthermore, workforce optimization applications provide the right information at the right time to enable the "Learning Organization," one that can quickly influence employees and react to market conditions.

The workforce optimization discussion is divided into the following sections:

- Using Workforce Optimization in Functional Areas
- Advantages of Workforce Optimization
- Workforce Optimization Components
- Tools for Implementing a Solution
- Elements of Internet-Based Workforce Optimization

Using Workforce Optimization in Functional Areas

You can use the core concepts of workforce optimization to create a knowledgeable, empowered workforce. The best companies do this across their entire organization, addressing business issues in many functional areas.

The first functional area is in *finance*. Applications that assist in both day-to-day business analysis and periodic business planning activities can be optimized as Internet business solutions. Financial data coupled with project management data, for example, allows detailed reporting and querying of daily, weekly, monthly, quarterly, and yearly metrics. Workforce optimization of financial business processes allows for detailed investigation of financial goals and operating costs.

Communications makes up the second functional area. Two-way communication and collaboration applications assist in the dissemination of corporate and product information and are an easy match for workforce optimization efforts. A company memo is a one-way informational broadcast, but corporate e-mail exchanges enable employee feedback and detailed Internet-based surveys. Analysis of communication networks within an organization is possible with Internet-based communication tools, such as e-mail, collaborative authoring software, and videoconferencing. Optimizing communication paths and groups represents a major opportunity to improve the health and vitality of a business.

Human resources represents the third functional area. Practices and applications that empower the workforce, improve the culture, perform administrative functions, and develop the leadership to optimize the effectiveness of your organization are all opportunities for human resources to take advantage of Internet technologies. For example, automated synchronization of employee information with benefits provider databases ensures a high level of service for employees with low levels of cost. Workforce optimization is also responsible for opening up secure access to HR databases so that employees can enter and update their own contact information, saving administrative overhead and increasing the data quality. In an emergency, being able to reliably contact each employee is an invaluable ability.

The fourth functional area encompasses *purchasing and expense management*. Applications that streamline an enterprise's repetitive, administrative, and operational tasks are a mainstay of workforce optimization initiatives. Previous databases of vendor names have given way to higher levels of integration. Internet business purchasing systems solutions now offer new levels of automatically updated purchase detail, such as serial numbers and support agreements. This data can be accessed along with requests for quotes for hardware, automatically keeping abreast of new models, and generally adding a greater level of detail to expense management opportunities.

IT services make up the fifth functional area. Workforce optimization of IT services means applications that enable employees to request, query, and update services without requiring help from other employees. The daily record detailing what is right and what is wrong with a business lives in the helpdesk ticket log. Identifying and incorporating solutions to the problems documented by helpdesk tickets enables an organization to quickly learn from its mistakes. If workforce optimization offers ways to change process for the better, the IT services optimization within an organization is certainly the best area to focus on before all others.

The sixth functional area is in *education and training*. Initiatives addressing learning within an organization focus on applications that enable optimization of all aspects of the training process. Self-guided, web-based training is exciting for your business learning needs. A workforce optimization project that introduces basic employee training quickly increases efficiencies within your business. By combining learning initiatives with a corporate extranet, vendors and third-party service providers can participate in your workforce optimization plans.

Company Profile: Verizon Communications Inc.

Workforce optimization provides many benefits for companies around the world. Verizon Communications Incorporated followed a workforce optimization solution because they needed to increase the productivity of their new sales hires. Verizon developed a web-based training tool, augmented by classroom training and a mentor. Not only did this solution reduce the training schedule from an 18-week program to 8 weeks, but it also resulted in a 25 percent reduction in the time until the first sale by a new hire.

The first sale also had twice the value of a sale by a traditionally trained sales hire. Carol Sabia, director of Verizon Learning Systems, said, "We had discussions with the sales managers. . . the quantitative changes were directly linked to the training."

Advantages of Workforce Optimization

Workforce optimization applications provide the right information at the right time to enable the "Learning Organization," one that quickly influences employees and reacts to market conditions. Figures 6-2 thru 6-8 contain reasons why a company might implement workforce optimization into their business practices.

The highlighted advantage in Figure 6-2 concerns Reduced Administrative Time (RAT).

Figure 6-2 *Reduced Administrative Time (RAT)*

R.A.T.	Coordination	Focus Change	Market Focus	Training	Centralization	Scalability

With business conducted on the Internet, an organization must react quickly. This haste means that the delays involved in administrative tasks must be minimized. The idea is to delegate more responsibility to the workforce.

Traditionally, a department is dedicated to administrative tasks, such as entering employee records in a database, keeping track of their hours and phone numbers, and keeping their personal files up to date. This activity adds overhead in the form of time. By allowing employees to enter the data themselves into a system that automates the manual processes, the middle layer can be minimized, if not fully eliminated. A smaller administrative workforce can now provide more effective services because it is freed from mundane tasks.

The highlighted advantage in Figure 6-3 concerns coordination.

Figure 6-3 *Coordination*

R.A.T.	Coordination	Focus Change	Market Focus	Training	Centralization	Scalability

In any organization, coordination is most important. This activity can be viewed in two ways: operational optimization and resource optimization. Operational optimization streamlines coordination between different groups employed to address a problem and optimize workforce functionality. This is usually the case in a service sector organization, where proper coordination between those in the field and those in the office must be established.

Resource optimization judges how many people to employ for a job, selects people with the proper background, and so on. Essentially, it manages workforce size. The distinction between these two kinds of optimization is important. The problem of optimizing the functionality is challenging because it presupposes proper understanding of organization dynamics.

The highlighted advantage in Figure 6-4 concerns focus change.

Figure 6-4 *Focus*

R.A.T.	Coordination	Focus Change	Market Focus	Training	Centralization	Scalability

The Internet provides a new paradigm in conducting business. The focus is changed from the product to the customer. By including the customer early in the lifecycle, quality service can be provided. With business conducted on the Internet, the gap between the customer and the company that provides the service or product is fairly small. Instead of developing a product and then finding a customer, a company can understand the needs of the customer first and then provide the service or product.

Understanding the customer's needs first, and providing a service or product to match has wide implications. The organization must be restructured to handle the situation. The Internet industry's production sector has created a solution called *just in time (JIT)*. The exact processes to harness JIT are specific to an organization but require highly structured information flow between various departments.

The highlighted advantage in Figure 6-5 concerns market focus awareness.

Figure 6-5 *Market Focus*

R.A.T.	Coordination	Focus Change	Market Focus	Training	Centralization	Scalability

You can understand the customer behavior patterns by using information gathered through feedback channels. This resource helps in market forecasting and is a proactive service to the customer. Feedback also helps in resource management and has been the domain of *enterprise resource planning (ERP)* solutions. Several powerful and mature, ready-made packages or solutions to accomplish enterprise resource planning are now available.

The highlighted advantage in Figure 6-6 concerns training.

Figure 6-6 *Training*

R.A.T.	Coordination	Focus Change	Market Focus	Training	Centralization	Scalability

Training is an important element in any major system deployment. This fact is especially true with workforce optimization. To properly maximize system use, each workgroup needs to be shown not only how to use the system, but also how it will make their work more efficient. Training can be directed on a module basis to the various users (human resources, finance, purchasing, and so on). Comprehensive training including many components can benefit support and operational groups.

The highlighted advantage in Figure 6-7 concerns centralization.

Figure 6-7 *Centralization*

R.A.T.	Coordination	Focus Change	Market Focus	Training	Centralization	Scalability

A centralized system containing mostly updated information can establish proper communication between the workforce, management, and customers. An automated response system reduces the overhead of extra workforce.

The highlighted advantage in Figure 6-8 concerns scalability.

Figure 6-8 *Scalability*

R.A.T.	Coordination	Focus Change	Market Focus	Training	Centralization	Scalability

Scalability is easily achieved at no extra cost. Every organization's dream is to "begin local and grow global" with a well-conceived service or product that caters to a small clientele and keeps increasing its reach. The workforce grows in the same proportion. The aim is to understand this growth problem at the inception level and address it. An automated workforce optimization system with well-conceived processes can cater to increases in volume.

Additional benefits to deploying Internet-powered workforce optimization follow:

- **Empowered employees**—Automated information systems are intuitively easy to use and allow employees to focus on the job, not the tools.

- **Increased profitability**—Every dollar saved through cost control can be reinvested in customer-focused initiatives or added directly to the bottom line.

- **High return on investment**—Significant returns are generated through cost reductions from decreased overhead and measurable productivity gains.

- **Ability to scale**—Through automation and self-service applications, employees can enter their own data and monitor their own activities. This shift reduces the manpower required to conduct daily business and frees administrative staff to focus on other valuable activities.

- **Increased employee satisfaction and loyalty**—By eliminating or reducing tedious administrative tasks and facilitating efficiency and productivity, employees feel more valued and more independent.

Workforce Optimization Components

Workforce optimization encompasses everything from facilitating routine administrative tasks, to managing complex business operations and decisions, to improving communications and learning — all enabled by an integrated, secure, global network. Four components keep all of this functional:

- Resource management
- Communication center

- Knowledge center
- Optimization engine

Resource Management

Resources can mean material resources or the workforce. When appropriate knowledge supports decision-making processes, material resources can be handled in a much better way. For example, inventory management is greatly benefited if you know in advance the proper estimation of requirements. This foreknowledge has traditionally been the focus of *enterprise resource planning (ERP)*, a well-addressed domain with many packages available. Depending on an organization's need, a specific package can be chosen.

Managing the other resource, workforce, is benefited by streamlining administration. By having a centralized database on the extranet, the employees can enter or retrieve information from any location, eliminating the need for the human resources department to intervene. The time gained there allows the human resources department to provide a value-added service. For example, consider a consulting company. The workforce is mobile most of the time. Saving time with an extranet-based workforce optimization package that handles time sheets and expense reports, the management can use the time to focus on quality service instead of addressing the logistic problems and paperwork. Presently, available packages address specific issues, such as web-based time reporting tools or web-based appointment calendars.

Communication Center

The communication center module provides universal information to the workforce and customers. Putting the information on the web establishes an open channel of communication. The medium can exchange both passive and active information. Depending on the need, users can get the information in the method of their choice. This capability brings transparency and increases the effectiveness of communication. Furthermore, this capability can include answering systems that satisfy questions from customers.

Knowledge Center

Employee effectiveness depends on their knowledge base, their systems use, and their sharing of experiences with others. The knowledge center module can provide the operational knowledge, access to the accumulated knowledge of previous experiences, and a mechanism to share the experiences with others. This training can be regular; for example, when you recruit a new staff member, or on an as-needed basis as the situation demands. A continuous upgrade of employee skills improves effectiveness. Spending less time on acquiring operational knowledge leaves more time to respond to a situation in a thoughtful way.

Another use of this module is knowledge interpretation. The optimization engine gathers information or knowledge, which can be put to good use if you have the ability to interpret it. For example, information on customer purchases can extract a customer behavior pattern. While patterns like the sale of more umbrellas during the rainy season are obvious, not so obvious connections and patterns can be discovered using sophisticated statistical pattern recognition tools. This is sometimes referred to as *data mining* or *data warehousing*.

Optimization Engine

The optimization engine forms the core of the activity. An autonomous system is designed that extracts the knowledge from the information and continues to grow in size over time. The effectiveness of the system mainly depends on the algorithms used to acquire the knowledge.

This module's responsibility is to build the knowledge base and use it effectively. Because this system grows autonomously scalability is a minor issue. If the organization supplies volume N, provided the processes are well conceived, the optimization engine can supply volume N + X. Building such an engine is an iterative exercise. The various factors involved in building this engine, such as algorithm or model choice and infrastructure, are subject to change within the requirements. Therefore, a transient time period occurs before the system stabilizes.

Tools for Implementing a Solution

The secret to success is building a strong network infrastructure to support current and future workforce optimization requirements. Without a solid network foundation to tie the workforce optimization solution components together, limitations and inefficiencies will prevail.

In addition to an appropriate network foundation, Internet tools and technologies are now used in developing all networked applications, regardless of whether those applications are accessed on an intranet or the Internet. Such tools and technologies include a common foundation, standards-based tools, platform-independent browsers, and network-facilitated communication and collaboration.

The following are Internet-based applications benefits:

- Reduced complexity
- Shorter development time
- Lower variable costs
- Instant task execution by a paperless, seamless, global process

Cisco Systems, Inc. workforce optimization solution consists of the following four elements:

- **Leading practices**—Broad range of comprehensive information on the strategies and tactics involved in deploying workforce optimization applications, including Cisco case studies, best practices, return-on-investment models, lessons learned, business process improvement, and end-to-end solution recommendations

- **Network foundation**—Recommendations on the most effective Internet technologies to deploy the solution, including security architecture, directory services, network quality and class-of-service, and application and policy requirements, which combine into layers of foundation and enabling technologies—providing a robust foundation for your business solutions

- **Packaged applications**—Information on independent software vendors (ISVs) who provide software applications to effectively deploy and maintain cost-effective, integrated workforce optimization applications

- **Consulting partners**—Information on consulting partners who provide consulting and implementation services based on the Cisco workforce optimization solution

Elements of Internet-Based Workforce Optimization

This section introduces the following elements that you should consider when implementing workforce optimization applications:

- Connectivity
- Capacity
- Availability
- Reliability
- Security
- Manageability

Connectivity in Internet-Based Workforce Optimization

Workforce optimization system connectivity requirements, like the Internet-based customer care systems, depend on the system requirements and overall design. Connectivity issues for third-party database integrations, such as vendor databases, human resources benefits provider databases, and outsourced application services, require analysis of data integration points.

Database fields and data type specifications must be documented before data conduits can be designed to exchange information between these systems. The frequency and breadth of data exchange dictates various options, such as the speed of the network link needed between systems, whether a dedicated private line is required or a VPN solution is adequate. Connectivity requirements also affect the choice of communication protocols, and whether error checking is performed within the application.

Capacity in Internet-Based Workforce Optimization

The workforce optimization system implementation must consider capacity from two perspectives. The system must have enough storage and processing power to handle the current user load and the next two years of service. This capability allows normal system growth but does not dedicate resources prematurely.

The physical systems (network, database, and application servers) used to implement the workforce optimization system must also be expandable. In addition, the system size must be scaled according to the customer requirements. Typically, these systems are purchased or developed on a modular basis, with capacities determined by the number of users. A workforce optimization project capacity plan should also take special peak usage periods into account. Beyond peak usage estimates for day-to-day operations, certain conditions, such as the close of a quarter, can cause greater system loads as more transactions are processed.

Availability in Internet-Based Workforce Optimization

The workforce optimization system must be available to its users during required business hours. If a global corporation is using this system, the opportunity for maintenance can shrink to nearly zero. However, because these are not mission-critical systems, maintenance windows (unavailable periods) are most likely acceptable. A read-only copy of the system (created by data replication) can be made available during the maintenance window. This action provides the secondary benefit of having a failover system.

Reliability in Internet-Based Workforce Optimization

The workforce optimization system should be implemented on a reliable system. However, the system does not require fault tolerance. The system must be well designed and tested. Likewise, the system must be capable of delivering accurate and reliable results. Sometimes, because a project is focused on a workforce optimization initiative, testing and quality assurance are not given a high priority. This usually results in a system that, once deployed and used by the actual employees, does not perform satisfactorily. For perceived reliability, systems and networks must be designed to meet the availability requirements when the system is under load.

Security in Internet-Based Workforce Optimization

Generally, the workforce optimization system handles sensitive information (employee records, customer information, and so on). A high security level must be present in the system to ensure that information is not available to unauthorized users. Encrypted passwords (with history tracking and periodic expiration), menu security, and database table access restriction by username create a minimal set of security features.

Security must be configurable to the needs of the customer and the system's current purpose. Security should not become a management burden. Much of the security must be centralized and implemented according to user roles defined in the system (administrator, human resources user, employee user, and so on). When implementing workforce optimization software and applications, take care when making use of role accounts. If a given role account for a finance project is created, an audit trail of access and use of the role account is a necessary security requirement. Password rotation schemes and periodic review of security event logs should be a part of the overall corporate or department security policy.

Manageability in Internet-Based Workforce Optimization

Workforce optimization system manageability includes maintenance and flexibility. Basic monitoring and systems status must be available at an administrative level. The workforce optimization system needs to be a maintainable system that requires little active, historical information cleanup. The applications must contain self-maintenance features to aid in system database maintenance. Furthermore, the system must be flexible and capable of growing from a functionality standpoint. Because most of these systems are modular, adding new areas of functionality is part of the design.

Internet-Based Supply Chain Management

The logistics of dealing with your upstream and downstream supply chain can become extremely complicated and convoluted as licensing agreements give way to near real-time fulfillment and delivery services. Not only have product management logistics become more complicated, but services are also growing in complexity, with multiple vendors taking part in the delivery of data services that will soon use millicent and micro payment systems. A supply chain manager's responsibility is to implement a supply chain management system, which requires the services of a CISS certified networking professional.

Supply chain management (SCM) encompasses all those activities associated with moving goods from the raw materials stage through to the end user. This activity includes sourcing and procurement, product design, production planning, materials handling, order processing, inventory management, transportation, warehousing, and customer service. It also includes the information systems necessary to communicate among supply chain partners. No universal standard exists for supply chain management applications—SCM requirements are different for each company. The organizations involved must respond to each other to become viable supply chain partners. Partners must develop and customize specific ways to handle customers—their orders, their shipments, and their invoices must be developed and customized.

Standardizing SCM data objects between participants is a first-step toward achieving strong SCM. XML (which is discussed elsewhere in this book) plays an important role in this area.

A supply chain management program coordinates and integrates the preceding activities into a seamless process. (It embraces and links the different partners in the chain.) In addition to the departments within the organization, these partners include suppliers, distributors, transportation carriers, third-party logistics companies, and information systems providers.

The remainder of this section discusses Internet-based supply chain management with the following topics:

- Supply Chain Management Focus
- Advantages of Supply Chain Management
- Supply Chain Management Implementation
- Elements of Supply Chain Management

Supply Chain Management Focus

SCM focuses intensely on actual customer demand, instead of forcing product into the market that might or might not sell quickly. Technology is a critical supply chain enabler. Professionals working in this field must become technologically proficient to achieve any measure of success. In addition, professionals must become knowledgeable about the kinds of technology that impact supply chain operations.

Supply chain managers must be intimately familiar with their corporate mission and determine how the supply chain can help achieve that mission. Supply chain managers should do the following:

- Think about the supply chain as a whole.
- Pursue tangible outcomes.

Advantages of Supply Chain Management

Supply chain management minimizes the flow of raw materials, finished product, and packaging materials, cutting inventory carrying costs across the chain. SCM can enhance revenue, control cost, improve asset utilization, and improve customer satisfaction. SCM determines what the customers want and how to coordinate efforts across the supply chain to meet those requirements faster, cheaper, and better.

With SCM, you can implement real-time processes, which mean faster time to market, lower inventory levels, lower obsolescence rates, faster fulfillment times, faster order-to-cash cycles, and satisfied customers. The advantages are better revenue and profit performance.

Supply chain management allows for the existence of the following (from the GartnerGroup—*Electronic Commerce Best Practice for SCM* by A. Mesher).

- Shared production schedules
  - Safety stock (extra stock in case of high demand) reductions
  - Lowered per-unit purchase price through inventory leveling by supplier
  - On-time performance
- Shared on-hand inventory
  - Increased sales because of fewer stock outs (backorders)
  - Increased item margins because of enhanced service level
- Shared in-transit inventory and manufacturing capacities
  - Measured lead-time metrics from safety stock variability adjustments
  - Increased throughput or asset return on assets
- Shared product designs
  - Increased new product cycle times
  - Lower product development cost
- Shared demand forecasts
  - Decreased inventory carrying cost
  - Increased order fill or customer service level

Supply Chain Management Implementation

Successfully implementing a supply chain management process depends on many factors. The following list details important bases upon which supply chain management must grow:

- Subdivide customers by need
- Tailor logistics
- Note market signals
- Make product distinctions

- Develop a strategic Plan
- Develop a technology strategy
- Develop performance measurements
- Understand trading partner capability

The text discusses each in turn.

Subdivide Customers by Need

Subdivide customers by their specific needs and develop a collection of services customized to various groups. Past customers were grouped by industry, product, or trade channel, and a one-size-fits-all approach was taken to serve them. Now, using advanced analytical techniques, such as cluster and conjoint analysis, to measure customer tradeoffs and predict the marginal profitability of each group, a more customized approach is called for. Surveys, interviews, and industry research are traditional tools for defining key component criteria. Apply a disciplined, cross-functional process to develop a list of supply chain program options, and create group-specific service packages that combine basic services for everyone with the services from the options list that have the greatest appeal to particular groups. The goal is to find the degree of division and variation needed to maximize profitability.

The service offering must turn a profit (many companies lack adequate financial understanding of their customers and their own costs to gauge forecasted profitability). Forecasted profitability knowledge is essential to correctly match accounts with service offerings, which translates into enhanced revenues through a combination of increases in volume and price. Only by understanding costs at the activity level and using that understanding to strengthen fiscal control can companies profitably deliver value to customers. Companies must analyze the profitability of the group, and evaluate the costs and benefits of alternate service offerings to ensure a reasonable return on their investment and the most profitable resource allocation.

For example, all the groups in Figure 6-9 value consistent delivery, but those in the lower left quadrant have little interest in the advanced supply chain management programs, such as customized packaging and advance shipment notification that appeal greatly to those in the upper-right quadrant.

Figure 6-9 *Needs-Based Segmentation*

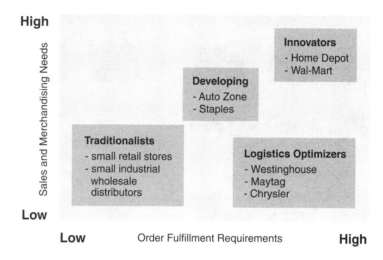

Tailor Logistics

The network requires more robust logistics planning enabled by real-time decision-support tools that can handle flow-through distribution and more time-sensitive approaches to managing transportation. Traditionally, companies have taken a monolithic approach to logistics network design, organizing inventory, warehouse, and transportation activities to meet a single standard. Logistics networks have been designed to meet the average service requirements of all customers. These satisfy the toughest requirements of a single customer group.

These approaches cannot achieve superior asset utilization or accommodate the group-specific logistics necessary for excellent supply chain management. The new logistics network has to be more flexible; therefore, it is more complex, involving alliances with third-party logistics providers. Essential changes in the mission, number, location, and ownership structure of warehouses will be necessary.

As shown in Figure 6-10, the food and packaged goods industry might well cut logistics costs by 42 percent per case, and reduce total days in the system by 73 percent by integrating logistics assets across the industry, with extensive participation by third-party logistics providers.

Figure 6-10 *Market-Level Logistics*

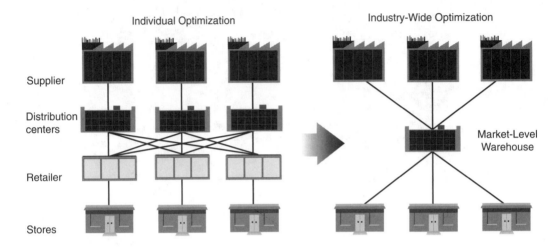

Note Market Signals

Sales and operations planning needs to develop early warning signals of supply chain demands hidden in customer promotions, ordering patterns, and restocking algorithms. They also need to take vendor and carrier capabilities, capacity, and constraints into account. Companies have traditionally used forecasts from multiple departments, independently creating projections for the same products using their own assumptions, measurements, and level of detail. Such companies consult the marketplace only informally, with minimal involvement of their major suppliers. Companies have allowed sales forecasts to envision growing demand while manufacturing second-guesses how much product the market actually wants. Self-centered forecasting is incompatible with excellent supply chain management.

Manufacturers must implement a cross-functional planning process supported by demand planning software. Excellent supply chain management calls for sales and operations planning to eclipse company boundaries, and involve every link of the supply chain in developing forecasts collaboratively. Then, they must maintain the required capacity across the operation.

Companies need to recognize that demand-based planning takes time to get right. Developing a leading-edge pilot program, such as vendor-managed inventory or jointly managed forecasting and replenishment, takes time. The development is conducted in conjunction with a few high-volume, sophisticated partners in the supply chain. As the partners refine their collaborative forecasting, planned orders become firm orders. The customer no longer sends a purchase order, and the manufacturer commits inventory from its available-to-promise stock. This activity formalizes the planning process, infrastructure, and measurements. The program expands to include other channel partners until enough are participating to facilitate significant improvement in using manufacturing and logistics assets and cost performance. Figure 6-11 shows the results of paying attention to market signals to stabilize distributor fluctuations.

Figure 6-11 *Market Signals*

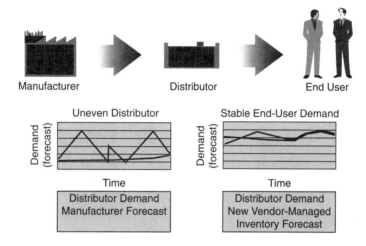

Make Product Distinctions

Manufacturers have traditionally based production goals on the demand projections for finished goods and have stockpiled inventory to offset forecasting errors. Manufacturers tend to view lead times in the system as fixed, with only a finite time in which to convert materials into products that meet customer requirements. However, manufacturers strengthen their ability to react to market signals by compressing lead times along the supply chain, speeding the conversion from raw materials to finished products tailored to customer requirements. This action enhances their flexibility to make product configuration decisions much closer to when demand occurs.

The key to just-in-time product differentiation is to locate the control point in the manufacturing process where the product is fixedly configured to meet a single requirement and assess options, such as postponement, modularized design, or manufacturing process modification, that can increase flexibility. Manufacturers must ask whether the control point can be pushed closer to actual demand.

Next, develop a mass customization strategy. Manufacturers must strive to meet individual customer needs efficiently and delay product differentiation to the last possible moment. The hardware manufacturer in the following figure solved the problem by determining the point at which a standard bracket turned into multiple *Standard Keeping Units (SKUs)*. The manufacturer further concluded that overall demand for these brackets is relatively stable and easy to forecast, while demand for the 16 SKUs is much more volatile. The solution was to make brackets in the factory but package them at the distribution center, within the customer order cycle. This strategy improved asset utilization by cutting inventory levels by more than 50 percent. Figure 6-12 details packaging postponement to create the possibility of mass customization.

Figure 6-12 *Packaging Postponement*

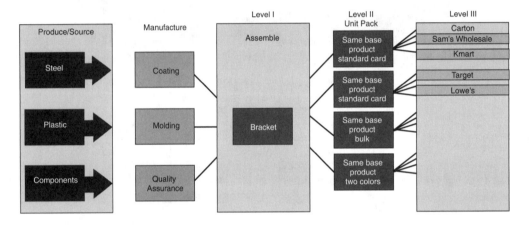

Develop a Strategic Plan

Manufacturers must cultivate friendly relationships with suppliers. Manufacturers must place high demands on suppliers, but realize that partners must share the goal of reducing costs across the supply chain. Considering a gain-sharing arrangement to reward everyone who contributes to the greater profitability is a must. Expanding network connectivity to accommodate the desire to track supply chain changes increases dependencies and can introduce latency and reliability issues. Companies must have sound knowledge of their entire supply chain integration points and commodity costs, not only for direct materials, but also for maintenance, repair, operating supplies, utility expenses, travel, temporary workers, and everything else in between.

Considering marketplace position and industry structure, manufacturers can decide how to approach suppliers. One approach might be soliciting short-term competitive bids. Entering into long-term contracts and strategic supplier relationships is another consideration. Outsourcing or integrating vertically is an additional approach. Excellent supply chain management calls for creativity and flexibility. Developing a strategic plan to manage supply sources warrants early attention because the savings that it can realize can fund additional initiatives. Figure 6-13 portrays the relation between time and price with an indexed pricing strategy.

Figure 6-13 *Indexed Pricing*

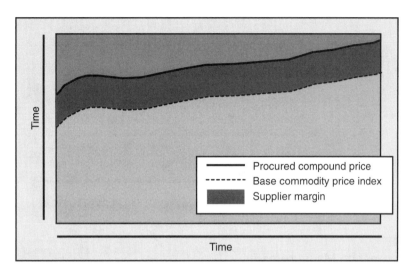

Develop a Technology Strategy

Implement an integrated enterprise-wide system based on a reasonable technology strategy. The system must handle day-to-day transactions and electronic commerce across the supply chain and help align supply and demand by sharing information on orders, payments, and daily scheduling. The system must facilitate planning and decision-making, and support the demand and shipment planning and master production scheduling needed to allocate resources efficiently. The system must facilitate strategic analysis by providing tools, such as an integrated network model that uses "what-if" scenario planning to help managers evaluate plants, distribution centers, suppliers, and third-party service alternatives. Figure 6-14 depicts the areas of technology strategy across an enterprise supply chain.

CAUTION   Many of today's enterprise-wide systems remain enterprise-bound, unable to share information that channel partners need to achieve mutual success across the supply chain. Many of these companies find themselves victims of the powerful new transactional systems they put in place. Unfortunately, many leading-edge information systems capture reams of data but cannot easily translate it into actionable intelligence that enhances real-world operations. System and network integration designs have to accommodate a wide range of back-end systems and disparate data formats to be successful.

Figure 6-14 *Technology Strategy Areas*

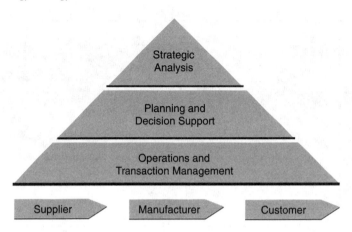

Develop Performance Measurements

A company should measure service in terms of the ideal order. The order arrives when promised, complete, undamaged, and priced and billed correctly. The ideal order determines true service profitability by identifying the actual costs and revenues of the activities required to serve an account. Traditional accounting applications tend to mask the real costs of the supply chain. They focus on cost type rather than the cost of activities. The general ledger organizes data according to a chart of accounts; it obscures the information needed for activity-based costing. Deriving maximum benefit from activity-based costing requires sophisticated information technology, specifically, a data warehouse. By maintaining data in discrete units, or data cubes, the data warehouse (data mart) provides ready access to this information. A company should develop a common report card to help partners locate and capitalize on synergies across the supply chain. Figure 6-15 shows an example.

Understand Trading Partner Capability

Because businesses are only as strong as their weakest link, they cannot afford the time it will take for each member of the trading community to become Internet-commerce-enabled on their own. Companies can speed up the process by providing economic incentive, acquire and deploy systems on their behalf, and incorporate Internet-based technology initiatives with web-based forms to collect data.

Figure 6-15 *Joint Performance Measures*

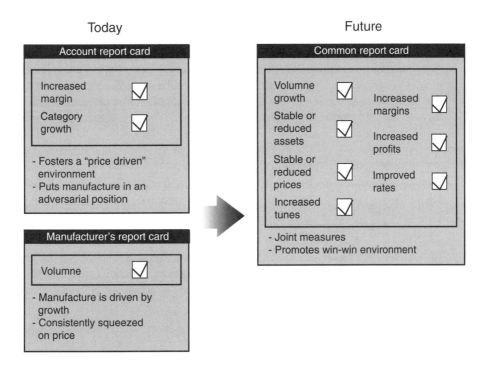

Elements of Supply Chain Management

Knowing what the customer wants, when the customers wants it, and delivering the goods or services without delay is critical to SCM's overall success. Speed, flexibility, and productivity are amplified by new technology and information-exchange capabilities.

To survive, a company's supply chain strategy should closely align with its overall business objectives and customer requirements. Such a strategy has the following components, each of which is discussed in turn:

- Configuration and Enabling Practices
- Supply Chain Network and Organizational Structure
- Information Technology Architecture
- Elements to Consider When Implementing SCM

Configuration and Enabling Practices

Overall supply chain configuration defines the asset base required to meet the needs of the end-to-end supply chain, including the suppliers and customers asset base. Creating data flow diagrams and network diagrams supports the configuration process.

These practices determine how the actual customer drives the supply chain. Is the model make-to-order or make-to-forecast? The ultimate goal is to create an environment where the customer drives the entire supply chain. Selecting the right mix of enabling practices dictates the supply chain's velocity.

Supply Chain Network and Organizational Structure

This network creates a horizontally integrated, virtual supply chain. To accomplish horizontal integration, an Internet-based SCM system must include complicated data feeds and data flows. These data feeds and flows require careful security designs and configurations, which the CISS professional will create and maintain.

Choose between decentralization and centralization. You must choose one that enables the supply chain strategy, as opposed to creating conflicting directions and objectives. Organizational structure does not dictate network structure, especially if components are outsourced instead of managed internally.

Information Technology Architecture

Fully integrated *enterprise resource planning (ERP)* packages or web technology offers real-time, information-sharing capabilities across the supply chain. Give ample time and resources to selecting and implementing an ERP package. Many features and components will not appear useful or necessary until an implementation has been attempted. Finding an experienced consultant familiar with your business sector will help you avoid the cost of having to re-implement or delay key features implementation.

SCM applications typically pull information from the company's enterprise resource planning system but must also pull information from one or more data warehouses. An SCM application is not just one application with lots of options; many different types of mathematical models can be involved. These applications can stand alone or operate in conjunction with other applications to compose a user interface. Accordingly, SCM requirements can either be very small or very large.

The question is, "Where is the data?" It might be all in-house or at an application service provider (ASP). Some might be stored at a customer site, some at a vendor site, or the information might be spread among all these locations.

Elements to Consider When Implementing SCM

You should consider the following six elements when implementing supply chain management:

- Connectivity
- Capacity
- Availability
- Reliability
- Security
- Manageability

Connectivity—To accommodate high information volume, enterprises must extend beyond their own brick and mortar, and move away from the traditional SCM system to a connected or networked SCM solution. A recent Forté-commissioned research report, conducted by Spikes Cavell, covered more than 300 large businesses across Europe. Seventy-seven percent of IT respondents and 70 percent of business respondents said lack of integration had a significant cost impact on the business. Business users almost unanimously agree on the importance of integration, with 95 percent rating application integration as important, and 87 percent citing application integration as increasing their business capabilities. Enterprises need a networked supply chain management system that enables process-driven integration. Process-driven integration allows existing applications to be reused as supporting steps in larger business activities.

Excellent communications are a superior supply chain management cornerstone. From the technical side, IT staffers look for connectivity ease. They want something that is more standards-based and does not require much custom coding, that is easier to connect, and that does not take much time, effort, or money. Web-based services that speak to one another using XML requests wrapped in *Simple Object Access Protocol (SOAP)* connections over secure sockets provide a standards-based solution typified by Microsoft's .NET strategy.

Capacity—Scalability and flexibility define capacity in the Internet environment. As a manufacturer, you cannot discuss Internet commerce, Internet business, or supply chain management without concerning yourself with how your network and business application are going to hold up under the strain of hundreds of thousands of transactions a day. Enterprises getting into the Internet business or Internet arena expect to drive revenues upward, and that means handling more transactions. High-speed connections to public systems and private systems must be factored into network capacity planning and requirements definitions.

Availability—Availability is fairly self-explanatory. Without it, your company cannot see where it is going. Internet availability has been reduced to a commodity; businesses expect greater than 99.9 percent uptime no differently than expecting to have 24-hour electricity available. Excellent communication is a critical element of progressive supply chain management. Mission-critical information must have top network priority over lower-level traffic. A high quality, integrated solution must prioritize network data traveling between supply chain components. Proprietary Cisco network protocols allow traffic-shaping rules to be applied on the network's data layer (layer 3), so shared network hardware is not bottlenecked by surges in other kinds of traffic.

CAUTION   The difference between 99.9 percent uptime and 99.99 percent uptime is significant in terms of hardware budgeting and network redundancy expense. As you approach continuous availability, the costs increase dramatically. Table 6-1 shows the downtime per year for several high-availability levels.

Table 6-1   *High Availability Downtime Calculations*

Percent Availability	Downtime per Year
99	87 hours, 36 minutes
99.5	43 hours, 48 minutes
99.9	8 hours, 30 minutes
99.95	4 hours, 23 minutes
99.99	53 minutes
99.999 (nearly continuous)	5 minutes

Reliability—A reliable, around-the-clock operation under heavy network traffic represents a key requirement. Web-based products must provide intelligent load balancing across multiple co-located servers.

In another context, web-based systems are crucial because many small and mid-size manufacturers in the far reaches of Asia, Latin America, and the Caribbean are relatively low-tech companies; they do not have the financial wherewithal or technological sophistication to handle *electronic data interchange (EDI)*. These companies usually phone, fax, or mail orders to their overseas manufacturers. This process is slow and error prone, and errors introduced at the beginning of the process may grow exponentially as wares move along the supply trail.

Security—No matter what application or process is used, security measures are high on the prerequisites list of every organization. Organizations demand proven security measures within their network. That includes hardware, software, and monitoring procedures. If a company is considering opening a port to its systems to the outside, first reviewing its security procedures and schemes is critical. For Internet business systems, in which multiple internal and external enterprise applications and data are linked into one integrated system, the security issue becomes even more critical. In fact, security determines how comfortable companies, their employees, and their customers are with conducting business on integrated Internet business systems.

Systematic security risk management processes customized to an Internet business environment create the best defenses for a company against security breaches. Regardless of how diligent company processes are, ensuring complete security is impossible for many reasons, including the complex nature of integrated systems, the lack of visibility into the source code supplied by vendors and partners, the changing nature of software, and the human factor.

Complex combinations of software applications and components make up Internet business systems. Software vendors provide some of these components; some are custom-developed; some are off-the-shelf applications, such as packaged ERPs or CRM suites; some come from ASPs; and business partners provide some through interconnected computer systems. This complexity makes evaluating the overall systems software in sufficient detail to discover and resolve all potential security exposures practically impossible. At best, an enterprise must depend on each software component being well designed from a security standpoint, and make sure to minimize exposures resulting from combining and integrating software. Although companies must accept that not all security holes can be plugged, they should nonetheless strive to define an acceptable level of risk at a reasonable cost.

Internet business security is not yet a mature area of business management. As a result, each company must set its own approach for risk management, without the benefit of industry-accepted benchmarks. Standards boards and committees are developing and proposing security standards, but significant differences of opinion and approach still exist. In addition, no well-understood economic model exists for evaluating the benefit of a marginal rate of risk reduction versus investment in security technology and management. Consequently, companies must operate in a setting without much guidance on their security budgets. Perhaps the most serious problem in managing security risk is the absence of an accepted industry-wide measurement system enabling managers to judge the risks embedded in their current Internet business systems to determine if investments related to reducing risks are warranted.

Companies can still set up internal systems to successfully manage risk. The ability to deal with computer security and information privacy assurance is critical to the future of Internet business. Although the technology community offers many new solutions to security problems, IT managers must put this technology through a systematic risk management process tailored to the unique needs and characteristics of an integrated Internet business system. See Chapter 5 , "Build or Buy?," for a more detailed discussion of security requirements for Internet business solutions.

Manageability—Regardless of chain complexity, when talking about the SCM application, application management is critical. This initiative expects highly trained individuals to implement and maintain the program. Both business managers and IT professionals must recognize that the process *is* the business—and that a clear understanding of business processes is the appropriate starting point to a successful Internet business strategy. The business requirement quickly translates into an IT requirement to integrate new application functionality with purchased application packages and previously built systems. The goal is to create a coordinated business applications portfolio that provides a high degree of responsiveness, while remaining flexible enough to accommodate further integration and evolution.

e-learning and e-publishing Systems

E-learning is Internet-enabled learning. Components can include content delivery in multiple formats, learning experience management, and a networked community of learners, content developers, and subject matter experts. E-learning provides faster learning at reduced costs, increased access to learning, and clear accountability for all participants in the learning process. Learners are free to study at their own pace, regardless of location.

E-publishing is a cornerstone of the web enabling almost all Internet business on some level. *E-publishing* as a strategic component encompasses the tools, business processes, and systems architecture necessary for an integrated Internet experience. E-publishing creates the rich experience that can be used to build valuable relationships with clients and partners. Without a solid e-publishing framework and document management processes providing control over the experience, you will be unable to leverage your Internet business efforts to build the advantage you need to stay competitive. Document management software and electronic workflow processes take advantage of the Internet to build robust and powerful e-publishing systems.

The Internet represents the world's largest content publication system ever devised. If the invention of the printing press by Gutenberg represented a revolution for literacy through a radical increase in the population of readers, the Internet has affected a revolution of similar scope by radically increasing the population of writers, authors, and learners.

To be successful in the modern hypercompetitive marketplace, organizations need an advantage. That advantage is Internet-based business initiatives like e-learning systems and e-publishing systems. For example, Cisco Systems, Inc. saves more than 825 million dollars every year as a direct result of its Internet-based business practices, allowing the company to stay competitive and invest in its future.

This section of the chapter discusses e-learning and e-publishing in terms of the following:

* Advantages
* Components
* Requirements
* Network designs

Advantages of e-learning and e-publishing

Information technology (IT) professionals face rapid changes in skill requirements. Executives worldwide need to know that their employees are prepared. With e-learning's power and efficiency, learners can turn fast-paced change into a key advantage for themselves and their organizations. Some of the benefits follow:

- Learners are free to study at their own pace, regardless of location.
- Learners are accountable through online testing and progress management.
- Learners obtain relevant information faster and more productively.
- Organizations can track learner performance to assess workforce preparation.
- E-learning content developers can receive immediate feedback on the performance of their learning tools and provide continual and timely improvements to their curriculum.
- Learners can access interactive, technology-based learning tools, including web-based platforms, and video and satellite broadcasts.
- Organizations see significant savings because they do not have to send employees to universities and training centers.
- Learners have access to content that is or can be customized to specific needs.
- Organizations provide integrated delivery to employees worldwide.
- Organizations can deliver new courses quickly.

E-publishing benefits are numerous. A few of those benefits follow:

- Increases customer satisfaction
- Improves content quality
- Simplifies the global publishing process
- Reduces IT operational costs
- Positions organizations for future growth
- Improves editorial control and asset management

e-learning and e-publishing Components

You should know and understand the components of e-learning and e-publishing. Toward that goal, the text covers the following:

- Educational objectives
- Content creation
- Assessment and management
- Delivery technologies

- Cisco and e-learning
- Content management
- Content delivery
- Cisco Systems, Inc. and e-publishing

Educational Objectives

The workforce continually needs new competencies. Employees must update their skills. With e-learning, employers provide rich educational experiences while controlling costs.

Content Creation

To maximize efficiency, content is stored and tagged as modules of information. It is then stored in a content management system, asset management system, or database, and dynamically pulled to create the learning materials. This allows a high degree of reuse. Reusable content can result in a lower cost to build the learning materials, faster development time, and content that targets a specific audience. With modularized content, updates can be made easily and consistently across numerous training materials. Simple and sophisticated commercial packages provide a range of content management tools for use with an e-learning system.

E-publishing enables the authoring and development of content into structured components or objects that can be stored, updated, and searched with relative ease. Unstructured content can also be developed and stored, but with greater difficulty in the areas of update and search capabilities.

Assessment and Management

With the right management tools, employers identify knowledge gaps, workforce benchmarks, and individual learning plans. They create an assessment process and user profiles, document learning histories, establish entitlement processes, and develop a custom learning agenda. Employers use these tools to maximize their workforce and obtain a competitive edge.

Delivery Technologies

Employers develop a technology plan that delivers the learning through the most effective vehicle, such as e-text, real-time collaboration, virtual labs, and interactive multimedia, content on demand, videoconferencing, broadcast video, or simulation.

Cisco and e-learning

Employers worldwide look for highly trained networking experts with demonstrated skills. The Cisco Career Certifications program allows individuals to certify their technical proficiency in network design and network support. These highly regarded certifications are available at the associate, professional, and expert levels. Achieving recognized industry certification represents one of the most important objectives of today's information technology professional. E-learning expands the learner's options for seeking certification.

Cisco customers, partners, and employees benefit from the extensive investment in the latest learning solutions, as illustrated in the following examples:

- The Cisco Networking Academy Program uses a complete e-learning system to bring information technology training to educational institutions worldwide.

- Through over 100 Cisco Training Partners, information technology professionals can use three new e-learning offerings for online instruction and web-based hands-on experiences.

- Responding to the need for Cisco's representatives throughout the world to keep pace with technology changes, a comprehensive e-learning system has been developed for sales and technical specialists.

E-publishing components can each be complete systems unto themselves. One or more of these components can involve multiple servers in multiple networks, as published content moves from development and staging networks and systems toward production systems. A company should agree upon an e-publishing business strategy before determining system requirements. In addition to the business strategy and process elements of using content to build relationships, an e-publishing solution has three primary components: content creation, content management, and content delivery.

Content Management

Content management systems come in different configurations and on several platforms. Validating, versioning, and deploying e-publishing content components are the content management systems' basic functions. A goal of content management tools is to allow users access to templates to create content for internal and external web sites. Some content management systems use web-based tools to generate HTML so that content producers do not need to know HTML themselves.

Content Delivery

Content delivery applications and web-based services recombine and distribute managed content into various mediums and data formats for all audiences across multiple display devices.

These components provide the building blocks for creating e-publishing systems across all phases of the e-publishing spectrum, from static to relationship-based. The right e-publishing model streamlines the development of new applications that transform relationships. This agility helps your business provide more services more quickly and cheaply to a broader audience. One-to-one marketing becomes possible with a well-integrated e-publishing system. Content personalization and user scenario profiling can be coded into these systems to provide a unique experience for each user according to their explicit and implicit preferences. If complex content delivery components are required for your project, application design and network architecture must accommodate the various ports and protocols used by the e-publishing systems to author, manage, and deliver content.

Cisco Systems, Inc. and e-publishing

Cisco Systems, Inc.'s e-publishing system, *Cisco Connection Enterprise Web Production (CCEWP),* is the largest electronic publishing system in the world. It empowers more than 20,000 Cisco employees to proactively manage more than 10 million Cisco web pages, enabling users to access specific content on demand, saving more than 125 million dollars and increasing customer satisfaction.

CCEWP is the content management solution for *Cisco Connection Online (CCO).* It consists of a publishing application, which is used by web authors to create and post content to CCO, and a server, which acts as a repository for all information published to, and removed from, the Cisco web site.

To understand how Cisco's e-publishing system works, think of a museum. Many items are on display for the public; many more are archived or stored, ready to be displayed at any time. In this analogy, CCO represents the collection of items on display; CCEWP is the museum itself—encompassing all the items on display, along with the archived or stored items. By combining a superior application with a powerful server, CCEWP delivers much greater functionality than the previous file server system, allowing authors to publish, control, and organize content more effectively. As a result, users can navigate the web site and find the critical information they need faster and easier than ever before. The CCEWP is one of the most sophisticated e-publishing systems available on the Internet, and results in a reliable site that gains the respect and regular use of networking professionals the world over.

Requirements of e-learning and e-publishing

The CISS professional should consider the nonfunctional requirements of e-learning initiatives and projects. Recall from Chapter 4, "Application Requirements," that nonfunctional requirements are factors, such as application features, that are not related to specific functionality. Case study number 3 in Chapter 8, "CISS Case Studies," provides a good example of each of these factors as they relate to network design for a streaming video project for a healthcare e-learning system.

E-publishing systems provide some of the most powerful examples of Internet business solutions. In fact, e-publishing was one impetus that led to the growth and development of the Internet itself. Scientific publication was once the sole domain of a few, well-respected publications and journals. Although this exclusivity provided a high level of quality through peer review and other lengthy publication processes, it may have also hindered the free flowing of new ideas into the scientific publication arena.

Scientific researchers were among the first users of e-mail and Internet networks. The content of their communications was not just personal discussions about sports teams and the weather. Researchers who wanted to share their prepublication material with other researchers immediately seized upon the power of the Internet. It is not hard to imagine that with the addition of potentially thousands of new scientific papers and authors, the quality of information might decline. The factors you consider when designing an e-publishing system should reflect this dynamic relationship between quality and quantity of information. The CISS professional's attention to network designs helps structure e-publishing systems to minimize the detrimental effects of opening closed authorship domains to the masses of aspiring authors.

Consider the following factors when implementing e-learning and e-publishing systems:

- Connectivity
- Capacity
- Availability
- Reliability
- Security
- Manageability

Connectivity in e-learning and e-publishing

The *e-learning system's (ELS)* connectivity requirements are dependent on the system requirements and overall design. Principal among the implications for network professionals is whether the system will use multicast or unicast routing. If the ELS is implemented on a thin client running on an intranet or the Internet using unicast routing, the connectivity is a factor of the number of users times the amount of data transfer between the client and the servers.

With a thin client running on a multicast network, the connectivity is only a factor of the number and bit size of the data streams. The format of data delivered to the users also influences connectivity requirements (such as, text, interactive documents, streaming video). You can lessen the bandwidth impact of adding e-learning streaming video to a business network with the appropriate use of multicast routing instead of unicast routing. Cisco network routers and switches are easily configured to support multicast routing required for high-quality, low bandwidth audio and video streams. For example, designing an *e-learning system* to make use of streaming content repeaters is another way to keep bandwidth usage within reasonable levels.

The *e-publishing system (EPS)* connectivity requirements are dependent on the system requirements and overall design. If the EPS is implemented on a thin client running on an intranet or the Internet, the connectivity is a factor of the number of users times the amount of data transfer between the client and the servers. The format of data delivered to the users also influences connectivity requirements (such as text, interactive documents, and streaming video). EPSs possess many of the same qualities as ELSs.

Capacity in e-learning and e-publishing

The ELS implementation must consider capacity from several perspectives. The system must have enough network, storage, and processing power to handle the current user load and estimated growth in audience over the next two years of service. On all accounts, e-learning systems require great quantities of network, storage, and processing resources. Building capability now for estimated future traffic levels allows the system to grow normally, without dedicating resources prematurely.

The physical systems (network, database, and application servers) that implement the ELS must also be expandable without a major network infrastructure overhaul. In addition, the system size must be scaled according to the project requirements. Typically, these systems are purchased or developed on a modular basis with capacities determined by the number of users and the volume of subjects. A fully switched, 100-Mbit Ethernet multicast-enabled network should support several independent Realtime Transport Protocol (RTP) applications and services at the same time. Streaming audio and video fidelity largely determines the actual number of concurrent broadcast sources.

In implementing the EPS, you must consider capacity from two perspectives. The system must have enough storage and processing power to handle the current user load, accommodate organization and data growth, and growth in the cycle of use over the next two years of service. The EPS's physical systems must present a network design that allows the addition of more servers as needed. E-publishing system capacity can rapidly grow to include unplanned additions, and care must be taken to avoid project scope creep once it has launched.

Availability in e-learning and e-publishing

Both the ELS and the EPS must be available to their users during the required business hours or on-demand for limited periods during the day. The maintenance opportunity for a global corporation using these systems or marketing them to clients around the world can shrink to nearly zero. However, because these are generally not mission-critical systems, periods of unavailability are most likely acceptable to the customer. A company can make a read-only copy of the systems (created by data replication) available to customers during the maintenance window. This activity can also provide the secondary benefit of having a fail-over system. With the EPS, this activity can also provide a limited testing environment where major system-level upgrades and patches are performed.

Reliability in e-learning and e-publishing

Generally, the ELS must be implemented on a reliable system. However, the systems do not necessarily require fault tolerance. Most e-learning and e-publishing applications and services rely up fault-tolerant protocols instead. The systems must be well designed, tested, and tuned to handle the additional bandwidth. Likewise, the systems must deliver accurate and reliable information by being available during high-network and system-load conditions.

The EPS must be implemented on a reliable system. The systems do not require total fault tolerance but must be well designed and tested. The systems must deliver accurate, reliable information and meet the system availability requirements.

Security in e-learning and e-publishing

The ELS and the EPS handle sensitive information (corporate proprietary information and intellectual property, employee records, customer information, and so on). A high system security level must be present to ensure that no information is available to unauthorized users. ELS and EPS security and privacy policies must accommodate copyright and intellectual property issues. Encrypted passwords (with history tracking and periodic expiration), menu security, and source content and database table access restrictions by username are a minimal set of security features. Security must be configurable to the needs of the customer and the systems' current purpose. Security must not become a management burden. Much of the security must be centralized and implemented according to user roles defined in the systems (administrator, education designer, employee user, and so on).

The resulting content produced by an e-publishing system represents potentially millions of hours of work. Guarding the security of this investment is an important task, and systems security testing should be extensive. See Chapter 4 for detailed discussions of system tests and the role of the CISS professional during the testing phase of software development.

Manageability in e-learning and e-publishing

ELS and EPS manageability includes maintenance and flexibility. Basic monitoring and systems status must be available at an administrative level. The ELS and EPS must be maintainable systems that require little active cleanup of historical information. In addition, the applications must contain self-maintenance features to aid in maintenance of the systems databases. The systems must be flexible and able to grow from a functionality standpoint. Because most of these systems are modular, adding new areas of functionality is part of the design. One key aspect of EPS manageability is the ability to revoke or revert select content elements, or entire releases. A good release management process takes full advantage of e-publishing software management tools.

Network Designs for e-learning and e-publishing

Case study 3 in Chapter 8, "CISS Case Studies," explores the network design of an ELS for a healthcare provider. The case study deals with an internal network design and does not take external networks into consideration. Not all ELSs and EPSs are for internal consumption only. A few different network design considerations to discuss when starting an e-learning or e-publishing project include the following:

- Content caching and proxies
- Mirrors and repeaters
- Interoperability

Content Caching and Proxies

Some e-learning or e-publishing projects warrant the use of content caching and proxy technologies. Caching and proxy servers attempt to reduce bandwidth and system resource load by maintaining a local copy of files and other data requests. For example, rather than having every request served by each server in a three-tiered architecture, the introduction of caching and proxy servers can respond from the server's own content cache.

A business must decide whether or not content caching and proxy services should be built in-house or outsourced to *Application Service Providers (ASPs)* to take advantage of their large caching server networks. The effective management of caches and proxies introduces some unique problems and opportunities for network design and management. Several different algorithms can provide dynamic routing to a caching server that is close to a user (close network-wise, as the server can be located geographically far away). Only certain kinds of content can be served through caching and proxy servers. Secure web traffic, for example, is not well suited to caching and proxying because it is encrypted and hard to cache or proxy. Applying caching and proxy servers is not always a good idea, and they are sometimes best implemented for only frequently accessed content that is sure to benefit from being served by a caching or proxy server.

Mirrors and Repeaters

Content mirrors and repeaters are another method to address the same problems of bandwidth usage and system resource load. *Content mirrors* act as complete and discrete copies of the content. *Content repeaters* act as relays of content and are used to move data to distant end-points on a network so that each branch office, for example, can receive content from a local repeater. With ELSs that incorporate streaming video, deploying content mirrors and repeaters can represent significant cost savings.

Interoperability

New technologies allowing e-learning to be leveraged beyond the corporate firewall to include supply chain partners, customers, and strategic partners. Some ELSs and EPSs have requirements that hinge on having interoperable systems that might not be owned and administered by one single department, business unit, or company. Synchronized Multimedia Integration Language (SMIL) is one XML-based language that is being developed to allow ELSs and EPSs to have high levels of interoperability. Web-based training makes use of regular telephone conferencing for the audio portion of the training. SMIL-enabled video streams can contain clickable objects within a presentation or broadcast. The next generation ELSs and EPSs will take advantage of not only these new technologies, but also of wider access to broadband network services to make highly immersive learning environments possible.

Summary

Now that you have completed this chapter, you should understand how the Internet can help your company deliver customer care, workforce optimization, supply chain management, and e-learning and e-publishing opportunities. You should be able to do the following after reading this chapter:

- Define customer care, more specifically, Internet-based customer care.
- Describe the benefits and advantages of integrating Internet-based customer care into a business solution.
- Describe the different components comprising Internet-based customer care.
- Describe the different components that comprise the lifecycle of Internet-based customer care. These include target, acquire, transact, deliver, retain, and grow.
- Explain the need for Internet-based customer care in businesses wanting to succeed with modern customers.
- Define workforce optimization.
- Describe why a company would need to integrate workforce optimization into its business solution.
- Explain the different components that can comprise a workforce optimization solution. These include resource management, communication centers, knowledge centers, and optimization engines.

- Describe the major considerations for workforce optimization applications to include connectivity, capacity, availability, reliability, security, and manageability.

- Define supply chain management (SCM) and describe the benefits of integrating supply chain management into a business solution.

- Discuss the main factors involved in implementing a successful supply chain management process, including subdividing customers by need; tailoring logistics, noting market signals, and making product distinctions; and developing a strategic plan, a technology strategy, and performance measurements; and understanding your partner's abilities.

- Describe the major considerations for SCM applications to include connectivity, capacity, availability, reliability, security, and manageability.

- Explain e-learning and e-publishing on a high-level, addressing issues such as its definition, components, factors to consider, and benefits.

- Describe the major considerations for e-learning and e-publishing applications to include connectivity, capacity, availability, reliability, security, and manageability.

- Define and describe the components of Content Management Systems and speak to the network design issues of caching and proxy servers, mirrors and repeaters, and interoperability.

Review Questions

1 Which main component distinguishes Internet-based customer care from traditional customer care?

   a. Call centers

   b. Being Internet-based

   c. Using IP-telephony

   d. Interacting person-to-person

2 Which benefit is not linked to customer care?

   a. Customer care boosts a company's valuation.

   b. Sales agents focus more time on customer satisfaction and less on administrative functions.

   c. Customers can enter and retrieve data using the same front-end application as customer service, sales or distribution, and have access to that data on a 24-hour basis.

   d. Everyone is informed when the need arises to respond quickly to an issue or concern that cannot be easily answered by a single contact person.

3 Which Internet-based customer care component represents the individual or company and the location where a product is being sold?

a. Account management

b. Contact management

c. Marketing management

d. Opportunity management

4 Which component is not part of the Internet-based customer care lifecycle?

a. Grow

b. Produce

c. Service

d. Target

5 Which term best defines the process that occurs when conflicting or incomplete information originates and is disseminated by different parts of the company?

a. Inconsistent sales and service levels

b. Missed sales opportunities

c. Inefficient business process

d. Fragmented customer messaging

6 Which time or cost has the Internet greatly reduced by allowing customers to compare competitive offerings and move to another supplier with relative ease?

a. Down time

b. Switching costs

c. Operating time

d. Cost options

7 What should be centralized and implemented according to user roles defined in the system?

a. Manageability

b. Security

c. Connectivity

d. Availability

8 Which item does workforce optimization NOT encompass?

  a. Accumulating more employees to help with administrative tasks

  b. Using the knowledge for market prediction and educating the customer

  c. Empowering the workforce with relevant knowledge

  d. Performing administrative tasks

9 Operational optimization streamlines coordination between different groups that have been employed to address a problem and optimize the _____ .

  a. Workforce functionality

  b. Workforce complexity

  c. Customer functionality

  d. Companies' dexterity

10 A centralized system that contains mostly updated information can establish proper communication between the workforce, management, and _____ .

  a. Employees

  b. Customers

  c. Maintenance

  d. Stakeholders

11 Which workforce optimization module provides universal information to workforce and customers?

  a. Optimization engine

  b. Communication center

  c. Knowledge center

  d. Resource management

12 With the New World network, what is built on universally available browser platforms that can reach a global audience without large incremental investments?

  a. Web-based applications

  b. Global network integration

  c. Secure access

  d. Database consolidation

13 Implementing the workforce optimization system requires capacity consideration from what two perspectives?

  a. Physical inventory and practicality

  b. Storage space and practicality

  c. Storage space and expandability

  d. Expandability and capability

14 Supply chain management encompasses all of the activities associated with moving goods from which stage to the end user?

  a. Production

  b. Distributor

  c. Raw materials

  d. Completed product

15 Which benefit is not linked to supply chain management?

  a. Faster time to market

  b. Lower obsolescence rates

  c. Higher inventory levels

  d. Satisfied customers

16 Which signal type is essential when applying demand planning across the supply chain?

  a. Supply

  b. Consumer

  c. Distribution

  d. Market

17 What determines how the actual customer drives the supply chain?

  a. Supply chain network

  b. Enabling practices

  c. Organizational structure

  d. Information technology architecture

18 Which factor bases its definition on scalability and flexibility?

   a. Reliability

   b. Security

   c. Capacity

   d. Connectivity

19 Which component is not a part of e-learning?

   a. Content creation

   b. Delivery objectives

   c. Assessment and management

   d. Delivery technologies

20 Which benefit is not a result of e-learning?

   a. Learners are accountable through online testing and progress management.

   b. Learners obtain relevant information faster and more productively.

   c. Learners are free to study at their own pace, but only at a central location.

   d. Organizations can track learner performance to assess workforce preparation.

21 Recombining and distributing managed components into various mediums for all audiences for e-publishing is called content _____ .

   a. Creation

   b. Delivery

   c. Management

   d. Proposal

22 Which strategic component encompasses the tools, business processes, and systems architecture necessary for an integrated Internet experience?

   a. E-commerce

   b. E-delivery

   c. E-learning

   d. E-publishing

23 Which factor includes basic monitoring and status of available systems at an administrative level?

a. Security

b. Connectivity

c. Availability

d. Manageability

Applied Solutions

Transacting business is at the heart of commerce. E-commerce is defined as electronic commerce exemplified by amazon.com and other retail institutions that have created on-line catalogs for on-line shopping and product information searches. Case study 1 and case study 4 involve on-line commerce and discuss the efforts of Yukon, Inc. to provide an electronic catalog and electronic commerce through the Internet.

M-commerce is defined as commerce performed through mobile electronic platforms, such as PDAs, WAP-enabled telephones, and other wireless devices. M-commerce represents the migration of e-commerce to newer, smaller platforms than the personal computer, and represents a rapidly growing market. Researchers expect to see one billion Internet-enabled phones by 2002 and that mobile computing will surpass hardwired Internet computer connections by the year 2006. As with most technological advances on the Internet, new standards and technologies do not actually ever replace old ones; they just add to them. Mobile computing will probably not replace workstations and laptops but provide one more access point to Internet-based services.

Scenario 1: Finance Industry

Problem

Financial services companies take their network security very seriously because reputation and consumer trust is an easy thing to lose with just one highly publicized lapse in security. My work in the financial services industry has covered securities and trading systems, as well as banking and mortgage systems. With one particular client project, I was tasked with designing a system that contained a disposable production environment. This was a result of disaster recovery plans that made the assumption that the production systems should contain no critical data but subscribe to data sources within the private, internal networks.

Solution

This disposable production environment design factor required a network with two complete production environments (similar to a network designed for geographic redundancy). Such network designs are discussed thoroughly elsewhere in books devoted entirely to the subject, and extensive planning to build Internet solutions for financial services projects should make good use of the experience and experimentation of others.

Solution Details

Another personal experience with the finance industry involved a large degree of third-party integration. Credit card verification services, multiple real-time data feeds, and cross-site session persistence were all features of this project. Testing and tuning the timings, timeouts, and error handling routines for this web site turned into a major QA effort. Debugging application, server, and network device error logs was required to resolve problems and defects. As for the multiple sites requiring cross-site session persistence, a solution was proposed to use low-level broadcast pings between sites to make the other sites aware of a user's temporary session ID and allow him to browse between discrete web properties without having to log in each time. The network professional overlaps with the application developer in performing tasks such as building hooks to accomplish site requirements. The CISS professional operates in this space, suggesting alternative solutions that match with existing and proposed services.

Scenario 2: Pharmaceutical Industry

Problem

The following example is quite short but carries a good deal of importance with regard to managing expectations.

A pharmaceutical site being built needed a fault-tolerant production environment. The problem was that the fault tolerance requirement was stipulated well into the project's development phase.

Solution

A fault-tolerant environment meant, among other things, ordering additional power circuits into the hosting facility cage so that dual power supply routers, switches, servers, and disk arrays could actually benefit from their redundant components. The network design also called for cross-hatched connectivity so that each web application and database server was either load-balanced, clustered, or had a hot standby system waiting to be switched into use.

Solution Details

This site's transactions were considered by the managers and executives to be of even higher security significance than that of banking because the databases involved contained not only credit card information, but also user medical profiles. Threats of government regulation and oversight justified the additional expense to build the system to these specifications. The hosting facility also provided tape backup services over its own private network connections, another perceived risk, so the site needed its own backup solution within the cage.

Scenario 3: Retail Business

Problem

"Approved and supported hardware and software only" was the mandate from a large retail business client. The client wanted a world-class e-commerce site to host a large catalog of products, and to have multiple paths to the products so that individual items would show up under several categories. The solution had to make use of a limited set of software applications (and not the latest software versions either, because its vendor had not officially approved the latest releases of the web server software, for example).

Solution

Rather than save licensing costs by using open source solutions (where doing so might otherwise have been proposed), certified and approved hardware and software vendors were solicited and purchased. One of the vendors, however, was selling a product that was based on the open source web server, Apache. The commercial product was simply a branded and approved-by-the-vendor version of the web server software used widely throughout the Internet (and for good reason; it is a great web server).

Solution Details

Problems arose when potential security exploits were identified with versions of the software released prior to the last three version revisions. The "vendor-approved" version was an exploitable release, but because the vendor was not able to respond quickly to the announcement of the security vulnerability, the site was forced to launch with the vulnerable Apache release. Not until some months later was the vendor able to update its approved software version after its own testing had verified what the ever-vigilant open source community had demonstrated several months earlier.

Despite technical and confirmed problems with a piece of software, in the end, the client is always right. At the very least, monitoring was set up to be triggered by any attempts to take advantage of the exploit and allow some advanced warning before a large security breach could be created. Luckily, no such trigger was ever tripped.

Scenario 4: Entertainment Business

Problem

"We want inventory changes to propagate from the on-line store all the way to the back-end systems, and we want it in realtime." This customer proposed a challenging supply chain management requirement. How realtime can we make it? Is once an hour adequate? "No," came the reply, "What we want is to be able to decrement our back-end inventory database for a given product when someone on the web site adds that product to their shopping cart." "What about abandoned shopping carts and broken dial-up connections because someone in the house picked up the telephone?" we asked. "That is understandable and your system needs to take that into account."

Solution

The details of how to design a realtime inventory into an e-commerce application and reliably synchronize it with back-end legacy database systems are not for discussion here, especially without a nondisclosure agreement between all parties involved, reader included. Suffice it to say that the site provides for this requirement, and I have never had a harder time getting out of the test phase in my entire Internet-based life.

Solution Details

Any application server failure in the business logic tier had to assume that the contents of the shopping carts it had created had to be released as inventory upon restart. The application server initialization process's startup environment used a unique token to establish whether the application server had restarted "cleanly" or whether it had failed and restarted.

On a lighter note, the site also required the creation of community-building sections and moderated discussion boards. This aspect of Internet-based customer care is often overlooked. Fan sites and discussion boards are often considered competition with the customer site, but the energy and enthusiasm found on discussion boards provides a great basis upon which to build a knowledge management system or a good FAQ for a product or service. After all, fan sites are really just customers who have taken e-publishing to heart and managed to find or build their own channel for communicating with others about a product or service.

PART III

Application Management and Support

Chapter 7   Application and System Management

CHAPTER **7**

Application and System Management

As the number of components and services that comprise CISS projects increases, possible interactions and dependencies also increase. Integrating all the components can sometimes seem like trying to fit square pegs into round holes. Application and system management involves a wide range of roles and responsibilities, with complex interactions and dependencies involving all sorts of third-party vendors and their services.

Application and system management's goal is not to solve a complex knot, but actually to tie a complex knot and make sure that it won't come apart under stress. This chapter presents the following:

- Application and System Management Overview
- Elements of Application and System Management
- Key Facts About Application Management
- Key Facts About System Management

Application and System Management Overview

Application management is composed of managing the application performance, application version, version levels, distribution, and functionality. System management allows system and network managers to monitor and control the remote workstation and server resources in a distributed network.

After completing this section, you will understand the following key elements:

- Participants in xSP business
- Application and system management benefits
- FCAPS model

Participants in xSP Business

With the advent of distributed client/server computing and web-based applications, the need to manage systems and applications has grown quickly and considerably. Currently, any organization that performs distributed network computing requires that system and application policies be implemented. Leading the growth in system and application management are Internet service providers (ISPs), application service providers (ASPs), management service providers (MSPs), and hosting services. Their business viability depends on the viability of the services that they offer their customers.

ISPs are businesses that provide Internet access of various types ranging from basic e-mail and web site hosting for individuals on shared servers to complete, large-scale hosting solutions for companies in multiple locations. ISPs have the equipment and telecommunications access to provide a point of presence on the Internet and make their money by reselling their high bandwidth access to multiple users and customers.

ASPs provide services over the Internet that might otherwise be run within a company or by individuals themselves. Remote access to applications using Internet protocols allows ASPs to market services to companies and individuals by charging for application and related services, such as managing those applications and the servers they run on.

MSPs monitor and manage their customer networks and systems, looking for problems. Like ASPs taking on an application problem, MSPs take on information technology (IT) management problems. MSPs recognize that merely providing application service might not be enough to satisfy potential customers. Managing the service is also important because, although the service might make the most sense economically to small companies, such customers do not usually have the required infrastructure or the IT staff to adequately manage their networks and systems.

Hosting providers provide a wide range of services, from full-featured, managed services for 100 percent of an application or service needs on dedicated or shared hardware, to minimum services, such as reliable electrical circuits and a network drop in a locked hosting cage. Depending on the skills present in your organization, and depending on which skills your organization wants to have present, the hosting provider can fill in any missing areas. System management can be built to suit your particular needs. See Chapter 5, "Build or Buy?," for a longer discussion of the advantages and disadvantages of using outsourced services.

The importance of an integrated management solution to any managed network service is vital to the success of the operation. When problems are encountered, determining if they are network or application related is often difficult. This requires integrated tools that can monitor all aspects of the network, system, and applications together.

Application and System Management Benefits

Typical application management benefits include the following:

- Measure application throughput
- Monitor application response time
- Understand the application topology and connectivity requirements
- Manage the application security requirements remotely
- Monitor and troubleshoot application and database processes remotely
- Secure Open System Interconnection (OSI) layer visibility

Typical server management benefits include the following:

- Control end devices remotely
- Monitor vital system performance metrics
- Manage software distribution
- Perform inventory management functions

Figure 7-1 shows the relationship between application management and system management and where server management comes into play.

Figure 7-1   *Relationship Between Application Management and Server Management*

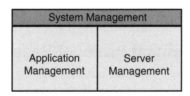

FCAPS Model

Application management is a key element of the FCAPS (Fault, Configuration, Accounting, Performance, Security) model. As with the other managed system elements, applications must be monitored and managed for faults, configuration, accounting, performance, and security. Each system element must be maintained and managed properly to deliver effective systems. If one element, such as application performance, fails to meet its individual goals, the system as a whole fails to achieve its goals.

The components of the FCAPS model can be described as levels in a hierarchy, as written in the following list:

- **F level**—Problem or fault identification in managed network or application
- **C level**—Configuration control and monitoring operations used to coordinate application and network maintenance and upgrades

- **A level**—Accounting for application or network resource distribution
- **P level**—Performance of an application or network elements, including methods to enhance overall performance
- **S level**—Security and identification of an application or network to ensure confidentiality of sensitive information

Elements of Application and System Management

As application and system management technology has developed, the complexity of the systems used to manage them has expanded exponentially. Several different approaches have been taken to create a method for the design of management architecture. Three of the most widely used methodologies are Simple Network Management Protocol (SNMP), Desktop Management Interface (DMI), and Object Management Architecture (OMA).

The discussion for this part of the chapter is broken into the following sections:

- Simple Network Management Protocol-Based Solutions
- Desktop Management Interface
- Object Management Architecture
- How Management Data Is Collected
- Processes for Managing Systems

Simple Network Management Protocol-Based Solutions

SNMP is the most widely used standard for managing distributed networks. However, the protocol was originally developed for networks, and the protocol foundation of MIBII was inadequate for managing systems and applications. To resolve this issue, public and private extensions to SNMP have been developed to meet these needs. SNMP uses "traps" to trigger monitoring events, and gathers groups of systems and applications into "communities." SNMP traps are messages from a managed node to the server and are sent unsolicited. SNMP communities are based on a simple plain-text password string used in SNMP get and set requests to managed nodes.

Desktop Management Interface

Application and system management is often defined in terms of proprietary services specific to a particular application. To bring a common standard to application management, the Desktop Management Task Force (DMTF) was founded in 1992. A major deliverable of this forum was a standardized method of managing desktop systems and applications called the DMI.

The following are key features that define the DMI:

- The application management model uses the concepts of a software product, software feature, software element, and application system.

- Software product is a collection of software features that can be acquired as a unit. Acquisition implies an agreement between the consumer and supplier, which can have licensing, support, or warranty implications.

- Software feature is a collection of software elements that performs the function or role of a software product. This level of granularity is intended to be meaningful to a consumer or user of the application. This concept allows software products or application systems to be decomposed into units that are meaningful to users, rather than units that reflect how the product or application was built (that is, software elements).

- Software element represents the level of granularity at which software features are managed. A software element is a collection of one or more files and associated details that are individually managed on a particular platform.

- Application system is a collection of software features that can be managed as an independent unit that supports a particular business function. The crucial component of the DMI is an element called the service provider (SP). The SP mediates between the management system and the client in a similar format to SNMP. Management information is exchanged at the management interface (MI).

The information model used to define the management information collected is called the Management Information File (MIF). The component interface (CI) is the interface to the system that executes the requests from the SP. To provide cross-platform compatibility, MIF information has been mapped directly to SNMP by a working group of the DMTF.

Object Management Architecture

As management solutions become more complex, various groups are promoting standardization. One of the largest groups, called the *Object Management Group (OMG)*, has defined the OMA. The OMA is a framework that standardizes the processes of network management system middleware. The most important specification of the OMA is the Common Object Request Broker Architecture, or CORBA, which defines the mechanisms that allow communications between managed objects using an Object Request Broker (ORB). The ORB is the procedure that allows communications between various system management objects transparently, independent of platform type.

CORBA has its own programming Interface Definition Language (IDL) that allows application developers to comply with the common keyword standards of OMA. CORBA is a framework that allows a degree of flexibility to developers when designing management systems. Examples of CORBA systems are IBM Tivoli and Openview CORBA compliant ORB extension. Figure 7-2 illustrates a typical CORBA framework.

Figure 7-2   *CORBA Framework*

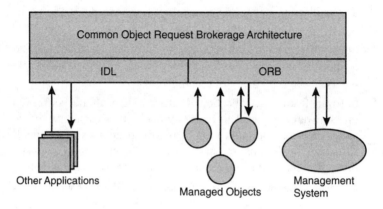

With the development of proprietary Management Information Bases (MIBs), you can manage almost every remote system device in the enterprise. In a large network, a system manager must be able to define what devices are critical to fulfill business requirements and what devices require active monitoring. In most cases, system management is reserved solely for servers, network devices, workstations, and their local resources. Server management varies depending on the operating systems and importance of the system. UNIX systems have different management requirements than Windows-based servers.

The following are common management requirements:

- Operational status
- Resource use
- Inventory management
- Software distribution
- Remote operation
- Security management

Application management is mostly focused on the following specifics:

- Application response time
- Number of simultaneous application sessions and application processes
- Download rates
- Application availability

Figure 7-3 shows how a management system can be composed of various server platforms and collect data about specific object properties or performance metrics.

Figure 7-3 *Management System*

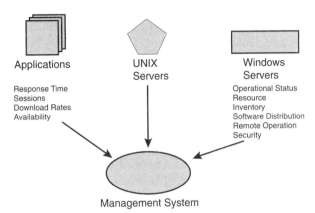

How Management Data Is Collected

Specific system information must be collected when managing distributed systems. An agent collects this information locally. SNMP agents are management software that resides on the local system. Agent software usually consists of a standard SNMP agent or a proprietary agent that is loaded on the system by either the product manufacturer or a system management application vendor. The collected data is stored in a local register as a single record or table. Information is sent to a central server or collector for analysis by an event trap or direct poll from the managing server.

Managing remote systems requires collecting and collating information stored on these devices. Typical SNMP statistics collected via the MIBII provide the administrator with basic information on the device being managed, such as the number and type of network interfaces and traffic volume. Other standard MIBs, such as the host MIB, have been developed, but these are not always available. To be able to understand the true nature of how a remote system is operating, many system vendors have their own private MIBs that provide information on the specific devices. System management organizations develop *agents* that can be loaded on the server. An example of a private MIB is Compaq Insight Agent for Compaq servers, and a common management agent is the BMC Patrol Agent.

To get a true understanding of how a remote network is being used, it is necessary to understand the functional status of the managed devices. The only way to do this is to interrogate the remote systems to discover the status of the resources. With this information, the network administrator can understand three vital components of system management, which are discussed in the following sections:

- Capacity planning
- Proactive operational management
- Performance management

Capacity Planning

Capacity planning is the understanding of the loads being experienced by an application or system and the expectations and changing business requirements of the application or system in the near and distant future.

Capacity planners need to understand the following types of critical data:

- The network environment and whether the bandwidth is sufficient to support the application
- The system resources, such as disk space, processing power, memory, and operating system
- Configurable application parameters, such as the number of users and the database size that versions of the application or system can support
- General robustness of the application or system to support future expansion and reuse

Key reasons to use capacity planning when implementing a system or application management solution include the following:

- **Speed of change**—Rapid growth in using systems and applications makes it necessary to monitor and plan for this growth before any overloads occur and cause serious performance problems or system crashes.
- **New services**—As new services are added, it is important to model the impact of these additions before implementation to avoid potential resource problems or conflicts with existing applications.
- **Cost of ownership**—Lost productivity of end users in critical business functions, overpaying for network equipment or services, and the costs of upgrading systems already in production more than justify the cost of capacity planning.

Capacity planning requires careful attention to system configuration capacities when purchasing hardware, such as the number of PCI slots in a computer, the maximum number of blades possible for a given class of router or switch, the maximum configuration of memory, and the total number of CPUs that can be added to a given model of server. While scalability addresses whether an application or service can be expanded without radical changes to its architecture to meet greater demands for capacity, capacity planning deals with the planned needs for expandability of existing components.

Proactive Operational Management

Proactive operational management is the understanding of the daily status of the remote systems being monitored. This knowledge incorporates understanding all the key features that are required to keep the system functional, available, and producing alarms, or sending event notifications to the network operations center (NOC) or system administrators if a device fails.

Performance Management

Performance management is closely linked to capacity planning and operations as items such as degrading performance are tied into operations management. Other aspects of performance, such as threshold exceptions, are often directly related to capacity issues. For example, disk space utilization reaching 90 percent can cause the performance management system to create an alarm notification that is tagged as a capacity issue and reported to the appropriate system.

Processes for Managing Systems

Most systems are managed through SNMP or the parsing of system log files. Management systems are commercially available in either part of a framework solution (for example, Tivoli) or specialized applications. Three processes are responsible for managing systems: polling, events (or traps), and thresholds.

Polling is generally performed by specific applications that have been developed for system management. Polling is done via an SNMP *get* request that queries a single or group of MIB variables (usually referred to as MIB *objects*) and imports them into a database. This information is then calculated and presented in a graphical format for the administrator to view. Historical information can be summarized and stored in a configurable repository to show trends and gradual changes.

Events or traps are proactive SNMP messages that are sent to a collector when a specific trigger occurs. An example of an event is the system creating a trap when a failure occurs on a local device such as a disk failure. These received events are fed into the network management system and produce a visual alarm that requires operator intervention. The alarms are given varying levels of priority dependent on the type of trap received.

Thresholds can occur at two points in the management process:

- **At the source**—The local agent monitors the status of various system components, and if a predetermined threshold is reached or exceeded, an SNMP trap is generated and sent to a collector or network management system for processing. The local agent can either be a private system, third party, Remote Monitoring (RMON), or a combination of all three. Typically, the local agent continues to notify the collector or management system until the situation is corrected. The collector or management system decides to notify system administrators based on its configuration and escalation policies. These events are usually weighted with a higher priority.

- **Remotely by a performance management system**—A performance management system polls the device and collects and calculates the data in its database against predefined thresholds. A performance management system creates thresholds for device information that require complex calculations. When the threshold is exceeded, a trap is generated and sent to the network management system, which identifies the source and problem type. Similar to local agents, the performance management system continues to notify the collector or management system until the situation is corrected. The collector or management system decides to notify system administrators based on its configuration and escalation policies. These thresholds are usually weighted with a lower priority than local server thresholds.

Care must be taken in designing a network management system so that the act of monitoring the components does not create an overly large burden on overall system capacity. Rather than polling objects every 5 seconds for example, a 20-second or 30-second polling interval has less impact on system resource availability and still provides adequate alert and notification triggers. The actual polling interval required to adequately monitor system health and availability varies depending upon your specific requirements.

It is also a good idea to combine both local and remote monitoring so that alerts and notifications can help isolate a problem as being specific to one set of systems or services or part of a much larger problem, such as widespread outages caused by interruptions in major carrier connectivity, such as MCI or AT&T failures.

Figure 7-4 illustrates how polling, performance, and thresholds feed a network management system for system administrators.

Figure 7-4   *Network Management System*

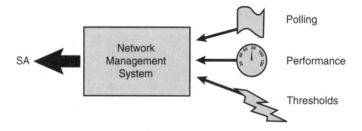

Key Facts About Application Management

Application management was, until recently, not as fully developed as the area of server management in terms of availability of sophisticated tools and services. Growth in application management in recent years is a result of the creation of new web-based applications and services in addition to the development of sophisticated tools to monitor and manage application functionality and performance.

NOTE   Remote application management of Windows applications has become easier with the introduction of Windows Terminal Services. With Windows 2000, Windows Terminal Services has finally brought the benefits of real multi-user server software to the Windows platform. Previously, it was necessary to use tools, such as PCAnywhere or Virtual Network

Computer (VNC), to remotely access and administer many important aspects of Windows applications. This caused a problem when more than one remote administrator needed to access a given server at the same time because only one console was available, giving rise to pointer contention. If two system administrators needed to access a machine, one would have to wait for the other to release the console before the second could establish a connection and begin to work.

Windows Terminal Services presents an important growth in the multi-user capabilities of Windows servers, allowing multiple login console windows to be accessed at the same time. It should be noted, however, that the security of Windows Terminal Services is, by the fact of being a new addition, unproven as yet. Additional security and authentication measures should be applied to restrict access to this useful new remote management tool.

Figure 7-5 shows application management's relationship to infrastructure management and its other elements.

Figure 7-5   *The Elements of Infrastructure Management*

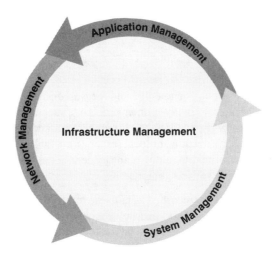

Application management is often described in broad terms and can mean different things to different people. For the context of this chapter, application management is discussed in the following four categories:

- Key Factors of Application Management
- Individuals Involved in Application Distribution and Configuration
- Application Configuration Management
- Application Performance Management

Key Factors of Application Management

Application management involves application-specific details *within* an application as well as configuration details *between* applications and environments. An important contribution that the CISS engineer makes to project development and application integration is to be aware of dependencies and integration points that restrict the range of possibilities. An example of this would be for a software engineer to be working with a software component such as Java that has been newly released for Windows the platform, but the same version has yet to be released for the Solaris platform being used on the production servers. In this case, the software engineer cannot proceed with code development on the new release until it becomes available for the production platform operating system.

To fully understand application management, begin by learning the basics about the following:

- Application faults
- Application distribution and configuration
- Application performance
- Application security

The following subsections discuss each key factor.

Application Faults

Application faults must be documented and measured as a part of the development cycle. Application faults can also indicate other problems, such as performance and security issues. Typically, every application fault is registered either centrally (thin client) or locally (thick client) on a user's machine or local server. If the fault information is stored locally, a sweep of this fault information (along with any central fault information) must occur to get the information back to software engineering.

Many application faults are recorded as numeric return codes. Such is the case with Oracle database server errors. In order to find out what any particular error code means, a special Oracle error message program needs to be run to find out the name of the error. In the worst case, applications simply dump core and exit without any error codes. In this case, using tools, such as stack traces and strings, is necessary to analyze the core file for clues as to why the application faulted. It is usually the case, however, that an application will have one or more levels of debug mode, which increase the verbosity of error messages, allowing for easier investigation and problem resolution.

Application Distribution and Configuration

Application distribution and configuration must be managed to allow for updates and new users on a continual basis. Automatically, the application version running must be checked to see if there is a newer version available. Likewise, new users need to have correct system and application settings to run the application. Application configuration and distribution must be verified periodically. Statistics about performance and frequency of distribution must also be measured.

Sometimes, the process of installing and configuring an application is a long and extended sequence of installation, reboot, and sequential patching repeated several times. Making use of disk cloning or disk images can often circumvent this tedious and error-prone process. Disk cloning is possible on servers with identical configurations of RAM, CPU, disk space, and processor speed. With disk cloning or disk images, it is possible to build and configure an application once, make a disk image of the entire hard drive, and then produce clones of this hard drive in minutes instead of days. The byte-by-byte cloning also reduces the possibility of configuration mismatches that might occur if the process were to be repeated manually every time a new server is built.

The ideal situation, however, is to not have to rebuild an entire computer's hard drive just to re-install an application, but to instead use a file-based operating system, in which the application, its code, and the application and system configurations can all be placed under version control. This allows code release and rollback to be completely controlled, making sure that application-specific code changes are checked into and out of software repositories along with the corresponding server and network hardware configurations.

Application Performance

Application performance is measured in availability and response time. Typically, response time is measured in processing time or event response time. Availability is the application's ability to be run in a correct manner within reasonable processing durations several times per day. Application performance must be measured and collected for trend analysis and historical reference. Some application performance tests should be performed locally, on the application server itself. But in the event that an error condition creates a situation that prevents an alert from leaving the server, it is a good idea to have some tests of application performance executed remotely.

Setting thresholds for alert triggers is necessary so that false alarms are not triggered because of periodic slowness experienced by a system during system backups or peak usage periods. Calibrating an application-performance monitoring tool is something that can only be done under actual conditions of stress, as it is not possible to know what kind of cascade interactions can occur. One must also be careful to not make application performance monitoring be a cause of application degradation. Too frequent monitoring is as risky as not monitoring at all.

Application Security

Application security ensures that only authorized users can only run the application. This model allows for open-ended generic (Internet) use, in addition to traditional user/password security. Application security also allows for access to specified application functions to groups of users.

Application security is typically verified periodically rather than continually measured. However, because of the vulnerability of most Internet applications, security must be tested frequently. Security policy compliance must also be fully tested when new services are added to existing applications, and new application security tests should be devised to ensure that services and features do not disappear without notice or alarm.

Individuals Involved in Application Distribution and Configuration

The people who are involved in this area are system administrators and software engineers. The system administrators manage the distribution and implementation of the operating plan for applications, and software engineers typically specify the operating configuration of applications.

An example of this relationship is for a software engineer to specify that a given application requires Java 2.1, and for the system administrator to install the Java 2.1 SDK on a computer and tell the software engineer what file system path to use to reference the installed Java 2.1 binary.

As a part of continuous improvement, software engineers use operational data obtained by automated or manual means by system administrators to improve future versions of applications as appropriate. Typically, this means after new releases of components, they are tested and validated before being released into a production environment.

NOTE   Application distribution and configuration falls within the configuration component of the FCAPS model.

Application Configuration Management

Initial application configuration occurs when software is first installed. The configuration management process includes maintaining and expanding application software and its configurations. When planning an application configuration, consider these four criteria:

- Where the application is located (local or remote).

- Physical storage of the application (on disks, in memory, or more recently in an application specific integrated circuit, which is a semiconductor chip customized for a specific application for a customer).

- Application configuration validation (Is the configuration static or dynamic? Does the application need to be stopped? Will stopping the application cause failover mechanisms to be triggered?)

- The type of interface available.

Figure 7-6 is a weighted representation of the elements of application configuration management.

Figure 7-6   *Elements of Application Configuration Management*

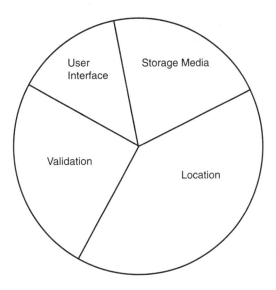

Application Performance Management

Application performance is the task of monitoring and measuring applications across a network. There are three key areas managed: application response time, server processing time, and the number of active sessions on a host.

Network administrators usually handle application performance, but in large organizations, responsibilities can fall to software developers and service level management (SLM) personnel.

Within the service provider market, especially ASPs, application performance is a key tool used in developing SLM tools and defining Service Level Agreements (SLAs) with customers. SLAs are defined as a set of key performance indicators and levels of acceptable performance. Response times for various degrees of malfunction are also defined in an SLA document, and for these reasons, the SLA becomes a fairly long and legally binding document. The SLA also stipulates the conditions under which notification for planned service outages need to be made so that adequate measures can be taken to minimize the effects of routine maintenance. The SLA is a contract and needs to be negotiated based on uptime requirements, fees paid for services, and response times for the particular needs of your application.

The following are two of the most important features of application performance:

- **Application response time**—This primarily includes transaction processing time and flight time across the network. Calculations are made for each of these indicators individually, and the combined values give a user's view of response time.

- **Application availability**—Application availability is measured using several criteria. These criteria include extensive delays in response time that cause applications to time out, loss of availability because of network outages or because of application or hardware failure, Denial of Service attacks, or virus infections.

You need to consider application performance in various situations, such as the following:

- Application performance over the network
- Application performance within the server
- Application performance across the network

The text discusses each in turn.

Application Performance over the Network

The first scenario is application performance over the network. Typically, application performance at the transport layer includes dropped connections because of insufficient ports or sockets. Some form of excessive usage of network, memory, or disk resources usually causes dropped connections. If the system is not able to support additional sessions, it is advisable to limit the number of connections at the network layers reducing system and network overhead. A typical example is a dial-up connection that connects to an application, finds no available ports, and drops the call. This situation can tie up the modems for several minutes.

Application Performance Within the Server

The second scenario is application performance within the server. Here are typical issues that affect application performance:

- Inadequate system resources.
- Poor design and poor programming techniques.
- Poorly developed interfaces at the transport layer between the application and network layers can cause extended timeouts.
- Inappropriate application tuning parameters or configurations for memory usage or session timeout settings.

Application Performance Across the Network

The third scenario is application performance across the network. Here is what generally causes poor performance:

- Network congestion, such as packet collisions on unswitched network segments
- Inadequate application timers that necessitate large numbers of retransmissions
- Bandwidth "hogging" by overdemanding applications such as FTP

Better application design can keep data processing at the server and thereby reduce the amount of data crossing the network. More efficient applications also take varying network performance into consideration; retransmissions are unnecessary because of slower response times. Applications must also be designed for limited network resources. If large amounts of data need to be transmitted, the transmission rate must vary according to available bandwidths (decreasing so that bandwidth is always available for other applications).

Key Facts About System Management

System management is not system administration in the traditional sense. Interpretation of system management varies depending on the environment and organizational processes being used. When put into the context of a job role, system management is usually shared between server administrators, network administrators, and operational database administrators. Typically, server administrators, network administrators, and database administrators are in similar IT organizations (if not the same departments). This commonality is because of the increasingly overlapping tasks between these roles.

The system administrator manager role is the next logical step in this system management evolution. The overlapping roles have a secondary purpose of providing a limited form of checks and balances. Furthermore, the system administrator is concerned with the local or end system's functionality in relation to local resources; whereas, the network administrator looks at the system functionality and how it affects the network resources.

Figure 7-7 shows the domain of System Management as it relates to both system administration and network administration.

Upon completing this section, you will be able to identify the key factors of system management and highlight the differentiators to system administration. In particular, you will learn about the following:

- Key responsibilities of system administrators
- Classes of system management
- Overview of key system management tools
- Practice of system management

Figure 7-7   *System Management Domain*

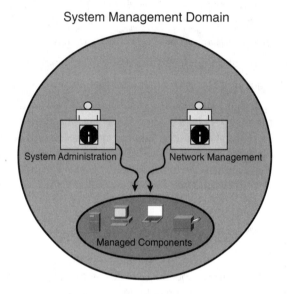

System Management Domain

Key Responsibilities of System Administrators

System administrators are looking for failures of components of a system or the whole system. The objective is to prevent failures rather than react to them. Prevention involves detailed monitoring of benchmarked key statistics for each component of the system. Benchmarking defines what is normal (performance, activity level, and so on) for the components of the system. As a characteristic, such as response time, falls out of the acceptable limits, preventive actions can be taken to correct any problems that might increase in severity over time.

Typically, preventive activities include data or file cleanups, compression, optimization, configuration of new features, implementing updated server software patches, and resolving conflicts in hardware or software components. It is important to understand that these functions are performed periodically, but not necessarily on a regular basis.

Operational personnel must handle repeatable functions that cover preventive maintenance. The system administrators must focus on preventing a problem from getting out of control. Part of that solution might be to add maintenance processes to the operational personnel.

System administrators must help determine the following:

- Server standards and configurations, such as server naming schemes, where to install various software components, how to track server configuration changes, and which services need to be added or removed beyond the initial OS installation

- Network standards and configurations, such as IP address schemes for nonrouted networks so that servers can easily be identified by their IP number as well as by hostname
- Database standards and configurations, such as directory structure, system kernel settings for semaphores and flags, when to generate stored procedures and table indices, and how often to perform various kinds of database backups

System administrators are also responsible for defining operational procedures for system maintenance. This information is often stored in something called a *run book* and needs to be kept up to date at all times. Furthermore, system administrators must be very involved with strategic planning to ensure proper delivery of system services to the customer.

Understanding what objects system management typically manages is an important factor in defining these functions:

- Server connectivity
- Disk and I/O management functions
- Application distribution functions
- Database maintenance and implementation
- Diagnostics by monitoring critical system information, database availability and performance, executing applications, or restarting individual workstations or services
- Security, such as configuring and monitoring access, to databases, servers, workstations, and other shared resources

Classes of System Management

The functional classes of system management, which are discussed in the next sections, are divided into four categories:

- System monitoring
- Software distribution
- Inventory management
- User administration

System Monitoring

System monitoring monitors the operational state of remote systems and their local resources. Monitoring tools poll or respond to traps from end systems and generate alarms based on a particular event or threshold exception. Monitoring also involves measuring the system performance, allowing the administrator to proactively assess the resources, and maintain an effective capacity-planning policy.

The best forms of system monitoring have minimal impact on the system availability. Where possible, monitoring hooks should be built into applications and systems that allow quick and simple application component connectivity queries, such as between an application server and database. In some cases, finding ways to have monitoring tests immediately drop or terminate sockets and connections immediately after the test is prudent. In the case of network devices that constantly monitor an application for specific request results, they can trigger failover conditions or automatically out-of-service an application or service. For these devices, discrete target pages or application requests should be written not only to maintain low impact on availability, but also to be able to distinguish monitoring-generated traffic in web and application logs.

Software Distribution

Because of the large number of remote systems involved in modern Internet business solutions, automated software distribution is now becoming mandatory. Over time, the variety of applications' versions and releases can become quite great, and the task of maintaining historical application downloads and install targets becomes unmanageable. Rather than have unique distribution download files for each version and release, put careful thought into structuring the download and installation URLs and mechanisms so that only a few URLs are needed which accept software distributions and versions as arguments passed to the URL. This long-term view and structured approach to software distribution also saves users from frustration of not being able to find links from older software distribution media that they are trying to use. The four processes involved in the distribution cycle follow:

1 **Predistribution administration**—Collecting software into a central source and defining the installation procedures to implement the software after it has been distributed. Additional processes include back-out procedures in the event of a problem.

2 **Target definition**—Identifying the remote systems where the software will be downloaded and mapping the systems to their respective applications.

3 **Software download**—Distributing the software and determining that it has reached the correct target without any errors.

4 **Software install**—Installing and configuring the software and the processes involved, making sure that the install was successful, and that all systems are operating correctly.

Inventory Management

The inventory database is a vital component when managing a distributed system. Without it, the other categories of system management will be ineffective. Inventory management involves keeping track of both hardware and software resources. Typically, a hardware database contains information on internal processor types and records of disk and memory allocation, in addition to information on peripheral devices, such as network cards and printers. A software database contains information on the operating system version, installed applications, licenses, and directory structures. Databases also have their own inventory databases, typically referred to as *meta-data*, or *data about the data*. These meta-data databases contain information about the servers, databases, database structures, and relationships.

Maintaining the inventory databases is crucial. An inventory database aids in successful disaster recover by allowing a rapid response and resolution of any incidents by making available lists of servers that are running affected software or services. Performing updates can be carried out manually or automatically by autodiscovery. Manual database updates are effective on small networks and systems that do not respond to autodiscovery probes. Autodiscovery is effective on large networks but can present problems with nonresponding devices and sifting through discovered devices that are not relevant to the database.

User Administration

Managing remote users generally falls in the security category of the FCAPS model. User administration is comprised of authorization, accounting of resources (sharing disk space), privileges, and the creation of roles. Although most user administration tools provide a mechanism for adding a user's full name or a comment, many administrators neglect to add any information. This is generally because it is considered obvious to the person creating the account who or what the account is for. The problem is that later, other administrators might not know what purpose a role or user account serves. Rather than risk breaking something that might depend on the account, these role accounts and temporary accounts never get removed, creating a security risk over time that really should not exist. Label temporary and role accounts with full name descriptions, and identify a city, office, or department with the account if possible.

Overview of Key System Management Tools

Because of the large number of remote systems that require management, it is nearly impossible to have an effective administrative policy without system management tools. Commercial system management tools can be either process specific or be included in a suite provided by frameworks solutions providers. Determining whether to use a framework or process-specific toolset usually depends on the network size, budget, and relationship to other management systems that are already in place. Upon completing this section, you will be able to discuss these key system management tools:

- Enterprise management
- Software distribution
- System monitoring
- User administration

Enterprise Management Tools

Enterprise management tools enable organizations to manage all IT resources, encompassing heterogeneous networks, systems, applications, and databases. Such tools must provide end-to-end management for TCP/IP, Systems Network Architecture (SNA), Internetwork Packet Exchange (IPX/SPX), Frame Relay and ATM networks, platforms such as Windows NT, Linux, BSD, AIX, Solaris, HP-UX, SCO, AS/400, Netware, mainframes, and databases such as Oracle, Sybase, DB2, Informix, Postgres, and Microsoft SQL Server. Fully integrated management solutions provide inventory management, network discovery, topology, performance, events and status, security, software distribution, storage, and workload for traditional, distributed, and n-tier computing environments.

Typically, these systems are a composite of specialized tools, which are integrated into a centralized management scheme. Unicenter TNG, HP Openview, and Tivoli are some examples of these enterprise management tools. These tools all have open and configurable interfaces to external systems that can be used as a replacement for a particular component. Such third-party systems must likewise support a common interface, such as SNMP.

A recent advancement in these tools has been the introduction of predictive management technology. These functions bring neural network-based self-learning and pattern-recognition that enable the tool to learn from past history and predict future behavior. This activity helps predict potential problems indicating when to take preventive action.

Software Distribution Tools

Applications and application data need to be stored on network servers. Using software distribution tools, the clients can be configured to load applications from the network, or the servers can push the applications to the clients. You can direct data to be managed locally and centrally. This provides for improved centralized control and management of both applications and data, allowing for easy upgrades of applications, as well as centralized backup and security. Upgrades to client operating systems can be managed on a remote basis. Most comprehensive tools include these functions as a modular option or component. Smaller toolsets, such as Microsoft SMS, also include these features.

System Monitoring Tools

System monitoring tools must gather and reconcile hardware, software, and database faults and alerts. Preemptive maintenance must be recommended and facilitated if possible. Operational and performance statistics must be kept (optionally and configurable) for each critical system element. You can specify criteria to generate alerts and notifications about different levels and types of system problems. Historical data can be exported to historical databases for later analysis.

Most comprehensive tools include features as a modular option for hardware, software, and databases. Smaller tool sets, such as Microsoft SMS, also include these features. If individual tools are used (such as a database monitor and a file server monitor), these tools must communicate (typically through an SNMP interface) with a centralized management system.

User Administration Tools

User administration tools need to have the capability to define user-computing resources, such as access to the Internet or intranet, which applications can be run, where data is stored, and desktop layouts. Typical user admin tools can create server shares and unattended client installations, predefined system policies, user profiles and roles, and desktop environment templates. These tools allow administrators to define remotely what applications can be run, where user data resides, and all levels of security. Most comprehensive tools include theses features as a modular option or component.

Practice of System Management

The practice of system management involves keeping up with a moving target. The moving target in this case is a secure, well-tuned system that accommodates changes in features and functionality as well as increases in system use. Seeking out OS patches, network software patches, and application patches and upgrades is an on-going responsibility of the CISS engineer.

Software applications and their configurations are not, however, the only things that need to be keep up to date. Operations documentation also needs to be maintained so that adequate operations procedures are available in the event that someone less familiar with the systems needs to perform basic or complex changes. It is tempting to think that the team of system and network administrators will always be on-hand to deal with any emergencies or issues that arise, but in actuality, everyone takes vacations, and the most knowledgeable and qualified system administrator will not always be available.

System management must also take into consideration the idea of program management. Here, program management is not meant to refer to computer programs and applications, but rather the "program" of having a web-based customer care application, or an online catalog. In the overall context of organizational initiatives, an online catalog application will have three kinds of stakeholders: marketing and communications, IT, and the users.

It is important to make sure that users' needs and perceptions are included as real stakeholders, soliciting their feedback with occasional surveys or opt-in questionnaires. Sometimes, the top-level program goals originating from marketing and communications are at odds with the desires and goals of IT, and so it should be the perspective of the actual catalog users that gives final direction in making program direction decisions. Often, the CISS engineer needs to find ways to accommodate the mixed needs and potentially unclear lines of authority that might exist in controlling an application.

Web server logfile analysis is crucial to learning user browsing patterns and behaviors and, therefore, a powerful tool in the practice of system management. A daily diary of what is right and what is wrong with all web page requests logged by a site or application web server exists in the traffic analysis. Because web server log files contain a large amount of information about site and application usability and performance, web server logfile analysis should be an essential component of any system maintenance agreement or contract.

Traffic analysis reports are not just used for finding and resolving server errors. The daily successes and measurements of key transactions occurring on the site are also present in the reports. How many users registered each day? How many users have started a purchase but then abandoned their shopping cart? At what stage in the checkout process did these abandoned carts occur? Traffic analysis can answer these questions and thereby provide vital information to support successful changes or additions to the online catalog shopping experience for users.

As an example of the utility of logfile analysis, a specific web ad banner marketing campaign can be measured for click-through from web server and application server logs to validate the numbers of click-throughs reported by the ad-serving agency. By creating a discrete entry point for the target URLs in your marketing campaigns, you can also directly measure marketing dollar ROI or test theories about browsing styles and keywords that attract users with intent to buy. System management and application management tools, such as logfile analysis, should be thought of as supporting and informing program management and system administration.

Summary

Application and system management uses key tools and design methodologies to satisfy the needs of an Internet business solution. Both system and network administration must configure and maintain servers and applications running on those servers, and so the distinction between network administrator and system administrator might not be meaningful depending on the size and organization of an IT department within a company.

The dependencies and possible interactions of application and system management tools and methodologies need to be considered to keep applications and server resources operating within desired performance levels.

The FCAPS model is a common approach to application management. A well-integrated application and system management architecture is also the major basis for performing the kinds of measurement and analysis needed to determine usability performance to quantify ROI.

Review Questions

1 Which function is not considered a system or application management function?

   a. Firewall intrusion detection

   b. Monitoring server CPU utilization

   c. Measuring system availability

   d. Software distribution

2 Which benefits are not attributed to application management?

   a. Understanding the application's topology and characteristics

   b. Monitoring application CPU/memory consumption

   c. The ability to measure an application throughput

   d. Remotely managing the applications security requirements

3 The task of monitoring and measuring applications across a network is called
_____ .

   a. Application servicing

   b. Service level management

   c. Application performance

   d. Application distribution

4 An example of application configuration management includes which of the
following?

   a. Calculating response times when changes are made

   b. Understanding what parameters need to be changed

   c. Knowing application performance

   d. Configuring application availability software

5 Which of the following does not affect application performance across the network?

   a. Traffic congestion

   b. Bandwidth utilization

   c. Router utilization

   d. Number of active sessions

6 DMI stands for _____ .

    a. Distributed Management Interface

    b. Dynamic Managed Integration

    c. Desktop Management Interface

    d. Digital Module Interface

7 Which of the following is not a typical measurement of application management?

    a. Application availability

    b. Operating system version

    c. Application response time

    d. Download rates

8 How does the speed of change affect capacity planning?

    a. It is linked to operations that are tied into the operations management.

    b. Rapid growth makes it necessary to monitor and plan for growth before any overloads occur and cause serious performance problems or system crashes.

    c. It is tied to all the key features that are required to keep the system working.

    d. It predicts if and when system saturation occurs.

9 Which of the following are two types of threshold system management?

    a. RMON and SNMP

    b. Immediate and historical

    c. Framework and best-of-breed

    d. Local and remote performance-based

10 Which of the following is key to system management?

    a. System management helps determine server standards and configurations.

    b. System management is not shared between server, network, or operational database administrators.

    c. System management interpretation varies, depending on the environment and organizational processes being used.

    d. System management is the same as system administration.

11 Why is the inventory database a vital component of system management?

   a. Without it, there would be no management capabilities.

   b. It provides a log of all routers and switches.

   c. It contains a directory of all managed components.

   d. It stores vital system statistics.

12 Which is not a key system management tools element?

   a. The tools can help identify the source and cause of the problem quickly and allow a rapid response.

   b. System management tools must gather and reconcile hardware, software, and database faults and alerts.

   c. Management tools enable organizations to manage all IT resources and encompassing heterogeneous networks, systems, applications, and databases.

   d. The tools do not have the capability to create server shares and unattended client installations.

Applied Solutions

The best advice my experience can offer in regards to application and system management is to move away from the defaults and take advantage of good shareware tools to make your job easier.

If you investigated the configurations of 100 web servers, not more than five or six would probably demonstrate anything other than pure default settings. Default configurations survive far too long in my experience, especially on Microsoft IIS web servers. The trouble seems to be that, out of the box, application performance seems adequate, and when resource contention issues do arise, the problem is usually solved by throwing money at the problem instead of digging in and looking around for information.

The Internet is full of information about how to tune and configure software to make it run better without having to add another server, CPU, or more memory. Today's laptop computers, for example, contain more processing power than the entire Apollo moon mission computers used by NASA. Are you really going to believe that your project or application has greater demands and technical requirements than launching astronauts into space, landing them thousands of miles away on the moon, and returning them safely to the earth?

Technical discussions on message boards, FAQs, and the other results of search engine queries represent hundreds of hours of other people's experiences and experimentations. These discussions of problems and solutions should not be thought of as answers per se, but rather indications of which components and settings have produced some kind of identifiable results. YMMV (Your Mileage May Vary) of course, but half the battle in moving your servers off their default settings is knowing which settings are worth tinkering with.

Scenario 1: Network and System Management

Problem

Providing network and systems management support for a project or several projects can take a varying amount of time. How can a single person maintain the systems and network configurations for a project without spending all his time managing the infrastructure instead of working on the project itself?

Solution

If there is one basic thing that separates the junior administrator from the senior administrator, it is the awareness of crafty shareware tools. By this I mean, don't go around researching, buying, training, and suffering from a need to always rely on commercial or custom-built software to solve problems. I can almost guarantee that any kind of problem that seems to require an expensive, complicated commercial software solution can usually be solved with a free, and often open source, simple solution.

Solution Details

Crafty shareware software is amazing. Whether it is a Perl module that someone has written that gives you libraries of functions to easily query and configure Cisco routers and switches, an extensive and long-running project like the Apache web server, or the more recent Apache Tomcat application server, shareware offers a myriad of tried-and-true solutions. The quality is often greater than that of commercial programs that purport to do the same thing because the inner workings of the problem are often open to inspection, making them open to customization and optimization for your own needs.

A shareware author feels no pressure to sell you code but offers it in the spirit of contribution and hopes that in return you will either help make it better by commenting on problems, requesting new features, or sending a couple of dollars because the program or code snippet put out a fire that would have taken you weeks to resolve had it not been for the shareware. The junior administrator hopes to find the time to write some cool code to handle a bug or compatibility issue; the senior administrator knows that it already exists and continues to look for it to find what is needed.

Application and system management can be a burden with only a handful of servers to manage and maintain, but it can also be simple with hundreds of computers under your care. The difference comes in the administrator's expectations. If you expect that ten servers are all you can handle, that's how many you'll be able to keep online and healthy. If, however, you expect that you can, with some clever and crafty scripts at your side, take on a server farm of 100 machines, your expectations too shall be met. Which of these two self-fulfilling prophecies do you want to pursue?

Scenario 2: Application Management

Problem

Microsoft IIS web server software configuration is, by default, set up to log web server requests in what is known as common logfile format. What other formats can IIS log in order to capture more information?

Solution

In the case of Microsoft IIS web servers, my advice is to make sure that you do one thing at the very least: change the default logfile format to extended logfile format. Two important fields get added right away: user agent and referring URL. (If your application or service makes use of session or persistent cookies, those should also be logged so that traffic analysis can do more accurate session counts instead of needing to model user sessions and estimate session counts.) Of all the data contained in web server log files, the referring URL and the user agent (or browser type) are perhaps the most useful and insightful.

Solution Details

The first web page request made by a user session contains a referring URL field with the link used to get to your site. If the referring URL is a search engine, as it often is, you can also learn what specific keywords that user used. Knowing what keywords are associated with users who are looking for your site is important and valuable information. Subsequent requests from a user session also contain referring URLs, but those URLs will be pages from your site. This, however, does not mean that these referring URLs are not interesting and important, as well. Without this information, path analysis and followed link reports are not possible.

Path analysis tells you how users navigate through your site. In the case of a site with registration, e-commerce, and detailed product information pages, path analysis is a direct lens into your customers' thoughts and experience. How many users experienced errors? Which pages led to those errors? Referring URLs make the answers to these questions possible.

The user agent field or browser type also provides knowledge about the kinds of users of your application or site. How many user agent varieties make their way to your application? How many of those are included in your requirements for compatibility and QA testing? Is your site compatible with WebTV (popular among the elderly because of less emphasis on arthritis-compounding keyboarding skills)? How many WAP-enabled telephones are trying to browse your site? Without the user agent field in the web server log files, your business is guessing that everything looks fine for every kind of visitor and user.

A preponderance of the last version of Microsoft Internet Explorer or other web browser software in the user agent field also tells you that you have a natural segment of early-adopters visiting your site. These users generally stay on top of the latest software releases and have machines with a full set of plug-ins to enable a rich media experience. Similarly, seeing ancient user agent versions, such as Mozilla 2.0 or MSIE 3.0, can indicate a less technically savvy group of users. If this user segment is a part of your target audience, make sure that the technology used on your site or in your application is of a lower common denominator that generally uses navigation elements with lower page weights for faster download times.

Other nondefault configuration options exist within the Microsoft IIS web server application and drastically impact server performance. The Windows registry also contains a slew of default settings, some of which are quite appropriate to a single server site getting less than 250,000 hits per day. Others are definitely at odds with a load-balanced server farm of five high-powered web servers that relegate most of the difficult work to another farm of application servers to provide dynamic content and business logic.

You can safely assume that application defaults cannot be suited to the purpose to which you designed. Default settings also represent a mixture of demands, striking a balance between several roles a server might be asked to serve. You must know, through tinkering and intelligent experimentation, which settings govern the application services and tasks for your situation.

Indeed, with the recent rise in network load balancing use and traffic shaping hardware and software, your application default settings might be at complete odds with your network architecture. The Cisco iQ initiative web site offers some good basic case studies and white papers that capture some of the principal forces at work in trying to build successful Internet solutions. You will do well to assume that someone has already tried to work out the detailed configurations of a networked computer application much like yours, and that time spent searching for an account of his thinking and testing is well worth the effort.

PART IV

CISS Case Studies

CHAPTER 8

CISS Case Studies

Case studies help make the CISS certification a more practical training experience. Without access to concrete situations involving web-based applications, sorting out the details of real-world experiences can be hard.

The five case studies detailed in this chapter from the CISS Solutions course include questions and exercises requiring you to translate information presented in earlier chapters into specific problem solving solutions. Although based on actual situations, the company names in these studies have been changed. In some cases, the type of business has also been changed to ensure that any proprietary or privileged knowledge is not divulged to protect Non-Disclosure Agreements and potential intellectual property rights.

Case Study 1: e-business

This case study's activities relate to the business modeling and requirements phase of the solutions development lifecycle. During the business modeling and requirements phase, the CISS aids in gathering, modeling, and analyzing business area information to help identify and prioritize requirements. Techniques, such as interviews and facilitated sessions, can be used to gather information about strategy, operations, processes, data, system performance, functionality, and costs. The CISS will likely be involved in all aspects of an Internet business solution project's business modeling and requirements phase. During this phase, the CISS has these three major responsibilities:

- Keep the requirements gathering focused on business, functional, and information models.
- Provide leadership on gathering system requirements.
- Validate completion of the business modeling and requirements phase.

Objectives for e-business

Identify a complete set of nonfunctional requirements based on the questions and answers from a client interview.

Scenario for e-business

Yukon, Inc., a national retailer, has established itself over the past forty years by selling merchandise through catalog orders and to in-store customers. Over the past few years, Yukon has experienced a significant decline in sales. After hiring a marketing firm to research current trends in the retail industry, it found that more shoppers choosing the convenience of shopping online caused the decline. To survive and stay competitive, Yukon is looking to expand its presence in the United States by putting its catalog on the Internet (seamless transition from catalog to online).

Assignment I for e-business

User satisfaction is critical to Yukon. It has done extensive research on similar e-business sites and is asking you to design an e-business solution. You are given the opportunity to interview the chief technology officer. Your goal for this meeting is to ask questions and gather information to identify nonfunctional requirements for the solution. (A nonfunctional requirement is one that does not pertain to an application's actual features and functionality. The basic CISS nonfunctional requirements areas are security, reliability and availability, scalability, performance, and manageability.)

In preparation, you create a list of questions that need to be asked to collect the necessary information about nonfunctional requirements.

Answer to Assignment I for e-business

The questions you created and asked are in the following list. Yukon's CTO provided the answers.

Q — *How many customers will access the site per month?*

A — We anticipate that 1000 to 5000 customers will access the site for the first few months, hopefully growing to 50,000 over the first year.

Q — *When are the peak periods and the low times?*

A — Peak times are seasonal, as with most other retailers—Thanksgiving to Christmas. As far as times go, we would expect an e-business site to have most of its business in the evening, probably 60 percent between the hours of 6 and 10 in the evening, after people get home from work. The remaining 40 percent will probably be spread through the day with a strong spike during the lunch hour.

Q — *What does a transaction look like?*

A — A complete e-business transaction requires multiple interactions with host servers. The customers search for products, enter them into a "shopping cart," and go through a "checkout" procedure. This involves a long transaction with many independent database queries and updates.

Q — *How many customers are just browsing, and how many actually buy/purchase?*

A — Typically, an e-business site has about a 50/50 split between customers browsing and purchasing. We want to do better than that—if customers comes to our site, we want to entice them to buy.

Q — *What do you know about the target demographics, such as age group or income level?*

A — Yukon has performed several market surveys to determine the target demographic for our products and services. The kinds of customers that we include in our target audience are young females, aged 15-20, in high-income households.

Q — *How many customer sessions per month, week, and day do you expect to receive?*

A — Initially, we would expect to see several hundred to a thousand sessions per day, growing to tens of thousands per week after a few months. By the end of the first year, we would like to see upward of 100,000 sessions per month.

Q — *How fast do you expect to grow?*

A — We are basing our e-business expectations on how other similar companies have done. We expect to start slow as customers learn about us and we begin to advertise—maybe 1000 to 5000 customer sessions the first few months. By the end of the second year, as a result of aggressive advertising, we want to grow to 10,000,000 customer sessions per year based on a peak load of 10,000 sessions per hour.

Q — *What is the average revenue value of a transaction?*

A — Based on industry experience and the relative value of our product line, a typical customer transaction will result in $165.00 in revenue. This is based on an average customer purchase of two and a half items per shopping trip.

Q — *How many transactions do you plan to conduct during a peak hour?*

A — After we get going, we expect to have 1000 transactions during a peak hour (approximately 25 percent of the transactions on a heavy day).

Q — *What kind of sensitive information goes across the wires in a transaction?*

A — Credit card numbers, personal identifiable information, such as names, addresses, phone numbers, and so on.

Q — *How will you store and protect the sensitive information?*

A — Sensitive information must be encrypted and/or access control mechanisms must be available to restrict access.

Q — *What other information about the system can you provide?*

A — The company's portion of the system should have close to zero impact on the customer's wait time. If voice is incorporated into the solution, "toll quality" should be the performance goal. If video is incorporated into the solution, the video can demonstrate MPFG quality. Some flickering and graininess are acceptable. Photos are acceptable if video is not feasible.

With an average transaction worth $165 and a peak transaction rate of 1000, our worst downtime case would cost us $165,000 per hour in direct revenue. It would cost us even more in lost repeat business from customers who are frustrated that their shopping cart was lost when the system failed.

Assignment II for e-business

Now that you have asked all the necessary questions, generate a list of nonfunctional requirements that the client wants for the solution. Think about how you would explain how you produced the list of nonfunctional requirements.

Proposed Answers to Assignment II for e-business

Come up with a list of requirements similar to those in Chapter 4, "Application Requirements," that includes performance, scalability, availability, and security. The following sections detail typical requirements for a solution.

Performance

The system must be able to initially support 1000 customer transactions per hour. Each transaction is complex, involving many database queries with graphic retrievals and multiple database updates as the customer fills their shopping cart and checks out.

Scalability

Although the system will start small with an expected customer transaction rate averaging about 1000 transactions during the peak hour, the rate is expected to grow tenfold over the first two years. From that point, the company hopes to increase by 15–25 percent per annum.

Availability

The system going down is unacceptable. A 99.99 percent availability (53 minutes of unplanned downtime per year) would be desirable. The maximum potential cost of downtime is $165,000 per hour during the initial year, increasing to over $1,000,000 per hour of unplanned downtime after the second year.

Security

Transaction data relating to checkout must be sufficiently secure to reduce risk to an acceptable level. Increased security costs must be balanced with a decision about the potential risk of data compromise. Extremely sensitive customer data involving credit card numbers and personal information will be passing over the network. Although absolute security is not possible, there must be no opportunity during the checkout period for interception.

Case Study 2: Application Architecture Design

The activities in this case study relate to the analysis and design phase of the solutions development lifecycle. During the analysis and design phase, the CISS further analyzes the information and requirements gathered during the business modeling and requirements phase, and works with the project team to plan and design the Internet business solution. The goal is to design a system that fulfills user requirements and is effective, usable, reliable, and maintainable.

The solutions development lifecycle's analysis and design phase is critical to successful development and implementation. Throughout this phase, the CISS has four major responsibilities:

- Analyze business requirements in relation to system architecture.
- Develop a project management plan.
- Design a robust and maintainable system.
- Design a system architecture and application solution that satisfies business requirements.

Objectives for Application Architecture Design

The objectives in this case include the following:

- Create an optimal application architecture design by placing the specified components (the browser client, web server, application server, and database server) within the geographical constraints.
- Explain your proposed application architecture's benefits.
- Propose a security design, in terms of identification, authentication, access controls, auditing, and accountability that addresses the company's security issues.

Scenario I for Application Architecture Design

Rupert Design Systems Incorporated (RDSI) has a number of major clients who, because of government regulations, demand that security restrictions be monitored more closely. RDSI has decided to implement a web campus and three satellite campuses. The main campus is located in the United States. The first remote campus is located in Asia with a low-speed, remote circuit line of 64 Kbps connecting it to the main campus. The second remote campus is located in Europe with a low-speed circuit line of 128 Kbps connecting it to the main campus. RDSI's third remote campus is located in the United States with a T1 circuit connecting it to the main campus.

Components of this packaged application include the following:

- Databases
- Application servers
- Web servers
- Browser clients
- Firewalls

Data analysis for a critical finance transaction shows the following dataflow and transaction size pairings:

- Oracle Database with application server: 2 MB
- Application server with web server: 180 KB
- Web server with browser client: 490 KB

Assignment I for Application Architecture Design

Create an optimal application architecture design by placing the specified components (browser client, web server, application server, database server, and firewalls) within the geographical constraints. Explain your proposed application architecture's benefits.

Answer to Assignment I for Application Architecture Design

Study Figure 8-1 to see one answer to the assignment.

You should locate database and application servers together. This placement provides an efficient data transfer between the application running on the application server and the Relational Database Management System (RDMS).

Figure 8-1   *Application Design Network Diagram*

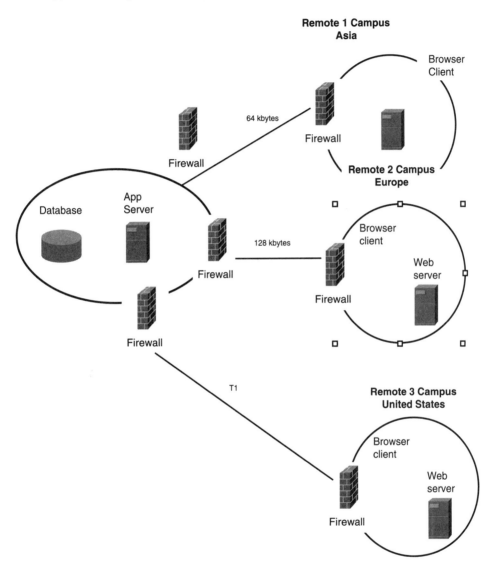

Note the following facts:

- The web server can be located with the application server or with the browser at each campus.

- Dataflow is faster if the web server is located with the browser.

- If the web server is located with the application server, you need only one server instead of four.

- Locate the application server with the database server, and not at a remote campus location.

- Place the firewalls on each side of the private links for the T1, 128 Kbps line, and 64 Kbps line if VPN tunnels are to be used on existing Internet connections to each campus. Firewalls are not necessarily required if the private links are long-haul carrier private connections that are not connected to the Internet.

- To avoid access control issues within the application introduced by the remote campus requirements, only the web servers can be located remotely from the application and database servers.

- A good solution will include a distributed authentication mechanism to allow each remote campus web server to authenticate users locally, and yet, allow network-wide replication of user accounts on a nightly basis, for example.

Scenario II for Application Architecture Design

The RDSI project is well underway by the time the CISS resource has been added to the project. The proposed three-remote-campus architecture in Figure 8-1 has been tested and is almost ready for production. You engage in a casual conversation with the project's primary business owner and discover that there are a couple of additional security concerns:

- The system allows end-users to log in with one shared user ID (all with a standard password) per company location. However, industry regulations require that every transaction must be associated with the identity of the requestor, along with the date, time, and location where the request was submitted. Audits will be conducted and all requestors will be held accountable for their individual transactions.

- The system also allows end-users to submit all available financial transactions through the application, instead of restricting high-value transactions to certain authorized managers.

The primary business owner is still willing to forge ahead with production rollout and rectify the security requirements later.

Assignment II for Application Architecture Design

Decide whether you are going to agree or disagree with the decision to continue the production rollout. Provide some supporting arguments for your position.

Answer to Assignment II for Application Architecture Design

Attention should have been given to security requirements during the initial business requirements interview sessions to address security requirements. If the primary business owner was not formally interviewed, care should have been taken to ensure that the list of interviewees was complete. The interview process should have addressed any regulatory requirements that might impact the application. After the security requirements were defined, they should have been included in the application's design and translated into technical solutions. In addition, all the extracted business requirements should have been presented and approved by all interested RDSI business units.

For identification purposes, the security design should allow assignment of unique user IDs to each end-user. For authentication purposes, use standard security passwords, which are encrypted with expirations (typically 30 to 90 days). This offers the level of reliability necessary to meet the regulatory requirements and enforce individual accountability.

In terms of access control, the security design should allow for mechanisms that control the different level of access privileges per the defined security profiles, and support auditing requirements, which are logging mechanisms that should be in place to record all the necessary data changes. Refer to Chapter 4 for more information on this.

Planning and designing security solutions must be based on business-defined security policies, standards, and procedures. You must also define budget and resource assignments during the planning process to ensure that sufficient support is available.

Basically, the purpose of planning and designing is to define a security roadmap that describes how things will get done. A design includes setting policies for who can access the system, what they are allowed to access, what methods will be used to protect the system, what standards will be used to implement security (passwords, hand scans, locks and keys, and so on), and implementation procedures for those security policies and standards (such as each person being required to enter a password when logging onto the system).

What if the client decides to continue without making your suggested changes?
Although the primary business owner might be willing to assume the risks (not meeting regulatory requirements), in the long term, the application will probably suffer from disruptions because of the efforts to rectify security. Additionally, the application might require significant revisions to accommodate the security design.

What if the client decides to continue without making your suggested changes at this time? Because the primary business owner is willing to assume the risks (not meeting regulatory requirements), have her sign a waiver explaining that the security is to be implemented at a specified later date. This allows the program to be released and subsequently changed after going through another development cycle (design, code, test, implement).

Case Study 3: Network Design

The following case study's activities relate to the analysis and design phase of the solutions development lifecycle. During the analysis and design phase, the CISS further analyzes the information and requirements gathered during the business modeling and requirements phase, and works with the project team to plan and design the Internet business solution. The goal is to design a system that fulfills user requirements and is effective, usable, reliable, and maintainable.

The analysis and design phase of the solutions development lifecycle is critical to successful development and implementation. Throughout this phase, the CISS has four major responsibilities:

- Analyze business requirements in relation to system architecture.
- Develop a project management plan.
- Design a robust and maintainable system.
- Design a system architecture and application solution that satisfies business requirements.

Not all customer projects will have hard and fast variables or requirements to use in creating an Internet business solution. A CISS will often be called upon to deal with fairly vague "wishes" and guide decision makers toward a solution by helping to set the requirements. This case study is an example of one such project.

Objectives for Network Design

The objectives include the following:

- Determine whether a proposed e-learning system meets a set of given nonfunctional requirements.
- Design a new e-learning system architecture given a set of nonfunctional requirements.

Scenario for Network Design

HealthCare, Inc., a large HMO, has intense training demands for internal staff. It needs to keep its sales staff at all 100 remote hospitals and clinics up-to-date with new medical procedure techniques and policies. HealthCare wants to provide streaming video for corporate communications and training. It also wants to make content on demand (Video on Demand) available on a just-in-time basis for medical and office staff. It further wants to enable training meetings for doctors, nurses, and office staff over its intranet.

The following set of mandatory requirements was derived from several meetings with key users and network professionals at HealthCare: quality of service (QoS), availability, performance, and security. A discussion of each requirement follows.

Quality of Service

The new network must deliver real-time broadcast video with no apparent latency transmission. Streaming video must demonstrate no flickering and no jitter. Virtual classes on the new network will use voice over HealthCare's intranet with no discernable jitter. Real-time e-learning applications, such as broadcast video classes and virtual classrooms, must be able to operate during prime business hours without interfering with HealthCare's business activities.

Availability

HealthCareInc.'s business will rely on the new network. Its network must be available a minimum of 99.99 percent of the time (unplanned downtime cannot exceed 53 minutes per year). Remote sites must have access to HealthCare's central site at all times.

Performance

When a HealthCare user wants to take content on demand (CoD) training, the CoD must be available to the user within several minutes. CoD cannot affect regular business traffic's response time.

Security

Because of the sensitive patient data which transverses the network, HealthCare requires a completely secure network. The new network must be impervious to threats from outside networks. Data traversing any non-HealthCare network must be assured of a high degree of security.

Assignment for Network Design

Examine Figure 8-2. Given the diagram depicting the e-learning components at HealthCare's planned central site and an example remote site, at least three areas exist where the proposed design does not meet HealthCare's nonfunctional requirements.

Figure 8-2 *Healthcare's E-learning Components*

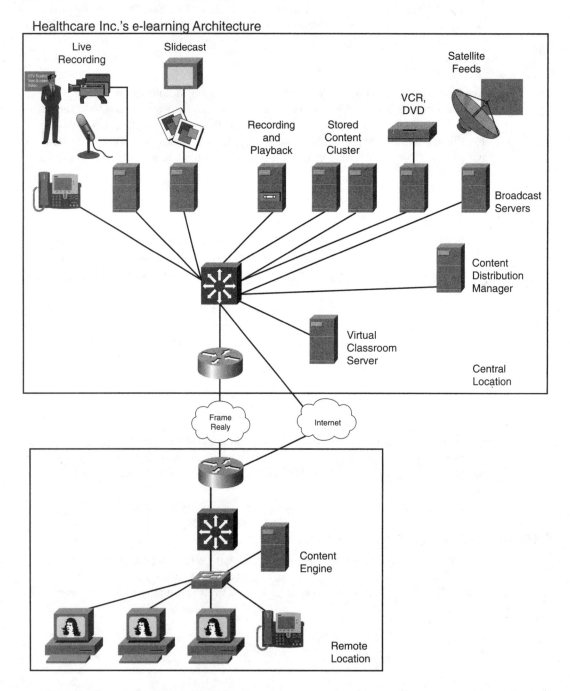

Healthcare Inc.'s e-learning Architecture

Use the following questions to help you analyze the diagram:

1 What are three obvious areas where the proposed design does not meet the nonfunctional requirements?

2 Can you modify the existing system architecture so that it meets the given nonfunctional requirements?

3 Can you identify any other areas of concern (nonfunctional requirements) that you would investigate that might not be immediately apparent from the system diagram? Can you identify any solutions that might be used to ensure that those areas are satisfied?

4 What can be done to protect the internal network from external Internet access? What can be done to protect any confidential data that is being transmitted across the Internet?

Answers for Assignment in Network Design

- Answer to question 1:
  - Add redundancy in terms of network equipment and links.
  - Add firewalls between the intranet and Internet.
  - Use Virtual Private Network (VPN) to enable the routers with connections to the Internet.
- Answer to question 2:
  - See "HealthCare, Inc.'s Modified Architecture" for sample answer, as shown in Figure 8-3.
- Answer to question 3:
  - Apply QoS through the intranet to ensure that voice and video can be transported. You can do this by using the QoS technologies explained in the CISS Architecture Essentials course to ensure that voice and video can be transmitted through the network.
  - Ensure the use of QoS to enable the transfer of CoD without interfering with mission-critical business. You can do this by using the QoS technologies explained in the CISS Architecture Essentials course to ensure the massive CoD files are transferred during network quiet times so that the CoD traffic does not interfere with mission-critical business.
  - Ensure that live video is not interfering with mission-critical traffic. Use QoS to ensure that the mission-critical traffic receives preferential treatment.

— Ensure that the bandwidth is big enough. Making sure that multicast routing is enabled on all intranet routers allows for reduced bandwidth consumption where possible. Employ buffered video signal repeater servers for links that need to travel over unicast network segments. Use network management tools to measure and monitor traffic on the network to proactively determine bandwidth requirements and add bandwidth before the lack of bandwidth impacts network performance.

— Ensure the availability of the Frame-Relay network. Obtain Service Level Agreements (SLAs) from the Frame Relay network service provider to guarantee the required availability. Because of the application's criticality, it might be desirable to enter into an SLA with a secondary back-up provider for "service-on-demand."

— Ensure that there are back-up links to the central site using a different medium. You can do this by using ISDN back-up links. (This might also be a consideration for the back-up service provider.)

- Answer to question 4:

  — Firewalls behind each router will protect the internal network from unauthorized access from the Internet. Enabling VPN capabilities on the routers will provide an encrypted tunnel to securely transit data over the Internet.

  — To assure that confidential data remains protected from unauthorized access from the Internet or unauthorized internal access, the use of firewalls is recommended. Additionally, to protect the confidential data as it traverses the Internet, some form of encryption is necessary.

Figure 8-3   *HealthCare Modified Diagram*

Healthcare Inc.'s e-learning Architecture

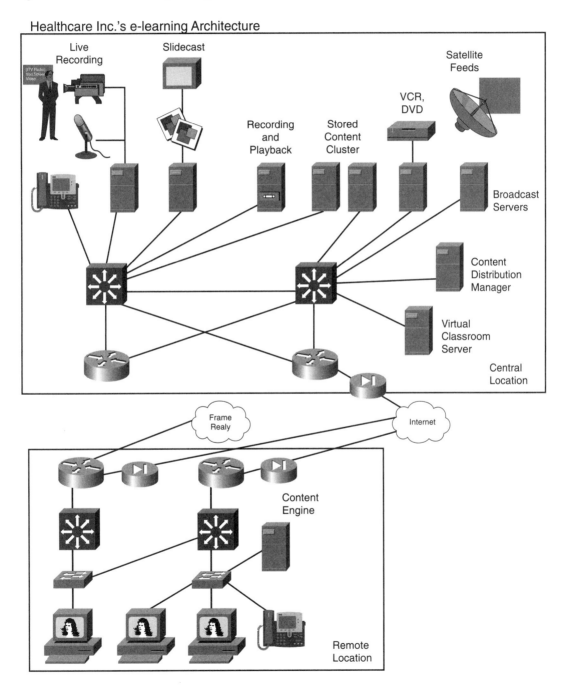

Case Study 4: Testing

The activities in this case study relate to the testing phase of the solutions development lifecycle. The test phase integrates the application's components and operations into a completed system, discovers and corrects any nonconformities between the developed system and the business requirements, as stated in the design document, and concludes with the formal acceptance of the system.

Few stages in the solutions development lifecycle are more important than testing. Good testing equals a better return on investment, higher levels of customer satisfaction, and most important, better solutions. Ensuring quality is critical, especially for an Internet business solution where the consequences of defects range from mere inconvenience and customer dissatisfaction to the loss of money and business.

The test phase varies in duration and difficulty depending on the proposed application system's dimensions and complexity. However, the test phase usually has four major stages: plan the test, run the test, analyze the test results, and perform acceptance testing. During each of these test phase stages, the CISS might perform the following responsibilities to ensure the success of the project:

- Confirm the test plan is sufficient to test the system requirements, as specified in the design document.
- Verify that testing is performed.
- Ensure that test results are analyzed.
- Collaborate with acceptance testing, as needed.

Objectives for Testing

The objectives include the following:

- Given a set of scenarios, identify the flaws and/or the completeness of the testing scenarios. Redesign any scenarios that are incorrect, and design any scenarios that need to be added for a complete and efficient testing phase.
- Given test results, compare the test results to the nonfunctional requirements for compliance. Identify any corrective action.

Load Test Scenario

Yukon is in the process of expanding its retail business by adding an online catalog. The application provides both browsing and buying capability. Both the application and network architecture are functional in a testing environment. The company plans to go live within 30 days and is currently validating its production environment for the expected number of peak users, security controls, and recovery time in the event of a failure.

Based on the information Yukon has from its current paper catalog sales, it has identified a nonfunctional requirement of 1000 users during peak usage at any one time. Another nonfunctional requirement is that any "Buy" transaction must be completed in two seconds or less (user think time not included because transactions are scripted). Yukon believes that most of its new Internet users will be browsing online catalog pages to start with, but it expects this to change in a short time to more buying than browsing. Figure 8-4 shows the proposed testing environment to test.

Figure 8-4   *Load Test Environment*

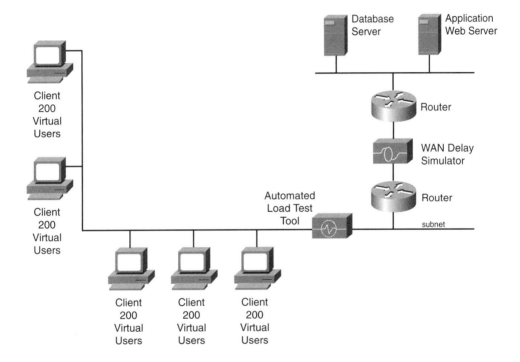

Figure 8-5 shows how Yukon plans on ramping up the users to 1000 simultaneous users:

The e-business lifecycle critical success factors include the following:

- Flexibility
- Security
- Performance
- Scalability
- Reliability
- Usability
- Cost and value

Figure 8-5   *Load Test Ramp Up*

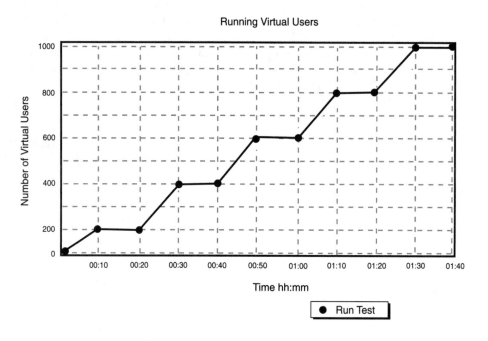

Assignment I Load Test Scenario

Identify the flaws and the completeness of the Yukon load test scenario. Redesign the scenario if incorrect, and add any new testing requirements that need to be added for a complete and efficient load testing for the peak of 1000 concurrent user sessions.

Answers to Assignment I for Load Test Scenario

The following are the flaws and additions for the load test scenario assignment:

1 Figure 8-4 has one major flaw—there is no control client to take performance measurements and access actual operation of the application.

2 Figure 8-5 shows that instead of 100 users at a time being added to the total virtual users on the way to 1000, 200 are being added at each step. This should be 100 at a time resulting in a slower ramp-up. This is important because if the users are ramped up too quickly, any failures could be anomalies.

3 The measurements that are going to be taken during the test should be mentioned: server performance monitors (OS-level), packet sniffer traces, and the measurements provided by the load test tool, such as transaction times and pass/fail status.

4 No mention is made of the transaction mix in the setup. This is a necessary element to the load testing design. In this case, exact information about the type of transactions or the mix is not available. There is, however, general information, so transaction types and a transaction mix will need to be created from this general information. Given the information in the scenario description, it would probably be good to test at least two transaction scenarios (there will usually be more) peaking at 1000 transactions at one time. The first is 80 percent browsing catalog pages and 20 percent buying. The second is 40 percent browsing catalog pages and 60 percent buying.

Changes Made to the Load Testing Scenario

After reviewing its load testing design with its CISS consultant, Yukon fixed the flaws and made the additions needed to have a solid and refillable test. Many measurements were taken and archived. The following figures show the results that Yukon used to diagnose the health of the system when the simultaneous usage reached 1000 users with the transaction type and mix being 40 percent browsing and 60 percent buying. When the system was tested at 1000 users with 80 percent browsing and 20 percent buying, all nonfunctional requirements were met successfully.

Assignment II of the Load Testing Scenario

Figures 8-6 through 8-11 show test results from just a small slice of time after the ramp-up to 1000 users was completed. Analyze these test results and document that the system meets the nonfunctional requirements for peak usage and maximum transaction response time. Also, document which testing tool (server performance tool, sniffer, or load test tool) most likely collected the data shown in each figure.

Figure 8-6   *Web Server CPU Utilization*

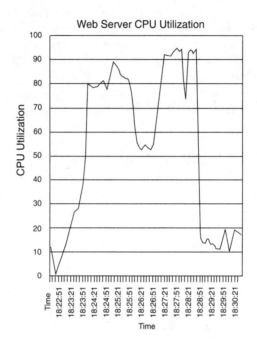

Figure 8-7   *Web Server Connections Per Second*

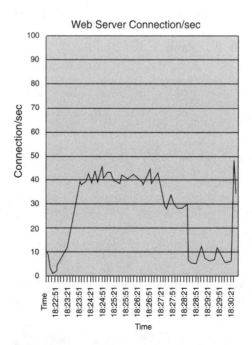

Figure 8-8   *Application Server Requests*

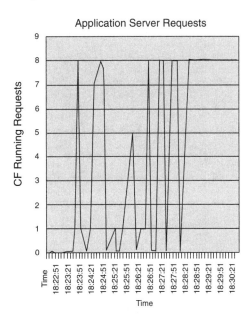

Figure 8-9   *Database Server Total CPU Utilization*

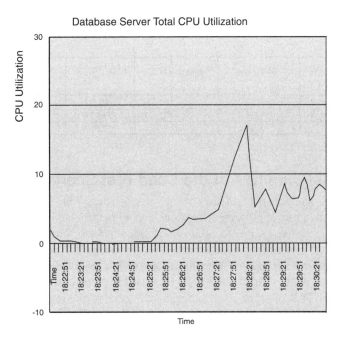

Figure 8-10 *Database Server Total Interrupts Per Second*

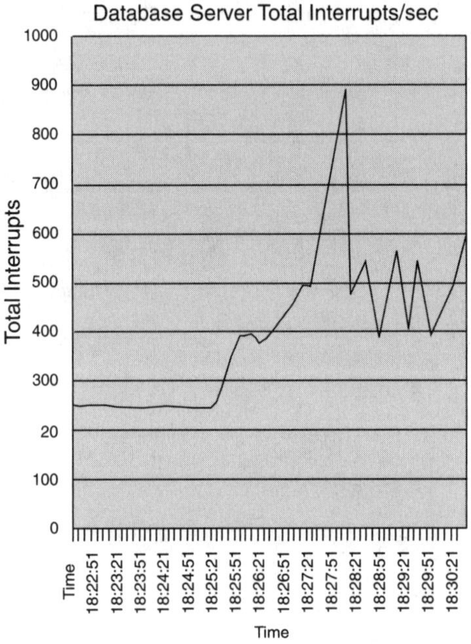

Database Server Total Interrupts/sec

Figure 8-11 *Control Client Performance*

Client Test Run	Duration (sec.)	Frames	Bytes	Avg. Frame	App. Turns	Time Captured
1000 Users_1	1.19	49	31,668	646.29	7	18:26:18
1000 Users_2	24.98	53	31,912	602.11	7	18:27:34
1000 Users_3	0.01	5	1251	250.2	2	18:30:18

Answers to Assignment II of the Load Test Scenario

Figures 8-6 through 8-11 do show a problem when the system is processing 1000 users with a transaction mix of 60 percent browsing and 40 percent buying. The "buy" transaction causes the database server to get involved more than the "browsing" transaction. The "browsing" transaction impacts the web server and application server (dynamic content) but not the database server. Therefore, the problem observed did not show up until the percentage of "buy" transactions was increased to 60 percent.

The following is the analysis that Yukon and its CISS consultant went through to diagnose the problem and to propose a fix:

1   Figure 8-6 shows that CPU Utilization is very high on the web server and then drops off suddenly—90 percent or more. A server performance tool most likely collected the data shown in Figure 8-6.

2   Figure 8-7 shows that the connections per second on the web server average about 40 connections per second, and then the connections drop suddenly at the same time that the CPU utilization dropped for this server. At this point the system is having problems accepting any new connections. A server performance tool most likely collected the data shown in Figure 8-7.

3   Figure 8-8 shows at about the same time that no new connections are being accepted. The application server is at its maximum of eight requests and the requests are not being served. These are requests to the database server. A server performance tool most likely collected the data shown in Figure 8-8.

4   Figures 8-9 and 8-10 show database server activity. The database CPU load is not too high, though it does go up at the time when the web server connections are dropping. The database interrupts per second were the highest just prior to the web server connections dropping. This could suggest that the database is not able to process the requests from the application server in a timely manner, and that is causing the system to reject any new requests requiring attention ("buy" transactions). A server performance tool most likely collected the data shown in Figures 8-9 and 8-10.

5   Figure 8-11 shows the control client's performance in executing a "buy" transaction at various times during the 1000 simultaneous users browsing and buying. This shows that prior to the connections starting to drop on the web server (18:26:18), the transaction time is below the nonfunctional requirement of 2 seconds—1.19 seconds. As the connections start to drop, the same transaction now takes 24.98 seconds—way beyond the nonfunctional requirement of 2 seconds. When the transaction is attempted during the time that the application server requests are at the maximum of 8 (18:30:18), the "buy" transaction connection is refused. This is determined by looking at the duration (0.1 seconds), frames (5) and bytes (1251) for this control client test (1000 Users_3). The control client's user observed that during this particular test an error was returned from the web server ("The Server Encountered an Error") instead of the "buy" transaction page. This is why the duration, frames, and byte count changed. A sniffer most likely collected the data shown in Figure 8-11.

The conclusion from this analysis is that the current configuration of the new online Yukon system does not support 1000 users with the transaction mix of 40 percent browsing and 60 percent buying. The fixes to these issues are not so easy to come up with. From the data collected and the analysis done, this could either be a web server/application server issue or a database issue. The data shown seems to point to the database not processing the application server requests quickly enough, causing the application server's request queue to max out, and the web server starts to drop connections. The CISS consultant and Yukon need to seek DBA help, as well as help from the web server's vendor and application server software's vendor.

The other issue to consider is whether the transaction mix was matched to reality. Sixty percent of the connected users buying at one time might not be a realistic assumption. Because the system behaved well when only 20 percent of the 1000 connected users were buying, maybe another test should be run with 40 percent of the connected users buying instead of 60 percent. If the system behaves well under this new scenario, Yukon would have valuable information about the "edge" of their system configurations and could decide if it wants to work further to analyze the failure at 60 percent or hope that a failure will never really happen.

Analyzing web server and application server log files after launch will reveal what the actual buy/browse mixture is. Take care to measure weekday versus weekend days, as the mixture might change significantly depending on the day of the week. The CISS consultant's job is to help Yukon with these tough decisions going forward.

Security Test Scenario

Security testing was performed in the following three areas: systems and network, applications, and operations.

Systems and Network

Security (nonfunctional) requirements:

- Hosts/servers must support established password management requirements; that is, passwords must be at least six characters, must not be the same as the six previous passwords, should contain a combination of letters, numerals, and possibly nonstandard characters like symbols, and must expire every 45 days.

- Assure the application's availability by preventing known Denial of Service (DoS) attacks.

A comprehensive series of security vulnerability testing activities were conducted on the hosts/servers and the network using scanning and probing security tools with the most recent vulnerability profiles. A few high-risk vulnerabilities were reported on the firewall located between the web server and the application server:

- Password never expires.
- Minimum password length is four.
- Do not keep password history.
- Successful logon to Administrator account with default password.
- Successful chargen (character generator service) DoS attack on Firewall Server XYZ.

Applications

Security (nonfunctional) requirement:

- Ensure that customers can only log in to the application after they have successfully registered for access. Customers can only access their own personal data and not data belonging to other customers. Each customer can only be assigned one unique User ID in the system.

Test scripts were created as follows:

- After successfully completing the registration process, attempt to create and log in with customer ID and password. Use a list of test customer IDs with unique registration data for each customer. Ensure that each test customer successfully completes the registration process and is able to create and log in with a test customer ID.
- After logging in with each customer ID, view or change personal data. Use the same list of test customer IDs.

Operations

Security (nonfunctional) requirement:

- Ensure that only personnel responsible for the application's system administration have physical access to the application hosts/servers.

Test procedures:

- Review and ensure that application hosts/servers are located in a secured area. (Entry points are secured under some form of lock and key.)
- Review the list of authorized personnel who require physical access to the application hosts/servers. Ensure that each has been granted the ability to access the secured area.

Assignment for Security Test Scenario

Execute the following tasks:

1 Based on the vulnerabilities reported, advise on corrective actions to take, or how to determine corrective actions.

2 Identify omissions/flaws in test scripts based on defined access control requirements for customers. Suggest improvements and explain how those improvements add value to the tests.

3 Identify omissions/flaws in test procedures based on defined physical access requirements. Suggest improvements and explain how those improvements add value to the tests.

Answers to Assignment for the Security Test Scenario

1 Make the following changes:

- Password expires every 45 days.

- Minimum password length is six and should contain a combination of letters, numerals, and possibly nonstandard characters like symbols.

- Keep password history for previous six passwords.

- Successfully log on to the Administrator account with a default password. Research security best practice (might find recommended actions in security tools or seek input from security experts). Depending on the operating system, corrective actions can range from assigning the Administrator account a strong password (eight characters with a combination of letters and numbers), to renaming and disabling/locking-out the Administrator account. For accountability purposes, each person responsible for system administration should be issued a personal account with the required administration privileges. Best practice security recommends that administrator accounts be accessed using encrypted logins, so that account information is not passed over internal or external networks in clear text. Remote access protocols, such as telnet and FTP, do not use encrypted login and should be replaced with secure shell (ssh) and secure copy (scp). Using encrypted logins for normal user accounts is advisable, as well, if possible.

- Successful chargen DoS attack on Firewall Server XYZ. The security tool used to identify this vulnerability should have some recommended corrective actions. If not, enlist the help of a security expert. The corrective actions can include disabling the chargen service, or applying a security patch to the known chargen vulnerability.

2 The test scripts did not test for assurance that each customer can only be assigned one unique customer ID. The first test script should have included an iteration of registering an existing customer with the same registration data. This iteration should have failed, notifying the customer that he already has an existing customer ID. Additionally, the first test script only checks for successfully completed registrations—it did not check for the results of erroneous registration attempts.

Test scripts should include erroneous registration attempts to verify that error handling routines are being properly invoked to prevent any security exposures in the application. The second test script makes no mention of performing a second iteration to ensure that any changes made in the first iteration were actually completed accurately for each customer. A step to verify the entered data, through a second iteration, would assure that changes were being made to the correct customer records.

3 The test procedures did not preclude the fact that personnel responsible for supporting other systems might have authorized access to the same secured area. The test should have included a review of all personnel who were authorized to access that secured area. Subsequently, a risk assessment would determine whether it was acceptable for the other personnel to have access to the target systems, or if the target systems should be further isolated in the same secured area or in an entirely different secured location.

Case Study 5: Supply Chain Management

The activities in this case study relate to the examination of a recently implemented network management strategy. Such an examination occurs in the maintenance phase of the solutions development lifecycle. The maintenance phase's purpose is to examine and modify the new system to sustain its operational capabilities and support the operation of the network management system installed during the implementation phase. If the analysis of the new system reveals that major changes must be made, these changes are not made in the maintenance phase. The maintenance phase does not redesign the system but does supply, as a major output, recommendations for change based on the continuing observation of system performance. These changes are made in the development phase, or, if changes are significant, they begin in the analysis and design phase. The CISS might be responsible for performing the following activities in the maintenance phase:

- Monitor system performance in accordance with an SLA.
- Verify that there are processes established to support maintenance of systems in production.
- Ensure that a tracking and reporting process is established to communicate production issues.
- Ensure that a continuous improvement process is established.

Objectives for Supply Chain Management

The objectives include the following:

- Identify potential gaps in a proposed network management strategy and suggest corrective actions.
- Identify the flaws that might have occurred while deploying the Intrusion Detection System (IDS).
- Explain how the appropriate deployment of the IDS should have occurred, and why the appropriate IDS deployment could have prevented a particular security incident.

Scenario for Supply Chain Management

XYZ Company has implemented a new, Internet-based supply chain management, as illustrated in Figure 8-12. The XYZ Company expects to reduce inventory and cut operational costs by using the supply chain management software with current and future vendors. Some of the current supply chain vendors make use of Internet-based tools, and their adoption of the new XYZ software tools will be fairly rapid and painless. For some, however, the supply chain change is going to present a problem. The company has created a network management strategy hoping that the network needs of all supply chain partners will be met to everyone's satisfaction.

Figure 8-12 *Supply Chain Management Network Diagram*

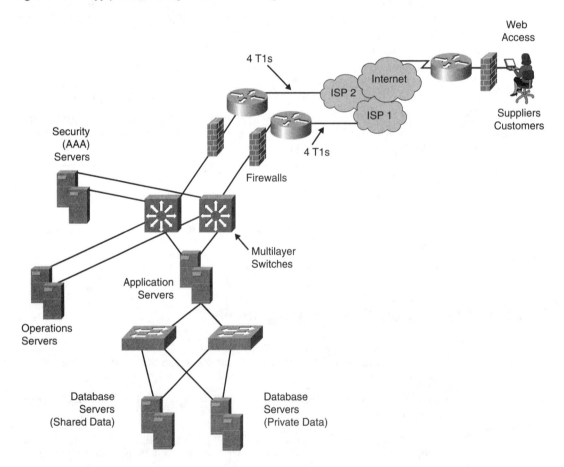

Assignment I for Supply Chain Management

Identify potential gaps in the Proposed Network Management Plan for XYZ Company and suggest corrective measures according to the following guidelines:

- Performance monitoring

  1 Capture statistics on an hourly basis.

  2 Examine the statistics weekly to determine problem areas and identify potential bottlenecks before they occur.

  3 Monitor the following servers:
     - Application servers
     - Database servers
     - Network management servers
     - Security server

  4 Monitor the following links:
     - Servers to switches
     - Switches to routers

  5 Monitor the following network devices:
     - Switches
     - Routers
     - Firewalls

- Fault management

  1 Capture all fault events in the log.

  2 Set the alarm to Network Operations Console (pager alerts to network personnel) on critical faults.

  3 Monitor links

  4 Monitor the following network devices:
     - Switches
     - Routers
     - Firewalls

  5 Monitor the following security device:
     - Firewalls

  6 Monitor the following servers:
     - Application servers
     - Data servers

- Security management

    1 Capture security breaches on logs.

    2 Examine logs on a weekly basis to identify and correct problems.

    3 Monitor external links.

    4 Monitor internal links.

    5 Monitor the following servers:

    — Application servers

    — Database servers (shared and private data servers)

- Accounting management

    1 Capture usage statistics by user and department.

    2 Capture usage statistics by using an external entity (company).

    3 Summarize and report weekly to finance so that departments and external entities can be charged (or notified), as appropriate

Answers to Assignment I for Supply Chain Management

The information obtained through network management must be examined more frequently than once a week. Overall, the gaps are very weak to be examining data on a weekly basis. The only place where problems are detected and alarmed is fault management. (This should also exist for performance and security management.)

A gap in performance could indicate that the NMS is not monitoring external links to Internet service providers (ISPs), only internal links between switches and routers. Setting up a monitoring policy to actively monitor the links to the two ISPs, reporting on performance, and alarming when an overutilization threshold is reached for a link, can rectify this problem.

A security gap could indicate that the NMS might not detect a security breach until a week after it occurs (issuing a warning after the horses have already escaped from the barn).

The proposed network diagram in Figure 8-12 does not make use of the "demilitarized zone (DMZ) by deploying firewalls not only after the Internet-accessible routers, but also in front of the application, database, and security servers. The DMZ is a neutral zone that affords an extra layer of security in the event that the front-line servers are compromised, making exposure of sensitive data by intruders more difficult.

Several things can be done to rectify this problem:

- Set up intrusion detection to actively search for security breaches.

- Monitor other security facilities, such as AAA server.

- Set up alarms for critical security breaches.
- Set up additional firewalls to create a DMZ.

A gap might indicate that some devices, in general, are not being monitored. (These devices might include operations servers, security server, and AAA servers). A fix is to set up monitoring on identified devices, such as operations servers, security server, AAA servers, and so on.

The Configuration Management area of network management is not included. It should contain the following parts:

- Maintain component configurations on operations servers.
- Maintain network device configurations.
- Maintain server configurations.
- Maintain line configurations.

Assignment II for Supply Chain Management

Given a set of problem events related to network management, identify where you think the problems could be and what you believe might have happened. Explain how the problem could be resolved.

- **Event 1**—A user complains that customer MMM successfully queried a private inventory database. Where and what happened?
- **Event 2**—Suppliers complain about excessive wait times for queries in shared databases. Where and why?
- **Event 3**—Someone hacked into the private database from outside the company. Where and why?
- **Event 4**—Excessive wait times exist for clients to update shared databases. Where and why?

Answers to Assignment II for Supply Chain Management

- Observations related to Event 1:
  - The Security (AAA) server is not set up correctly. Perhaps external users are blocked from changing private data, but not from viewing the private data.
  - The Security (AAA) server has no alarms set. Maybe the action was recorded in the log, but no one looked at the log, and no one will look at the log until the log's weekly review time arrives.
  - The application-level security on the server is not set up correctly.

- — The database security is not set up correctly. The user views are not correctly allowing customer entry.

- — There is no firewall on the link between switches and private database servers.

- Resolution to Event 1:

  - — Check security on the security server and make certain external users are not allowed ANY type of access to private data.

  - — Check security logs to see if a breach was recorded. If a breach has been recorded, set up alarms on the server so that when a breach occurs again, the correct people are immediately notified.

  - — Check the application security setting. Does the server block nonusers from viewing company private data? Is any security set up on the applications? If there is no security set up on the applications, set it up, and use an additional security layer, such as placing a firewall between the switches and the private database servers.

  - — Check the database security settings. Is private data protected from any type of access from an outside user? Correct the settings.

  - — Add a firewall between the switches for the private database servers. This will deny access to anyone without an internal network ID.

- Observations related to Event 2:

  - — Excessive wait times are taking place at the shared database servers. Further monitoring shows that the shared database servers are not overloaded. The problem could still be inefficient database design, the lack of sufficient indices, improper configuration of the application server, and so on, that make data access slow. Perhaps there are bottlenecks in the database design at which all users must queue, waiting for a single database resource.

  - — Excessive wait times are taking place at the router to Internet connection. If further monitoring shows that utilization of the router connecting to the Internet is acceptable (55 percent), the problem cannot be the router.

  - — Excessive wait times are taking place at the switch to the shared database servers. If further monitoring shows that utilization of the switch connecting to the database servers is acceptable (55 percent), the problem is not the switch.

  - — Excessive wait times are taking place at the links to the Internet through the ISP. These links are not being monitored (gap in NM plan). Checking these links shows that the links are over utilized, and are causing a bandwidth problem, four T1 links each.

- Resolution to Event 2:

  — Redesign the database.

  — Increase the links to the Internet to a T3 link each to improve bandwidth (pays to go to T3 after six T1s).

- Observations related to Event 3:

  — The firewall is not set up correctly. An intruder gains entrance by masquerading as another user using a hacked password.

- Resolution to Event 3:

  — Set up the firewall (or firewalls in the case of a DMZ architecture) correctly. Ensure that only the application servers are allowed to make connections to the database servers. Make sure that only encrypted login is used for user accounts and administrator accounts. Add an IDS and use one-time passwords (OTP), such as SecurID and CryptoCard. (The intruder could have masqueraded as another user to gain initial access.)

- Observations related to Event 4:

  — The shared servers are overloaded. If monitoring shows that the shared servers are not overloaded (65 percent busy), the links between the servers and the switches could be the culprit. If many collisions show in the logs, 100 MB link to servers has too much contention.

- Resolution to Event 4:

  — High-end UNIX servers can provide 300 MB output, but have half-duplex Network Interface Cards (NICs).

  — Upgrade the servers to full-duplex NICs to get rid of collisions.

Security Exercise Scenario for Supply Chain Management

To ensure that the new supply chain management (SCM) system is not threatened by intrusions, the requirement to deploy the host-based and network-based IDS was included in the network management implementation.

Approximately six months after the host-based and network-based IDS were deployed, an incident occurred involving a successful Distributed Denial of Service (DDoS) attack launched from the SCM server and several other servers. As a result, the SCM server was down for three days. This sparked an immediate investigation on both the IDS platforms. The investigation revealed that the host-based IDS logs contained one-week old alarms, which indicated that several critical files on the SCM server were tampered with. Unfortunately, no apparent actions were taken in response to the alarms as they occurred. Furthermore, the launch occurred through a vulnerable segment of the network that did not have an IDS sensor installed.

Assignment for Security in Supply Chain Management

From a design and operational support perspective (IDS and incident response policies, procedures, personnel roles, and responsibilities), identify the flaws that might have occurred during the IDS deployment. Explain how the appropriate deployment of the IDS should have occurred, and why that could have prevented the incident.

Answers to Assignment on Security for Supply Chain Management

No incident response policies or procedures were defined. Incident response personnel roles and responsibilities were either nonexistent or unclear. If incident response personnel roles and responsibilities did exist, they were not being enforced. The network-based IDS's design was not thorough enough, because an exposure in one of the vulnerable network segments occurred in a location with no IDS sensor installed.

When designing the IDS, the incident response handling policies and procedures should be clearly defined. These policies and procedures should include an enforceable incident notification process and a clear description of the designated personnel's roles and responsibilities. This would have ensured that someone received the alarm when it occurred, and that the appropriate action was taken to prevent the DDoS from spreading to other servers and from being successfully launched. Further, the installation of an IDS sensor on the vulnerable segment of the network could have detected the DDoS behavior as it was being launched, and immediately sent alarms to stop the activities before it was too late.

Summary

These case studies only begin to introduce the kinds of situations requiring the knowledge and techniques of a CISS. Search the Internet for more examples of case studies, and to try to understand how application essentials presented in this study guide would apply to those situations. More important than the details of each case study is the approach to problem solving, and applying best practices to customer projects and applications. In analyzing the case study scenarios, there are generally several correct responses or options to pursue. In the end, your ability to understand the implications of various "correct" options will make a your contribution to a project increasingly valuable.

CISS Exams

CHAPTER 9

CISS Applications Essentials Sample Exam Questions

This chapter offers sample exam questions like those found on the CISS Applications Essentials certification examination. The test questions in this chapter are intended to help you prepare for the exam by becoming familiar with the test format and the level of detail required to master each of the topics that the exam covers. The questions focus on the course content for CISS Applications Essentials. The answers to these questions are in Appendix B.

Courses 1 and 2, "Architecture Essentials" and "Applications Essentials," can be taken interchangeably; they are not sequential. If you have an experienced background in architecture or applications, you may choose to take the exam for Course 1 and/or Course 2 to qualify to take only Course 3, the "Solutions" course. The Solutions course is a required course.

Exam Description

The Cisco Internet Solutions Specialist Applications Essentials exam is the second of three exams that lead to a Cisco Internet Solutions Specialist designation.

As of this writing, the CISS Applications Essentials exam has the following characteristics and features:

- Exam Number: 9E0-801
- Associated Certifications: Cisco Internet Solutions Specialist
- Duration: 90 Minutes (60–70 questions)
- Languages Available: English

Exam Topics

The topics for this exam match the topics covered in the recommended training, Cisco Internet Solutions Specialist — Applications Essentials. However, other related topics may also appear on any specific delivery of the exam. Note the following topics:

- Application architecture concepts
- Application concepts
- Application design and development
- Application factors to consider
- Sourcing models
- Internet-based business initiatives
- Application and system management

Sample Exam Questions

1 In a distributed application architecture, the web browser participates in which tier?

   a. Business logic

   b. Data source

   c. Presentation

   d. Distributed

2 A logical layer of a distributed system that represents a computer running a DBMS is the _____ tier.

   a. Data source

   b. Middle

   c. Client

   d. Security

3 Companies searching to stay competitive develop a distributed application in order to take advantage of _____ .

   a. Less expensive labor

   b. Scalability

   c. Feasibility

   d. Centralization

4 Middleware addresses the needs of the networked enterprise to create, integrate, and manage large-scale, distributed applications in _____ environments.

   a. Heterogeneous

   b. Homogenous

   c. Scripted

   d. Development

5 With a client/server application architecture, the server _____ .

   a. Brokers and queues messages from other servers

   b. Is customized by client service requests

   c. Supplies requested services to peers

   d. Supplies requested services to clients

6 _____ architecture allows organizations to modify business rules without changing the whole system.

   a. Client/server

   b. Peer-to-peer

   c. Client-to-peer

   d. Peer/server

7 In a "thick" client/server environment, a majority of the application processing occurs on the _____ .

   a. Client side

   b. Server side

   c. Database backend

   d. Web frontend

8 Which of the following is not a benefit of client/server application architecture?

   a. Client/server architecture is aligned with both the user view and the business process view.

   b. A change to the GUI does not require any changes to the other layers.

   c. Developers create components that can be reused in other applications.

   d. In general, client/server applications are less expensive to develop and implement.

9 In a typical web application, business logic should be performed by which of the following scripts?

   a. Client

   b. Server

   c. Backup

   d. Monitoring

10 JSPs are not usually run on _____ servers.

   a. Search

   b. Web

   c. Database

   d. Application

11 The three common transaction models are _____ .

   a. Flat, nested, and chained

   b. Atomic, one-way, and two-way

   c. Required, core, and context

   d. On-demand, batch, and synchronous

12 Which one of the following is not used to ensure transaction integrity?

   a. Triggers

   b. Rollbacks

   c. Journaling

   d. Access control

13 Three common types of application transactions are _____ .

   a. Electronic, printed, and pending

   b. Limited, guaranteed, and unlimited

   c. Lookup, update, and add

   d. Serial, parallel, and threaded

14 In the commit phase of a distributed transaction, which of the following is true?

   a. Not all nodes need to respond to the coordinator that they are prepared to commit.

   b. Only nodes that cannot commit are asked to rollback the transaction.

    c. Individual nodes do not have to wait until changes are committed on the other nodes.

    d. The initiating node asks all nodes to commit the transaction simultaneously.

15 Which of the following is not a type of database?

    a. Clustered

    b. Hierarchical

    c. Object-oriented

    d. Networked

16 The components of an SQL database are _____ .

    a. Data elements, rows, and columns

    b. Screens, tables, and views

    c. Schemas, tables, and views

    d. Selects, joins, and deletes

17 The Unified Modeling Language (UML) has become an industry standard because _____ .

    a. It joins the concepts of Booch, the Object Modeling Technique, Object-Oriented Software Engineering, and other methods.

    b. It makes a strong break with previous practices for object-oriented modeling languages.

    c. It does not attempt to make a common language for modeling large and complex systems.

    d. It synthesizes data collection, data distribution, and data warehousing.

18 A green thread is implemented by the Java runtime system itself, while a native thread is specific to the underlying operating system. Which of the following statements is false?

    a. Green threads must be trapped to prevent I/O from suspending.

    b. Green threads take advantage of built-in operating support.

    c. Native threads are less safe because anything is likely to happen.

    d. Native threads depend on a good implementation of threading in the underlying operating system.

19 Hardware drivers are responsible for _____ .

    a. Device naming and mapping symbolic device names onto the proper drivers

    b. Keeping users from accessing devices they are not supposed to access

    c. Providing read and write buffers so that data is written in blocks

    d. All of the above

20 Which definition states the main function of the Basic Lifecycle Model?

    a. The Basic Lifecycle Model provides decision makers with a guide to creating structured project documentation.

    b. The Basic Lifecycle Model defines the order in which a project specifies, implements, tests, and performs its activities.

    c. The Basic Lifecycle Model determines the mean time before failure (MTBF) for system components.

    d. The Basic Lifecycle Model defines the testing methods generally acknowledged as best practices.

21 When do web-based projects benefit from adopting a lifecycle model?

    a. When business decision makers and application specialists can capture, organize, and visualize the application as if it were functioning within their business

    b. When the business model remains constant throughout the entire project lifecycle so that subsequent outputs do not affect the model

    c. When the project can avoid selecting a tangible structure for the business model until potential damage is assessed

    d. When a business need demonstrates a projected loss for the product or service

22 An application with small gain opportunity but very high feasibility _____ to be accepted.

    a. Has great potential

    b. Requires strategic advice

    c. Meets the minimum requirements

    d. Has little potential

23 A relevant baseline _____ .

    a. Is not part of the business model outputs

    b. Can be taken from comparisons with government-owned applications

    c. May be derived either from current company performance in acquiring an application or from similar business organizations in the industry

    d. Does not have to list the criteria against which to compare application performance

24 Which of the following specifications is not included in the analysis and design phase?

   a. System

   b. Testing

   c. Networking

   d. Database

25 The main focus of the analysis and design phase should be to concentrate on _____ .

   a. Providing a complete specification of every application detail

   b. Gathering more information about the application specification designated in the business model

   c. Finding the basic features needed by the application in order to achieve minimal functionality

   d. Determining which application tests can be run before the test phase has begun

26 The purpose of the development phase is to _____ .

   a. Translate the application system specification into an application installation package

   b. Reshape customer desires into already existing application packages

   c. Start a fresh cycle of analysis and design of customer requirements

   d. Provide a budget for training and conferences

27 The primary input to the development phase of the Basic Lifecycle Model is the system _____ .

   a. Test plan

   b. Operation manual

   c. Monitoring configuration

   d. Specification

28 Which of these would not be tested during the Test Phase?

   a. Maintenance procedures

   b. Application requirements

   c. Investor support

   d. Authentication

29 The Test Phase verifies which set of objectives?

  a. Hardware and software licensing and support agreements

  b. Content, structure, and interaction of operational mechanisms

  c. Adherence to standards and project programming style guides

  d. Content creation, distribution, and management

30 Formal written customer acceptance should be obtained in the _____ phase.

  a. Analysis and design

  b. Implementation

  c. Maintenance

  d. Test

31 Which of the following is not a distinct type of manual?

  a. Test

  b. System

  c. Program

  d. Data

32 The application maintenance team must monitor which of the following functions?

  a. Base lining, prototyping, and unit testing

  b. Business capabilities, model presentation, and identification of critical success factors

  c. Expense reporting, benefits administration, and other business-context processes

  d. Resource utilization, system security, and downtime

33 Upgrades to application capacity are performed _____ .

  a. After unplanned downtime occurs

  b. Only in a clustered environment

  c. During the maintenance phase

  d. Every two years

34 The _____ lifecycle model does not repeat any phase.

  a. prototype

  b. waterfall

  c. iterative

  d. spiral

35 Which is not a weakness of the Waterfall Lifecycle Model?

  a. The model provides a rigid structure that enforces a strict order of accomplishing phase objectives.

  b. The model has no feedback loops.

  c. Delay in one stage of the project results in delays in all the stages that follow.

  d. It needs all requirements to be stated by the customer in the initial phase.

36 Repeating the sequence of lifecycle phases until the desired application is achieved _____ .

  a. Is the definition of the Iterative Lifecycle Model

  b. Is the definition of the Waterfall Lifecycle Model

  c. Does not permit adding higher level functions during design and development

  d. Is a disorganized method for application development

37 The Rapid Application Development (RAD) Lifecycle Model is characterized by _____ .

  a. A series of evolving executable prototypes

  b. Modularized application system components

  c. The ability to schedule unlimited change requests

  d. A compromise in quality and completeness of the end product in exchange for quick delivery on a tight schedule

38 The lifecycle model that boasts a low error rate is the _____ model.

  a. Spiral

  b. Rapid Application Development (RAD)

  c. Clean Room

  d. Prototype

39 Which lifecycle model consists of four steps: plan, design, review, and assess risk?

  a. Prototype

  b. Spiral

  c. Linear Sequential

  d. Waterfall

40 Which one of the following is not a common security technology enabling web-based applications?

   a. Biometric Authentication System (BAS)

   b. Secure Sockets Layer (SSL) encryption

   c. Public Key Infrastructure (PKI)

   d. Virtual Private Networks (VPNs)

41 Site _____ increases availability by means of a replica of an existing site.

   a. Indexing

   b. Updating

   c. Mirroring

   d. Striping

42 Which one of the following is not a high-availability technology?

   a. Hot swappable CPU

   b. Server clustering

   c. Small Computer Integrated Services (SCSI) drives

   d. RAID 5 disk array

43 A Service Level Agreement (SLA) defines _____ .

   a. Health, availability, and accountability assurances for service provider services

   b. Third-party review of backup procedures

   c. Price checks and balances for service provider services

   d. Supply chain management system requirements

44 Storage Area Networks (SANs) are increasingly popular because _____ .

   a. RAID arrays cannot use redundant power supplies.

   b. Campus-wide distances are too great for peripheral channels to handle.

   c. They are connected exclusively through fiber channels.

   d. Large amounts of data are shared using peripheral channels instead of overburdened networks.

45 Software is, on average, becoming _____ as software applications grow in complexity and size.

   a. Less reliable

   b. More reliable

   c. Less profitable

   d. More profitable

46 Which database design factors can affect an Internet business application's performance?

   a. Mixed uppercase and lowercase table names

   b. Indexing, normalization, and stored procedures

   c. Four or more accounts with administrative privileges

   d. Use of weak passwords with less than five characters

47 What percentage of a software applications budget is typically devoted to maintenance activity over the life of the software?

   a. 20 to 40 percent

   b. 40 to 70 percent

   c. 5 to 20 percent

   d. 5 to 10 percent

48 Network management is concerned with all the following except _____.

   a. Collecting system usage statistics and generating reports

   b. Updating network management, application configurations documentation

   c. Implementing and maintaining database security

   d. Controlling network management system configurations

49 In an application integration strategy, _____ is concerned with enabling data to be consolidated from a variety of disparate data sources into a single view.

   a. Database middleware

   b. Conceptual data modeling

   c. Object-oriented design

   d. Centralized computing

50 Enterprise Resource Planning (ERP) is defined as _____ .

    a. Using mainly proprietary software tools instead of packaged software within an enterprise

    b. An information system dedicated for use with human resources departments

    c. Any resource planning software that uses Enterprise JavaBeans (EJB)

    d. An integrated information system that serves all departments within an enterprise

51 What is the major disadvantage of using an insourcing model for implementing a business application?

    a. The company may be the only provider in a core business area.

    b. The company must acquire and maintain the personnel expertise and equipment required for the application.

    c. Senior management is relieved of delivery accountability.

    d. The company will retain control over the project implementation.

52 Under the _____ model, companies developing a new business application undergo a heightened risk of the application solution becoming obsolete before they realize the anticipated return on investment.

    a. insourcing

    b. outsourcing

    c. ASP

    d. MSP

53 A project that pursues outsourcing an application to a service provider gains all of the following benefits except _____ .

    a. Time to market

    b. Application cost reduction

    c. Retaining full control

    d. Technology leveraging

54 When outsourcing business-context processes, data encryption should be employed for sensitive customer information _____ .

    a. Only if required by the service provider

    b. Just for remotely accessed services

    c. Prior to a security audit

    d. Always

55 An ASP's ability to continuously increase or decrease capacity to accommodate growth is known as _____ .

    a. Short-term use

    b. Availability

    c. Scalability

    d. Customization

56 A disadvantage to the ASP outsourcing model is that _____ .

    a. The ASP may decide to merge with another company that could lead to leasing a business application from a direct competitor.

    b. The ASP has a greater probability of successfully implementing an application based on standard applications.

    c. The ASP may provide multiple firewalls and data encryption so the customer data is isolated.

    d. By spreading equipment, software, and expertise expenses over many users, the ASP can readily customize applications to suit customer needs.

57 Which sourcing model could best be adapted to high levels of application customization?

    a. Outsourcing

    b. Insourcing

    c. Application service provider

    d. In-line sourcing

58 The advantage of avoiding large up-front costs associated with developing an application is known as _____ .

    a. Total cost of ownership (TCO)

    b. Time-to-money ratio

    c. Rapid application development (RAD)

    d. The cost of money

59 Which is the first stage in the Internet-based customer care lifecycle?

    a. Target.

    b. Acquire.

    c. Transact.

    d. None of the above; the stages are simultaneous.

60 Which of the following is not an example of a workforce optimization initiative?

   a. Web-based time reporting tools

   b. Self-service expense report application

   c. Inventory leveling

   d. On-demand training materials

61 A workforce optimization system should be designed to have sufficient storage and processing power to handle _____ .

   a. The current user load

   b. The current user load and the load over the next two years

   c. Twice the current user load

   d. 110 percent of the current user load

62 A Supply Chain Management program encompasses all the following except _____ .

   a. Customer service

   b. Content versioning

   c. Inventory reduction

   d. Improved demand forecasting

63 An Internet-driven Supply Chain Management system groups customers by _____ .

   a. Industry

   b. Product

   c. Need

   d. Trade channel

64 Which of the following is not true of e-learning tools?

   a. Learners are free to study at their own pace.

   b. Lack of accountability is a disadvantage of e-learning systems.

   c. Developers of e-learning tools may receive immediate feedback to improve the curriculum.

   d. Organizations can track learner performance.

65 An e-publishing solution addresses which of the following areas?

    a. Content creation

    b. Content management

    c. Content delivery

    d. All of the above

66 Devices are _____ for information in system management applications such as SNMP.

    a. Polled

    b. Peeked

    c. Poked

    d. Interrupted

67 Which area is not a key area of application performance management?

    a. Application response time

    b. Server processing time

    c. Application security

    d. Number of active sessions

68 Which networks benefit most from inventory management?

    a. Heterogeneous networks

    b. Distributed networks

    c. Large networks

    d. All of the above

69 Which set makes up the four categories of system management?

    a. Remote operation, security management, version control, and operational status

    b. Proactive, reactive, selective, and exclusive

    c. System monitoring, software distribution, inventory management, and user administration

    d. Requirements gathering, design, implementation, and maintenance

CHAPTER 10

CISS Solutions Sample Exam Questions

The Cisco Internet Solutions Specialist Solutions exam is the third of three exams required to achieve a Cisco Internet Solutions Specialist designation.

This chapter offers sample exam questions like those found on the CISS Solutions certification examination. The test questions in this chapter are intended to help you prepare for the exam by becoming familiar with the test format and the level of detail required to master each of the topics that the exam covers. The questions focus on the course content for CISS Solutions. The answers to these questions are in Appendix C.

Courses 1 and 2, "Architecture Essentials" and "Applications Essentials," can be taken interchangeably; they are not sequential. If you have an experienced background in architecture or applications, you can choose to take the exam for Course 1 or Course 2 and then take the required Course 3, the "Solutions" course.

Exam Description

As of this writing, the CISS Solutions exam has the following characteristics and features:

- Exam Number: 9E0-802
- Associated Certifications: Cisco Internet Solutions Specialist
- Duration: 120 Minutes (70–80 questions)
- Languages Available: English

Exam Topics

The topics for this exam match the topics covered in the recommended training, "Cisco Internet Solutions Specialist—Solutions" (other related topics might also appear on any specific delivery of the exam):

- Testing and validation
- Responsibilities of a CISS and tools that may be used in the basic software lifecycle model

Sample Exam Questions

1 The business modeling and requirements phase of the software development life cycle gathers _____ .

   a. Functional requirements and information

   b. Nonfunctional requirements and information

   c. Functional and nonfunctional requirements and information

   d. Packaged software and open source software information

2 Which statement correctly defines the purpose of the testing and validation phase of the Basic Life Cycle Model?

   a. Testing is the process of setting up and executing test scenarios in a controlled setting, and validation is the process of validating or confirming that the testing results meet certain business requirements.

   b. Testing is the process of identifying functional and non-functional requirements, and validation is the process of tracking software changes that contain business logic.

   c. Testing is the sequence of virtual user scripts executed in concurrent test scenarios, and validation is the process of confirming that the original business requirements have avoided scope creep.

   d. Testing is the sequence of all unit tests run against an application under development, and validation is the sequence of all unit tests run against an application after it has been deployed.

3 All of the following, except _____ testing, are common types of software testing.

   a. Application performance

   b. Security

   c. User load

   d. Hardness

4 The _____ phase has been consistently rated as the most important phase in the software development lifecycle.

   a. Testing and validation

   b. Analysis and design

   c. Maintenance

   d. Development

5 "Stress Testing" is also known as _____ testing.

   a. Application performance

   b. User load

   c. Hardness

   d. Security

6 A key characteristic of application performance testing is testing _____ .

   a. Multi-user response times

   b. Single-user response times

   c. Concurrent virtual user response times

   d. Application fault tolerance

7 Which of the following is a measure of application throughput?

   a. Branches per second

   b. Builds per second

   c. Bits per second

   d. Boxes per second

8 To ensure that an application performs as expected with real users, user load testing measures _____ .

   a. Server CPU use

   b. Server memory use

   c. Network packets per second

   d. All of the above

9 Which of the following is not a network component metric in availability testing?

   a. Router CPU use

   b. Load-balanced connections

   c. Image server caching

   d. Firewall memory use

10 Network implications of proposed user transactions are assessed by _____ .

   a. Determining where users are located, how many users are at each location, and how frequently users are expected to perform various transactions

   b. Gathering comprehensive requirements, understanding user learning styles, and the ratio of users to network printers

c. Data modeling, object-oriented application design, and various Java class transaction properties

d. Initial "best guess" estimates, cross-office collaboration tools, and careful transaction prototyping

11 Which answer lists the four-step application performance testing process in the correct order?

a. Application assessment, development environment setup, data collection for transactions, and testing results analysis

b. Development environment setup, test environment setup, data collection, and testing results analysis

c. Control client setup, data collection, data translation, and results analysis

d. Application assessment, test environment setup, data collection, and results analysis

12 Which of the following is not a consideration during the application assessment process?

a. How the application will be deployed to users and servers

b. Software licensing model options and cost-per-seat calculations

c. Transactions representative of how the application will be used

d. Effects on existing traffic flows in the application network environment

13 An application test environment component that inserts delays to simulate network traffic is called a WAN _____ Simulator.

a. Network

b. Decay

c. Delay

d. Circuit

14 Application performance testing includes capturing data for _____ .

a. A network protocol, network addresses, and network port numbers

b. A network subnet, a network route, and a network mask

c. A top-level domain name, a second-level domain name, and a hostname

d. A horizontal refresh rate, a vertical refresh rate, and interleave settings

15 Which of the following best states the definition of how to calculate end-to-end response times?

  a. Add the process times for the client and servers.

  b. Add the process times for the client, servers, and network.

  c. Add the process times for the client and servers, and then subtract the network process times.

  d. Add the process times for the client and servers, and then divide by two.

16 Security testing of an Internet business solution involving outsourced service providers should involve _____ .

  a. Only service provider environments

  b. All systems and environments

  c. Only production systems and environments

  d. Only those systems and environments with sensitive information

17 Which step is not part of the simple four-step security architecture testing process?

  a. Perform iterative tests.

  b. Configure and enable the security systems.

  c. Coordinate the trusted domain relationships.

  d. Coordinate the installation of security systems.

18 The ultimate goal of security testing is to _____ .

  a. Protect information assets

  b. Make an application harder to use

  c. Determine customer account administration procedures

  d. Create functional security vulnerabilities

19 Which of the follows provides the comprehensive set of areas that must be validated and corrected in security testing?

  a. Systems, networks, and applications

  b. Policies, procedures, and access lists

  c. Identity, authorization, and nonrepudiation

  d. Operations, systems, networks, and applications

20 The number of simultaneous users predicted for peak usage is _____ if there are 2000 total users and 10 concurrent users.

    a. 20

    b. 200

    c. 2000

    d. 20,000

21 Which of the following is not a user load-testing tool?

    a. An intrusion-detection system

    b. WAN Delay Simulator

    c. A packet sniffer

    d. A control client

22 Software development load testing collects measurement data for _____ .

    a. Only successful transaction scenarios

    b. Only failed transaction scenarios

    c. Minimum, average, and maximum response times

    d. Minimum response times

23 A hits-per-second report evaluates the load placed by virtual users on the _____ .

    a. Control client

    b. Web server

    c. Database server

    d. Application server

24 Availability testing for an Internet business solution can best be defined as _____ .

    a. Testing where fault tolerant components are deliberately failed in a number of ways to verify reliability

    b. Testing where network components are deliberately failed in a number of ways to verify that the network architecture is secure

    c. Testing that deliberately fails components in a number of ways to verify that the designed level of availability is achieved

    d. Testing where virtual users follow deliberately failed test scenarios to verify that application transactions are sufficiently robust

25 Unplanned downtime is counted against the application availability requirements as outlined in _____ .

  a. The Service Level Agreement

  b. An availability test plan

  c. The development documentation

  d. An enterprise resource model

26 Which scenario is not a network connectivity failure?

  a. A cut LAN cable

  b. A loopback interface

  c. A dropped VPN connection

  d. A dead ISP circuit

27 A company has set an availability goal for their web-based e-learning system of 99.9 percent uptime. The goal has been met if the system is down for _____ per year.

  a. 12 hours

  b. 8 days

  c. 8 hours

  d. 600 minutes

28 Availability testing is built on the results of _____ testing.

  a. Security

  b. LAN-to-WAN

  c. White box

  d. Load

29 Availability test results analysis provides answers to which question?

  a. Does the redundant device take over for the failed device?

  b. Can the development environment communicate with the production environment?

  c. How many test-team members are required to verify test failures?

  d. Which software patches can be applied to the router?

30 In documenting testing and validation results, the test team must _____ .

   a. Diagram the test environment

   b. Describe the test methodology

   c. List the test objectives

   d. All of the above

31 Which of the following demonstrates the correct order of the steps in an application performance test process?

   a. Application assessment, test environment setup, data collection for transactions, and testing results analysis

   b. Application assessment, data collection for transactions, test environment setup, and testing results analysis

   c. Data collection for transactions, test environment setup, application assessment, and testing results analysis

   d. Test environment setup, application assessment, data collection for transactions, and testing results analysis

32 Security tests and documentation must address _____ .

   a. Network, systems, applications, and operations security results

   b. Minimum, average, and maximum transaction response times

   c. Mirroring, clustering, and multiprocessor application design

   d. Memory and CPU utilization with 1000 virtual users

33 Typical activities that a CISS might perform in an Internet business project would generally not include _____ .

   a. Project facilitation, project management, and project leadership

   b. Test-plan writing, plan implementation, and plan maintenance

   c. Marketing, communications, and advertising

   d. Application performance testing, security research, and operations documentation

34 The three major responsibilities of a CISS during the business modeling and requirements phase of the life cycle model are to _____ .

   a. Attend weekly project meetings, take meeting notes, and verify business hours of operation

   b. Keep requirements gathering focused, provide leadership, and validate completion of the phase

    c. Design the look and feel of user interface, provide color palette standards, and develop global navigation artwork

    d. Publish the project plan, track testing issues, and obtain sign-off from the client for the finished application

35 A CISS can use all the following business modeling and requirements tools on a project except _____ .

    a. Case models

    b. Packet sniffer

    c. Data flow diagrams

    d. Entity relationship diagrams

36 If requirements gathering is to remain focused on business, functional, and information models, a CISS must _____ .

    a. Interview stakeholders and telephone helpdesk support

    b. Communicate expectations, adopt client phrases of speech, and create opportunities for social interaction with team members

    c. Use Internet search engines, spell-check project correspondence, and assess the environmental impact of the business model

    d. Communicate the methodology, perform research, and quantify impact at a high level

37 Gathering system requirements includes all the following responsibilities except _____ .

    a. Assessing legal implications of trademarks and service marks

    b. Defining nonfunctional system requirements

    c. Defining system expectations

    d. Assessing the current system, processes, users, and tools

38 Which of the following is not a design constraint that might emerge from the requirements and modeling phase?

    a. Project code name

    b. Database resource limits

    c. Required security policies

    d. Implementation language

39 Being able to perform a walkthrough of _____ signifies the completion of the business modeling and requirements phase.

    a. Storyboard concepts, logo treatments, and narrative style

    b. Release procedures, services monitoring, and problem escalation

    c. The business model, functional requirements, and nonfunctional requirements

    d. Potential areas of reusability, the systems inventory database, and database recovery

40 Shadowing is _____ .

    a. A technique used for low-level data replication

    b. A technique used to gather information about project requirements

    c. The practice of making text and images appear three-dimensional

    d. The practice of making a virtual interface respond to requests

41 Throughout the analysis and design phase, a CISS is responsible for analyzing _____ .

    a. Disclosure requirements, developing a test plan, designing a prototype system, and designing a system architecture that satisfies business requirements

    b. Business requirements, developing a project management plan, designing a robust and maintainable system, and designing a system architecture that satisfies business requirements

    c. Funding sources, testing disaster recovery mechanisms, and reducing system functionality by 50 percent before development begins

    d. The profit margin, predicting project feasibility, identifying strategic partnerships, and generating a design document

42 A robust system is one that _____ .

    a. Performs single-user operations within normal conditions and parameters

    b. Performs multi-user operations, but locks up frequently

    c. Has thorough documentation and has been indexed recently

    d. Is thoroughly tested and has built-in safeguards against system failure

43 During the analysis and design phase, the process of validating the data flow diagrams, data modeling, and data dictionary is known as _____ .

    a. A major task in analyzing business requirements in relation to system architecture

    b. A technique for documenting hours in the project budget

    c. A technique for analyzing business concepts that are hard to visualize

    d. A major obstacle to starting the development phase

44 Data modeling tools provide database administrators with a means of _____ .

   a. Testing data models to discover errors or inefficiencies in database schema

   b. Exporting data from one database to another by converting each schema into a shared or common model

   c. Creating an application foundation by graphically depicting the organization of business processes and data requirements, and how they relate to each other

   d. Creating a functioning application by embedding commands and program code within a database

45 Which of the following is not an approach for implementing a software application?

   a. Phased

   b. Osmosis

   c. Parallel

   d. Immediate cut-over

46 Which of the following is generally not a characteristic of a maintainable system?

   a. Ad-hoc configuration settings

   b. Detailed documentation

   c. Modular design

   d. Change management process

47 Which of the following is not a technique that a CISS might apply in the analysis and design phase?

   a. Structured walkthrough

   b. Abstraction

   c. Code branching

   d. Project management software

48 A "proof of concept prototype" is commonly developed during the analysis and design phase to _____ .

   a. Boost morale and show initial evidence that the application will work as expected

   b. Test unknown or suspect areas; the prototype is discarded after the answers are obtained

   c. Test known areas of application functionality, as needed

   d. Build a set of nonreusable models to find the right solution

49 Which of the following is not a responsibility of a CISS during the implementation phase?

   a. Perform comprehensive implementation planning

   b. Gather comprehensive application requirements

   c. Verify that users will be trained on new functionality

   d. Document detailed installation procedures

50 As physical integration begins in the development phase, a CISS will contribute to the integration of architecture components by _____ .

   a. Verifying security policies

   b. Developing an upgrade schedule

   c. Reviewing the Service Level Agreement

   d. Sizing hardware

51 For projects in which a CISS works closely with the project manager, a collaboration to ensure adequate development resources might require _____ .

   a. Learning how to negotiate under pressure with customers and end users to achieve a realistic balance of schedule and functionality

   b. Learning about development methodologies that favor speed over rigor

   c. Contracting optional formal training early in the budget period

   d. Contracting outside developers to reduce total project costs

52 Software change control and version control systems are applicable to _____ .

   a. Configuration files

   b. Code updates

   c. Design specifications

   d. All of the above

53 Which of the following is not a responsibility of a CISS during the development phase?

   a. Determine hardware sizing requirements

   b. Define nonfunctional business requirements

   c. Verify that development resources are adequate

   d. Verify that change control process can handle code updates

54 Joint Application Development (JAD) is a structured development methodology typified by _____ .

    a. Analyzing and resolving any problems in the connection points or "joints" of a system before working on other defects

    b. Bringing users and developers together for intensive, highly productive, facilitated sessions to resolve the task at hand

    c. Bringing internal and external developers together to best determine which components can be subcontracted to external development teams

    d. Bringing internal and external developers together by introducing a structured correspondence through e-mail to document all discussions and ideas

55 A design document can become stale and inaccurate unless _____ .

    a. Each deliverable is developed and tested by a different person

    b. Informal conversations are encouraged to promote better collaboration

    c. Each deliverable is reviewed with a team walkthrough to ensure adherence to the stated design document criteria

    d. The document is maintained and edited outside of version control restrictions

56 _____ is designed to simulate a number of users or transactions and to demonstrate the system's performance.

    a. A test impact analyzer

    b. A test data generator

    c. Load testing software

    d. A WAN delay simulator

57 System component availability testing includes all the following except _____ .

    a. Operating system failure

    b. Cut LAN cable

    c. Application server power failure

    d. Database cluster node failure

58 A drawback to web-enabled workflow automation tools used during project development is based on the fact that _____ .

    a. Explanations and analyses of defects and metrics are not readily available to the customer

    b. Customers have to wait for project status updates

    c. Customers cannot observe design reviews

    d. Customers cannot track defects or critical problems

59 A test plan describes all of the following except _____ .

    a. Resources

    b. Test objectives

    c. Test environment constraints

    d. Project maintenance documentation

60 Which of the following is the correct definition of black box testing?

    a. Black box testing is testing that includes performance/availability, scalability, security, and disaster recovery.

    b. Black box testing is functional testing that includes reviewing the internal parts of the system based on the logic and calculations.

    c. Black box testing is testing systems behavior and performance under excessive demands and resource utilization.

    d. Black box testing is integration testing of a string of units that accomplish a specific function in the application.

61 _____ testing is the first stage in which all parts of the application are assembled and presented as a system.

    a. Regression

    b. Thread

    c. Availability

    d. Integration

62 System testing is largely dependent upon _____ .

    a. A four-step process that configures, enables, installs, and documents the system security architecture

    b. Verifying the accuracy of system installation and configuration documentation

    c. Identifying a comprehensive list of maintenance phase defects that need to be iteratively tested until resolved

    d. A balanced and realistic mixture of functionally diverse test scenarios

63 One of the final responsibilities of a CISS during the test phase is _____ .

    a. Creating a defect tracking system

    b. Creating a final test plan

   c. Gaining formal acceptance of the system by the customer

   d. Gaining formal acceptance of the requirements from the customer

64 Which of the following does not describe a responsibility that a CISS might have in the test phase?

   a. Perform verify testing

   b. Ensure test results are analyzed

   c. Develop a project management plan

   d. Confirm that the test plan will sufficiently test the system requirements

65 A test case records all of the following test attributes *except* _____ .

   a. Test objectives, test constraints, and test inputs

   b. Expected results, actual results, and results analysis

   c. Test constraints, entry criteria, and exit criteria

   d. Server memory utilization, server CPU utilization, and disk I/O performance metrics

66 Changes to application code can affect previously tested functionality. For this reason, testing groups often perform _____ testing throughout the test phase to verify that all known bugs are fixed and stay fixed.

   a. Regression

   b. Integration

   c. Backward

   d. Redundant

67 Processor architectures that support highly scalable applications are _____ .

   a. Parallel Server Instance (PSI) and Load Performance Guard (LPG)

   b. Symmetric Multiprocessing (SMP) and Massively Parallel Processing (MPP)

   c. Processor Group Awareness (PGA) and Conjoint-Gated Systems (CGS)

   d. Modular Memory Architecture (MMA) and Distributed Node Locking (DNL)

68 A test impact analyzer is a tool used during the software development life cycle that _____ .

   a. Automatically compares different versions of a file and reports on the differences

   b. Allows a project manager to track the resolution of problems and provide metrics on the progress of problem resolution

   c. Creates meaningful test data that meets given criteria

   d. Can gauge the impact of a code change before actually making the change

69 A responsibility of a CISS during the implementation phase of a project is to ensure that _____ .

   a. there is a back-out or contingency plan in place

   b. the project plan identifies project dependencies

   c. there is adequate documentation of project scope

   d. data flow diagrams are validated against the data model

70 An implementation benefit of a packaged version and controlled releases is that

   _____ .

   a. An installation is smaller in size than the source components, runs faster, and takes less time to test

   b. Each software application component is updated only if changes have been made to that component

   c. A uniform installation is consistent and simplified because all associated files are released simultaneously and contained within the package

   d. A packaged version application does not have to be stopped and restarted because the process occurs entirely in RAM

71 Which of the following tasks cannot be used to ensure that there is a comprehensive implementation plan in place?

   a. Confirm that a notification plan is in place for downtimes and for communicating scheduled updates or changes.

   b. Ensure that training environment requirements are developed and documented as a separate project.

   c. Ensure that well-defined migration procedures are in place that have been tested and verified.

   d. Determine how to verify that the new solution is in place and functioning.

72 A user documentation update _____ .

   a. Is an optional feature of a software application that allows users to submit documentation suggestions and comments

   b. Contains detailed steps for the implementation team to use while installing the application

   c. Replaces traditional printed documentation by relying on a centralized server and ensures that user documentation is always up to date

   d. Includes any functionality changes or additions to the application that are not described in previous user documentation

73 Why should a CISS be involved in ensuring that the training environment reflects the released system?

   a. CISS involvement ensures that additional time required to complete the training environment can be used to cover schedule slippage.

   b. If the CISS is not involved, training and implementation support will be inconsistent and possibly incomplete.

   c. The training environment does not need to demonstrate production-level stability because real transactions with actual customer data are not being supplied.

   d. Support personnel do not need to be notified or trained on the new system because their fresh approach to solving problems will generate novel ways of using the application.

74 One of the responsibilities of a CISS during the maintenance phase of a project is _____ .

   a. Removing the defect tracking and reporting processes after the application or service has been deployed

   b. Tuning the WAN delay simulator so that production systems are not overloaded with WAN traffic

   c. Monitoring system performance in accordance with the Service Level Agreement (SLA)

   d. All of the above

75 If key performance indicators begin to degrade for an application or service, all the following steps can be taken, *except* to _____ .

   a. Identify which system components are degraded and determine whether transaction accuracy or security has been impacted

   b. Investigate firewall, web, application, and database server logs to see if components are reaching licensed limits

   c. Reconfigure the monitoring thresholds so key performance targets are in line with the degraded performance

   d. Recommend the purchase of additional hardware resources, such as memory, CPU number and speed, or disk space, if average utilization is consistently above 80 percent

76 An important part of supporting the maintenance phase of a project is _____ .

   a. Validating back-up and recovery procedures

   b. Making ad hoc and frequent changes to configurations to maintain the application

   c. Fragmenting disk drives so that data is spread across multiple disk sectors

   d. Performing system maintenance during peak usage periods to measure how quickly systems reach nominal levels

77 In reviewing and analyzing system performance and transaction summary reports, problem trends should be _____ .

   a. Tracked and cataloged so that corrective measures can be implemented

   b. Compared with test scenarios from the testing phase so that only anticipated problems get prioritized for resolution

   c. Used as a basis for deducing which developers were responsible so that project managers can avoid using those developers

   d. Allowed to accumulate for at least one year so that sufficient statistical significance is achieved before allocating any resources to problem analysis and resolution

78 Which of the following is not a task associated with the process of continuous improvement?

   a. Interacting with end users through e-mail or in person

   b. Identifying targets of opportunity through regular reviews of potential new application features

   c. Monitoring real-world application use so that future development can focus on orienting application features and tasks appropriately

   d. Creating a test plan and validating the successful completion of each test scenario

79 SNMP stands for _____ .

   a. Simple Network Monitoring Protocol

   b. Simple Network Management Protocol

   c. Security Network Monitoring Protocol

   d. Software Network Management Problem

80 It is the goal of _____ to keep organizations within legal compliance of copyright law.

   a. Database management systems

   b. Intrusion detection systems

   c. Software license management tools

   d. Peer-to-peer software

PART **VI**

Appendixes

Recommended Further Reading

Bourke, Tony. *Server Load Balancing,* Second Edition. O'Reilly & Associates, 2001. (ISBN: 0596000502)

Chaudhury, Abhijit and Jean-Pierre Kuilboer. *E-Business & E-Commerce Infrastructure: Technologies Supporting the E-Business Initiative.* McGraw-Hill Higher Education, 2001. (ISBN: 0072478756)

Cockcroft, Adrian, Richard Pettit, and Sun Microsystems. *Sun Performance and Tuning: Java and the Internet,* Second Edition. Prentice Hall PTR, 1998. (ISBN: 0130952494)

Dart, Susan. *Configuration Management: The Missing Link in Web Engineering.* Artech House, 2000. (ISBN: 1580530982)

Ford, Warwick and Michael Baum. *Secure Electronic Commerce: Building the Infrastructure for Digital Signatures and Encryption,* Second Edition. Prentice Hall PTR, 2000. (ISBN: 0130272760)

Garfinkel, Simson, Debby Russell, and Gene Spafford. *Web Security, Privacy and Commerce,* Second Edition. O'Reilly & Associates, 2002. (ISBN: 0596000456)

Harmon, Paul, Michael Rosen, and Michael Guttman. *Developing E-Business Systems and Architectures: A Manager's Guide.* Morgan Kaufmann Publishers, 2000. (ISBN: 1558606653)

Harnedy, Sean. *Web-Based Management: For the Enterprise.* Prentice Hall PTR, 1998. (ISBN: 0130960187)

Huston, Geoff, Vinton G. Cerf, and Lyman Chapin. *Internet Performance Survival Guide: QoS Strategies for Multiservice Networks.* John Wiley & Sons, 2000. (ISBN: 0471378089)

Killelea, Patrick and Linda Mui. *Web Performance Tuning: Speeding Up the Web.* O'Reilly & Associates, 1998. (ISBN: 1565923790)

Larson, Eric and Brian Stephens. *Administrating Web Servers, Security, & Maintenance Interactive Workbook.* Prentice Hall PTR, 1999. (ISBN: 0130225347)

Limoncelli, Thomas and Christine Hogan. *The Practice of System and Network Administration.* Addison-Wesley Pub Co., 2001. (ISBN: 0201702711)

Marcus, Evan and Hal Stern. *Blueprints for High Availability: Designing Resilient Distributed Systems.* John Wiley & Sons, 2000. (ISBN: 0471356018)

Marshall, Steve, Ryszard Szarkowski, and Billie Shea. *Making E-Business Work: A Guide to Software Testing in the Internet Age.* Newport Press Publications, 2000. (ISBN: 0970133103)

Mason, Andrew and Mark J. Newcomb. *Cisco Secure Internet Security Solutions.* Cisco Press, 2001. (ISBN: 1587050161)

Mauro, Douglas R. and Kevin J. Schmidt. *Essential SNMP.* O'Reilly & Associates, 2001. (ISBN: 0596000200)

Menasce, Daniel A. and Virgilio A. F. Almeida. *Capacity Planning for Web Performance: Metrics, Models. and Methods.* Prentice Hall PTR, 1998. (ISBN: 0136938221)

Menasce, Daniel A. and Virgilio A. F. Almeida. *Scaling for E-Business: Technologies, Models, Performance, and Capacity Planning.* Prentice Hall PTR, 2000. (ISBN: 0130863289)

Nguyen, Hung Quoc. *Testing Applications on the Web: Test Planning for Internet-Based Systems.* John Wiley & Sons, 2000. (ISBN: 047139470X)

Norberg, Stefan and Deborah Russell. *Securing Windows NT/2000 Servers for the Internet.* O'Reilly & Associates, 2000. (ISBN: 1565927680)

Rajput, Wasim. *E-Commerce Systems Architecture and Applications.* Artech House, 2000. (ISBN: 1580530850)

Sharma, Vivek and Rajiv Sharma. *Developing e-Commerce Sites: An Integrated Approach.* Addison-Wesley Pub Co., 2000. (ISBN: 0201657643)

Stallings, William. *Cryptography & Network Security: Principles & Practice,* Second Edition. Prentice Hall, 1998. (ISBN: 0138690170)

Ware, Scott, et al. *Professional Web Site Optimization.* Wrox Press, Inc., 1997. (ISBN: 186100074X)

Wong, Brian L. *Configuration and Capacity Planning for Solaris Servers.* Prentice Hall PTR, 1997. (ISBN: 0133499529)

Solutions to CISS Applications Essentials Sample Exam

Sample Exam Questions from Chapter 9 and Answers

1 In a distributed application architecture, the web browser participates in which tier?

a. Business logic

b. Data source

c. Presentation

d. Distributed

Answer: C

2 A logical layer of a distributed system that represents a computer running a DBMS is the _____ tier.

a. Data source

b. Middle

c. Client

d. Security

Answer: A

3 Companies searching to stay competitive develop a distributed application in order to take advantage of _____ .

a. Less expensive labor

b. Scalability

c. Feasibility

d. Centralization

Answer: B

4 Middleware addresses the needs of the networked enterprise to create, integrate, and manage large-scale, distributed applications in _____ environments.

a. Heterogeneous

b. Homogenous

c. Scripted

d. Development

Answer: A

5 With a client/server application architecture, the server _____ .

a. Brokers and queues messages from other servers

b. Is customized by client service requests

c. Supplies requested services to peers

d. Supplies requested services to clients

Answer: D

6 _____ architecture allows organizations to modify business rules without changing the whole system.

a. Client/server

b. Peer-to-peer

c. Client-to-peer

d. Peer/server

Answer: A

7 In a "thick" client/server environment, a majority of the application processing occurs on the _____ .

a. Client side

b. Server side

c. Database backend

d. Web frontend

Answer: A

8 Which of the following is not a benefit of client/server application architecture?

   a. Client/server architecture is aligned with both the user view and the business process view.

   b. A change to the GUI does not require any changes to the other layers.

   c. Developers create components that can be reused in other applications.

   d. In general, client/server applications are less expensive to develop and implement.

Answer: D

9 In a typical web application, business logic should be performed by which of the following scripts?

   a. Client

   b. Server

   c. Backup

   d. Monitoring

Answer: B

10 JSPs are not usually run on _____ servers.

   a. Search

   b. Web

   c. Database

   d. Application

Answer: C

11 The three common transaction models are _____ .

   a. Flat, nested, and chained

   b. Atomic, one-way, and two-way

   c. Required, core, and context

   d. On-demand, batch, and synchronous

Answer: A

12 Which one of the following is not used to ensure transaction integrity?

    a. Triggers

    b. Rollbacks

    c. Journaling

    d. Access control

    Answer: D

13 Three common types of application transactions are _____ .

    a. Electronic, printed, and pending

    b. Limited, guaranteed, and unlimited

    c. Lookup, update, and add

    d. Serial, parallel, and threaded

    Answer: C

14 In the commit phase of a distributed transaction, which of the following is true?

    a. Not all nodes need to respond to the coordinator that they are prepared to commit.

    b. Only nodes that cannot commit are asked to rollback the transaction.

    c. Individual nodes do not have to wait until changes are committed on the other nodes.

    d. The initiating node asks all nodes to commit the transaction simultaneously.

    Answer: D

15 Which of the following is not a type of database?

    a. Clustered

    b. Hierarchical

    c. Object-oriented

    d. Networked

    Answer: A

16 The components of an SQL database are _____ .

    a. Data elements, rows, and columns

    b. Screens, tables, and views

    c. Schemas, tables, and views

    d. Selects, joins, and deletes

    Answer: C

17 The Unified Modeling Language (UML) has become an industry standard because
_____ .

    a. It joins the concepts of Booch, the Object Modeling Technique, Object-Oriented Software Engineering, and other methods.

    b. It makes a strong break with previous practices for object-oriented modeling languages.

    c. It does not attempt to make a common language for modeling large and complex systems.

    d. It synthesizes data collection, data distribution, and data warehousing.

Answer: A

18 A green thread is implemented by the Java runtime system itself, while a native thread is specific to the underlying operating system. Which of the following statements is false?

    a. Green threads must be trapped to prevent I/O from suspending.

    b. Green threads take advantage of built-in operating support.

    c. Native threads are less safe because anything is likely to happen.

    d. Native threads depend on a good implementation of threading in the underlying operating system.

Answer: B

19 Hardware drivers are responsible for _____ .

    a. Device naming and mapping symbolic device names onto the proper drivers

    b. Keeping users from accessing devices they are not supposed to access

    c. Providing read and write buffers so that data is written in blocks

    d. All of the above

Answer: D

20 Which definition states the main function of the Basic Lifecycle Model?

    a. The Basic Lifecycle Model provides decision makers with a guide to creating structured project documentation.

    b. The Basic Lifecycle Model defines the order in which a project specifies, implements, tests, and performs its activities.

    c. The Basic Lifecycle Model determines the mean time before failure (MTBF) for system components.

    d. The Basic Lifecycle Model defines the testing methods generally acknowledged as best practices.

Answer: B

21 When do web-based projects benefit from adopting a lifecycle model?

   a. When business decision makers and application specialists can capture, organize, and visualize the application as if it were functioning within their business

   b. When the business model remains constant throughout the entire project lifecycle so that subsequent outputs do not affect the model

   c. When the project can avoid selecting a tangible structure for the business model until potential damage is assessed

   d. When a business need demonstrates a projected loss for the product or service

   Answer: A

22 An application with small gain opportunity but very high feasibility _____ to be accepted.

   a. Has great potential

   b. Requires strategic advice

   c. Meets the minimum requirements

   d. Has little potential

   Answer: D

23 A relevant baseline _____ .

   a. Is not part of the business model outputs

   b. Can be taken from comparisons with government-owned applications

   c. May be derived either from current company performance in acquiring an application or from similar business organizations in the industry

   d. Does not have to list the criteria against which to compare application performance

   Answer: C

24 Which of the following specifications is not included in the analysis and design phase?

   a. System

   b. Testing

   c. Networking

   d. Database

   Answer: B

25 The main focus of the analysis and design phase should be to concentrate on
_____ .

   a. Providing a complete specification of every application detail

   b. Gathering more information about the application specification designated in the business model

   c. Finding the basic features needed by the application in order to achieve minimal functionality

   d. Determining which application tests can be run before the test phase has begun

Answer: B

26 The purpose of the development phase is to _____ .

   a. Translate the application system specification into an application installation package

   b. Reshape customer desires into already existing application packages

   c. Start a fresh cycle of analysis and design of customer requirements

   d. Provide a budget for training and conferences

Answer: A

27 The primary input to the development phase of the Basic Lifecycle Model is the system _____ .

   a. Test plan

   b. Operation manual

   c. Monitoring configuration

   d. Specification

Answer: D

28 Which of these would not be tested during the Test Phase?

   a. Maintenance procedures

   b. Application requirements

   c. Investor support

   d. Authentication

Answer: C

29 The Test Phase verifies which set of objectives?

   a. Hardware and software licensing and support agreements

   b. Content, structure, and interaction of operational mechanisms

   c. Adherence to standards and project programming style guides

   d. Content creation, distribution, and management

   Answer: B

30 Formal written customer acceptance should be obtained in the _____ phase.

   a. Analysis and design

   b. Implementation

   c. Maintenance

   d. Test

   Answer: B

31 Which of the following is not a distinct type of manual?

   a. Test

   b. System

   c. Program

   d. Data

   Answer: A

32 The application maintenance team must monitor which of the following functions?

   a. Base lining, prototyping, and unit testing

   b. Business capabilities, model presentation, and identification of critical success factors

   c. Expense reporting, benefits administration, and other business-context processes

   d. Resource utilization, system security, and downtime

   Answer: D

33 Upgrades to application capacity are performed _____ .

   a. After unplanned downtime occurs

   b. Only in a clustered environment

   c. During the maintenance phase

   d. Every two years

   Answer: C

34 The _____ Lifecycle Model does not repeat any phase.

   a. Prototype

   b. Waterfall

   c. Iterative

   d. Spiral

   Answer: B

35 Which is not a weakness of the Waterfall Lifecycle Model?

   a. The model provides a rigid structure that enforces a strict order of accomplishing phase objectives.

   b. The model has no feedback loops.

   c. Delay in one stage of the project results in delays in all the stages that follow.

   d. It needs all requirements to be stated by the customer in the initial phase.

   Answer: A

36 Repeating the sequence of lifecycle phases until the desired application is achieved _____ .

   a. Is the definition of the Iterative Lifecycle Model

   b. Is the definition of the Waterfall Lifecycle Model

   c. Does not permit adding higher level functions during design and development

   d. Is a disorganized method for application development

   Answer: A

37 The Rapid Application Development (RAD) Lifecycle Model is characterized by _____ .

   a. A series of evolving executable prototypes

   b. Modularized application system components

   c. The ability to schedule unlimited change requests

   d. A compromise in quality and completeness of the end product in exchange for quick delivery on a tight schedule

   Answer: D

38 The lifecycle model that boasts a low error rate is the _____ model.

a. Spiral

b. Rapid Application Development (RAD)

c. Clean Room

d. Prototype

Answer: C

39 Which lifecycle model consists of four steps: plan, design, review, and assess risk?

a. Prototype

b. Spiral

c. Linear Sequential

d. Waterfall

Answer: B

40 Which one of the following is not a common security technology enabling web-based applications?

a. Biometric Authentication System (BAS)

b. Secure Sockets Layer (SSL) encryption

c. Public Key Infrastructure (PKI)

d. Virtual Private Networks (VPNs)

Answer: A

41 Site _____ increases availability by means of a replica of an existing site.

a. Indexing

b. Updating

c. Mirroring

d. Striping

Answer: C

42 Which one of the following is not a high-availability technology?

a. Hot swappable CPU

b. Server clustering

c. Small Computer Integrated Services (SCSI) drives

d. RAID 5 disk array

Answer: C

43 A Service Level Agreement (SLA) defines _____ .

    a. Health, availability, and accountability assurances for service provider services

    b. Third-party review of backup procedures

    c. Price checks and balances for service provider services

    d. Supply chain management system requirements

    Answer: A

44 Storage Area Networks (SANs) are increasingly popular because _____ .

    a. RAID arrays cannot use redundant power supplies.

    b. Campus-wide distances are too great for peripheral channels to handle.

    c. They are connected exclusively through fiber channels.

    d. Large amounts of data are shared using peripheral channels instead of overburdened networks.

    Answer: D

45 Software is, on average, becoming _____ as software applications grow in complexity and size.

    a. Less reliable

    b. More reliable

    c. Less profitable

    d. More profitable

    Answer: A

46 Which database design factors can affect an Internet business application's performance?

    a. Mixed uppercase and lowercase table names

    b. Indexing, normalization, and stored procedures

    c. Four or more accounts with administrative privileges

    d. Use of weak passwords with less than five characters

    Answer: B

47 What percentage of a software applications budget is typically devoted to maintenance activity over the life of the software?

   a. 20 to 40 percent

   b. 40 to 70 percent

   c. 5 to 20 percent

   d. 5 to 10 percent

Answer: B

48 Network management is concerned with all the following except _____ .

   a. Collecting system usage statistics and generating reports

   b. Updating network management, application configurations documentation

   c. Implementing and maintaining database security

   d. Controlling network management system configurations

Answer: C

49 In an application integration strategy, _____ is concerned with enabling data to be consolidated from a variety of disparate data sources into a single view.

   a. Database middleware

   b. Conceptual data modeling

   c. Object-oriented design

   d. Centralized computing

Answer: A

50 Enterprise Resource Planning (ERP) is defined as _____ .

   a. Using mainly proprietary software tools instead of packaged software within an enterprise

   b. An information system dedicated for use with human resources departments

   c. Any resource planning software that uses Enterprise JavaBeans (EJB)

   d. An integrated information system that serves all departments within an enterprise

Answer: D

51 What is the major disadvantage of using an insourcing model for implementing a business application?

a. The company may be the only provider in a core business area.

b. The company must acquire and maintain the personnel expertise and equipment required for the application.

c. Senior management is relieved of delivery accountability.

d. The company will retain control over the project implementation.

Answer: B

52 Under the _____ model, companies developing a new business application undergo a heightened risk of the application solution becoming obsolete before they realize the anticipated return on investment.

a. Insourcing

b. Outsourcing

c. ASP

d. MSP

Answer: A

53 A project that pursues outsourcing an application to a service provider gains all the following benefits except _____ .

a. Time to market

b. Application cost reduction

c. Retaining full control

d. Technology leveraging

Answer: C

54 When outsourcing business-context processes, data encryption should be employed for sensitive customer information _____ .

a. Only if required by the service provider

b. Just for remotely accessed services

c. Prior to a security audit

d. Always

Answer: D

55 An ASP's ability to continuously increase or decrease capacity to accommodate growth is known as _____ .

   a. Short-term use

   b. Availability

   c. Scalability

   d. Customization

Answer: C

56 A disadvantage to the ASP outsourcing model is that _____ .

   a. The ASP may decide to merge with another company that could lead to leasing a business application from a direct competitor.

   b. The ASP has a greater probability of successfully implementing an application based on standard applications.

   c. The ASP may provide multiple firewalls and data encryption so the customer data is isolated.

   d. By spreading equipment, software, and expertise expenses over many users, the ASP can readily customize applications to suit customer needs.

Answer: A

57 Which sourcing model could best be adapted to high levels of application customization?

   a. Outsourcing

   b. Insourcing

   c. Application service provider

   d. In-line sourcing

Answer: B

58 The advantage of avoiding large up-front costs associated with developing an application is known as _____ .

   a. Total cost of ownership (TCO)

   b. Time-to-money ratio

   c. Rapid application development (RAD)

   d. The cost of money

Answer: D

59 Which is the first stage in the Internet-based customer care lifecycle?

    a. Target.

    b. Acquire.

    c. Transact.

    d. None of the above; the stages are simultaneous.

    Answer: D

60 Which of the following is not an example of a workforce optimization initiative?

    a. Web-based time reporting tools

    b. Self-service expense report application

    c. Inventory leveling

    d. On-demand training materials

    Answer: C

61 A workforce optimization system should be designed to have sufficient storage and processing power to handle _____ .

    a. The current user load

    b. The current user load and the load over the next two years

    c. Twice the current user load

    d. 110 percent of the current user load

    Answer: A

62 A Supply Chain Management program encompasses all the following except _____ .

    a. Customer service

    b. Content versioning

    c. Inventory reduction

    d. Improved demand forecasting

    Answer: B

63 An Internet-driven Supply Chain Management system groups customers by
_____ .

    a. Industry

    b. Product

    c. Need

    d. Trade channel

    Answer: C

64 Which of the following is not true of e-learning tools?

    a. Learners are free to study at their own pace.

    b. Lack of accountability is a disadvantage of e-learning systems.

    c. Developers of e-learning tools may receive immediate feedback to improve the curriculum.

    d. Organizations can track learner performance.

    Answer: B

65 An e-publishing solution addresses which of the following areas?

    a. Content creation

    b. Content management

    c. Content delivery

    d. All of the above

    Answer: D

66 Devices are _____ for information in system management applications such as SNMP.

    a. Polled

    b. Peeked

    c. Poked

    d. Interrupted

    Answer: A

67 Which area is not a key area of application performance management?

  a. Application response time

  b. Server processing time

  c. Application security

  d. Number of active sessions

Answer: C

68 Which networks benefit most from inventory management?

  a. Heterogeneous networks

  b. Distributed networks

  c. Large networks

  d. All of the above

Answer: D

69 Which set makes up the four categories of system management?

  a. Remote operation, security management, version control, and operational status

  b. Proactive, reactive, selective, and exclusive

  c. System monitoring, software distribution, inventory management, and user administration

  d. Requirements gathering, design, implementation, and maintenance

Answer: C

Solutions to CISS Solutions Sample Exam

Sample Exam Questions from Chapter 10 and Answers

1 The business modeling and requirements phase of the software development life cycle gates _____ .

   a. Functional requirements and information

   b. Nonfunctional requirements and information

   c. Functional and nonfunctional requirements and information

   d. Packaged software and open source software information

Answer: C

2 Which statement correctly defines the purpose of the testing and validation phase of the Basic Life Cycle Model?

   a. Testing is the process of setting up and executing test scenarios in a controlled setting, and validation is the process of validating or confirming that the testing results meet certain business requirements.

   b. Testing is the process of identifying functional and nonfunctional requirements, and validation is the process of tracking software changes that contain business logic.

   c. Testing is the sequence of virtual user scripts executed in concurrent test scenarios, and validation is the process of confirming that the original business requirements have avoided scope creep.

   d. Testing is the sequence of all unit tests run against an application under development, and validation is the sequence of all unit tests run against an application after it has been deployed.

Answer: A

3 All of the following, except _____ testing, are common types of software testing.

   a. Application performance

   b. Security

   c. User load

   d. Hardness

   Answer: D

4 The _____ phase has been consistently rated as the most important phase in the software development lifecycle.

   a. Testing and validation

   b. Analysis and design

   c. Maintenance

   d. Development

   Answer: A

5 Stress Testing is also known as _____ testing.

   a. Application performance

   b. User load

   c. Hardness

   d. Security

   Answer: B

6 A key characteristic of application performance testing is testing _____ .

   a. Multi-user response times

   b. Single-user response times

   c. Concurrent virtual user response times

   d. Application fault tolerance

   Answer: B

7 Which of the following is a measure of application throughput?

   a. Branches per second

   b. Builds per second

   c. Bits per second

   d. Boxes per second

   Answer: C

8 To ensure that an application performs as expected with real users, user load testing measures _____ .

    a. Server CPU use

    b. Server memory use

    c. Network packets per second

    d. All of the above

Answer: D

9 Which of the following is not a network component metric in availability testing?

    a. Router CPU use

    b. Load-balanced connections

    c. Image server caching

    d. Firewall memory use

Answer: C

10 Network implications of proposed user transactions are assessed by _____ .

    a. Determining where users are located, how many users are at each location, and how frequently users are expected to perform various transactions

    b. Gathering comprehensive requirements, understanding user learning styles, and the ratio of users to network printers

    c. Data modeling, object-oriented application design, and various Java class transaction properties

    d. Initial "best guess" estimates, cross-office collaboration tools, and careful transaction prototyping

Answer: A

11 Which answer lists the four-step application performance testing process in the correct order?

    a. Application assessment, development environment setup, data collection for transactions, and testing results analysis

    b. Development environment setup, test environment setup, data collection, and testing results analysis

    c. Control client setup, data collection, data translation, and results analysis

    d. Application assessment, test environment setup, data collection, and results analysis

Answer: D

12 Which of the following is not a consideration during the application assessment process?

   a. How the application will be deployed to users and servers

   b. Software licensing model options and cost-per-seat calculations

   c. Transactions representative of how the application will be used

   d. Effects on existing traffic flows in the application network environment

Answer: B

13 An application test environment component that inserts delays to simulate network traffic is called a WAN _____ Simulator.

   a. Network

   b. Decay

   c. Delay

   d. Circuit

Answer: C

14 Application performance testing includes capturing data for _____ .

   a. A network protocol, network addresses, and network port numbers

   b. A network subnet, a network route, and a network mask

   c. A top-level domain name, a second-level domain name, and a hostname

   d. A horizontal refresh rate, a vertical refresh rate, and interleave settings

Answer: A

15 Which of the following best states the definition of how to calculate end-to-end response times?

   a. Add the process times for the client and servers.

   b. Add the process times for the client, servers, and network.

   c. Add the process times for the client and servers, and then subtract the network process times.

   d. Add the process times for the client and servers, and then divide by two.

Answer: B

16 Security testing of an Internet business solution involving outsourced service providers should involve _____ .

  a. Only service provider environments

  b. All systems and environments

  c. Only production systems and environments

  d. Only those systems and environments with sensitive information

Answer: B

17 Which step is not part of the simple four-step security architecture testing process?

  a. Perform iterative tests.

  b. Configure and enable the security systems.

  c. Coordinate the trusted domain relationships.

  d. Coordinate the installation of security systems.

Answer: C

18 The ultimate goal of security testing is to _____ .

  a. Protect information assets

  b. Make an application harder to use

  c. Determine customer account administration procedures

  d. Create functional security vulnerabilities

Answer: A

19 Which of the follows provides the comprehensive set of areas that must be validated and corrected in security testing?

  a. Systems, networks, and applications

  b. Policies, procedures, and access lists

  c. Identity, authorization, and nonrepudiation

  d. Operations, systems, networks, and applications

Answer: D

20 The number of simultaneous users predicted for peak usage is _____ if there are 2000 total users and 10 concurrent users.

  a. 20

  b. 200

  c. 2000

  d. 20,000

Answer: D

21 Which of the following is not a user load-testing tool?

 a. An intrusion-detection system

 b. WAN Delay Simulator

 c. A packet sniffer

 d. A control client

 Answer: A

22 Software development load testing collects measurement data for _____ .

 a. Only successful transaction scenarios

 b. Only failed transaction scenarios

 c. Minimum, average, and maximum response times

 d. Minimum response times

 Answer: C

23 A hits-per-second report evaluates the load placed by virtual users on the _____ .

 a. Control client

 b. Web server

 c. Database server

 d. Application server

 Answer: B

24 Availability testing for an Internet business solution can best be defined as _____ .

 a. Testing where fault tolerant components are deliberately failed in a number of ways to verify reliability

 b. Testing where network components are deliberately failed in a number of ways to verify that the network architecture is secure

 c. Testing that deliberately fails components in a number of ways to verify that the designed level of availability is achieved

 d. Testing where virtual users follow deliberately failed test scenarios to verify that application transactions are sufficiently robust

 Answer: C

25 Unplanned downtime is counted against the application availability requirements as outlined in _____ .

   a. The Service Level Agreement

   b. An availability test plan

   c. The development documentation

   d. An enterprise resource model

   Answer: A

26 Which scenario is not a network connectivity failure?

   a. A cut LAN cable

   b. A loopback interface

   c. A dropped VPN connection

   d. A dead ISP circuit

   Answer: B

27 A company has set an availability goal for their web-based e-learning system of 99.9 percent uptime. The goal has been met if the system is down for _____ per year.

   a. 12 hours

   b. 8 days

   c. 8 hours

   d. 600 minutes

   Answer: C

28 Availability testing is built on the results of _____ testing.

   a. Security

   b. LAN-to-WAN

   c. White box

   d. Load

   Answer: D

29 Availability test results analysis provides answers to which question?

   a. Does the redundant device take over for the failed device?

   b. Can the development environment communicate with the production environment?

   c. How many test-team members are required to verify test failures?

   d. Which software patches can be applied to the router?

   Answer: A

30 In documenting testing and validation results, the test team must _____ .

   a. Diagram the test environment

   b. Describe the test methodology

   c. List the test objectives

   d. All of the above

   Answer: D

31 Which of the following demonstrates the correct order of the steps in an application performance test process?

   a. Application assessment, test environment setup, data collection for transactions, and testing results analysis

   b. Application assessment, data collection for transactions, test environment setup, and testing results analysis

   c. Data collection for transactions, test environment setup, application assessment, and testing results analysis

   d. Test environment setup, application assessment, data collection for transactions, and testing results analysis

   Answer: A

32 Security tests and documentation must address _____ .

   a. Network, systems, applications, and operations security results

   b. Minimum, average, and maximum transaction response times

   c. Mirroring, clustering, and multiprocessor application design

   d. Memory and CPU utilization with 1000 virtual users

   Answer: A

33 Typical activities that a CISS might perform in an Internet business project would generally not include _____ .

 a. Project facilitation, project management, and project leadership

 b. Test-plan writing, plan implementation, and plan maintenance

 c. Marketing, communications, and advertising

 d. Application performance testing, security research, and operations documentation

Answer: C

34 The three major responsibilities of a CISS during the business modeling and requirements phase of the life cycle model are to _____ .

 a. Attend weekly project meetings, take meeting notes, and verify business hours of operation

 b. Keep requirements gathering focused, provide leadership, and validate completion of the phase

 c. Design the look and feel of user interface, provide color palette standards, and develop global navigation artwork

 d. Publish the project plan, track testing issues, and obtain sign-off from the client for the finished application

Answer: B

35 A CISS can use all the following business modeling and requirements tools on a project except _____ .

 a. Case models

 b. Packet sniffer

 c. Data flow diagrams

 d. Entity relationship diagrams

Answer: B

36 If requirements gathering is to remain focused on business, functional, and information models, a CISS must _____ .

 a. Interview stakeholders and telephone helpdesk support

 b. Communicate expectations, adopt client phrases of speech, and create opportunities for social interaction with team members

 c. Use Internet search engines, spell-check project correspondence, and assess the environmental impact of the business model

 d. Communicate the methodology, perform research, and quantify impact at a high level

Answer: D

37 Gathering system requirements includes all the following responsibilities except
_____ .

   a. Assessing legal implications of trademarks and service marks

   b. Defining nonfunctional system requirements

   c. Defining system expectations

   d. Assessing the current system, processes, users, and tools

   Answer: A

38 Which of the following is not a design constraint that might emerge from the
requirements and modeling phase?

   a. Project code name

   b. Database resource limits

   c. Required security policies

   d. Implementation language

   Answer: A

39 Being able to perform a walkthrough of _____ signifies the completion of
the business modeling and requirements phase.

   a. Storyboard concepts, logo treatments, and narrative style

   b. Release procedures, services monitoring, and problem escalation

   c. The business model, functional requirements, and nonfunctional requirements

   d. Potential areas of reusability, the systems inventory database, and database recovery

   Answer: C

40 Shadowing is _____ .

   a. A technique used for low-level data replication

   b. A technique used to gather information about project requirements

   c. The practice of making text and images appear three-dimensional

   d. The practice of making a virtual interface respond to requests

   Answer: B

41 Throughout the analysis and design phase, a CISS is responsible for analyzing
_____ .

    a. Disclosure requirements, developing a test plan, designing a prototype system, and designing a system architecture that satisfies business requirements

    b. Business requirements, developing a project management plan, designing a robust and maintainable system, and designing a system architecture that satisfies business requirements

    c. Funding sources, testing disaster recovery mechanisms, and reducing system functionality by 50 percent before development begins

    d. The profit margin, predicting project feasibility, identifying strategic partnerships, and generating a design document

Answer: B

42 A robust system is one that _____ .

    a. Performs single-user operations within normal conditions and parameters

    b. Performs multi-user operations, but locks up frequently

    c. Has thorough documentation and has been indexed recently

    d. Is thoroughly tested and has built-in safeguards against system failure

Answer: D

43 During the analysis and design phase, the process of validating the data flow diagrams, data modeling, and data dictionary is known as _____ .

    a. A major task in analyzing business requirements in relation to system architecture

    b. A technique for documenting hours in the project budget

    c. A technique for analyzing business concepts that are hard to visualize

    d. A major obstacle to starting the development phase

Answer: A

44 Data modeling tools provide database administrators with a means of _____ .

    a. Testing data models to discover errors or inefficiencies in database schema

    b. Exporting data from one database to another by converting each schema into a shared or common model

    c. Creating an application foundation by graphically depicting the organization of business processes and data requirements, and how they relate to each other

    d. Creating a functioning application by embedding commands and program code within a database

Answer: C

45 Which of the following is not an approach for implementing a software application?

a. Phased

b. Osmosis

c. Parallel

d. Immediate cut-over

Answer: B

46 Which of the following is generally not a characteristic of a maintainable system?

a. Ad-hoc configuration settings

b. Detailed documentation

c. Modular design

d. Change management process

Answer: A

47 Which of the following is not a technique that a CISS might apply in the analysis and design phase?

a. Structured walkthrough

b. Abstraction

c. Code branching

d. Project management software

Answer: C

48 A "proof of concept prototype" is commonly developed during the analysis and design phase to _____ .

a. Boost morale and show initial evidence that the application will work as expected

b. Test unknown or suspect areas; the prototype is discarded after the answers are obtained

c. Test known areas of application functionality, as needed

d. Build a set of nonreusable models to find the right solution

Answer: B

49 Which of the following is not a responsibility of a CISS during the implementation phase?

a. Perform comprehensive implementation planning

b. Gather comprehensive application requirements

c. Verify that users will be trained on new functionality

d. Document detailed installation procedures

Answer: B

50 As physical integration begins in the development phase, a CISS will contribute to the integration of architecture components by _____ .

a. Verifying security policies

b. Developing an upgrade schedule

c. Reviewing the Service Level Agreement

d. Sizing hardware

Answer: D

51 For projects in which a CISS works closely with the project manager, a collaboration to ensure adequate development resources might require _____ .

a. Learning how to negotiate under pressure with customers and end users to achieve a realistic balance of schedule and functionality

b. Learning about development methodologies that favor speed over rigor

c. Contracting optional formal training early in the budget period

d. Contracting outside developers to reduce total project costs

Answer: A

52 Software change control and version control systems are applicable to _____ .

a. Configuration files

b. Code updates

c. Design specifications

d. All of the above

Answer: D

53 Which of the following is not a responsibility of a CISS during the development phase?

   a. Determine hardware sizing requirements

   b. Define nonfunctional business requirements

   c. Verify that development resources are adequate

   d. Verify that change control process can handle code updates

Answer: B

54 Joint Application Development (JAD) is a structured development methodology typified by _____ .

   a. Analyzing and resolving any problems in the connection points or "joints" of a system before working on other defects

   b. Bringing users and developers together for intensive, highly productive, facilitated sessions to resolve the task at hand

   c. Bringing internal and external developers together to best determine which components can be subcontracted to external development teams

   d. Bringing internal and external developers together by introducing a structured correspondence through e-mail to document all discussions and ideas

Answer: B

55 A design document can become stale and inaccurate unless _____ .

   a. Each deliverable is developed and tested by a different person

   b. Informal conversations are encouraged to promote better collaboration

   c. Each deliverable is reviewed with a team walkthrough to ensure adherence to the stated design document criteria

   d. The document is maintained and edited outside of version control restrictions

Answer: C

56 _____ is designed to simulate a number of users or transactions and to demonstrate the system's performance.

   a. A test impact analyzer

   b. A test data generator

   c. Load testing software

   d. A WAN delay simulator

Answer: C

57 System component availability testing includes all the following except
_____ .

a. Operating system failure

b. Cut LAN cable

c. Application server power failure

d. Database cluster node failure

Answer: B

58 A drawback to web-enabled workflow automation tools used during project development is based on the fact that _____ .

a. Explanations and analyses of defects and metrics are not readily available to the customer

b. Customers have to wait for project status updates

c. Customers cannot observe design reviews

d. Customers cannot track defects or critical problems

Answer: A

59 A test plan describes all of the following except _____ .

a. Resources

b. Test objectives

c. Test environment constraints

d. Project maintenance documentation

Answer: D

60 Which of the following is the correct definition of black box testing?

a. Black box testing is testing that includes performance/availability, scalability, security, and disaster recovery.

b. Black box testing is functional testing that includes reviewing the internal parts of the system based on the logic and calculations.

c. Black box testing is testing systems behavior and performance under excessive demands and resource utilization.

d. Black box testing is integration testing of a string of units that accomplish a specific function in the application.

Answer: A

61 _____ testing is the first stage in which all parts of the application are assembled and presented as a system.

   a. Regression

   b. Thread

   c. Availability

   d. Integration

Answer: D

62 System testing is largely dependent upon _____ .

   a. A four-step process that configures, enables, installs, and documents the system security architecture

   b. Verifying the accuracy of system installation and configuration documentation

   c. Identifying a comprehensive list of maintenance phase defects that need to be iteratively tested until resolved

   d. A balanced and realistic mixture of functionally diverse test scenarios

Answer: B

63 One of the final responsibilities of a CISS during the test phase is _____ .

   a. Creating a defect tracking system

   b. Creating a final test plan

   c. Gaining formal acceptance of the system by the customer

   d. Gaining formal acceptance of the requirements from the customer

Answer: C

64 Which of the following does not describe a responsibility that a CISS might have in the test phase?

   a. Perform verify testing

   b. Ensure test results are analyzed

   c. Develop a project management plan

   d. Confirm that the test plan will sufficiently test the system requirements

Answer: C

65 A test case records all of the following test attributes *except* _____ .

   a. Test objectives, test constraints, and test inputs

   b. Expected results, actual results, and results analysis

   c. Test constraints, entry criteria, and exit criteria

   d. Server memory utilization, server CPU utilization, and disk I/O performance metrics

   Answer: D

66 Changes to application code can affect previously tested functionality. For this reason, testing groups often perform _____ testing throughout the test phase to verify that all known bugs are fixed and stay fixed.

   a. Regression

   b. Integration

   c. Backwards

   d. Redundant

   Answer: A

67 Processor architectures that support highly scalable applications are _____ .

   a. Parallel Server Instance (PSI) and Load Performance Guard (LPG)

   b. Symmetric Multiprocessing (SMP) and Massively Parallel Processing (MPP)

   c. Processor Group Awareness (PGA) and Conjoint-Gated Systems (CGS)

   d. Modular Memory Architecture (MMA) and Distributed Node Locking (DNL)

   Answer: B

68 A test impact analyzer is a tool used during the software development life cycle that _____ .

   a. Automatically compares different versions of a file and reports on the differences

   b. Allows a project manager to track the resolution of problems and provide metrics on the progress of problem resolution

   c. Creates meaningful test data that meets given criteria

   d. Can gauge the impact of a code change before actually making the change

   Answer: D

69 A responsibility of a CISS during the implementation phase of a project is to ensure that _____ .

  a. There is a back-out or contingency plan in place

  b. The project plan identifies project dependencies

  c. There is adequate documentation of project scope

  d. Data flow diagrams are validated against the data model

Answer: A

70 An implementation benefit of a packaged version and controlled releases is that

_____ .

  a. An installation is smaller in size than the source components, runs faster, and takes less time to test

  b. Each software application component is updated only if changes have been made to that component

  c. A uniform installation is consistent and simplified because all associated files are released simultaneously and contained within the package

  d. A packaged version application does not have to be stopped and restarted because the process occurs entirely in RAM

Answer: C

71 Which of the following tasks cannot be used to ensure that there is a comprehensive implementation plan in place?

  a. Confirm that a notification plan is in place for downtimes and for communicating scheduled updates or changes.

  b. Ensure that training environment requirements are developed and documented as a separate project.

  c. Ensure that well-defined migration procedures are in place that have been tested and verified.

  d. Determine how to verify that the new solution is in place and functioning.

Answer: B

72 A user documentation update _____ .

    a. Is an optional feature of a software application that allows users to submit documentation suggestions and comments

    b. Contains detailed steps for the implementation team to use while installing the application

    c. Replaces traditional printed documentation by relying on a centralized server and ensures that user documentation is always up to date

    d. Includes any functionality changes or additions to the application that are not described in previous user documentation.

Answer: D

73 Why should a CISS be involved in ensuring that the training environment reflects the released system?

    a. CISS involvement ensures that additional time required to complete the training environment can be used to cover schedule slippage.

    b. If the CISS is not involved, training and implementation support will be inconsistent and possibly incomplete.

    c. The training environment does not need to demonstrate production-level stability because real transactions with actual customer data are not being supplied.

    d. Support personnel do not need to be notified or trained on the new system because their fresh approach to solving problems will generate novel ways of using the application.

Answer: B

74 One of the responsibilities of a CISS during the maintenance phase of a project is _____ .

    a. Removing the defect tracking and reporting processes after the application or service has been deployed

    b. Tuning the WAN delay simulator so that production systems are not overloaded with WAN traffic

    c. Monitoring system performance in accordance with the Service Level Agreement (SLA)

    d. All of the above

Answer: C

75 If key performance indicators begin to degrade for an application or service, all the following steps can be taken, *except* to _____ .

a. Identify which system components are degraded and determine whether transaction accuracy or security has been impacted

b. Investigate firewall, web, application, and database server logs to see if components are reaching licensed limits

c. Reconfigure the monitoring thresholds so key performance targets are in line with the degraded performance

d. Recommend the purchase of additional hardware resources, such as memory, CPU number and speed, or disk space, if average utilization is consistently above 80 percent

Answer: C

76 An important part of supporting the maintenance phase of a project is

_____ .

a. Validating back-up and recovery procedures

b. Making ad hoc and frequent changes to configurations to maintain the application

c. Fragmenting disk drives so that data is spread across multiple disk sectors

d. Performing system maintenance during peak usage periods to measure how quickly systems reach nominal levels

Answer: A

77 In reviewing and analyzing system performance and transaction summary reports, problem trends should be _____ .

a. Tracked and cataloged so that corrective measures can be implemented

b. Compared with test scenarios from the testing phase so that only anticipated problems get prioritized for resolution

c. Used as a basis for deducing which developers were responsible so that project managers can avoid using those developers

d. Allowed to accumulate for at least one year so that sufficient statistical significance is achieved before allocating any resources to problem analysis and resolution

Answer: A

78 Which of the following is not a task associated with the process of continuous improvement?

   a. Interacting with end users through e-mail or in person

   b. Identifying targets of opportunity through regular reviews of potential new application features

   c. Monitoring real-world application use so that future development can focus on orienting application features and tasks appropriately

   d. Creating a test plan and validating the successful completion of each test scenario

   Answer: D

79 SNMP stands for _____ .

   a. Simple Network Monitoring Protocol

   b. Simple Network Management Protocol

   c. Security Network Monitoring Protocol

   d. Software Network Management Problem

   Answer: B

80 It is the goal of _____ to keep organizations within legal compliance of copyright law.

   a. Database management systems

   b. Intrusion detection systems

   c. Software license management tools

   d. Peer-to-peer software

   Answer: C

Answers to Chapter Review Questions

This appendix contains the answers to the chapter review questions. The original questions are included for your convenience. The answers are in bold.

Chapter 2

1 Which definition best describes a distributed application?

    a. PC user accessing application from the server

    b. Cooperative processing

    c. Retail channel sales of software applications

    d. Web browser

    Answer: A

2 Which is not a key benefit of moving to distributed applications?

    a. Reliability

    b. Cost-saving

    c. Scalability

    d. Reusability

    Answer: B

3 Which is not a purpose of middleware in relation to addressing the needs of networked enterprises?

    a. Migrating distributed applications

    b. Developing distributed applications

    c. Integrating distributed applications

    d. Managing distributed applications

    Answer: A

4 Which is not one of the five categories of middleware classifications?

   a. RPC

   b. MOM

   c. TPM

   d. OMG

   e. ORB

Answer: D

5 Which statement is false?

   a. A client usually waits for a server to initiate requests.

   b. A client relies on servers for resources, such as files, devices, and processing power.

   c. A client manages the user-interface portion of the client/server application.

   d. A client workstation usually has a graphics user interface.

Answer: A

6 Which is not a client/server application?

   a. Ping

   b. Internet Explorer browser

   c. Nslookup

   d. MS Access

Answer: D

7 Client/server computing is the logical extension of modular programming. With this architecture, what requests a service?

   a. The user

   b. The server

   c. The client

   d. The system administrator

Answer: C

8 Which layer allows you to tell the difference between an order entry application and an inventory control application?

   a. Presentation

   b. Business logic

   c. Data

   d. Enhanced data streams

Answer: B

9 Which is not an advantage of a three-tier architecture over a two-tier architecture?

   a. Improved performance for groups with a large number of users

   b. Greater flexibility to update business rules

   c. Easier code programming

   d. Enhanced capability to implement load balancing

Answer: C

10 Which example typifies a thin client?

   a. A UNIX-based workstation

   b. JavaStations

   c. A VMS terminal

   d. A traditional PC

Answer: B

11 Which company develops network computers?

   a. Oracle

   b. Microsoft

   c. Cisco

   d. Sun Microsystems

Answer: D

12 Which statement about web applications is false?

   a. Every web site is a web application.

   b. An online store is an example of web applications.

   c. Web applications have the capacity to provide extensive collaboration or interactivity.

   d. A web application uses a web site as the front end to a more typical application.

Answer: A

13 Web applications are developed to display on what?

a. Client/servers

b. Browsers

c. Mainframes

d. High-end PCs

Answer: B

14 Which is not a key component of the web application architecture?

a. Server components

b. Web pages

c. Web forms

d. Graphical user interface (GUI)

Answer: D

15 Which component of the web application architecture is mainly used to collect user input?

a. Frame

b. Form

c. Client Component

d. Server Component

Answer: B

16 A Java servlet engine is a _____ .

a. Search engine

b. Program

c. Web server

d. Web application

Answer: B

17 Which web application language is not a programming language?

a. Perl

b. ActiveX

c. JAVA

d. HTML

Answer: B

18 CGI can be written in many languages, but the most popular one is _____ .

   a. Visual Basic

   b. Perl

   c. C

   d. Java

   Answer: B

19 In which scenario is a transaction considered illegal?

   a. Goods or services are incorrectly shipped or performed.

   b. Integrity constraint cannot be met.

   c. One of the B2B partners rejects the transaction.

   d. Data is passed between distributed components.

   Answer: B

20 When an update to a row can be performed quickly and with little overhead, this is called _____ .

   a. Indirect update

   b. Deferred update

   c. Update in place

   d. None of the above

   Answer: C

21 Query transactions are not used to create _____ .

   a. Terminal outputs

   b. Records

   c. Printed reports

   d. Transaction summaries

   Answer: B

22 Which statement about distributed transactions is false?

   a. A distributed transaction is more complex than a traditional transaction in terms of management.

   b. A distributed transaction is a transaction that involves multiple transaction resources running on two or more distinct nodes.

    c. Distributed transactions are important in maintaining consistency across multiple resource managers.

    d. A distributed transaction is different from a traditional transaction in that it does not have to conform to the ACID rule.

Answer: D

23 What transaction model does not need an explicit begin_transaction command to start a new transaction?

    a. Chained transactions

    b. Nested transaction

    c. Flat transaction

    d. Team transaction

Answer: A

24 Which statement is FALSE?

    a. Database management systems allow multiple users to simultaneously retrieve a record.

    b. Database engines are the parts of database management systems that actually perform the storing and data retrieving functions.

    c. Databases are collections of information organized to make data easily retrievable.

    d. Database management systems allow multiple users to simultaneously update a record.

Answer: D

25 Which element is not a component of a typical DBMS?

    a. Data Description Language

    b. Data Manipulation Language

    c. Data dictionary

    d. Query Language

    e. Data

Answer: E

26 Which one is not an advantage of a relational database?

    a. It reduces redundancy. Because the data between tables can be easily connected, the relational model provides a minimum level of controlled redundancy to eliminate most of the redundancies commonly found in file systems.

    b. It is faster than the other database systems because it requires minimum hardware and operating system overhead.

    c. It is simple and easy to maintain. You can modify or add new entities, attributes, or tables at any time without restructuring the entire database.

    d. It is easy to design the database because the relational model achieves both data and structural independence.

Answer: B

27 What statement about backup is false?

    a. An incremental backup alone is necessary to restore a database in case of failures.

    b. A full backup must be performed offline.

    c. An incremental backup creates a copy of only the journal files that have changed since the last backup.

    d. A full backup archives the entire database providing a copy of all data and journal files.

Answer: A

28 What situation does not limit the performance, efficiency, and cost-effectiveness of traditional RAID storage?

    a. Performance versus data protection

    b. Large versus small data transfers

    c. Read versus write performance

    d. Centralized versus distributed data management

Answer: D

29 What statement about object-oriented design is false?

    a. In object-oriented design, data and function are not separated.

    b. Objects are the central focus throughout object-oriented design.

    c. Object-oriented design indicates a top-down design process from the beginning of the class construction.

    d. Object-oriented design is based on a uniform underlying representation (classes and objects).

Answer: C

30 What language is the first object-oriented language?

   a. Eiffel

   b. Simula

   c. SmallTalk

   d. C++

Answer: B

31 What statement is not a benefit of object-oriented design?

   a. Fundamental infrastructure

   b. Reduced development time because of data structure reuse

   c. Superior quality because programs are created out of existing and tested elements

   d. Uncomplicated preservation of the scheme because changes to existing systems can be made by restoring the system

Answer: D

32 What statement about object and class is false?

   a. The class definition specifies the set of attributes and allowed operations for objects of the class.

   b. Polymorphism has the ability to take many forms as a single message to execute a specific function.

   c. An object is a self-contained entity that consists of both data and procedures to manipulate the data.

   d. A class is an abstraction of a real-world entity that can be either concrete or abstract.

   e. Instances are the individual items that are created using the class's creation mechanism.

Answer: B

33 What statement about the CASE tool is false?

   a. CASE technology is an important tool for large schemes.

   b. CASE tools were once considered an easy approach, but are now a necessity.

   c. CASE tools are hindered by their narrow mixture of techniques.

   d. CASE tools methodologies provide a way to present sophisticated processes.

Answer: C

34 What definition best describes a parallel computing pattern?

    a. A central modeling technique that runs through nearly all object-oriented methods

    b. A full lifecycle of analysis, design, coding, testing, and integration

    c. A reusable code-skeleton for quick and reliable development of correlative applications

    d. Indications between blocks and input and output from the environment

Answer: C

35 What definition best describes the difference between structured programming and OO programming?

    a. Structured programming discipline allows reasonable structure on large software systems based on the idea of encapsulation and inheritance, while object-oriented programming discipline limits control transfers to a small set.

    b. In object-oriented programming, all the data is usually placed before any of the functions are written.

    c. In object-oriented programming, the information and tasks are kept apart, while in structured programming they are combined into one unit.

    d. In structured programming, information and tasks are maintained independently, while in object-oriented programming they are kept together.

Answer: D

36 What language is not an object-oriented programming language?

    a. Java

    b. C++

    c. Perl

    d. SmallTalk

Answer: C

37 What statement about data models is false?

    a. A data model is a specification of the data structures needed to support a business area.

    b. A data model is to a database designer what blueprints are to a builder.

    c. A data model is built to map business concepts into relational objects.

    d. A data model is a miniature of the actual data itself.

Answer: D

38 What element is not a key component of a data model?

   a. Integrity rules

   b. Cost

   c. Data structure types

   d. Operators

Answer: B

39 What attribute is not essential to a good data model?

   a. Effectiveness

   b. Reusability

   c. Abstraction

   d. Transparency

Answer: B

40 What statement is not a benefit of data modeling?

   a. Data modeling allows each department to be accountable for its portion of the data.

   b. It leads to better system design that is understandable, flexible, and stable.

   c. It facilitates requirements clarification and documentation.

   d. It facilitates communication among knowledge workers.

   e. It reduces the cost of change.

Answer: A

41 What model is both software and hardware dependent?

   a. Conceptual model

   b. Logical model

   c. Physical model

   d. Transaction model

Answer: C

42 What model allows many-to-many relationships?

   a. Conceptual model

   b. Physical model

   c. Logical model

   d. Transaction model

Answer: A

43 What element is not one of the three components of an ER model?

a. Relationship

b. Cardinality

c. Entity

d. Attribute

Answer: B

44 The important ingredients of data modeling consist of which set?

a. Entity type, instance, and attributes

b. Domain, relationship, and cardinality

c. Relationship, entities, and attributes

d. Unary, binary, and ternary

Answer: C

45 What method is used as a system development methodology in which enterprise models, data models, and process models are built up in a comprehensive knowledge base and are used to create and maintain data processing systems?

a. Information engineering

b. IDEF1X

c. ORM

d. Entity relationship method

Answer: A

46 In what modeling method is it difficult to describe entities independently from relationships?

a. Entity relationship method

b. Information engineering

c. IDEF1X

d. ORM

Answer: D

47 What item does not fit in with IDEF1X?

   a. Relational systems

   b. Object-oriented systems

   c. No-Repeat Rule

   d. No-Null Rule

   Answer: B

48 Why is a thread sometimes called "lightweight"?

   a. It runs within the context of fully developed programs.

   b. It is an inexpensive code.

   c. It is easy to use.

   d. The design is not important.

   Answer: A

49 What statement about threads is false?

   a. Multithreaded models allow a single process to handle multiple tasks.

   b. Multithreaded programs can have several threads running through different code paths simultaneously.

   c. Multithreaded designs divide tasks into multiple processes and coordinates with signal handlers to provide concurrency.

   d. Multithreaded programs can avoid blocked input/output (I/O) by scheduling the next read while the previous write is finishing.

   Answer: C

50 What disadvantage is there to a multithreaded design?

   a. Complex learning curve

   b. CPU is inactive until the task is completed

   c. Set up to operate independently

   d. Expensive

   Answer: A

51 What statement is true?

    a. A program with many conditional functions can be modified as a thread.

    b. An advantage to using a single-threaded design is that the essential part of the OS that is responsible for the resource allocation is affected.

    c. Single-threaded program requests must wait for one job to complete before another can begin.

    d. Native threads are implemented by a Java runtime system instead of the operating system.

Answer: C

52 What device does not make I/O requests to hardware drivers?

    a. Monitor

    b. Printer

    c. Telephone

    d. Keyboard

    e. Disk drive

Answer: E

53 What function is not fundamental to hardware device software?

    a. Deny access to some devices

    b. Capture misbehaved requests

    c. Sponsor dissimilar interface to the user-level software

    d. Allocate and release dedicated devices

Answer: C

Chapter 3

1 Which word best describes the quality that a lifecycle model adds to an application project?

    a. Cost

    b. Location

    c. Order

    d. Time

Answer: C

2 The application development lifecycle became a tool to help businesses respond to greater competition in which manner?

a. More quickly

b. More honestly

c. More leisurely

d. More publicly

Answer: A

3 Which grouping of application development lifecycle phases is in the order in which they normally occur?

a. Analysis and design, development, test, implementation

b. Implementation, maintenance, business modeling and requirements

c. Business modeling and requirements, maintenance, development, implementation

d. Development, implementation, maintenance, test

Answer: A

4 Which is the definition of the business modeling and requirements phase of the application development lifecycle?

a. A demonstration of the application that allows the production specialists to determine the quality of the product or service resulting from use of the application

b. A simulation of the application, without the expense of actual performance to the application, which allows the marketing personnel to determine the potential for revenue generation during the lifecycle of the application

c. A requisition for contracting the application that allows the administration to determine the cost and schedule of implementation of that application

d. A representation of the application that allows the decision makers and application specialists in the business to capture, organize, and visualize the web-based application as if it were functioning within their business

Answer: D

5 Which feature is not a purpose of the Application Development Lifecycle Model?

a. Providing the basis for future application development

b. Supplying the specifications to which the application will be built

c. Organizing the knowledge of the people conducting business

d. Discussing the impact the system would have on company personnel requirements

Answer: B

6 Which set of inputs is required for developing a business model to present to the potential user of an application?

   a. Business need, business organization, company capabilities

   b. Business need, business organization, equipment inventory

   c. Business need, company capabilities, equipment inventory

   d. Business organization, company capabilities, equipment inventory

Answer: A

7 Which set of desired outputs reflects the business modeling and requirements phase?

   a. Customized procedures documentation, feasibility of the application, product or service

   b. Customized procedures documentation, feasibility of the application, gain or loss potential

   c. Customized procedures documentation, gain or loss potential, product or service

   d. Feasibility of the application, gain or loss potential, product or service

Answer: D

8 Which phase of the application development lifecycle does the business modeling and requirements phase provide input?

   a. Analysis and design

   b. Development

   c. Implementation

   d. All phases

Answer: D

9 Which does the business modeling and requirements phase treat the model as?

   a. Cost estimate

   b. Dynamic specification

   c. Equipment specification

   d. Marketing tool

Answer: B

10 Which of the following is not a part of the typical application specification that results from the analysis and design phase?

   a. Quotation response request

   b. Software and database specifications

   c. Networking specifications

   d. Equipment specifications

   Answer: A

11 Which accurately describes the analysis and design phase of the application development lifecycle?

   a. Produces a more detailed technical description of the system affecting and supporting the application

   b. Analyzes only the data received from the business modeling and requirements phase but restates it for technical clarity

   c. Attempts to reduce the requirements identified in the business modeling and requirements phase

   d. Modifies the intent of the business model from the business modeling and requirements phase

   Answer: A

12 Which set of analysis and design phase inputs assist the analysis and design team in developing the application system design?

   a. Cost analyses, existing applications, and training requirements

   b. Cost analyses, existing applications, and validation test requirements

   c. Cost analyses, training requirements, and validation test requirements

   d. Existing applications, training requirements, and validation test requirements

   Answer: D

13 Which phrase describes the output from the analysis and design phase of the application development lifecycle?

   a. Prototype of the application and all the technical specifications from which the developers can create the application

   b. Prototype of the application and basic technical information from which the developers can create the application

c. System design and all the technical specifications from which the developers can create the application

d. System design and basic technical information from which the developers can create the application

Answer: D

14 Which statement describes the level of design detail required during the analysis and design phase of the application development lifecycle?

a. The design specification should provide sufficient technical design detail that the developers will not need to develop any additional technical specification.

b. The design specification should provide sufficient technical design detail that the developer can develop the application but not so much that the developer cannot make necessary adjustments for the application environmental differences.

c. The design specification should provide general design information and wait until the development phase personnel request approval of their design.

d. The design specification should provide general design information and appropriately pass responsibility for finishing the design to the development engineers and the customer interface personnel.

Answer: B

15 What does the size and importance of the development phase do with an increase in size of the application?

a. Increases exponentially

b. Increases in proportion

c. Remains the same

d. Varies randomly

Answer: A

16 The purpose of the development phase is to translate the application system specification into an application implementation package that allows the application to work effectively _____ .

a. In the customer environment

b. In the development laboratory

c. On turnover to the implementation phase personnel

d. Under standard industry conditions

Answer: A

17 Which is the primary input to the development phase of the application development lifecycle?

   a. Customer contact point

   b. Equipment operating parameter

   c. Local regulation

   d. System specification

Answer: D

18 Besides the completed application design, the development phase output includes what set of additional pieces of data?

   a. Customer contracted cost, customer validation criteria

   b. Implementation schedule, customer contracted cost

   c. Implementation schedule, customer validation criteria

   d. Prototype operating parameters, customer validation criteria

Answer: C

19 What are the objectives of the analysis and design team and the implementation team, respectively?

   a. Designing the most technically efficient application; implementing to satisfy customer desire

   b. Designing to use company current equipment; implementing high reliability systems

   c. Designing to accommodate customer desire; providing the most technically efficient application

   d. Designing to use high profit margin systems; installing company current equipment

Answer: C

20 Which statement does not describe a benefit of testing and validation?

   a. Testing and validation ensures customer satisfaction.

   b. Testing and validation involves setting up the test scenarios and executing the test scenarios in a controlled manner.

   c. Testing and validation is a nice-to-have step that is dispensable for some Internet business solution projects.

   d. Testing and validation is the process of ensuring that the solution meets the business requirements.

Answer: C

21 Which does not represent a function of the test phase of the application development lifecycle?

a. Corrects the application system specification

b. Discovers any nonconformances to the application system specification

c. Integrates the application components and operations

d. Prepares for the formal acceptance of the application

Answer: A

22 Which is the purpose of the test phase of the application development lifecycle?

a. Ensuring the adequacy of the test plan provided by the customer

b. Preparing a formal final acceptance testing procedure

c. Limiting the test size by including only the application system specification

d. Proposing to the customer additional features for economical system performance enhancements

Answer: B

23 The test phase must acquire any inputs necessary to ensure that it can fully define
_____ .

a. Test objectives, test procedures, and test schedules

b. Test appeal to customer, test objectives, and test schedules

c. Test appeal to customer, test objectives, and test procedures

d. Test appeal to customer, test procedures, and test schedules

Answer: A

24 What must be satisfied before an application implementation is complete in the test phase?

a. Delivery milestones

b. Cost restrictions

c. Application requirements

d. Service successes

Answer: C

25 Which group is in the correct order of function?

    a. Application system specification, work priority, initial customer intent

    b. Initial customer intent, work priority, application system specification

    c. Initial customer intent, application system specification, work priority

    d. Application system specification, initial customer intent, work priority

Answer: C

26 Which is the most important objective of testing an application prior to implementing it?

    a. Ensuring that each function performs to specification

    b. Obscuring weak portions of the application by emphasizing the robust portions

    c. Ensuring that test personnel use time-saving software to do evaluation

    d. Testing how the application works within the end-to-end business process that it supports

Answer: D

27 Which of the following is not a type of testing that is usually performed in the testing and validation phase?

    a. User load testing

    b. Availability testing

    c. Application performance testing

    d. Functional testing

    e. Security testing

Answer: D

28 The purpose of application performance testing is to ensure that the application meets the _____ .

    a. Functional requirements

    b. Functional requirements in a single-user environment

    c. Nonfunctional requirements

    d. Nonfunctional requirements in a single-user environment

Answer: D

29 Which item does not need to be measured in application performance testing?

a. Process time

b. Traffic size

c. Throughput

d. GUI friendliness

Answer: D

30 Security testing is the process of _____ .

a. Applying assessment methodologies and tools that measure the cost of security components that are required to implement the designed security architecture across the entire Internet business infrastructure

b. Validating that the implemented security components across the entire Internet business security infrastructure are manageable

c. Applying assessment methodologies and tools across the entire security architecture to ensure that all security mechanisms are installed and configured to protect the information resources as designed and intended

d. Validating that the assessment methodologies and tools used on the entire security architecture are reliable and capable of measuring the performance of each security component

Answer: C

31 Which statement does not define user load testing?

a. User load testing is a type of testing that ensures that the application and system perform as expected when accessed by the maximum number of authorized users in the production environment.

b. User load testing is essential to verify that the application and system do meet the Service Level Agreement under excessive usage.

c. User load testing is a type of testing where you test the manageability of the application and system.

d. User load testing allows you to observe the application and system behavior under load conditions.

Answer: C

32 Which of the following is not a device on which you need to collect measurements during availability testing?

   a. WAN simulator

   b. Servers

   c. Control clients

   d. Network components

   Answer: A

33 The output of an application assessment is a/an _____ .

   a. Application architecture diagram of the application that will be deployed

   b. Network architecture diagram of the network in which the application will be run

   c. Set of typical transactions that are representative of the way that the application will be used by users

   Answer: C

34 Which consideration is not needed when determining how an application will be deployed on a network during application assessment?

   a. Locations of users and servers

   b. Frequency with which users execute the application transactions

   c. Number of users at each location

   d. Number of servers at each location

   Answer: D

35 Which component is not in a typical lab environment?

   a. WAN simulator

   b. Client

   c. Production circuit

   d. Server

   e. Data collection device

   Answer: C

36 Which type of data does not need to be collected in application performance testing?

   a. Throughput

   b. Network errors

   c. Menu options for the GUI

   d. Quantity of data

   e. Process time for each server and client

   Answer: C

37 Which tool is not a data collection tool in application performance testing?

   a. Traffic analyzer

   b. Netsys

   c. Sniffer

   d. Test inputs

   Answer: B

38 Which tool is an example of a performance analysis tool that analyzes metrics for collected data?

   a. RMON probe

   b. Optimal application expert

   c. Network modeling tool

   d. Prototype user

   Answer: B

39 Which metric do you not need to obtain after the final results analysis in application performance testing?

   a. Transaction sizes for each tier of the transaction

   b. Processing time for each server and client component

   c. Average think time for a user

   d. Total transaction response time

   Answer: C

40 Which step is the first in the recommended approach for security testing?

   a. Install and configure security components.

   b. Review security requirements.

   c. Set up testing lab environments.

   d. Generate test scenarios.

Answer: B

41 Which environment is not one of the three final target environments that are recommended in the best-practice security testing approach?

   a. Production environment

   b. Development environment

   c. Lab environment

   d. QA environment

Answer: C

42 Implementing and testing a security architecture in a lab environment can be a staging process for promoting it to a development, QA, or production environment. Which advantage best describes the staging process?

   a. It provides an assurance that all three target environments have identical security components installed.

   b. It provides an isolated and controlled lab environment where iterative security tests can be performed without interference from unexpected variables.

   c. It provides ample time to ensure that testing occurs iteratively and accurately prior to promoting the security architecture.

   d. It provides an identical replication of a real-world environment for the security testing to produce accurate and reliable results.

Answer: B

43 The verification process essentially requires that the functionality of security components be validated and corrected across the entire Internet business infrastructure. Which statement best describes why this verification process is essential?

   a. It ensures that the security controls are successfully achieving the protection of the intended information resources.

   b. It ensures that the operational framework is manageable and scalable.

c. It ensures that the systems, network, applications, and operations infrastructures are all assessed with a single security methodology.

d. It ensures that the application components are free of threats and vulnerabilities.

Answer: A

44 Which of the following is not a purpose of user load testing?

a. To verify that application functionality meets user requirements

b. To verify that performance in terms of response time for the user of the application meets SLA goals under load conditions

c. To determine whether current capability is sufficient for SLA goals

d. To measure the individual user experience as overall user load is increased on the system

Answer: A

45 There are four steps in a user load testing process:

Set up testing environments and select measurement tools.

Analyze results.

Determine user load testing scenarios.

Execute testing and collect measurement.

Which order of steps is correct?

a. A-B-C-D

b. A-D-B-C

c. C-A-D-B

d. A-C-D-B

Answer: C

46 Which of the following describes the two elements of a user load testing scenario?

a. Maximum number of users and transaction mix

b. Average number of users and transaction mix

c. Transaction mix and transaction distribution

d. Target population and concurrency rate

Answer: A

47 Which of the following describes a good practice to follow when testing?

    a. Rapidly increase the load on the target system incrementally.

    b. Have a fast ramp-up of users—1000+ at one time.

    c. Always start with the peak number of users.

    d. Ramp up slowly to the number of users to be tested.

Answer: D

48 Which of the following is not a component of the user load testing environment?

    a. Control client

    b. LoadRunner

    c. Knowledgeable users

    d. Virtual users

Answer: C

49 Which device collects data on virtual users?

    a. Virtual users

    b. LoadRunner

    c. Control client

    d. Traffic analyzer

Answer: B

50 In a load testing, you need to collect two types of data for virtual users. One is response time and the other one is _____ .

    a. CPU use

    b. Throughput

    c. Memory use

    d. Pass and fail of each transaction

Answer: D

51 When analyzing load testing results, you need to first look at the data collected to see if there is a problem. Which one of the following is not a type of data that you should examine at this point?

    a. User perception data

    b. Application performance data for control client (response time for client, server, network)

c. Response time for each transaction executed by virtual users

d. Pass and fail of each transaction

Answer: A

52 Which description is not appropriate for availability testing?

a. Availability testing is to ensure that unplanned downtime is kept to a minimum.

b. Availability testing is to ensure that security controls are operating correctly.

c. Availability testing is to verify that application performance meets SLA goals under certain failure conditions.

d. Availability testing involves breaking a stable system and observing what happens.

Answer: B

53 Which of the following is not a typical failure scenario?

a. System components failure

b. Network components failure

c. User-error/process failure

d. Network connectivity failure

Answer: C

54 Which of the following is not a network connectivity failure?

a. Database server LAN connection failure

b. Dedicated WAN circuit failure

c. Database query failure

d. ISP connection failure

Answer: C

55 Which of the following is not a measurement that you need to collect in availability testing?

a. Application functionality

b. Whether the redundant device is operating correctly

c. The overall performance after the system is stable again

d. The time for the switch-over to take place

Answer: A

56 Which of the following is not a task that you need to execute in availability testing?

    a. Fail components that have the most impact first.

    b. Test in a single-user environment.

    c. Apply the peak number of virtual users.

    d. None of the above.

Answer: B

57 A sniffer is generally used to collect data on _____ .

    a. Servers

    b. Routers

    c. The control client

    d. DVirtual users

Answer: C

58 Which of the following is not a conclusion that you are trying to draw in an availability testing results analysis?

    a. Whether the response time meets the SLA goals under different load conditions

    b. Whether the speed of convergence is acceptable

    c. Whether any user connectivity is lost because of slow response

    d. Whether traffic is rerouted when a path fails

Answer: A

59 Which of the following is not a typical type of chart to be put in an application performance testing report?

    a. Transaction response time chart

    b. Total bytes per transaction chart

    c. Total number of users supported chart

    d. User perception report

Answer: C

60 Which of the following is not a conclusion that you are trying to draw in an application performance testing results analysis?

    a. Whether any user connectivity is lost because of slow response

    b. Whether the response time meets the SLA goals under different load conditions

   c. Whether the speed of convergence is acceptable

   d. Whether traffic is rerouted when a path fails

Answer: B

61 Which set of requirements is not a critical part of the documentation for security testing?

   a. Security standard and functional security requirements for systems and network

   b. Security policies and procedures, and user account administration

   c. User perceptions toward security requirements

   d. Functional security requirements for applications

Answer: C

62 Which chart is not a typical test results chart for user load testing?

   a. The database server interrupts per second chart

   b. User perception chart

   c. The web server CPU utilization chart

   d. The control client performance metrics table

Answer: B

63 Which of the following is not a typical test results chart for availability testing?

   a. Database CPU utilization chart

   b. Control client performance metrics table

   c. Web server number of connections per second chart

   d. Control client memory utilization chart

Answer: D

64 Which of the following is not a phase in the software development lifecycle?

   a. Operation

   b. Test

   c. Analysis and design

   d. Business modeling and requirements implementation

Answer: A

65 Which set of three components makes up the development phase?

a. Technical, functional, creative

b. Internet, extranet, intranet

c. Support preparation, market effectiveness, best practices

d. Master technology plan, operations strategy IT strategy, marketing strategy, business strategy enterprise's vision

Answer: A

66 Which of the following is not an activity that a CISS typically performs in an Internet business solution project?

a. Implementation plan

b. Security assessment

c. Application architecture design

d. Financial audit

Answer: D

67 Which of the following is not an activity that a CISS typically performs in an Internet business solution project?

a. Testing scenarios validation

b. Network and system management planning

c. Nonfunctional requirements identification

d. Router and switch configuration

e. Current network assessment

Answer: D

68 What statement is not a responsibility of a CISS in the business modeling and requirements phase?

a. Validate completion of the business modeling and requirements phase.

b. Lay out design and implementation details.

c. Keep the requirements gathering focused on business, functional, and information models.

d. Provide leadership on gathering system requirements.

Answer: B

69 Which of the following statements is not accurate?

a. A CISS does not participate in requirements gathering.

b. Functional requirements describe the core activities that the system must perform.

c. Nonfunctional requirements describe constraints on the system such as availability or security.

d. Business modeling and requirements is the first phase of the software development lifecycle.

Answer: A

70 Which statement does not describe the tasks involved in gathering systems requirements?

a. Analyzing functional requirements data helps the CISS understand the specific functions, tasks, or behaviors that the system must support.

b. Assessing current system, processes, people, and tools provides input to the planning process.

c. Defining all nonfunctional requirements can be done without knowing the functional requirements.

d. Defining system performance expectations can include elements such as security, availability, and space efficiency.

Answer: C

71 Which statement reflects the major tasks involved in validating completion of the business modeling and requirements phase?

a. Walkthrough of SLA, identify reusable components, provide input on order of magnitude, define nonfunctional requirements

b. Walkthrough of business models and requirements, identify potential areas of reusability, develop project plan, generate a system concept

c. Walkthrough of business models and requirements, ensure SLA components are in place, identify reusable components, generate the system concept

d. Ensure SLA components are in place, define system requirements, identify reusable components, develop project plan

Answer: C

72 Which of the following statements is not a major responsibility of the CISS during the analysis and design phase of the software development lifecycle?

   a. Analyze return on investment (ROI) data.

   b. Design a robust and maintainable system.

   c. Analyze business requirements in relation to system architecture.

   d. Design a system architecture and application solution that satisfies business requirements.

   e. Develop a project management plan.

   Answer: A

73 Which task is not involved in analyzing business requirements in relation to system architecture?

   a. Validate data flow diagrams, data dictionary, and data modeling against requirements.

   b. Specify hardware and software requirements.

   c. Assess the current system architecture relative to requirements.

   d. Verify process modeling and process descriptions against requirements.

   Answer: B

74 Which task is not one of the tasks involved in designing a robust and maintainable system?

   a. Ensure that the disaster recovery and backup process is in place.

   b. Provide input on prototyping and testing strategies.

   c. Verify that security issues are addressed.

   d. Ensure that the disaster recovery and backup process is in place.

   e. Redefine nonfunctional requirements.

   Answer: E

75 Which set of tasks comprises the responsibility of designing a system architecture and application solution that meets business requirements?

   a. Verify that the design fulfills requirements, develop the application, specify the hardware and software needed, and generate the design document.

   b. Lead architecture and application design, verify that the design fulfills requirements, specify the hardware and software needed, and generate the design document.

c. Verify that the design fulfills requirements, participate in prototyping, specify the hardware and software needed, and generate the design document.

d. Lead architecture and application design, specify the hardware and software, verify that the design meets requirements, and develop the application.

Answer: B

76 Which of the following is not a responsibility that a CISS can perform during the development phase?

a. Ensure that the design document is adhered to.

b. Confirm that change control processes exist.

c. Verify that all necessary resources exist to perform development.

d. Confirm that quality assurance testing has been performed.

e. Ensure that documentation is created.

Answer: D

77 Which task is not necessary for a CISS to perform when contributing to the physical integration of the architecture components defined in the design document?

a. Ensure that a change control process exists.

b. Determine hardware sizing.

c. Review design document strategies with the appropriate administrators and staff.

Answer: A

78 Which set of data does the CISS have to determine hardware sizing for?

a. Number of servers, amount of memory, number of users

b. Number of CPUs, number of servers, appropriate bandwidth

c. Number of users, appropriate bandwidth, number of servers

d. Amount of memory, number of users, number of CPUs

Answer: B

79 When reviewing the design document implementation strategies with the appropriate administrators and staff, the CISS might need to _____ .

a. Develop the preliminary maintenance schedule.

b. Determine the impact of the test phase.

c. Design a change control process.

d. Determine the implementation approach.

Answer: D

80 Which statement is not an activity included in Internet business project management during the development phase?

a. Learning to negotiate with customers and end users to achieve a balance between schedule and functionality

b. Using triage to focus on critical functionality and features

c. Learning about effective light methodologies

d. Contracting with outside vendors for support of application server pages

Answer: D

81 Which statement about a change control process is false?

a. The change control process tracks who has a document checked out.

b. After a document has been checked out, a change control process prohibits anyone else from checking out the same document until it has been returned.

c. The person who checks out a document updates the version number before returning the document.

d. The change control process saves the updated document after it has been returned.

Answer: C

82 Which data is the change control process not used to track changes in?

a. Updates to configuration files

b. Results of running test case scenarios

c. Modifications to the design document

d. Changes to code

Answer: B

83 Which statement is not valid about the tasks that a CISS performs while ensuring that the design document is being adhered to during the development phase?

a. Confirm that a process exists to do walkthroughs of deliverables.

b. Establish regular information exchange sessions.

c. Ensure that the code delivery is meeting scheduled deadlines.

d. Monitor and verify project progress against the design document.

Answer: C

84 Which task might a CISS not perform while confirming that each individual development group is performing adequate unit testing during the development phase?

   a. Ensure that unit test activities are included in the project plan.

   b. Confirm design specifications of test scenarios.

   c. Review unit test scenarios and results.

   d. None of the above.

Answer: B

85 A set of rules, processes, and procedures that are followed by all members of a project team during the development phase is a _____ .

   a. Network change control process

   b. Prototyping tool

   c. Structured development methodology

   d. None of the above

Answer: C

86 Which methodology is not a major structured development methodology?

   a. Rapid application development

   b. Change control process

   c. Joint application development

   d. Light methodologies

Answer: B

87 Which category of tools might a CISS not use during the development phase?

   a. Application assessment tools

   b. Documentation tools

   c. Application development tools

   d. None of the above

Answer: A

88 A new approach used by some organizations to create documentation is _____ .

 a. Version tracking all the project team's documents

 b. Audio taping conference calls

 c. Video taping the project's technical meetings

 d. None of the above

 Answer: C

89 Which statement is not an application development tool?

 a. Debugger

 b. Scalability tool

 c. Editor

 d. Compiler

 Answer: B

90 Which statement is not a responsibility that a CISS performs during the test phase?

 a. Resolve testing issues by updating the design document.

 b. Confirm that the test plan is sufficient to test the system requirements as specified in the design document.

 c. Verify that testing is performed.

 d. Ensure that test results are analyzed.

 Answer: A

91 Which task is not necessary for a CISS to perform while confirming that the test plan is sufficient to test for the system requirements, as specified in the design document?

 a. Verify that sufficient resources are available for the test environment.

 b. Confirm that test cases are written and executed.

 c. Discuss the various approaches/techniques that can validate an application.

 d. Guarantee that the complete scope of the project is considered when developing the test plan.

 e. Ensure that all requirements, as specified in the design document, have been identified.

 Answer: B

92 When examining the scope of a project, be sure to consider _____ .

a. Performance testing

b. Staffing requirements

c. Testing schedule

d. Filtered power needs

Answer: A

93 Which resource is not necessary when verifying that sufficient resources are available for a test environment?

a. Support services

b. People requirements

c. System and support software

d. Help desk scripts

e. Client and server hardware

Answer: D

94 When creating test cases, which consideration is not needed?

a. Find those things that are wrong.

b. Discard test cases after testing.

c. Capture the maximum number of errors in the most cost effective way.

d. Use walkthroughs of test cases and inspections of test data.

Answer: B

95 Which task is not necessary for a CISS to execute while verifying that testing is performed?

a. Review the design document to identify functional and nonfunctional requirements.

b. Verify that documentation is validated.

c. Ensure that integration, system, and regression testing are performed.

d. Confirm that an incident/problem reporting process is in place and being used.

Answer: A

96   The incident problem reporting process is important because it can _____ .

    a. Solve compilation errors

    b. Help identify problem issues and trends

    c. Create test scenarios to test discrepancies

    d. None of the above

    Answer: B

97   Which statement does not apply to documentation?

    a. User documentation should be verified while using the associated test scenarios.

    b. Software program documentation is part of the configuration documentation.

    c. Documentation of installation instructions should be validated during the building of the test environment.

    d. Help desk scripts can include when and how issues should be escalated.

    Answer: B

98   Which task is not necessary for a CISS to perform while ensuring that test results are analyzed?

    a. Verify that incidents/problems are resolved.

    b. Confirm that actual test results match expected results.

    c. Identify documentation to include in the test.

    d. None of the above.

    Answer: C

99   Which task is not necessary for a CISS to perform while collaborating with acceptance testing?

    a. Ensure that incidents/problems are resolved.

    b. Guarantee that developers perform acceptance testing.

    c. Verify that the acceptance test plan exists.

    d. None of the above.

    Answer: B

100 Which statement does not apply to acceptance testing criteria?

   a. Developers establish the completion criteria.

   b. The actual customer team that is running the developed system in the customer environment must perform hands-on testing and acceptance.

   c. The actual software and hardware configuration must be tested.

   d. The actual procedures and documentation that will exist and that will be required to meet the stated objectives of the system must be used in the test.

   Answer: A

101 Which of the following might a customer receive during the implementation phase?

   a. Marketing tools

   b. Documentation

   c. Design parameters

   d. Business plan

   Answer: B

102 What does the implementation team specify in the implementation phase?

   a. Implementation activities

   b. Application system specification

   c. Acceptance criteria

   d. Performance criteria

   Answer: A

103 The inputs to the implementation phase consist of specifications and instructions that are required to perform what functions?

   a. Install, maintain, and test the application

   b. Install, obtain acceptance for, and maintain the application

   c. Install, obtain acceptance for, and test the application

   d. Maintain, obtain acceptance for, and test the application

   Answer: C

104 The application provider gives the customer, as an output of the implementation phase of the applications development lifecycle, manuals and other items needed to operate and maintain the application _____ .

   a. Automatically

   b. Bimodally

   c. Experimentally

   d. Independently

Answer: D

105 The implementation phase links to the development phase to provide _____ .

   a. Implementation schedule changes

   b. Potential application additions

   c. Recommendations for change

   d. Reports of implementation progress

Answer: C

106 Which is an important responsibility of implementation phase personnel?

   a. Customizing the application to accommodate customer changes

   b. Completing the application implementation process with good business advantage

   c. Concluding their own company business as quickly as possible

   d. Satisfying all the expressed customer desires

Answer: B

107 Which task is not necessary for the CISS to ensure is in place during the implementation phase?

   a. Secure training environments for support personnel.

   b. Secure a comprehensive implementation plan.

   c. Secure a comprehensive requirements analysis.

   d. Secure training environments for users.

Answer: C

108 Which item does a CISS not need to verify is in place in a comprehensive implementation plan?

a. Notification plan

b. Development process

c. Contingency plan

d. Migration process

e. Installation procedures

Answer: B

109 Which statement associated with verifying that the appropriate parties receive their required deliverables is true?

a. All solution components have identical installation procedures.

b. Solution components never need to follow a specified order for distribution.

c. Verification that all the deliverables required to move into implementation is critical to a successful implementation.

d. A tracking process for the solution versions can ease the installation process by distributing the required solution files to separate locations.

Answer: C

110 Which statement is false?

a. A CISS must assist in developing plans and strategies to address training requirements.

b. Production environments must have more stability than the training environment.

c. Availability and accuracy of training environments can be critical in an Internet business application implementation.

d. CISS must be involved in ensuring that the training environment reflects the released system.

Answer: B

111 A site survey checklist is used to do which of the following?

a. Provide metrics including performance, storage capacity, and memory use.

b. Provide all parties in the improvement endeavor a chance to examine the resources, implementation plan, and implementation process.

    c. Distribute software to all desktops and servers on the network from a central location.

    d. Identify gaps in required hardware, software, and support for a new solution.

Answer: D

112 Which is a benefit for the customer of the maintenance phase?

    a. Maintenance of the application environment after implementation

    b. Support for the application during implementation

    c. Support for the operation of the application during the test phase

    d. Sustaining the application from acceptance until no further changes occur

Answer: D

113 Which is not a purpose of the maintenance phase of the application development lifecycle?

    a. Redesigning the application to improve output

    b. Sustaining the application operational capabilities

    c. Making corrections to the application system

    d. Upgrading the application capacity to support the changing needs of the user

Answer: A

114 Which is the characteristic of the maintenance phase that is different from the input process in the other phases that are involved in the process of getting inputs?

    a. Monitoring

    b. Codifying

    c. Sanitizing

    d. Purchasing

Answer: A

115 Which represents an output of the maintenance phase of the application development lifecycle?

    a. Tuning the application for improved effectiveness

    b. Application servicing

    c. Repair activity

    d. Recommendation for change of application

Answer: D

116 Which of the following is not a major handover criterion?

    a. Completed performances within the maintenance phase

    b. All documentation conforms to standards

    c. Smoothly operating system

    d. Complete and consistent source documentation

Answer: A

117 Which of the following is not an item that the CISS might be responsible for ensuring is in place in the maintenance phase?

    a. Tracking and reporting process

    b. Requirements analysis document

    c. Continuous improvement process

    d. Processes in place to support maintenance of systems in production

Answer: B

118 The CISS ensures that systems:

    a. Are available

    b. Perform within acceptable criteria

    c. Are in compliance

    d. All of the above

    e. None of the above

Answer: D

119 Production systems should be backed up on a regular basis.

    a. True

    b. False

Answer: A

120 DRPs should be validated daily.

    a. True

    b. False

Answer: B

121 Change management prevents change from occurring.

    a. True

    b. False

Answer: B

122 Production systems require maintenance.

    a. True

    b. False

Answer: T

123 Which statement is a benefit of tracking and cataloging problems?

    a. Problems can be prioritized.

    b. Problems are documented so that they can be resolved.

    c. Appropriate personnel are notified when there is a problem.

    d. All of the above.

    e. None of the above.

Answer: D

124 Which term distinguishes the Waterfall Lifecycle Model from the Basic Lifecycle Model?

    a. Sequential

    b. Repeating

    c. Coincident

    d. Parallel

Answer: A

125 The Waterfall Lifecycle Model came into existence to deal with which problem in the software development process?

    a. Overly structured business processes

    b. Disorganized attempts at development

    c. Lack of focus the customer desires

    d. Tendency to develop documentation before code development

Answer: B

126 Which statement about the inputs to the Waterfall Lifecycle Model is true?

   a. The inputs to the phases of the Waterfall Lifecycle Model are the same as those for the same phases in the Basic Lifecycle Model.

   b. The inputs to all the phases of the Waterfall Lifecycle Model must be gathered before beginning the project because the process is sequential.

   c. The Waterfall Lifecycle Model has no inputs because of the random variable concept that enhance development options.

   d. The inputs to the Waterfall Lifecycle Model accrue as the various phases repeat during the development process.

Answer: A

127 Which sentence describes the outputs associated with the Waterfall Lifecycle Model?

   a. The outputs from each phase of the Waterfall Lifecycle Model become a unique section of the implementation plan.

   b. No outputs from any phase serve as feedback input to any earlier phase.

   c. Each phase outputs its own input data after modification for accuracy.

   d. The Waterfall Lifecycle Model has no outputs from any phase except the implementation phase because of the random development process employed.

Answer: B

128 Which is a weakness of the Waterfall Lifecycle Model?

   a. Produces something deliverable during each phase of the lifecycle

   b. Enforces a strict order of accomplishing phase objectives

   c. Provides no feedback loops

   d. Attempts to randomly develop the application

Answer: C

129 The Iterative Lifecycle Model forces which of the following development processes?

   a. Customer involvement avoidance

   b. Cost analysis based on continually upgraded engineering estimates

   c. Application requirements freezing after lifecycle starts

   d. Continual adjustment of plans based on risk analysis

Answer: D

130 Which three functions are purposes of the Iterative Lifecycle Model?

    a. Avoids continual assessment processes, corrects the problems associated with the Waterfall Lifecycle Model, and facilitates the communication of requirements among developers

    b. Allows recursion during the course of design and development, avoids continual assessment processes, and facilitates the communication of requirements among developers

    c. Allows recursion during the course of design and development, corrects the problems associated with the Waterfall Lifecycle Model, and facilitates the communication of requirements among developers

    d. Avoids continual assessment processes, corrects the problems associated with the Waterfall Lifecycle Model, and facilitates the communication of requirements among developers

Answer: C

131 Besides the usual inputs required by other business lifecycle models, the Iterative Lifecycle Model requires which input?

    a. A set of assumptions about the number of iterations allowed in the development process

    b. An expected rate of decline in application improvement for each additional iteration

    c. An estimate of the operational longevity of the initial prototype

    d. A firm definition of the end product of the iterative process

Answer: A

132 Which is a unique output of each iteration of the Iterative Lifecycle Model?

    a. Statement of remaining development budget

    b. Comparison of the current iteration goal with that of the previous iterations

    c. Plan that identifies the goal of the next iteration

    d. Assessment of differences in the final application and the current prototype

Answer: C

133 Which aspect of the Iterative Lifecycle Model can assist with assessing the contribution required of each lifecycle phase team for an application development?

   a. Process architecture

   b. Projected number of prototypes

   c. Client business organization

   d. Average of development team estimates

Answer: A

134 Which set of lifecycles has sequential phases?

   a. RAD and Waterfall

   b. Cleanroom and Spiral

   c. Iterative and Waterfall

   d. Iterative and Prototype

Answer: A

135 Which description characterizes the Cleanroom Lifecycle Model?

   a. Extensive modeling of the product

   b. Numerous development iterations

   c. Quick development

   d. Rigorous adherence to specifications

Answer: D

136 Which set of characteristics best match, in order, the Spiral, Prototype, Cleanroom, and RAD Lifecycle Models?

   a. Useful application during development, little maintenance, less initial cost, risk management

   b. Less initial cost, risk management, useful application during development, little maintenance

   c. Little maintenance, less initial cost, risk management, useful application during development

   d. Risk management, useful application during development, little maintenance, less initial cost

Answer: D

137   Which lifecycle model would you use if you did a research project but did not know all the requirements, options, and constraints at the start of the project?

   a. Iterative

   b. RAD

   c. Spiral

   d. Waterfall

   Answer: C

138   Which lifecycle model tends to produce applications needing the least maintenance?

   a. Spiral

   b. Cleanroom

   c. Iterative

   d. Waterfall

   Answer: B

139   Which set of three lifecycle models emphasizes repeating application development lifecycle activities until the application meets requirements?

   a. Waterfall, Iterative, Spiral

   b. Iterative, Spiral, Prototype

   c. Prototype, Cleanroom, RAD

   d. Spiral, Prototype, Cleanroom

   Answer: B

140   Which application development lifecycle model requires a large fraction of the development budget at the beginning of the lifecycle?

   a. Spiral

   b. RAD

   c. Prototype

   d. Iterative

   Answer: C

141 Which set of two application development lifecycle models requires multitalented developers with high levels of expertise?

a. Iterative and Waterfall

b. Iterative and Prototype

c. Spiral and Prototype

d. Cleanroom and RAD

Answer: D

142 Which lifecycle model would you not use if you desired to avoid the probability of the customer identifying additional application requirements during development?

a. Spiral

b. Waterfall

c. Prototype

d. Cleanroom

Answer: C

143 Which application development lifecycle model would an application provider use if they knew that they would need to attract funding before they could finish development of the application?

a. RAD

b. Spiral

c. Iterative

d. Prototype

Answer: D

144 Which application development lifecycle model can result in your meeting all the major project specifications and the customer still feeling somewhat dissatisfied with the application received?

a. Spiral

b. Iterative

c. Prototype

d. RAD

Answer: D

145 Which application development lifecycle model can produce several useful applications of lesser value while developing and implementing the final application?

a. Spiral

b. RAD

c. Iterative

d. Prototype

Answer: D

Chapter 4

1 Which statement is a common approach when designing an application's authentication structure?

a. Focus on creating and building the authentication structure within the application.

b. Rely on the application's team to design and implement the authentication services.

c. Focus on selecting the simplest and most cost-effective solution.

d. Rely on external authentication services that are available to the application.

Answer: D

2 Access control mechanisms within an application should be able to support some basic objectives. Which of the following objectives is not an achievable objective?

a. Detecting when end users share their access privileges

b. Encrypting stored data

c. Assigning a security profile to each end user

d. Managing user accounts and policies

Answer: A

3 Data confidentiality and data integrity can be achieved through appropriately implementing authentication and access control mechanisms. Which of the following implementations does not support either of these two goals?

a. Performing periodic audit log reviews to prevent security breaches

b. Including edit checks, such as date checks and valid ranges, in data entry panels

c. Assigning access to sensitive data only to end users with a need to know

d. Enabling data encryption services within the application

Answer: A

4 To support auditing requirements, applications must provide certain logging conditions. Which of the following is not considered an essential condition?

  a. Log the data, time, and location for all significant events.

  b. Log all modifications, additions, or deletions made against the database.

  c. Log all inquiries made against the database.

  d. Log the identity of the user or process that performed an action.

Answer: C

5 What is the purpose of security technologies?

  a. To make an application more accessible and available through security

  b. To provide an application with a safer and more secure image

  c. To enhance the look and feel of the application

  d. To ensure that an application is completely protected from threats

Answer: A

6 An effective tool that monitors events in an application log for attacks, anomalous activities, resource utilization, and availability is an example of _____ .

  a. Directory services

  b. Virtual Private Networks

  c. Public key infrastructure

  d. Intrusion-detection systems

Answer: D

7 What is the correct definition of reliability?

  a. Reliability is the probability that a system or a system's capability functions without failure for a specified time.

  b. Reliability is the ability to service a component in the system without shutting down the entire operation.

  c. Reliability is when the state of an executing program is periodically saved to a disk file from which it can be recovered.

  d. Reliability is the ability to continue to perform a specified task even when a hardware failure occurs.

Answer: A

8 What is the correct definition of availability?

a. Availability is the process of restoring a backup because of a planned business situation or an unplanned event.

b. Availability is the probability that a system functions satisfactorily in a specified environment.

c. Availability is a way to store the same data in different places on multiple hard disks.

d. Availability provides a means for easier management of your computing resources, while not restricting the systems' potential capabilities.

Answer: B

9 Which of these choices is not a method used to achieve reliability and availability?

a. SLAs

b. Outage

c. Backup and recovery

d. Clustering

Answer: B

10 Which statement does not describe a scalability characteristic?

a. Scalability is the ease with which a system or component is modified to fit a problem area.

b. Scalability is a combination of things, including good database management.

c. Scalability refers to how well a hardware or software system can adapt to increased demands.

d. Scalability will not change in size or configuration to suit changing conditions.

Answer: D

11 Which question is not a factor to consider for scalability?

a. How many records can the system hold?

b. How well does the application grow?

c. How many users can use the system at one time?

d. How long can each user be on the system?

Answer: D

12 In relation to scalable software solutions, software components should be distributed across what type of platform?

    a. Multithreaded

    b. Single

    c. Threaded

    d. Multiple

Answer: D

13 Which method should not be considered to ensure a scalable network?

    a. Increasing the number of CPUs on your web servers

    b. Express forwarding

    c. DistributedDirector

    d. Tag switching

Answer: D

14 Which service allows enterprises and service providers to conserve valuable IP addresses by hiding internal IP address from public networks?

    a. DistributedDirector

    b. Tag switching

    c. Network Address Translation

    d. NetFlow switching

Answer: C

15 If you double the number of processors on your web server, performance should _____ .

    a. Decrease by half

    b. Increase, but less than double

    c. Increase exponentially by a factor of four

    d. Double

Answer: B

16 Which factor is not important for application performance?

   a. User productivity

   b. Application being up

   c. Perception

   d. Logic

Answer: D

17 What workload growth is related to increased transactions and more component access?

   a. User population

   b. Transaction complexity

   c. Component allocation

   d. Application population

Answer: A

18 What design factor determines how a database can affect performance?

   a. Workload growth

   b. Transaction complexity

   c. Indexing

   d. Application population

Answer: C

19 Which of these statements describes a multi-user operating system?

   a. It allows two or more users to run programs at the same time. Some operating systems permit hundreds or thousands of concurrent users.

   b. The operating system supports running a program on more than one CPU.

   c. It allows multiple programs to run concurrently.

   d. The operating system allows different parts of a single program to run concurrently.

Answer: A

20 Which of these actions is not a reason to support software maintenance?

   a. Performing enhancements to optimize

   b. Correcting errors in the software

   c. Adapting to change in the operational environment

   d. Adding an Internet interface to a legacy billing application

Answer: D

21 Application services administration can affect application manageability by which of these means?

   a. Taking care of the database design and implementation

   b. Not maintaining documentation and standards

   c. Working without a team

   d. Capacity planning

Answer: A

22 Which of these services is not typically provided by the operations management team?

   a. Changing the application code to add new functionality

   b. Providing console services

   c. Retaining an onsite maintenance staff

   d. Operating a help desk service

Answer: A

23 Which of these features is not required to support an application's manageability?

   a. Architecture

   b. Environments that perform stress and volume testing

   c. Global clientele

   d. Distribution and management

Answer: C

24 Which statement is not a description of application integration?

   a. Application integration is about interoperability and information synchronization across multiple applications.

   b. Application integration is about bringing together multiple disparate applications so that they work together, as if they were one application.

   c. Application integration provides the path and traffic management for message flow between integrated resources.

   d. Application integration must have a tool or methodology in place to facilitate this process.

Answer: C

25 What benefit is not linked to application integration?

   a. 10 to 15 percent reduction in IT budget

   b. 25 to 50 percent reduction in time-to-market for new applications

   c. Increased efficiency through consistent and accurate information available in real time

   d. Reduced cost and complexity compared to custom point-to-point integration

Answer: A

26 What question should not be asked when considering application integration?

   a. What resources are available to address the problem?

   b. How much space is on the hard drive?

   c. What entry points are available into the applications being integrated?

   d. How many applications need to be integrated?

Answer: B

Chapter 5

1 For which business category would an organization use an insourcing model?

   a. Administration

   b. Context

   c. Core

   d. Personnel

Answer: C

2 Which reason explains why companies tend to underestimate the resources they use to support an internally sourced business application?

a. Because the business application is new, accounting has no established accounts to debit for the application expenses.

b. Only resources used by the developing application's final version get counted, and the development costs get assigned to overhead account categories.

c. Some parts of the new business application support get charged to existing operating budgets.

d. The department in charge of implementing the new business application wants to disguise the actual application costs.

Answer: C

3 Which of the following are associated with using an insourcing model for business application development and implementation?

a. Application development failure, changed solution need, noncompetitive application

b. Changed solution need, noncompetitive application, premature implementation

c. Application development failure, noncompetitive application, premature implementation

d. Application development failure, changed solution need, premature implementation

Answer: A

4 Which statement best explains why the insourcing model allows the business application the most secure environment of all the sourcing models?

a. Customers sign standard nondisclosure statements before doing application business.

b. The insourcing model retains application elements within the company.

c. The internally sourced application model generates little product to compromise.

d. With the insourcing model, only customers have access to company application information.

Answer: B

5 When companies use the insourcing model for business applications, to whom do they assign delivery accountability?

   a. Chief executive officer

   b. Customer representative assigned to the customer buying the application product or service

   c. Manager in charge of the applicable core business area

   d. Manager in charge of the business application

Answer: D

6 Which explanation best demonstrates why a company would want to use an insourcing model for a business application directly related to one of their core business interests?

   a. Increasing accuracy of accounting resources expended on the application

   b. Maintaining complete control of the business application

   c. Reducing costs associated with the application

   d. Retaining its personnel currently working in a core business area

Answer: B

7 Which areas of day-to-day operation do companies with technical, core business areas tend to outsource?

   a. Basic technical research

   b. Product customization

   c. Product development

   d. Record archiving

Answer: D

8 Which business application resource requirement consideration is favorable to outsourcing the application?

   a. Allowing immediate write-off of up-front application costs

   b. Boosting morale by not having to include existing personnel in the design process

   c. Increasing application data security by using public facilities

   d. Making resources otherwise required for the application available to support core business activity

Answer: D

9 Which risk is not linked to a company outsourcing a business application to a provider?

    a. Failure of a new application provider

    b. Intermediate manager resistance in the company

    c. Provider incompatibility

    d. Trial before obtaining the application

Answer: D

10 Which set of security measures is normally used to prevent customer information compromise in an outsourced business application?

    a. Digital certificates, encryption, and multiple firewalls

    b. Encryption, multiple firewalls, and private data lines

    c. Digital certificates, multiple firewalls, and private data lines

    d. Digital certificates, encryption, and private data lines

Answer: A

11 Which statement describes the difference between a business application's delivery responsibility using the insourcing model and a business application using the outsourcing model?

    a. With the outsourcing model, both the oversight of the application and the delivery responsibility occur at a much higher level of management.

    b. With the outsourcing model, both the oversight of the application and the delivery responsibility occur at a lower level of management.

    c. With the outsourcing model, the oversight of the application occurs at a lower level of management, and the delivery responsibility escalates to the chief executive officer.

    d. With the outsourcing model, the oversight of the application occurs at a lower level of management, and delivery responsibility stays with the same managers as with the insourcing model.

Answer: D

12 Which set of advantages does outsourcing deliver?

    a. Bandwidth requirements and innovation development time

    b. Remote access and innovation development time

    c. Remote access and download time

    d. Bandwidth requirements and remote access

Answer: B

13 Which set of three reasons drive companies to use ASPs?

a. Best practices, emerging technology, and industry excess IT expertise

b. Best practices, emerging technology, and increasing global competition

c. Best practices, industry excess IT expertise, and increasing global competition

d. Emerging technology, industry excess IT expertise, and increasing global competition

Answer: B

14 Which set of resource requirements would a company expect the ASP to supply?

a. Internet connection, licenses, and networking

b. Licenses, networking, and servers

c. Internet connection, networking, and servers

d. Internet connection, licenses, and servers

Answer: B

15 Which risk is involved when using an ASP to obtain a business application?

a. ASP failure

b. Leveraged ASP capabilities

c. Performance monitoring tools

d. Service Level Agreements

Answer: A

16 Which security issue provides the greatest objection of business application users to obtaining the application from an ASP?

a. Unable to determine the ability of ASP employees

b. Compromise of customer data

c. Cost of leased data lines

d. Need to keep user employees occupied with the application

Answer: B

17 Which statement best describes the way the ASP accepts responsibility from the user company for the delivery of the product or service the ASP provides?

a. It guarantees the application performance.

b. It returns the ASP fee to the user for the default period.

c. It returns the ASP fee both to the user and to any customer for the default period.

d. It takes no responsibility.

Answer: A

18 Which advantage does not result from obtaining a business application from an ASP?

a. Eliminating obsolescence

b. Providing universal accessibility

c. Reducing risk

d. Scheduling updates

Answer: D

19 Which sourcing model tends to require a company to maintain a larger staff of employees?

a. ASP

b. Contracting

c. Insourcing

d. Outsourcing

Answer: C

20 Which commodity does a company exchange for the risk associated with business application implementation in the process of using an outsourcing arrangement?

a. Payment

b. Profit

c. Time

d. Trust

Answer: D

21 Which causes the perceived loss of customer data security associated with forms of outsourcing models?

  a. Data encryption

  b. Employees leaving employment

  c. Loss of data control

  d. User tokens

Answer: C

22 Which statement best explains why companies assign business application delivery responsibility to lower levels of management if the company outsources the application?

  a. The company CEO has no responsibility for outsourced applications.

  b. The company has less direct management and supervisory activity.

  c. Outsourcing's cost-saving philosophy dictates less management involvement.

  d. The provider prefers a lower level point of contact with the user company.

Answer: B

23 Which major impact results from a company insourcing its context business?

  a. Allows leveraging of provider company skills and expertise for core business

  b. Prevents context business procedures from becoming obsolete

  c. Requires employees to work on context business at the expense of core business

  d. Requires employees to work on core business at the expense of context business

Answer: C

Chapter 6

  1 Which main component distinguishes Internet-based customer care from traditional customer care?

  a. Call centers

  b. Being Internet-based

  c. Using IP-telephony

  d. Interacting person-to-person

Answer: B

2 Which benefit is not linked to customer care?

   a. Customer care boosts a company's valuation.

   b. Sales agents focus more time on customer satisfaction and less on administrative functions.

   c. Customers can enter and retrieve data using the same front-end application as customer service, sales or distribution, and have access to that data on a 24-hour basis.

   d. Everyone is informed when the need arises to respond quickly to an issue or concern that cannot be easily answered by a single contact person.

   Answer: A

3 Which Internet-based customer care component represents the individual or company and the location where a product is being sold?

   a. Account management

   b. Contact management

   c. Marketing management

   d. Opportunity management

   Answer: A

4 Which component is not part of the Internet-based customer care lifecycle?

   a. Grow

   b. Produce

   c. Service

   d. Target

   Answer: B

5 Which term best defines the process that occurs when conflicting or incomplete information originates and is disseminated by different parts of the company?

   a. Inconsistent sales and service levels

   b. Missed sales opportunities

   c. Inefficient business process

   d. Fragmented customer messaging

   Answer: D

6 Which time or cost has the Internet greatly reduced by allowing customers to compare competitive offerings and move to another supplier with relative ease?

   a. Down time

   b. Switching costs

   c. Operating time

   d. Cost options

   Answer: B

7 What should be centralized and implemented according to user roles defined in the system?

   a. Manageability

   b. Security

   c. Connectivity

   d. Availability

   Answer: B

8 Which item does workforce optimization not encompass?

   a. Accumulating more employees to help with administrative tasks

   b. Using the knowledge for market prediction and educating the customer

   c. Empowering the workforce with relevant knowledge

   d. Performing administrative tasks

   Answer: A

9 Operational optimization streamlines coordination between different groups that have been employed to address a problem and optimize the _____ .

   a. Workforce functionality

   b. Workforce complexity

   c. Customer functionality

   d. Companies' dexterity

   Answer: A

10 A centralized system that contains mostly updated information can establish proper communication between the workforce, management, and _____ .

  a. Employees

  b. Customers

  c. Maintenance

  d. Stakeholders

Answer: B

11 Which workforce optimization module provides universal information to workforce and customers?

  a. Optimization engine

  b. Communication center

  c. Knowledge center

  d. Resource management

Answer: B

12 With the New World network, what is built on universally available browser platforms that can reach a global audience without large incremental investments?

  a. Web-based applications

  b. Global network integration

  c. Secure access

  d. Database consolidation

Answer: A

13 Implementing the workforce optimization system requires capacity consideration from what two perspectives?

  a. Physical inventory and practicality

  b. Storage space and practicality

  c. Storage space and expandability

  d. Expandability and capability

Answer: C

14 Supply chain management encompasses all of the activities associated with moving goods from which stage to the end user?

    a. Production

    b. Distributor

    c. Raw materials

    d. Completed product

Answer: C

15 Which benefit is not linked to supply chain management?

    a. Faster time to market

    b. Lower obsolescence rates

    c. Higher inventory levels

    d. Satisfied customers

Answer: C

16 Which signal type is essential when applying demand planning across the supply chain?

    a. Supply

    b. Consumer

    c. Distribution

    d. Market

Answer: D

17 What determines how the actual customer drives the supply chain?

    a. Supply chain network

    b. Enabling practices

    c. Organizational structure

    d. Information technology architecture

Answer: B

18 Which factor bases its definition on scalability and flexibility?

  a. Reliability

  b. Security

  c. Capacity

  d. Connectivity

  Answer: C

19 Which component is not a part of e-learning?

  a. Content creation

  b. Delivery objectives

  c. Assessment and management

  d. Delivery technologies

  Answer: D

20 Which benefit is not a result of e-learning?

  a. Learners are accountable through online testing and progress management.

  b. Learners obtain relevant information faster and more productively.

  c. Learners are free to study at their own pace, but only at a central location.

  d. Organizations can track learner performance to assess workforce preparation.

  Answer: C

21 Recombining and distributing managed components into various mediums for all audiences for e-publishing is called content _____ .

  a. Creation

  b. Delivery

  c. Management

  d. Proposal

  Answer: B

22 Which strategic component encompasses the tools, business processes, and systems architecture necessary for an integrated Internet experience?

a. E-commerce

b. E-delivery

c. E-learning

d. E-publishing

Answer: D

23 Which factor includes basic monitoring and status of available systems at an administrative level?

a. Security

b. Connectivity

c. Availability

d. Manageability

Answer: D

Chapter 7

1 Which function is not considered a system or application management function?

a. Firewall intrusion detection

b. Monitoring server CPU utilization

a. Measuring system availability

a. Software distribution

Answer: A

2 Which benefits are not attributed to application management?

a. Understanding the application's topology and characteristics

b. Monitoring application CPU/memory consumption

c. The ability to measure application throughput

d. Remotely managing the applications security requirements

Answer: B

3 The task of monitoring and measuring applications across a network is called
_____ .

   a. Application servicing

   b. Service level management

   c. Application performance

   d. Application distribution

Answer: C

4 An example of application configuration management includes which of the following?

   a. Calculating response times when changes are made

   b. Understanding what parameters need to be changed

   c. Knowing application performance

   d. Configuring application availability software

Answer: B

5 Which of the following does not affect application performance across the network?

   a. Traffic congestion

   b. Bandwidth utilization

   c. Router utilization

   d. Number of active sessions

Answer: C

6 DMI stands for _____ .

   a. Distributed Management Interface

   b. Dynamic Managed Integration

   c. Desktop Management Interface

   d. Digital Module Interface

Answer: C

7 Which of the following is not a typical measurement of application management?

    a. Application availability

    b. Operating system version

    c. Application response time

    d. Download rates

Answer: B

8 How does the speed of change affect capacity planning?

    a. It is linked to operations that are tied into the operations management.

    b. Rapid growth makes it necessary to monitor and plan for growth before any over-loads occur and cause serious performance problems or system crashes.

    c. It is tied to all the key features that are required to keep the system working.

    d. It predicts if and when system saturation occurs.

Answer: B

9 Which of the following are two types of threshold system management?

    a. RMON and SNMP

    b. Immediate and historical

    c. Framework and "best of breed"

    d. Local and remote performance-based

Answer: D

10 Which of the following is key to system management?

    a. System management helps determine server standards and configurations.

    b. System management is not shared between server, network, or operational data-base administrators.

    c. System management interpretation varies, depending on the environment and organizational processes being used.

    d. System management is the same as system administration.

Answer: C

11 Why is the inventory database a vital component of system management?

   a. Without it, there would be no management capabilities.

   b. It provides a log of all routers and switches.

   c. It contains a directory of all managed components.

   d. It stores vital system statistics.

Answer: C

12 Which is not a key system management tools element?

   a. The tools can help identify the source and cause of the problem quickly and allow a rapid response.

   b. System management tools must gather and reconcile hardware, software, and database faults and alerts.

   c. Management tools enable organizations to manage all IT resources and encompassing heterogeneous networks, systems, applications, and databases.

   d. The tools do not have the capability to create server shares and unattended client installations.

Answer: D

Public-Key Infrastructure

A public key infrastructure (PKI) enables users of an unsecure public network, such as the Internet, to securely and privately exchange data and money using a public and a private cryptographic key pair that is obtained and shared through a trusted authority. The public-key infrastructure provides a digital certificate that identifies an individual or an organization and directory services that can store and, when necessary, revoke the certificates. Although the components of a PKI are generally understood, a number of vendor approaches and services are emerging. Meanwhile, an Internet standard for PKI is being developed.

Components of PKI

The PKI assumes the use of *public-key cryptography*, which is the most common method on the Internet for authenticating a message sender or encrypting a message. Traditional cryptography usually involves creating and sharing a secret key to encrypt and decrypt messages. This secret, or private, key system has a significant flaw. If the key is discovered or intercepted by someone else, messages can easily be decrypted. For this reason, public-key cryptography with the PKI is the preferred approach on the Internet. (The private-key system is sometimes known as symmetric cryptography, and the public-key system is also called *asymmetric cryptography*.)

A public-key infrastructure consists of the following:

- A certificate authority (CA) that issues and verifies digital certificates; a certificate includes the public key or information about the public key
- A registration authority (RA) that acts as the verifier for the certificate authority before a certificate authority can issue digital certificates to a requestor
- One or more directories that house the certificates and their public keys
- A certificate management system

How Public- and Private-Key Cryptography Works

In public-key cryptography, a public key and a private key are created simultaneously using the same algorithm (a popular one is known as RSA) by a certificate authority (CA). The private key is given only to the requesting party, and the public key is made publicly available (as part of a digital certificate) in a directory that all parties can access. The private key is never shared with anyone or sent across the Internet.

You use the private key to decrypt text that has been encrypted with your public key by someone else. If I want to send you a message, I can find out your public key (but not your private key) from a central administrator and encrypt a message to you using your public key. When you receive the message, you decrypt it with your private key. In addition to encrypting messages (which ensures privacy), you can authenticate yourself to me (so I know that you really originated the message) by using your private key to encrypt a digital certificate. When I receive your encrypted digital certificate, I can use your public key to decrypt it.

Table E-1 provides an outline of the encryption process.

Table E-1   *Encryption Process*

Action	By Using	Belonging to This Person
Sending an encrypted message	Public key	Receiver
Sending an encrypted signature	Private key	Sender
Decrypting an encrypted message	Private key	Receiver
Authenticating a send (decrypt an encrypted signature)	Public key	Sender

Who Provides the Infrastructure?

A number of available products enable a company, or group of companies, to implement a PKI. The acceleration of e-commerce and business-to-business commerce over the Internet has increased the demand for PKI solutions. Related ideas are the Virtual Private Network (VPN) and the IP Security (IPSec) standard.

Leading PKI manufacturers include the following:

- RSA has developed the main algorithms used by PKI vendors.
- Verisign acts as a certificate authority and sells software that allows a company to create its own certificate authorities.
- GTE CyberTrust provides a PKI implementation methodology and consultation service that it plans to vend to other companies for a fixed price.
- Xcert's, Web Sentry product checks the revocation status of certificates on a server using the Online Certificate Status Protocol (OCSP).

- Netscape's Directory Server product is said to support 50 million objects and process 5000 queries per second; Secure E-Commerce allows a company or extranet manager to manage digital certificates; and Meta-Directory can connect all corporate directories into a single directory for security management.

Pretty Good Privacy

Pretty Good Privacy (PGP) is a popular program used to encrypt and decrypt e-mail over the Internet. PGP can also send an encrypted digital signature that lets the receiver verify the sender's identity and that message integrity is intact (was not changed en route).

PGP is one of the most widely used privacy-ensuring programs by individuals, and it is also used by many corporations. Developed by Philip R. Zimmermann in 1991 and released as freeware, PGP has become a de facto standard for e-mail security. PGP can also encrypt stored files so that they are unreadable by unauthorized users or intruders.

How Pretty Good Privacy Works

PGP uses a variation of the public-key system. Each user has a publicly known encryption key and a private key known only to that user. You encrypt a message you send to someone else using his public key. When he receives it, he decrypts it using his private key.

Because encrypting an entire message can be time-consuming, PGP uses a faster (shorter) encryption algorithm to encrypt the message, and then uses the public key to encrypt the shorter key that encrypted the entire message. Both the encrypted message and the short key are sent to the receiver, who first uses the receiver's private key to decrypt the short key, and then uses that key to decrypt the message.

PGP Versions

PGP comes in two public key versions—Rivest-Shamir-Adleman (RSA) and Diffie-Hellman. The RSA version, for which PGP must pay a license fee to RSA, uses the IDEA algorithm to generate a short key for the entire message and RSA to encrypt the short key. The Diffie-Hellman version uses the CAST algorithm for the short key to encrypt the message and the Diffie-Hellman algorithm to encrypt the short key.

The Role of Algorithms

To send digital signatures, PGP uses an efficient algorithm that generates a hash (or mathematical summary) from the user's name and other signature information. This hash code is then encrypted with the sender's private key. The receiver uses the sender's public key to decrypt the hash code. If it matches the hash code sent as the digital signature for the message, the receiver is sure that the message has arrived securely from the stated sender. PGP's RSA version uses the MD5 algorithm to generate the hash code. PGP's Diffie-Hellman version uses the SHA-1 algorithm to generate the hash code.

Preparing to Use PGP

To use PGP, you must download it and install it on your computer system. PGP software typically contains a user interface that works with your customary e-mail program. You also need to register the public key that your PGP program provides with a PGP public-key server so that people you exchange messages with will be able to find your public key. Network Associates maintains an LDAP/HTTP public-key server with 300,000 registered public keys. This server has mirror sites around the world. Several versions of PGP are in use. Add-ons can be installed to allow backward-compatibility for newer RSA versions with older versions. However, the Diffie-Hellman and RSA versions of PGP do not work with each other because they use different algorithms.

Restrictions on PGP

Originally, the U.S. government restricted the exportation of PGP technology. Today, however, you can exchange PGP encrypted e-mail with users outside the United States if you have the correct versions of PGP at both ends. Unlike most other encryption products, the international version is just as secure as the domestic version.

Current Status of PGP

Network Associates bought the commercial rights to PGP from Zimmerman in 1997, but the software is available free for personal use. In March of 2002, Network Associates stopped selling the software when it was unable to find a buyer for the technology.

GLOSSARY

A

American Standard Code for Information Interchange (ASCII). Developed by the American National Standards Institute (ANSI) in 1958, the modern version was adopted in 1967. Only 128 character codes exist in ASCII, and its sparse, clean form reflects the extreme lack of bandwidth in all forms of hardware and software at the time ASCII was created.

access control list (ACL). A table that tells a computer or network operating system which access rights each user has to a particular system object, such as a file directory, individual file, or network connection. Each object has a security attribute that identifies its access control list.

accountability. The condition of willingness or obligation to accept responsibility or to account for one's actions; and the ability to audit the actions of all parties and processes that interact with information.

ActiveX. The name Microsoft has given to a set of "strategic," object-oriented programming technologies. The main technology is the Component Object Model (COM).

American National Standards Institute (ANSI). ANSI is the primary organization for fostering the development of technology standards in the United States.

application service provider (ASP). A company that offers individuals or enterprises access to applications and related services over the Internet that would otherwise have to be located in their own personal or enterprise computers.

application integration. Multiple, dissimilar applications working together as one application.

application program interface (API). A set of definitions that govern the ways one piece of computer software communicates with another. It is a method of achieving abstraction, usually (but not necessarily) between lower-level and higher-level software.

authentication. Authentication is the process of verifying that an entity's identity is truly what it claims to be.

authorization. The administrative granting of rights by an established body responsible for security or access control.

B

backup. A copy of data. A full backup creates a copy of all data and files, while an incremental backup creates a copy of only those files that have changed since the last backup.

bandwidth. Bandwidth describes the width of a band of frequencies. Bandwidth applies to hardwire connections, as well as wireless connections.

baselining. Taking measurements of key performance indicators at regular intervals, over a long enough period of time, to encompass both normal and busy times, in order to establish a value (the baseline). This value is a performance metric against which resulting changes in the metric can be meaningfully compared.

business model. An architecture for the definition of all business activities related to providing goods or services. A business model includes a description of a business, business roles, potential benefits of various business activities, and a description of revenue sources, risks, and challenges.

byte. A byte is a unit of data that is eight binary digits (ones and zeros) long, and, in most computer systems, represents a character, such as a letter, number, or typographic symbol (for example, m, 4, or @).

C

cache. A temporary storage unit. Computers and network devices employ caching at various levels, including network caches of web page requests, disk caches of files, and RAM caches of data in memory.

certificate authority (CA). An authority that issues and manages security credentials and public keys for message encryption. As part of a public-key infrastructure (PKI), a CA checks with a registration authority (RA) to verify information provided by the requestor of a digital certificate. If the RA verifies the requestor's information, the CA can issue a certificate.

change control. Change control (or version control) is the tracking and management of changes made to a program or data file.

child. A child is a descendant node or process that is linked to a parent node or process.

class. In object-oriented programming, a class is a template definition of the methods and variables in a specific object. An object is a specific instance of a class.

client-server architecture. In client-server applications and services, the client makes requests and the server responds to requests.

clustering. Clustering is the connection of many (usually low-cost) computers using special software so they can be used as one larger computer.

Common Object Request Broker Architecture (CORBA). An architecture and specification for creating, distributing, and managing distributed program objects in a network. CORBA allows programs, at different locations and developed by different vendors, to communicate in a network through an "interface broker."

Common Gateway Interface (CGI). A standard way for a web server to pass a request to an application program and to receive data to forward to the user.

component object model (COM). Microsoft's framework for developing and supporting program component objects, aimed at providing similar capabilities to those defined in CORBA.

compiler. A special program that processes statements written in a particular programming language and turns them into machine language, or code, that a computer's processor uses.

computer-aided software engineering (CASE). The use of a computer-assisted method to organize and control the development of software, especially on large, complex projects involving many software components and people. Using CASE allows designers, code writers, testers, planners, and managers to share a common view of where a project stands at each stage of development.

concurrent versions system (CVS). A program that lets a code developer save and retrieve different development versions of source code. CVS also lets a team of developers share control of different file versions in a common repository of files.

content management system (CMS). A system used to manage the content of a web site. Typically, a CMS consists of two elements: the content management application (CMA) and the content delivery application (CDA).

customer relationship management (CRM). An information industry term for methodologies, software, and, usually, Internet capabilities that help an enterprise manage customer relationships in an organized way.

D

data description language (DDL). Enables the structure and instances of a database to be defined in a human-readable and machine-readable form. XML and Abstract Syntax Notation (ASN) are examples of data description languages.

data dictionary. A data dictionary is a collection of descriptions of the data objects or items in a data model for the benefit of programmers and those needing a reference.

data flow diagram (DFD). Depicts the processes, data stores, data flows, and external agents in a business area. DFD specifies how data flows among these components at one level of a decomposition of activities.

data manipulation language (DML). Provides a means for applications and/or end users to manipulate data in a database. SQL, for example, contains DML commands, such as INSERT, UPDATE, and DELETE.

data mining. Sorting through data to identify patterns and establish relationships.

data modeling. Analyzing data objects used in a business or other context and identifying the relationships among these data objects. Data modeling is a first step in object-oriented programming.

data warehousing. Keeping a copy of transaction data specifically structured for querying and reporting.

database management system (DBMS). A program allowing one or more computer users to create and access data in a database. The DBMS manages user requests (and requests from other programs) so that users and other programs don't have to understand where the data is physically located on storage media, or in a multi-user system, who else might be accessing the data.

debugger. Software with extensive facilities to trace the execution of another software program and monitor and change the values of variables of that program. A debugger is a diagnostic tool used by developers.

digital certificate. Usually an attachment to an electronic message that establishes your credentials when doing business or other transactions on the web. A digital certificate is issued by a certificate authority (CA). It contains your name, a serial number, expiration dates, a copy of the certificate holder's public key (used for encrypting messages and digital signatures), and the certificate-issuing authority's digital signature so a recipient can verify that the certificate is real.

disaster recovery. A plan for recovery from a disaster. Appropriate plans vary from one enterprise to another, depending on the type of business, the processes involved, and the level of security needed.

documentation. In computer hardware and software product development, documentation is information that describes the product to its users. It consists of the product technical manuals and online resources (including online versions of the technical manuals and help facility descriptions).

E

e-commerce. The buying and selling of goods and services over networks, especially the World Wide Web. In practice, this term and the newer term, e-business, are often used interchangeably. For online retail selling, the term e-tailing is sometimes used.

e-learning. Covers a wide set of applications and processes, such as web-based learning, computer-based learning, virtual classrooms, and digital collaboration. It includes the delivery of content by the Internet, intranet/extranet (LAN/WAN), audio- and videotape, satellite broadcast, interactive TV, and CD-ROM.

e-publishing. Publishing method that creates, archives, maintains and distributes an electronic document by means of computers. The entire life cycle of the document is electronic.

encapsulation. In object-oriented programming, encapsulation is the inclusion within a program object of all the resources needed for the object to function.

encryption. The conversion of data into a ciphertext form that cannot be easily understood by unauthorized people. Decryption converts encrypted data back into its original form so it can be understood.

enterprise resource planning (ERP). The broad set of activities supported by multimodule application software that helps a manufacturer (or other enterprise) manage the important parts of its business, including product planning, parts purchasing, maintaining inventories, interacting with suppliers, providing customer service, and tracking orders.

entity-relationship diagram (ERD). A data modeling technique that creates a graphical representation of the entities, and the relationships between entities, within an information system.

Ethernet. The most widely installed LAN technology. Specified in, IEEE 802.3, Ethernet was originally developed by Xerox, and developed further by Xerox, DEC, and Intel.

Extensible Markup Language (XML). A flexible way to create common information formats and share both the format and the data on the World Wide Web, intranets, and elsewhere. For example, computer manufacturers might agree on a standard or common way to describe the information about a computer product (processor speed, memory size, and so forth), and describe the product information format with XML. This standard way of describing data enables a user to send an intelligent agent (a program) to each computer maker's web site, gather data, and make a valid comparison. XML can be used by any individual, group of individuals, or companies that want to share information in a consistent way.

F

failover. A backup operational mode in which the functions of a system component (such as a processor, server, network, or database, for example) are assumed by secondary system components when the primary component becomes unavailable because of failure or scheduled down time.

fault-management, configuration, accounting, performance, and security model (FCAPS). A categorical, five-level model of the working objectives of network management. Levels include the fault-management level (F), the configuration level (C), the accounting level (A), the performance level (P), and the security level (S).

fault-tolerant. Describes a computer system or component designed so that, in the event a component fails, a backup component or procedure can immediately take its place with no loss of service. Fault tolerance can be provided with software, embedded in hardware, or provided by some combination.

File Transfer Protocol (FTP). A standard Internet protocol that is the simplest way to exchange files between computers on the Internet. It uses the Internet's TCP/IP protocols. It is commonly used to download programs and other files to your computer from other servers.

firewall. A set of related programs, located at a network gateway server, that protects the resources of a private network from users from other networks. (The term also implies the security policy that is used with the programs.)

flowchart. A formalized graphic representation of a program logic sequence, work or manufacturing process, organization chart, or similar formalized structure. In computer programming, flowcharts were formerly used to describe each processing path in a program (the main program and various subroutine branches).

G - H

graphical user interface (GUI). A graphical (rather than textual) user interface to a computer. Applications typically use the elements of the GUI that come with the operating system and add their own graphical user interface elements and functionality.

high availability. A system or component that is continuously operational for a desirably long time. Availability can be measured relative to "100 percent operational" or "never failing." A widely-held but difficult-to-achieve standard of availability for a system or product is known as "five 9s" (99.999 percent) availability.

hot swap. The replacement of a hard drive, CD-ROM drive, power supply, or other device with a similar device while the computer system using it remains in operation.

Hypertext Markup Language (HTML). The set of markup symbols or codes inserted in a file to display on a World Wide Web browser page. The markup tells the Web browser how to display a web page's words and images for the user.

Hypertext Transfer Protocol (HTTP). The set of rules for exchanging files (text, graphic images, sound, video, and other multimedia files) on the World Wide Web. HTTP is an application protocol. An essential concept of HTTP is the idea that files can contain references to other files whose selection will elicit additional transfer requests.

Hypertext Transfer Protocol over Secure Socket Layer HTTPS). A web protocol developed by Netscape and built into its browser that encrypts and decrypts user page requests, as well as the pages that are returned by the web server.

I

indexing. A process for improving the time it takes to access data in a database. The proper or improper use of indexing on columns within a database can greatly affect the performance of that database.

inheritance. In object-oriented programming, when a class of objects is defined, any defined subclass can inherit the definitions of one or more general classes. For the programmer, this means that an object in a subclass need not carry its own definition of data and methods that are generic to the class (or classes) of which it is a part.

insourcing model. Provides a framework in which a company controls, configures, and administers all parts of a business application.

integrity. The assurance that information has remained unchanged from its source. Measures taken to ensure integrity include controlling the physical environment of networked terminals and servers, restricting access to data, and maintaining rigorous authentication practices.

interface. A user interface consists of the devices provided by a computer or program to allow the user to communicate and use the computer or program. A programming interface consists of the ways of expressing program instructions and data provided by a program or language. Interface can also mean to communicate with another person or object.

Internet service provider (ISP). A company that provides individuals and other companies with access to the Internet and other related services, such as web site building and virtual hosting.

Intrusion detection system (IDS). A security management system for computers and networks. An IDS gathers and analyzes information from various areas within a computer or network to identify possible security breaches, which include both intrusions (attacks from outside the organization) and misuse (attacks from within the organization).

J - K

Java. An object-oriented programming language created by engineers at Sun Microsystems. Java was officially announced on May 23, 1995, at SunWorld. The Java programming platform is based on the Java language, the Java Virtual Machine (JVM), and the Java API.

Java API. An extensive collection of library routines (written in the Java programming language or in native code) that perform basic tasks, such as GUI display and manipulation, sorting, and countless others.

Java Virtual Machine (JVM). Software that simulates a CPU that runs Java byte codes.

journaling file system. A fault-tolerant file system that ensures data integrity because updates to directories and bitmaps are constantly written to a serial log on disk before the original disk log is updated. In the event of a system failure, a full journaling file system ensures that the data on the disk has been restored to its pre-crash configuration. It also recovers unsaved data and stores it in the location where it would have gone if the computer had not crashed, making it an important feature for mission-critical applications.

key. In cryptography, a key is a variable value applied using an algorithm to a string or block of unencrypted text to produce encrypted text, or to decrypt encrypted text. The length of the key is a factor in considering how difficult it will be to decrypt the text in a given message.

knowledge management. A concept in which an enterprise consciously and comprehensively gathers, organizes, shares, and analyzes its knowledge in terms of resources, documents, and people skills. In the late 90s, few enterprises actually had a comprehensive knowledge management practice (by any name) in operation.

L - M - N

legacy application. Legacy applications and data are those that have been inherited from earlier languages, platforms, techniques, and technologies. Most enterprises that use computers have legacy applications and databases that serve critical business needs.

Lightweight Directory Access Procotol (LDAP). A software protocol for enabling anyone to locate organizations, individuals, and other resources, such as files and devices in a network, whether on the public Internet or on a corporate intranet.

local-area network (LAN). A group of computers and associated devices that share a common communications line and, typically, share the resources of a single processor or server within a small geographic area (for example, within an office building). A LAN can serve as few as two or three users (for example, in a home network) or many thousands of users (for example, in an FDDI network).

Metropolitan Area Exchange (MAE). A MAE (pronounced MAY), originally an abbreviation for Metropolitan Area Exchange and now a service mark of MCI WorldCom, is a major center in the United States for switch traffic between Internet service providers (ISPs). The two major MAEs are MAE-East, in the Washington, D.C. area and MAE-West, in the San Jose, California area.

managed service provider (MSP). Delivers and manages network-based services, applications, and equipment to enterprises, residences, or other service providers. MSPs can be hosting companies or access providers that offer fully outsourced network management arrangements, including advanced features like IP telephony, messaging, call center, Virtual Private Networks (VPNs), managed firewalls, and network server monitoring and reporting.

middleware. A general, computer industry term for any programming that "glues together" or mediates between two separate and, usually, already existing programs. A common application of middleware is to allow programs written for access to a particular database to access other databases.

mirroring. Also known as port mirroring, this method of monitoring network traffic forwards a copy of each incoming and outgoing packet from one network switch port to another port where the packet can be studied. A network administrator uses port mirroring as a diagnostic tool or debugging feature, especially when fending off an attack.

Network Address Translation (NAT). The translation of an Internet Protocol address (IP address) from one network to a different IP address known within another network. One network is designated the inside network and the other is the outside network.

normalization. Normalization within a database is a technique used to organize the contents of the tables for transactional databases and data warehouses. Without normalization, database systems can be inaccurate, slow, and inefficient.

O

Object-oriented programming (OOP). A revolutionary concept that changed the rules in computer program development, OOP is organized around objects rather than actions, data rather than logic. OOP takes the view that what users really care about are the objects they want to manipulate, rather than the logic required to manipulate them.

object request broker (ORB). In Common Object Request Broker Architecture (CORBA), ORB is the programming that acts as a broker between a client request for a service from a distributed object or component and the completion of that request. Having ORB support in a network means that a client program can request a service without having to understand where the server is in a distributed network, or exactly what the interface to the server program looks like.

Open Database Connectivity (ODBC). An open standard application programming interface (API) that accesses a database. By using ODBC statements in a program, you can access files in a number of different databases. In addition to the ODBC software, a separate module or driver is needed for each database to be accessed. Microsoft is the main proponent and supplier of ODBC programming support.

Open System Interconnection (OSI). A standard description or reference model for how messages should be transmitted between any two points in a telecommunication network. OSI guides product implementers so that their products will consistently work with other products. The reference model defines seven layers of functions that take place at each end of a communication.

operating system (OS). An OS is a program that, after being loaded into the computer by a boot program, manages all the other programs in a computer.

outsourcing. A company provides services for another company that could also be, or traditionally have been, provided in-house. Outsourcing is a trend that is becoming more common in information technology and other industries for services that have usually been regarded as intrinsic to managing a business.

P

packet. A unit of data that is routed between an origin and a destination on the Internet or any other packet-switched network. When any file (e-mail message, HTML file, Graphics Interchange Format file, Uniform Resource Locator request, and so forth) is sent from one place to another on the Internet, the Transmission Control Protocol (TCP) layer of TCP/IP divides the file into appropriately sized data segments for routing.

packet sniffer. A packet sniffer (or just sniffer) is a dedicated device using a software package designed to monitor network traffic to recognize and decode certain packets of interest. The packet sniffer is normally used by system administrators for network management and diagnostics, but it is occasionally used by hackers for illicit purposes, such as stealing a user's password or credit-card number.

parallel processing. The processing of program instructions by dividing them among multiple processors with the objective of running a program in less time than it would take to process them as a whole. In the earliest computers, only one program ran at a time. A computation-intensive program that took one hour to run and a tape-copying program that took one hour to run would take a total of two hours to run. An early form of parallel processing allowed the interleaved execution of both programs together.

password. A sequence of characters used to determine that a computer user requesting access to a system is really that user. Typically, users of a multiuser or securely protected, single-user system claim a unique name (often called a user ID) that can be generally known. To verify that someone entering that user ID really is that person, a second identification, the password, known only to that individual and to the system itself, is entered by the user.

patch. Sometimes called a fix, this is a quick-repair job for a piece of programming. During a software product's beta test distribution or try-out period, and after the product is formally released, problems (called bugs) will invariably be found. A patch provides an immediate solution to users; the patch is not necessarily the best solution for the problem, and product developers often find a better solution to provide when they package the product for its next release.

practical extraction report language (PERL). A script programming language invented by Larry Wall that is similar in syntax to the C language and includes a number of popular UNIX facilities, such as SED, awk, and tr. Perl is an interpreted language that can optionally be compiled just before execution into either C code or cross-platform bytecode. When compiled, a Perl program is almost as fast as a fully precompiled C language program.

PL/SQL. In Oracle database management, PL/SQL is a procedural language extension to Structured Query Language (SQL). PL/SQL combines database language and procedural programming language. The basic unit in PL/SQL is called a block, which is made up of three parts: a declarative part, an executable part, and an exception-building part. Because PL/SQL allows you to mix SQL statements with procedural constructs, you can use PL/SQL blocks and subprograms to group SQL statements before sending them to Oracle for execution.

process. An instance of a program running in a computer. In UNIX and some other operating systems, a process is started when a program is initiated (either by a user entering a shell command or by another program). A process is a running program with which a particular set of data is associated so the process can be kept track of. At some stage in execution, an application that is being shared by multiple users will generally have one process for each user.

proxy server. In an enterprise that uses the Internet, a proxy server acts as an intermediary between a workstation user and the Internet so that the enterprise can ensure security, administrative control, and caching service. A proxy server is associated with, or part of, a gateway server that separates the enterprise network from the outside network, and a firewall server that protects the enterprise network from outside intrusion.

public-key infrastructure (PKI). Enables users of an insecure public network, such as the Internet, to securely and privately exchange data and money through the use of a public and a private cryptographic key pair obtained and shared through a trusted authority. The public key infrastructure provides for digital certificates that identify an individual or an organization, and directory services that store and, when necessary, revoke the certificates. Although the fundamental components of a PKI are generally understood, a number of different vendor approaches and services are emerging.

public and private key cryptography. A public key and a private key are created simultaneously by a certificate authority (CA) using the same algorithm (a popular one is RSA). The private key is given only to the requesting party, and the public key is made publicly available (as part of a digital certificate) in a directory that all parties can access. The private key is never shared with anyone or sent across the Internet. You use the private key to decrypt text that has been encrypted with your public key by someone else.

Pretty Good Privacy (PGP). A popular program used to encrypt and decrypt e-mail over the Internet. PGP can also be used to send an encrypted digital signature that lets the receiver verify the sender's identity and know that the message was not changed en route. PGP is one of the most widely used privacy-ensuring programs by individuals, and it is also used by many corporations.

Q - R

quality assurance (QA). Actions taken to ensure that standards and procedures are adhered to, and that delivered products or services meet performance requirements. Additionally, QA is concerned with the policies, procedures, and systematic actions established in an enterprise to provide and maintain a specified degree of confidence in data integrity and accuracy throughout the lifecycle of the data, which includes input, update, manipulation, and output.

quality of service (QoS). The idea that transmission rates, error rates, and other characteristics on the Internet and in other networks can be measured, improved, and, to some extent, guaranteed in advance. QoS is of particular concern for the continuous transmission of high-bandwidth video and multimedia information. Transmitting this kind of content dependably is difficult in public networks using ordinary "best effort" protocols.

remote-procedure call (RPC). A protocol that one program can use to request a service from a program located in another computer in the same network without having to understand network details. RPC uses the client/server model. The requesting program is a client and the service-providing program is the server. Like a regular or local procedure call, an RPC is a synchronous operation requiring the requesting program to be suspended until the results of the remote procedure are returned. However, the use of lightweight processes or threads that share the same address space allows multiple RPCs to be performed concurrently.

repeater. In telecommunication networks, a repeater is a device that receives a signal on an electromagnetic or optical transmission medium, amplifies the signal, and retransmits it along the next leg of the medium. Repeaters overcome the attenuation caused by free-space electromagnetic-field divergence or cable loss.

run book. A written set of procedures for the routine and exceptional operation of a computer system or network by an administrator or operator. Typically, a run book contains procedures for starting, stopping, and monitoring the system or network; for handling special requests such as the mounting of a storage device containing archived material; and for handling problems that may arise.

S

schema. In computer programming, a schema is the organization or structure for a database. The activity of data modeling leads to a schema.

Secure Socket Layer (SSL). A commonly used protocol for managing the security of a message transmission on the Internet. SSL has recently been succeeded by Transport Layer Security (TLS), which is based on SSL. It uses a program layer located between the Internet's Hypertext Transfer Protocol (HTTP) and Transport Control Protocol (TCP) layers. SSL is included as part of both the Microsoft and Netscape browsers and most web server products.

Service Level Agreement (SLA). A contract between a network service provider and a customer that specifies, usually in measurable terms, what services the network service provider will furnish. Many Internet service providers (ISPs) provide their customers with an SLA. More recently, IS departments in major enterprises have adopted the practice of writing an SLA so that services for their customers (users in other departments within the enterprise) can be measured, justified, and compared with those of outsourcing network providers.

Service Advertising Protocol (SAP). Part of Novell's NetWare suite, SAP is a protocol residing in OSI layers 4 through 7, which is used for servers in a NetWare network to advertise what services they offer. By default, SAP broadcasts occur every 60 seconds and consist of packets up to 576 bytes, containing up to 7 entries (services). Each entry is a hexadecimal number corresponding to a specific service offered; 4 is a file server, 7 is a print server, 26B is a time-sync server, and so on. These SAP broadcasts can become a major problem for network administrators, as they consume considerable bandwidth.

servlet. A small program that runs on a server. The term was coined in the context of the Java applet, a small program that is sent as a separate file along with a web (HTML) page. Java applets, usually intended to run on a client, can, for example, perform a calculation for a user or position an image based on user interaction.

Simple Network Management Protocol (SNMP). A protocol governing network management and the monitoring of network devices and their functions that is not necessarily limited to TCP/IP networks. SNMP is described formally in the Internet Engineering Task Force (IETF) Request for Comment (RFC) 1157, and in a number of other related RFCs.

single sign on. In any client/server relationship, single sign on is a session/user authentication process that permits a user to enter one name and password to access multiple applications. The single sign on, which is requested at the initiation of the session, authenticates the user to access all the applications he has been given the rights to on the server, and eliminates future authentication prompts when the user switches applications during that particular session.

Simple Object Access Protocol (SOAP). A protocol that allows a program running in one kind of operating system (such as Windows 2000) to communicate with a program in the same or another kind of operating system (such as Linux) by using the World Wide Web's Hypertext Transfer Protocol (HTTP) and its Extensible Markup Language (XML) as the mechanisms for information exchange. Because web protocols are installed and available for use by all major operating system platforms, HTTP and XML provide an already at-hand solution to the problem of how programs running under different operating systems in a network can communicate with each other.

storage area network (SAN). A high-speed, special-purpose network (or subnetwork) that interconnects different kinds of data storage devices with associated data servers on behalf of a larger network of users. Typically, a SAN is part of the overall network of computing resources for an enterprise. A SAN is usually clustered in close proximity to other computing resources, such as IBM S/390 mainframes, but may also extend to remote locations for backup and archival storage using wide-area network carrier technologies, such as asynchronous transfer mode or Synchronous Optical Networks.

stored procedure. A set of Structured Query Language (SQL) statements with an assigned name that's stored in the database in compiled form so that it can be shared by a number of programs. Using stored procedures can be helpful in controlling access to data (end-users may enter or change data but do not write procedures), preserving data integrity (information is entered in a consistent manner), and improving productivity (statements in a stored procedure only need to be written one time).

Structured Query Language (SQL). SQL is a standard, interactive, and programming language that gets information from and updates a database. Although SQL is both an ANSI and an ISO standard, many database products support SQL with proprietary extensions to the standard language. Queries take the form of a command language that lets you select, insert, update, find the location of data, and so forth. There is also a programming interface.

Synchronized Multimedia Integration language (SMIL). SMIL is a language that allows web site creators to easily define and synchronize multimedia elements (video, sound, and still images) for web presentation and interaction. On today's Web, although you can send moving and still images and sound to a web user, each element is separate from the others and can't be coordinated with other elements without elaborate programming. SMIL (pronounced "smile") lets site creators send multiple movies, still images, and sound separately but coordinate their timing.

T

threads. On the Internet in Usenet newsgroups and similar forums, a thread is a sequence of responses to an initial message posting. This enables you to follow or join an individual discussion in a newsgroup from among the many discussions that may be there. A thread is usually shown graphically as an initial message and successive messages "hung off" the original message. As a newsgroup user, you contribute to a thread by specifying a reference topic as part of your message. In computer programming, a thread is placeholder information associated with a single use of a program that handles multiple concurrent users.

Total Cost of Ownership (TCO). A type of calculation designed to help consumers and enterprise managers assess both direct and indirect costs and benefits related to the purchase of an IT component. The intention is to arrive at a final figure that reflects the effective cost of purchase, all things considered.

Transmission Control Protocol/Internet Protocol (TCP/IP). TCP/IP is the basic communication language, or protocol, of the Internet. It is also used as a communications protocol in a private network (either an intranet or an extranet). When you are set up with direct access to the Internet, your computer is provided with a copy of the TCP/IP program. Every other computer that you might send messages to, or get information from, also has a copy of TCP/IP.

trigger. In a database, a trigger is a set of Structured Query Language (SQL) statements that automatically "fires off" an action when a specific event, such as changing data in a table, occurs. A trigger consists of an event (an INSERT, DELETE, or UPDATE statement issued against an associated table) and an action (the related procedure). Triggers preserve data integrity by checking on or changing data in a consistent manner.

U

Universal Description, Discovery, and Integration (UDDI). An XML-based, Internet registry in which businesses worldwide list themselves. UDDI's ultimate goal is to streamline online transactions by enabling companies to find one another on the Web and make their systems interoperable for e-commerce. UDDI is often compared to a telephone book's white, yellow, and green pages. The project allows businesses to list themselves by name, product, location, or the web services they offer. Microsoft, IBM, and Ariba spearheaded UDDI.

use case. A methodology used in system analysis to identify, clarify, and organize system requirements. The use case consists of a set of possible sequences of interactions between systems and users in a particular environment and related to a particular goal. It consists of a group of elements (for example, classes and interfaces) that can be used together in a way that has an effect larger than the sum of the separate elements. The use case should contain all system activities that are significant to the users. A use case can be thought of as a collection of possible scenarios related to a particular goal; indeed, the use case and goal are sometimes considered to be synonymous.

V - W

Virtual Private Network (VPN). A private data network that uses the public telecommunication infrastructure, maintaining privacy through the use of a tunneling protocol and security procedures. A VPN can be contrasted with a system of owned or leased lines that can be used only by one company. VPN technology is embraced by companies as a secure solution for providing employees with remote access to corporate systems.

Visual Basic script (VBScript). Visual Basic (VB) is a programming environment from Microsoft in which a programmer uses a graphical user interface to choose and modify preselected sections of code written in the BASIC programming language. Because Visual Basic is easy to learn and fast to write code with, it's sometimes used to prototype an application that will later be written in a more difficult but efficient language. Visual Basic is also widely used to write working programs. Microsoft reports that at least three million developers use Visual Basic. VBScript is designed for use with Microsoft's Internet Explorer browser and other programming that runs at the client, including ActiveX controls, automation servers, and Java applets.

wide-area network (WAN). A geographically dispersed telecommunications network that distinguishes a broader telecommunication structure than a local-area network (LAN). A WAN can be privately owned or rented, but the term usually connotes the inclusion of public (shared user) networks. An intermediate form of network in terms of geography is a metropolitan-area network (MAN).

INDEX

Numerics

1NF (First Normal Form) normalization, 108
2NF (Second Normal Form) normalization, 108
3NF (Third Normal Form) normalization, 108

A

A level, 474
abstraction
    applications, 173
    data modeling, 98
acceptance testing, 200
access
    controlling, 322–324
    e-business sites, 506
    databases, 343
    devices, 121
    Internet, 472
    remote, 385
Access Control Lists (ACLs), 382
accountability
    applications, 326
    delivery
        ASPs, 396
        insourcing, 375
        outsourcing, 384
accounts (user), 323
ACID properties, 70–71
ACLs (Access Control Lists), 382
acquire lifecycle component, 420
actions (autonomous), 21
Active X controls, 47
Active X Server Framework, 47
add transactions, 78
administration (users), 491–493
administrators, system, 488–489
advantages
    ASPs, 396–397
    data warehousing, 64
    e-learning, 449
    e-publishing, 449
    hierarchical databases, 52
    insourcing, 375

Internet-based customer care, 414, 417
Internet-based workforce optimization, 425–428
multithreaded applications, 119
network databases, 54
object-oriented databases, 58
OOP, 93
outsourcing, 384–385
relational databases, 56
SCM, 434–435
web applications, 37
after-image journaling, 74
agreements
    maintenance, 354
    service-level, 390
algorithms, 324
allocations
    components, 343
    dedicated devices, 122
    storage, 122
alternate keys (IDEFIX), 112
Analysis and Design Phase (Basic Lifecycle Model), 142, 161
    abstraction, 173
    data dictionaries, 166–173
    data modeling, 166
    DFDs, 165
    inputs, 162
    issues, 163
    outputs, 162–163
    overview, 277
    project management tools, 174
    prototypes, 173
    responsibilities, 164–165
    system modeling tools, 174
    techniques, 173
analyzing
    traffic, 207–208
    trend analysis, 264
    user load testing results, 226
answers
    application architecture design, 510, 513
    e-business case study, 506–508
    load testing, 522, 526–528
    network design, 517–518

Q

S

CISCO SYSTEMS

IF YOU'RE USING

CISCO PRODUCTS,

YOU'RE QUALIFIED

TO RECEIVE A

FREE SUBSCRIPTION

TO CISCO'S

PREMIER PUBLICATION,

PACKET™ MAGAZINE.

Packet delivers complete coverage of cutting-edge networking trends and innovations, as well as current product updates. A magazine for technical, hands-on Cisco users, it delivers valuable information for enterprises, service providers, and small and midsized businesses.

Packet is a quarterly publication. To start your free subscription, click on the URL and follow the prompts: www.cisco.com/go/packet/subscribe

☐ **YES!** I'm requesting a **free** subscription to *Packet™* magazine.

☐   No. I'm not interested at this time.

☐ Mr.
☐ Ms.

First Name (Please Print) | Last Name

Title/Position (Required)

Company (Required)

Address

City | State/Province

Zip/Postal Code | Country

Telephone (Include country and area codes) | Fax

E-mail

Signature (Required) | Date

☐ I would like to receive additional information on Cisco's services and products by e-mail.

1. Do you or your company:
- A ☐ Use Cisco products
- B ☐ Resell Cisco products
- C ☐ Both
- D ☐ Neither

2. Your organization's relationship to Cisco Systems:
- A ☐ Customer/End User
- B ☐ Prospective Customer
- C ☐ Cisco Reseller
- D ☐ Cisco Distributor
- E ☐ Integrator
- F ☐ Non-Authorized Reseller
- G ☐ Cisco Training Partner
- I ☐ Cisco OEM
- J ☐ Consultant
- K ☐ Other (specify): _____

3. How many people does your entire company employ?
- A ☐ More than 10,000
- B ☐ 5,000 to 9,999
- C ☐ 1,000 to 4,999
- D ☐ 500 to 999
- E ☐ 250 to 499
- F ☐ 100 to 249
- G ☐ Fewer than 100

4. Is your company a Service Provider?
- A ☐ Yes
- B ☐ No

5. Your involvement in network equipment purchases:
- A ☐ Recommend
- B ☐ Approve
- C ☐ Neither

6. Your personal involvement in networking:
- A ☐ Entire enterprise at all sites
- B ☐ Departments or network segments at more than one site
- C ☐ Single department or network segment
- F ☐ Public network
- D ☐ No involvement
- E ☐ Other (specify): _____

7. Your Industry:
- A ☐ Aerospace
- B ☐ Agriculture/Mining/Construction
- C ☐ Banking/Finance
- D ☐ Chemical/Pharmaceutical
- E ☐ Consultant
- F ☐ Computer/Systems/Electronics
- G ☐ Education (K–12)
- U ☐ Education (College/Univ.)
- H ☐ Government—Federal
- I ☐ Government—State
- J ☐ Government—Local
- K ☐ Health Care
- L ☐ Telecommunications
- M ☐ Utilities/Transportation
- N ☐ Other (specify): _____

CPRESS

PACKET

Packet magazine serves as the premier publication linking customers to Cisco Systems, Inc. Delivering complete coverage of cutting-edge networking trends and innovations, *Packet* is a magazine for technical, hands-on users. It delivers industry-specific information for enterprise, service provider, and small and midsized business market segments. A toolchest for planners and decision makers, *Packet* contains a vast array of practical information, boasting sample configurations, real-life customer examples, and tips on getting the most from your Cisco Systems' investments. Simply put, *Packet* magazine is straight talk straight from the worldwide leader in networking for the Internet, Cisco Systems, Inc.

We hope you'll take advantage of this useful resource. I look forward to hearing from you!

Cecelia Glover
Packet Circulation Manager
packet@external.cisco.com
www.cisco.com/go/packet

PACKET